M000195353

Langenscheidt

Universal Norwegian Dictionary

Norwegian – English
English – Norwegian

edited by the
Langenscheidt editorial staff

Langenscheidt

New York · Berlin · Munich · Vienna · Zurich

Neither the presence nor the absence of a designation indicating that any entered word constitutes a trademark should be regarded as affecting the legal status thereof.

© 2008 Langenscheidt KG, Berlin and Munich
Printed in Germany

Contents
Innhold

Preface

In selecting the vocabulary and phrases for this dictionary, the editors have had the traveller's needs foremost in mind. This book will prove a useful companion to casual tourists and business travellers alike who appreciate the reassurance a small and practical dictionary can provide. It offers them – as well as beginners and students – all the basic vocabulary they will have to encounter and have to use, giving the key words and expressions to allow them to cope in everyday situations.

This dictionary is designed to slip into pocket or purse, and thus have a role as a handy companion at all times.

Besides just about everything you normally find in dictionaries, there are these bonuses:

- simplified pronunciation after each foreign-word entry, making it easy to read and enunciate words whose spelling may look forbidding

- useful information on how to tell the time and how to count, on conjugating irregular verbs, commonly seen abbreviations and converting to the metric system, in addition to basic phrases.

While no dictionary of this size can pretend to completeness, we are confident this dictionary will help you get most out of your trip abroad.

Forord

I valget av ordforråd og uttrykk til denne ordboken har vi først og fremst tatt sikte på å dekke den reisendes behov. Denne boken vil derfor være en god følgesvenn for både turister og forretningsreisende som setter pris på den tryggheten en hendig ordbok gir. Også de som vil lære språket, nybegynnere såvel som viderekomne, finner her de grunnleggende ordforråd de vil komme i berøring med, dertil nøkkelord og – uttrykk som gjør det mulig å klare seg i dagligdagse situasjoner.

Ordboken er laget for å kunne tas med i en veske eller lomme. Vi håper at den ved sitt praktiske format vil tiltale mange og være til god hjelp i alle situasjoner.

Foruten alt det en ordbok vanligvis inneholder, finner du følgende bonustillegg:

- imitasjon av uttalen etter hver oppføring på fremmedspråket, noe som gjør det enkelt å lese ordet og å bruke ord med en komplisert stavemåte

- en rekke praktiske opplysninger som tallord, vanlige forkortelser, hvordan man angir klokkeslett, bøyning av uregelmessige verb, samt et avsnitt med nyttige uttrykk.

Det sier seg selv at en ordbok av dette format ikke kan gjøre krav på å være fullstendig. Allikevel er vi overbevist om at denne ordboken vil være til uvurderlig hjelp når det gjelder å få det beste ut av utenlandsreisen din.

Introduction

This dictionary has been designed to take account of your practical needs. Unnecessary linguistic information has been avoided. The entries are listed in alphabetical order, regardless of whether the entry is printed in a single word or in two or more separate words. As the only exception to this rule, a few idiomatic expressions are listed alphabetically as main entries by the most significant word of the expression. When an entry is followed by sub-entries, such as expressions and locutions, these are also listed in alphabetical order*.

Each main-entry word is followed by a phonetic transcription (see guide to pronunciation). Following the transcription, the part of speech of the entry word is indicated, whenever applicable. If an entry word is used as more than one part of speech, the translations are grouped together after the respective part of speech.

In the regular indefinite plural, both common, masculine and neuter nouns take an -(e)r ending. Exceptions: masculine nouns ending in -er take ～e (e.g.: arbeider, pl arbeidere), and monosyllabic neuter nouns remain unchanged (e.g.: barn, pl barn).

All irregular plural forms of nouns not conforming to these rules are given in brackets after the part of speech.

Whenever an entry word is repeated in irregular forms or sub-entries, a tilde (～) is used to represent the full word. In plurals of long words, only the part that changes is written out fully, whereas the unchanged part is represented by a hyphen (-).

Entry word: mus *c* (pl ～)   Plural: mus
      vidunder *nt* (pl ～, ～e)   vidunder, vidundere
      antibiotikum *nt* (pl -ka)   antibiotika

An asterisk (*) in front of a verb indicates that it is irregular. For more detail, refer to the list of irregular verbs.

---

* Note that the Norwegian alphabet comprises 29 letters; æ, ø and å are considered independent characters and come after z, in that order.

Veiledning

Ved utarbeidelsen av denne ordboken har vi først og fremst tatt sikte på å gjøre den så praktisk og anvendelig som mulig. Mindre viktige språklige opplysninger er utelatt. Oppslagsordene står i alfabetisk rekkefølge uansett om uttrykket skrives i ett ord, med bindestrek, eller i to eller flere ord. Det eneste unntaket fra denne regelen er noen få idiomatiske uttrykk, som du vil finne under det meningsbærende ordet. Når et oppslagsord følges av flere sammensetninger eller uttrykk, er også disse satt i alfabetisk rekkefølge.

Hvert hovedoppslagsord er fulgt av lydskrift (se Uttale), og vanligvis av ordklasse. I fall et oppslagsord tilhører flere ordklasser, er oversettelsene gruppert sammen etter de respektive ordklassene.

Dersom et substantiv har uregelmessig flertallsform, er denne angitt. I tilfeller der det kan oppstå tvil, har vi gitt eksempler på bruken.

Bølgestrek (~) er brukt som gjentagelsestegn for oppslagsordet når dette forekommer senere i artikkelen (f.eks. ved uregelmessig flertallsform, sammensatte ord, etc.).

Når det gjelder uregelmessig flertallsform av sammensatte ord, er bare den delen som forandres, skrevet helt ut; en kort strek (–) står for den uforandrede delen.

En stjerne (*) foran et verb betyr at verbet er uregelmessig. Bøyningsmønster finner du i listen over uregelmessige verb.

I denne ordboken har vi anvendt vanlig engelsk stavemåte. Alle ord som må regnes som amerikanske, er merket *Am* (se listen over forkortelser).

Guide to Pronunciation

Each main entry in this part of the dictionary is followed by a phonetic transcription which shows you how to pronounce the words. This transcription should be read as if it were English. It is based on Standard British pronunciation, though we have tried to take account of General American pronunciation also. Below, only those letters and symbols are explained which we consider likely to be ambiguous or not immediately understood.

The syllables are separated by hyphens, and stressed syllables are printed in *italics*.

Of course, the sounds of any two languages are never exactly the same, but if you follow carefully our indications, you should be able to pronounce the foreign words in such a way that you'll be understood. To make your task easier, our transcriptions occasionally simplify slightly the sound system of the language while still reflecting the essential sound differences.

Consonants

g	always hard, as in **g**o
kh	quite like **h** in **h**uge, but with the tongue raised a little higher
r	rolled in the front of the mouth, except in south-western Norway, where it's pronounced in the back of the mouth
s	always hard, as in **s**o

The consonants **d, l, n, s, t**, if preceded by **r**, are generally pronounced with the tip of the tongue turned up well behind the upper front teeth. The **r** then ceases to be pronounced.

Vowels and Diphthongs

aa	long **a**, as in c**a**r, without any **r**-sound
ah	a short version of **aa**; between **a** in c**a**t and **u** in c**u**t
aw	as in r**aw** (British pronunciation)
æ	like **a** in c**a**t
ǣæ	a long **æ**-sound
eh	like **e** in g**e**t
er	as in oth**er**, without any **r**-sound
ew	a "rounded **ee**-sound". Say the vowel sound **ee** (as in s**ee**), and while saying it, round your lips as for **oo** (as in s**oo**n), without moving your tongue; when your lips are in the **oo** position, but your tongue is in the **ee** position, you should be pronouncing the correct sound
igh	as in s**igh**
o	always as in h**o**t (British pronunciation)
ou	as in l**ou**d
ur	as in f**ur**, but with rounded lips and no **r**-sound

1) A bar over a vowel symbol (e.g. $\overline{\text{ew}}$) shows that this sound is long.
2) Raised letters (e.g. ʸ**aa**, **ew**ᵉᵉ) should be pronounced only fleetingly.

Tones

In Norwegian there are two "tones": one is rising, the other consists of a falling pitch followed by a rise. As these tones are complex and very hard to copy, we do not indicate them, but mark their position as stressed.

Uttale

I denne delen av ordboken er hvert stikkord fulgt av internasjonal lydskrift (IPA). Hvert enkelt tegn i denne fonetiske skriften står for en bestemt lyd. Tegn som her ikke er nærmere forklart, uttales omtrent som de tilsvarende norske bokstavene.

Konsonanter

ð	en slags lespende, stemt **s**-lyd; uttales med tungespissen løftet mot overtennene
g	alltid som i **gå**, aldri som i **gi**
k	alltid som i **ku**, aldri som i **kinn**
ŋ	som **ng** i la**ng**
r	en stemt **r**-lyd som dannes ved at tungebladet heves mot den bakre del av gommene
ʃ	som **sj** i øst- og nordnorsk **sjø**
θ	en slags lespende, stemmeløs **s**-lyd
w	som **o** i **o**st, men meget svak
z	stemt **s**-lyd
ʒ	stemt **sj**-lyd

Merk: Transkripsjonen [sj] skal alltid uttales som en **s** fulgt av en **j**-lyd, ikke som i øst- og nordnorsk **sjø**.

Vokaler

ɑ	som **a** i f**a**r
æ	omtrent som **æ** i l**æ**rd
ʌ	omtrent som **a** i k**a**tt
e	som i t**e**legram
ɛ	som **e** i p**e**nn
ə	som **e** i g**a**te
ɔ	som **o** i t**o**lv
u	som **o** i **o**st

1) Et kolon [ː] etter en vokal angir lang vokallyd.
2) Noen franske låneord har nasalert vokal (dvs. at ved uttalen går luften ut både gjennom munn og nese); dette er angitt med en tilde over vokalen (f. eks. [ãʃ]).

Diftonger

En diftong består av to vokaler hvorav den ene er sterk (betont) og den andre svak (ubetont), og uttales som en glidende lyd som bare utgjør én stavelse, som f. eks. **ei** i st**ei**n. I engelske diftonglyder er det alltid den andre vokalen som er svak. Dersom diftongen etterfølges av en [ə] medfører dette en ytterligere svekkelse av den andre vokalen.

Trykk

Tegnet ['] står foran den trykksterke stavelsen, [ˌ] foran stavelser med bitrykk.

Amerikansk uttale

Lydskriften her i boken følger britisk uttale. Selv om amerikansk uttale varierer sterkt fra den ene delen av USA til den annen, kan en sette opp visse regler for forskjellen mellom amerikansk og britisk uttale. Her er noen av dem:

1) I motsetning til på britisk engelsk uttales **r** både når den etterfølges av konsonant og på slutten av ord.
2) I mange ord (f. eks. *ask, castle, laugh*, osv.) blir [ɑː] til [æ].
3) Lyden [ɔ] uttaler amerikanerne som [ɑ] eller [ɔː].
4) I ord som *duty, tune, new*, osv. utelates ofte [j]-lyden som på britisk engelsk går forut for [uː].
5) Mange ord har trykkforskyvning i forhold til britisk uttale.

Abbreviations
Forkortelser

adjective	*adj*	adjektiv
adverb	*adv*	adverb
American	*Am*	amerikansk
article	*art*	artikkel
common gender	*c*	felleskjønn
conjunction	*conj*	konjunksjon
masculine	*m*	hankjønn
noun	*n*	substantiv
noun (American)	*nAm*	substantiv (amerikansk)
neuter	*nt*	intetkjønn
numeral	*num*	tallord
past tense	*p*	imperfektum
plural	*pl*	flertall
plural (American)	*plAm*	flertall (amerikansk)
past participle	*pp*	perfektum partisipp
present tense	*pr*	presens
preposition	*prep*	preposisjon
pronoun	*pron*	pronomen
verb	*v*	verb
verb (American)	*vAm*	verb (amerikansk)

Norwegian – English
Norsk – Engelsk

A

-a (*aa*) *art* the

abbedi (ah-ber-*dee*) *nt* abbey

abonnement (ah-boo-ner-*mahng*ng) *nt* subscription

abonnent (ah-boo-*nehnt*) *m* subscriber

abort (ah-*bott*) *m* abortion; miscarriage

abort-tilhenger (ah-*bott* til-hehng-er) *c* (pl -e) pro life

abortmotstander (ah-*bott*-moot-stahnd-er) *c* (pl -e) pro choice

absolutt (ahp-soo-*lewtt*) *adj* very, sheer; *adv* absolutely

abstrakt (ahp-*strahkt*) *adj* abstract

absurd (ahp-*sewrd*) *adj* absurd

adapter (ah-*dap*-terr) *m* adaptor

addisjon (ah-di-*shoon*) *m* addition

adekvat (ah-deh-*kvaat*) *adj* adequate

adel (*aa*-derl) *m* nobility

adelig (*aa*-der-li) *adj* belonging to nobility

adgang (*aad*-gahng) *m* admission, entrance,

admittance, entry; ~ forbudt no entry, no admittance

adjektiv (*ahd*-ᵛehk-tiv) *nt* adjective

adkomst (*aad*-komst) *m* access

*adlyde (*aad*-lēw-der) *v* obey

administrasjon (ahd-mi-ni-strah-*shoon*) *m* administration

administrerende (ahd-mi-ni-*stray*-rer-ner) *adj* administrative; executive

adoptere (ah-doop-*tay*-rer) *v* adopt

adressat (ahd-reh-*saat*) *m* addressee

adresse (ah-*drehss*-ser) *c* address

adressere (ahd-reh-*say*-rer) *v* address

advare (*aad*-vaa-rer) *v* caution, warn

advarsel (*aad*-vah-sherl) *m* (pl -sler) warning

adverb (ahd-*værb*) *nt* adverb

advokat (ahd-voo-*kaat*) *m* lawyer, barrister; solicitor, attorney

affektert (ah-fehk-*tāyt*) *adj* affected

affære (ah-*fææ*-rer) *m* affair

Afrika (*aaf*-ri-kah) Africa

afrikaner (ahf-ri-*kaa*-nerr) *m* African

afrikansk (ahf-ri-*kaansk*) *adj* African

aftensmat (*ahf*-terns-maat) *m* supper

agent (ah-*gehnt*) *m* agent

agentur (ah-gehn-*tēwr*) *nt* agency

aggressiv (*ah*-greh-seev) *adj* aggressive

agn (ahngn) *nt* bait

agurk (ah-*gewrk*) *m* cucumber

AIDS (ayds) AIDS

airbag (*ehr*-bæg) *m* airbag

akademi (ah-kah-day-*mee*) *nt* academy

akkompagnere (ah-koom-pahn-*ӯay*-rer) *v* accompany

akkreditiv (ah-kreh-di-*teev*) *nt* letter of credit

akkurat (ah-kew-*raat*) *adj* just; exact; *adv* exactly

aksel (*ahk*-serl) *m* (pl aksler) axle

akselerere (*ahk*-ser-ler-*rāy*-rer) *v* accelerate

aksent (ahk-*sahngng*) *m* accent

akseptere (ahk-sehp-*tāy*-rer) *v* accept

aksje (*ahk*-sher) *m* share, stock

aksjon (ahk-*shōōn*) *m* action

akt (ahkt) *m* act; nude

akte (*ahk*-ter) *v* esteem

aktelse (*ahk*-terl-ser) *m* respect; esteem

akterspeil (*ahk*-ter-shpayl) *nt* (pl ∼) stern, rear

aktiv (*ahk*-tiv) *adj* active

aktivitet (ahk-ti-vi-*tāyt*) *m* activity

aktuell (ahk-tew-*ehll*) *adj* topical; current

akutt (ah-*kewtt*) *adj* acute

akvarell (ahk-vah-*rehll*) *m* watercolo(u)r

alarm (ah-*lahrm*) *m* alarm

alarmere (ah-lahr-*māy*-rer) *v* alarm

albue (*ahl-bēw*-er) *m* elbow

album (*ahl*-bewm) *nt* album

alder (*ahl*-derr) *m* (pl ∼e, aldrer) age

alderdom (*ahl*-der-dom) *m* old age, age

aldri (*ahl*-dri) *adv* never

alene (ah-*lāy*-ner) *adv* alone; only

ale opp (*aa*-ler) *v* *breed, raise

alfabet (ahl-fah-*bāyt*) *nt* alphabet

algebra (*ahl*-geh-brah) *m* algebra

Algerie (ahl-sheh-*ree*) Algeria

algerier (ahl-*shāy*-ri-err) *m* Algerian

algerisk (ahl-*shāy*-risk) *adj* Algerian

alkohol (ahl-koo-*hōōl*) *m*

alcohol, *colloquial* booze
alkoholholdig (ahl-koo-*hōōl*-hol-di) *adj* alcoholic;
alkoholholdige drikker spirits
all (ahll) *adj* all
allé (ah-*lāy*) *m* avenue
allerede (ah-ler-*rāy*-der) *adv* already
allergi (ahl-ær-*gee*) *m* allergy
allianse (ah-li-*ahng*-ser) *m* alliance
allierte (ah-li-*āy*-ter) *pl* Allies *pl*
allikevel (ah-*lee*-ker-vehl) *conj* yet
allmektig (*ahl*-mehk-ti) *adj* omnipotent
allmenn (*ahl*-māyn) *adj* public; general
alltid (*ahl*-ti) *adv* always; ever; **for ~** forever, for ever
allting (*ahl*-ting) *pron* everything
alm (ahlm) *m* elm
almanakk (ahl-mah-*nahkk*) *m* diary
alminnelig (ahl-*min*-ner-li) *adj* plain, customary, common
alt (ahlt) *pron* everything; *adj* all; *m* alto
alter (*ahl*-terr) *nt* (pl altre) altar
alternativ (ahl-tæ-nah-teev) *nt* alternative
altfor (*ahlt*-for) *adv* too
altså (*ahlt*-so) *adv* consequently

alv (ahlv) *m* elf
alvor (*ahl*-vor) *nt* seriousness, gravity
alvorlig (ahl-*vaw*-li) *adj* serious, bad, grave
ambassade (ahm-bah-*saa*-der) *m* embassy
ambassadør (ahm-bah-sah-*dūrr*) *m* ambassador
ambisiøs (ahm-bi-si-*ūrss*) *adj* ambitious
ambulanse (ahm-bew-*lahng*-ser) *m* ambulance
Amerika (ah-*māy*-ri-kah) America
amerikaner (ah-meh-ri-*kaa*-nerr) *m* American
amerikansk (ah-meh-ri-*kaansk*) *adj* American
ametyst (ah-mer-*tewst*) *m* amethyst
amme (*ahm*-mer) *v* nurse
amnesti (ahm-ner-*stee*) *nt* amnesty
amulett (ah-mew-*lehtt*) *m* lucky charm, charm
analfabet (ahn-nahl-fah-*bāyt*) *m* illiterate
analyse (ahn-ah-*lew*-ser) *m* analysis
analysere (ahn-ah-lew-*sāy*-rer) *v* analyse
analytiker (ahn-ah-*lewt*-ti-kerr) *m* analyst
ananas (*ahn*-nah-nahss) *m* pineapple
anarki (ahn-ahr-*kee*) *nt* anarchy
anatomi (ahn-ah-too-*mee*) *m* anatomy

anbefale

anbefale (*ahn-beh-faa-ler*) *v* recommend

anbefaling (*ahn-beh-faa-ling*) *c* recommendation

and (ahnn) *c* (pl ender) duck

ane (*aa-ner*) *v* suspect, guess

anelse (*aa-nerl-ser*) *m* notion; suspicion

anemi (ahn-eh-*mee*) *m* anaemia

anerkjenne (*ahn-nær-kheh-ner*) *v* recognize, acknowledge

anerkjennelse (*ahn-nær-kheh-nerl-ser*) *m* recognition

anfall (*ahn-fahl*) *nt* (pl ~) fit

anfører (*ahn-fūr-rerr*) *m* leader

anførselstegn (*ahn-fur-sherls-tayn*) *pl* quotation marks

anger (*ahng-ngerr*) *m* repentance

*angi (*ahn-*Yee*) *v* indicate

angre (*ahng-rer*) *v* regret, repent

angrep (*ahn-grāyp*) *nt* (pl ~) attack; raid

*angripe (*ahn-gree-per*) *v* attack, assault

angst (ahngst) *m* fright

*angå (*ahn-gaw*) *v* concern

angående (*ahn-gaw-erner*) *prep* regarding, about, as regards, concerning

ankel (*ahng-kerl*) *m* (pl ankler) ankle

anker (*ahn-kerr*) *nt* (pl ankre) anchor

anklage¹ (*ahn-klaa-ger*) *v* accuse, charge

anklage² (*ahn-klaa-ger*) *m* charge

anklagede (*ahn-klaa-ger-der*) accused

*ankomme (*ahn-ko-mer*) *v* arrive

ankomst (*ahn-komst*) *m* arrival

ankomsttid (*ahn-komst-teed*) *c* time of arrival

anledning (*ahn-lāyd-ning*) *m* chance, opportunity; *ha ~ til* afford

anlegg (*ahn-lehg*) *nt* (pl ~) aptitude; construction

anliggende (*ahn-li-ger-ner*) *nt* affair, concern

anmassende (*ahn-mah-ser-ner*) *adj* presumptuous

anmelde (*ahn-meh-ler*) *v* report; review

anmeldelse (*ahn-meh-lerl-ser*) *m* review

anmode (*ahn-mōō-der*) *v* request

anmodning (*ahn-mōōd-ning*) *m* request

anneks (ah-*nehks*) *nt* annex

annektere (ah-nehk-*tāy-rer*) *v* annex

annen (*aa-ern*) *num* second; *pron* other

annerledes (*ahn-ner-lāy-derss*) *adv* otherwise; *adj* different

annetsteds (*aa-ern-stehss*) *adv* elsewhere

annonse (ah-*nong-ser*) *m*

advertisement

annullere (ah-new-*lay*-rer) *v* cancel; recall

anonym (ah-noo-*newm*) *adj* anonymous

ansatt (*ahn*-saht) *m* (pl ~e) employee

***anse** (ahn-*say*) *v* consider, regard

anseelse (ahn-*say*-erl-ser) *m* reputation

anselig (ahn-*say*-li) *adj* considerable, substantial

***ansette** (*ahn*-seh-ter) *v* engage

ansikt (*ahn*-sikt) *nt* face

ansiktskrem (*ahn*-sikts-kraym) *m* face cream

ansiktstrekk (*ahn*-sikts-trehk) *nt* feature

ansjos (ahn-*shōōss*) *m* anchovy

anskaffe (*ahn*-skah-fer) *v* *buy, *get

anskaffelse (*ahn*-skah-ferl-ser) *m* purchase

anspennelse (*ahn*-speh-nerl-ser) *m* strain

anspent (*ahn*-spehnt) *adj* tense

anspore (*ahn*-spōō-rer) *v* incite

anstendig (ahn-*stehn*-di) *adj* decent

anstendighet (ahn-*stehn*-di-hāyt) *c* decency

anstrengelse (*ahn*-strayng-erl-ser) *m* effort, strain

anstrenge seg (*ahn*-strehng-nger) labo(u)r; try

anstøt (ahn-*stūrt*) *nt* (pl ~) offense *Am*, offence

anstøtelig (ahn-*stūrt*-eli) *adj* offensive

ansvar (*ahn*-svahr) *nt* liability, responsibility

ansvarlig (ahn-*svaa*-li) *adj* liable, responsible; ~ for in charge of

***anta** (*ahn*-taa) *v* assume, suppose; guess

antakelig (ahn-*taa*-ker-li) *adj* presumable

antall (*ahn*-tahl) *nt* (pl ~) number; quantity

antenne (ahn-*tehn*-ner) *c* aerial

antibiotikum (ahn-ti-bi-*ōō*-ti-kewm) *nt* (pl -ka) antibiotic

antikk (ahn-*tikk*) *adj* antique

antikvitet (ahn-ti-kvi-*tāyt*) *m* antique

antikvitetshandler (ahn-ti-kvi-*tāyts*-hahnd-lerr) *m* antique dealer

antipati (ahn-ti-pah-*tee*) *m* dislike

antyde (*ahn*-tēw-der) *v* indicate; imply; hint

antydning (*ahn*-tēw-dning) *m* hint

anvende (*ahn*-veh-ner) *v* employ, apply; utilize

anvendelig (ahn-*vehn*-ner-li) *adj* usable

anvendelse (*ahn*-veh-nerl-ser) *m* application

anvise (*ahn*-vee-ser) *v*

indicate

ape (*aa*-per) *c* monkey

aperitiff (ah-peh-ri-*tiff*) *m* aperitif

apotek (ah-poo-*tayk*) *nt* pharmacy, chemist's; drugstore *nAm*

apoteker (ah-poo-*tay*-kerr) *m* chemist

apparat (ah-pah-*raat*) *nt* apparatus; machine; appliance; gadget

appell (ah-*pehll*) *m* appeal

appelsin (ah-perl-*seen*) *m* orange

appetitt (ah-per-*titt*) *m* appetite

appetittlig (ah-per-*tit*-li) *adj* appetizing

appetittvekker (ah-per-*tit*-veh-kerr) *m* appetizer

applaudere (ahp-lou-*day*-rer) *v* clap, applaud

applaus (ah-*plouss*) *m* applause

aprikos (ahp-ri-*kōōss*) *m* apricot

april (ah-*preel*) April

araber (ah-*raa*-berr) *m* Arab

arabisk (ah-*raa*-bisk) *adj* Arab

arbeid (*ahr*-bay) *nt* labo(u)r, work; employment

arbeide (ahr-*bay*-der) *v* work

arbeider (ahr-*bay*-derr) *m* labo(u)rer, worker, workman

arbeidsbesparende (ahr-

bayss-beh-spaa-rer-ner)
adj labo(u)r-saving

arbeidsdag (ahr-bayss-daag) *m* working day

arbeidsformidling (ahr-bayss-for-mid-ling) *c* employment exchange

arbeidsgiver (ahr-bayss-ʸee-verr) *m* employer

arbeidsledig (ahr-bayss-lay-di) *adj* unemployed, jobless

arbeidsledighet (ahr-bayss-lay-di-hayt) *c* unemployment

arbeidsløs (ahr-bayss-lūrss) *adj* unemployed, jobless

arbeidsløshet (ahr-bayss-lūrss-hayt) *c* unemployment

arbeidstillatelse (ahr-bayss-ti-laa-terl-ser) *m* work permit; labor permit *Am*

arbeidsnarkoman (ahr-bayss-nahr-kōō-mahn) *c* workaholic

areal (ah-reh-*aal*) *nt* area

Argentina (ahr-gern-*tee*-nah) Argentina

argentiner (ahr-gern-*tee*-nerr) *m* Argentinian

argentinsk (ahr-gern-*teensk*) *adj* Argentinian

argument (ahr-gew-*mehnt*) *nt* argument

argumentere (ahr-gew-mehn-*tay*-rer) *v* argue

ark (ahrk) *nt* sheet

arkade (ahr-*kaa*-der) *m*

arcade

arkeolog (ahr-keh-oo-*lawg*) *m* archaeologist

arkeologi (ahr-keh-oo-loo-gee) *m* archaeology

arkitekt (ahr-ki-*tehkt*) *m* architect

arkitektur (ahr-ki-tehk-*tewr*) *m* architecture

arkiv (ahr-*keev*) *nt* archives *pl*

arm (ahrm) *m* arm; **arm i arm** arm-in-arm

armbånd (*ahrm*-bon) *nt* (pl ~) bracelet

armbåndsur (*ahrm*-bons-ewr) *nt* (pl ~) wrist-watch

armé (ahr-*māy*) *m* army

aroma (ah-*rōō*-mah) *m* aroma

arr (ahrr) *nt* scar

arrangere (ah-rahng-*shāy*-rer) *v* arrange

arrestasjon (ah-reh-stah-*shōōn*) *m* arrest, capture

arrestere (ah-reh-*stāy*-rer) *v* arrest

art (ahtt) *m* species

artikkel (ah-*tik*-kerl) *m* (pl artikler) article

artisjokk (ah-ti-*shokk*) *m* artichoke

artistisk (ah-*tiss*-tisk) *adj* artistic

arv (ahrv) *m* inheritance

arve (*ahr*-ver) *v* inherit

arvelig (*ahr*-ver-li) *adj* hereditary

arving (*ahrv*-ing) *m* heir; heiress

asbest (ahss-*behst*) *m* asbestos

asfalt (*ahss*-fahlt) *m* asphalt

Asia (*aa*-si-ah) Asia

asiat (ah-si-*aat*) *m* Asian

asiatisk (ah-si-*aa*-tisk) *adj* Asian

aske (*ahss*-ker) *c* ash

askebeger (*ahss*-ker-bāy-gerr) *nt* (pl -gre) ashtray

asparges (ah-*spahr*-gerss) *m* (pl ~) asparagus

aspekt (ah-*spehkt*) *nt* aspect

aspirin (ahss-pi-*reen*) *m* aspirin

assistanse (ah-si-*stahng*-ser) *m* assistance

assistent (ah-si-*stehnt*) *m* assistant

astma (*ahst*-mah) *m* asthma

astronomi (ah-stroo-noo-mee) *m* astronomy

asyl (ah-*sēwl*) *nt* asylum

at (ahtt) *conj* that

ateist (ah-teh-*ist*) *m* atheist

Atlanterhavet (aht-*lahn*-terr-haa-ver) Atlantic

atlet (aht-*lāyt*) *m* athlete

atmosfære (aht-mooss-*fææ*-rer) *m* atmosphere

atom (ah-*tōōm*) *nt* atom; **atom-** atomic

atskillelse (*aat*-shi-lerl-ser) *m* separation

atskillige (aht-*shil*-li-er) *adj* several

atskilt (*aat*-shilt) *adj* separate; *adv* apart

atspredelse (*aat*-sprāy-derl-ser) *m* amusement,

diversion; recreation
atten (*aht*-tern) *num*
eighteen
attende (*aht*-terner) *num*
eighteenth
atter (*aht*-terr) *adv* again
attest (ah-*tehst*) *m*
certificate
attestere (ah-tehs-*tāy*-rer) *v*
attest
attraksjon (ah-trahk-*shōōn*)
m attraction
attråverdig (*aht*-raw-vær-di)
adj desirable
aubergine (o-behr-*sheen*) *m*
eggplant
auditorium (ou-di-*tōō*-ri-
ewm) *nt* (pl -ier)
auditorium
august (ou-*gewst*) August
auksjon (ouk-*shōōn*) *m*
auction
Australia (ou-*straa*-li-ah)
Australia
australier (ou-*straa*-li-err)
m Australian
australsk (ou-*straalsk*) *adj*
Australian
autentisk (ou-*tehn*-tisk) *adj*
authentic
automat (ou-too-*maat*) *m*
slot machine; vending
machine
automatisering (ou-too-
mah-ti-*sāy*-ring) *c*
automation
automatisk (ou-too-*maa*-
tisk) *adj* automatic
automobilklubb (ou-too-
moo-*beel*-klewb) *m*

automobile club
autorisasjon (ou-too-ri-
sah-*shōōn*) *m*
authorization
autoritet (ou-too-ri-*tāyt*) *m*
authority
autoritær (ou-too-ri-*tæær*)
adj authoritarian
av (aav) *prep* by, of, for,
with, from; *adv* off, ~ **og til**
sometimes, occasionally
avansert (ah-vahng-*sāyt*)
adj advanced
avbestille (*aav*-beh-sti-ler)
v cancel
avbestilling (*aav*-beh-sti-
ling) *c* cancellation
avbetale (*aav*-beh-tah-ler) *v*
*pay on account; *pay
instalments on
avbetalingskjøp (*aav*-beh-
tah-lings-khúrp) *nt* (pl ~)
hire purchase, *Am*
instalment plan
*****avbryte** (*aav*-brēw-ter) *v*
interrupt
avbrytelse (*aav*-brēwt-erl-
ser) *m* interruption
avdekke (*aav*-deh-ker) *v*
uncover
avdeling (ahv-*dāy*-ling) *c*
department; division,
section
avdrag (*aav*-draag) *nt* (pl ~)
instalment
aveny (ah-ver-*nēw*) *m*
avenue
avfall (*aav*-fahl) *nt* rubbish,
refuse, garbage, litter
avfatte (*aav*-fah-ter) *v*

*draw up; compose

avføringsmiddel (*aav-fÜr*-rings-mi-derl) *nt* (pl -midler) laxative

avgang (*aav-gahng*) *m* departure

avgangstid (*aav-gahngs*-teed) *c* time of departure

avgifter (*aav-ʸif*-terr) *pl* dues *pl*

***avgjøre** (*aav-ʸÜr*-rer) *v* decide

avgjørelse (*aav-ʸÜr*-rerl-ser) *m* decision

avgud (*aav-gÉwd*) *m* idol

avhandling (*aav-hahnd*-ling) *c* essay, treatise

avhengig (*aav-heh*-ngi) *adj* dependant

avhente (*aav-hehn*-ter) *v* collect, fetch

***avholde seg fra** (*aav-ho*-ler) abstain from

avis (ah-*veess*) *c* newspaper

aviskiosk (ah-*veess*-khosk) *m* newsstand

avlang (*aav-lahng*) *adj* oblong

avleiring (*aav-lay*-ring) *c* deposit

avlevere (*aav-leh-vÁy*-rer) *v* deliver

avling (*ahv*-ling) *c* harvest, crop

avløp (*aav-lÜrp*) *nt* (pl ∼) drain

avløse (*aav-lÜr*-ser) *v* relieve

avreise (*aav-ray*-ser) *c* departure

avrundet (*aav*-rew-nert) *adj* rounded

avsende (*aav-seh*-ner) *v* dispatch, dispatch

avsender (*aav-seh*-nerr) *m* sender

avsides (*aav*-see-derss) *adj* out of the way, remote

avskaffe (*aav-skah*-fer) *v* abolish

avskjed (*aav-shÁyd*) *m* parting; resignation

avskjedige (*aav-shÁy*-di-er) *v* dismiss, fire

avskjedssøknad (*aav-shÁyds-sÚrk*-nah) *m* resignation

avskrekke (*aav-skrehk*-ker) *v* discourage

avsky[1] (*aav-shÉw*) *v* hate, dislike, detest

avsky[2] (*aav-shÉw*) *m* dislike, disgust

avskyelig (ahv-*shÉw*-er-li) *adj* hideous, horrible, disgusting

avslag (*aav-shlaag*) *nt* (pl ∼) refusal; discount, reduction

avslapning (*aav-shlahp*-ning) *m* relaxation

avslappet (*aav-shlah*-pert) *adj* easy-going; relaxed

avslutning (*aav-shlewt*-ning) *m* ending

avslutte (*aav-shlew*-ter) *v* stop, finish; settle

avsløre (*aav-shlÜr*-rer) *v* reveal; expose

avsløring (*aav-shlÜr*-ring) *c*

revelation

*avslå (*aav*-shlaw) *v* refuse

avsnitt (*aav*-snit) *nt* (pl ~) paragraph; passage

avspark (*aav*-spahrk) *nt* kick-off

avstamning (*aav*-stahm-ning) *m* origin

avstand (*aav*-stahn) *m* distance; space; way

avstandsmåler (*aav*-stahns-maw-lerr) *m* range finder

avstemning (*aav*-stehm-ning) *m* vote

*avta (*aav*-taa) *v* decrease

avtale (*aav*-taa-ler) *m*

agreement, engagement; date, appointment

avtrekker (*aav*-treh-kerr) *m* trigger

avtrykk (*aav*-trewk) *nt* (pl ~) print

avveksling (*aav*-vehks-ling) *c* variation

avvente (*aa*-vehn-ter) *v* await

avverge (*aa*-vær-ger) *v* prevent

*avvike (*aa*-vee-ker) *v* deviate

avvise (*aa*-vee-ser) *v* reject

B

babord (*baa*-boor) port

baby (*bay*-bi) *m* baby

babybag (*bay*-bi-bæg) *m* carry-cot

bacon (*bay*-kern) *nt* bacon

bad (baad) *nt* bath, bathroom

bade (*baa*-der) *v* bathe; swim

badebukse (*baa*-der-book-ser) *c* swimming-trunks *pl*, bathing suit

badedrakt (*baa*-der-drahkt) *c* swimsuit, swimming suit *Am*, bathing suit

badehette (*baa*-der-heh-ter) *c* bathing cap

badehåndkle (*baa*-der-hong-kler) *nt* (pl -lær) bath towel

badekåpe (*baa*-der-kaw-per) *c* bathrobe

badested (*baa*-der-stāy) *nt* seaside resort

badevakt (*baa*-der-vakt)*c*pool attendant

badeværelse (*baa*-der-væl-ser) *nt* bathroom

badstue (*bahss*-tēwer) *c* sauna

bagasje (bah-*gaa*-sher) *m* luggage, baggage

bagasjehylle (bah-*gaa*-sher-hew-ler) *c* luggage rack

bagasjeoppbevaring (bah-*gaa*-sher-oop-ber-*vaa*-ring) *c* left luggage office; *Am* baggage deposit office

bagasjerom (bah-*gaa*-sher-

23 **bare**

room) *nt* (pl ~) boot; *nAm* trunk

bagasjevogn (bah-*gah*-sher-vongn) *c* luggage van

bak (baak) *prep* behind; *adv* behind; *m* bottom

bake (*baa*-ker) *v* bake

baker (*baa*-kerr) *m* baker

bakeri (bah-ker-*ree*) *nt* bakery

bakgrunn (*baak*-grewn) *m* background

bakhold (*baak*-hol) *nt* (pl ~) ambush

bakke (*bahk*-ker) *m* hill; earth

bakketopp (*bahk*-ker-top) *m* hilltop

baklengs (*baak*-lehngs) *adv* backwards

baklykt (*baak*-lewkt) *c* rear light

baklys (*baak*-le͞wss) *nt* (pl ~) tail-light

bakside (*baak*-see-der) *c* rear; reverse

bakterie (bahk-*tāy*-ri-er) *c* bacterium

bakvaskelse (*baak*-vahss-kerl-ser) *c* slander

bakverk (*baak*-værk) *nt* bakegoods; finere ~ pastry

balanse (bah-*lahng*-ser) *c* balance

balkong (bahl-*kongng*) *m* balcony; dress circle

ball (bahll) *m* ball; *nt* ball

ballett (bah-*lehtt*) *m* ballet

ballong (bah-*longng*) *m* balloon

banan (bah-*naan*) *m* banana

bandasje (bahn-*daa*-sher) *m* bandage

bande (bahn-der) *m* gang

bane (*baa*-ner) *m* track

bank (bahngk) *m* bank; *m/ nt* tap; *sette i banken* deposit

banke (*bahng*-ker) *v* knock, tap

bankett (bahng-*kehtt*) *m* banquet

bankhvelv (bahngk-vehlv) *nt* (pl ~) vault

bankkonto (*bahng*-kon-too) *m* (pl ~er, -ti) bank account

banne (*bahn*-ner) *v* curse, *swear

banner (*bahn*-nerr) *nt* (pl ~, ~e) banner

banning (*bahn*-ning) *c* curse

bar (baar) *adj* bare, naked; neat; *m* bar, saloon

barberblad (bahr-*bāyr*-blaa) *nt* (pl ~) razor blade

barbere seg (bahr-*bāy*-rer) shave

barberhøvel (bahr-*bair*-hur-verl) *m* (pl -vler) safety razor, razor

barberkost (bahr-*bāyr*-koost) *m* shaving brush

barbermaskin (bahr-*bāyr*-mah-sheen) *m* electric razor, shaver

barberskum (bahr-*bāyr*-skoomm) *nt* shaving foam

bare (*baarer*) *adv* only,

merely

bark (bahrk) *m* bark

barm (bahrm) *m* bosom

barmhjertig (bahrm-ʸæ-ti) *adj* merciful

barmhjertighet (bahrm-ʸæ-ti-hāyt) *c* mercy

barn (baan) *nt* child; kid; **foreldreløst** ~ orphan

barnebarn (baa-ner-baan) *nt* grandchild

barnehage (baa-ner-haa-ger) *m* kindergarten

barnepike (baa-ner-pee-ker) *m* nurse

barnevakt (baa-ner-vahkt) *c* babysitter

barnevogn (baa-ner-voangn) *c* pram; baby carriage *Am*

barneværelse (baa-ner-næ-vææ-rerl-ser) *nt* nursery

barokk (bah-rokk) *adj* baroque

barometer (bah-roo-māy-terr) *nt* (pl -tre) barometer

barriere (bah-ri-ǣæ-rer) *m* barrier; crash barrier

barsk (bahshk) *adj* bleak; tough

bart (bahtt) *m* moustache

bartender (baa-tehn-derr) *m* bartender

baryton (bahr-ri-ton) *m* baritone

basar (bah-saar) *m* fair

base (baa-ser) *m* base

basere (bah-sāy-rer) *v* base

basilika (bah-see-li-kah) *m* basilica

basill (bah-sill) *m* germ

basis (baa-siss) *m* basis, base

bass (bahss) *m* bass

bastard (bah-stahrd) *m* bastard

batteri (bah-ter-ree) *nt* battery

*be (bāy) *v* ask; beg; pray

bebo (beh-bōō) *v* inhabit

beboelig (beh-bōō-er-li) *adj* habitable, inhabitable

beboer (beh-bōō-err) *m* occupant, inhabitant

bebreide (beh-bray-der) *v* blame, reproach

bebreidelse (beh-bray-derl-ser) *m* blame, reproach

bedervelig (beh-dær-ver-li) *adj* perishable

*bedra (beh-draa) *v* deceive

bedrag (beh-draag) *nt* (pl ~) deceit

bedrageri (beh-drah-ger-ree) *nt* fraud

bedre (bāyd-rer) *adj* better; superior

bedrift (beh-drift) *m* concern; feat

bedring (bāyd-ring) *c* recovery

bedrøvelig (beh-drūr-ver-li) *adj* sad, dreary

bedrøvet (beh-drūr-vert) *adj* sad

bedyre (beh-dēw-rer) *v* affirm

bedømme (beh-durm-mer) *v* judge

bedøvelse (beh-dūr-verl-

beite

ser) *m* anaesthesia

bedøvelsesmiddel (beh-*dūr*-verl-serss-mi-derl) *nt* (pl -midler) anaesthetic

bedårende (beh-*daw*-rer-ner) *adj* enchanting

befale (beh-*faa*-ler) *v* command

befaling (beh-*faa*-ling) *c* order, command

befalshavende (beh-*faals*-haa-ver-ner) *m* commander

befolkning (beh-*folk*-ning) *m* population

befrielse (beh-*free*-erl-ser) *m* liberation

befruktning (beh-*frewkt*-ning) *m* conception; fertilization

begavelse (beh-*gaa*-verl-ser) *m* talent, faculty

begavet (beh-*gaa*-vert) *adj* gifted, talented; clever, brilliant

begeistret (beh-*gayss*-trert) *adj* keen, enthusiastic

begge (behg-ger) *pron* both; either

begivenhet (beh-*ʸee*-vern-hāyt) *c* event, happening

begjær (beh-*ʸæær*) *nt* desire; lust

begjære (beh-*ʸææ*-rer) *v* desire

begrave (beh-*graa*-ver) *v* bury

begravelse (beh-*graa*-verl-ser) *m* funeral; burial

begrense (beh-*grehn*-ser) *v* limit

begrenset (beh-*grehn*-sert) *adj* limited

begrep (beh-*grāyp*) *nt* notion, idea

*begripe** (beh-*gree*-per) *v* *see, *understand

begunstige (beh-*gewns*-ti-er) *v* favo(u)r

begynne (beh-*ʸewn*-ner) *v* start, commence, *begin; ~ igjen recommence

begynnelse (beh-*ʸewn*-nerl-ser) *m* beginning; i begynnelsen at first; originally

*begå** (beh-*gaw*) *v* commit

behagelig (beh-*haa*-ger-li) *adj* agreeable, pleasing, enjoyable

behandle (beh-*hahnd*-ler) *v* handle, treat

behandling (beh-*hahnd*-ling) *c* treatment

*beholde** (beh-*hol*-ler) *v* *keep

beholder (beh-*hol*-lerr) *m* container

behov (beh-*hōōv*) *nt* (pl ~) need; want

behøve (beh-*hūr*-ver) *v* need; demand

behå (beh-ho) *m* bra

beige (bāysh) *adj* beige

bein (bayn) *nt* (pl ~) leg; bone

beinskinne (*bāyn*-shi-ner) *c* splint

beite (*bay*-ter) *nt* pasture; *v* graze

bekjempe (beh-*khehm*-per) *v* combat

bekjenne (beh-*kheh*-ner) *v* confess

bekjent (beh-*khehnt*) *m* acquaintance

*bekjentgjøre (beh-*khehnt*-ȳūr-rer) *v* announce

bekjentgjørelse (beh-*khehnt*-ȳūr-rerl-ser) *m* announcement; bulletin

bekk (behkk) *m* stream, brook

bekken (*behk*-kern) *nt* pelvis

beklage (beh-*klaager*) *v* regret

beklagelse (beh-*klaa*-gerl-ser) *m* regret

beklager! (beh-*klaa*-gerr) sorry!

bekrefte (beh-*krehf*-ter) *v* confirm; acknowledge; affirm

bekreftelse (beh-*krehf*-terl-ser) *m* confirmation

bekreftende (beh-*krayf*-ter-ner) *adj* affirmative

bekvem (beh-*kvehmm*) *adj* comfortable; easy, convenient

bekvemmelighet (beh-*kvehm*-mer-li-hȳayt) *c* comfort

bekymre seg (beh-*khewm*-rer) worry; **bekymre seg om** care about

bekymret (beh-*khewm*-rert) *adj* concerned, worried

bekymring (beh-*khewm*-ring) *c* anxiety, worry; concern, care

belastning (beh-*lahst*-ning) *m* load, strain

beleilig (beh-*lay*-li) *adj* convenient

beleiring (beh-*lay*-ring) *c* siege

Belgia (*behl*-gi-ah) Belgium

belgier (*behl*-gi-err) *m* Belgian

belgisk (*behl*-gisk) *adj* Belgian

beliggende (beh-*lig*-ger-ner) *adj* situated

beliggenhet (beh-*lig*-gern-hȳayt) *c* location, site

belte (*behl*-ter) *nt* belt

belyse (beh-*lȳew*-ser) *v* illuminate

belysning (beh-*lȳewss*-ning) *m* lighting, illumination

belønne (beh-*lurn*-ner) *v* reward

belønning (beh-*lurn*-ning) *c* reward; prize

beløp (beh-*lȳūrp*) *nt* (pl ∼) amount

*beløpe seg til (beh-*lȳūr*-per) amount to

bemerke (beh-*mær*-ker) *v* note, notice; remark

bemerkelsesverdig (beh-*mær*-kerl-serss-vær-di) *adj* noticeable, remarkable

bemerkning (beh-*mærk*-ning) *m* remark

benekte (beh-*nehk*-ter) *v* deny

benektende (beh-*nehk*-ter-ner) *adj* negative

benevnelse (beh-*nehv*-nerl-ser) *m* name, designation, denomination

benk (behngk) *m* bench

bensin (behn-*seen*) *m* fuel, petrol; gas *nAm*, gasoline *nAm*; **blyfri ~** unleaded petrol

bensinpumpe (behn-*seen*-poom-per) *c* petrol pump; fuel pump *Am*

bensinstasjon (behn-*seen*-stah-*shōōn*) *m* service station, petrol station, filling station; gas station *Am*

bensintank (behn-*seen*-tahngk) *m* petrol tank, gas tank *Am*

benytte (beh-*newt*-ter) *v* use, make use of

benådning (beh-*nawd*-ning) *m* pardon

beordre (beh-*or*-drer) *v* order

beredt (beh-*reht*) *adj* prepared

beregne (beh-*ray*-ner) *v* calculate

berettiget (beh-*reht*-ti-ert) *adj* justified

berg (bærg) *nt* mountain

berglendt (*bærg*-lehnt) *adj* mountainous

berolige (beh-*rōō*-li-er) *v* reassure, calm down

beroligende (beh-*rōō*-li-er-ner) *adj* restful; **~ middel** sedative, tranquillizer

bero på (beh-*rōō*) depend on

beruset (beh-*rēw*-sert) *adj* intoxicated, drunk

beryktet (beh-*rewk*-tert) *adj* notorious

berømmelse (beh-*rurm*-merl-ser) *m* fame, glory, celebrity

berømt (beh-*rurmt*) *adj* famous

berøre (beh-*rūr*-rer) *v* touch

berøring (beh-*rūr*-ring) *c* touch

besatt (beh-*sahtt*) *adj* possessed

beseire (beh-*say*-rer) *v* conquer

***besette** (beh-*seht*-ter) *v* occupy

besettelse (beh-*seht*-terl-ser) *m* obsession

besittelse (beh-*sit*-terl-ser) *m* possession

beskatning (beh-*skaht*-ning) *m* taxation

beskjed (beh-*shēr*) *m* message

beskjeden (beh-*shāy*-dern) *adj* modest

beskjedenhet (beh-*shāy*-dern-hāyt) *c* modesty

beskjeftige (beh-*shehf*-ti-er) *v* employ, occupy

beskjeftigelse (beh-*shehf*-ti-erl-ser) *m* employment, occupation

***beskrive** (beh-*skree*-ver) *v* describe

beskrivelse (beh-*skree*-

beskylde

verl-ser) *m* description

beskylde (beh-*shewl*-ler) *v* accuse

beskytte (beh-*shewt*-ter) *v* protect

beskyttelse (beh-*shewt*-terl-ser) *m* protection

*beslaglegge (beh-*shlaag*-leh-ger) *v* confiscate

beslektet (beh-*shlehk*-tert) *adj* related

beslutning (beh-*shlewt*-ning) *m* decision

beslutsom (beh-*shlewt*-som) *adj* resolute

best (behst) *adj* best

bestanddel (beh-*stahn*-dāyl) *m* element, ingredient

bestefar (*behss*-ter-faar) *m* (pl -fedre) grandfather, granddad

besteforeldre (*behss*-ter-fo-rehl-drer) *pl* grandparents *pl*

bestemme (beh-*stehm*-mer) *v* define, determine; designate, destine

bestemmelse (beh-*stehm*-merl-ser) *m* regulation

bestemmelsessted (beh-*stehm*-merl-serss-stāy) *nt* destination

bestemor (*behss*-ter-mōōr) *m* (pl -mødre) grandmother

bestemt (beh-*stehmt*) *adj* definite; resolute

*bestige (beh-*stee*-ger) *v* ascend; mount

bestikk (beh-*stikk*) *nt* cutlery; silverware *nAm*

*bestikke (beh-*stik*-ker) *v* corrupt, bribe

bestikkelse (beh-*stik*-kerl-ser) *m* corruption, bribery; bribe

bestille (beh-*stil*-ler) *v* order; book, engage, reserve

bestilling (beh-*stil*-ling) *c* order; booking; laget på ~ made to order

bestrebelse (beh-*strāy*-berl-ser) *m* effort

*bestride (beh-*stree*-der) *v* dispute

bestyre (beh-*stēw*-rer) *v* manage

bestyrer (beh-*stew*-rer) *m* manager

bestå (beh-*staw*) *v* exist; pass a test; ~ av consist of

besvare (beh-*svaa*-rer) *v* answer

besvime (beh-*svee*-mer) *v* faint

besvær (beh-*svæær*) *nt* trouble, inconvenience

besværlig (beh-*svææ*-li) *adj* inconvenient

besøk (beh-*sūrk*) *nt* (pl ~) call, visit

besøke (beh-*sūr*-ker) *v* call on, visit

besøkende (beh-*sūr*-ker-ner) *m* visitor

besøkstid (beh-*sūrks*-teed) *c* visiting hours

betagende (beh-*taa*-ger-

ner) *adj* moving; beautiful
betalbar (beh-*taal*-bahr) *adj*
due; payable
betale (beh-*taa*-ler) *v* *pay
betaling (beh-*taa*-ling) *c*
payment
betegnende (beh-*tay*-ner-
ner) *adj* characteristic
betenkt (beh-*tehngkt*) *adj*
uneasy
betennelse (beh-*tehn*-nerl-
ser) *m* inflammation; *gå ~
i *become septic
betingelse (beh-*ting*-ngerl-
ser) *m* term; stipulation
betingelsesløs (beh-*ting*-
ngerl-serss-*lûrss*) *adj*
unconditional
betinget (beh-*ting*-ngert)
adj conditional
betjene (beh-*t^yay*-ner) *v*
attend on; serve
betjening (beh-*t^yay*-ning) *c*
service
betong (beh-*tongng*) *m*
concrete
betoning (beh-*tōō*-ning) *c*
accent
betrakte (beh-*trahk*-ter) *v*
consider, regard; view,
watch; **i betraktning av**
considering
betraktelig (beh-*trahk*-ter-
li) *adj* considerable
betro (beh-*trōō*) *v* confide
in
betvile (beh-*tvee*-ler) *v*
query, doubt
bety (beh-*tēw*) *v* *mean
betydelig (beh-*tēw*-der-li)

adj considerable
betydning (beh-*tēwd*-ning)
m sense; importance;
*være av ~ matter
betydningsfull (beh-*tēwd*-
nings-fewl) *adj* important;
significant
beundre (beh-*ewn*-drer) *v*
admire
beundrer (beh-*ewn*-drerr)
m fan
beundring (beh-*ewn*-dring)
c admiration
bevare (beh-*vaa*-rer) *v*
*keep; *uphold
bevege (beh-*vāy*-ger) *v*
move
bevegelig (beh-*vāy*-ger-li)
adj mobile
bevegelse (beh-*vāy*-gerl-
ser) *m* motion, movement
bever (*bāy*-verr) *m* beaver
beverte (beh-*væ*-ter) *v*
entertain, treat
bevilge (beh-*veel*-ger) *v*
extend, grant; allow
bevis (beh-*veess*) *nt* proof,
evidence; token
bevise (beh-*vee*-ser) *v*
prove; demonstrate, *show
bevisst (beh-*vist*) *adj*
conscious
bevissthet (beh-*vist*-hāyt) *c*
consciousness
bevisstløs (beh-*vist*-lûrss)
adj unconscious
bevitne (beh-*vit*-ne) *v* attest
bevokte (beh-*vok*-ter) *v*
watch, guard
bevæpne (beh-*vāyp*-ner) *v*

arm
bevæpnet (beh-*vayp*-nert)
adj armed
bibel (*bee*-berl) *m* (pl
bibler) bible
bibliotek (bi-bli-oo-*tayk*) *nt*
library
bidrag (*bee*-draag) *nt* (pl ~)
contribution; allowance
bie (*bee*-er) *c* bee
bielv (*bee*-ehlv) *c* tributary
bifalle (*bee*-fah-ler) *v*
consent; applaud
biff (bif) *m* steak
bikube (*bee*-kew-ber) *m*
beehive
bil (beel) *m* automobile, car
bilde (*bil*-der) *nt* picture,
image
bildemelding (*bil*-der-
mehl-ling) *c* photo
message
bile (*bee*-ler) *v* motor
bilhorn (*beel*-hoon) *nt* (pl ~)
hooter
bilisme (bi-*liss*-mer) *m*
motoring
bilist (bi-*list*) *m* motorist
biljard (bil-*yaad*) *m* billiards
pl
bille (*bil*-ler) *m* beetle; bug
billedhogger (*bil*-lerd-ho-
gerr) *m* sculptor
billett (bi-*lehtt*) *m* ticket
billettautomat (bi-*lehtt*-ou-
too-maat) *m* ticket
machine
billettkontor (bi-*leht*-koon-
toor) *nt* box office
billettluke (bi-*leht*-lew-ker)

c box office window
billettpris (bi-*leht*-preess) *m*
fare; admission fee
billig (*bil*-li) *adj* cheap,
inexpensive
billigbok (*bil*-li-book) *c*
paperback
bilpanser (*beel*-pahn-serr)
nt bonnet; hood *nAm*
bilran (*beel*-rahn) *c*
carjacking
bilutleie (*beel*-oot-lay-er) *c*
car hire; car rental *Am*
bind (binn) *nt* volume;
sanitary napkin *Am*,
sanitary towel
***binde** (*bin*-ner) *v* **bind;
tie; ~ sammen bundle
bindestrek (*bin*-ner-strayk)
m hyphen
biologi (bi-oo-loo-*gee*) *m*
biology
biologisk nedbrytbar (bee-
oo-*loo*-isk nayd-*brewt*-
bahr) *adj* biodegradable
bipolar (bee-poo-*laar*) *adj*
bipolar
biskop (*biss*-kop) *m* bishop
***bistå** (*bee*-staw) *v* assist,
aid
bit (beet) *m* bit, piece; scrap,
morsel; bite
***bite** (*bee*-ter) *v* **bite
bitter (*bit*-terr) *adj* bitter
bjelke (*b*ʸ*ehl*-ker) *m* beam
bjelle (*b*ʸ*ehl*-ler) *c* small
bell
bjørk (b*y*urrk) *c* birch
bjørn (b*y*ūrn) *m* bear
bjørnebær (*b*ʸ*ūr*-ner-bæær)

nt (pl ~) blackberry

Blackberry® (*blæk-bahr-ēē*) *c* Blackberry®

blad (blaa) *nt* leaf; blade

bladgull (*blaa-gewl*) *nt* gold leaf

bladsalat (*blaa-sah-laht*) *m* lettuce

blakk (blahkk) *adj* broke

blande (*blahn-ner*) *v* mix; ~ **seg inn** I interfere with

blandet (*blahn-nert*) *adj* mixed

blanding (*blahn-ning*) *c* mixture

blank (blahngk) *adj* glossy; blank

blankett (blahng-*kehtt*) *m* form

blant (blahnt) *prep* amid; among; ~ **annet** among other things

bleie (*blay-er*) *c* nappy; diaper *nAm*

blek (blāyk) *adj* pale

bleke (*blāy-ker*) *v* bleach

blekk (blehkk) *nt* ink

blekksprut (*blehk-sprēwt*) *m* octopus

blekne (*blāyk-ner*) *v* fade; *grow pale

blemme (*blehm-mer*) *c* blister

blende (*blehn-ner*) *v* blind

blendende (*blehn-ner-ner*) *adj* glaring

***bli** (blee) *v* *become, *be, *get, *grow; stay; ~ **igjen** remain

blikk (blikk) *nt* glance, look;

kaste et ~ glance

blind (blinn) *adj* blind

blindgate (*blin-gaa-ter*) *c* cul-de-sac

blindtarm (*blin-tahrm*) *m* appendix

blindtarmbetennelse (*blin-tahrm-beh-teh-nerl-ser*) *c* appendicitis

blinklys (*blingk-lēwss*) *nt* (pl ~) trafficator; blinker *nAm*

blitzlampe (*blits-lahm-per*) *c* flash bulb

blod (blōō) *nt* blood

blodforgiftning (*blōō-for-ʸift-ning*) *m* blood poisoning

blodkar (*blōō-kaar*) *nt* (pl ~) blood vessel

blodomløp (*blōō-oom-lūrp*) *nt* (pl ~) circulation

blodtrykk (*blōō-trewk*) *nt* (pl ~) blood pressure

blogg (blawg) *c* blog

blokk (blokk) *c* block

blokkere (blo-*kāy-rer*) *v* block

blomkål (*blom-kawl*) *m* cauliflower

blomst (blomst) *m* flower, blossom

blomsterbed (*blom-sterr-behd*) *nt* (pl ~) flowerbed

blomsterforretning (*blom-sterr-for-reht-ning*) *c* flower shop

blomsterhandler (*blom-sterr-hahnd-lerr*) *m* florist

blomsterløk (*blom-sterr-*

lūrk) *m* bulb

blomstre (*blom*-strer) *v* flower, blossom

blond (blonn) *adj* fair, blond

blondine (blon-*dee*-ner) *c* blonde

*****blottlegge** (*blott*-leh-ger) *v* expose

bluse (*blēw*-ser) *c* blouse

bly (blēw) *nt* lead

blyant (*blēw*-ahnt) *m* pencil

blyantspisser (*blēw*-ahnt-spi-serr) *m* pencil sharpener

blyg (blēwg) *adj* timid

blære (*blææ*-rer) *c* bladder

blø (blūr) *v* *****bleed

blødning (*blūrd*-ning) *m* h(a)emorrhage

bløt (blūrt) *adj* mellow

bløte (*blūr*-ter) *v* soak

*****bløtgjøre** (*blūrt*-ȳūr-rer) *v* soften

blå (blaw) *adj* blue; **blått merke** bruise

blåse (*blaw*-ser) *v* *****blow; ~ **opp** inflate

blåsende (*blaw*-ser-ner) *adj* gusty

blåskjell (*blo*-shehl) *nt* (pl ~) mussel

bo (bōō) *v* live, reside

bobil (*bōō*-beel) *m* camper, caravan

boble (*bob*-ler) *c* bubble

bok (bōōk) *c* (pl bøker) book

bokbind (*bōōk*-bin) *nt* (pl ~) binding

bokføre (*bōōk*-fūr-rer) *v* enter, book

bokhandel (*bōōk*-hahn-derl) *m* (pl -dler) bookstore

bokhandler (*bōōk*-hahnd-lerr) *m* bookseller

boks (boks) *m* can, tin

bokse (*bok*-ser) *v* box

boksekamp (*bok*-ser-kahmp) *m* boxing match

bokstav (book-*staav*) *m* letter; **stor** ~ capital letter

boksåpner (*boks*-awp-nerr) *m* can opener

bolig (*bōō*-li) *m* house, residence

Bolivia (boo-*lee*-vi-ah) Bolivia

bolivianer (boo-li-vi-*aa*-nerr) *m* Bolivian

boliviansk (boo-li-vi-*aansk*) *adj* Bolivian

bolle (*bol*-ler) *m* bowl; basin; bun

bolt (bolt) *m* bolt

bom (boomm) *m* barrier; miss

bombardere (boom-bah-*dāy*-rer) *v* bomb

bombe (*boom*-ber) *c* bomb

bomme (*boom*-mer) *v* miss

bompenger (*boomm*-peh-ngerr) *pl* toll

bomull (*boom*-mewl) *m* cotton; **bomulls-** cotton

bomullsfløyel (*boom*-mewls-flur^ew-erl) *m* velveteen

bomvei (*boom*-vay) *m*

turnpike *nAm*

bonde (*boon*-ner) *m* (pl bønder) peasant, farmer

bondegård (*boon*-ner-gawr) *m* farm

bondekone (*boon*-ner-kōō-ner) *c* farmer's wife

bong (bong) *m* voucher

bopel (*bōō*-payl) *m* domicile

bor (borr) *nt* drill

bord (bōōr) *nt* table

bordell (boo-*dehll*) *m*/*nt* brothel

bordtennis (*bōō*-teh-niss) *m* ping-pong, table tennis

bore (*bōō*-rer) *v* bore, drill; ~plattform drilling platform

borg (borg) *c* castle

borger (*bor*-gerr) *m* citizen; borger- civic

borgerlig (*bor*-ger-li) *adj* middle-class

borgermester (*bor*-ger-mehss-terr) *m* (pl -tre) mayor

bort (boott) *adv* away; *gå ~ *leave, *go away

borte (*boot*-ter) *adv* gone; off

bortenfor (*boot*-tern-for) *adv* beyond; *prep* off; beyond

bortsett fra (*boot*-seht) apart from

bosatt (*bōō*-saht) *adj* resident

boss (boss) *m* boss

bot (bōōt) *c* (pl bøter) fine

botanikk (boo-tah-*nikk*) *m* botany

botemiddel (*bōō*-ter-mi-derl) *nt* (pl -midler) remedy

bowlingbane (*bov*-ling-baa-ner) *m* bowling alley

bra (braa) *adj* good; *colloquial* super; bra! all right!

brann (brahn) *m* fire

brannalarm (*brahn*-nah-lahrm) *m* fire alarm

brannmann (*brahn*-mahn) *m* firefighter

brannmannskap (*brahn*-mahn-skaap) *nt* firefighter

brannmur (*brahn*-mēwr) *c* firewall

brannsikker (*brahn*-si-kerr) *adj* fireproof

brannslokker (*brahn*-shloo-kerr) *m* fire extinguisher

brannsår (*brahn*-sawr) *nt* (pl ~) burn

branntrapp (*brahn*-trahp) *c* fire escape

brannvesen (*brahn*-vāy-sern) *nt* fire brigade

Brasil (brah-*seel*) Brazil

brasilianer (brah-si-li-*aa*-nerr) *m* Brazilian

brasiliansk (brah-si-li-*aansk*) *adj* Brazilian

bratt (brahtt) *adj* steep

bred (brāy) *adj* wide, broad

bredbånd (*brehd*-bawn) *nt* broadband

bredd (brehdd) *m* shore, bank; embankment

bredde (*brehd*-der) *m*
width, breadth

breddegrad (*brehd*-der-graad) *m* latitude

*brekke (brehk-ker) *v*
fracture; ~ seg vomit

brekkjern (*brehk-*ʸæn) *nt*
crowbar

bremse (*brehm*-ser) *c*
brake; *v* slow down

bremselys (*brehm*-ser-lēwss) *pl* brake lights

bremsetrommel (*brehm*-ser-troo-merl) *m* (pl -tromler) brake drum

*brenne (*brehn*-ner) *v*
*burn

brennemerke (*brehn*-ner-mær-ker) *nt* brand; stigma

brennpunkt (*brehn*-poongkt) *nt* focus

brensel (*brehn*-sherl) *nt*
fuel

brenselolje (*brehn*-sherl-ol-ʸer) *c* fuel oil

brett (brehtt) *nt* tray

brette (*breht*-ter) *v* fold; ~ ut
unfold

brev (*brāyv*) *nt* letter;
rekommandert ~
registered letter

brevpapir (*brāyv*-pah-peer) *nt* notepaper

brevveksle (*brāyvehk*-shler) *v* correspond

brevveksling (*brāyvehk*-shling) *c* correspondence

brikke (*brik*-ker) *c* chip;
piece

briller (*bril*-lerr) *pl*

spectacles, glasses

*bringe (*bring*-nger) *v*
*bring; ~ tilbake *bring
back

bringebær (*bring*-nger-bæær) *nt* (pl ~) raspberry

bris (breess) *m* breeze

*briste (*briss*-ter) *v* *burst

brite (*brit*-ter) *m* Briton

britisk (*brit*-tisk) *adj* British

bro (brōō) *c* bridge

brodere (broo-*dāy*-rer) *v*
embroider

broderi (broo-der-*ree*) *nt*
embroidery

brokk (brokk) *m/nt* hernia

*brolegge (*brōō*-leh-ger) *v*
pave

bronkitt (broong-*kitt*) *c*
bronchitis

bronse (*brong*-sher) *m*
bronze; bronse- bronze

bror (brōōr) *m* (pl brødre)
brother

brorskap (*brōōsh*-kaap) *m/ nt* fraternity, brotherhood

brosje (*brosh*-sher) *c*
brooch

brosjyre (bro-*shēw*-rer) *c*
brochure

brud (brēwd) *c* bride

brudd (brewdd) *nt* fracture,
break

bruddstykke (*brewd*-stew-ker) *nt* fragment

brudgom (*brewd*-gom) *m*
(pl ~mer) groom,
bridegroom

bruk (brewk) *m* use

brukbar (*brēwk*-baar) *adj*

useful

bruke (brew-ker) v apply, use; *spend; ~ opp use up

bruker (brew-kerr) m user

bruksanvisning (brewks-ahn-viss-ning) m directions for use

brukt (brewkt) adj second-hand

brumme (broom-mer) v growl

brun (brewn) adj brown; tanned

brunette (brew-neht-ter) m brunette

brunfarge (brewn-fahr-ger) m suntan

brus (brewss) m fizz; m lemonade; soft drink Am

bruse (brew-ser) v roar

brusk (brewsk) m cartilage

brutal (broo-taal) adj brutal

brutto (brewt-too) adj gross

bry (brew) v trouble; bother; ~ seg bother; ~ seg om mind; care for

brydd (brewdd) adj embarrassed; *gjøre ~ embarrass

brygge (brewg-ger) v brew

bryggeri (brew-ger-ree) nt brewery

bryllup (brewl-lewp) nt wedding

bryllupsdag (brewl-lewps-daag) m anniversary

bryllupsreise (brewl-lewps-ray-ser) c honeymoon

brysom (brew-som) adj

bryst (brewst) nt chest,

breast; bosom

brystholder (brewst-ho-lerr) m bra

brystkasse (brewst-kah-ser) c chest

brystsvømming (brewst-svur-ming) c breaststroke

*bryte (brew-ter) v *break; ~ sammen collapse

bryter (brew-terr) m switch

brød (brur) nt bread; loaf; ristet ~ toast

brøkdel (brurk-dayl) m fraction

brøl (brurl) nt roar

brøle (brur-ler) v roar

brønn (brurnn) m well

bråk (brawk) nt din; fuss

bu (bew) c booth

bud (bewd) nt messenger; bid; sende ~ etter *send for

budsjett (bewd-shehtt) nt budget

bue (bew-er) m bow; arch

bueformet (bew-er-for-mert) adj arched

buegang (bew-er-gahng) m arcade

buet (bew-ert) adj curved

bukett (bew-kehtt) m bouquet, bunch

bukk (bookk) m buck

bukke (book-ker) v bow; ~ under succumb

bukse (book-ser) c trousers pl; pants plAm

buksedrakt (book-ser-drahkt) c pant suit

buksedress (book-serdrehss) *m* pant suit

bukseseler (*book*-ser-sāȳ-lerr) *pl* braces *pl*; suspenders *plAm*

buksesmekk (*book*-ser-smehk) *m* fly

bukt (bookt) *c* bay

buktet (*book*-tert) *adj* winding

bulder (*bewl*-derr) *nt* noise

bulgarer (bewl-*gaa*-rerr) *m* Bulgarian

Bulgaria (bewl-*gaa*-ri-ah) Bulgaria

bulgarsk (bewl-*gaashk*) *adj* Bulgarian

bulk (bewlk) *m* dent

bunad (*boo*-nahd) *m* (Norwegian) national costume, national dress

bunke (*boong*-ker) *m* batch

bunn (bewnn) *m* bottom

bunnfall (bewn-fahl) *nt* (pl ~) deposit; sediment

bunt (bewnt) *m* bundle

bunte (*bewn*-ter) *v* bundle

buntmaker (*bewnt*-maa-kerr) *m* furrier

bur (bēw) *nt* cage

***burde** (bēw-der) *v* *ought to

busk (bewsk) *m* bush; shrub

buss (bewss) *m* bus; coach

butikk (bew-*tikk*) *m* shop; boutique

butikkeier (bew-*tikk*-ay-err) *m* tradeswoman, tradesman

butikkselger (bew-*tikk*-sehl-gerr) *m* shop assistant

butt (bewtt) *adj* blunt

by (bēw) *m* town, city; by-urban

***by** (bēw) *v* bid

byfolk (*bēw*-folk) *pl* townspeople *pl*

bygd (bewgd) *c* village

bygg (bewgg) *nt* barley; building

bygge (*bewg*-ger) *v* construct, *build

byggekunst (*bewg*-ger-kewnst) *m* architecture

bygning (*bewg*-ning) *m* construction, building

byll (bewll) *m* abscess, boil

byrde (*bewrr*-der) *m* burden; charge

byrå (bew-*raw*) *nt* agency

byråkrati (bew-ro-krah-*tee*) *nt* bureaucracy

byste (*bewss*-ter) *c* bust

bytte (*bewt*-ter) *v* exchange, swap; *nt* exchange

bær (bæær) *nt* berry

bærbar PC (*bæær*-baar peh-seh) *c* laptop

***bære** (*bææ*-rer) *v* carry, *bear; support

bærer (*bææ*-rerr) *m* porter

bøddel (*burd*-derl) *m* (pl bødler) executioner

bøk (būrk) *m* beech

bølge (*burl*-ger) *c* wave

bølgelengde (*burl*-ger-lehng-der) *c* wave-length

bølget (*burl*-gert) *adj* wavy

bølle (*burl*-ler) *m* brute

bøllete (*burl*-ler-ter) *adj* rowdy

bønn (burnn) *m* prayer

bønne (*burn*-ner) *v* beg

*bønnfalle (*burn*-fah-ler) *v* beg

bør (būrr) *c* load

børs (būrsh) *m* stock exchange

børste (*bursh*-ter) *v* brush; *m* brush

bøyd (bur^{ew}d) *adj* bent

bøye (*burew*-er) *v* *bend; *m* buoy; ~ seg *bend down

bøyelig (*burew*-er-li) *adj* flexible, supple

bøyning (*burew*-ning) *m* bend

både ... og (*baw*-der aw) both ... and

bål (bawl) *nt* bonfire

bånd (bonn) *nt* band; ribbon; tape; leash

bås (bawss) *m* booth

båt (bawt) *m* boat

C

campe (kæm-*per*) *v* camp

camping (*kæm*-ping) *m* camping

campinggjest (*kæm*-ping-^yehst) *m* camper

campingplass (*kæm*-ping-plahss) *m* camping site

campingvogn (*kæm*-ping-vongn) *c* caravan; trailer n*Am*

Canada (*kahn*-nah-dah) Canada

CD (*seh*-deh) *m* CD

CD-ROM (seh-deh-*romm*) *m* CD-ROM

CD-spiller (*seh*-deh-spil-ler) *c* CD player

celle (*sehl*-ler) *c* cell

cello (*chel*-lo, *sel*-lo) *m* cello

celsius (*sehl*-si-ewss) centigrade

cembalo (*shehm*-bah-loo) *m* harpsichord

centimeter (*sehn*-ti-māy-

terr) *m* (pl ~) centimeter *Am*, centimetre

champagne (shahm-*pahn*-^yer) *m* champagne

charterflygning (chaa-terr-flēwg-ning) *m* charter flight

Chile (*chee*-ler) Chile

chilener (chi-*lāy*-nerr) *m* Chilean

chilensk (chi-*lāynsk*) *adj* Chilean

cirka (*seer*-kah) *adv* approximately

clutch (klurch) *m* clutch

cocktail (*kok*-tayl) *m* cocktail

Colombia (koo-*loom*-bi-ah) Colombia

colombianer (koo-loom-bi-aa-nerr) *m* Colombian

colombiansk (koo-loom-bi-aansk) *adj* Colombian

container (koon-*tay*-nerr)

m container
cricket (*kri*-kertt) *m* cricket
cruise (krēwss) *nt* (pl ~)

cruise
Cuba (*kēw*-bah) Cuba

D

da (daa) *conj* when; *adv*
then
daddel (*dahd*-derl) *m* (pl
dadler) date
dag (daag) *m* day; i ~ today;
om dagen by day; per ~
per day
dagbok (*daag*-bōōk) *c* (pl
-bøker) diary
daggry (*daa*-grēw) *nt*
daybreak, dawn
daglig (*daag*-li) *adj*
everyday, daily
dagligdags (*daag*-li-dahks)
adj ordinary
dagligstue (*daag*-li-stēw-er)
c living room
dagsavis (*dahks*-ahveess) *c*
daily newspaper
dagslys (*dahks*-lēwss) *nt*
daylight
dagsorden (*dahk*-so-dern)
m agenda
dagspa (*daag*-spaa) *c* day
spa
dagstur (*dahks*-tēwr) *m* day
trip
dal (daal) *m* valley
dam (dahmm) *m* (pl ~mer)
pond; pool
dame (*daa*-mer) *c* lady
dameundertøy (*daa*-mer-
ew-ner-tur^(ew)) *nt* lingerie

damp (dahmp) *m* steam,
vapo(u)r
dampskip (*dahmp*-sheep)
nt (pl ~) steamer
damspill (*dahm*-spil) *nt* (pl
~) draughts; checkers
plAm
Danmark (*dahn*-mahrk)
Denmark
dans (dahns) *m* dance
danse (*dahn*-ser) *v* dance
dansk (dahnsk) *adj* Danish
danske (*dahn*-sker) *m* Dane
dask (dahsk) *m* smack
datamaskin (*daa*-tah-mah-
sheen) *m* computer
dato (*daa*-too) *m* date
datter (*daht*-terr) *c* (pl
døtre) daughter
de (dee) *pron pl* (c den, nt
det) those, they
debatt (deh-*baht*) *m* debate,
discussion
debattere (deh-bah-*tāy*-rer)
v argue, discuss
debet (*dāy*-bert) *m* debit
debetkort (*dāy*-bert-kott) *nt*
debit card
defekt (deh-*fehkt*) *m* fault;
adj faulty
definere (deh-fi-*nāy*-rer) *v*
define
definisjon (deh-fi-ni-shōōn)

m definition

deg (day) *pron* yourself; you

deig (day) *m* batter, dough

deilig (*day*-li) *adj* enjoyable, delicious; pleasant

dekk (dehkk) *nt* tire, tyre; deck; øverste ~ main deck

dekke (*dehk*-ker) *v* cover

deklarasjon (dehk-lah-rah-*shōōn*) *m* declaration

deklarere (dehk-lah-*rāy*-rer) *v* declare

dekorasjon (deh-koo-rah-*shōōn*) *m* decoration

del (dāyl) *m* part; share

dele (*dāy*-ler) *v* divide; share; ~ seg fork; ~ ut *deal

delegasjon (deh-leh-gah-*shōōn*) *m* delegation

delikat (deh-li-*kaat*) *adj* delicate

delikatesse (deh-li-kah-*tehss*-ser) *m* delicatessen

deling (*dāy*-ling) *c* division

*delta** (*dāyl*-taa) *v* participate

deltakelse (*dāyl*-taa-kerl-ser) *m* participation

deltakende (*dāyl*-taa-ker-ner) *adj* sympathetic

deltaker (*dāyl*-taa-kerr) *m* participant

delvis (*dāyl*-veess) *adv* partly; *adj* partial

dem (dehmm) *pron* them

demning (*dehm*-ning) *m* dam; dike

demokrati (deh-moo-krah-*tee*) *nt* democracy

demokratisk (deh-moo-*kraa*-tisk) *adj* democratic

demonstrasjon (deh-moon-strah-*shōōn*) *m* demonstration

demonstrere (deh-moon-*strāy*-rer) *v* demonstrate

den (dehnn) *pron* (nt det, pl de) it; that

denne (*dehn*-ner) *pron* (nt dette) this; *adj* this

dens (dehnns) *pron* its

deodorant (deh-oo-doo-*rahnt*) *m* deodorant

departement (deh-pah-ter-*mahngng*) *nt* department; ministry

deponere (deh-poo-*nāy*-rer) *v* deposit

depositum (deh-*pōō*-si-tewm) *nt* (pl -ta) deposit

depresjon (deh-preh-*shōōn*) *m* depression

deprimere (deh-pri-*māy*-rer) *v* depress

deprimerende (deh-pri-*māy*-rer-ner) *adj* depressing

deprimert (deh-pri-*māyt*) *adj* depressed

deputert (deh-pew-*tāyt*) *m* deputy

der (dær) *adv* there; ~ borte over there

dere (*dāy*-rer) *pron* you, yourselves

deres (*dāy*-rerss) *pron* your, yours; their, theirs

derfor (*dær*-for) *adv* therefore

dersom (*dæ*-shom) *conj* if, in case

desember (deh-*sehm*-berr) December

desertere (deh-sæ-*tāy*-rer) *v* desert

desimalsystem (deh-si-*maal*-sewss-*tāym*) *nt* decimal system

desinfisere (dehss-sin-fi-*sāy*-rer) *v* disinfect; **desinfiserende middel** disinfectant

dessert (deh-*sæær*) *m* dessert; sweet

dessuten (deh-*sēw*-tern) *adv* moreover, also, furthermore, besides

dessverre (dehss-*væ*-rer) *adv* unfortunately

det (dāy) *pron* (c den, pl de) it; that

detalj (deh-*tahlʸ*) *m* detail

detaljert (deh-tahl-*ʸāyt*) *adj* detailed

detaljhandel (deh-*tahlʸ*-hahn-derl) *m* (pl -dler) retail trade

detektiv (*deht*-tehk-teev) *m* detective

dets (dehts) *pron* its

devaluere (deh-vah-lew-*āy*-rer) *v* devalue

devaluering (deh-vah-lew-*āy*-ring) *c* devaluation

diabetes (di-ah-*bāy*-terss) *m* diabetes

diabetiker (di-ah-*bāy*-ti-kerr) *m* diabetic

diagnose (di-ahg-*nōō*-ser) *m* diagnosis; **stille en ~** diagnose

diagonal (di-ah-goo-*naal*) *m* diagonal; *adj* diagonal

diagram (di-ah-*grahm*) *nt* (pl ⁓mer) chart, graph, diagram

dialekt (di-ah-*lehkt*) *m* dialect

diamant (di-ah-*mahnt*) *m* diamond

diaré (di-ah-*rāy*) *m* diarrh(o)ea

diesel (*dee*-serl) *m* diesel

diett (di-*ehtt*) *m* diet

difteri (dif-ter-*ree*) *m* diphtheria

digital (di-gī-*tahl*) *adj* digital

digital prosjektor (di-gī-*tahl* proo-*shek*-turr) *c* digital projector

digitalbilde (di-gī-*tahl*-bil-der) *nt* digital photo

digitalkamera (di-gī-*tahl*-kaa-mer-rah) *nt* digital camera

dikt (dikt) *nt* poem

diktator (dik-*taa*-toor) *m* dictator

dikter (*dik*-terr) *m* poet

diktere (dik-*tāy*-rer) *v* dictate

dimensjon (di-mehn-*shōōn*) *m* size; dimension

din (deen) *pron* your, yours

dine (*dee*-ner) *pron* your, yours

diplom (di-*plōōm*) *nt* certificate, diploma

dose

diplomat (dip-loo-*maat*) *m*
diplomat

direksjon (deer-ehk-*shoon*)
m board of directors

direkte (di-*rehk*-ter) *adj*
direct

direktiv (di-rehk-*teev*) *nt*
directive; direction

direktør (di-rehk-*türr*) *m*
executive, manager,
director

dirigent (di-ri-*gehnt*) *m*
conductor

dirigere (di-ri-*gay*-rer) *v*
conduct

dirre (*deer*-rer) *v* tremble

dis (deess) *m* mist, haze

disig (*dee*-si) *adj* hazy;
misty

disiplin (di-si-*pleen*) *m*
discipline

disk (disk) *m* counter

diskonto (diss-*kon*-too) *m*
bank rate

diskstasjon (disk-stah-
shoon) *c* disk drive

diskusjon (diss-kew-*shoon*)
m discussion; argument

diskutere (diss-kew-*tay*-rer)
v discuss; argue

disponibel (diss-poo-*nee*-
berl) *adj* available

disposisjon (diss-poo-si-
shoon) *m* disposal

disse (*diss*-ser) *pron* these

distrikt (diss-*trikt*) *nt* district

dit (deet) *adv* there

diverse (di-*væsh*-sher) *adj*
miscellaneous, various

djerv (dᵛærv) *adj* fearless,
bold

djevel (dᵛ*ay*-verl) *m* (pl
-vler) devil

do (doo) *m*/*nt colloquial*
toilet

dobbel (*dob*-berl) *adj*
double

dobbeltseng (*dob*-berlt-
sehng) *c* double bed

dokk (dokk) *m* dock

***dokksette** (*dok*-seh-ter) *v*
dock

doktor (*dok*-toor) *m* doctor

dokument (doo-kew-*mehnt*)
nt certificate, document

dokumentmappe (doo-
kew-*mehnt*-mah-per) *c*
attaché case, briefcase

dollar (*dol*-lar) *m* dollar,
colloquial buck

dom (domm) *m* (pl ⁓mer)
judgment; verdict,
sentence

domfellelse (*dom*-feh-lerl-
ser) *m* conviction

domfelt (*dom*-fehltt) *m* (pl
⁓e) convict

dominere (doo-mi-*nay*-rer)
v dominate

domkirke (*dom*-kheer-ker)
c cathedral

dommer (*dom*-merr) *m*
judge; magistrate; umpire

domstol (*dom*-stool) *m*
court, law court

donasjon (doo-nah-*shoon*)
m donation

dongeribukse (dongh-ri-
book-se) *c* jeans

dose (*doo*-ser) *m* dose

dott (dott) *m* wisp; tuft; wad

doven (*daw*-vern) *adj* lazy

***dra** (draa) *v* pull; travel,
*go; ~ **av sted** *set out

drake (*draa*-ker) *m* kite;
dragon

drakt (drahkt) *c* costume

dram (drahmm) *m* drink of
liquor

drama (*draa*-mah) *nt* drama

dramatisk (drah-*maa*-tisk)
adj dramatic

drap (draap) *nt*
manslaughter, homicide

dreie (*dray*-er) *v* turn,
resolve

dreining (*dray*-ning) *m* turn

drenere (dreh-*nāȳ*-rer) *v*
drain

drepe (*drāȳ*-per) *v* kill

dress (drehss) *m* suit

dressere (dreh-*sāȳ*-rer) *v*
train

dressjakke (*drehss-ᵞ*ahk-
ker) *c* jacket

dreven (*drāȳ*-vern) *adj*
skilled, clever

drikk (drikk) *m* drink;
beverage; **alkoholfri ~** soft

***drikke** (*drik*-ker) *v* *drink

drikkelig (*drik*-ker-li) *adj*
drinkable

drikkepenger (*drik*-ker-
peh-ngerr) *pl* tip, gratuity

drikkevann (*drik*-ker-vahn)
nt drinking water

drink (dringk) *m* drink

dristig (*driss*-ti) *adj* bold,
daring; risky

dristighet (*driss*-ti-hāȳt) *c*
daring

dritt (dritt) *m vulgar* crap

***drive frem** (*dree*-ver)
propel

drivhus (*dreev*-hewss) *nt* (pl
~) greenhouse

drivkraft (*dreev*-krahft) *c*
driving force

dronning (*droan*-ning) *c*
queen

drosje (*drosh*-sher) *c* cab,
taxi

drosjeholdeplass (*drosh*-
sher-ho-ler-plahss) *m* taxi
rank; taxi stand *Am*

drosjesjåfør (*drosh*-sher-
sho-fūrr) *m* cab driver, taxi
driver

druer (*drēw*-err) *pl* grapes
pl

drukne (*drook*-ner) *v* *be
drowned; drown

dryppe (*drewp*-per) *v* drip

drøm (drurmm) *m* (pl
~mer) dream

drømme (*drurm*-mer) *v*
*dream

dråpe (*draw*-per) *m* drop

du (dēw) *pron* you

due (*dēw*-er) *c* pigeon

duft (dewft) *m* scent

dugg (dewgg) *m* dew

duk (dēwk) *m* table-cloth

dukke (*dewk*-ker) *v* dive; *c*
doll

dukketeater (*dewk*-ker-teh-
aa-terr) *nt* (pl ~, -tre)
puppet-show

dum (doomm) *adj* stupid,

dumb; foolish, silly

dun (dewn) *nt* down

dunke (*doong*-ker) *v* thump, bump

dunkel (*doong*-kerl) *adj* dim

dur (dewr) *m* roar; major

dusin (dew-*seen*) *nt* (pl ~) dozen

dusj (dewshsh) *m* shower

duskregn (*dewsk*-rehngn) *nt* drizzle

DVD (*deh*-veh-deh) *c* DVD

DVD-rom (*deh*-veh-deh-rawm) *c* (pl ~mer) DVD-rom

dverg (dværg) *m* dwarf

dybde (*dewb*-der) *m* depth

dyd (dewd) *m* virtue

dykke (*dewk*-ker) *v* dive

dykkermaske (*dew*-ker-mahss-ker) *c* goggles *pl*

dyktig (*dewk*-ti) *adj* able, capable, skil(l)ful

dyktighet (*dewk*-ti-hayt) *c* ability, skill

dynamo (dew-*naa*-moo) *m* dynamo

dyne (*dew*-ner) *c* eiderdown

dyp (dewp) *adj* deep; low

dypfryser (*dewp*-frew-serr) *m* deep-freeze

dypfryst mat (*dewp*-frewst maat) frozen food

dypsindig (*dewp*-sin-di) *adj* profound

dyr (dewr) *nt* beast, animal; *adj* expensive

dyrebar (*dew*-rer-baar) *adj* precious; dear

dyrekretsen (*dew*-rer-kreht-sern) zodiac

dyrke (*dewr*-ker) *v* raise, cultivate, *grow

dyrlege (*dewr*-lāy-ger) *m* veterinary surgeon

dyster (*dewss*-terr) *adj* gloomy, somber *Am*, sombre

dytt (dewtt) *m* push

dø (dūr) *v* die

død (dūr) *adj* dead; *m* death

dødelig (*dūr*-der-li) *adj* mortal, fatal

dødsfall (*durts*-fahl) *nt* (pl ~) death

dødsstraff (*durt*-strahf) *m* death penalty

døgn (durngn) *nt* twenty-four hours

dømme (*durm*-mer) *v* sentence; judge

døpe (*dūr*-per) *v* baptize, christen

dør (dūr) *c* door

dørslag (*dūr*-shlaag) *nt* (pl ~) strainer

dørvokter (*dūr*-vok-terr) *m* door-keeper

døv (dūrv) *adj* deaf

dåd (dawd) *m* exploit, achievement

dåkalv (*daw*-kahlv) *m* fawn

dåp (dawp) *m* christening, baptism

dårlig (*daw*-li) *adj* ill, bad; poor; ~ luft stale air

E

ebbe (*ehb*-ber) *m* ebb

e-billett (*ēh*-bi-*lehtt*) *c* e-
-ticket

Ecuador (ehk-vah-*dawr*)
Ecuador

ecuadorianer (ehk-vah-do-
ri-*aa*-nerr) *m* Ecuadorian

ed (āyd) *m* oath, vow

edderkopp (*ehd*-derr-kop)
m spider

eddik (*ehd*-dik) *m* vinegar

edel (*āy*-derl) *adj* noble

edelstein (*āy*-derl-stāyn) *m*
gem, precious stone

edru (*āyd*-rēw) *adj* sober

effekt (eh-*fehkt*) *m* effect

effektiv (*ehf*-fehk-tiv) *adj*
effective; efficient

eføy (*āy*-fur^(ew)) *m* ivy

egen (*āy*-gern) *adj* own;
peculiar, odd

egenskap (*āy*-gern-skaap)
m quality, characteristic

egentlig (*āy*-gernt-li) *adv*
really

egg (ehgg) *nt* egg

eggeplomme (*ehg*-ger-plo-
mer) *c* yolk, egg yolk

egn (ayn) *m* region

egnet (*ay*-nert) *adj*
convenient, suitable, fit

egoisme (eh-goo-*iss*-mer)
m selfishness

Egypt (eh-*gewpt*) Egypt

egypter (eh-*gewp*-terr) *m*
Egyptian

egyptisk (eh-*gewp*-tisk) *adj*
Egyptian

ei (ay) *art* a; *num* one

eie (*ay*-er) *v* own; possess, *nt*
possession; eiendeler
belongings *pl*

eiendom (*ay*-ern-dom) *m*
(pl ~mer) property; estate;
premises *pl*

eiendommelig (ay-ern-
dom-li) *adj* peculiar;
quaint

eiendommelighet (ay-ern-
dom-li-hāyt) *c* peculiarity

eiendomsmegler (ay-ern-
doms-*mehg*-lerr) *m* house-
-agent; realtor *nAm*

eier (*ay*-err) *m* owner,
proprietor

eik (ayk) *c* oak

eike (*ay*-ker) *m* spoke

eikenøtt (*ay*-ker-nurt) *c*
acorn

ekkel (*ehk*-kerl) *adj* nasty

ekko (*ehk*-koo) *nt* echo

ekorn (*ehk*-koon) *nt* squirrel

eksakt (eh-*sahkt*) *adj* exact

eksamen (ehk-*saa*-mern) *m*
exam *colloquial*,
examination; *ta ~
graduate

eksem (ehk-*sāym*) *m/nt*
eczema

eksempel (ehk-*sehm*-perl)
nt (pl -pler) example,
instance; for ~ for instance,

for example

eksemplar (ehk-sehm-*plaar*) *nt* specimen; copy

eksentrisk (ehk-*sehn*-trisk) *adj* eccentric

eksil (ehk-*seel*) *nt* exile

eksistens (ehk-si-*stehns*) *m* existence

eksistere (ehk-si-*stay*-rer) *v* exist

eksklusiv (ehks-klew-*seev*) *adj* exclusive

eksos (ehk-*sōōss*) *m* exhaust gases

eksospotte (ehk-*sōōss*-po-ter) *c* silencer; muffler *nAm*

eksosrør (ehk-*sōōss*-rürr) *nt* (pl ~) exhaust pipe

eksotisk (ehk-*sōō*-tisk) *adj* exotic

ekspedisjon (ehk-sper-di-*shōōn*) *m* expedition

ekspansjon (ehk-spang-*shōōn*) *m* expansion

ekspeditør (ehk-sper-di-*tūrr*) *m* shop assistant, salesman

eksperiment (ehk-speh-ri-*mehnt*) *nt* experiment

eksperimentere (ehk-speh-ri-mehn-*tay*-rer) *v* experiment

ekspert (ehk-*spæt*) *m* expert

eksplodere (ehk-sploo-*day*-rer) *v* explode, blow up

eksplosiv (ehk-sploo-*seev*) *adj* explosive

eksplosjon (ehk-sploo-*shōōn*) *m* blast, explosion

eksponere (ehk-spoo-*nay*-rer) *v* expose

eksponering (ehk-spoo-*nay*-ring) *c* exposure

eksportere (ehk-spo-*tay*-rer) *v* export

ekspress- (ehk-*sprehss*) express

ekstase (ehk-*staa*-ser) *m* ecstasy

ekstra (*ehk*-strah) *adj* additional, extra; spare

ekstravagant (ehk-strah-vah-*gahnt*) *adj* extravagant

ekstrem (ehk-*straym*) *adj* extreme

ekte (*ehk*-ter) *adj* genuine, authentic, true; *v* marry

ektemann (*ehk*-ter-mahn) *m* (pl -menn) husband

ektepar (*ehk*-ter-paar) *nt* married couple

ekteskap (*ehk*-teh-skaap) *nt* matrimony, marriage

ekvator (ehk-*vaa*-toor) *m* equator

elastisk (eh-*lahss*-tisk) *adj* elastic

eldre (*ehl*-drer) *adj* older; elderly; eldst eldest

elefant (eh-ler-*fahnt*) *m* elephant

eleganse (eh-ler-*gahng*-ser) *m* elegance

elegant (eh-ler-*gahnt*) *adj* elegant

elektriker (eh-*lehk*-tri-kerr) *m* electrician

elektrisitet (eh-lehk-tri-si-*tayt*) *m* electricity

elektrisk (eh-*lehk*-trisk) *adj*
electric

elektronisk (eh-lehk-*trōō*-
nisk) *adj* electronic

element (eh-ler-*mehnt*) *nt*
element

elementær (eh-ler-mehn-
tæær) *adj* primary

elendig (eh-*lehn*-di) *adj*
miserable

elendighet (eh-*lehn*-di-
hāyt) *c* misery

elev (eh-*lāyv*) *m* pupil

elfenbein (*ehl*-fern-bayn) *nt*
ivory

elg (ehlg) *m* moose, elk

eliminere (eh-li-mi-*nāy*-rer)
v eliminate

eller (*ehl*-lerr) *conj* or;
enten ... eller either ... or;
om ... eller whether ... or

ellers (*ehl*-lersh) *adv*
otherwise; else

elleve (*ehl*-ver) *num* eleven

ellevte (*ehl*-lerf-ter) *num*
eleventh

elske (*ehl*-sker) *v* love

elsker (*ehl*-skerr) *m* lover

elskerinne (ehl-sker-*rin*-
ner) *c* mistress

elsket (*ehl*-skert) *adj*
beloved

elskling (*ehlsk*-ling) *m*
sweetheart

elv (elv) *c* river

elvebredd (*el*-ver-brehd) *m*
river bank, riverside

elvemunning (*el*-ver-mew-
ning) *m* estuary

emalje (eh-*mahl*-Yer) *m*
enamel

emaljert (eh-mahl-*Yāyt*) *adj*
enamelled

embete (*ehm*-ber-ter) *nt*
civil service office

embetsmann (*ehm*-berts-
mahnn) *m* (pl -menn) civil
servant

emblem (ehm-*blāym*) *nt*
emblem

emigrant (eh-mi-*grahnt*) *m*
emigrant

emigrasjon (eh-mi-grah-
shōōn) *m* emigration

emne (*ehm*-ner) *nt* topic,
theme

en (āyn) *art* a; *num* one; **-en**
the *art*

enakter (*āyn*-ahk-terr) *m*
one-act play

ende (*ehn*-ner) *m* end

endelig (*ehn*-der-li) *adv*
finally; eventually

endestasjon (*ehn*-ner-stah-
shōōn) *m* terminal

endetarm (*ehn*-ner-tahrm)
m rectum

endossere (ahng-do-*sāy*-
rer) *v* endorse

endre (*ehn*-drer) *v* alter;
modify

endring (*ehn*-dring) *c*
alteration; change

eneforhandler (*āy*-ner-for-
hahnd-lerr) *m* sole
distributor

energi (eh-nær-*gee*) *m*
power, energy

energisk (eh-*nær*-gisk) *adj*
energetic

eneste (*ay*-nerss-ter) *adj*
sole, only

enestående (*ay*-ner-sto-er-ner) *adj* exceptional,
unique; singular

eng (ehngng) *c* meadow

engangs- (*ayn*-gahngs)
disposable

engel (*ehng*-ngerl) *m* (pl
engler) angel

engelsk (*eh*-ngerlsk) *adj*
English

engelskmann (*eh*-ngerlsk-mahn) *m* (pl -menn)
Englishman; Briton

England (*ehng*-lahn)
England

engroshandel (ahng-*graw*-hahn-derl) *m* (pl -dler)
wholesale-trade

engstelig (*ehng*-ster-li) *adj*
anxious; afraid

engstelse (*ehng*-sterl-ser)
m fear

enhet (*ayn*-hāyt) *m* unity;
unit

enhver (ehn-*væær*) *pron*
anyone; everybody,
everyone

enig (*ay*-ni) *adj* unanimous,
agreed; *være ~ agree

enke (*ehng*-ker) *c* widow

enkel (*ehng*-kerl) *adj*
simple; plain; single

enkelt (*ehng*-kerlt) *adj*
individual

enkelte (*ehng*-kerl-ter) *pron*
some

enkeltperson (*ehng*-kerlt-pæ-shōōn) *m* individual

enkeltrom (*ehng*-kerlt-room) *nt* (pl ~) single room

enkemann (*ayng*-ker-mahn)
m (pl -menn) widower

enn (ehnn) *conj* than

ennå (ehn-naw) *adv* yet

enorm (eh-*norm*) *adj*
enormous; huge, immense,
gigantic

ensartet (*ayn*-saa-tert) *adj*
uniform

ensidig (*ayn*-see-di) *adj*
one-sided

ensom (*ayn*-som) *adj* lonely

enstemmig (*ayn*-steh-mi)
adj unanimous

entall (*ayn*-tahl) *nt* singular

entrénøkkel (ahng-*trāy*-nur-kerl) *m* (pl -nøkler)
latchkey

entreprenør (ahng-trer-preh-*nūrr*) *m* contractor

entusiasme (ehn-tew-si-*ahss*-mer) *m* enthusiasm

entusiastisk (ehn-tew-si-*ahss*-tisk) *adj* enthusiastic

enveiskjøring (*ayn*-vayss-khūr-ring) *c* one-way
traffic

epidemi (eh-pi-der-*mee*) *m*
epidemic

epilepsi (eh-pi-lehp-*see*) *m*
epilepsy

epilog (eh-pi-*lawg*) *m*
epilogue

episk (*ay*-pisk) *adj* epic

episode (eh-pi-*sōō*-der) *m*
episode

eple (*ehp*-ler) *nt* apple

epos (*ay*-pooss) *nt* epic

e-post (*ay*-poost) *m* e-mail

erfare (*ær-faa*-rer) *v* experience

erfaren (*ær-faa*-rern) *adj* experienced

erfaring (*ær-faa*-ring) *c* experience

ergerlig (*ær*-ger-li) *adj* annoying

ergre (*ær*-grer) *v* annoy; irritate

ergrelse (*ær*-grerl-ser) *m* annoyance

erindre (eh-*rin*-drer) *v* recall

erindring (eh-*rin*-dring) *c* remembrance

erkjenne (*ær-khehn*-ner) *v* acknowledge; confess, admit

erklære (*ær-klææ*-rer) *v* declare; state

erklæring (*ær-klææ*-ring) *c* declaration, statement

erme (*ær*-mer) *nt* sleeve

erobre (*æ-rōōb*-rer) *v* conquer; capture

erobrer (*æ-rōōb*-rerr) *m* conqueror

erobring (*æ-rōōb*-ring) *c* conquest; capture

erstatning (*æ-shtaht*-ning) *m* indemnity; substitute

erstatte (*æ-shtaht*-ter) *v* replace, substitute

ert (ætt) *c* pea

erte (*æ*-ter) *v* tease

erverve (*ær-vær*-ver) *v* acquire; obtain

ervervelse (*ær-vær*-verl-ser) *m* acquisition

esel (*ay*-serl) *nt* (pl esler) donkey

eske (*ehss*-ker) *c* box

eskorte (ehss-*kot*-ter) *c* escort

eskortere (ehss-ko-*tay*-rer) *v* escort

essay (*ehss*-say) *nt* (pl ~, ~s) essay

essens (eh-*sehns*) *m* essence

et (*ayt*) *art* a; *num* one; -et the *art*

etablere (eh-tah-*blay*-rer) *v* establish

etappe (eh-*tahp*-per) *m* stage, leg

etasje (eh-*taa*-sher) *m* stor(e)y, floor; første ~ ground floor

eter (*ay*-terr) *m* ether

etikett (eh-ti-*kehtt*) *m* label

Etiopia (eh-ti-*ōō*-pi-ah) Ethiopia

etiopier (eh-ti-*ōō*-pi-err) *m* Ethiopian

etiopisk (eh-ti-*ōō*-pisk) *adj* Ethiopian

etsteds (eht-*stehss*) *adv* somewhere

etter (*eht*-terr) *prep* after; ~ at after

etterforske (*eht*-terr-fosh-ker) *v* investigate

etterforskning (*eht*-terr-foshk-ning) *m* inquiry, investigation

*etterfølge (*eht*-terr-fur-ler) *v* succeed

etterkommer (*eht-terr-ko-merr*) *m* descendant

*etterlate (*eht-ter-laa-ter*) *v* *leave behind; *leave

etterligne (*eht-ter-ling-ner*) *v* copy, imitate

etterligning (*eht-ter-ling-ning*) *c* imitation

ettermiddag (*eht-terr-mi-dah*) *m* afternoon; i ~ this afternoon

etternavn (*eht-ter-nahvn*) *nt* (pl ~) family name, surname

etterpå (*eht-terr-paw*) *adv* afterwards

ettersende (*eht-ter-sheh-ner*) *v* forward

ettersom (*eht-ter-shom*) *conj* as, because

etterspore (*eht-ter-shpoo-rer*) *v* trace

etterspørsel (*eht-ter-shpur-sherl*) *m* demand

etui (eh-tew-*ee*) *nt* case

EU (eh-ew) EU

euro (ou-roo) *m* Euro

Europa (ou-*roo*-pah) Europe

europeer (ou-roo-*pay*-err) *m* European

europeisk (ou-roo-*pay*-isk) *adj* European

evakuere (eh-vah-kew-*ay*-rer) *v* evacuate

evangelium (eh-vahng-*gay*-li-ewm) *nt* (pl -ier) gospel

eventuell (eh-vehn-tew-*ehll*) *adj* possible

eventyr (*ay*-vern-tewr) *nt* (pl ~) fairytale; tale; adventure

evig (*ay*-vi) *adj* eternal

evighet (*ay*-vi-hayt) *c* eternity

evne (*ehv*-ner) *c* faculty, gift; ability, capacity

evolusjon (eh-voo-lew-*shoon*) *m* evolution

F

fabel (*faa*-berl) *m* (pl fabler) fable

fabrikant (fahb-ri-*kahnt*) *m* manufacturer

fabrikk (fahb-*rikk*) *m* works *pl*, mill, plant, factory

fabrikkere (fahb-ri-*kay*-rer) *v* manufacture

faen (*fa*-ahrn) *colloquial* damn!

fag (faag) *nt* profession

fagforening (*faag*-fo-reh-ning) *c* trade union; union

fagmann (*faag*-mahnn) *m* (pl -menn) expert

fakkel (*fahk*-kerl) *m* (pl fakler) torch

faks (fahks) *m* fax; sende en ~ send a fax

faktisk (*fahk*-tisk) *adv* as a matter of fact, really, actually, in effect, in fact;

adj actual, factual

faktor (*fahk*-toor) *m* factor

faktum (*fahk*-tewm) *nt* (pl -ta) fact

faktura (fahk-*tew*-rah) *m* invoice

fakturere (fahk-tew-*ray*-rer) *v* bill

fakultet (fah-kewl-*tayt*) *nt* faculty

fald (fahll) *m* hem

falk (fahlk) *m* hawk

fall (fahll) *nt* fall; **i alle ~ at** any rate; **i hvert ~** anyway, at any rate

***falle** (*fahl*-ler) *v* *fall; ~ **sammen med** coincide; ***la ~ drop**

falleferdig (*fahl*-ler-fæ-di) *adj* ramshackle

fallitt (fah-*litt*) *adj* bankrupt

falme (*fahl*-mer) *v* fade

falsk (fahlsk) *adj* false

familie (fah-*mee*-li-er) *m* family

familiær (fah-mi-li-*ær*) *adj* familiar

fanatisk (fah-*naa*-tisk) *adj* fanatical

fang (fahng) *nt* lap

fange (*fahng*-nger) *v* capture; *catch; *m* prisoner; ***ta til ~** capture

fangenskap (*fahng*-ngern-skaap) *nt* imprisonment

fangst (fahngst) *m* catch

fantasi (fahn-tah-*see*) *m* fantasy, imagination, fancy

fantasifoster (fahn-tah-*seefooss*-terr) *nt* illusion

fantastisk (fahn-*tahss*-tisk) *adj* fantastic

fantom (fahn-*toom*) *nt* phantom

far (faar) *m* (pl fedre) father; dad

fare (*faa*-rer) *m* peril, danger; risk

farfar (*fahr*-faar) *m* (pl -fedre) grandfather

farge (*fahr*-ger) *m* colo(u)r; dye; *v* dye; **~ av** discolo(u)r

fargeblind (*fahr*-ger-blin) *adj* colo(u)r-blind

fargerik (*fahr*-ger-reek) *adj* colo(u)rful; gay

farget (*fahr*-gert) *adj* colo(u)red

farlig (*faa*-li) *adj* dangerous

farmakologi (fahr-mah-koo-loo-*gee*) *m* pharmacology

farmor (*fahr*-moor) *c* (pl -mødre) grandmother

fart (fahtt) *m* rate, speed; **i full ~** in a hurry; **saktne farten** slow down; **øke farten** accelerate

fartsgrense (*fahts*-grehn-ser) *c* speed limit

fartsmåler (*fahts*-maw-lerr) *m* speedometer

fartøy (*faa*-tur^(ew)) *nt* vessel

fasade (fah-*saa*-der) *m* façade

fasan (fah-*saan*) *m* pheasant

fascisme (fah-*shiss*-mer) *m* fascism

fascist (fah-*shist*) *m* fascist

fascistisk (fah-*shiss*-tisk) *adj* fascist

fase (*faa*-ser) *m* stage, phase

fast (fahst) *adj* firm; fixed; permanent; *adv* tight

fastboende (*fahst*-bōō-er-ner) *m* (pl ~) resident

*****fastholde** (*fahst*-ho-ler) *v* insist

fastland (*fahst*-lahn) *nt* mainland

*****fastsette** (*fahst*-seh-ter) *v* determine; stipulate

*****fastslå** (*fahst*-shlo) *v* establish; ascertain

fat (faat) *nt* dish; cask; barrel

fatal (fah-*taal*) *adj* fatal

fatning (*faht*-ning) *m* composure

fatøl *nt* draught beer

fatte (*faht*-ter) *v* *understand, grasp

fattig (*faht*-ti) *adj* poor

fattigdom (*faht*-ti-dom) *m* poverty

fattigslig (*faht*-tik-sli) *adj* poor

favoritt (fah-voo-*ritt*) *m* favo(u)rite

fe (fāy) *m* fairy

feber (*fāy*-berr) *m* fever

feberaktig (*fāy*-berr-ahk-ti) *adj* feverish

februar (feh-brew-*aar*) February

fedme (*fehd*-mer) *m* obesity

fedreland (*fāy*-drer-lahn) *nt* native country

feie (*fay*-er) *v* *sweep

feig (fayg) *adj* cowardly

feiging (*fay*-ging) *m* coward

feil (fayl) *m* (pl ~) fault, error, mistake; *adj* incorrect; *ta ~ *be mistaken

feilaktig (fayl-*ahk*-ti) *adj* mistaken

feile (*fay*-ler) *v* err

feilfri (*fayl*-free) *adj* faultless

feiltakelse (fayl-*taa*-kerl-ser) *m* mistake, error

feiltrinn (*fayl*-trin) *nt* slip

feire (*fay*-rer) *v* celebrate

feiring (*fay*-ring) *c* celebration

fekte (*fehk*-ter) *v* fence

fele (*fai*-ler) *c* fiddle

felg (fehlg) *m* rim

felle (*fehl*-ler) *c* trap

felles (*fehl*-lerss) *adj* common; joint; i **fellesskap** jointly

fellesprosjekt *nt* joint venture

felt (fehlt) *nt* field

feltkikkert (*fehlt*-khi-kert) *m* field glasses

feltseng (*fehlt*-sehng) *c* camp bed; cot *nAm*

fem (fehmm) *num* five

feminin (feh-mi-*neen*) *adj* feminine

femte (*fehm*-ter) *num* fifth

femten (*fehm*-tern) *num* fifteen

femtende (*fehm*-ter-ner) *num* fifteenth

femti (*fehm*-ti) *num* fifty

fengsel (*fehng*-sherl) *nt* (pl -sler) jail, prison

fengsle (*fehng*-shler) *v* imprison; fascinate

ferdig (*fær*-di) *adj* finished

ferdselsåre (*færd*-serls-*aw*-rer) *c* thoroughfare

ferge (*fær*-ger) *c* ferry-boat

ferie (*fāy*-ri-er) *m* vacation, holiday; på ~ on holiday

ferieleir (*fāy*-ri-er-layr) *m* holiday camp

feriested (*fāy*-ri-er-stāy) *nt* holiday resort

ferje (*fær*-ᵞer) *c* ferry-boat

fersk (fæshk) *adj* fresh

fersken (*fæsh*-kern) *m* peach

ferskvann (*fæshk*-vahn) *nt* fresh water

fest (fehst) *m* feast, party

feste (*fehss*-ter) *v* attach, fasten; ~ med nål pin

festeinnretning (*fehss*-ter-in-reht-ning) *m* fastener

festival (fehss-ti-*vaal*) *m* festival

festlig (*fehst*-li) *adj* festive

festning (*fehst*-ning) *m* fortress; stronghold

fet (fāyt) *adj* fat, obese

fett (fehtt) *nt* grease, fat

fetter (*feht*-terr) *m* cousin

fettet (*feht*-tert) *adj* greasy

fettfri (*fehtt*-frēē) *adj* fat free

fettholdig (*feht*-hol-di) *adj* fatty

fettsuging (*fehtt*-sēwg-ing) *c* liposuction

fiasko (fi-*ahss*-koo) *m* failure

fiber (*fee*-berr) *m* (pl fibrer) fibre

fiende (*fee*-ern-der) *m* enemy

fiendtlig (*fee*-ern-tli) *adj* hostile

figur (fi-*gēwr*) *m* figure

fik (feek) *m* slap, blow

fike (*fee*-ker) *v* slap

fiken (*fee*-kern) *m* fig

fiks (fiks) *adj* smart

fil (feel) *m* file; lane

filial (fi-li-*aal*) *m* branch

filipens (fi-li-*pehns*) *m* acne

Filippinene (fi-li-*pee*-ner-ner) Philippines *pl*

filippinsk (fi-li-*peensk*) *adj* Philippine

fille (*fil*-ler) *c* rag

film (film) *m* movie, film

filme (*fil*-mer) *v* film

filmkamera (*film*-kaa-mer-rah) *nt* camera

filmlerret (*film*-lær-rert) *nt* screen

filosof (fi-loo-*sōōf*) *m* philosopher

filosofi (fi-loo-soo-*fee*) *m* philosophy

filt (filt) *m* felt

filter (*fil*-terr) *nt* (pl -tre) filter

fin (feen) *adj* fine

finanser (fi-*nahng*-serr) *pl* finances *pl*

finansiell (fi-nahng-si-*ehll*) *adj* financial

finansiere (fi-nahng-si-*āy*-

rer) *v* finance

finger (*fing*-ngerr) *m* (pl -gre) finger

fingeravtrykk (*fing*-ngerr-ahv-trewk) *nt* (pl ~) fingerprint

fingerbøl (*fing*-ngerr-burl) *nt* (pl ~) thimble

finhakke (*feen*-hah-ker) *v* mince

finke (*fing*-ker) *m* finch

Finland (*fin*-lahn) Finland

finmale (*feen*-maa-ler) *v* *grind

finne¹ (*fin*-ner) *m* Finn

*finne² (*fin*-ner) *v* *find; ~ igjen recover; ~ skyldig convict; ~ sted *take place

finsk (finsk) *adj* Finnish

fint! (feent) all right!, okay!

fiol (fi-*ool*) *m* violet

fiolett (fi-oo-*lehtt*) *adj* violet

fiolin (fi-oo-*leen*) *m* violin

fire (*fee*-rer) *num* four

firfisle (*feer*-fis-ler) *c* lizard

firma (*feer*-mah) *nt* firm, company

fisk (fisk) *m* fish

fiske (*fiss*-ker) *v* fish; angle

fiskebein (*fiss*-ker-bayn) *nt* bone, fishbone

fiskeforretning (*fiss*-ker-fo-reht-ning) *c* fish shop

fiskegarn (*fiss*-ker-gaan) *nt* (pl ~) fishing net

fiskekort (*fiss*-ker-kot) *nt* (pl ~) fishing license *Am*, fishing licence

fiskekrok (*fiss*-ker-krook) *m* fishing hook

fisker (*fiss*-kerr) *m* fisherman

fiskeredskap (*fiss*-ker-rehss-kaap) *nt* fishing tackle

fiskeri (fiss-ker-*ree*) *nt* fishing industry

fiskesnøre (*fiss*-ker-snūr-rer) *nt* fishing line

fiskestang (*fiss*-ker-stahng) *c* (pl -stenger) fishing rod

fiskeutstyr (*fiss*-ker-ewt-stēwr) *nt* fishing gear

fjell (f³ehll) *nt* mountain

fjellendt (f³ehl-lent) *adj* mountainous

fjellkjede (f³ehl-khāy-der) *m* mountain range

fjellklatring (f³ehl-klaht-ring) *c* mountaineering

fjerde (f³ǣ-rer) *num* fourth

fjern (f³ǣn) *adj* far, distant, remote, far-off

fjerne (f³ǣ-ner) *v* *take away, remove

fjerning (f³ǣ-ning) *c* removal

fjernkontroll (f³ǣn-koon-troll) *c* remote control

fjernsyn (f³ǣn-sēwn) *nt* television, *colloquial* telly

fjernsynsapparat (f³ǣn-sēwn-sah-pah-raat) *nt* television set

fjollet (f³ol-lert) *adj* foolish

i fjor (ee f³ōōr) last year

fjord (f³ōōr) *m* fjord

fjorten (f³oot-tern) *num* fourteen; ~ dager fortnight

fjortende (*f⁰oot*-ter-ner)
num fourteenth

fjær (f⁹ær) *c* (pl ~) feather;
spring

fjære (f⁹ææ-rer) *c* low tide

fjæring (f⁹ææ-ring) *c*
suspension

fjærkre (f⁹ær-krāy) *nt* (pl
~) fowl, poultry

flagg (flahgg) *nt* flag

flakke (*flahk*-ker) *v* wander

flamingo (flah-*ming*-goo)
m flamingo

flamme (*flahm*-mer) *m*
flame

flanell (flah-*nehll*) *m*
flannel

flaske (*flahss*-ker) *c* bottle;
flask

flaskehals (*flahss*-ker-
hahls) *m* bottleneck

flaskeåpner (*flahss*-ker-
awp-nerr) *m* bottle opener

flass (flahss) *nt* dandruff

flat (flaat) *adj* flat; plane

flekk (flehkk) *m* spot, stain;
speck, blot

flekke (*flehk*-ker) *v* stain

flekket (*flehk*-kert) *adj*
spotted

flekkfjerner (*flehk*-f⁹æ-
nerr) *m* stain remover

flere (*flāy*-rer) *adj* several;
flest most

flerkinoanlegg (*flāyr*-khee-
nōō-ahn-*lehgg*) *nt*
multiplex (theater)

flertall (*flāy*-tahl) *nt*
majority; plural

flid (fleed) *m* diligence

flink (flingk) *adj* clever,
skil(l)ful, smart

flintstein (*flint*-stayn) *m*
flint

flis (fleess) *c* chip; tile

flittig (*fli*-ti) *adj* diligent;
industrious

flo (floo) *m* flood

flokk (flokk) *m* herd, flock;
bunch

flott (flott) *adj* swell;
colloquial super

flottør (flo-*türr*) *m* float

flue (*flew*-er) *c* fly

flukt (flewkt) *c* escape

fluktstol (*flewkt*-stool) *m*
deck chair

fly (flew) *nt* aeroplane,
airplane *nAm*

*fly (flew) *v* *fly

flybensin (*flew*-behn-seen)
m kerosene

flygel (*flew*-gerl) *nt* (pl
-gler) grand piano

flykaptein (*flew*-kahp-tayn)
m captain

flykte (*flewk*-ter) *v* escape,
flee

flyktig (*flewk*-ti) *adj* casual

flyktning (*flewkt*-ning) *m*
refugee

flyndre (*flewnd*-rer) *c* sole

flyplass (*flew*-plahss) *m*
airport, airfield

flyselskap (*flew*-sehl-
skaap) *nt* airline

*flyte (*flew*-ter) *v* flow; float

flytende (*flew*-ter-ner) *adj*
fluent; fluid, liquid

flyttbar (*flewt*-baar) *adj*

movable

flytte (*flewt*-ter) v move

flytur (*flew*-tewr) m flight

flyulykke (*flew*-ew-lew-ker) c plane crash

flyvert (*flew*-væt) m steward

flyvertinne (*flew*-væ-ti-ner) c stewardess

fløte (*flur*-ter) m cream

fløteaktig (*flur*-ter-ahk-ti) adj creamy

fløyel (*flurew*-erl) m velvet

fløyte (*flurew*-ter) c flute; whistle

flå (flaw) v fleece

flåte (*flaw*-ter) m raft; fleet; navy

fnise (*fnee*-ser) v giggle

foajé (foa-ah-ʾay) m foyer, lobby

fold (foll) m crease, fold

folde (*fol*-ler) v fold; ~ sammen fold; ~ ut v unfold

foldekniv (*fol*-ler-kneev) m clasp-knife

folk (folk) nt people, nation; pl people; folke- popular; national

folkedans (*fol*-ker-dahns) m folk dance

folkemengde (*fol*-ker-mehng-der) m crowd

folkerik (*fol*-ker-reek) adj populous

folkeslag (fol-ker-*shlaag*) nt (pl ~) people

folkevise (*fol*-ker-vee-ser) c folk song

folklore (folk-*law*-rer) m

folklore

fond (fonn) nt fund

fondsbørs (*fons*-būrsh) m stock exchange

fondsmarked (*fons*-mahr-kerd) nt stock market

fonetisk (foo-*nay*-tisk) adj phonetic

for¹ (forr) conj for; prep for; ~ hånden available; ~ å in order to, to

fôr² (toōr) nt lining; fodder

forakt (for-*ahkt*) m scorn, contempt

forakte (for-*ahk*-ter) v despise, scorn

foran (*for*-rahn) prep before, ahead of, in front of

forandre (for-*ahn*-drer) v change; vary, alter

forandring (for-*ahn*-dring) c variation, change; alteration

foranledning (*for*-rahn-lāyd-ning) m occasion

foranstaltning (*for*-rahn-stahlt-ning) m measure

forargelse (for-*ahr*-gerl-ser) m indignation

forbanne (for-*bahn*-ner) v curse

forbause (for-*bou*-ser) v astonish; amaze, surprise

forbauselse (for-*bou*-serl-ser) m astonishment; amazement

forbausende (for-*bou*-ser-ner) adj astonishing; amazing

forbedre (for-*bāyd*-rer) v

improve

forbedring (for-*bayd*-ring) *c* improvement

forbehold (*for*-ber-hol) *nt* qualification; reservation

forberede (*for*-ber-*ray*-der) *v* prepare

forberedelse (*for*-ber-*ray*-derl-ser) *m* preparation

forberedende (*for*-ber-*ray*-der-ner) *adj* preliminary

forbi (for-*bee*) *prep* past, beyond, past; *ga ~ pass by

***forbinde** (for-*bin*-ner) *v* connect, link, join; dress; associate

forbindelse (for-*bin*-nerl-ser) *m* connection; relation, reference

forbipasserende (for-*bee*-pah-*say*-rer-ner) *m* (pl ~) passer-by

***forbli** (for-*blee*) *v* remain

forbløffe (for-*blurf*-fer) *v* astonish

forbokstav (*for*-book-staav) *m* initial

forbruk (for-*brewk*) *nt* expenditure; consumption

forbruke (for-*brew*-ker) *v* consume

forbruker (for-*brew*-kerr) *m* consumer

forbrytelse (for-*brew*-terl-ser) *m* crime

forbryter (for-*brew*-terr) *m* criminal

forbrytersk (for-*brew*-tershk) *adj* criminal

forbud (*for*-bewd) *nt* (pl ~) prohibition

forbudt (for-*bewtt*) *adj* prohibited; **forbikjøring forbudt** no passing *Am*

forbund (for-bewn) *nt* (pl ~) league, union; **forbunds-** federal

forbundsfelle (*for*-bewns-feh-ler) *m* associate

forbundsstat (*for*-bewn-staat) *m* federation

***forby** (for-*bew*) *v* *forbid, prohibit

fordampe (for-*dahm*-per) *v* evaporate

fordel (fo-*dayl*) *m* benefit, advantage, profit; *ha ~ av benefit; til ~ for for the benefit of

fordelaktig (fo-*dayl*-ahk-ti) *adj* advantageous

fordele (fo-*day*-ler) *v* divide

fordi (fo-*dee*) *conj* as, because; since

fordom (*fo*-dom) *m* (pl ~mer) prejudice

fordreid (fo-*drayd*) *adj* crooked, twisted

fordring (*fod*-ring) *c* claim

***fordrive** (fo-*dree*-ver) *v* expel; chase

fordum (*fo*-dewm) *adv* formerly

fordømt (fo-*dømt*) *adv* damned; *colloquial* bloody

fordøye (fo-*durew*-er) *v* digest

fordøyelig (fo-*durew*-er-li) *adj* digestible

fordøyelse (fo-*durew*-erl-

ser) *m* digestion; dårlig ~
indigestion

forebygge (*faw-rer-bew-ger*) *v* prevent

forebyggende (*faw-rer-bew-ger-ner*) *adj* preventive

foredrag (*faw-rer-draag*) *nt* (pl ~) lecture

*****foregi** (*faw-rer-ʸee*) *v* pretend

*****foregripe** (*faw-rer-gree-per*) *v* anticipate

foregående (*faw-rer-gaw-er-ner*) *adj* preceding, previous

*****forekomme** (*faw-rer-ko-mer*) *v* occur

forelder (*for-ehl-derr*) *m* parent

foreldet (*for-ehl-dert*) *adj* out of date

foreldre (*for-ehl-drer*) *pl* parents *pl*

*****forelegge** (*faw-rer-leh-ger*) *v* present

forelesning (*faw-rer-layss-ning*) *m* lecture

forelsket (*for-ehl-skert*) *adj* in love

foreløpig (*faw-rer-lūr-pi*) *adj* provisional, temporary

forene (*for-āy-ner*) *v* join, unite

forening (*for-āy-ning*) *c* association; club, society

forent (*for-āynt*) *adj* joint; De forente stater (di for-āyn-ter staa-terr) the States, United States

*****foreskrive** (*faw-rer-skree-ver*) *v* prescribe

*****foreslå** (*faw-rer-shlaw*) *v* propose, suggest

*****forespørre** (*faw-rer-spur-rer*) *v* inquire, query, enquire

forespørsel (*faw-rer-spur-sherl*) *m* (pl -sler) inquiry, query, enquiry

forestille (*faw-rer-sti-ler*) *v* represent; ~ seg conceive; imagine, fancy

forestilling (*faw-rer-sti-ling*) *c* show, performance; idea, conception

foretak (*faw-rer-taak*) *nt* undertaking; concern

*****foretrekke** (*faw-rer-treh-ker*) *v* prefer; å ~ preferable

forfader (*for-faa-derr*) *m* (pl -fedre) ancestor

forfallen (*for-fahl-lern*) *adj* dilapidated

forfalske (*for-fahl-sker*) *v* counterfeit, forge

forfalskning (*for-fahlsk-ning*) *m* fake

forfalt (*for-fahlt*)*adj*overdue

forfatter (*for-faht-terr*) *m* author, writer

forfengelig (*for-fehng-nger-li*) *adj* vain

forferdelig (*for-fæ-der-li*) *adj* awful, dreadful, frightful, terrible

forfremme (*for-frehm-mer*) *v* promote

forfremmelse (*for-frehm-*

merl-ser) *m* promotion

forfriske (for-*friss*-ker) *v* refresh

forfriskende (for-*friss*-ker-ner) *adj* refreshing

forfriskning (for-*frisk*-ning) *c* refreshment

***forfølge** (for-*furl*-ler) *v* pursue, chase

forføre (for-*fūr*-rer) *v* seduce

forgasser (for-*gahss*-serr) *m* carburettor

forgifte (for-*ʸif*-ter) *v* poison

forgjenger (for-*ʸeh*-ngerr) *m* predecessor

forgjeves (for-*ʸay*-verss) *adv* in vain; *adj* vain

forglemmelse (for-*glehm*-merl-ser) *m* oversight

forgrunn (for-*grewn*) *m* foreground

forgylt (for-*ʸewlt*) *adj* gilt

i forgårs (ee for-*gosh*) the day before yesterday

***forgå seg** (for-*gaw*) offend

forhandle (for-*hahnd*-ler) *v* negotiate

forhandler (for-*hahnd*-lerr) *m* dealer

forhandling (for-*hahnd*-ling) *c* negotiation

forhastet (for-*hahss*-tert) *adj* rash; premature

forhenværende (for-*hehn*-væe-rer-ner) *adj* former

forhindre (for-*hin*-drer) *v* prevent; inhibit

forhold (for-hol) *nt* (pl ~) relation; affair

forholdsmessig (for-hols-meh-si) *adj* proportional

forhør (for-*hūr*) *nt* (pl ~) interrogation, examination

forhøre (for-*hūr*-rer) *v* interrogate; ~ seg inquire

på forhånd (po for-hon) in advance

forhåndsbetalt (for-hons-beh-tahlt) *adj* prepaid

forhåndsvisning (for-hons-visning) *m* preview

forkaste (for-*kahss*-ter) *v* reject, turn down

forkjemper (for-*khehm*-perr) *m* champion

forkjærlighet (for-khææ-li-hāyt) *c* preference

forkjølelse (for-*khūr*-lerl-ser) *m* cold; ***bli forkjølet** *catch a cold

forkjørsrett (for-*khūrsh*-reht) *m* right of way

forklare (for-*klaa*-rer) *v* explain

forklaring (for-*klaa*-ring) *c* explanation

forkle (for-kler) *nt* (pl -lær) apron

forkledning (for-*klāyd*-ning) *m* disguise

forkle seg (for-*klāy*) disguise

forkorte (for-*kot*-ter) *v* shorten

forkortelse (for-*ko*-terl-ser) *m* abbreviation

forlange (fo-*lahng*-nger) *v* demand

59   **fornye**

*forlate (fo-*laa*-ter) v check
out, *leave; desert

forleden (fo-*lay*-dern) adv
recently

forlegen (fo-*lay*-gern) adj
embarrassed; *gjøre ~
embarrass

forlegenhet (fo-*lay*-gern-
hayt) c embarrassment

*forlegge (fo-*leh*-ger) v
*mislay

forlegger (fo-*leh*-gerr) m
publisher

forlenge (fo-*lehng*-nger) v
lengthen; extend

forlengelse (fo-*lehng*-ngerl-
ser) m extension

forlovede (fo-*law*-ver-der)
m fiancé; fiancée

forlovelse (fo-*law*-verl-ser)
m engagement

forlovelsesring (fo-*law*-
verl-serss-ring) m
engagement ring

forlovet (fo-*law*-vert) adj
engaged

forlystelse (fo-*lewss*-terl-
ser) m entertainment,
amusement

*forløpe (fo-*lūr*-per) v pass

form (form) c form, shape

formalitet (for-mah-li-*tayt*)
m formality

formane (for-*maa*-ner) v
urge

formann (for-*mahn*) m (pl
-menn) president,
chairman, chairwoman;
foreman

format (for-*maat*) nt size

forme (for-mer) v shape,
model, form

formel (for-merl) m (pl
-mler) formula

formell (for-*mehll*) adj
formal

formiddag (for-mi-dah) m
morning

formiddagsmat (for-mi-
dahks-maat) m lunch

forminske (for-*min*-sker) v
lessen

formodning (for-*mood*-
ning) m guess

formue (for-moo-er) m
fortune

formynder (for-*mewn*-derr)
m guardian

formynderskap (for-*mewn*-
der-shkaap) nt custody

formørkelse (for-*murr*-kerl-
ser) m eclipse

formål (for-mawl) nt (pl ~)
purpose, objective, object

formålstjenlig (for-mawls-
t*yayn*-li) adj appropriate

fornavn (fo-*nahvn*) nt (pl ~)
first name, Christian name

fornemme (fo-*nehm*-mer) v
perceive

fornemmelse (fo-*nehm*-
merl-ser) m perception;
sensation

fornuft (fo-*newft*) m reason,
sense

fornuftig (fo-*newf*-ti) adj
reasonable, sensible

fornybar (fo-*new*-baar) adj
renewable

fornye (fo-*new*-er) v renew

fornærme (fo-*nær*-mer) v offend; insult

fornærmelse (fo-*nær*-merl-ser) m offense *Am*, offence; insult

fornøyd (for-*nurewd*) adj pleased; glad

fornøyelse (fo-*nurew*-erl-ser) m pleasure

forpakte bort (for-*pahk*-ter bot) lease

forpaktning (for-*pahkt*-ning) m lease

forplikte (for-*plik*-ter) v oblige; ~ seg engage; *være forpliktet til *be obliged to

forpliktelse (for-*plik*-terl-ser) m engagement

forresten (for-*rehss*-tern) adv besides; by the way

forretning (fo-*reht*-ning) c store, shop; business

forretninger (fo-*reht*-ni-ngerr) pl business; i ~ on business

forretningskvinne (fo-*reht*-nings-kvin-ner) c businesswoman

forretningsmann (fo-*reht*-nings-mahn) m (pl -menn) businessman

forretningsmessig (fo-*reht*-nings-meh-si) adj business-like

forretningsreise (fo-*reht*-nings-ray-ser) c business trip

forretningssenter (fo-*reht*-ning-sehn-terr) nt (pl -trer) shopping centre, mall *nAm*

forrett (*for*-reht) hors d'œuvre

forrige (*for*-*y*er) adj previous, last, past

forræder (fo-*rāy*-derr) m traitor

forræderi (fo-reh-der-der-*ree*) nt treason

forråd (*foar*-rawd) nt (pl ~) supply

forråde (fo-*raw*-der) v betray

forsamling (fo-*shahm*-ling) c assembly, rally

forseelse (fo-*shāy*-erl-ser) m offense *Am*, offence, misdemeanour

forsere (fo-*shāy*-rer) v force

forside (fo-*shee*-der) c front

forsikre (fo-*shik*-rer) v assure; insure

forsikring (fo-*shik*-ring) c insurance

forsikringspolise (fo-*shik*-rings-poo-lee-ser) m insurance policy

forsikringspremie (fo-*shik*-rings-*prāy*-mi-er) m premium

forsiktig (fo-*shik*-ti) adj careful, cautious; gentle; wary; *være ~ watch out

forsiktighet (fo-*shik*-ti-hāyt) c caution, precaution

forsinke (fo-*shing*-ker) v delay

forsinkelse (fo-*shing*-kerl-ser) m delay

forsinket (fo-*shing*-kert) adj

61
forsømme

overdue

forskjell (*fo*-shehl) *m*
distinction, difference;
*gjøre ~ distinguish

forskjellig (fo-*shehl*-li) *adj*
different, unlike, distinct;
*være ~ vary, differ

forskning (*foshk*-ning) *m*
research

forskole (fo-shkoo-ler) *m*
kindergarten

forskrekke (fo-*shkrehk*-ker)
v frighten; *bli forskrekket
*be frightened

forskrekkelig (fo-*shkrehk*-
ker-li) *adj* frightful

forskudd (*fo*-shkewd) *nt* (pl
~) advance; betale på ~
advance; på ~ in advance

forslag (*fo*-shlaag) *nt* (pl ~) *m*
proposal, suggestion,
proposition; motion

forsoning (fo-shoo-ning) *c*
reconciliation

***forsove seg** (fo-*shaw*-ver)
*oversleep

forsprang (*fo*-shprahng) *nt*
(pl ~) lead

forstad (fo-shtaad) *m* (pl
-steder) suburb; forstads-
suburban

forstand (fo-*shtahnn*) *m*
reason; brain, wits *pl*,
intellect

forstavelse (fo-shtaa-ver-l-
ser) *m* prefix

forstmann (*fosht*-mahn) *m*
(pl -menn) forester

forstoppelse (fo-*shtop*-
perl-ser) *m* constipation

forstue (fo-*shtew*-er) *v*
sprain

forstuing (fo-*shtew*-ing) *c*
sprain

forstyrre (fo-*shtewr*-rer) *v*
disturb; *upset

forstyrrelse (fo-*shtewr*-rerl-
ser) *m* disturbance

forstørre (fo-*shturr*-rer) *v*
enlarge; magnify

forstørrelse (fo-*shturr*-rerl-
ser) *m* enlargement

forstørrelsesglass (fo-
shturr-rerl-serss-glahss) *nt*
(pl ~) magnifying glass

***forstå** (*fo*-shtaw) *v*
*understand; *see

forståelse (fo-*shtaw*-erl-
ser) *m* understanding

forsvar (fo-*shvaar*) *nt*
defense *Am*, defence

forsvare (fo-*shvaa*-rer) *v*
defend

forsvarstale (*fo*-shvaa-sh-
taa-ler) *m* plea

***forsvinne** (fo-*shvin*-ner) *v*
disappear, vanish

forsvunnet (fo-*shvewn*-
nert) *adj* lost

forsyne (fo-*shew*-ner) *v*
provide, furnish, supply; ~
med furnish with

forsyning (fo-*shew*-ning) *c*
stock

forsøk (fo-*shürk*) *nt* (pl ~)
try, attempt; trial;
experiment

forsøke (fo-*shür*-ker) *v* try,
attempt

forsømme (fo-*shurm*-mer)

v neglect; fail

forsømmelse (fo-*shurm*-merl-ser) *m* neglect

fort (foott) *adv* quickly

***forta seg** (fo-*taa*) *wear away

fortau (fo-tou) *nt* (pl ~) pavement; sidewalk *nAm*

fortauskant (fo-*touss*-kahnt) *m* curb

fortelle (fo-*tehl*-ler) *v* *tell; relate

fortelling (fo-*tehl*-ling) *c* story, tale

forte seg (*foot*-ter) hurry

fortid (*for*-teed) *c* past

fortjene (fo-*t'ay*-ner) *v* deserve, merit

fortjeneste (fo-*t'ay*-nerss-ter) *m* profit, gain; merit

fortred (fo-*trayd*) *m* harm, mischief

fortrinnsrett (fo-trins-reht) *m* priority

fortryllelse (fo-*trewl*-lerl-ser) *m* spell

fortryllende (fo-*trewl*-ler-ner) *adj* charming

***fortsette** (*fot*-seh-ter) *v* continue; *keep on, carry on, *go on, proceed, *go ahead

fortsettelse (*fot*-seh-terl-ser) *m* sequel

fortvile (fo-*tvee*-ler) *v* despair

fortvilet (fo-*tvee*-lt) *adj* desperate

fortynne (fo-*tewn*-ner) *v* dilute

forundre (for-*ewn*-drer) *v* amaze

forundring (for-*ewn*-dring) *c* wonder

forurense (for-rew-rehn-ser) *v* pollute

forurensning (for-rew-rehns-ning) *m* pollution

forurolige (for-rew-*rōō*-li-er) *v* alarm

foruroligende (for-rew-*rōō*-li-er-ner) *adj* scary

foruten (for-*ēw*-tern) *prep* besides

forutgående (for-rewt-gaw-er-ner) *adj* prior

forutsatt at (for-*ēwt*-sahtt ahtt) provided that, supposing that

***forutse** (for-*rēwt*-sāy) *v* anticipate

***forutsi** (for-rewt-see) *v* predict, forecast

forutsigelse (for-rewt-see-erl-ser) *m* prediction

forvaltende (for-*vahl*-ter-ner) *adj* administrative

forvaltningsrett (for-vahlt-nings-reht) *m* administrative law

forvandle (for-*vahnd*-ler) *v* transform; **forvandles til** turn into

forvaring (for-*vaa*-ring) *c* custody

forveksle (for-*vehk*-shler) *v* *mistake, confuse

forventning (for-*vehnt*-ning) *m* expectation

forvirre (for-*veer*-rer) *v*

confuse

forvirret (for-*veer*-rert) *adj* confused

forvirring (for-*veer*-ring) *c* confusion; disturbance; muddle

forårsake (*for*-o-shaa-ker) *v* cause

foss (foss) *m* waterfall

fossestryk (*foss*-ser-strēwk) *nt* (pl ~) rapids *pl*

fot (tōōt) *m* (pl føtter) foot; til **fots** on foot, walking

fotball (*foot*-bahl) *m* soccer; football

fotballkamp (*foot*-bahl-kahmp) *m* football match

fotbrems (*fōōt*-brehms) *m* foot brake

fotgjenger (*fōōt*-ᵞehng-err) *m* pedestrian

fotgjengerovergang (*fōōt*-ᵞayng-err-aw-verr-gahng) *m* crossing, pedestrian crossing; crosswalk *nAm*

fotoforretning (*fōō*-too-fo-reht-ning) *c* camera shop

fotograf (*foo*-too-*graaf*) *m* photographer

fotografere (foo-too-grah-*fay*-rer) *v* photograph

fotografering (foo-too-grah-*fay*-ring) *c* photography

fotografi (foo-too-grah-*fee*) *nt* photograph, photo

fotografiapparat (foo-too-grah-*fee*-ah-pah-raat) *nt* camera

fotokopi (*foot*-too-koo-pee)

m photocopy

fotokopiere (*fōō*-too-koo-pee-*āy*-rer) *v* photocopy

fottur (*foot*-tēwr) *m* hike

fra (fraa) *prep* from; out of; as from; ~ **og med** from, as from

fradrag (*fraa*-draag) *nt* (pl ~) deduction; rebate

fraflytte (*fraa*-flew-ter) *v* vacate

frakk (frahkk) *m* coat, overcoat

frakt (frahkt) *c* cargo, freight

frankere (frahng-*kāy*-rer) *v* stamp

franko (*frahng*-koo) *adv* post-paid

Frankrike (*frahngk*-ree-ker) France

fransk (frahnsk) *adj* French

franskmann (*frahnsk*-mahn) *m* (pl -menn) Frenchman

fraråde (*fraa*-raw-der) *v* dissuade from

frastøtende (*fraa*-stūr-ter-ner) *adj* revolting, repellent, repulsive

*****frata** (*fraa*-taa) *v* deprive of

*****fratre** (*fraa*-trāy) *v* resign

fravær (*fraa*-væær) *nt* (pl ~) absence

fraværende (*fraa*-væææ-rer-ner) *adj* absent

fred (frāyd) *m* peace

fredag (*frāy*-dah) *m* Friday

fredelig (*frāy*-der-li) *adj* peaceful

frekk (frehkk) *adj* insolent, bold, *colloquial* cheeky

frekkhet (frehk-hāyt) *c* impertinence

frekvens (freh-*kvehns*) *m* frequency

frelse (frehl-ser) *v* redeem, save; *m* salvation

frem (frehmm) *adv* forward

fremad (frehm-maad) *adv* forward

fremadstrebende (frehm-maad-strāy-ber-ner) *adj* go-ahead

***frembringe** (frehm-bring-er) *v* effect

fremdeles (frehm-*dāy*-lerss) *adv* still

fremgang (frehm-gahng) *m* prosperity

fremgangsmåte (frehm-gahngs-maw-ter) *m* approach; method, process, procedure

***fremgå** (frehm-gaw) *v* appear

fremkalle (frehm-kah-ler) *v* develop

fremme (frehm-mer) *v* promote

fremmed (frehm-merd) *adj* strange; foreign; *m* stranger

fremover (frehm-maw-verr) *adv* onwards, ahead

fremragende (frehm-raa-ger-ner) *adj* outstanding, excellent

fremskritt (frehm-skrit) *nt* (pl ~) progress; advance;

***gjøre** ~ ***get on**, advance

fremstille (frehm-sti-ler) *v* produce

fremstående (frehm-staw-er-ner) *adj* distinguished

fremtid (frehm-tee) *c* future

fremtidig (frehm-tee-di) *adj* future

fremtoning (frehm-tōō-ning) *m* appearance

***fremtre** (frehm-trāy) *v* appear

fremtredende (frehm-trāy-der-ner) *adj* outstanding, distinguished

fremvise (frehm-vee-ser) *v* exhibit

fri (free) *adj* free

fribillett (free-bi-leht) *m* free ticket

frifinnelse (free-fi-nerl-ser) *m* acquittal

frigjørelse (free-*ȳur*-rerl-ser) *m* emancipation

frihet (free-hāyt) *c* freedom, liberty

friidrett (free-id-reht) *m* athletics *pl*

friksjon (frik-*shōōn*) *m* friction

frikvarter (free-kvah-tāyr) *nt* break; recess *nAm*

frimerke (free-mær-ker) *nt* postage stamp, stamp

frimerkeautomat (free-mær-ker-ou-too-maat) *m* stamp machine

frisk (frisk) *adj* well; bli ~ recover

frist (frist) *m* term

fullsatt

friste (*friss*-ter) v tempt

fristelse (*friss*-terl-ser) m temptation

frisyre (fri-*sew*-rer) m hair-do

frisør (fri-*surr*) m hairdresser

*frita (*free*-taa) v exempt; ~ for discharge of

fritak (*free*-taak) nt exemption

fritatt (*free*-taht) adj exempt

fritid (*free*-teed) c spare time; leisure

frivillig¹ (*free*-vi-li) adj voluntary

frivillig² (*free*-vi-li) m (pl ~e) volunteer

frokost (*froo*-kost) m breakfast

from (fromm) adj pious

frontlys (*front*-lewss) nt (pl ~) headlamp; headlight

frontrute (*front*-rew-ter) c windscreen; windshield nAm

frosk (frosk) m frog

frossen (*fross*-sern) adj frozen

frost (frost) m frost

frotté (fro-*tay*) m towel(l)ing, terry(cloth)

frue (*frew*-er) c madam; mistress

frukt (frewkt) m fruit

fruktbar (*frewkt*-baar) adj fertile

frukthage (*frewkt*-haa-ger) m orchard

fruktsaft (*frewkt*-sahft) m squash

fryd (frewd) m delight, joy

frykt (frewkt) m fear, dread

frykte (*frewk*-ter) v fear, dread

fryktelig (*frewk*-ter-li) adj terrible, dreadful

frynse (*frewn*-ser) c fringe

fryse (*frew*-ser) v *freeze

*fryse (*frew*-ser) v *freeze

fryseboks (*frew*-ser-boks) m freezer

frysepunkt (*frew*-ser-pewngt) nt freezing point

fryser (*frew*-serr) m freezer

frysevæske (*frew*-ser-vehss-ker) c antifreeze

frø (frur) nt seed

fugl (fewl) m bird

fukte (*fook*-ter) v moisten, damp

fuktig (*fook*-ti) adj wet, damp, humid, moist

fuktighet (*fook*-ti-hayt) c damp, humidity, moisture

fuktighetskrem (*fook*-ti-hayts-kraym) m moisturizing cream

full (fewll) adj full; drunk

fullende (*fewl*-leh-ner) v accomplish, complete, finish

fullføre (*fewl*-fur-rer) v complete

fullkommen (*fewl*-ko-mern) adj perfect

fullkommenhet (*fewl*-ko-mern-hayt) c perfection

fullsatt (*fewl*-saht) adj full up

fullstappet (*fewl*-stah-pert) *adj* chockfull

fullstendig (fewl-*stehn*-di) *adv* altogether, *adj* total; utter, whole, complete

fundament (fewn-dah-*mehnt*) *nt* base

fundamental (fewn-dah-mehn-*taal*) *adj* fundamental

fungere (fewng-*gaȳ*-rer) *v* work

funklende (*foongk*-ler-ner) *adj* sparkling

funksjon (fewngk-*shōōn*) *m* function; operation

funksjonshemmet (fewngk-*shōōns*-hemmert) *m* disabled

fure (*few*-rer) *m* groove

furu (*few*-rew) *c* pine

fusjon (few-*shōōn*) *m* fusion; merger

fusjonere (few-shōōn-*aȳ*-rer) *v* fusion; merge

fy! (*few*) shame!

fyldig (*fewl*-di) *adj* bulky; plump

fylke (*fewl*-ker) *nt* province

fyll (fewll) *nt* filling

fylle (*fewl*-ler) *v* fill; ~ **opp** fill up; ~ **ut** fill in; fill out *Am*

fyllepenn (*fewl*-ler-pehn) *m* fountainpen

fylt (fewlt) *adj* stuffed

fyr (fēwr) *m* chap, fellow

fyring (*fēw*-ring) *c* heating

fyrstikk (*fewsh*-tik) *m* match

fyrstikkeske (*fewsh*-ti-kehss-ker) *c* match-box

fyrtårn (*fēw*-tawn) *nt* (pl ~) lighthouse

fysiker (*fēw*-si-kerr) *m* physicist

fysikk (few-*sikk*) *m* physics

fysiologi (few-si-oo-loo-*gee*) *m* physiology

fysisk (*fēw*-sisk) *adj* physical

føde (*fūr*-der) *c* nourishment

fødested (*fūr*-der-stāȳd) *nt* place of birth

fødsel (*furt*-serl) *m* (pl -sler) birth; childbirth

fødselsdag (*furt*-serls-daag) *m* birthday

fødselsveer (*furt*-serls-vāȳ-err) *pl* labo(u)r pains

født (furtt) *adj* born

følbar (*fūrl*-baar) *adj* tangible

føle (*fūr*-ler) *v* *feel

følelig (*fūr*-ler-li) *adj* perceptible

følelse (*fūr*-lerl-ser) *m* sensation, feeling; emotion

følelsesløs (*fūr*-lerl-serss-lūrss) *adj* numb

følesans (*fūr*-ler-sahns) *m* touch

følge (*furl*-ler) *m* consequence; result; *v* **følge *holde ~ med** *keep up with

*følge (*furl*-ler) *v* follow, accompany

følgende (*furl*-ger-ner) *adj*

subsequent, following
følsom (*fūrl*-som) *adj*
sensitive
før (fūrr) *conj* before; *prep*
before
føre (*fū*-rer) *v* *lead,
conduct
fører (*fū*-rerr) *m* leader;
driver, conductor
førerhund (*fū*-rerr-hewn)
m guide dog
førerkort (*fū*-rerr-kot) *nt*
(pl ~) driving licence,
driver's license *Am*
førerskap (*fū*-rer-shkaap)
nt leadership
først (fursht) *adv* at first; ~
og fremst especially,
essentially
første (*fursh*-ter) *num* first;
adj foremost, primary
førstehjelp (*fursh*-ter-

ᵞehlp) *c* first aid
førstehjelpsskrin (*fursh*-
ter-*ᵞehlp*-skreen) *nt* first
aid kit
førstehjelpsstasjon (*fursh*-
ter-*ᵞehlp*-stah-shōōn) *m*
first aid post
førsteklasses (*fursh*-ter-
klah-serss) *adj* first-class,
first-rate
førsterangs (*fursh*-ter-
rahngs) *adj* first-rate
forti (*furt*-ti) *num* forty
føydal (fur*ᵉʷ*-*daal*) *adj*
feudal
få (faw) *adj* few
***få** (faw) *v* *get; obtain,
receive; *have; ~ **til å** cause
to
fårekjøtt (*faw*-rer-khurtt) *nt*
mutton

G

gaffel (*gahf*-ferl) *m* (pl
gafler) fork
gal (gaal) *adj* wrong, false;
mad, crazy
galge (*gahl*-ger) *m* gallows
pl
galle (*gahl*-ler) *m* bile, gall
galleblære (*gahl*-ler-blæær-
rer) *c* gall bladder
galleri (gah-ler-*ree*) *nt*
gallery
gallestein (*gahl*-ler-stayn)
m gallstone
galopp (gah-*lopp*) *m* gallop

galskap (*gaal*-skaap) *m*
madness
gammel (*gahm*-merl) *adj*
ancient, old; aged;
gammelt brød stale bread
gammeldags (*gahm*-merl-
dahks) *adj* ancient, old-
-fashioned; quaint
gang[1] (gahng) *m* time; **en ~**
once; some time, some
day; **en ~ til** once more; **for
en gangs skyld** for once;
gang på gang time and
again; ***gå i ~ med**

*undertake; med en ~ straight away; nok en ~ once more

gang² (gahngng) *m* aisle; hallway

gangsti (*gahng*-sti) *m* footpath

ganske (*gahn*-sker) *adv* quite, fairly, pretty, rather

gap (gaap) *nt* mouth, throat

garantere (gah-rahn-*tay*-rer) *v* guarantee

garanti (gah-rahn-*tee*) *m* guarantee

garasje (gah-*raa*-sher) *m* garage

garderobe (gahr-der-*rōō*-ber) *m* (pl ~) wardrobe; checkroom *nAm*, cloakroom

garderobeskap (gahr-der-*rōō*-ber-skaap) *nt* (pl ~) wardrobe, closet *nAm*

gardin (gah-*deen*) *m/nt* curtain

garn (gaan) *nt* yarn, knitting wool; net

gartner (*gaht*-nerr) *m* gardener

gasje (*gaa*-sher) *m* pay, salary

gass (gahss) *m* gas

gasskomfyr (*gahss*-koom-fēw) *m* gas cooker

gassovn (*gahss*-ovnn) *m* gas oven

gasspedal (*gahss*-peh-daal) *m* accelerator

gassverk (*gahss*-værk) *nt* gasworks

gate (*gaa*-ter) *c* street, road

gatekryss (*gaa*-ter-krewss) *nt* (pl ~) crossroads

gave (*gaa*-ver) *c* present, gift

gavekort (*gāāv*-er-kott) *nt* (pl ~) gift card

gavl (gahvl) *m* gable

gavmild (*gaav*-mil) *adj* liberal, generous

gavmildhet (*gaav*-mil-hāyt) *c* generosity

gebiss (geh-*biss*) *nt* denture, false teeth

geit (ᵞayt) *c* goat

gelé (sheh-*lāy*) *m* jelly

gelender (geh-*lehn*-derr) *nt* (pl -dre) railing, rail

gemen (geh-*māyn*) *adj* foul, mean

general (geh-ner-*raal*) *m* general

generasjon (geh-ner-rah-*shōōn*) *m* generation

generator (geh-ner-*raa*-toor) *m* generator

generell (sheh-ner-*rehll*) *adj* universal, general

generøs (sheh-ner-*rūrss*) *adj* generous

geni (sheh-*nee*) *nt* genius

genser (*gehn*-serr) *m* sweater, jersey, pullover, sweatshirt

geografi (geh-oo-grah-*fee*) *m* geography

geologi (geh-oo-loo-*gee*) *m* geology

geometri (geh-oo-meh-*tree*) *m* geometry

gest (shehst) *m* gesture

gestikulere (gehss-ti-kew-*lay*-rer) *v* gesticulate

gevinst (geh-*vinst*) *m* prize

gevær (geh-*væær*) *nt* rifle, gun

***gi** (ᵞee) *v* *give; ~ etter indulge, *give in; ~ opp *give up; ~ seg *give in

gift (ᵞift) *c* poison

gifte seg (ᵞif-ter) marry

giftig (ᵞif-ti) *adj* toxic, poisonous

gikt (ᵞikt) *c* gout

gips (ᵞips) *m* plaster

gir (geer) *nt* gear; **skifte ~** change gear

girkasse (*geer*-kah-ser) *c* gear-box

girstang (*gee*-shtahng) *c* (pl -stenger) gear lever

gissel (*giss*-serl) *nt* (pl gisler) hostage

gitar (gi-*taar*) *m* guitar

gjedde (ᵞayd-der) *c* pike

gjeld (ᵞehll) *c* debt

***gjelde** (ᵞehl-ler) *v* concern, apply

gjelle (ᵞehl-ler) *c* gill

gjemme (ᵞehm-mer) *v* *hide

gjenforene (ᵞehn-fo-*ray*-ner) *v* reunite

gjeng (ᵞehngng) *m* gang

gjenlyd (ᵞehn-*lewd*) *m* echo

gjennom (ᵞehn-noom) *prep* through; *gå ~ pass through

gjennombløte (ᵞehn-noom-*blur*-ter) *v* soak

gjennombore (ᵞehn-noom-*boo*-rer) *v* pierce

***gjennomgå** (ᵞehn-noom-gaw) *v* *go through, suffer

gjennomreise (ᵞehn-noom-ray-ser) *c* passage

gjennomsiktig (ᵞehn-noom-sik-ti) *adj* sheer, transparent

gjennomsnitt (ᵞehn-noom-snit) *nt* (pl ~) average, mean; **i ~** on the average

gjennomsnittlig (ᵞehn-noom-snit-li) *adj* average, medium

gjennomtrenge (ᵞehn-noom-treh-nger) *v* penetrate

gjenvinnbar (ᵞenn-vinn-*bāhr*) *adj* recyclable

gjenopplivelse (ᵞehn-noop-lee-verl-ser) *m* revival

***gjenoppta** (ᵞehn-*nop*-taa) *v* resume

gjensidig (ᵞehn-see-di) *adj* mutual

gjenstand (ᵞehn-stahn) *m* object; article

***gjenta** (ᵞehn-taa) *v* repeat

gjentakelse (ᵞehn-taa-kerl-ser) *m* repetition

gjerde (ᵞææ-der) *nt* fence

gjerne (ᵞææ-ner) *adv* willingly, gladly

gjerning (ᵞææ-ning) *c* deed

gjerrig (ᵞær-ri) *adj* stingy

gjespe (ᵞehss-per) *v* yawn

gjest (ᵞehst) *m* guest

gjesteværelse (ᵞehss-tervææ-rerl-ser) *nt* guest room

gjestfri (*ˈehst*-free) *adj* hospitable

gjestfrihet (*ˈehst*-fri-hāyt) *c* hospitality

gjeter (*ˈāy*-terr) *m* shepherd

gjette (*ˈeht*-ter) *v* guess

gjær (*ˈyæær*) *m* yeast

gjære (*ˈyææ*-rer) *v* ferment

gjø (*ˈyur*) *v* bark, bay

gjødsel (*ˈyurt*-serl) *c* manure, dung

gjøk (*ˈyurk*) *m* cuckoo

*gjøre (*ˈyur*-rer) *v* *do

glad (glaa) *adj* cheerful, glad, joyful, happy; *være ~ I love

glans (glahns) *m* gloss

glansløs (*glahns*-lūrss) *adj* mat

glass (glahss) *nt* glass; glass- glass

glassmaleri (*glahss*-maa-ler-ree) *nt* stained glass window

glasur (glah-*sewr*) *m* icing, frosting

glede (*glāy*-der) *c* gladness, joy, delight; *v* please, delight; **ha ~ av* enjoy; *med ~* gladly

glemme (*glehm*-mer) *v* *forget

glemsom (*glehm*-som) *adj* forgetful

*gli (glee) *v* *slide, glide; skid, slip

glidefly (*glee*-der-flew) *nt* (pl ~) glider

glidelås (*glee*-der-lawss) *m* zip, zipper

glimrende (*glim*-rer-ner) *adj* splendid

glimt (glimt) *nt* flash; glimpse

glinse (*glin*-ser) *v* *shine

glis (gleess) *nt* grin

glise (glee-ser) *v* grin

global oppvarming (*gloo-bāal* opp-*vahrm*-ing *c* global warming

globalisere (*gloo-bāal*-ee-*sāyr*-eh) *v* globalize

globalisering (*gloo-bāal*-ee-*shéer*-ing) *c* globalization

globalt posisjonssystem (*gloo-bahlt* poo-sish-*oons*-sews-*taym*) *nt* (pl ~mer) global positioning system (GPS)

globus (*gloo*-bewss) *m* globe

gløde (*glūrd*) *m* glow

gløde (*glūr*-der) *v* glow

*gni (gnee) *v* rub

gnist (gnist) *m* spark

gobelin (goo-beh-*lehngng*) *nt* tapestry

god (goo) *adj* good; kind

godkjenne (*goo*-kheh-ner) *v* approve of, approve

godkjennelse (*goo*-kheh-nerl-ser) *m* approval

godlynt (*goo*-lewnt) *adj* good-humo(u)red

godmodig (*goo-moo*-di)

adj good-tempered, good-natured

godskrive (*gōō*-skree-ver) *v* credit

godstog (*goots*-tawg) *nt* (pl ~) goods train; freight train *Am*

godsvogn (*goots*-vongn) wag(g)onm (goods)wagon; freight car *Am*

godt (gott) *adv* well

godter (got-terr) *pl* candy *nAm*, sweets

godtgjøre (*got*-^yur-rer) *v* *make good

godtgjørelse (*got*-^yur-rerl-ser) *m* remuneration

godtroende (*gōō*-trōō-er-ner) *adj* credulous

godvilje (*gōō*-vil-^yer) *m* goodwill

golf (golf) *m* golf; gulf

golfbane (*golf*-baa-ner) *m* golf links, golf course

gondol (gon-*dōōl*) *m* gondola

grad (graad) *m* degree; grade; i den ~ so

gradvis (*graad*-veess) *adv* gradually; *adj* gradual

grafisk (*graa*-fisk) *adj* graphic; ~ fremstilling diagram

gram (grahmm) *nt* gram

grammatikk (grah-mah-*tikk*) *m* grammar

grammatisk (grah-*maa*-tisk) *adj* grammatical

gran (graan) *c* fir tree

granitt (grah-*nitt*) *m* granite

granne (*grahn*-ner) *m* neighbo(u)r

grapefrukt (*grayp*-frewkt) *c* grapefruit

grasiøs (grah-si-*ūrss*) *adj* graceful

gratis (*graa*-tiss) *adj* free, gratis; free of charge

gratulasjon (grah-tew-lah-*shōōn*) *m* congratulation

gratulere (grah-too-*lāy*-rer) *v* congratulate

grav (graav) *c* tomb, grave

grave (*graa*-ver) *v* *dig; ~ ned bury

gravere (grah-*vāy*-rer) *v* engrave

gravid (grah-*veed*) *adj* pregnant

gravlund (*graav*-lewn) *c* cemetery

gravstein (*graav*-stayn) *m* tombstone, gravestone

gravør (grah-*vūrr*) *m* engraver

gre (greh) *v* comb

grei (gray) *adj* nice; det er greit that's fine; OK

greie (*gray*-er) *v* cope

greker (*grāy*-kerr) *m* Greek

gren (grayn) *c* branch

grense (*grehn*-ser) *c* limit, bound, boundary; frontier, border

grenseløs (*grehn*-ser-lūrss) *adj* unlimited

grep (grāyp) *nt* grasp; clutch, grip

gresk (grāysk) *adj* Greek

gress (grehss) *nt* grass

gresshoppe (*grehss*-ho-per) *c* grasshopper

gresslok (*grehss*-lūrk) *m* chives *pl*

gressplen (gehss-*plāyn*) *m* lawn

gresstrå (*greh*-straw) *nt* (pl ~) blade of grass

greve (*grāy*-ver) *m* earl, count

grevinne (greh-*vin*-ner) *c* countess

grevskap (*grāy*v-skaap) *nt* county

gribb (gribb) *m* vulture

grille (*gril*-ler) *v* grill; barbecue

grind (grinn) *c* gate

*gripe (*gree*-per) *v* *take, *catch, grasp, seize, grip; ~ **inn** intervene, interfere

gris (greess) *m* pig

grisk (grisk) *adj* greedy

griskhet (*grisk*-hāyt) *c* greed

grop (grōōp) *c* pit

grossist (groos-*sist*) *m* wholesale dealer

grotte (*grot*-ter) *c* cave, grotto

grov (grawv) *adj* coarse, gross

grovsmed (*grawv*-smāy) *m* blacksmith

gru (grēw) *m* horror

grundig (*grewn*-di) *adj* thorough

grunn[1] (grewnn) *m* ground; reason; cause; **på ~ av** owing to, because of, for,

on account of

grunn[2] (grewnn) *adj* shallow

grunnlag (*grewn*-laag) *nt* (pl ~) basis; basics

*grunnlegge (*grewn*-leh-ger) *v* found

grunnleggende (*grewn*-leh-ger-ner) *adj* basic

grunnlov (*grewn*-lawv) *m* constitution

grunnsetning (*grewn*-seht-ning) *m* principle

grunntall (*grewn*-tahll) *nt* cardinal number

gruppe (*grewp*-per) *c* group; party

gruppere (grew-*pāy*-rer) *v* classify

grus (grēwss) *m* gravel, grit

grusom (*grēw*-som) *adj* cruel, harsh; terrible, horrible, grim

gruve (*grēw*-ver) *c* pit, mine

gruvearbeider (*grēw*-ver-ahr-bay-derr) *m* miner

gruvedrift (*grēw*-ver-drift) *c* mining

gryte (*grēw*-ter) *c* pot

grøft (grurft) *c* ditch

grønn (grurnn) *adj* green; **grønt kort** green card

grønnsak (*grurn*-saak) *c* vegetable

grønnsakhandler (*grurn*-saak-hahnd-lerr) *m* greengrocer; vegetable man

grøt (grūrt) *m* porridge

grå (graw) *adj* grey

grådig (*graw*-di) *adj* greedy

gåtefull

*gråte (graw-ter) v *weep,
cry
gud (gewd) m god
guddommelig (gew-dom-
mer-li) adj divine
gudfar (gēw-faar) m (pl
-fedre) godfather
gudinne (gew-din-ner) c
goddess
gudstjeneste (gewts-t'ay-
nerss-ter) m worship,
service
guide (gighd) m guide
gul (gēwl) adj yellow
gull (gewll) nt gold
gullsmed (gewll-smāy) m
jeweller, goldsmith
gulrot (gēwl-rōōt) c (pl
-røtter) carrot
gulsott (gēwl-sot) m
jaundice
gulv (gewlv) nt floor
gulvteppe (gewlv-teh-per)
nt carpet
gummi (gewm-mi) m
rubber, gum
gunstig (gewn-sti) adj
favo(u)rable; cheap
gurgle (gewr-gler) v gargle
gutt (gewtt) m boy; lad
guvernør (gew-veh-nūrr) m
governor
gyldig ('ewl-di) adj valid
gyllen ('ewl-lern) adj
golden
gymnastikk (gewm-nah-
stikk) m physical
education, PE; gymnastics

pl
gymnastikksal (gewm-nah-
stik-saal) m gymnasium
gynekolog (gew-ner-koo-
lawg) m gynaecologist
gynge ('ewng-nger) v rock
gys ('ewss) nt shudder
gøy (gur^ew) m/nt fun
gøyal (gurew-ahl) adj
amusing
*gå (gaw) v *go, walk; pull
out; ~ bort *leave, *go
away; pass away; ~ forbi
pass by; ~ forut for
precede; ~ fottur hike; ~
fra borde disembark; ~
gjennom pass through; ~
hjem *go home; ~
igjennom *go through; ~ i
land land; ~ inn enter, *go
in; ~ med på agree; ~ ned
descend; ~ om bord
embark; ~ over cross; ~ sin
vei depart; ~ tilbake *get
back; ~ til verks proceed; ~
ut *go out; ~ videre *go
ahead, *go on
i går (i-gawr) yesterday
gårdsplass (gawsh-plahss)
m backyard, courtyard
gås (gawss) c (pl gjess)
goose
gåsehud (gaw-ser-hēwd) c
goose flesh
gåte (gaw-ter) c puzzle,
enigma, riddle
gåtefull (gaw-ter-fewl) adj
mysterious

H

*ha (haa) v ***have;** ~ **noe imot** mind; ~ **på seg** ***wear;** ~ **det!** bye-bye

hage (haa-ger) m garden

hagl (haghl) nt hail; buckshot

hai (high) m shark

haike (high-ker) v hitchhike

haiker (high-kerr) m hitchhiker

hake (haa-ker) c chin

hakke (hahk-ker) v chop

hale (haa-ler) m tail

hallo! (hah-lōō) hello!

halm (hahlm) m straw

halmtak (hahlm-taak) nt (pl ~) thatched roof

hals (hahls) m throat, neck

halsbrann (hahls-brahn) m heartburn

halsbånd (hahls-bon) nt (pl ~) collar

halsesyke (hahl-ser-sēw-ker) m sore throat

halskjede (hahls-khāy-der) nt necklace

halt (hahlt) adj lame

halte (hahl-ter) v limp

halv (hahll) adj half; **halv-** semi-

halvdel (hahl-dāyl) m half

halvere (hahl-vāy-rer) v halve

halvsirkel (hahl-seer-kerl) m (pl -kler) semicircle

halvt (hahlt) adv half

halvtid (hahl-teed) c half time

halvveis (hahl-vayss) adv halfway

halvøy (hahl-lur^ew) c peninsula

ham (hahmm) pron him

hamburger (hahmm-bur-gerr) m hamburger, beefburger, burger

hammer (hahm-merr) m hammer

hamp (hahmp) m hemp

han (hahnn) pron he, him; **hann-** male

handel (hahn-derl) m (pl -dler) commerce, business, trade; deal; ***drive ~** trade; **handels-** commercial

handelsmann (hahn-derls-mahn) m (pl -menn) tradesman

handelsrett (hahn-derls-reht) m commercial law

handelsvare (hahn-derls-vaa-rer) m merchandise

handikap (hahn-di-kapp) nt handicap

handle (hahnd-ler) v shop; act; ~ **med** *deal with

handlebag (hahnd-ler-bæg) m shopping bag

handlende (hahnd-ler-ner) m (pl ~) dealer

handling (hahnd-ling) c action, act, deed; plot

hane (haa-ner) m cock

hans (hahns) pron his

hanske (*hahn*-sker) *m* glove

hard (haar) *adj* hard

harddisk (*haar*-disk) *m* hard disk

hardnakket (*haanah*-kert) *adj* obstinate

hare (*haa*-rer) *m* hare

harmoni (hahr-moo-*nee*) *c* harmony

harpe (*hahr*-per) *c* harp

harsk (hahshk) *adj* rancid

hasselnøtt (*hahss*-serl-nurt) *c* hazelnut

hast (hahst) *m* haste

hastig (*hahss*-ti) *adj* hasty

hastighet (*hahss*-ti-hāyt) *c* speed

hastverk (*hahst*-værk) *nt* hurry

hat (haat) *nt* hatred, hate

hate (*haa*-ter) *v* hate, detest

hatt (hahtt) *m* hat

haug (hou) *m* pile, heap; mound

hauk (houk) *m* hawk

hav (haav) *nt* ocean

havmåke (*haav*-maw-ker) *c* seagull

havn (hahvn) *c* port, harbour

havnearbeider (*hahv*-ner-ahr-bay-derr) *m* docker

havneby (*hahv*-ner-bēw) *m* seaport

havre (*hahv*-rer) *m* oats *pl*

hebraisk (heh-*braa*-isk) *nt* Hebrew

hedensk (*hāy*-dernsk) *adj* pagan, heathen

heder (*hāy*-derr) *m* glory

hederlig (*hāy*-der-li) *adj* honourable

hedning (*hāyd*-ning) *m* pagan, heathen

hedre (*hāy*-drer) *v* honour

heftig (*hehf*-ti) *adj* severe, violent, fierce

hegre (*hāy*-grer) *m* heron

hei (hay) *c* heath

heis (hayss) *m* lift; elevator *nAm*

heise (*hay*-ser) *v* hoist

heisekran (*hay*-ser-kraan) *m* crane

hekk (hehkk) *m* hedge

hekle (*hehk*-ler) *v* crochet

heks (hehks) *c* witch

hel (hāyl) *adj* entire, whole

helbrede (*hehl*-brāy-der) *v* cure, heal

helbredelse (*hehl*-brāy-derl-ser) *m* recovery, cure

heldig (*hehl*-di) *adj* lucky, fortunate

heldigvis (*hehl*-di-vis) *adv* luckily, fortunately

hele (*hāy*-ler) *nt* whole; i det ~ altogether

helg (hehlg) *c* weekend

helgen (*hehl*-gern) *m* saint

helgenskrin (*hehl*-gern-skreen) *nt* (*pl* ~) reliquary

helikopter (hehll-ee-*kopp*-terr) *nt* helicopter

helkornbrød (*hāyl*-kōōn-brŪr) *nt* (*pl* ~) wholemeal bread

hell (hehll) *nt* luck

Hellas (*hehl*-lahss) Greece

helle (*hehl*-ler) *v* pour; slope

heller (*hehl-lerr*) *adv* sooner, rather

hellig (*hehl-li*) *adj* holy, sacred

helligbrøde (*hehl-li-brūr-der*) *m* sacrilege

helligdag (*hehl-li-daag*) *m* holiday, Sunday

helligdom (*hehl-li-dom*) *m* (pl ~mer) shrine

helling (*hehl-ling*) *c* gradient

helse (*hehl-ser*) *c* health

helseattest (*hehl-ser-ah-tehst*) *m* health certificate

helt¹ (*hehlt*) *m* hero

helt² (*hāylt*) *adv* wholly, entirely, quite, completely

heltinne (hehlt-*inn*-ner) *c* heroine

helvete (*hehl-ver-ter*) *nt* hell

hemme (*hehm-mer*) *v* inhibit

hemmelig (*hehm-li*) *adj* secret

hemmelighet (*hehm-li-hāyt*) *c* secret

hemorroider (heh-moo-*ree-*derr) *pl* piles *pl*, haemorrhoids *pl*

hende (*hehn-ner*) *v* happen, occur

hendelse (*hehn-nerl-ser*) *m* incident, happening, occurrence

hendig (*hehn-di*) *adj* handy

***henge** (*hehng-nger*) *v* *hang

hengebro (*hehng-nger-brōō*) *c* suspension bridge

hengekøye (*hehng-nger-kur*ᶜʷ-*er*) *c* hammock

hengelås (*heh-nger-lawss*) *m* padlock

henger (*hehng-ngerr*) *m* hanger

hengiven (*hehn-ʸee-vern*) *adj* affectionate

hengivenhet (*hehn-ʸee-vern-hāyt*) *c* affection

hengsel (*hehng-sherl*) *nt* (pl -sler) hinge

henne (*hehn-ner*) *pron* her

hennes (*hehn-nerss*) *pron* her, hers

henrettelse (*hehn-reh-terl-ser*) *m* execution

henrivende (*hehn-ree-ver-ner*) *adj* adorable, delightful, enchanting

henrykt (*hehn-rewkt*) *adj* delighted

hensikt (*hehn-sikt*) *m* intention, purpose, design; *ha til ~ intend

henstand (*hehn-stahn*) *m* respite

hensyn (*hehn-sēwn*) *nt* regard; med ~ til as regards, regarding

hensynsfull (*hehn-sēwns-fewl*) *adj* considerate

hensynsfullhet (*hehn-sēwns-fewl-hāyt*) *c* consideration

hente (*hehn-ter*) *v* fetch; *get, pick up, collect

henvende seg til (*hehn-veh-ner*) address

henvise til (*hehn-vee-ser*)
refer to

henvisning (*hehn-veess-
ning*) *m* reference

her (*hær*) *adv* here

heretter (*hææ-reh-terr*) *adv*
from now on

herkomst (*hæær-komst*) *m*
origin

herlig (*hææ-li*) *adj*
wonderful, lovely,
delightful

hermetikk (*hær-mer-tikk*) *m*
tinned food

hermetikkboks (*hær-mer-
tik-boks*) *m* tin; can *nAm*

hermetikkåpner (*hær-mer-
tik-awp-nerr*) *m* tin opener

hermetisere (*hær-mah-ti-
sāy-rer*) *v* preserve

herre (*hær-rer*) *m*
gentleman

herredømme (*hær-rer-dur-
mer*) *nt* dominion

herregård (*hær-rer-gawr*) *m*
mansion, manor house

herretoalett (*hær-rer-too-
ah-leht*) *nt* men's room

herske (*hæsh-ker*) *v* reign,
rule

hersker (*hæsh-kerr*) *m*
sovereign

hertug (*hæt-tewg*) *m* duke

hertuginne (*hæ-tew-gin-
ner*) *c* duchess

hes (*hāyss*) *adj* hoarse

hest (*hehst*) *m* horse

hestekraft (*hehss-ter-
krahft*) *c* (pl -krefter)
horsepower

hestesko (*hehss-ter-skōō*)
m (pl ~) horseshoe

hesteveddeløp (*hehss-ter-
veh-der-lūrp*) *nt* (pl ~)
horserace

het (*hāyt*) *adj* hot

hete (*hāy-ter*) *m* heat

*hete (*hāy-ter*) *v* *be called

heteroseksuell (*hāy-ter-
roo-sehk-sew-ehl*) *adj*
heterosexual

hette (*heht-ter*) *c* hood

heve (*hāy-ver*) *v* raise;
*draw, cash

hevelse (*hāy-verl-ser*) *m*
swelling

hevn (*hehvn*) *m* revenge

hi (*hee*) *nt* den

hierarki (*hi-eh-rahr-kee*) *nt*
hierarchy

hikke (*hik-ker*) *m* hiccup

hilse (*hil-ser*) *v* greet;
salute; ~ på say hello to

hilsen (*hil-sern*) *m* greeting

himmel (*him-merl*) *m* (pl
himler) sky; heaven

hindre (*hin-drer*) *v* hinder,
impede

hindring (*hin-dring*) *c*
obstacle, impediment

hinsides (*heen-see-derss*)
prep beyond

hint (*hinnt*) *nt* hint; *v* ~e
hint

hiphop (*hipp-hopp*) *c* hip-
-hop

hissig (*hiss-si*) *adj* hot-
-tempered, quick-tempered

historie (*hiss-tōō-ri-er*) *c*
history

historiker (hiss-_tōō_-ri-kerr) *m* historian

historisk (hiss-_tōō_-risk) *adj* historic, historical

hittegods (_hit_-ter-goots) *nt* lost and found

hittegodskontor (_hit_-ter-goots-koon-_tōōr_) *nt* lost property office

hittil (_heet_-til) *adv* so far

hjelm (ʸehlm) *m* helmet

hjelp (ʸehlp) *c* aid, assistance, help; relief

*__hjelpe__ (ʸehl-per) *v* help, aid; support, assist

hjelper (ʸehl-perr) *m* helper

hjelpsom (ʸehlp-som) *adj* helpful

hjem (ʸehmm) *nt* home

hjemlengsel (ʸehm-lehng-serl) *m* homesickness

hjemme (ʸehm-mer) *adv* at home

hjemmelaget (ʸehm-mer-laa-gert) *adj* home-made

hjemover (ʸehm-maw-verr) *adv* homeward

hjemreise (ʸehm-ray-ser) *c* return journey

hjerne (ʸææ-ner) *m* brain

hjernerystelse (ʸæ-ner-rewss-terl-ser) *m* concussion

hjerte (ʸæt-ter) *nt* heart

hjerteanfall (ʸæt-ter-ahn-fahl) *nt* (pl ~) heart attack

hjerteklapp (ʸæt-ter-klahp) *m* palpitation

hjertelig (ʸæt-li) *adj* cordial, hearty

hjerteløs (ʸæt-ter-lūrss) *adj* heartless

hjort (ʸott) *m* deer

hjul (ʸewl) *nt* wheel

hjørne (ʸūr-ner) *nt* corner

hode (_hōō_-der) *nt* head; **på hodet** upside down

hodepine (_hōō_-der-pee-ner) *c* headache

hodepute (_hōō_-der-pēw-ter) *c* pillow

hoff (hoff) *nt* court

hofte (_hof_-ter) *c* hip

hold (holl) *nt* stitch

*__holde__ (_hol_-ler) *v* *hold; *keep; ~ **oppe** *hold up; ~ **opp med** stop; ~ **på** *hold; ~ **på med** *keep at; ~ **seg borte fra** *keep away from; ~ **seg fast** *hold on; ~ **tilbake** keep back, *withhold ~ **ut** *keep up; *bear, endure; ~ **utkikk etter** watch for

holdeplass (_hol_-ler-plahss) *m* stop

holdning (_hold_-ning) *m* position, attitude

Holland (_hol_-lahn) Holland

hollandsk (_hol_-lahnsk) *adj* Dutch

hollender (_hol_-lehn-derr) *m* Dutchman

homofil (_hōō_-moo-_feel_) *adj* homosexual, gay *colloquial*; lesbian

honning (_hon_-ning) *m* honey

honorar (hoo-noo-_raar_) *nt* fee

hop (hoop) *m* lot; heap

hopp (hopp) *nt* jump, leap, hop

hoppe¹ (*hop*-per) *v* jump; skip, hop; *leap; ~ over skip

hoppe² (*hop*-per) *c* mare

hore (*hoo*-rer) *c* whore

horisont (hoo-ri-*sont*) *m* horizon

horisontal (hoo-ri-son-*taal*) *adj* horizontal

horn (hoon) *nt* horn

hornorkester (*hoo*-nor-kehss-terr) *nt* (pl -tre) brass band

hos (hooss) *prep* with; at

hospital (hooss-pi-*taal*) *nt* hospital

hoste (*hooss*-ter) *v* cough; *m* cough

hotell (hoo-*tehll*) *nt* hotel

hov (hoov) *m* hoof

hoved- (*hoo*-verd) capital, cardinal, chief, main, primary, principal

hovedgate (*hoo*-verd-gaa-ter) *c* main street

hovedkvarter (*hoo*-verd-kvah-tayr) *nt* headquarters *pl*

hovedledning (*hoo*-verd-layd-ning) *m* mains *pl*

hovedsakelig (*hoo*-verd-saa-ker-li) *adv* mainly

hovedstad (*hoo*-verd-staad) *m* (pl -steder) capital

hovedvei (*hoo*-verd-vay) *m* thoroughfare, main road

hoven (*haw*-vern) *adj* snooty

hovmester (*hawv*-mehss-terr) *m* (pl -tre) head waiter

hovmodig (hov-*moo*-di) *adj* haughty; proud

hud (hewd) *c* skin

hudfarge (*hewd*-fahr-ger) *m* complexion

hukommelse (hew-*kom*-merl-ser) *m* memory

hul (hewl) *adj* hollow

hule (*hew*-ler) *c* cave, cavern

hull (hewll) *nt* hole

hulrom (*hewl*-room) *nt* (pl ~) cavity

humle (*hoom*-ler) *c* bumblebee; *m* hops

hummer (*hoom*-merr) *m* lobster

humor (*hew*-moor) *m* humo(u)r

humoristisk (hew-moo-*riss*-tisk) *adj* humorous

humpet (*hoom*-pert) *adj* bumpy

humør (hew-*mūrr*) *nt* mood; spirits

hun (hewnn) *pron* she; hunn- female

hund (hewnn) *m* dog

hundehus (*hewn*-ner-hewss) *nt* (pl ~) kennel

hunderem (*hewn*-ner-rehmm) *c* (pl ~mer) lead

hundre (*hewn*-drer) *num* hundred

hurtig (*hewt*-ti) *adj* fast,

quick, rapid

hurtigtaster (*hewt*-ti-tahs-ter) *c* (pl ~e) speed dial(ing)

hurtigtog (*hewt*-ti-tawg) *nt* (pl ~) through train, express train

hus (*hewss*) *nt* house; **hus-domestic**

husarbeid (*hewss*-ahr-bayd) *nt* housework

husbåt (*hewss*-bawt) *m* houseboat

husdyr (*hewss*-dewr) *nt* (pl ~) domestic animal

huse (*hew*-ser) *v* lodge

huseier (*hewss*-ay-err) *m* landlord

hushjelp (*hewss*-ᵞerlp) *c* maid, housemaid

husholderske (*hewss*-ho-lersh-ker) *m* housekeeper

husholdning (*hewss*-hol-ning) *m* housekeeping

huske (*hewss*-ker) *v* remember; recollect; *swing; *m* swing

huslærer (*hewss*-læ-rerr) *m* tutor

husmor (*hewss*-mōōr) *c* (pl -mødre) housewife

husrom (*hewss*-room) *nt* accommodation; **skaffe ~** accommodate

husstand (*hew*-stahn) *m* household

husvert (*hewss*-vært) *m* landlord, landlady

hutre (*hewt*-rer) *v* shiver

hva (vaa) *pron* what; **~ enn**

whatever; **~ som helst** anything

hval (vaal) *m* whale

hvelv (vehlv) *nt* arch

hvelving (*vehl*-ving) *m* vault

hvem (vehmm) *pron* who; **~ som enn** whoever; **~ som helst** anybody; **til ~** whom

hver (væær) *adj* every, each

hverandre (væ-*rahn*-drer) *pron* each other

hverdag (*væ*-daag) *m* weekday

hvete (*vaȳ*-ter) *m* wheat

hvetebolle (*vaȳ*-ter-bo-ler) *m* bun

hvetebrødsdager (*vaȳ*-ter-brüss-daa-gerr) *pl* honeymoon

hvile (*vee*-ler) *v* rest; *m* rest

hvilehjem (*vee*-ler-ᵞehm) *nt* (pl ~) rest home

hvilken (*vil*-kern) *pron* which; **~ som helst** whichever; **hvilke som helst** any

hvin (veen) *nt* shriek

hvis (viss) *conj* if; in case

hviske (*viss*-ker) *v* whisper

hvisking (*viss*-king) *c* whisper

hvit (veet) *adj* white

hvitløk (*veet*-lük) *m* garlic

hvitting (*vit*-ting) *m* whiting

hvor (vōōr) *adv* where; how; **~ enn** wherever; **~ mange** how many; **~ mye** how much; **~ som helst** anywhere

hvordan (*voo*-dahn) *adv*
how

hvorfor (*voor*-for) *adv* why;
what for

hyggelig (*hewg*-ger-li) *adj*
pleasant, enjoyable

hygiene (hew-gi-*āy*-ner) *m*
hygiene

hygienisk (hew-gi-*āy*-nisk)
adj hygienic

hykler (*hewk*-lerr) *m*
hypocrite

hykleri (hewk-ler-*ree*) *nt*
hypocrisy

hyklersk (*hewk*-lehshk) *adj*
hypocritical

hyl (hēwl) *nt* scream, yell

hyle (*hēw*-ler) *v* scream, yell

hylle (*hewl*-ler) *c* shelf; *v*
*pay tribute to

hyllest (*hewl*-lerst) *m*
homage, tribute

hymne (*hewm*-ner) *m* hymn

hypotek (hew-poo-*tāyk*) *nt*
mortgage

hyppig (*hewp*-pi) *adj*
frequent

hyppighet (*hewp*-pi-hāyt) *c*
frequency

hyssing (*hewss*-sing) *m*
twine

hysterisk (hewss-*tāy*-risk)
adj hysterical

hytte (*hewt*-ter) *c* cabin,
hut; chalet, lodge; cottage

hæl (hæl) *m* heel

høflig (*hurf*-li) *adj* polite,
civil

høne (*hūr*-ner) *c* hen

hørbar (*hūrr*-baar) *adj*

audible

høre (*hūr*-rer) *v* *hear

hørsel (*hursh*-sherl) *m*
hearing

høst (hurst) *m* autumn; fall
nAm

høste (*hurss*-ter) *v* gather

høvding (*hurv*-ding) *m*
chieftain

høvisk (*hūr*-visk) *adj*
courteous

høy¹ (hur^{ew}) *adj* tall, high;
loud

høy² (hur^{ew}) *nt* hay

høyde (*hurew*-der) *m*
height; altitude, rise

høydepunkt (*hurew*-der-
poongt) *nt* zenith, height

høyderygg (*hurew*-der-
rewgg) *m* ridge

høyere (*hurew*-er-rer) *adj*
superior, higher

høyland (*hurew*-lahn) *nt* (pl
~) uplands *pl*

høylydt (*hurew*-lewt) *adj*
loud

høyre (*hurew*-rer) *adj* right;
right-hand; på ~ side
right-hand

høyrød (*hurew*-rūr) *adj*
crimson

høysesong (*hurew*-seh-
song) *m* peak season, high
season

høyslette (*hurew*-shleh-ter)
c plateau

høysnue (*hurew*-snew-er)
m hay fever

høyst (hur^{ew}st) *adv* at most

høyt (hur^{ew}t) *adv* aloud

høytalertelefon (*hurew-tāal-er-tel-e-foōn*) *c* speaker phone

høytidelig (hur^{ew}-*tee*-der-li) *adj* solemn

høyttaler (*hurew-taa-lerr*) *m* loud-speaker

høyvann (*hurew-vahn*) *nt* high tide

hån (hawn) *m* mockery, scorn

hånd (honn) *c* (pl hender) hand; *ta ~ om attend to

håndarbeid (*hon-nahr-bayd*) *nt* needlework; handwork

håndbagasje (*hon-bah-gaa-sher*) *m* hand luggage; hand baggage *Am*

håndbok (*hon-bōōk*) *c* (pl -bøker) handbook, manual

håndbrems (*hon-brehms*) *m* hand-brake

håndflate (*hon-flaa-ter*) *c* palm

håndfull (*hon-fewl*) *m* handful

håndholdt (hon-*holt*) *adj* hand held

håndjern (*hon-^yæærn*) *pl* handcuffs *pl*

håndkle (*hong-kler*) *nt* (pl -lær) towel

håndkrem (*hon-krāym*) *m* hand cream

håndlaget (*hon-laa-gert*) *adj* hand-made

håndledd (*hon-lehd*) *nt* (pl ~) wrist

håndskrift (*hon-skrift*) *c* handwriting

håndtak (*hon-taak*) *nt* (pl ~) handle

håndtere (hon-*tāy*-rer) *v* handle

håndterlig (hon-*tāy*-li) *adj* manageable

håndtrykk (*hon-trewk*) *nt* (pl ~) handshake

håndvask (*hon-vahsk*) *m* wash-basin; hand wash

håndverk (*hon-værk*) *nt* (pl ~) handicraft

håndveske (*hon-vehss-ker*) *c* bag, handbag

håne (*haw*-ner) *v* mock

håp (hawp) *nt* hope

håpe (*haw*-per) *v* hope

håpefull (*haw*-per-fewl) *adj* hopeful

håpløs (*hawp*-lūrss) *adj* hopeless

håpløshet (*hawp*-lūrss-hāyt) *c* despair

hår (hawr) *nt* hair

hårbalsam (*hawr-bahl-sahm*) *m* conditioner

hårbørste (*hawr-bursh-ter*) *m* hairbrush

håret (*haw*-rert) *adj* hairy

hårfrisyre (*hawr-fri-sēw-rer*) *m* hair-do

hårgelé (*hawr-sheh-lay*) *m* hair gel

hårklipp (*hawr-klip*) *m* haircut

hårlakk (*haw-lahk*) *m* hair spray

hårskill (*haw-shil*) *m* parting

hårspenne (*haw*-shpeh-ner) *c* hair-pin; bobby pin *Am*

hårtørrer (*haw*-turr-rerr) *m* hairdrier, hairdryer

I

i (ee) *prep* in; for, at

***iaktta** (i-*ahk*-tah) *v* observe, watch

iakttakelse (i-*ahk*-taa-kerl-ser) *m* observation

ibenholt (*ee*-bern-holt) *m/nt* ebony

idé (i-*day*) *m* idea

ideal (i-deh-*aal*) *nt* ideal

ideell (i-deh-*ehll*) *adj* ideal

identifisere (i-dehn-ti-fi-*say*-rer) *v* identify

identifisering (i-dehn-ti-fi-*say*-ring) *c* identification

identisk (i-*dehn*-tisk) *adj* identical

identitet (i-dehn-ti-*tayt*) *m* identity

identitetskort (i-dehn-ti-*tayts*-kot) *nt* (pl ~) identity card, ID

idiom (i-di-*oom*) *nt* idiom

idiomatisk (i-di-oo-*maa*-tisk) *adj* idiomatic

idiot (i-di-*oot*) *m* idiot

idiotisk (i-di-*oo*-tisk) *adj* idiotic

idol (i-*dool*) *nt* idol

idrettsmann (*eed*-rehts-mahn) *m* (pl -menn) sportsman

idrettskvinne (*eed*-rehts-kvin-ner) *c* sportswoman

ifølge (i-*furl*-ger) *prep* according to

igjen (i-*³ehnn*) *adv* again

ignorere (ig-noo-*ray*-rer) *v* ignore

ikke (*ik*-ker) *adv* not

ikke-røyker (*ik*-ker-rurew-kerr) *m* non-smoker

ikon (i-*koon*) *m/nt* icon

ild (ill) *m* fire

ildfast (*il*-fahst) *adj* fireproof, ovenproof

ildsfarlig (*ils*-faa-li) *adj* inflammable

ildsted (*il*-stayd) *nt* hearth

illegal (*il*-leh-gaal) *adj* illegal

illeluktende (*il*-ler-look-ter-ner) *adj* smelly

illevarslende (*il*-ler-vahsh-ler-ner) *adj* sinister, ominous

illusjon (i-lew-*shoon*) *m* illusion

illustrasjon (i-lew-strah-*shoon*) *m* illustration; picture

illustrere (i-lew-*stray*-rer) *v* illustrate

imens (i-*mehns*) *adv* meanwhile, in the meantime

imidlertid (i-*mid*-ler-ti) *adv*

though; in the meantime

imitasjon (i-mi-tah-*shōōn*) *m* imitation

imitere (i-mi-*tāy*-rer) *v* imitate

immigrant (i-mi-*grahnt*) *m* immigrant

immigrasjon (i-mi-grah-*shōōn*) *m* immigration

immigrere (i-mi-*grāy*-rer) *v* immigrate

immun: *gjøre ~ (ʸūr-rer i-mēwn*) immunize

immunitet (i-mew-ni-*tāyt*) *m* immunity

imperium (im-*pāy*-ri-ewm) *nt* (pl -ier) empire

imponere (im-poo-*nāy*-rer) *v* impress

imponerende (im-poo-*nāy*-rer-ner) *adj* impressive, imposing

import (im-*pott*) *m* import

importavgift (im-*pot*-taav-ʸift) *c* import duty

importere (im-po-*tāy*-rer) *v* import

importvarer (im-*pot*-vaa-rerr) *pl* imported goods

importør (im-po-*tūrr*) *m* importer

impotens (im-poo-*tehns*) *m* impotence

impotent (im-poo-*tehnt*) *adj* impotent

improvisere (im-proo-vi-*sāy*-rer) *v* improvise

impuls (im-*pewls*) *m* impulse

impulsiv (*im*-pewl-seev) *adj*

impulsive

imøtekommende (i-*mūr*-ter-ko-mer-ner) *adj* obliging

indeks (*in*-dehks) *m* index

inder (*in*-derr) *m* Indian

India (*in*-di-ah) India

indianer (in-di-*aa*-nerr) *m* Indian

indiansk (in-di-*aansk*) *adj* Indian

indirekte (*in*-di-rehk-ter) *adj* indirect

indisk (*in*-disk) *adj* Indian

individ (in-di-*veed*) *nt* individual

individuell (in-di-vi-dew-*ehll*) *adj* individual

Indonesia (in-doo-*nāy*-si-ah) Indonesia

indonesier (in-doo-*nāy*-si-err) *m* Indonesian

indonesisk (in-doo-*nāy*-sisk) *adj* Indonesian

indre (*in*-drer) *adj* internal; inside, inner

industri (in-dew-*stree*) *m* industry

industriell (in-dew-stri-*ehll*) *adj* industrial

industriområde (in-dew-stree-om-raw-der) *nt* industrial area

infanteri (in-fahn-ter-*ree*) *nt* infantry

infeksjon (in-fehk-*shōōn*) *m* infection

infinitiv (in-*fin*-ni-teev) *m* infinitive

infisere (in-fi-*sāy*-rer) *v*

infect

inflasjon (in-flah-*shōōn*) *m*
inflation

influensa (in-flew-*ehn*-sah)
m flu, influenza

informasjon (in-for-mah-*shōōn*) *m* information

informasjonskontor (in-for-mah-*shōōns*-koon-tōōr) *nt* inquiry office, information bureau

informere (in-for-*māy*-rer) *v* inform

inline rulleskøyter (inn-*læin* rew-ler-shurew-ter) *pl* Rollerblade

infrarød (in-frah-*rūr*) *adj* infra-red

ingefær (*ing*-nger-fæær) *m* ginger

ingen (*ing*-ngern) *pron* nobody, no one; none; *adj* no; ~ av dem neither

ingeniør (in-shern-*yūrr*) *m* engineer

ingensteds (*ing*-ngern-stehss) *adv* nowhere

ingenting (*ing*-ngern-ting) *pron* nil, nothing

ingrediens (ing-greh-di-*ehns*) *m* ingredient

initiativ (i-nit-si-ah-*teev*) *nt* initiative

injeksjon (in-*y*ehk-*shōōn*) *m* injection

inkludert (in-klew-*dāyt*) *adj* included; alt ~ all included

inklusive (*in*-klew-seever) *adv* inclusive

inkompetent (*in*-kom-per-

tehnt) *adj* incompetent

inn (inn) *adv* in; ~ i into

innbefatte (*in*-beh-fah-ter) *v* comprise, include

innbille seg (*in*-bi-ler) *v* imagine

innbilsk (*in*-bilsk) *adj* conceited

innbilt (*in*-bilt) *adj* imaginary

innblande (*in*-blah-ner) *v* involve

innblandet (*in*-blah-nert) *adj* concerned, involved

innblanding (*in*-blah-ning) *c* interference

innbringende (*in*-bri-nger-ner) *adj* profitable

innbrudd (*in*-brewd) *nt* burglary

innbruddstyv (*in*-brewds-tēwv) *m* burglar

innby (*in*-bēw) *v* ask; invite

innbydelse (in-*bēw*-derl-ser) *m* invitation

innbygger (*in*-bew-gerr) *m* inhabitant

inndele (in-*dāy*-ler) *v* *break down, divide into

inne (*in*-ner) *adv* indoors; inside

innebære (*in*-ner-bææ-rer) *v* imply

innehaver (*in*-ner-haa-verr) *m* owner, bearer

inneholde (*in*-ner-ho-ler) *v* contain

innen (*in*-nern) *prep* inside; within

innendørs (*in*-nern-dūrsh)

adj indoor

innenfor (*in*-nern-for) *prep*
inside; within

innenlands (*in*-nern-lahns)
adj domestic

innfall (*in*-fahl) *nt* (pl ~)
idea; whim; brain wave

innfatning (*in*-faht-ning) *m*
frame

innflytelse (*in*-flēw-terl-ser)
m influence

innflytelsesrik (*in*-flēw-
terl-serss-reek) *adj*
influential

innfødt (*in*-furt) *m* (pl ~e)
native

innføre (*in*-fūr-rer) *v*
import; introduce; initiate

innførsel (*in*-fur-sherl) *m*
import

innførselstoll (*in*-fur-sherls-
tol) *m* duty

inngang (*in*-gahng) *m*
entrance, entry; way in

inngangspenger (*in*-
gahngs-peh-ngerr) *pl*
entrance fee

innhold (*in*-hol) *nt* contents
pl

innholdsfortegnelse (*in*-
hols-fo-tay-nerl-ser) *m*
table of contents

inni (*in*-ni) *adv prep* within;
inside

innkassere (*in*-kah-sāy-rer)
v collect

innledende (*in*-lāy-der-ner)
adj preliminary

innledning (*in*-lāyd-ning) *m*
introduction

innlemme (*in*- lāym -mer) *v*
integrate

innlysende (*in*-lēw-ser-ner)
adj obvious

innover (*in*-naw-verr) *adv*
inwards

innpakning (*in*-pahk-ning)
m packing, wrapping

innpakningspapir (*in*-
pahk-nings-pah-peer) *nt*
wrapping paper

innrede (*in*-reh-der) *v*
furnish; decorate

innredning (*in*-reh-dning)
m furnishing, decoration

innrette (*in*-reht-ter) *v*
arrange

innretning (*in*-reht-tning)
m facilities; gadget

innrømme (*in*-rur-mer) *v*
acknowledge, admit

innsamler (*in*-sahm-lerr) *m*
collector

innsats (*in*-sahts) *m*
achievement; contribution;
stake

innsatt (*in*-saht) *m* (pl ~e)
prisoner

*****innse** (*in*-sāy) *v* realize,
*see

innside (*in*-see-der) *c*
inside; interior

innsikt (*in*-sikt) *m* insight

innsirkle (*in*-seer-kler) *v*
encircle

innsjø (*in*-shūr) *m* lake

innskipning (*in*-ship-ning)
m embarkation

innskrenkning (*in*-
skrehngk-ning) *m*

reduction, restriction

*innskrive (*in*-skree-ver) *v*
list, enter, register; ~ seg
register

*innskyte (*in*-shēw-ter) *v*
insert

innskytelse (*in*-shēw-terl-
ser) *m* impulse

innsprøyte (*in*-sprur^{ew}-ter)
v inject

innstendig (in-*stehn*-di) *adj*
urgent

inntekt (*in*-tehkt) *c* income,
earnings

inntektsskatt (*in*-tehkt-
skaht) *m* income tax

inntil (*in*-til) *conj* until, till;
prep till

inntreden (*in*-trāy-dern) *m*
entrance

inntrengende (*in*-treh-nger-
ner) *adj* pressing

inntrykk (*in*-trewk) *nt*
impression; *gjøre ~ på
impress

innvende (*in*-veh-ner) *v*
object; ~ mot object to

innvendig (*in*-vehn-di) *adv*
within

innvending (*in*-veh-ning) *c*
objection

innviklet (*in*-vik-lert) *adj*
complex, complicated

innvilge (*in*-vil-ger) *v* grant

innvoller (*in*-vo-lerr) *pl*
insides, entrails

innånde (*in*-no-ner) *v*
inhale

insekt (*in*-sehkt) *nt* insect;
bug *nAm*

insektmiddel (*in*-sehkt-mi-
derl) *nt* (pl -midler)
insecticide, insect
repellent

insinuere (in-si-new-āy-rer)
v hint, insinuate

insistere (in-si-*stay*-rer) *v*
insist

inskripsjon (in-skrip-
shōōn) *m* inscription

inspeksjon (in-spehk-
shōōn) *m* inspection

inspektør (in-spayk-*tūrr*) *m*
inspector

inspirere (in-spi-*rāy*-rer) *v*
inspire

inspisere (in-spi-*sāy*-rer) *v*
inspect

installasjon (in-stah-lah-
shōōn) *m* installation

installere (in-stah-*lāy*-rer) *v*
install

instinkt (in-*stingt*) *nt*
instinct

institusjon (in-sti-tew-
shōōn) *m* institution

institutt (in-sti-*tewtt*) *nt*
institution, institute

instruktør (in-strewk-*tūrr*)
m instructor

instrument (in-strew-
mehnt) *nt* instrument

instrumentbord (in-strew-
mehnt-bōōr) *nt* (pl ~)
dashboard

intakt (in-*tahkt*) *adj* intact;
unbroken

integrere (in-teh-*grēy*-rer) *v*
integrate

intellekt (in-teh-*lehkt*) *nt*

intellect

intellektuell (in-teh-lehk-tew-*ehll*) *adj* intellectual

intelligens (in-teh-li-*gehns*) *m* intelligence

intelligent (in-teh-li-*gehnt*) *adj* intelligent; clever

intens (in-*tehns*) *adj* intense

interessant (in-ter-reh-*sahngng*) *adj* interesting

interesse (in-ter-*rehss*-ser) *m* interest

interessere (in-ter-reh-*sāy*-rer) *v* interest

interessert (in-ter-reh-*sāyt*) *adj* interested

internasjonal (*in*-ter-nah-shoo-naal) *adj* international

Internett (*in*-terr-nett*l*) Internet

intervall (in-terr-*vahl*) *nt* interval

intervju (in-terr-*v*ʸ*ew*) *nt* interview

intet (*in*-tert) *nt* nothing

intetkjønn (*in*-tert-khurn) neuter

intetsigende (*in*-tert-see-er-ner) *adj* insignificant, petty

intim (in-*teem*) *adj* intimate

intrige (in-*tree*-ger) *m* intrigue

introduksjonsskriv (in-troo-dewk-*shoon*-skreev) *nt* (pl ∼) letter of recommendation

introdusere (in-troo-dew-*sāy*-rer) *v* introduce

invadere (in-vah-*dāy*-rer) *v*

invade

invasjon (in-vah-*shoon*) *m* invasion

investere (in-vehss-*tāy*-rer) *v* invest

investering (in-vehss-*tāy*-ring) *c* investment

invitere (in-vi-*tāy*-rer) *v* invite

Irak (i-*raak*) Iraq

iraker (i-*raa*-kerr) *m* Iraqi

irakisk (i-*raa*-kisk) *adj* Iraqi

Iran (i-*raan*) Iran

iraner (i-*raa*-nerr) *m* Iranian

iransk (i-*rahnsk*) *adj* Iranian

Irland (*eer*-lahn) Ireland

ironi (i-roo-*nee*) *m* irony

ironisk (i-*rōō*-nisk) *adj* ironical

irritabel (i-ri-*taa*-berl) *adj* irritable

irritere (i-ri-*tāy*-rer) *v* irritate; annoy

irriterende (i-ri-*tāy*-rer-ner) *adj* annoying

irsk (eeshk) *adj* Irish

is (eess) *m* ice

isbre (*eess*-brāy) *m* glacier

iskald (*eess*-kahl) *adj* freezing

iskrem (*eess*-krāym) *m* ice cream

Island (*eess*-lahn) Iceland

islandsk (*eess*-lahnsk) *adj* Icelandic

islending (*eess*-leh-ning) *m* Icelander

isolasjon (i-soo-lah-*shoon*) *m* isolation; insulation

isolator (i-soo-*laa*-toor) *m*

insulator
isolere (i-soo-*lay*-rer) *v*
insulate; isolate
isolert (i-soo-*layt*) *adj*
isolated
Israel (*eess*-rah-ehl) Israel
israeler (iss-rah-*ay*-lerr) *m*
Israeli
israelsk (iss-rah-*ayls*k) *adj*
Israeli
istedenfor (i-*stay*-dern-for)
prep instead of

isvann (*eess*-vahn) *nt* iced
water
især (i-*sær*) *adv* especially
Italia (i-*taa*-li-ah) Italy
italiener (i-tah-li-*ay*-nerr) *m*
Italian
italiensk (i-tah-li-*aynsk*) *adj*
Italian
iver (*ee*-verr) *m* zeal
ivrig (*eev*-ri) *adj* zealous;
anxious, eager

J

ja (*ya*) yes; ~ vel! well!;
OK!
jade (*yaa*-der) *m* jade
jage (*yaa*-ger) *v* hunt, chase;
~ bort chase
jakke (*yahk*-ker) *c* jacket
jakt (*yahkt*) *c* hunt; chase
jakte (*yahk*-ter) *v* hunt
jamre (*yahm*-rer) *v* moan
januar (*yah*-new-*aar*)
January
Japan (*yaa*-pahn) Japan
japaner (*yah*-*paa*-nerr) *m*
Japanese
japansk (*yaa*-pahnsk) *adj*
Japanese
japp (yahpp) *c* yuppie
jeg (*yay*) *pron* I
jekk (*yehk*k) *m* jack
jeksel (*yehk*-serl) *m* (pl
-sler) molar
jente (*yehn*-ter) *c* girl
jern (*yæn*) *nt* iron
jernbane (*yæn*-baa-ner) *m*

railway; railroad *nAm*
jernbaneferje (*yæn*-baa-
ner-fær-*y*er) *c* train ferry
jernbaneovergang (*yæn*-
baa-ner-aw-verr-gahng) *m*
crossing
jernbanevogn (*yæn*-baa-
ner-vongn) *c* coach
jernvarehandel (*yæn*-vaa-
rer-hahn-derl) *m* (pl -dler)
hardware store
jernvarer (*yæn*-vaa-rerr)
pl hardware
jersey (*yæsh*-shi) *m* jersey
jetfly (*yeht*-flew) *nt* (pl ~) jet
jetlag (*yett*-læg) *c* jet lag
jevn (*yehvn*) *adj* level;
smooth, even
jo (*yoo*) *adv* yes; certainly;
jo ... jo the ...
jobb (*yobb*) *m* job
jockey (*yok*-ki) *m* jockey
jod (*yodd*) *m* iodine
jogge (*yogg*-er) *v* go

jogging, go running

joggesko (ʸogg-er-skoo) *pl* running shoes; sneakers; tennis shoes

jolle (ʸol-ler) *c* dinghy

jomfru (ʸom-frew) *c* virgin

jonglere (ʸon-gler-rer) *v* juggle

jonglør (ʸon-glur) *m* juggler

jord (ʸoor) *c* earth; ground, soil

Jordan (ʸoo-dahn) Jordan

jordaner (ʸoo-daa-nerr) *m* Jordanian

jordansk (ʸoo-daansk) *adj* Jordanian

jordbruk (ʸoor-brewk) *nt* agriculture

jordbunn (ʸoor-bewn) *m* soil

jordbær (ʸoor-bæær) *nt* (pl ~) strawberry

jordklode (ʸoor-kloo-der) *m* globe

jordmor (ʸoor-moor) *c* (pl -mødre) midwife

jordskjelv (ʸoor-shehlv) *m/nt* (pl ~) earthquake

jordsmonn (ʸoosh-mon) *nt* soil

journalist (shoo-nah-*list*) *m* journalist

journalistikk (shoor-nah-li-*stikk*) *m* journalism

jubileum (ʸew-bi-*lay*-ewm) *nt* (pl -eer) jubilee; anniversary

jukse (ʸook-ser) *v* cheat

jul (ʸewl) *c* Christmas, Xmas; gledelig ~! Merry Christmas!

juli (ʸew-li) July

juling (ʸew-ling) *c* spanking

jungel (ʸoong-ngerl) *m* jungle

juni (ʸew-ni) June

junior (ʸew-ni-oor) *adj* junior

juridisk (ʸew-ree-disk) *adj* legal

jurisdiksjon (ʸew-ris-dik-*shoon*) *m* jurisdiction

jurist (ʸew-*rist*) *m* lawyer

jury (ʸew-ri) *m* jury

justere (ʸewss-*tay*-rer) *v* adjust

juvel (ʸew-*vayl*) *m* gem

jøde (ʸur-der) *m* Jew

jødisk (ʸur-disk) *adj* Jewish

K

kabaret (kah-bah-*ray*) *m* cabaret

kabel (*kaa*-berl) *m* (pl kabler) cable; ~TV cable tv

kabelfjernsyn (*kaa*-berl-fʸææn-*sewn*) *nt* cable television

kabin (kah-*been*) *m* cabin

kabinett (kah-bi-*nehtt*) *nt* cabinet

kafé (kah-*fay*) *m* café

kafeteria (kah-feh-*tay*-ri-ah) *m* cafeteria; self-service restaurant

kaffe (*kahf*-fer) *m* coffee

kaffein (kah-feh-*een*) *m* caffeine

kaffeinfri (kah-feh-*een*-free) *adj* decaffeinated

kaffetrakter (*kahf*-fer-trahk-terr) *m* percolator

kai (kigh) *c* dock, quay

kajakk (kah-*yahkk*) *m* kayak

kake (*kaa*-ker) *c* cake

kaki (*kaa*-ki) *m* khaki

kald (kahll) *adj* cold

kalender (kah-*lehn*-derr) *m* (pl -drer) calendar

kalk (kahlk) *m* lime

kalkulator (*kahl*-koo-lah-toor) *m* calculator

kalkun (kahl-*kewn*) *m* turkey

kalle (*kahl*-ler) *v* call, name

kalori (kah-loo-*ree*) *m* calorie

kalsium (*kahl*-si-ewm) *nt* calcium

kalv (kahlv) *m* calf

kalvekjøtt (*kahl*-ver-khurt) *nt* veal

kalveskinn (*kahl*-ver-shin) *nt* (pl ~) calf skin

kam (kahmm) *m* (pl ~mer) comb

kamerat (kah-mer-*raat*) *m* friend, buddy

kamp (kahmp) *m* fight, battle, combat; struggle; match

kampanje (kahm-*pahn*-[y]er) *m* campaign

kanadier (kah-*naa*-di-err) *m* Canadian

kanadisk (kah-*naa*-disk) *adj* Canadian

kanal (kah-*naal*) *m* channel, canal; Den engelske ~ English Channel

kanarifugl (kah-*naa*-ri-fewl) *m* canary

kandidat (kahn-di-*daat*) *m* candidate

kanel (kah-*nayl*) *m* cinnamon

kanin (kah-*neen*) *m* rabbit

kano (*kaa*-noo) *m* canoe

kanon (kah-*noon*) *m* gun

kanskje (*kahn*-sher) *adv* perhaps, maybe

kant (kahnt) *m* edge, verge, rim, border

kantine (kahn-*tee*-ner) *c* canteen

kaos (*kaa*-oss) *nt* chaos

kaotisk (kah-*oo*-tisk) *adj* chaotic

kapasitet (kah-pah-si-*tayt*) *m* capacity

kapell (kah-*pehll*) *nt* chapel

kapellan (kah-peh-*laan*) *m* chaplain

kapital (kah-pi-*taal*) *m* capital

kapitalanbringelse (kah-pi-*taal*-ahn-bri-ngerl-ser) *m* investment

kapitalisme (kah-pi-tah-*liss*-mer) *m* capitalism

kapitulasjon (kah-pi-tew-lah-*shōōn*) m capitulation

kapp (kahpp) nt cape

kappe (*kahp*-per) c coat, cloak

kapplop (*kahp*-lūrp) nt race

kapre (*kaap*-rer) v hijack

kaprer (*kaap*-rerr) m hijacker

kapsel (*kahp*-serl) m (pl -sler) capsule

kaptein (kahp-*tayn*) m captain

kar (kaar) nt vessel; m guy

karakter (kah-rahk-*tāyr*) m character; mark

karakterisere (kah-rahk-teh-ri-*sāy*-rer) v characterize

karakteristisk (kah-rahk-teh-*riss*-tisk) adj characteristic

karaktertrekk (kah-rahk-*tāy*-trehk) nt (pl ~) characteristic

karamell (kah-rah-*mehll*) m caramel

karantene (kah-rahn-*tāy*-ner) m quarantine

karat (kah-*raat*) m carat

kardinal (kahr-di-*naal*) m cardinal

karneval (*kaa*-ner-vahl) nt carnival

karosseri (kah-ro-ser-*ree*) nt bodywork; body nAm

karpe (*kahr*-per) m carp

karri (*kahr*-ri) m curry

karriere (kah-ri-*æœ*-rer) m career

kart (kahtt) nt map

kartong (kah-*tongng*) m carton; kartong-cardboard

karusell (kah-rew-*sehll*) m merry-go-round

kaserne (kah-*sææ*-ner) m barracks pl

kasino (kah-*see*-noo) nt casino

kasjmir (kahsh-*meer*) cashmere

kasse (*kahss*-ser) c pay desk; crate

kassere (kah-*sāy*-rer) v discard

kasserer (kah-*sāy*-rerr) m cashier; treasurer; teller nAm

kasserolle (kah-ser-*rol*-ler) m saucepan

kassett (kah-*sett*) m cassette

kassettspiller (kah-*sett*-spi-lerr) m recorder

kast (kahst) nt throw, cast

kastanje (kah-*stahn*-ᶦer) m chestnut

kaste (*kahss*-ter) v *cast, *throw; toss; ~ opp vomit

katakombe (kah-tah-*koom*-ber) m catacomb

katalog (kah-tah-*lawg*) m catalogue

katarr (kah-*tahrr*) m catarrh

katastrofal (kah-tah-stroo-*faal*) adj disastrous

katastrofe (kah-tah-*strōō*-fer) m catastrophe, calamity, disaster

katedral (kah-ter-*draal*) m cathedral

kategori (kah-ter-goo-*ree*) *m* category

kateter (kah-*tay*-terr) *nt* (pl -tre) desk; catheter

katolsk (kah-*toolsk*) *adj* catholic

katt (kahtt) *m* cat

kausjon (kou-*shoon*) *m* bail, security; guarantee

kaviar (kah-vi-*aar*) *m* caviar

keiser (*kay*-serr) *m* emperor

keiserdømme (*kay*-ser-dur-mer) *nt* empire

keiserinne (kay-ser-*rin*-ner) *c* empress

keiserlig (*kay*-ser-li) *adj* imperial

keivhendt (*khayv*-hehnt) *adj* left-handed

kelner (*kehl*-nerr) *m* waiter, waitress

kenguru (*kehng*-gew-rew) *m* kangaroo

kennel (*kehn*-nerl) *m* kennel

Kenya (*kehn*-ᵞah) Kenya

keramikk (kheh-rah-*mikk*) *m* ceramics *pl*; pottery

kikke (*khik*-ker) *v* peep

kikkert (*khik*-kert) *m* binoculars *pl*

kilde (*khil*-der) *m* fountain, source, well, spring; **kildesortering** *c* waste separation

kile (*khee*-ler) *v* tickle; *m* wedge

kilo (*khee*-loo) *m*/*nt* kilogram

kilometer (*khil*-loo-*may*-terr) *m* (pl ~) kilometer *Am*, kilometre

kilometertall (*khil*-loo-*may*-ter-tahl) *nt* (pl ~) distance in kilometres (*Am* kilometers)

kim (kheem) *m* germ

Kina (*khee*-nah) China

kineser (khi-*nay*-serr) *m* Chinese

kinesisk (khi-*nay*-sisk) *adj* Chinese

kinn (khinn) *nt* cheek

kinnbein (*khin*-bayn) *nt* (pl ~) cheek-bone

kinnskjegg (*khin*-shehg) *nt* sideburns *pl*, whiskers *pl*

kino (*khee*-noo) *m* cinema, pictures; movies *plAm*, movie theater *Am*

kiosk (khosk) *m* kiosk

kirke (*kheer*-ker) *c* church; chapel

kirkegård (*kheer*-ker-gawr) *m* graveyard, churchyard

kirketårn (*kheer*-ker-tawn) *nt* (pl ~) steeple

kirsebær (*khish*-sher-bæær) *nt* (pl ~) cherry

kirurg (khi-*rewrg*) *m* surgeon

kirurgi (khi-rewg-*ee*) *c*: **rekonstruktiv** ~ reconstructive surgery

kiste (*khiss*-ter) *c* chest; coffin

kjede (*khay*-deh) *v* bore

kjedelig (*khay*-der-li) *adj* dull, boring

kjeft (khehft) *m* mouth

kjeks (khehks) *m* (pl ~) cookie; biscuit

kjele (*khāy*-ler) *m* kettle

kjelke (*khæl*-ker) *m* sledge, sleigh

kjeller (*khehl*-lerr) *m* cellar

kjelleretasje (*khehl*-lerr-eh-taa-sher) *m* basement

kjemi (kheh-*mee*) *m* chemistry

kjemisk (*khāy*-misk) *adj* chemical

kjempe (*khehm*-per) *v* combat, *fight, struggle, battle; *m* giant

kjenne (*khehn*-ner) *v* *know; ~ igjen recognize

kjennelse (*khehn*-nerl-ser) *m* verdict

kjennemerke (*khehn*-ner-mær-ker) *nt* feature

kjenner (*khehn*-nerr) *m* connoisseur

kjennetegn (*khehn*-ner-tayn) *nt* (pl ~) characteristic

kjennetegne (*khehn*-ner-tay-ner) *v* mark, characterize

kjennskap (*khehn*-skaap) *nt* knowledge

kjent (khehnt) *adj* noted

kjepphest (*khehp*-hehst) *m* hobby-horse

kjerne (*khææ*-ner) *m* pip; heart, essence, core, nucleus; nuclear

kjernehus (*khææ*-ner-hēwss) *nt* (pl ~) fruit core

kjernekraft (*khææ*-ner-krahft) *c* nuclear energy

kjerre (*khær*-rer) *c* cart

kjertel (*khæt*-terl) *m* (pl -tler) gland

kjetting (*kheht*-ting) *m* chain

kjeve (*khāy*-ver) *m* jaw

kjole (*khōō*-ler) *m* gown, dress; frock; lang ~ robe

kjæledyr (*khāy*-ler-dēwr) *nt* (pl ~) pet

kjælenavn (*khāy*-ler-nahvn) *nt* (pl ~) nickname

kjær (khæær) *adj* dear

kjæreste (*khææ*-rerss-ter) *m* darling, girlfriend, boyfriend

kjærlig (*khææ*-li) *adj* affectionate

kjærlighet (*khææ*-li-hāyt) *c* love

kjærlighetshistorie (*khææ*-li-hāyts-hiss-tōō-ri-er) *c* love story

kjøkken (khurk-kern) *nt* kitchen

kjøkkenhage (khurk-kern-haager) *m* kitchen garden

kjøkkenhåndkle (khurk-kern-hong-kler) *nt* (pl -lær) kitchen towel

kjøkkenredskap (t*v*urk-kehn-reh-skaap) *nt* utensil

kjøkkensjef (khurk-kern-shāyf) *m* chef

kjøl (khūrl) *m* keel

kjøleskap (khūr-ler-skaap) *nt* (pl ~) refrigerator, fridge

kjølig (*khūr*-li) *adj* chilly, cool

kjønn (khurnn) *nt* sex; gender; **kjønns-** genital

kjønnssykdom (*khurn-sēwk*-dom) *m* venereal disease

kjøp (khūrp) *nt* purchase; **godt ~** buy

kjøpe (*khūr*-per) *v* purchase, *buy

kjøper (*khūr*-perr) *m* purchaser, buyer

kjøpesenter (*khūr*-per-senterr) *nt* shopping centre, mall *nAm*

kjøpesum (*khūr*-per-sewm) *m* (pl ~mer) purchase price

kjøpmann (*khūr*p-mahn) *m* (pl -menn) shopkeeper; trader, merchant

***kjøpslå** (*khūr*p-shlo) *v* bargain

kjøre (*khūr*-rer) *v* *drive; *ride; **~ forbi** *overtake; **pass** *vAm*; **~ for fort** *speed

kjørebane (*khūr*-rer-baa-ner) *m* carriageway; roadway *nAm*

kjøretur (*khūr*-rer-tēwr) *m* drive

kjøretøy (*khūr*-rer-tur^(ew)) *nt* vehicle

kjøtt (khurtt) *nt* meat; flesh

klage (*klaa*-ger) *v* complain; *m* complaint

klagebok (*klaa*-ger-bōōk) *c* (pl -bøker) complaints book

klamre (*klahm*-rer) *v*: **~ seg til** cling to

klandre (*klahn*-drer) *v* blame

klang (klahngng) *m* tone; sound

klappe (*klahp*-per) *v* clap, applaud

klar (klaar) *adj* clear; serene; ready; **ha klart for seg** realize; **~ over** aware

***klargjøre** (*klaar*-^(y)ūr-rer) *v* elucidate, clarify

***klarlegge** (*klaar*-leh-ger) *v* clarify

klart (klaart) *adv* certainly

klasse (*klahss*-ser) *c* class; form

klassekamerat (*klahss*-ser-kah-mer-raat) *m* class-mate

klasseværelse (*klahss*-ser-væær-rerl-ser) *nt* classroom

klassifisere (klah-si-fi-*sāy*-rer) *v* classify, class

klassisk (*klahss*-sisk) *adj* classical

klatre (*klaht*-rer) *v* climb

klatring (*klaht*-ring) *c* climb

klausul (*klou*-sewl) *m* clause

kle (klāy) *v* *become; suit; **~ av seg** undress; **~ på seg** dress; **~ seg** dress; **~ seg om** change

klebe (*klāy*-beh) *v* *stick

klebrig (*klāy*b-ri) *adj* sticky

klem (klehm) *m* (pl ~mer) hug

klemme (*klehm*-mer) *v*

squeeze; cuddle, hug

klenge (*klehng*-er) *v* cling

klenodie (kleh-*nōō*-di-er) *nt* gem

kleshenger (*klāyss*-heh-ngerr) *m* coat hanger

klesskap (*klāy*-skaap) *nt* (pl ∼) wardrobe, closet *nAm*

klient (kli-*ehnt*) *m* client

klikk (klik) *m* set, clique; *nt* click

klikke (klik-ker) *v* click; ∼ på plass click into place

klima (*klee*-mah) *nt* climate

klinikk (kli-*nikk*) *m* clinic

klinkekule (*kling*-ker-kōō-ler) *c* marble

klippe (*klip*-per) *v* *cut; *m* cliff, rock; ∼ av *cut off

klistre (*kliss*-trer) *v* paste; cling; ∼merke *nt* sticker

klo (klōō) *c* (pl klør) claw

kloakk (kloo-*ahkk*) *m* sewer

klok (klōōk) *adj* clever, wise

klokke (klok-ker) *c* clock; bell; **klokken ... at ...** o'clock

klokkerem (*klok*-ker-rehm) *c* (pl ∼mer) watch-strap

klokkespill (*klok*-ker-spil) *nt* chimes *pl*

klone (*klōō*-neh) *v* clone

kloning (*kloon*-ing) *c* clone

klor (klōōr) *m* chlorine

kloss (kloss) *m* block

klosset (*kloss*-sert) *adj* awkward, clumsy

kloster (kloss-terr) *nt* (pl -tre) convent, monastery, cloister

klovn (klovn) *m* clown

klubb (klewbb) *m* club

klubbe (*klewb*-ber) *c* club

klukke (*klook*-ker) *v* chuckle

klump (kloomp) *m* lump

klumpet (*kloom*-pert) *adj* lumpy

klut (klewt) *m* cloth

***klype** (*klēw*-per) *v* pinch

klær (klæær) *pl* clothes *pl*

klø (klūr) *v* itch

kløe (*klūr*-er) *m* itch

kløft (klurft) *c* chasm, cleft

kløver (klurv-verr) *m* clover

kløyve (klurew-ver) *v* *split

knagg (knahgg) *m* peg

knapp (knahpp) *m* button; *adj* scarce

knappe (*knahp*-per) *v* button; ∼ opp unbutton

knappenål (*knahp*-per-nawl) *c* pin

knapphet (*knahp*-hāyt) *c* scarcity, shortage

knapphull (*knahp*-hewl) *nt* buttonhole

knapt (knahpt) *adv* scarcely

kne (knāy) *nt* (pl knær) knee

kneipe (*knay*-per) *c* pub

***knekke** (*knehk*-ker) *v* crack; break

knekt (knehkt) *m* knave

knele (*knāy*-ler) *v* *kneel

knep (knāyp) *nt* trick

kneskål (*knāy*-skawl) *c* kneecap

knipetang (*knee*-per-tahng) *c* (pl -tenger) pincers *pl*

komma

knipling (*knip*-ling) *m* lace

knirke (*kneer*-ker) *v* creak

kniv (kneev) *m* knife

knoke (*kn\overline{oo}*-ker) *m* knuckle

knopp (knopp) *m* bud

knott (knott) *m* knob

knulle (*knewl*-ler) *v vulgar* fuck

knurre (*knewr*-rer) *v* grumble

knuse (*kn\overline{ew}*ser) *v* *break; smash

knust (kn\overline{ew}st) *adj* broken

knute (*kn\overline{ew}*-ter) *m* knot

knutepunkt (*kn\overline{ew}*-ter-poongt) *nt* junction

knytte (*kn\overline{ew}*-ter) *v* tie, knot; ~ til attach to; ~ opp untie

knytteneve (*knewt*-n\overline{ay}-ver) *m* fist

knytteneveslag (*knewt*-n\overline{ay}-ver-shlaag) *nt* (*pl* ~) punch

koagulere (koo-ah-gew-*l\overline{ay}*-rer) *v* coagulate

kobbe (*kob*-ber) *m* seal

kode (*k\overline{oo}*-der) *m* code

koffert (*koof*-fert) *m* case, suitcase; trunk

kokain (koo-kah-*een*) *m*/*nt* cocaine

koke (*k\overline{oo}*-ker) *v* boil

kokebok (*k\overline{oo}*-ker-b\overline{oo}k) *c* (*pl* -bøker) cookery book; cookbook *nAm*

kokk (kokk) *m* cook

kokosnøtt (*kook*-kooss-nurt) *c* coconut

koldtbord (*kolt*-b\overline{oo}r) *nt* (*pl* ~) buffet

kolje (*kol*-$^\text{y}$er) *c* haddock

kolle (*kol*-ler) *m* hill, peak

kollega (koo-*l\overline{ay}*-gah) *m* colleague

kolleksjon (kol-lerk-*sh\overline{oo}n*) *n* collection *m*

kollektiv (*kol*-lerk-teev) *adj* collective

kollidere (koo-li-*d\overline{ay}*-rer) *v* collide, crash

kollisjon (koo-li-*sh\overline{oo}n*) *n* crash, collision

koloni (koo-loo-*nee*) *m* colony

kolonne (koo-*lon*-ner) *m* column

kolossal (koo-loo-*saal*) *adj* enormous, tremendous

koma (*k\overline{oo}*-mah) *m* coma

kombinasjon (koom-bi-nah-*sh\overline{oo}n*) *m* combination

kombinere (koom-bi-*n\overline{ay}*-rer) *v* combine

komedie (koo-*m\overline{ay}*-di-er) *m* comedy

komfort (koom-*fawr*) *m* comfort

komfortabel (koom-fo-*taa*-berl) *adj* comfortable

komfyr (koom-*f\overline{ew}r*) *m* cooker; stove

komiker (*k\overline{oo}*-mi-kerr) *m* comedian

komisk (*k\overline{oo}*-misk) *adj* funny, comic

komité (koo-mi-*t\overline{ay}*) *m* committee

komma (*kom*-mah) *nt* comma

komme (*kom-*mer) *nt*
coming

****komme** (*kom-*mer) *v*
*come; ~ **an på** depend; ~
over *come across; ~ **på**
*think of; ~ **seg** recover; ~
tilbake return

kommende (*kom-*mer-ner)
adj oncoming

kommentar (koo-mehn-
taar) *m* comment

kommentere (koo-mehn-
tāy-rer) *v* comment

kommersiell (koo-mæ-shi-
ehll) *adj* commercial

kommisjon (koo-mi-*shoon*)
m commission

kommode (koo-*mōō*-der)
m chest of drawers; bureau
nAm

kommunal (koo-mew-*naal*)
adj municipal

kommune (koo-*mēw*-ner)
m local authority,
municipality

kommunestyre (koo-*mēw*-
ner-stēw-rer) *nt* local
council

kommunikasjon (koo-
mew-ni-kah-*shoon*) *m*
communication

kommuniké (koo-mew-ni-
kāy) *nt* communiqué

kommunisme (koo-mew-
niss-mer) *m* communism

kommunist (koo-mew-*nist*)
m communist

kompakt (koom-*pahkt*) *adj*
compact

kompani (koom-pah-*nee*) *nt*

company

kompanjong (koom-pahn-
ʸongng) *m* partner,
associate

kompass (koom-*pahss*) *m* /
nt compass

kompensasjon (koom-
pehn-sah-*shoon*) *m*
compensation

kompensere (koom-pehn-
sāy-rer) *v* compensate

kompetent (koom-per-
tehnt) *adj* qualified;
capable

kompleks (koom-*plehks*) *nt*
complex

komplett (koom-*plehtt*) *adj*
complete

kompliment (koom-pli-
mahngng) *m* compliment

komplimentere (koom-pli-
mehn-*tāy*-rer) *v*
compliment

komplisert (koom-pli-*sāyt*)
adj complicated

komplott (koom-*plott*) *nt*
plot

komponist (koom-poo-*nist*)
m composer

komposisjon (koom-poo-
si-*shoon*) *m* composition

kompromiss (koom-proo-
miss) *nt* compromise

kondisjon (koon-di-*shoon*)
m physical fitness

konditori (koon-di-too-*ree*)
nt pastry shop

kondom (koon-*dom*) *nt*
condom

kone (*kōō*-ner) *c* wife

konfekt (koon-*fehkt*) *m*
chocolate

konferanse (koon-fer-*rahng*-ser) *m* conference

konfidensiell (koon-fi-dehn-si-*ehll*) *adj*
confidential

konfiskere (koon-fiss-*kāy*-rer) *v* confiscate

konflikt (koon-*flikt*) *m*
conflict

konfrontere (kon-fron-*tāy*-rer) *v* face, confront

konge (*kong*-nger) *m* king

kongelig (*kong*-nger-li) *adj*
royal

kongerike (*kong*-nger-ree-ker) *nt* kingdom

kongress (kong-*grehss*) *m*
congress

konjakk (kon-*ᵞahkk*) *m*
cognac

konklusjon (koong-klew-*shōōn*) *m* conclusion

konkret (koong-*krāyt*) *adj*
concrete

konkurranse (koong-kew-*rahng*-ser) *m* contest, competition; rivalry

konkurrent (koong-kew-*rehnt*) *m* rival, competitor

konkurrere (koong-kew-*rāy*-rer) *v* compete

konkurs (koong-*kēwsh*) *adj*
bankrupt

konsekvens (kon-ser-*kvehns*) *m* consequence

konsentrasjon (koon-sehn-trah-*shōōn*) *m*
concentration

konsentrere (koon-sehn-*trāy*-rer) *v* concentrate

konsert (koon-*sætt*) *m*
concert

konsertsal (koon-*sæt*-saal) *m* concert hall

konservativ (koon-*sær*-vah-teev) *adj* conservative

konservatorium (koon-sær-vah-*tōō*-ri-ewm) *nt* (pl -ier)
music academy

konservere (kon-sær-*vāy*-rer) *v* preserve

konservering (kon-sær-*vāy*-ring) *c* preservation

konsesjon (koon-seh-*shōōn*) *m* license *Am*,
licence; concession

konsis (koon-*seess*) *adj*
concise

konstant (koon-*stahnt*) *adj*
constant; even

konstatere (koon-stah-*tāy*-rer) *v* note; diagnose,
ascertain

konstruere (koon-strew-*āy*-rer) *v* construct

konstruksjon (koon-strewk-*shōōn*) *m*
construction

konsul (*kon*-sewl) *m* consul

konsulat (kon-sew-*laat*) *nt*
consulate

konsultasjon (kon-sewl-tah-*shōōn*) *m* consultation

konsum (koon-*sewm*) *nt*
consumption

konsument (koon-sew-*mehnt*) *m* consumer

konsumere (koon-sew-

meh-rer) *v* consume

kontakt (koon-*tahkt*) *m*
touch, contact

kontakte (koon-*tahk*-ter) *v*
contact

kontaktlinser (koon-*tahkt*-
lin-serr) *pl* contact lenses

kontanter (koon-*tahn*-terr)
pl cash

kontinent (koon-ti-*nehnt*) *nt*
continent

kontinental (koon-ti-nehn-
taal) *adj* continental

kontinuerlig (koon-ti-new-
āy-li) *adj* continuous

konto (*kon*-too) *m* (pl ~er,
-ti) account

kontor (koon-*tōōr*) *nt* office

kontortid (koon-*tōō*-teed) *c*
office hours, business
hours

kontra (*kon*-trah) *prep*
versus

kontrakt (koon-*trahkt*) *m*
contract; agreement; pact

kontrast (koon-*trahst*) *m*
contrast

kontroll (koon-*troll*) *m*
control; inspection

kontrollere (koon-troo-*lāy*-
rer) *v* verify, check, control

kontrollør (koon-troo-*lūrr*)
m supervisor

kontroversiell (kon-troo-
væ-shi-*ehll*) *adj*
controversial

kontur (kon-*tōōr*) *m* outline

konversasjon (koon-væ-
shah-*shōōn*) *m*
conversation

konvolutt (koon-voo-*lewtt*)
m envelope

kooperativ (koo-*op*-rah-
teev) *adj* co-operative

koordinasjon (koo-o-di-
nah-*shōōn*) *m* co-
-ordination

kopi (koo-*pee*) *m* copy

kopiere (koo-pi-*āy*-rer) *v*
copy

kople (*kop*-ler) *v* connect; ~
til connect

kopp (kopp) *m* cup

kopper (*kop*-perr) *pl*
smallpox; *nt* copper

kor (kōōr) *nt* choir

korall (koo-*rahll*) *m* coral

kordfløyel (*kawd*-flur ᶜʷ-
erl) *m* corduroy

kork (kork) *m* cork; stopper

korketrekker (*kor*-ker-treh-
kerr) *m* corkscrew

korn (kōōn) *nt* grain, corn

kornåker (*kōō*-naw-kerr) *m*
(pl -krer) cornfield

korpulent (kor-pew-*lehnt*)
adj stout, corpulent

korrekt (koo-*rehkt*) *adj*
correct

korrespondanse (koo-rer-
spoon-*dahng*-ser) *m*
correspondence

korrespondent (koo-rer-
spoon-*dehnt*) *m*
correspondent

korridor (koo-ri-*dōōr*) *m*
corridor

korrigere (koo-ri-*gāy*-rer) *v*
correct

korrupt (koo-*rewpt*) *adj*

corrupt

kors (koshsh) *nt* cross

korsett (ko-*shehtt*) *nt* corset

korsfeste (kosh-*fehss*-ter) *v* crucify

korsfestelse (kosh-*fehss*-terl-ser) *m* crucifixion

korstog (*kosh*-tawg) *nt* (pl ~) crusade

korsvei (*kosh*-vay) *m* road fork

kort (kott) *adj* short; brief; *nt* card

kortfattet (*kot*-fah-tert) *adj* brief

kortslutning (*kot*-slewt-ning) *m* short circuit

kortstokk *m* pack

kortvarig (*kot*-vaa-ri) *adj* momentary

koselig (*kōō*-ser-li) *adj* cosy; nice

kosmetika (koss-meh-*tikk* pl cosmetics *pl*

kost[1] (kost) *m* fare; ~ og losji room and board, bed and board, board and lodging

kost[2] (koost) *m* broom

kostbar (*kost*-baar) *adj* expensive; precious

koste (*koss*-ter) *v* *cost

kostfri (*kost*-free) *adj* free of charge

kostnad (*kost*-nah) *m* cost

kotelett (ko-ter-*lehtt*) *m* chop

krabbe (*krahb*-ber) *v* crawl; *c* crab

kraft (krahft) *c* (pl krefter) force; energy; power

kraftig (*krahf*-ti) *adj* strong

kraftverk (*krahft*-værk) *nt* power station

krage (*kraa*-ger) *m* collar

kragebein (*kraa*-ger-bayn) *nt* (pl ~) collarbone

krampe (*krahm*-per) *m* cramp; clamp

krampetrekning (*krahm*-per-trehk-ning) *m* convulsion

kran (kraan) *c* crane; tap

krangel (*krahng*-ngerl) *m*/*nt* (pl -gler) dispute, row, quarrel

krangle (*krahng*-ler) *v* quarrel

krater (*kraa*-terr) *nt* crater

kratt (krahtt) *nt* scrub

krav (kraav) *nt* demand; claim; requirement

kreativ (kreh-atieev) *adj* creative

kreditor (krāy-di-toor) *m* creditor

kreditt (kreh-*ditt*) *m* credit

kredittkort (kreh-*dit*-kot) *nt* (pl ~) credit card

kreere (kreh-āy-rer) *v* create

kreft (krehft) *m* cancer

krem (krāym) *m* cream

kremere (kreh-māy-rer) *v* cremate

kremgul (krāy-m-gēwl) *adj* cream

krenke (*krehng*-ker) *v* offend, injure; trespass

krenkelse (*krehng*-kerl-ser) *m* violation

krenkende (*krehng*-ker-ner) *adj* offensive

kresen (*kray*-sern) *adj* particular

krets (krehts) *m* ring, circle

kretsløp (*krehts*-lūrp) *nt* (pl ~) cycle

kreve (*kray*-ver) *v* require, claim; charge

krig (kreeg) *m* war

krigsfange (*kriks*-fah-nger) *m* prisoner of war

krigsmakt (*kriks*-mahkt) *c* armed forces

krigsskip (*krik*-sheep) *nt* warship

krim (kri-m) *m* detective story

kriminalitet (kri-mi-nah-li-*tayt*) *m* criminality

kriminell (kri-mi-*nehll*) *adj* criminal

kringkaste (*kring*-kahss-ter) *v* *broadcast

kringkasting (*kring*-kahss-ting) *c* broadcast

krise (*kree*-ser) *c* crisis

kristen[1] (*kriss*-tern) *m* (pl -tne) Christian

kristen[2] (*kriss*-tern) *adj* Christian

Kristus (*kriss*-tewss) Christ

kritiker (*kree*-ti-kerr) *m* critic

kritikk (kri-*tikk*) *m* criticism

kritisere (kri-ti-*say*-rer) *v* criticize

kritisk (*kree*-tisk) *adj* critical

kritt (kritt) *nt* chalk

kro (krōō) *c* pub, tavern

krok (krōōk) *m* hook

kroket (krōō-kert) *adj* crooked

krokodille (kroo-koo-*dil*-ler) *c* crocodile

kronblad (*krōōn*-blaa) *nt* (pl ~) petal

krone (*krōō*-ner) *c* crown; *v* crown

kronisk (*krōō*-nisk) *adj* chronic

kronologisk (kroo-noo-*law*-gisk) *adj* chronological

kropp (kropp) *m* body

krukke (*krook*-ker) *c* jar; pitcher

krum (kroomm) *adj* curved

krumning (*kroom*-ning) *m* bend; curve

krus (krēwss) *nt* mug

krusifiks (krew-si-*fiks*) *nt* crucifix

krutt (krewtt) *nt* gunpowder

krybbe (*krewb*-ber) *c* manger

krydder (*krewd*-derr) *nt* (pl ~) spice

krydderier (krew-der-*ree*-err) *pl* spices

krydret (*krewd*-rert) *adj* spiced, spicy

krykke (*krewk*-ker) *c* crutch

krympe (*krewm*-per) *v* *shrink

krympefri (*krewm*-per-free) *adj* shrinkproof

krypdyr (*krēwp*-dēwr) *nt* (pl ~) reptile

***krype** (*krēw*-per) *v* *creep

kryss (krewss) *nt* cross

krysse (krewss-ser) *v* cross

krysse av (krewss-ser) tick off

krystall (krew-stahll) *m/nt* crystal; **krystall-** *adj* crystal

krøll (krurll) *m* curl

krølle (krurl-ler) *v* curl; crease

krøllet (krurl-lert) *adj* curly

kråke (kraw-ker) *c* crow

ku (kew) *c* (pl ~er, kyr) cow

kubaner (kew-baa-nerr) *m* Cuban

kubansk (kew-baansk) *adj* Cuban

kubbe (kewb-ber) *m* log

kube (kew-ber) *m* cube

kul¹ (kewl) *m* lump

kul² (kewl) *adj colloquial* super, cool

kulde (kewl-ler) *c* cold

kuldegysning (kewl-ler-gewss-ning) *m* chill

kule (kew-ler) *c* bullet; sphere

kulepenn (kew-ler-pehn) *m* ballpoint pen, Biro

kull (kewll) *nt* coal; litter

kult (kewlt) *adj colloquial* super, cool

kultivert (kewl-ti-vayt) *adj* cultured

kultur (kewl-tewr) *m* culture

kun (kewnn) *adv* only

kunde (kewn-der) *m* client, customer

***kunne** (kewn-ner) *v* *can, *be able to; *may, *might

***kunngjøre** (kewn-ʸur-rer)

v announce; proclaim

kunngjøring (kewn-ʸur-ring) *c* announcement; notice

kunst (kewnst) *m* art; ~ **og håndverk** arts and crafts; **skjønne kunster** fine arts

kunstakademi (kewnst-ah-kah-deh-mee) *nt* art school

kunstferdig (kewnst-fææ-di) *adj* elaborate

kunstgalleri (kewnst-gah-ler-ree) *nt* gallery, art gallery

kunsthistorie (kewnst-hiss-tōō-ri-er) *c* art history

kunsthåndverk (kewnst-hon-værk) *nt* (pl ~) handicraft

kunstig (kewn-sti) *adj* artificial

kunstner (kewnst-nerr) *m* artist

kunstnerisk (kewnst-ner-risk) *adj* artistic

kunstsamling (kewnst-sahm-ling) *c* art collection

kunstutstilling (kewnst-ewt-sti-ling) *c* art exhibition

kunstverk (kewnst-værk) *nt* work of art

kupé (kew-pay) *m* compartment

kupert (kew-payt) *adj* hilly

kupong (kew-pongng) *m* coupon

kuppel (kewp-perl) *m* (pl kupler) dome

kur (kewr) *m* cure

kurs (kēwsh) *nt* course; *m* course

kursted (*kēw*-shtāy) *nt* spa

kurv (kewrv) *m* basket; hamper

kurve (kewr-ver) *m* curve

kusine (kew-*see*-ner) *c* cousin

kusma (kewss-mah) *m* mumps

kutt (kewtt) *nt* cut

kuvertavgift (kew-væær-raav-ỳift) *c* cover charge

kuøye (*kēw*-ur^(ew)-er) *m* porthole

kvadrat (kvah-*draat*) *nt* square

kvadratisk (kvah-*draa*-tisk) *adj* square

kvaksalver (*kvahk*-sahl-verr) *m* quack

kvalifikasjon (kvah-li-fi-kah-*shōon*) *m* qualification

kvalifisere seg (kvah-li-fi-*sāy*-rer) qualify

kvalifisert (kvah-li-fi-*sāyt*) *adj* qualified

kvalitet (kvah-li-*tāyt*) *m* quality

kvalm (kvahlm) *adj* sick

kvalme (*kvahl*-mer) *m* nausea; sickness

kvantitet (kvahn-ti-*tāyt*) *m* quantity

kvart (kvahtt) quarter

kvartal (kvah-*taal*) *nt* quarter; house block *Am*; kvartals- quarterly

kvarter (kvah-*tāyr*) *nt* quarter of an hour;

district; quarter

kveg (kvāyg) *nt* cattle *pl*

kveite (kvay-ter) *c* halibut

kveld (kvehll) *m* evening

kvele (*kvāy*-ler) *v* choke; strangle

kveles (*kvāy*-lerss) *v* choke

kveste (kvehss-ter) *v* injure

kvestelse (kvehss-terl-ser) *m* injury

kvikksølv (*kvik*-surl) *nt* mercury

kvinne (kvin-ner) *c* woman

kvinnelege (*kvin*-ner-lāy-ger) *m* gynaecologist

kvise (*kvee*-ser) *c* pimple

kvist (kvist) *m* twig

kvitt (kvit) *adj*: bli ~ get rid of

kvittering (kvi-*tāy*-ring) *c* receipt

kvote (*kvōo*-ter) *m* quota

kylling (*khewl*-ling) *m* chicken

kyndig (*khewn*-di) *adj* skilled, skil(l)ful

kysk (khewsk) *adj* chaste

kyss (khewss) *nt* kiss

kysse (*khewss*-ser) *v* kiss

kyst (khewst) *m* coast; seashore, shore, seaside

kø (kūr) *m* line; queue; *stå i ~ queue; stand in line *Am*

kølle (*kurl*-ler) *c* club; mallet

køye (kurew-er) *c* bunk

kål (kawl) *m* cabbage

kåpe (*kaw*-per) *c* coat

*la (laa) *v* *let; allow to; ~ være *keep off

L

laboratorium (lah-boo-rah-_tōō_-ri-ewm) *nt* (pl -ier) laboratory

labyrint (lah-bew-_rint_) *m* labyrinth; maze

ladning (lahd-ning) *m* charge

lag (laag) *nt* layer; team

lage (_laa_-ger) *v* *make

lagerbeholdning (_laa_-gerr-beh-hold-ning) *m* stock

lagerbygning (_laager_-bewg-ning) *m* store house, warehouse

lagerplass (_laa_-gerr-plahss) *m* depot

lagre (_laag_-rer) *v* store; stock

lagring (_laag_-ring) *c* storage

lagune (lah-_gew_-ner) *m* lagoon

laken (_laa_-kern) *nt* sheet

lakk (lahkk) *m* varnish, lacquer

lakkere (lah-_kāy_-rer) *v* varnish

lakris (_lahk_-riss) *m* liquorice

laks (lahks) *m* salmon

laktose (lahk-_tōōs_-er) *c* lactose

laktoseintolerant (lahk-_tōōs_-er-inn-tōōl-er-_ahnkt_) *adj* lactose intolerant

lam (lahmm) *nt* lamb; *adj* lame

lamme (_lahm_-mer) *v* paralyse

lammekjøtt (_lahm_-mer-khurt) *nt* lamb

lampe (_lahm_-per) *c* lamp

lampeskjerm (_lahm_-per-shærm) *m* lampshade

land (lahnn) *nt* country, land; *gå i ~ disembark, land; i ~ ashore; på landet in the country

landbruk (_lahn_-brewk) *nt* agriculture

lande (_lahn_-ner) *v* land

landemerke (_lahn_-ner-mær-ker) *nt* landmark

landflyktig *m* (pl ~e) exile

landgang (_lahn_-gahng) *m* gangway

landlig (_lahn_-li) *adj* rural

landområde (lahnn-om-_raw_-der) *nt* country

landsby (_lahns_-bew) *m* village

landsens (_lahn_-serns) *adj* rustic

landskap (_lahn_-skaap) *nt* scenery, landscape

landsmann (_lahns_-mahn) *m* (pl -menn) countryman

landsted (_lahn_-stāy) *nt* country house

landstryker (_lahn_-strew-kerr) *m* tramp

lang (lahngng) *adj* long; tall

langs (lahngs) *prep* past, along; på ~ lengthways

langsom (*lahng*-som) *adj*
slow

langvarig (*lahng*-vaa-ri) *adj*
longlasting

lapp (lahp) *m* patch, scrap,
note

larm (lahrm) *m* noise

last (lahst) *c* freight, cargo,
load; bulk

laste (*lahss*-ter) *v* charge,
load

laste opp (*lahss*-ter awpp) *v*
upload

lastebil (*lahss*-ter-beel) *m*
lorry; truck *nAm*

lasterom (*lahss*-ter-room)
nt (pl ~) hold

lat (laat) *adj* idle; lazy

***late som** (*laa*-ter somm)
pretend

***late til** (*laa*-ter till) seem

Latin-Amerika (lah-*teen*-
ah-*māy*-ri-kah) Latin
America

latinamerikansk (lah-*tee*-
nah-*māy*-ri-kaansk) *adj*
Latin-American

latter (*laht*-terr) *m* laughter,
laugh

latterlig (*laht*-ter-li) *adj*
ridiculous; ludicrous

***latterliggjøre** (*laht*-ter-li-
ȳur-rer) *v* ridicule

lav (laav) *adj* low

lavland (*laav*-lahn) *nt* (pl ~)
lowlands *pl*

lavsesong (*laav*-seh-song)
m low season

lavtrykk (*laav*-trewk) *nt* (pl
~) low pressure;
depression

lavvann (*laa*-vahn) *nt* low
tide

***le** (lāy) *v* laugh

ledd[1] (lehdd) *nt* joint; **gått
av** ~ dislocated

ledd[2] (lehdd) *nt* link

lede (*lāy*-der) *v* *lead, head

ledelse (*lāy*-derl-ser) *m*
management,
administration; lead

ledende (*lāy*-der-ner) *adj*
leading

ledig (*lāy*-di) *adj* vacant,
unoccupied

ledning (*lāyd*-ning) *m* flex;
electric cord

ledsager (*lāyd*-saa-gerr) *m*
companion

legal (leh-*gaal*) *adj* legal

legalisering (leh-gah-li-*sāy*-
ring) *c* legalization

legasjon (leh-gah-*shōōn*) *m*
legation

legat (leh-*gaat*) *nt* legacy

lege (*lāy*-ger) *m* physician,
doctor; *v* cure, heal;
allmennpraktiserende ~
general practitioner

legekontor (*lāy*-ger-koon-
tōōr) *nt* surgery

legeme (*lāy*-ger-mer) *nt*
body

legemiddel (*lāy*-ger-mi-
derl) *nt* (pl -midler)
remedy, medicine

legevitenskap (*lāy*-ger-vee-
tern-skaap) *m* medical
science

legg (lehgg) *m* calf

*legge (lehg-ger) v *put,
  *lay; pave; ~ **igjen** *leave;
  ~ **sammen** add; ~ **seg** *go
  to bed; ~ **seg ned** *lie
  down
lei av (lay) fed up with, tired
  of
leie (lay-er) v hire, rent,
  lease; m rent; ~ **ut** *let;
  lease; **til** ~ for hire
leieboer (lay-er-bōō-err) m
  lodger, tenant
leiegård (lay-er-gawr) m
  block of flats; apartment
  house Am
leiekontrakt (lay-er-koon-
  trahkt) m tenancy
  agreement
lei for (lay) sorry
leilighet (lay-li-hayt) c flat,
  apartment nAm; occasion,
  opportunity
leir (layr) m camp
leire (lay-rer) c clay
lek (layk) m play
leke (lay-ker) v play
lekeplass (lay-ker-plahss)
  m recreation ground,
  playground
leketøy (lay-ker-turew) nt
  toy
leketøysforretning (lay-
  ker-turewss-fo-reht-ning) c
  toyshop
lekk (lehkk) adj leaky
lekkasje (leh-kaa-sher) m
  leak
lekke (lehk-ker) v leak
lekker (lehk-kerr) adj
  delicious, nice

lekkerbisken (lehk-kerr-
  biss-kern) m delicacy
lekmann (layk-mahn) m (pl
  -menn) layman
leksikon (lehk-si-kon) nt (pl
  ~, ~er, -ka)
  encyclop(a)edia
leksjon (lehk-shōōn) m
  lesson
lektor (lehk-toor) m master,
  teacher
lem (lehmm) nt (pl ~mer)
  limb
lene seg (lāy-ner) v *lean
lenestol (lāy-ner-stōōl) m
  armchair; easy chair
lengde (lehng-der) c length
lengdegrad (lehng-der-
  graad) m longitude
lenge (lehng-er) adv long
lengsel (lehng-serl) m (pl
  -sler) longing; wish
lengte etter (lehng-ter) long
  for
lenke (lehn-ker) c link
leppe (lehp-per) c lip
leppepomade (lehp-per-
  poo-maa-der) m lip balm
leppestift (lehp-per-stift) m
  lipstick
lerke (lær-ker) c lark
lerret (lær-rert) nt canvas;
  screen
lesbisk (les-bisk) adj
  lesbian
lese (lāy-ser) v *read
leselampe (lāy-ser-lahm-
  per) c reading lamp
leselig (lāy-ser-li) adj
  legible

lesesal (*lay*-ser-saal) *m*
reading room

lesning (*layss*-ning) *m*
reading

lesse av (*lehss*-ser)
discharge, unload

lete etter (*lee*-ter) look for,
search; hunt for

leting (*lay*-ting) *c* search

lett (lehtt) *adj* light; easy;
gentle

lette (*leht*-ter) *v* *take off

lettelse (*leht*-terl-ser) *m*
relief

letthet (*leht*-hāyt) *c* ease

leve (*lay*-ver) *v* live

levebrød (*lay*-ver-brūr) *nt*
livelihood, living

levende (*lay*-ver-ner) *adj*
alive, live

lever (*lehv*-verr) *c* liver

leveranse (leh-ver-*rahng*-
ser) *m* delivery

levere (leh-*vāy*-rer) *v*
deliver

levering (leh-*vāy*-ring) *c*
delivery; supply

levestandard (*lay*-ver-
stahn-dahr) *m* standard of
living

levetid (*lay*-ver-teed) *c*
lifetime

levning (*lehv*-ning) *m*
remnant

li (lee) *c* hillside

libaneser (li-bah-*nāy*-serr)
m Lebanese

libanesisk (li-bah-*nāy*-sisk)
adj Lebanese

Libanon (*lee*-bah-non)
Lebanon

liberal (li-beh-*raal*) *adj*
liberal

Liberia (li-*bāy*-ri-ah)
Liberia

liberier (li-*bāy*-ri-err) *m*
Liberian

liberisk (li-*bāy*-risk) *adj*
Liberian

***lide** (*lee*-der) *v* suffer

lidelse (*lee*-derl-ser) *m*
suffering

lidenskap (*lee*-dern-skaap)
m passion

lidenskapelig (lee-dern-
skaa-per-li) *adj* passionate

liga (*lee*-gah) *m* league

***ligge** (*lig*-ger) *v* *lie

lighter (*ligh*-terr) *m* lighter

lik[1] (leek) *adj* alike, like;
equal; *være ~ equal

lik[2] (leek) *nt* corpse

like (*lee*-ker) *v* *be fond of,
fancy, like; *adv* equally, as;
adj even

likedan (*lee*-ker-dahn) *adv*
alike; *adj* alike

likefrem (*lee*-ker-frehm) *adj*
direct; simple

likegyldig (*lee*-ker-ᵞewl-di)
adj indifferent; careless

likeledes (*lee*-ker-*lāy*-derss)
adv likewise; also

likesinnet (*lee*-ker-si-nert)
adj like-minded

likestrøm (*lee*-ker-strurm)
m direct current

likeså (*lee*-ker-so) *adv*
likewise

likevekt (*lee*-ker-vehkt) *m*

balance

likevel (*lee*-ker-vehl) *adv* yet, however; still

likhet (*leek*-hāyt) *c* equality; resemblance, similarity

likne (*lik*-ner) *v* resemble

liknende (*lik*-ner-ner) *adj* similar

liksom (*lik*-som) *conj* like, as

liktorn (*leek*-tōōn) *m* corn

likør (li-*kūrr*) *m* liqueur

lilje (*lil*-^yer) *c* lily

lilla (*lil*-lah) *adj* purple, mauve, violet

lillefinger (*lil*-ler-fi-ngerr) *m* (pl -gre) little finger

lim (leem) *nt* gum, glue

limbånd (*leem*-bon) *nt* (pl ∼) adhesive tape

limett (li-*mehtt*) *m* lime

limonade (li-moo-*naa*-der) *m* lemonade

lind (linn) *m* lime

lindetre (*lin*-der-trāy) *nt* (pl -trær) limetree

lindre (*lin*-drer) *v* relieve

lindring (*lin*-dring) *c* relief

line (*lee*-ner) *c* line

linjal (lin-^y*aal*) *m* ruler

linje (*lin*-^yer) *c* line; extension

linse (*lin*-ser) *c* lens

lintøy (*leen*-tur^{ew}) *nt* linen

lisens (li-*sehns*) *m* license Am, licence

lisse (*liss*-ser) *c* lace

list (list) *c* cunning, ruse

liste (*liss*-ter) *c* list

lite (*lee*-ter) *adj* little

liten (*lee*-tern) *adj* (pl små) small, little; short; petty, minor; bitte ∼ tiny, minute

liter (*lee*-terr) *m* (pl ∼) liter Am, litre

litt (litt) *pron* some

litteratur (li-ter-rah-*tewr*) *m* literature

litterær (li-ter-*rœrr*) *adj* literary

liv (leev) *nt* life

livbelte (*leev*-behl-ter) *nt* lifebelt

livfull (*leev*-fewl) *adj* vivid

livlig (*liv*-li) *adj* lively, brisk

livmor (*leev*-mōōr) *c* womb

livsfarlig (*lishs*-faa-li) *adj* perilous

livsforsikring (*lifs*-fo-shik-ring) *c* life insurance

livvakt (*lee*-vahkt) *m* bodyguard

lodd (lodd) *m* destiny, lot

loddrett (*lod*-reht) *adj* perpendicular

loft (loft) *nt* attic

logikk (loo-*gikk*) *m* logic

logisk (*lōō*-gisk) *adj* logical

lojal (loo-^y*aal*) *adj* loyal

lokal (loo-*kaal*) *adj* local

lokalisere (loo-kah-li-*sāy*-rer) *v* locate

lokaltog (loo-*kaal*-tawg) *nt* (pl ∼) local train

lokk (lokk) *nt* cover, lid, top

lokomotiv (loo-koo-moo-*teev*) *nt* engine, locomotive

lomme (*loom*-mer) *c* pocket

lommebok (*loom*-mer-bōōk) *c* (pl -bøker) wallet,

pocketbook

lommekalkulator (*loom-mer-kahl-koo-lah-too*) *m* (pocket) calculator

lommekniv (*loom-mer-kneev*) *m* penknife, pocket-knife

lommelykt (*loom-mer-lewkt*) *c* torch, flash-light

lommeregner (*loom-mer-ray-nerr*) *m* (pocket) calculator

lommetørkle (*loom-mer-turr-kler*) *nt* (pl ~lær) handkerchief

lord (lord) *m* lord

los (lōōss) *m* pilot

losji (loo-*shee*) *nt* accommodation, lodgings *pl*

loslitt (*lōō*-shlit) *adj* threadbare

losse (*loss*-ser) *v* discharge

lotteri (lo-ter-*ree*) *nt* lottery

lov (lawv) *m* law; permission; *ha ~ til *be allowed to

love (*law*-ver) *v* promise

lovlig (*lawv*-li) *adj* lawful, legitimate

lubben (*lewb*-bern) *adj* plump

lue (*lewer*) *c* cap

luft (lewft) *c* air; sky; **luft**-pneumatic

lufte (*lewf*-ter) *v* air; ventilate; ~ **ut** ventilate

lufthavn (*lewft*- hahvn) *c* airport

luftig (*lewf*-ti) *adj* airy

luftkondisjonering (*lewft-koon-di-shoo-nāy*-ring) *c* air conditioning

luft-kondisjonert (*lewft-koon-di-shoo-nāyt*) *adj* air-conditioned

luftpost (*lewft*-post) *m* airmail

luftsyke (*lewft-sēw*-ker) *c* air-sickness

lufttett (*lewf*-teht) *adj* airtight

lufttrykk (*lewft*-trewkk) *nt* (pl ~) atmospheric pressure

lugar (lew-*gaar*) *m* cabin

luke (*lēw*-ker) *c* hatch

lukke (*look*-ker) *v* close, *shut; ~ **opp** unlock

lukket (*look*-kert) *adj* closed, shut

luksuriøs (lewk-sew-ri-*ūrss*) *adj* luxurious

luksus (*lewk*-sewss) *m* luxury

lukt (lookt) *c* odo(u)r, smell

lukte (*look*-ter) *v* *smell

lumbago (loom-*baa*-goo) *m* lumbago

lund (lewnn) *m* grove

lune (*lēw*-ner) *nt* mood, humo(u)r

lunge (*loong*-nger) *c* lung

lungebetennelse (*loong*-nger-beh-teh-nerl-ser) *m* pneumonia

lunken (*loong*-kern) *adj* lukewarm, tepid

lunsj (lurnsh) *m* luncheon, dinner, lunch

lunte (lewn-ter) c fuse

lur (lewr) m nap; adj smart, cunning

lus (lewss) c (pl ~) louse

ly (lew) nt shelter, cover; *gi ~ shelter

lyd (lewd) m sound; noise

lydbånd (lewd-bonn) nt (pl ~) tape

*lyde (lew-der) v sound

lydig (lew-di) adj obedient

lydighet (lew-di-hāyt) c obedience

lydpotte (lewd-po-ter) c silencer; muffler nAm

lydtett (lewd-teht) adj soundproof

lykke (lewk-ker) c happiness, fortune; ~ til! good luck!

lykkelig (lewk-li) adj happy

lykkes (lewk-kerss) v manage, succeed

lykkønskning (lewk-kurnsk-ning) m congratulation

lykt (lewkt) c lantern

lyn (lewn) nt lightning

lyng (lewngng) m heather

lynmelding (lewn-mehl-ling) c instant message

lys (lewss) nt light; adj light; pale; skarpt ~ glare

lysbilde (lewss-bil-der) nt slide

lysende (lew-ser-ner) adj luminous

lyserød (lew-ser-rūr) adj pink

lyshåret (lewss-haw-rert)

adj fair

lyskaster (lewss-kahss-terr) m searchlight

lyske (lewss-ker) m groin

lysmåler (lewss-maw-lerr) m exposure meter

lysning (lewss-ning) m clearing

lyspære (lewss-pææ-rer) c light bulb

lyst (lewst) c desire; zest; *ha ~ til *feel like, fancy

lystbåt (lewst-bawt) m yacht

lystig (lewss-ti) adj cheerful, jolly

lystspill (lewst-spil) nt (pl ~) comedy

lytt (lewtt) adj noisy

lytte (lewt-ter) v listen; eavesdrop

lytter (lewt-terr) m listener

*lyve (lew-wer) v lie, *tell a lie

lær (lær) nt leather; lær-leather

lærd (lærd) adj scholarly

lære (lææ-rer) v *learn; *teach; c teachings pl; ~ utenat memorize

lærebok (lææ-rer-bōōk) c (pl -bøker) textbook

lærer (lææ-rerr) m master, teacher, schoolmaster, schoolteacher

lærerik (lææ-rer-reek) adj instructive

lærling (læær-ling) m apprentice; trainee

løfte (lurf-ter) m lift; nt vow; promise

løgn (lur^{ew}n) *c* lie
løk (lurk) *m* onion
løkke (*lurk*-ker) *c* loop
lønn (lurnn) *m* salary, pay, wages *pl*; maple
lønne (*lurn*-ner) *v* *pay; ~ seg *be worthwhile
lønnsom (*lurn*-som) *adj* profitable
lønnstaker (*lurns*-taa-kerr) *m* employee
lønnstillegg (*lurns*-ti-lehg) *nt* (pl ~) *pay rise; raise *nAm*
løp (lūrp) *nt* course
*løpe (*lūr*-per) *v* *run
løper (*lūr*-perr) *m* runner
lørdag (*lūr*-dah) *m* Saturday
løs (lūrss) *adj* loose

løse (*lūr*-ser) *v* solve; unfasten; ~ opp *undo
løsepenger (*lūr*-ser-peh-ngerr) *pl* ransom
løsne (lurss-ner) *v* unfasten, detach; loosen
løsning (*lūrss*-ning) *m* solution
løve (*lūr*-ver) *m* lion
løvetann (*lūr*-ver-tahn) *c* dandelion
lån (lawn) *nt* loan
låne (*law*-ner) *v* borrow; ~ bort *lend
lår (lawr) *nt* thigh
lås (lawss) *m* lock
låse (*law*-ser) *v* lock; ~ inne lock up; ~ opp unlock
låve (*law*-ver) *m* barn

M

madrass (mahd-*rahss*) *m* mattress
mage (*maa*-ger) *m* stomach; belly; **mage-** gastric
mager (*maa*-gerr) *adj* lean, thin
magesår (*maa*-ger-sawr) *nt* (pl ~) gastric ulcer
magi (mah-*gee*) *m* magic
magisk (*maa*-gisk) *adj* magic
magnetisk (mahng-*nāy*-tisk) *adj* magnetic
mai (migh) May
mais (mighss) *m* maize; corn *nAm*
maiskolbe (*mighss*-kol-ber)

m corn on the cob
major (mah-^y*ōōr*) *m* major
makrell (mah-*krehll*) *m* mackerel
makt (mahkt) *c* might, power; rule
maktesløs (*mahk*-terss-lūrss) *adj* powerless
malaria (mah-*laa*-ri-ah) *m* malaria
Malaysia (mah-*ligh*-si-ah) Malaysia
malaysier (mah-*ligh*-s^yerr) *m* Malay
malaysisk (mah-*ligh*-sisk) *adj* Malaysian
male (*maa*-ler) *v* paint;

marmor

*grind

maler (*maa-lerr*) *m* painter

maleri (*mah-ler-ree*) *nt* picture, painting

malerisk (*maa-ler-risk*) *adj* picturesque

malerskrin (*maa-ler-shkreen*) *nt* (pl ~) paint-box

maling (*maa-ling*) *c* paint

malm (*mahlm*) *m* ore

malplassert (*maal-plah-sāyt*) *adj* misplaced

mamma (*mahm-mah*) *f*mom, mommy

man (*mahnn*) *pron* one

mandag (*mahn-dah*) *m* Monday

mandarin (*mahn-dah-reen*) *m* tangerine, mandarin

mandat (*mahn-daat*) *nt* mandate

mandel (*mahn-derl*) *m* (pl -dler) almond

mandler (*mahn-dlerr*) *pl* tonsils *pl*; betente ~ tonsilitis

manerer (*mah-nāy-rerr*) *pl* manners *pl*

manesje (*mah-nāy-sher*) *m* ring

manet (*mah-nāyt*) *m* jelly-fish

mange (*mahng-nger*) *pron* many; much

mangel (*mahng-ngerl*) *m* (pl -gler), want, lack, deficiency; shortage

mangelfull (*mahng-ngerl-fewl*) *adj* faulty, defective

mangle (*mahng-ler*) *v* fail, lack

manglende (*mahng-ler-ner*) *adj* missing, lacking

mani (*mah-nee*) *m* craze

manikyr (*mah-ni-kēwr*) *m* manicure

manikyrere (*mah-ni-kew-rāy-rer*) *v* manicure

mann (*mahnn*) *m* (pl menn) man; husband

mannekeng (*mah-ner-kehngng*) *m* model

mannskap (*mahn-skaap*) *nt* crew

mansjett (*mahn-shehtt*) *m* cuff

mansjettknapper (*mahn-sheht-knah-perr*) *pl* cuff links *pl*

manuskript (*mah-noo-skript*) *nt* manuscript

marg (*mahrg*) *m* margin; marrow

margarin (*mahr-gah-reen*) *m* margarine

marine- (*mah-ree-ner*) naval

maritim (*mah-ri-teem*) *adj* maritime

mark (*mahrk*) *m* worm; *c* field

marked (*mahr-kerd*) *nt* market

markere (*mahr-kāy-rer*) *v* mark; score

marmelade (*mahr-mer-laa-der*) *m* marmalade

marmor (*mahr-moor*) *m* marble

marokkaner (mah-ro-*kaa*-nerr) *m* Moroccan

marokkansk (mah-ro-*kaansk*) *adj* Moroccan

Marokko (mah-*rok*-koo) Morocco

mars (mahshsh) March

marsj (mahshsh) *m* march

marsjere (mah-*shāy*-rer) *v* march

marsjfart (mahsh-faht) *c* cruising speed

marsvin (*maa*-shveen) *nt* (pl ~) guinea pig

martyr (*maa*-tewr) *m* martyr

mas (maass) *nt* fuss

maske (*mahss*-ker) *c* mask; mesh

maskin (mah-*sheen*) *m* machine, engine

maskineri (mah-shi-ner-ree) *nt* machinery

maskinskade (mah-*sheen*-skaa-der) *m* breakdown

maskulin (*mahss*-kew-leen) *adj* masculine

massasje (mah-*saa*-sher) *m* massage

masse (*mahss*-ser) *m* bulk

masseproduksjon (mahss-ser-proo-dewk-*shōōn*) *m* mass production

massere (mah-*sāy*-rer) *v* massage

masseødeleggelsesvåpen (*mahss*-ser-urd-eh-leh-gel-sehs-*vāwp*-ehn) *nt* (pl ~) WMD

massiv (mah-*seev*) *adj*

massive; solid

massør (mah-*sūrr*) *m* masseur

mast (mahst) *c* mast

mat (maat) *m* food; **lage ~** cook

mate (*maa*-ter) *v* *feed

matematikk (mah-ter-mah-*tikk*) *m* mathematics

matematisk (mah-ter-*maa*-tisk) *adj* mathematical

materiale (mah-ter-ri-*aa*-ler) *nt* material

materiell (mah-ter-ri-*ehll*) *adj* material

matforgiftning (*maat*-for-ᵞift-ning) *m* food poisoning

matlyst (*maat*-lewst) *c* appetite

matolje (*maat*-ol-ᵞer) *c* salad-oil

matt (mahtt) *adj* mat, dull, dim

matte (*maht*-ter) *c* mat

matvareforretning (*maat*-vaa-rer-fo-reht-ning) *c* grocer's

matvarehandler (*maat*-vaa-rer-hahnd-lerr) *m* grocer

matvarer (*maat*-vaa-rerr) *pl* foodstuffs *pl*, groceries *pl*

maur (mour) *m* ant

mausoleum (mou-soo-*lāy*-ewm) *nt* (pl -eer) mausoleum

med (māy) *prep* with; by; **~ mindre** unless

medalje (meh-*dahl*-ᵞer) *m* medal

*medbringe (*māy*-bri-nger)

v *bring
meddele (*māy*-day-ler) *v* communicate, inform; notify
meddelelse (*māy*-day-lerlser) *m* information, communication
medfødt (*māy*-furt) *adj* inborn
medfølelse (*māyd*-fūr-lerlser) *m* sympathy
medfølende (*māyd*-fūr-lehner) *adj* sympathetic
medisin (meh-di-*seen*) *m* medicine; drug
medisinsk (meh-di-*seensk*) *adj* medical
meditere (meh-di-*tāy*-rer) *v* meditate
medlem (*māyd*-lehm) *nt* (pl ~mer) member, associate
medlemskap (*māyd*-lehmskaap) *nt* membership
medlidenhet (mehd-*lee*-dern-hāyt) *c* pity; *ha ~ med pity
medregne (*māyd*-ray-ner) *v* include, count in
medvirkning (*māyd*-veerkning) *m* co-operation
meg (may) *pron* me, myself
meget (*māy*-gert) *adv* very; far
megle (*mehg*-ler) *v* mediate
megler (*mehg*-lerr) *m* mediator; broker
meieri (may-er-*ree*) *nt* dairy
meisel (*may*-serl) *m* (pl -sler) chisel
mekaniker (meh-*kaa*-ni-

kerr) *m* mechanic
mekanisk (meh-*kaa*-nisk) *adj* mechanical
mekanisme (meh-kah-*niss*-mer) *m* mechanism
meksikaner (mehks-i-*kaa*-nerr) *m* Mexican
meksikansk (mehks-i-*kaansk*) *adj* Mexican
mektig (*mehk*-ti) *adj* powerful, mighty
mel (māyl) *nt* flour
melankoli (meh-lahng-koo-*lee*) *m* melancholy
melde (*mehl*-ler) *v* report; bid; ~ seg report
melding (*mehl*-ling) *c* report
melk (mehlk) *c* milk
melkaktig (*mehl*-kahk-ti) *adj* milky
mellom (*mehl*-lom) *prep* between; among
mellommann (*mehl*-loo-mahn) *m* (pl -menn) intermediary
mellomrom (*mehl*-loom-room) *nt* (pl ~) space
mellomspill (*mehl*-loom-spil) *nt* (pl ~) interlude
mellomste (*mehl*-loom-ster) *adj* middle
mellomtid (*mehl*-loom-teed) *c* interim; i mellomtiden meanwhile
melodi (meh-loo-*dee*) *m* tune; melody
melodisk (meh-*lōō*-disk) *adj* tuneful
melodrama (meh-loo-*draa*-

mah) *nt* melodrama

melon (meh-*lōōn*) *m* melon

membran (mehm-*braan*) *m* diaphragm

memorandum (meh-moo-*rahn*-dewm) *nt* (pl -da) memo

men (mehnn) *conj* but; only

mene (*māy*-ner) *v* *mean; consider

mened (*māyn*-āyd) *m* perjury

mengde (mehng-der) *m* lot, amount, mass; crowd

menighet (*māy*-ni-hāyt) *c* congregation

mening (*māy*-ning) *m* opinion; meaning, sense

meningsløs (*māy*-nings-lūrss) *adj* meaningless, senseless

meningsmåling (*māy*-nings-maw-ling)*c* poll

menneske (*mehn*-sker) *nt* human being, man

menneskehet (*mehn*-sker-hāyt) *c* humanity, mankind

menneskelig (*mehn*-sker-li) *adj* human

mens (mehns) *conj* while

menstruasjon (mehn-strew-ah-*shōōn*) *m* menstruation

mental (mehn-*taal*) *adj* mental

meny (meh-*new*) *m* menu

mer (māyr) *adj* more; litt ~ some more

merkbar (*mærk*-baar) *adj* perceptible, noticeable

merke[1] (*mær*-ker) *v* mark; *nt* tick, mark; brand

merke[2] (*mær*-ker) *v* sense; notice; *legge ~ til notice

merkelapp (*mær*-ker-lahp) *m* tag; *sette ~ på label

merkelig (*mær*-ker-li) *adj* funny, queer

merknad (*mærk*-nah) *m* note

merkverdig (mærk-*vær*-di) *adj* curious, strange

meslinger (mehsh-li-ngerr) *pl* measles

messe (*mehss*-ser) *m* Mass

messing (*mehss*-sing) *m* brass

mester (*mehss*-terr) *m* (pl ~e, -trer) master; champion

mesterverk (*mehss*-terr-vayrk) *nt* masterpiece

mestre (*mehss*-trer) *v* cope

metall (meh-*tahll*) *nt* metal; **metall-** metal

metalltråd (meh-*tahl*-traw) *m* wire

meter (*māy*-terr) *m* (pl ~) metre

metode (meh-*tōō*-der) *m* method

metodisk (meh-*tōō*-disk) *adj* methodical

metrisk (*māyt*-risk) *adj* metric

Mexico (*mehk*-si-koo) Mexico

middag (*mid*-dah) *m* dinner; midday; **spise ~** dine

minnestein

middel (*mid*-derl) *nt* (pl
    midler) means
middelalderen (*mid*-derl-
    ahld-rern) Middle Ages
middelaldersk (*mid*-derl-
    ahl-dershk) *adj* mediaeval
Middelhavet (*mid*-derl-haa-
    vert) Mediterranean
middelklasse (*mid*-derl-
    klah-ser) *c* middle class
middelmådig (*mid*-derl-
    maw-di) *adj* average,
    commonplace
middels (*mid*-derls) *adj*
    medium
midje (*mid*-ʸe) *c* waist
midlertidig (*mid*-ler-tee-di)
    adj temporary
midnatt (*mid*-nahtt) *c*
    midnight
midte (*mit*-ter) *m* midst,
    middle
midtpunkt (*mit*-poongt) *nt*
    center *Am*, centre
midtsommer (*mit*-so-merr)
    m midsummer
migrene (mig-*rāy*-ner) *m*
    migraine
mikrobølgeovn (*mik*-roo-
    burl-ge-ovnn) *m*
    microwave oven
mikrofon (mik-roo-*foōn*) *m*
    microphone
mikser (*mik*-serr) *m* mixer
mild (mill) *adj* mild; gentle
milestein (*mee*-ler-stayn) *m*
    milestone
militær- (mi-li-*tæær*)
    military
miljø (mil-*ʸūr*) *nt* milieu;

environment
miljøvern (mil-*ʸūr*-væən) *nt*
    environmental protection
milliard (mil-*ʸard*) *m* billion
million (mil-*ʸoōn*) *m* million
millionær (mil-*ʸoo-næær*)
    m millionaire
min (meen) *pron* my
mindre (*min*-drer) *adv* less;
    adj minor; ikke desto ~
    nevertheless
mindretall (*min*-drer-tahll)
    nt (pl ~) minority
mindreverdig (*min*-drer-
    væær-di) *adj* inferior
mindreårig (*min*-drer-aw-
    ri) *m* (pl ~e) minor
mineral (mi-ner-*raal*) *nt*
    mineral
mineralvann (mi-ner-*raal*-
    vahn) *nt* mineral water;
    soda (pop); lemonade
miniatyr (mi-ni-ah-*tēwr*) *m*
    miniature
minibank (*miin*-i-bahnk) *c*
    automatic teller machine
    (ATM)
minimum (*mee*-ni-moom)
    nt (pl -ima) minimum
mink (mingk) *m* mink
minke (*ming*-ker) *v*
    decrease
minne (*min*-ner) *nt*
    remembrance, memory; ~
    på remind
minnes (*min*-nerss) *v* recall
minnesmerke (*min*-nerss-
    mæer-ker) *nt* monument
minnestein (*min*-nerstayn)
    m memorial

minneverdig (*min*-ner-vær-di) *adj* memorable

minoritet (mi-noo-ri-*tayt*) *c* minority

minske (*min*-sker) *v* lessen, reduce, decrease

minst (minst) *adj* least; *adv* at least; **i det minste** at least

minus (*mee*-newss) *adv* minus

minutt (mi-*newtt*) *nt* minute

mirakel (mi-*raa*-kerl) *nt* (pl -kler) miracle

mirakuløs (mi-rah-kew-*lürss*) *adj* miraculous

misbillige (*miss*-bi-li-er) *v* disapprove

misbruk (*miss*-brewk) *nt* abuse, misuse

misdannet (*miss*-dahn-nert) *adj* deformed

misfornøyd (*miss*-fo-nur^(ew)d) *adj* discontented

*misforstå (*miss*-fo-shtaw) *v* *misunderstand

misforståelse (*miss*-fo-shtaw-erl-ser) *m* misunderstanding

mislike (*miss*-lee-ker) *v* dislike

mislykkes (*miss*-lew-kerss) *v* fail

mislykket (*miss*-lew-kert) *adj* unsuccessful

mistanke (*miss*-tahng-ker) *m* suspicion

miste (*miss*-ter) *v* miss; *lose

mistenke (*miss*-tehng-ker) *v* suspect

mistenkelig (miss-*tehng*-ker-li) *adj* suspicious

mistenksom (miss-*tehngk*-som) *adj* suspicious

mistenksomhet (*miss*-*tehngk*-som-hayt) *c* suspicion

mistenkt (*miss*-tehngt) *m* suspect

mistro (*miss*-troo) *v* mistrust

mistroisk (*miss*-troo-isk) *adj* distrustful

misunne (mi-*sewn*-ner) *v* envy; grudge

misunnelig (mi-*sewn*-li) *adj* envious

misunnelse (mi-*sewn*-nerl-ser) *m* envy

mobil (moo-*beel*) *adj* mobile

mobil(-telefon) (moo-*beel*-(teh-ler-*foon*)) *m* cellphone, mobile (phone)

modell (moo-*dehll*) *m* model

modellere (moo-der-*lay*-rer) *v* model

modem (*moo*-dem)*nt* modem

moden (*moo*-dern) *adj* ripe, mature

modenhet (*moo*-dern-hayt) *c* maturity

moderat (moo-der-*raat*) *adj* moderate

moderne (moo-*dææ*-ner) *adj* modern; fashionable; trendy

modifisere (moo-di-fi-*sáy*-rer) *v* modify

modig (*móo*-di) *adj* courageous, brave, plucky

moll (*moll*) *m* minor

molo (*móo*-loo) *m* jetty

molte (*mol*-ter) *c* cloudberry

moms (merverdiomsetningsavgift) (*mooms*) *m* purchase tax, turnover tax, sales tax

monark (moo-*nahrk*) *m* monarch, ruler

monarki (moo-nahr-*kee*) *nt* monarchy

monolog (moo-noo-*lawg*) *m* monologue

monopol (moo-noo-*póol*) *nt* monopoly

monoton (moo-noo-*tóon*) *adj* monotonous

monter (*moon*-terr) *m* (pl -trer) show-case

monument (moo-new-*mehnt*) *nt* monument

moped (moo-*páyd*) *m* moped; motorbike *nAm*

mor (*móor*) *c* (pl mødre) mother

moral (moo-*raal*) *m* morality; moral

moralsk (moo-*raalsk*) *adj* moral

mord (moord) *nt* assassination, murder

morder (*moor*-derr) *m* murderer

more (*móo*-rer) *v* amuse; entertain

morfar (*moor*-faar) *m* (pl -fedre) grandfather

morfin (moor-*feen*) *m* morphine

morgen (*maw*-ern) *m* morning; i ~ tomorrow; i morges this morning

morgenavis (*maw*-ern-ah-veess) *c* morning paper

morgenkåpe (*maw*-ern-kaw-per) *c* dressing gown

morgenutgave (*maw*-ern-ēwt-gaa-ver) *c* morning edition

mormor (*moor*-móor) *c* (pl -mødre) grandmother

moro (*moor*-roo) *c* fun

morsmål (*móosh*-mawl) *nt* mother tongue, native language

morsom (*moosh*-shom) *adj* enjoyable, entertaining; humorous

mort (moot) *m* roach

mosaikk (moo-sah-*ikk*) *m* mosaic

mose (*móo*-ser) *m* moss; *v* mash

moské (mooss-*káy*) *m* mosque

moskito (mooss-*kee*-too) *m* mosquito

mot[1] (*móot*) *prep* against; towards

mot[2] (*móot*) *nt* courage; **ta motet fra** *v* discourage

motbydelig (moot-*bēw*-der-li) *adj* disgusting, revolting

mote (*móo*-ter) *m* fashion

motell (moo-*tehll*) *nt* motel

motgang (*mōōt*-gahng) *m* adversity, hardship

motiv (moo-*teev*) *nt* motive; pattern

motivere (moo-tee-*vay*-rer) *v* motivate

motor (*mōō*-toor) *m* motor, engine

motorbåt (*mōō*-toor-bawt) *m* motor-boat

motorstopp (*mōō*-toor-stop) *m/nt* (pl ~) breakdown

motorsykkel (*mōō*-toor-sew-kerl) *m* (pl -sykler) motor-cycle

motorvei (*mōō*-toor-vay) *m* motorway; highway *nAm*

motsatt (*mōōt*-saht) *adj* opposite, contrary; reverse; det motsatte the contrary

motsetning (*mōōt*-seht-ning) *m* contrast; reverse

**motsette seg (*mōōt*-seh-ter) oppose

**motsi (*mōōt*-see) *v* contradict

motstand (*mōōt*-stahn) *m* resistance

motstander (*mōōt*-stahn-derr) *m* opponent

motstridende (*mōōt*-stree-der-ner) *adj* contradictory

motsvarende (*mōōt*-svaa-rer-ner) *adj* equivalent

**motta (*mōō*-taa) *v* receive; accept

mottakelse (*mōō*-taa-kerl-ser) *m* reception, receipt

motto (*moot*-too) *nt* motto

motvilje (*mōōt*-vil-ᵉer) *m* aversion, dislike; antipathy

mugg (mewgg) *m* mildew

mugge (mewg-ger) *c* jug

muggen (mewg-gern) *adj* mouldy

muldyr (mewl-dewr) *nt* (pl ~) mule

mulesel (mewl-ay-serl) *nt* (pl -sler) mule

mulig (mēw-li) *adj* possible; eventual; realizable

muligens (mēw-li-erns) *adv* perhaps

mulighet (mēw-li-hayt) *c* possibility

mulkt (mewlkt) *c* fine

multe (*mool*-ter) *c* cloudberry

multikulturell (mool-ti-kewl-tewr-ehll) *adj* multicultural

multiplex (*mōōl*-ti-plehks) *c* multiplex

multiplikasjon (mool-ti-pli-kah-*shōōn*) *m* multiplication

multiplisere (mool-ti-pli-*say*-rer) *v* multiply

munk (moongk) *m* monk

munkeorden (*moong*-ker-or-dern) *m* monastic order

munn (mewnn) *m* mouth

munning (mewn-ning) *m* outlet; estuary; muzzle

munnvann (mewn-vahn) *nt* mouthwash

munter (mewn-terr) *adj* merry, gay

muntlig (*mewnt*-li) *adj* oral, verbal

mur (*mewr*) *m* brick wall

mure (*mew*-rer) *v* *lay bricks

murer (*mew*-rerr) *m* bricklayer

murpuss (*mewr*-pewss) *m* plaster

murstein (*mewr*-shtayn) *m* brick

mus (*mewss*) *c* (pl ∼) mouse; ∼matte *c* mouse pad

museum (mew-*say*-ewm) *nt* (pl -eer) museum

musikal (*mew*-si-kaarl) *m* musical

musikalsk (mew-si-*kaalsk*) *adj* musical

musiker (*mew*-si-kerr) *m* musician

musikk (mew-*sikk*) *m* music

musikkinstrument (mew-*sikk*-in-strew-mehnt) *nt* musical instrument

musikkspill (mew-*sikk*-spil) *nt* (pl ∼) musical comedy

muskatnøtt (mewss-*kaat*-nurt) *c* nutmeg

muskel (*mewss*-kerl) *m* (pl -kler) muscle

muskuløs (mewss-kew-*lūrss*) *adj* muscular

muslim (mewss-*lim*) *m* Muslim

musserende (mew-*say*-rer-ner) *adj* sparkling

mutter (*mewt*-terr) *m* (pl

∼e, mutrer) nut

mye (*mew*-er) *adj* much; *adv* much; like ∼ as much

mygg (mewgg) *m* (pl ∼) mosquito

myggnett (*mewg*-neht) *nt* (pl ∼) mosquito net

myk (*mewk*) *adj* supple, smooth, soft; tender

mynde (mewn-der) *m* greyhound

myndig (*mewn*-di) *adj* of age

myndighet (*mewn*-di-*hāyt*) *c* authority; utøvende ∼ executive; myndigheter authorities *pl*

mynt (mewnt) *m* coin

mynte (*mewn*-ter) *c* mint

myntenhet (*mewnt*-āyn-hāyt) *m* monetary unit

myr (*mewr*) *c* swamp, bog

myrde (*mewr*-der) *v* murder

mysterium (mewss-*tay*-ri-ewm) *nt* (pl -ier) mystery

mystisk (*mewss*-tisk) *adj* mysterious

myte (*mew*-ter) *m* myth

mytteri (mew-ter-*ree*) *nt* mutiny

møbler (*mūrb*-lerr) *pl* furniture

møblere (murb-*lay*-rer) *v* furnish

møll (murll) *m* (pl ∼) moth

mølle (*murl*-ler) *c* mill

mønster (*murn*-sterr) *nt* (pl -tre) pattern

mør (*mūrr*) *adj* tender

mørk (murrk) *adj* obscure,

dark

mørke (*murr*-ker) *nt* dark; gloom

møte (*mūr*-ter) *v* encounter, *meet; *nt* encounter, meeting; appointment

møtende (*mūr*-ter-ner) *adj* oncoming

møtested (*mūr*-ter-stāy) *nt* meeting place

måke (*maw*-ker) *c* gull

mål (*mawl*) *nt* measure; goal; target; tongue, language

målbevisst (*mawl*-beh-vist) *adj* determined

måle (*maw*-ler) *v* measure

målebånd (*maw*-ler-bon) *nt* (pl ~) tape measure

måleinstrument (*maw*-ler-in-strew-mehnt) *nt* gauge

måler (*maw*-lerr) *m* meter

målestokk (*maw*-ler-stok)

m scale

mållinje (*mawl*-lin-ʸer) *c* finish

målløs (*mawl*-lūrss) *adj* speechless

målmann (*mawl*-mahn) *m* (pl -menn) goalkeeper

måltid (*mawl*-teed) *nt* meal

måne (*maw*-ner) *m* moon

måned (*maw*-nerd) *m* month

månedlig (*maw*-nerd-li) *adj* monthly

måneskinn (*maw*-ner-shin) *nt* moonlight

måte (*maw*-ter) *m* fashion, way, manner; **på hvilken som helst ~** any way; **på ingen ~** by no means

***måtte** (*mot*-ter) *v* *must, *have to; *be bound to; need, need to

N

nabo (*naa*-boo) *m* neighbo(u)r

nabolag (*naa*-boo-laag) *nt* (pl ~) vicinity, neighbo(u)rhood

naiv (*nah-eev*) *adj* naïve

naken (*naa*-kern) *adj* nude, bare, naked

nakke (*nahk*-ker) *m* nape of the neck

narkoman (*nahr*-koo-*mahn*) *m* drug addict

narkose (nahr-*kōō*-ser) *m*

narcosis

narkotika (nahr-*kōō*-ti-kah) *m* (pl ~) drug; **narkotisk middel** narcotic

narre (*nahr*-rer) *v* fool

nasjon (nah-*shōōn*) *m* nation

nasjonal (nah-shoo-*naal*) *adj* national

nasjonaldrakt (nah-shoo-*naal*-drahkt) *c* national dress

nasjonalisere (nah-shoo-

nah-li-*say*-rer) v
nationalize

nasjonalitet (nah-shoo-
nah-li-*tayt*) m nationality

nasjonalpark (nah-shoo-
naal-pahrk) m national
park

nasjonalsang (nah-shoo-
naal-sahng) m national
anthem

natt (nahtt) c (pl netter)
night; i ~ tonight; **om
natten** by night

nattergal (*naht*-terr-gaal) m
nightingale

nattklubb (*naht*-klewb) m
cabaret, nightclub

nattkrem (*naht*-kraym) m
night cream

nattlig (*naht*-li) adj nightly

natt-takst (*naht*-tahkst) m
night rate

natt-tog (*naht*-tawg) nt (pl
~) night train

natur (nah-*tewr*) m nature

naturlig (nah-*tew*-li) adj
natural

naturligvis (nah-*tew*-li-
veess) adv of course,
naturally

naturskjønn (nah-*tew*-
shurn) adj scenic

naturvitenskap (nah-*tewr*-
vee-tern-skaap) m natural
science

navigasjon (nah-vi-gah-
shoon) m navigation

navigere (nah-vi-*gay*-rer) v
navigate

navle (*nahv*-ler) m navel

navn (nahvn) nt name; **i ...s
~ on behalf of, in the name
of**

nebb (nehbb) nt beak

ned (*nayd*) adv down;
downstairs

nedbetale (*nayd*-beh-taa-
ler) v *pay off

nedbetaling (*nayd*-beh-taa-
ling) c down payment

nedbør (*nayd*-burr) m
precipitation

nede (*nay*-der) adv below,
downstairs

nedenfor (*nay*-dern-for)
prep under, below

nedenunder (*nay*-dern-ew-
nerr) adv underneath

nederlag (*nay*-der-laag) nt
(pl ~) defeat

Nederland (*nay*-der-lahn)
the Netherlands

nederlandsk (*nay*-der-
lahnsk) adj Dutch

nederlender (*nay*-der-leh-
nerr) m Dutchman

nedgang (*nayd*-gahng) m
decrease; depression

nedkomst (*nayd*-komst) m
delivery

nedlasting (nayd-*lahs*-ting)
c download

nedover (*nay*-do-verr) adv
down, downwards

nedre (*nayd*-rer) adj
inferior, lower

nedrivning (*nayd*-reev-
ning) m demolition

nedslått (*nayd*-shlot) adj
down

nedstemt (*nāyd*-stehmt) *adj* depressed

nedstigning (*nāyd*-steeg-ning) *m* descent

nedtrykt (*nāyd*-trewkt) *adj* depressed

negativ (*nāy*-gah-teev) *adj* negative; *nt* negative

negl (nayl) *m* nail

neglefil (*nay*-ler-feel) *c* nail file

neglelakk (*nay*-ler-lahk) *m* nail polish

neglesaks (*nay*-ler-sahks) *c* nail scissors *pl*

nei (nay) no

nekte (*nehk*-ter) *v* deny

nemlig (*nehm*-li) *adv* namely

neppe (*nehp*-per) *adv* hardly

nerve (*nær*-ver) *m* nerve

nervøs (nær-*vūrss*) *adj* nervous

nese (*nāy*-ser) *c* nose

neseblod (*nāy*-ser-blōō) *nt* nosebleed

nesebor (*nāy*-ser-bōōr) *nt* (pl ~) nostril

nesevis (*nāy*-ser-veess) *adj* impertinent

neshorn (*nāyss*-hōōn) *nt* (pl ~) rhinoceros

neste (*nehss*-ter) *adj* next; following

nesten (*nehss*-tern) *adv* nearly, almost

nestleder (*nehsst*-lāyd*-err) *c* (pl ~e) executive assistant

nett (nehtt) *nt* net; Internet;

adj neat

netthinne (*neht*-hi-ner) *c* retina

netto (*neht*-too) *adv* net

nettopp (*neht*-top) *adv* just

nettsted (*nehtt*-stāy) *nt* (pl ~er) website

nettverk (*neht*-værk) *nt* network

nettverksbygging (*neht*-værks-*bewgg*-ing) *c* networking

nevne (*nehv*-ner) *v* mention

nevralgi (nehv-rahl-*gee*) *m* neuralgia

nevrose (nehv-*rōō*-ser) *m* neurosis

nevø (neh-*vūr*) *m* nephew

ni (nee) *num* nine

niende (*nee*-er-ner) *num* ninth

niese (ni-*āy*-ser) *c* niece

nifs (nifs) *adj* creepy

Nigeria (ni-*gāy*-ri-ah) Nigeria

nigerianer (ni-geh-ri-*aa*-nerr) *m* Nigerian

nigeriansk (ni-geh-ri-*aansk*) *adj* Nigerian

nikk (nikk) *nt* nod

nikke (*nik*-ker) *v* nod

nikkel (*nik*-kerl) *m* nickel

nikotin (ni-koo-*teen*) *m* nicotine

nitten (*nit*-tern) *num* nineteen

nittende (*nit*-ter-ner) *num* nineteenth

nitti (*nit*-ti) *num* ninety

nivellere (ni-ver-*lāy*-rer) *v*

level

nivå (ni-*vaw*) *nt* level

noe (*noo*-er) *pron*
something

noen (*noo*-ern) *pron*
somebody, someone;
some; ~ **gang** ever

nok (nokk) *adv* enough

også (*nok*-so) *adv* fairly,
somewhat

nominasjon (noo-mi-nah-
shoon) *nt* nomination

nominell (noo-mi-*nehll*) *adj*
nominal

nominere (noo-mi-*nay*-rer)
v nominate

nonne (*non*-ner) *c* nun

nonsens (*non*-serns) *nt*
nonsense

nord (noor) *m* north

nordlig (*noo*-li) *adj* north,
northern

nordmann (*noor*-mahn) *m*
(pl -menn) Norwegian

Nordpolen (*noor*-poo-lern)
North Pole

nordvest (noor-*vehst*) *m*
north-west

nordøst (noor-*urst*) *m*
north-east

Norge (*nor*-ger) Norway

norm (norm) *m* standard

normal (noor-maal) *adj*
normal; regular

norsk (noshk) *adj*
Norwegian

nota (*noo*-tah) *m* bill

notar (noo-*taar*) *m* notary

notat (noo-*taat*) *nt* note

notere (noo-*tay*-rer) *v* note

notis (noo-*teess*) *m* note

notisblokk (noo-*teess*-blok)
c note pad

notisbok (noo-*teess*-book) *c*
(pl -bøker) notebook

november (noo-*vehm*-berr)
November

null (newll) *nt* zero, nought

nummer (*noom*-merr) *nt*
(pl numre) number; act

nummerskilt (*noom*-mer-
shilt) *nt* registration plate;
licence plate *Am*

nummervisning (*nomm*-
ehr-*veess*-nee-ning) *c*
caller id

ny (new) *adj* new; recent

nyanse (new-*ahng*-ser) *m*
nuance; shade

nybegynner (*new*-beh-[y]ew-
nerr) *m* beginner; learner

nybygger (*new*-bew-gerr)
m pioneer

nyhet (*new*-hayt) *c* news;
nyheter *pl* news

nykke (*newk*-ker) *nt* whim

nylig (*new*-li) *adv* recently,
lately

nynne (*newn*-ner) *v* hum

nyre (*new*-rer) *c* kidney

***nyse** (*new*-ser) *v* sneeze

nysgjerrig (new-*shær*-ri)
adj curious; inquisitive;
nosy *colloquial*

nysgjerrighet (new-*shær*-ri-
hāyt) *c* curiosity

***nyte** (*new*-ter) *v* enjoy

nytelse (*new*-terl-ser) *m*
enjoyment

nytte (*newt*-ter) *c* utility,

use; *v* *be of use
nytteløs (*newt-ter-lūrss*) *adj*
idle
nyttig (*newt-ti*) *adj* useful
nyttår (*newt-tawr*) *nt* New
Year
Ny-Zealand (*new-say-lahn*)
New Zealand
nær (*næær*) *adv* near; *adj*
close, near
nærende (*nææ-rer-ner*) *adj*
nourishing, nutritious
nærhet (*næær-hayt*) *c*
vicinity
næring (*næær-ing*) *c*
nourishment; industry;
economy; **næringsliv**
economy
nærliggende (*nææ-li-ger-
ner*) *adj* neighbo(u)ring,
nearby
nærme seg (*nær-mer*) *v*
approach
nærsynt (*nææ-shewnt*) *adj*
short-sighted
nærvær (*næær-væær*) *nt*
presence
nød (*nūd*) *c* misery, distress
nøde (*nū-der*) *v* compel;
*være nødt til *be obliged
to
nødsignal (*nūrd-sing-naal*)
nt distress signal
nødssituasjon (*nūrd-si-
tew-ah-shoon*) *m*
emergency
nødstilfelle (*nūrds-til-feh-
ler*) *nt* emergency
nødtvunget (*nūrd-tvoo-
ngert*) *adv* by force

nødutgang (*nūrd-ewt-
gahng*) *m* emergency exit
nødvendig (*nurd-vehn-di*)
adj necessary
nødvendighet (*nurd-vehn-
di-hayt*) *c* necessity, need
nøkkel (*nurk-kerl*) *m* (pl
nøkler) key
nøkkelhull (*nurk-kerl-hewl*)
nt keyhole
nøktern (*nurk-tern*) *adj*
down-to-earth, sober
nøle (*nū-ler*) *v* hesitate
nøtt (*nurtt*) *c* nut
nøtteknekker (*nurt-ter-
kneh-kerr*) *m* nutcrackers
pl
nøtteskall (*nurt-ter-skahl*)
nt (pl ~) nutshell
nøyaktig (*nur^{ew}-ahk-ti*) *adj*
accurate, precise, exact;
careful
nøyaktighet (*nur^{ew}-ahk-ti-
hayt*) *c* correctness
nøye seg med (*nurew-er*)
*make do with
nøytral (*nur^{ew}-traal*) *adj*
neutral
nå^1 (*naw*) *v* reach; *catch;
*make
nå^2 (*naw*) *adv* now; ~ og da
occasionally, now and then
nåde (*naw-der*) *m* mercy,
grace
nål (*nawl*) *c* needle
nåletre (*naw-ler-tray*) *nt* (pl
-rær) firtree
når (*norr*) *adv* when; *conj*
when; ~ enn whenever
nåtid (*naw-teed*) *c* present

nåtildags (*naw*-til-dahks)
   adv nowadays

nåværende (*naw*-væe-er-ner) *adj* current, present

O

oase (oo-*aa*-ser) *m* oasis
obduksjon (ob-dewk-*shōōn*) *m* autopsy
oberst (*ōō*-bersht) *m* colonel
objekt (oob-ᵞ*ehkt*) *nt* object
objektiv (ob-ᵞehk-*teev*) *adj* objective
obligasjon (ob-li-gah-*shōōn*) *m* bond
obligatorisk (oob-li-gah-*tōō*-risk) *adj* obligatory, compulsory
observasjon (op-sehr-vah-*shōōn*) *m* observation
observatorium (op-sehr-vah-*tōō*-ri-ewm) *nt* (pl -ier) observatory
observere (op-sehr-*vāy*-rer) *v* observe
offensiv (*of*-fahng-seev) *adj* offensive; *m* offensive
offentlig (*of*-fernt-li) *adj* public
*****offentliggjøre** (*o*-fernt-li-ᵞ*ūr*-rer) *v* publish
offentliggjørelse (*of*-fernt-li-ᵞ*ūr*-rerl-ser) *m* publication
offer (*of*-ferr) *nt* (pl ofre) victim; casualty; sacrifice
offiser (o-fi-*sāyr*) *m* (pl ~er) officer
offisiell (o-fi-si-*ehll*) *adj*

official
ofre (*of*-rer) *v* sacrifice
ofte (*of*-ter) *adv* frequently, often
og (o) *conj* and
også (*oss*-so) *adv* also; as well, too
okkupasjon (o-kew-pah-*shōōn*) *m* occupation
okse (*ook*-ser) *m* ox
oksekjøtt (*ook*-ser-khurt) *nt* beef
oksygen (ok-sew-*gāyn*) *nt* oxygen
oktober (ok-*tōō*-berr) October
olabukse (*ōō*-lah-book-se) *c* jeans
oliven (oo-*lee*-vern) *m* (pl ~, ~er) olive
olivenolje (oo-*lee*-vern-ol-ᵞer) *c* olive oil
olje (*ol*-ᵞer) *c* oil
oljebrønn (*ol*-ᵞer-brurn) *m* oil well
oljefilter (*ol*-ᵞer-fil-terr) *nt* (pl -tre) oil filter
oljemaleri (*ol*-ᵞer-maa-ler-ree) *nt* oil painting
oljeraffineri (*ol*-ᵞer-rah-fi-ner-ree) *nt* oil refinery
oljet (*ol*-ᵞert) *adj* oily
oljetrykk (*ol*-ᵞer-trewk) *nt* (pl ~) oil pressure

om (oomm) *prep* round; about; in; *conj* whether, if

om bord (om bōōr) aboard

omdanne (*oom*-dah-ner) *v* transform

omdreining (om-dray-ning) *m* revolution

omegn (*oom*-mayn) *m* surroundings *pl*

omelett (oo-mer-*lehtt*) *m* omelette

omfang (*oom*-fahng) *nt* extent

omfangsrik (*oom*-fahngsreek) *adj* big, bulky, extensive

omfatte (*oom*-fah-ter) *v* comprise, include

omfattende (*oom*-fah-terner) *adj* comprehensive, extensive

omfavne (*oom*-fahv-ner) *v* embrace, hug

omfavnelse (*oom*-fahvnerl-ser) *m* embrace

omgang (*oom*-gahng) *m* round; half time

*omgi (*oom*-ʸee) *v* encircle, circle, surround

omgivelser (*oom*-ʸee-verlserr) *pl* environment; setting

*omgå (*oom*-gaw) *v* by-pass

omgående (*oom*-gaw-erner) *adj* prompt

*omgås (*oom*-gawss) *v* associate with; ~ med mix with

omhyggelig (oom-*hew*-gerli) *adj* careful, thorough

omkjøring (*oom*-khūr-ring) *c* detour, diversion

*omkomme (*oom*-ko-mer) *v* perish

omkostninger (*oom*-kostni-ngerr) *pl* expenses *pl*

omkring (*oom*-*kringng*) *prep* round, around; *adv* about

omkringliggende (om-*kring*-li-ger-ner) *adj* surrounding

omløp (*oom*-lūrp) *nt* circulation; orbit

omregne (*oom*-ray-ner) *v* convert

omregningstabell (*oom*-ray-nings-tah-behll) *m* conversion chart

omringe (*oom*-ri-nger) *v* encircle, circle, surround

omriss (*oom*-riss) *nt* (pl ~) contour, outline; gi et ~ av outline

område (*oom*-raw-der) *nt* zone, area, territory, region; sphere

omsetning (*oom*-seht-ning) *m* turnover

omslag (*oom*-shlaag) *nt* reverse; sleeve; jacket

omslutte (*oom*-shlewt-ter) *v* envelop

omsorg (*oom*-sorg) *c* care

omstendighet (*oom-stehn*-di-hāyt) *c* condition, circumstance

omstridt (*oom*-strit) *adj* controversial

omtale (*oom*-taa-ler) *m*

mention

omtanke (*oom*-tahng-ker) *m* consideration

omtenksom (oom-*tehngk*-som) *adj* thoughtful

omtrent (oom-*trehnt*) *adv* approximately; about

omtrentlig (oom-*trehnt*-li) *adj* approximate

omvei (*oom*-vay) *m* detour

omvende (*oom*-veh-ner) *v* convert

ond (oonn) *adj* wicked, ill, evil

ondartet (*oon*-naa-tert) *adj* malignant

onde (*oon*-der) *nt* evil

ondsinnet (*oon*-si-nert) *adj* evil

ondskapsfull (*oon*-skaaps-fewl) *adj* vicious, spiteful, malicious

onkel (*oong*-kerl) *m* (pl onkler) uncle

onsdag (*oons*-dah) *m* Wednesday

onyks ($\overline{oo}$-newks) *m* onyx

opal (oo-*paal*) *m* opal

opera (*oo*-per-rah) *m* opera; opera house

operasjon (oo-per-rah-*shōōn*) *m* surgery, operation

operatør (oo-per-rah-*tūūr*)*m*operator

operere (oo-per-*rāy*-rer) *v* operate

opp (oopp) *adv* up

oppblåsbar (*oop*-blawss-baar) *adj* inflatable

oppdage (*oop*-daa-ger) *v* discover, detect; notice

oppdagelse (*oop*-daa-gerl-ser) *m* discovery

oppdikte (*oop*-dík-ter) *v* invent

*****oppdra** (*oop*-draa) *v* educate; *bring up; raise; rear

oppdrag (*oop*-draag) *nt* (pl ~) assignment

oppdragelse (*oop*-draa-gerl-ser) *m* up-bringing

oppdrette (*oop*-dreh-ter) *v* *breed

oppfatning (*oop*-faht-ning) *m* opinion, view

oppfatte (*oop*-fah-ter) *v* conceive

*****oppfinne** (*oop*-fi-ner) *v* invent

oppfinnelse (*oop*-fi-nerl-ser) *m* invention

oppfinner (*oop*-fi-nerr) *m* inventor

oppfinnsom (oop-*fin*-som) *adj* inventive

oppfostre (*oop*-fost-rer) *v* educate; *bring up; raise; rear

oppføre (*oop*-fūr-rer) *v* construct; ~ seg act, behave

oppførelse (*oop*-fūr-rerl-ser) *m* show; construction

oppførsel (*oop*-fur-sherl) *m* conduct, behavio(u)r

oppgave (*oop*-gaa-ver) *c* duty; task; exercise

*****oppgi** (*oop*-ʸee) *v* declare;

*give up
opphav (*oop*-haav) *nt* origin
opphisse (*oop*-hi-ser) *v* excite
opphisselse (*oop*-hi-serl-ser) *m* excitement
opphisset (*oop*-hi-sert) *adj* excited
opphold (*oop*-hol) *nt* (pl ~) stay
***oppholde seg** (*oop*-ho-ler) stay
oppholdstillatelse (*oop*-hols-ti-laa-terl-ser) *m* residence permit
opphøre (*oop*-hūr-rer) *v* finish, cease, discontinue, expire, end
oppkalle (*oop*-kahl-ler) *v* name after
opplag (*oop*-laag) *nt* (pl ~) edition
opplagt (*oop*-lahkt) *adj* fit; self-evident
oppleve (*oop*-lāy-ver) *v* experience
opplyse (*oop*-lēw-ser) *v* inform; illuminate
opplysning (*oop*-lēwss-ning) *m* information
oppløp (*oop*-lūrp) *nt* (pl ~) riot
oppløse (*oop*-lūr-ser) *v* dissolve
oppløselig (oop-lūr-ser-li) *adj* soluble
oppløsning (*oop*-lūrss-ning) *m* solution
oppmerksom (oop-*mærk*-som) *adj* attentive; ***være ~**

*pay attention; ***være ~ på** attend to, *pay attention to
oppmerksomhet (oop-*mærk*-som-*hāyt*) *c* notice, attention
oppmuntre (*oop*-mewn-trer) *v* encourage; cheer up
oppnå (*oop*-naw) *v* achieve, attain
oppnåelig (oop-*naw*-er-li) *adj* attainable; obtainable
opponere (oo-poo-*nāy*-rer) *v* oppose
opposisjon (oo-poo-si-*shōōn*) *m* opposition
oppover (*oop*-paw-verr) *adv* up, upwards
oppreist (*oop*-rayst) *adj* erect
opprette (*oop*-reh-ter) *v* found; institute
***opprettholde** (*oop*-reht-ho-ler) *v* maintain
oppriktig (oop-*rik*-ti) *adj* sincere, honest
oppringning (*oop*-ring-ning) *m* call
opprinnelig (oop-*rin*-ner-li) *adj* original, initial
opprinnelse (oop-*rin*-nerl-ser) *m* origin, source
opprør (*oop*-rūrr) *nt* (pl ~) revolt, rebellion; ***gjøre ~** revolt
opprørende (oop-*rūr*-rer-ner) *adj* revolting
opprørt (*oop*-rūrt) *adj* *upset
oppsiktsvekkende (*oop*-sikts-veh-ker-ner) *adj*

sensational, striking
oppskrift (*oop*-skrift) *c*
recipe
oppslag (*oop*-slag) *nt*
bulletin
oppslagstavle (oop-shlaks-
tahv-ler) *c* message board
oppspore (*oop*-spoo-rer) *v*
trace
oppstand (*oop*-stahn) *m*
rising, rebellion, revolt
oppstigning (*oop*-steeg-
ning) *m* ascent; rise
oppstyr (*oop*-stewr) *nt* fuss
*oppstå (*oop*-staw) *v* *arise
oppsyn (*oop*-sēwn) *nt* (pl ~)
supervision
oppsynsmann (*oop*-sēwns-
mahn) *m* (pl -menn)
warden
*oppta (*oop*-taa) *v* *take up;
occupy
opptak¹ (*oop*-taak) *nt* (pl ~)
recording
opptak² (*oop*-taak) *nt*
admission
opptatt (*oop*-taht) *adj* busy,
engaged; occupied
opptog (*oop*-tawg) *nt* (pl ~)
procession
opptre (oop-trāy) *v* perform
opptreden (*oop*-trāy-dern)
m appearance
oppvakt (*oop*-vahkt) *adj*
bright
oppvarte (*oop*-vah-ter) *v*
wait on
oppvask (*oop*-vahsk) *m*
washing-up; dirty dishes
oppvaskmaskin (*oop*-

vahsk-mah-sheen) *m*
dishwasher
oppvise (*oop*-vee-ser) *v*
exhibit, show
oppå (*oop*-po) *prep* on top
of
optiker (*oop*-ti-kerr) *m*
optician
optimisme (oop-ti-*miss*-
mer) *m* optimism
optimist (oop-t-*mist*) *m*
optimist
optimistisk (oop-ti-*miss*-
tisk) *adj* optimistic
oransje (oo-*rahng*-sher) *adj*
orange
ord (oor) *nt* word
ordbok (*oor*-book) *c* (pl
-bøker) dictionary
orden (*o*-dern) *m* order; **i ~**
in order
ordentlig (*o*-dernt-li) *adj*
tidy; neat
ordforråd (*oor*-fo-rawd) *nt*
vocabulary
ordinær (o-di-*næær*) *adj*
vulgar
ordliste (*oor*-liss-ter) *c* word
list
ordne (*oord*-ner) *v* arrange,
settle; sort; fix
ordning (*oord*-ning) *c*
arrangement, method;
settlement
ordre (*oord*-rer) *m* order
ordspill (*oor*-spil) *nt* (pl ~)
pun
ordspråk (*oor*-sprawk) *nt*
(pl ~) proverb
ordstrid (*oor*-streed) *m*

dispute

ordveksling (*ōōr*-vehk-shling) *c* argument

organ (or-*gaan*) *nt* organ

organisasjon (or-gah-ni-sah-*shōōn*) *m* organization

organisere (or-gah-ni-*sāy*-rer) *v* organize

organisk (or-*gaa*-nisk) *adj* organic

orgel (*or*-gerl) *nt* (pl orgler) organ

orientalsk (o-ri-ehn-*taalsk*) *adj* oriental

Orienten (o-ri-*ehn*-tern) Orient

orientere seg (o-ri-ehn-*tāy*-rer) orientate

original (o-ri-gi-*naal*) *adj* original

orkan (or-*kaan*) *m* hurricane

orke (*or*-ker) *v* sustain

orkester (or-*kehss*-terr) *nt* (pl -tre) orchestra; band

orkesterplass (or-*kehss*-terr-plahss) *m* stall; orchestra seat *Am*

ornament (o-nah-*mehnt*) *nt* ornament

ornamental (o-nah-mehn-*taal*) *adj* ornamental

ortodoks (o-too-*doks*) *adj* orthodox

oss (oss) *pron* us, ourselves

ost (oost) *m* cheese

outsource (*awt*-sour-ser) *v* outsource

ouverture (oo-ver-*tēw*-rer) *m* overture

oval (oo-*vaal*) *adj* oval

ovenfor (*aw*-vern-for) *prep* above, over; *adv* above, overhead

ovenpå (*aw*-vern-paw) *adv* upstairs

over (*aw*-verr) *prep* across, over; *adv* over; **over-** upper; ~ **ende** down, over

overall (*aw*-ver-rol) *m* overalls *pl*

overalt (o-ver-*rahlt*) *adv* everywhere, throughout

overanstrenge (*aw*-ver-rahn-streh-nger) *v* strain; ~ **seg** overwork

overbevise (*aw*-verr-beh-vee-ser) *v* convince, persuade

overbevisning (*aw*-verr-beh-veess-ning) *m* conviction, persuasion

overdreven (*aw*-*drāy*-vern) *adj* extravagant, excessive

***overdrive** (*aw*-ver-dree-ver) *v* exaggerate; magnify; overdo

overdrivelse (*aw*-verr-driv-erl-ser) *m* exaggeration

overenskomst (*aw*-ver-rehns-komst) *m* settlement, agreement

overensstemmelse (*aw*-ver-rehns-steh-merl-ser) *m* agreement; **i ~ med** in accordance with, according to

overfall (*aw*-verr-fahl) *nt* (pl ~) attack; robbery; hold-up

overfart (*aw*-verr-faht) *m*

crossing, passage

overfladisk (aw-verr-flaa-disk) adj superficial

overflate (aw-verr-flaa-ter) c surface

overflod (aw-verr-flōōd) m abundance; plenty

overflødig (aw-verr-flūr-di) adj superfluous; redundant

overfor (aw-verr-for) prep opposite, facing; towards

overfylt (aw-verr-fewlt) adj crowded

overføre (aw-verr-fūr-rer) v transfer; remit

overgang (aw-verr-gahng) m transition

*overgi seg** (aw-verr-ʸee) surrender

overgivelse (aw-verr-ʸee-verl-ser) m surrender

overgrodd (aw-verr-grood) adj overgrown

*overgå** (aw-verr-gaw) v exceed, *outdo

overhale (aw-verr-haa-ler) v overhaul

overhodet (o-verr-hōō-der) adv at all

overlagt (aw-ver-lahkt) adj deliberate

*overlate** (aw-ver-laa-ter) v *leave to; entrust

overlegen (aw-ver-lāy-gern) adj superior, haughty

overleve (aw-ver-lāy-ver) v survive

overlærer (aw-ver-læ-rerr) m headmaster, head teacher

overmodig (aw-verr-mōō-di) adj presumptuous

overoppsyn (awv-err-op-sēwn) nt supervision

overraske (aw-ver-rahss-ker) v surprise

overraskelse (aw-ver-rahss-kerl-ser) m surprise

*overrekke** (aw-ver-reh-ker) v hand, *give

overrumple (aw-ver-roomp-ler) v *catch

*overse** (aw-ver-shāy) v overlook

*oversette** (aw-ver-sheh-ter) v translate

oversettelse (aw-ver-sheh-terl-ser) m translation; version

oversetter (aw-ver-sheh-terr) m translator

overside (aw-ver-shee-der) c top side, top

oversikt (aw-ver-shikt) m survey

oversjøisk (aw-ver-shūr-isk) adj overseas

*overskride** (aw-ver-shkree-der) v exceed

overskrift (aw-ver-shkrift) c heading; headline

overskudd (aw-ver-shkewd) nt (pl ~) surplus

overskyet (aw-ver-shēw-ert) adj overcast, cloudy

overspent (aw-ver-shpehnt) adj overstrung

overstrømmende (aw-ver-shtrur-mer-ner) adj exuberant

oversvømmelse (aw-ver-shvur-merl-ser) *m* flood

*overta (aw-ver-taa) *v* *take over

overtale (aw-ver-taa-ler) *v* persuade

overtrekk (aw-ver-trehkk)*nt* overdraft

overtrett (aw-ver-trehtt) *adj* over-tired

overtro (aw-ver-trōō) *c* superstition

overveie (aw-verr-vay-er) *v* consider; deliberate

overveielse (aw-verr-vay-erl-ser) *m* consideration; deliberation

overvekt (aw-verr-vehkt) *c* overweight; predominance

overvelde (aw-verr-veh-ler) *v* overwhelm

*overvinne (aw-verr-vi-ner) *v* *overcome; defeat

*overvære (aw-verr-vææ-rer) *v* attend

overvåke (awv-err-vaw-ker) *v* supervise; patrol

overvåking (awv-err-vaw-king)*c*surveillance

ovn (ovnn) *m* stove, furnace

ozon (oo-sōōn) *nt* ozone

P

padde (pahd-der) *c* toad

padleåre (pahd-ler-aw-rer) *c* paddle

Pakistan (pah-ki-staan) Pakistan

pakistaner (pah-ki-staa-nerr) *m* Pakistani

pakistansk (pah-ki-staansk) *adj* Pakistani

pakke[1] (pahk-ker) *c* package, parcel

pakke[2] (pahk-ker) *v* pack; ~ inn wrap; envelop ~ ned pack up; ~ opp unpack, unwrap

pakkhus (pahk-hēwss) *nt* (pl ~) warehouse

pakt (pahkt)*c*pact

palass (pah-lahss) *nt* palace

palme (pahl-mer) *m* palm

panel (pah-nāyl) *nt* panel

panelverk (pah-nāyl-værk) *nt* panelling

panikk (pah-nikk) *m* scare, panic

panne (pahn-ner) *c* forehead; pan

panser (pahn-serr) *nt* bonnet; hood *nAm*

pant (pahnt) *m* deposit

pantelån (pahn-ter-lawn) *nt* mortgage

pantelåner (pahn-ter-lawnerr) *m* pawnbroker

*pantsette (pahnt-seh-ter) *v* pawn

papegøye (pah-per-gurewer) *m* parrot; parakeet

papir (pah-peer) *nt* paper; **papir-** paper

pasifist

papirhandel (pah-*peer*-hahn-derl) *m* (pl -dler) stationer's

papirkniv (pah-*peer*-kneev) *m* paper knife

papirkurv (pah-*peer*-kewrv) *m* wastepaper basket

papirlommetørkle (pah-*peer*-loo-mer-turr-kler) *nt* (pl -lær) tissue

papirpose (pah-*peer*-pōō-ser) *m* paper bag

papirserviett (pah-*peer*-sær-vi-eht) *m* paper napkin

papirvarer (pah-*peer*-vaa-rerr) *pl* stationery

papp (pahpp) *m* cardboard

pappa (*pahp*-pah) *m* dad, daddy

par (paar) *nt* pair; couple

parabol (pah-rah-*bōōl*) *c* satellite dish

parade (pah-*raa*-der) *m* parade

parabolantenne (pah-raa-bōōl-ahn-*tehn*-ner) *c* satellite dish

paradis (pah-raa-*dis*) *nt* paradise

parafin (pah-rah-*feen*) *m* paraffin

parallell (pah-rah-*lehll*) *m* parallel; *adj* parallel

paraply (pah-rah-*plēw*) *m* umbrella

parasoll (pah-rah-*soll*) *m* sunshade

parat (pah-*raat*) *adj* ready

parfyme (pahr-*fēw*-mer) *m* perfume

park (pahrk) *m* park; **offentlig parkanlegg** public garden

parkere (pahr-*kāy*-rer) *v* park

parkering (pahr-*kāy*-ring) *c* parking; ~ **forbudt** no parking

parkeringsavgift (pahr-*kāy*-rings-aav-ʾift) *c* parking fee

parkeringslys (pahr-*kāy*-rings-lēwss) *nt* (pl ~) parking light

parkeringsplass (pahr-*kāy*-rings-plahss) *m* car park; parking lot *Am*

parkeringssone (pahr-*kāy*-ring-sōō-ner) *c* parking zone

parkometer (pahr-koo-*māy*-terr) *nt* (pl ~, -tre) parking meter

parlament (pahr-lah-*mehnt*) *nt* parliament; **parlamentarisk** *adj* parliamentary

parlør (pahr-*lūrr*) *m* phrase book

parti (pahr-*tee*) *nt* party; side

partisk (*paa*-tisk) *adj* partial

partner (*paat*-nerr) *m* partner; associate

parykk (pah-*rewkk*) *m* wig

pasient (pah-si-*ehnt*) *m* patient

pasifisme (pah-si-*fiss*-mer) *m* pacifism

pasifist (pah-si-*fist*) *m* pacifist

pasifistisk (pah-si-*fiss*-tisk) *adj* pasifist

pass (pahss) *nt* passport; mountain pass

passasje (pah-*saa*-sher) *m* passage

passasjer (pah-sah-*shayr*) *m* passenger

passasjerbåt (pah-sah-*shayr*-bawt) *m* liner

passe (*pahss*-er) *v* fit, suit; tend; look after; ~ **på** mind, *take care of; ~ **seg for** mind, look out; ~ **til** match

passende (*pahss*-ser-ner) *adj* appropriate, convenient, adequate; proper, just

passere (pah-*say*-rer) *v* pass

passfoto (*pahss*-fōō-too) *nt* (pl ~) passport photograph

passiv (*pahss*-seev) *adj* passive

passkontroll (*pahss*-koon-trol) *m* passport control

passord (*pahss*- ōōr) *m* password

pasta (*pahss*-tah) *m* paste; noodles

patent (pah-*tehnt*) *nt* patent

pater (*paa*-terr) *m* Father

patriot (paht-ri-ōōt) *m* patriot

patron (paht-*rōōn*) *m* cartridge

patrulje (pah-*rewl*-ʸer) *m* patrol

patruljere (pah-trewl-ʸ*ay*-

rer) *v* patrol

pattedyr (*paht*-ter-dēwr) *nt* (pl ~) mammal

pause (*pou*-ser) *m* pause; intermission, interval

pave (*paa*-ver) *m* pope

paviljong (pah-vil-ʸ*oangng*) *m* pavilion

peanøtt (*pee*-ah-nurt) *c* peanut

pedal (peh-*daal*) *m* pedal

peis (payss) *m* fireplace

peke (*pay*-ker) *v* point

pekefinger (*pay*-ker-fi-ngerr) *m* (pl -grer) index finger

pelikan (peh-li-*kaan*) *m* pelican

pels (pehls) *m* fur

pelskåpe (pehls-kaw-per) *c* fur coat

pen (payn) *adj* good-looking, handsome, pretty; fine, nice

pendler (*pehnd*-lerr) *m* commuter

pengeanbringelse (pehng-nger-ahn-bri-ngerl-ser) *m* investment

pengepung (pehng-nger-poong) *m* purse

penger (pehng-ngerr) *pl* money

pengeseddel (pehng-nger-seh-derl) *m* (pl -sedler) banknote

pengeskap (pehng-nger-skaap) *nt* (pl ~) safe

pengeutpresning (pehng-nger-ēwt-prehss-ning) *m*

blackmail; **presse penger
av** blackmail
penicillin (peh-ni-si-*leen*) *nt*
penicillin
penn (pehnn) *m* pen
pensel (*pehn*-serl) *m* (pl
-sler) paint-brush, brush
pensjon (pahng-*shoon*) *m*
pension; board;
retirement; **full ~** full
board, board and lodging,
bed and board; **gå av med
~** retire
pensjonat (pahng-shoo-
naat) *nt* boarding-house,
guest-house, pension
pensjonatskole (pahng-
shoo-*naat*-skoo-ler) *m*
boarding school
pensjonert (pahng-shoo-
nāyt) *adj* retired
pepper (*pehp*-perr) *m*
pepper
peppermynte (peh-perr-
mewn-ter) *c* peppermint
pepperrot (*pehp*-per-root) *c*
horseradish
per, pr. (pær) *prep* per
perfeksjon (pær-fehk-
shoon) *m* perfection
perfekt (pær-*fehkt*) *adj*
perfect; faultless
periode (peh-ri-*oo*-der) *m*
period
periodevis (peh-ri-*oo*-der-
veess) *adj* periodical
perle (*pææ*-ler) *c* pearl,
bead
perlekjede (*pææ*-ler-khāy-
der) *nt* beads *pl*

perlemor (*pææ*-ler-moor)
nt mother of pearl
perm (pærm) *m* cover
permisjon (pær-mi-*shoon*)
m leave; permit
perrong (peh-*rongng*) *m*
platform
perser (*pæsh*-sherr) *m*
Persian
Persia (*pæsh*-shi-ah) Persia
persienne (pæ-shi-*ehn*-ner)
m blind, shutter
persille (pæ-*shil*-ler) *c*
parsley
persisk (*pæsh*-shisk) *adj*
Persian
person (pæ-*shoon*) *m*
person; **per ~** per person
personale (pæ-shoo-*naa*-
ler) *nt* personnel, staff
personlig (pæ-*shoon*-li) *adj*
personal; private
personlighet (pæ-*shoon*-li-
hāyt) *c* personality
persontog (pæ-*shoon*-tawg)
nt (pl ~) passenger train
perspektiv (pæsh-pehk-
teev) *nt* perspective
pertentlig (pæ-*tehnt*-li) *adj*
precise
pese (*pāy*-ser) *v* pant
pessimisme (peh-si-*miss*-
mer) *m* pessimism
pessimist (peh-si-*mist*) *m*
pessimist
pessimistisk (peh-si-*miss*-
tisk) *adj* pessimistic
petisjon (peh-ti-*shoon*) *m*
petition
petroleum (peht-*roo*-leh-

ewm) *m* petroleum;
kerosene

pianist (piah-*nist*) *m* pianist

piano (pi-*aa*-noo) *nt* piano

pigg (pigg) *m* spike; peak

pigge (*pigg*-ger) *v* spike;
prod

piggtråd (*pigg*-traw) *m*
barbed wire

pikant (pi-*kahnt*) *adj*
savo(u)ry

pike (*pee*-ker) *m* girl

pikenavn (*pee*-ker-nahvn)
nt (pl ~) maiden name

pikkolo (*pik*-koo-loo) *m*
bellboy

piknik (*pik*-nik) *m* picnic;
*dra på ~ picnic

pil (peel) *c* arrow; willow

pilegrim (*pil*-grim) *m*
pilgrim

pilegrimsreise (*pil*-grims-
ray-ser) *m* pilgrimage

pille (*pil*-ler) *c* pill

pilot (pi-*lōōt*) *m* pilot

pimpstein (*pimp*-stayn) *m*
pumice stone

pine (*pee*-ner) *v* torment; *c*
torment

pingvin (ping-*veen*) *m*
penguin

PIN kode (pinn-*kōō*-der) *c*
PIN; personal
identification number

pinlig (*peen*-li) *adj*
embarrassing, awkward

pinnsvin (*pin*-sveen) *nt* (pl
~) hedgehog

pinse (*pin*-ser) *c* Pentecost

pinsett (pin-*sehtt*) *m*

tweezers *pl*

pipe (*pee*-per) *c* pipe

pipetobakk (*pee*-per-too-
bahk) *m* pipe tobacco

pisk (pisk) *m* whip

pistol (piss-*tōōl*) *m* pistol

pittoresk (pi-too-*rehsk*) *adj*
picturesque

plage (*plaa*-ger) *v* bother;
m nuisance

plagg (plahgg) *nt* garment

plakat (plah-*kaat*) *m* poster,
placard

plan (plaan) *m* scheme,
project, plan; map; *nt*
level; *adj* even, flat, level

planet (plah-*nāyt*) *m* planet

planetarium (plah-neh-*taa*-
ri-ewm) *nt* (pl -ier)
planetarium

planke (*plahng*-ker) *m*
board, plank

***planlegge** (*plaan*-leh-ger)
v plan

planovergang (*plaa*-naw-
verr-gahng) *m* level
crossing

plantasje (plahn-*taa*-sher)
m plantation

plante (*plahn*-ter) *m* plant;
v plant

planteskole (*plahn*-ter-
skōōler) *m* nursery

plass (plahss) *m* square;
room; seat

plassere (plah-*sāy*-rer) *v*
*put, *lay

plaster (*plah*-sterr) *nt* (pl ~,
-tre) plaster

plastikk (plahss-*tikk*) *m*

plastic; **plastikk-** plastic
plate (plaa-ter) c plate;
sheet; record
platespiller (plaa-ter-spi-
lerr) m record player
platina (plaa-ti-nah) m
platinum
pleie (play-er) v *be in the
habit of; nurse
pleieforeldre (play-er-fo-
rehl-drer) pl foster parents
pl
pleiehjem (play-er-³ehm) nt
(pl ⁓) foster-home
plettfri (pleht-free) adj
spotless, stainless
plikt (plikt) c duty
plog (plōōg) m plough
plombe (ploom-ber) m
filling
plomme (ploom-mer) c
plum
plugge inn (plewg-er-in)
plug in
plukke (plook-ker) v pick
pluss (plewss) adv plus
plutselig (plewt-ser-li) adj
suddenly; sudden
plyndring (plewn-dring) c
robbery
plystre (plewss-trer) v
whistle
pløye (plurew-er) v plough
poengsum (po-ehng-sewm)
m (pl ⁓mer) score
poesi (poo-eh-see) m poetry
pokal (poo-kaal) m cup
Polen (pōō-lern) Poland
polere (poo-lāy-rer) v
polish

polio (pōō-li-oo) m polio
polise (poo-lee-ser) m
policy
politi (poo-li-tee) nt police
pl
politibetjent (poo-li-tee-
beh-t³ehnt) m policeman,
policewoman
politiker (poo-lee-ti-kerr) m
politician
politikk (poo-li-tikk) m
politics; policy
politisk (poo-lee-tisk) adj
political
politistasjon (poo-li-tee-
stah-shōōn) m police
station
polsk (pōōlsk) adj Polish
polstre (pol-strer) v
upholster
pommes frites (pom fritt)
chips; French fries Am
ponni (pon-ni) m pony
popmusikk (pop-mew-sik)
m pop music
populær (poo-pew-læær)
adj popular
porselen (poo-sher-lāyn) nt
china, porcelain
porsjon (poo-shōōn) m
portion; helping
port (poott) m gate
portier (poo-ti-æær) m (pl
⁓er) doorman
portner (poot-nerr) m
porter
porto (poot-too) m postage
portrett (poot-rehtt) nt
portrait
Portugal (poo-tew-gahl)

Portugal

portugiser (poo-tew-*gee*-serr) *m* Portuguese

portugisisk (poo-tew-*gee*-sisk) *adj* Portuguese

pose ($p\overline{oo}$-ser) *m* bag

posisjon (poo-si-*shoon*) *m* position; station

positiv ($p\overline{oo}$-si-teev) *adj* positive

post (post) *m* mail, post; item; **ledig ~** vacancy; **poste restante** poste restante

postbud (*post*-b$\overline{ew}$d) *nt* (pl ~) postman

poste (*poss*-ter) *v* mail, post

postei (*poewss*-tei) *m* pasty

poster (*poewss*-terr) *m* poster

postkasse (*post*-kah-ser) *c* pillar-box, letter-box; mailbox *nAm*

postkontor (*post*-koon-t$\overline{oo}$r) *nt* post-office

postkort (*post*-kot) *nt* (pl ~) postcard

postnummer (*post*-noo-merr) *nt* (pl -numre) zip code *Am*

postvesen (*post*-v$\overline{ay}$-sern) *nt* postal service

pote ($p\overline{oo}$-ter) *m* paw

potet (poo-*t$\overline{ay}$t*) *c* potato; **~stappe** *c* mashed potatoes

praksis (*prahk*-siss) *m* practice

prakt (prahkt) *m* splendo(u)r

praktfull (*prahkt*-fewl) *adj* magnificent, gorgeous, splendid

praktisere (prahk-ti-*s$\overline{ay}$*-rer) *v* practise

praktisk (*prahk*-tisk) *adj* practical; **~ talt** practically

prat (praat) *m*/*nt* chat

prate (*praa*-ter) *v* chat

preke (*pr$\overline{ay}$*-ker) *v* preach

preken (*pr$\overline{ay}$*-kern) *m* sermon

prekestol (*pr$\overline{ay}$*-ker-st$\overline{oo}$l) *m* pulpit

premie (*pr$\overline{ay}$*-mi-er) *m* prize

preposisjon (preh-poo-si-*shoon*) *m* preposition

presang (preh-*sahngng*) *m* gift, present

presentasjon (preh-sahng-tah-*shoon*) *m* introduction, presentation

presentere (preh-sahng-*t$\overline{ay}$*-rer) *v* present, introduce

president (preh-si-*dehnt*) *m* president

presis (preh-*seess*) *adj* punctual, precise

press (prehss) *nt* pressure

presse (*prehss*-ser) *v* press; squeeze; *c* press

pressekonferanse (*prehss*-ser-koon-feh-rahng-ser) *m* press conference

presserende (preh-*s$\overline{ay}$*-rer-ner) *adj* urgent, pressing

prest (prehst) *m* clergyman, parson; rector, minister; **katolsk ~** priest

prestasjon (prehss-tah-*shōōn*) *m* feat, achievement

prestegård (*prehss*-ter-gawr) *m* vicarage, parsonage

prestere (prehss-*tāy*-rer) *v* achieve

prestisje (prehss-*tee*-sher) *m* prestige

prevensjonsmiddel (preh-vahng-*shōōns*-mi-derl) *nt* (pl -midler) contraceptive

prikk (prik) *m* dot

primær (pri-*mæær*) *adj* primary

prins (prins) *m* prince

prinsesse (prin-*sehss*-ser) *c* princess

prinsipp (prin-*sipp*) *nt* principle

prioritet (pri-oo-ri-*tāyt*) *m* priority

pris (preess) *m* cost, price; charge, rate; award

prisfall (*preess*-fahl) *nt* drop in price, slump

prisliste (*preess*-liss-ter) *c* price list

privat (pri-*vaat*) *adj* private

privatliv (pri-*vaat*-leev) *nt* privacy

privilegere (pri-vi-leh-*gāy*-rer) *v* favo(u)r

privilegium (pri-vi-*lāy*-gi-ewm) *nt* (pl -ier) privilege

problem (proo-*blāym*) *nt* problem; question

produksjon (proo-dook-*shōōn*) *m* production;

output

produkt (proo-*dewkt*) *nt* product; produce

produsent (proo-dew-*sehnt*) *m* producer

produsere (proo-dew-*sāy*-rer) *v* produce

profesjon (proo-feh-*shōōn*) *m* profession

profesjonell (proo-feh-shoo-*nehll*) *adj* professional

professor (proo-*fehss*-soor) *m* professor

profet (proo-*fāyt*) *m* prophet

program (proo-*grahmm*) *nt* (pl ⁓mer) programme

programvare (proo-*grahmm*-vaarer) *m* software

progressiv (*proog*-reh-seev) *adj* progressive

promenade (proo-mer-*naa*-der) *m* promenade

pronomen (proo-*nōō*-mern) *nt* pronoun

propaganda (proo-pah-*gahn*-dah) *m* propaganda

propell (proo-*pehll*) *m* propeller

proporsjon (proo-poo-*shōōn*) *m* proportion

prosent (proo-*sehnt*) *m* percent

prosentsats (proo-*sehnt*-sahts) *m* percentage

prosesjon (proo-seh-*shōōn*) *m* procession

prosess (proo-*sehss*) *m*

process
prosjekt (proo-*shehkt*) nt
project
prosjektør (proo-shehk-*tūrr*) m spotlight
prospekt (proo-*spehkt*) nt
prospectus
prospektkort (proo-*spehkt*-kot) nt (pl ~) picture
postcard, postcard
prostituert (proo-sti-tew-*āyt*) m prostitute
protein (proo-teh-*een*) nt
protein
protest (proo-*tehst*) m
protest
protestantisk (proo-ter-*stahn*-tisk) adj Protestant
protestere (proo-ter-*stāy*-rer) v protest; object
protokoll (proo-too-*koll*) m
record
proviant (proo-vi-*ahnt*) m
provisions pl
provins (proo-*vins*) m
province
provinsiell (proo-vin-si-*ehll*) adj provincial
prute (*prew*-ter) v bargain
prøve (*prūr*-ver) v try,
attempt; try on; rehearse; c
specimen; test; rehearsal
prøverom (*prūr*-ver-room)
nt (pl ~) fitting room
psykiater (sew-ki-*aa*-terr)
m psychiatrist
psykisk (*sēw*-kisk) adj
psychic
psykoanalytiker (sew-koo-ah-nah-*lewt*-ti-kerr) m

analyst, psychoanalyst
psykolog (sew-koo-*lawg*) m
psychologist
psykologi (sew-koo-loo-gee) m psychology
psykologisk (sew-koo-*law*-gisk) adj psychological
publikum (*pewb*-li-kewm)
nt audience, public
publisitet (pewb-li-si-*tāyt*)
m publicity
pudder (*pewd*-derr) nt
powder
puff (pewff) m push
pule (*pew*-ler) v vulgar fuck
puls (pewls) m pulse
pulsåre (pewls-aw-rer) c
artery
pult (pewlt) m desk
pumpe (*poom*-per) v pump;
c pump
pund (pewnn) nt pound
pung (poongng) m purse;
pouch
punkt (poongt) nt point;
item
punktering (poong-*tāy*-ring) c puncture, blow-out;
flat tyre
punktert (poong-*tāyt*) adj
punctured
punktlig (*poongt*-li) adj
punctual
punktum (*pewng*-tewm) nt
full stop, period, dot
pur (pēwr) adj sheer
purpurfarget (*pewr*-pewr-fahr-gert) adj purple
pusekatt (*pēw*-ser-kaht) m
pussy-cat

pusle (*pewsh*-ler) *v* potter; busy oneself

puslespill (*pewsh*-ler-spil) *nt* (pl ~) jigsaw puzzle

pusse (*pewss*-ser) *v* polish

pussig (*pewss*-si) *adj* funny

pust (pewst) *m* breath

puste (*pewss*-ter) *v* breathe; ~ **ut** expire, exhale

pute (*pew*-ter) *c* cushion; pillow; pad

putevar (*pew*-ter-vaar) *nt* (pl ~) pillow-case

putte (*pewt*-ter) *v* *put

pyjamas (pew-*shaa*-mahss) *m* pyjamas *pl*

pynt (pewnt) *m* decoration

pynte (*pewn*-ter) *v* decorate

pytt (pewtt) *m* puddle

pære (*pææ*-rer) *c* pear

pæreholder (*pææ*-rer-hoa-lerr) *m* socket

pølse (*purl*-ser) *c* sausage

på (paw) *prep* upon, on, at; to

***pådra seg** (*paw*-draa) contract

påfallende (*paw*-fah-ler-ner) *adj* striking

påfugl (*paw*-fewl) *m* peacock

påkrevd (*paw*-krehvd) *adj* requisite

pålegg (*paw*-lehg) *nt* (pl ~) rise; sandwich spread, cold cuts

***pålegge** (*paw*-lehg-er) *v* raise, charge

pålitelig (po-*lee*-ter-li) *adj* sound, reliable, trustworthy

påske (*pawss*-ker) *c* Easter

påskelilje (*pawss*-ker-lil-Yer) *c* daffodil

påskjønne (*paw*-shur-ner) *v* appreciate

påskudd (*paw*-skewd) *nt* (pl ~) pretext, pretence

***påstå** (*paw*-staw) *v* claim

***påta seg** (*paw*-taa) *take charge of

påvirke (*paw*-veer-ker) *v* affect, influence

R

rabalder (rah-*bahl*-derr) *nt* racket

rabarbra (rah-*bahr*-brah) *m* rhubarb

rabatt (rah-*bahtt*) *m* discount, rebate

rabies (*raa*-bi-ehss) *m* rabies

racket (*rehk*-ket) *m* racket

rad (raad) *m* row

radering (rah-*dāy*-ring) *c* etching

radiator (rah-di-*aa*-toor) *m* radiator

radikal (rah-di-*kaal*) *adj* radical

radio (*raa*-di-oo) *m* radio

radius (*raa*-di-ewss) *m* (pl

-ier) radius

raffineri (rah-fi-ner-*ree*) *nt* refinery

rak (raak) *adj* straight

rake (*raa*-ker) *c* rake

rakett (rah-*kehtt*) *m* rocket

ramme (*rahm*-mer) *c* frame; *v* *hit

rampe (*rahm*-per) *c* ramp

ran (raan) *nt* robbery

rand (rahnn) *m* (pl render) brim

rane (*raa*-ner) *v* rob

rang (rahngng) *m* rank

ransake (*rahn*-saa-ker) *v* search

ransel (*rahn*-serl) *m* (pl -sler) satchel

ransmann (*raans*-mahn) *m* (pl -menn) robber

rap (ræp) *c* rap

rapphøne (*rahp*-hūr-ner) *c* partridge

rapport (rah-*pott*) *m* report

rapportere (rah-po-*tāy*-rer) *v* report

rar (raar) *adj* odd

rase (*raa*-ser) *v* race; breed; *v* rage; **rase-** racial

rasende (*raa*-ser-ner) *adj* mad, furious

raseri (raa-ser-*ree*) *nt* rage, anger

rasjon (rah-*shōōn*) *m* ration

rask (rahsk) *adj* swift, fast; *nt* trash

raspe (*rahss*-per) *v* grate

rastløs (*rahst*-lūrss) *adj* restless

rastløshet (*rahst*-lūrss-hāyt)

c unrest

ratt (rahtt) *nt* steering wheel

rattstamme (*raht*-stah-mer) *m* steering column

rav (raav) *nt* amber

ravn (rahvn) *m* raven

reagere (reh-ah-*ga***y-rer) *v* react

reaksjon (reh-ahk-*shōōn*) *m* reaction

realisere (reh-ah-li-*sāy*-rer) *v* realize

realistisk (reh-ah-*liss*-tisk) *adj* matter-of-fact

redaktør (reh-dahk-*tūrr*) *m* editor

redd (rehdd) *adj* afraid; *være ~ *be afraid

redde (*rehd*-der) *v* rescue, save

reddik (*rehd*-dik) *m* radish

rede (*rāy*-der) *nt* nest

redegjørelse (*rāy*-der-ᵞ*ūr*-rerl-ser) *m* account

redigere (reh-dig-*ehrer*) *v* edit

redning (*rehd*-ning) *m* rescue

redsel (*reht*-serl) *m* (pl -sler) terror, horror

redselsfull (*reht*-serls-fewl) *adj* awful, horrible

redskap (*rehss*-kaap) *nt* utensil, tool

reduksjon (reh-dewk-*shōōn*) *m* reduction

redusere (reh-dew-*sāy*-rer) *v* reduce

referanse (reh-fer-*rahng*-ser) *m* reference

reisebyrå

referat (reh-fer-raat) *nt*
minutes

refill (ri-*fill*) *m* (pl ~) refill

refleks (reh-*flehks*) *m*
reflection

reflektere (rehf-lehk-*tay*-
rer) *v* reflect

reflektor (reh-*flehk*-toor) *m*
reflector

Reformasjonen (reh-for-
mah-*shoo*-nern) the
Reformation

refundere (reh-fewn-*day*-
rer) *v* refund

regatta (reh-*gaht*-tah) *m*
regatta

regel (*ray*-gerl) *m* (pl
regler) rule; regulation;
som ~ in general, as a rule

regelmessig (*ray*-gerl-meh-
si) *adj* regular

regent (reh-*gehnt*) *m* ruler

regi (reh-*shee*) *c* direction,
staging

regime (reh-*shee*-mer) *nt*
régime

regional (reh-gi-oo-*naal*)
adj regional

regissere (reh-shi-*sai*-rer) *v*
direct

regissør (reh-shi-*surr*) *m*
director

register (reh-*giss*-terr) *nt*
(pl ~, -tre) index

registrere (reh-gi-*stray*-rer)
v record

registrering (reh-gi-*stray*-
ring) *c* registration

registreringsnummer
(reh-gi-*stray*-rings-noo-

merr) *nt* (pl -numre)
registration number;
licence number *Am*

regjere (reh-*yay*-rer) *v*
govern, rule

regjering (reh-*yay*-ring) *c*
government; rule

regjeringstid (reh-*yay*rings-
teed) *c* reign

regn (rayn) *nt* rain

regnbue (*rayn*-bew-er) *m*
rainbow

regne[1] (*ray*-ner) *v* rain

regne[2] (*ray*-ner) *v* reckon; **~
ut** calculate

regnfrakk (*rayn*-frahk) *c*
raincoat, mackintosh

regnfull (*rayn*-fewl) *adj*
rainy

regning (*ray*-ning) *c*
arithmetic; bill; check
nAm

regnskur (*rayn*-skoor) *m*
shower

regulere (reh-gew-*lay*-rer) *v*
regulate

regulering (reh-gew-*lay*-
ring) *c* regulation; brace

rehabilitering (reh-hah-bi-
li-*tay*-ring) *c* rehabilitation

reinsdyr (*rayns*-dewr) *nt* (pl
~) reindeer

reise[1] (*ray*-ser) *v* travel; *c*
voyage, journey, trip; **~
bort** depart

reise[2] (*ray*-ser) *v* erect; **~
seg** *rise

reisebyrå (*ray*-ser-bew-raw)
nt travel agency, travel
agent

reiseforsikring (*ray*-ser-fo-shik-ring) *c* travel insurance

reisehåndbok (*ray*-ser-hon-bōōk) *c* (pl -bøker) travel guide

reisende (*ray*-ser-ner) *m* (pl ∼) travel(l)er

reiseplan (*ray*-ser-plaan) *m* itinerary

reiserute (*ray*-ser-rēw-ter) *c* itinerary

reisesjekk (*ray*-ser-shehk) *m* travel(l)er's cheque

reiseutgifter (*ray*-ser-ēwt-Ÿif-terr) *pl* travelling expenses

reke (*rāy*-ker) *c* shrimp; prawn

rekke (*rehk*-ker) *c* rank, file; chain

***rekke** (*rehk*-ker) *v* pass, *catch

rekkefølge (*rehk*-ker-furl-ler) *m* sequence, order

rekkevidde (*rehk*-ker-vi-der) *c* reach; range

rekkverk (*rehk*-værk) *nt* railing

reklame (reh-*klaa*-mer) *m* advertising; commercial

rekommandere (reh-koo-mahn-*day*-rer) *v* register

rekord (reh-koord) *c* record

rekreasjon (rehk-reh-ah-*shōōn*) *m* recreation

rekreasjonssenter (reh-kreh-ah-*shōōn*-sehn-terr) *nt* (pl -trer) recreation

centre (*Am* center)

rekrutt (rehk-*rewtt*) *m* recruit

rektangel (rehk-*tahng*-ngerl) *nt* (pl -gler) oblong, rectangle

rektangulær (rehk-tahng-gew-*lǣr*) *adj* rectangular

rektor (*rehk*-toor) *m* headmaster, principal

relativ (*rehl*-lah-teev) *adj* comparative, relative

relieff (reh-li-*ehff*) *nt* relief

religion (reh-li-gi-*ōōn*) *m* religion

religiøs (reh-li-gi-*ūrss*) *adj* religious

relikvie (re-*leek*-vi-er) *m* relic

rem (rehmm) *c* (pl ∼mer) strap

remisse (reh-*miss*-ser) *m* remittance

ren (rāyn) *adj* clean; pure; **gjøre rent** clean

rengjøring (*rāyn*-Ÿūr-ring) *c* cleaning

rengjøringsmiddel (*rāyn*-Ÿūr-rings-mi-derl) *nt* (pl -midler) detergent

rennestein (*rehn*-ner-stayn) *m* gutter

rense (*rehn*-ser) *v* clean

rensemiddel (*rehn*-ser-mi-derl) *nt* (pl -midler) cleaning fluid

renseri (rehn-ser-*ree*) *nt* dry cleaner's

renslig (*rāyn*-shli) *adj* clean, cleanly

rente (rehn-ter) *c* interest

rep (rāyp) *nt* rope

reparasjon (reh-pah-rah-*shōōn*) *m* reparation, repair

reparere (reh-pah-*rāy*-rer) *v* repair; mend, fix

repertoar (reh-peh-too-*aar*) *nt* repertory

reporter (reh-*paw*-terr) *m* reporter

representant (reh-preh-sern-*tahnt*) *m* agent

representasjon (reh-preh-sern-tah-*shōōn*) *m* representation

representativ (reh-preh-*sehn*-tah-teev) *adj* representative

representere (reh-preh-sern-*tāy*-rer) *v* represent

reproduksjon (reh-proo-dewk-*shōōn*) *m* reproduction

reprodusere (reh-proo-dew-*sāy*-rer) *v* reproduce

republikansk (reh-pewb-li-*kaansk*) *adj* republican

republikk (reh-pew-*blikk*) *m* republic

resepsjon (reh-sehp-*shōōn*) *m* reception office

resepsjonist (reh-sehp-*shōōn*-ist) *m* receptionist

resept (reh-*sehpt*) *m* prescription

reservasjon (reh-sær-vah-*shōōn*) *m* reservation, booking

reserve (reh-*sær*-ver) *m* reserve; **reserve-** spare

reservedekk (reh-*sær*-ver-dehk) *nt* (pl ∼) spare tyre

reservedel (reh-*sær*-ver-dāyl) *m* spare part

reservehjul (reh-*sær*-ver-ẙewl) *nt* (pl ∼) spare wheel

reservere (reh-sær-*vāy*-rer) *v* reserve; book

reservert (reh-sær-*vāyt*) *adj* reserved

reservoar (reh-sær-voo-*aar*) *nt* reservoir

resirkulerbar (reh-seer-kew-*lāy*-bahr) *adj* recyclable

resirkulere (reh-seer-kew-*lāy*-rer) *v* recycle

resonnere (reh-soo-*nāy*-rer) *v* reason

respekt (rehss-*pehkt*) *m* esteem, respect; regard

respektabel (rehss-pehk-*taa*-berl) *adj* respectable

respektere (rehss-pehk-*tāy*-rer) *v* respect

respektiv (rehss-pehk-teev) *adj* respective

rest (rehst) *m* rest; remainder, remnant

restaurant (rehss-tew-*rahngng*) *m* restaurant

resterende (rehss-*tāy*-rer-ner) *adj* remaining

resultat (reh-sewl-*taat*) *nt* result; outcome, issue

resultere (reh-sewl-*tāy*-rer) *v* result

resymé (reh-sew-*māy*) *nt* résumé

retning (*reht*-ning) *m* direction; way

retningslinje (*rehtt*-nings-lin-ᵉyer) *c* guideline

retningsnummer (*rehtt*-nings-noom-merr) *nt* area code

rett[1] (rehtt) *m* dish, course

rett[2] (rehtt) *m* law, justice; *adj* right; appropriate; *adv* straight; *ha ~* *be right; ~ frem* straight on, straight ahead

rette[1] (*reht*-ter) *v* correct; *med ~* rightly

rette[2] (*reht*-ter) *v* direct; *~ mot* aim at

rettelse (*reht*-terl-ser) *m* correction

rettergang (*reht*-terr-gahng) *m* trial

rettferdig (reht-*fær*-di) *adj* just, fair, right

rettferdiggjøre (reht-*fær*-di-ᵞur-rer) *v* justify

rettferdighet (reht-*fær*-di-hāyt) *c* justice

rettighet (*reht*-ti-hāyt) *c* right

rettslig (*reht*-shli) *adj* legal

rettssak (*reht*-saak) *c* lawsuit, trial

returnere (reh-tewr-*nāy*-rer) *v* *send back

reumatisme (rehv-mah-*tiss*-mer) *m* rheumatism

rev (rāyv) *m* fox; *nt* reef

revers (reh-*væshsh*) *m* reverse

revidere (reh-vi-*dāy*-rer) *v* revise

revisjon (reh-vi-*shōōn*) *m* revision

revolusjon (reh-voo-lew-*shōōn*) *m* revolution

revolusjonær (reh-voo-lew-shoo-*nǽr*) *adj* revolutionary

revolver (reh-*vol*-verr) *m* gun, revolver

revy (reh-*vēw*) *m* revue

revyteater (reh-vēw-teh-aa-terr) *nt* (pl ~, -tre) music hall

ribbein (*rib*-bayn) *nt* (pl ~) rib

ridder (*rid*-derr) *m* knight

ride (*ree*-der) *v* *ride

rideskole (*ree*-der-skōō-ler) *m* riding school

ridning (*reed*-ning) *m* riding

rift (rift) *c* tear

rik (reek) *adj* wealthy, rich

rikdom (*reek*-dom) *m* (pl ~mer) wealth, riches *pl*

rike (*reeker*) *nt* kingdom

rikelig (*ree*-ker-li) *adj* plentiful; abundant

rikelighet (*reek*-li-hāyt) *c* plenty

riksvei (*riks*-vay) *m* highway

riktig (*rik*-ti) *adj* correct, just, right; proper; *adv* rather

rim (reem) *nt* rhyme

rimelig (*ree*-mer-li) *adj* reasonable

ring (ring) *m* ring

ringe (*ring*-nger) *v* *ring; *adj* small; *v* call; ring up,

phone; call up *Am*
ringeakt (*ring*-nger-ahkt) *m*
contempt, disdain
ringeklokke (*ring*-nger-klo-
ker) *c* doorbell, bell
ringvei (*ring*-vay) *m* by-pass
rips (rips) *m* (pl ~)
(red)currant
ris (reess) *m* rice
risikabel (ri-si-*kaa*-berl) *adj*
risky; precarious, critical
risikere (ri-si-*kāy*-rer) *v* risk
risiko (*riss*-si-koo) *m* risk;
hazard, chance
risp (risp) *nt* scratch
rispe (*riss*-per) *v* scratch
rist (rist) *c* grate
riste (*riss*-ter) *v* roast;
*shake; toast
rival (ri-*vaal*) *m* rival
rivalisere (ri-vah-li-*sāy*-rer)
v rival
rivalitet (ri-vah-li-*tāyt*) *m*
rivalry
*rive (*ree*-ver) *v* *tear; ~ i
stykker rip; ~ ned
demolish
rivjern (*reev*-ᵞærn) *nt* (pl ~)
grater
ro¹ (*rōō*) *m* quiet; falle til ~
calm down; roe seg calm
down; ~ og mak leisure
ro² (*rōō*) *v* row
robust (roo-*bewst*) *adj*
robust
robåt (*rōō*-bawt) *m* rowing
boat
rogn (rongn) *c* roe
rolig (*rōō*-li) *adj* quiet, calm,
tranquil; serene

rom (roomm) *nt* room,
chamber; space
roman (roo-*maan*) *m* novel
romanforfatter (roo-*maan*-
for-faht-terr) *m* novelist
Romania (roo-*maa*-ni-ah)
Rumania
romantisk (roo-*mahn*-tisk)
adj romantic
romerbad (*rōō*-merr-baad)
nt (pl ~) Turkish bath
romersk-katolsk (*rōō*-
mersh-kah-tōōlsk) *adj*
Roman Catholic
romferge (*rōōm*-fær-ger),
romferje (*rōōm*-fær-ᵞer) *c*
space shuttle
romme (*room*-mer) *v*
contain
rommelig (*room*-mer-li) *adj*
spacious, roomy; large
rop (rōōp) *nt* call, cry; shout
rope (*rōō*-per) *v* cry, call;
shout
ror (rōōr) *nt* helm, rudder
rorgjenger (*rōōr*-ᵞeh-ngerr)
m helmsman
rormann (*rōōr*-mahn) *m* (pl
-menn) helmsman
ros (rōōss) *m* glory, praise
rosa (*rōō*-sah) *adj* rose
rose (*rōō*-ser) *c* rose; *v*
praise
rosenkrans (*rōō*-sern-
krahns) *m* beads *pl*, rosary
rosenkål (*rōō*-sern-kawl) *m*
sprouts *pl*
rosin (roo-*seen*) *c* raisin
rot¹ (rōōt) *c* (pl røtter) root
rot² (rōōt) *nt* muddle, mess

rote   150

rote (*rōō*-ter) *v* muddle; ~ **til**
  mess up
rotte (*rot*-ter) *c* rat
rouge (*rōōsh*) *m* rouge
rovdyr (*rawv-dewr*) *nt* (pl ~)
  beast of prey
ru (*rew*) *adj* rough; harsh
rubin (*rew-been*) *m* ruby
rubrikk (*rew-brikk*) *m*
  column
ruin (*rew-een*) *c* ruins
rulett (*rew-lehtt*) *c* roulette
rull (*rewll*) *m* roll
rulle (*rewl-ler*) *v* roll
rullegardin (*rewl-ler-gah-
  deen*) *m/nt* blind
rulleskøyteløping (*rewl-
  ler-shur*ᵉʷ*-ter-lürp-ing*) *c*
  roller-skating
rullestein (*rewl-ler-stayn*) *m*
  boulder
rullestol (*rewl-ler-stōōl*) *m*
  wheelchair
rulletrapp (*rewl-ler-trahp*) *c*
  escalator
rumener (*roo-māy-nerr*) *m*
  Rumanian
rumensk (*roo-māynsk*) *adj*
  Rumanian
rumpeballe (*room-per-bah-
  ler*) *m* buttock
rund (*rewnn*) *adj* round
runde (*rewn-der*) *m* round;
  lap
rundhåndet (*rewn-ho-nert*)
  adj generous
rundkjøring (*rewn-khür-
  ring*) *c* roundabout
rundreise (*rewn-ray-ser*) *c*
  tour

rundspørring (*rewn-spur-
  ring*) *c* enquiry; poll
rundstykke (*rewn-stew-ker*)
  nt roll; bun *nAm*
rundt (*rewnt*) *prep* about;
  adv around
rushtid (*rursh-teed*) *m* rush
  hour, peak hour
russer (*rewss-serr*) *m*
  Russian
russisk (*rewss-sisk*) *adj*
  Russian
Russland (*rewss-lahn*)
  Russia
rust (*rewst*) *m* rust
rusten (*rewss-tern*) *adj* rusty
rustning (*rewst-ning*) *m*
  armour
rute (*rēw-ter*) *c* check; pane;
  route
ruteplan (*rēw-ter-plaan*) *c*
  schedule
rutine (*rew-tee-ner*) *m*
  routine
rutsjebane (*rewt-sher-baa-
  ner*) *m* slide
rydde opp (*rewd-der*) tidy
  up
rydde vekk (*rewd-der
  vehkk*) *put away
rye (*rēw-er*) *c* rug
rygg (*rewgg*) *m* back
rygge (*rewg-ger*) *v* reverse
ryggrad (*rewg-raad*) *c*
  spine, backbone
ryggsekk (*rewg-sehk*) *m*
  knapsack, rucksack
ryggsmerter (*rewg-smæ-
  terr*) *pl* backache
rykk (*rewkk*) *nt* wrench, tug

rykte (*rewk*-ter) *nt* rumour; reputation, fame

rynke (*rewng*-ker) *c* wrinkle; crease

ryste (*rewss*-ter) *v* *shake

rytme (*rewt*-mer) *m* rhythm

rytter (*rewt*-terr) *m* horseman, rider

rød (rūr) *adj* red

rødbete (*rūr*-bāy-ter) *c* beetroot

rødme (*rurd*-mer) *v* blush

rødspette (*rūr*-speh-ter) *c* plaice

rødstrupe (*rūr*-strēw-per) *m* robin

røkelse (*rūr*-kerl-ser) *m* incense

rømling (*rurm*-ling) *m* runaway

rømme¹ (*rurm*-mer) *m* sour cream

rømme² (*rurm*-mer) *v* escape, flee

røntgenbilde (*runt*-kern-bil-der) *nt* X-ray

røntgenfotografere (*runt*-kern-foo-too-grah-fāy-rer) *v* X-ray

røpe (*rūr*-per) *v* *give away

rør (rūr) *nt* tube, pipe; cane

røre (*rūr*-rer) *v* touch; stir; ~ seg move

rørende (*rūr*-rer-ner) *adj* touching

rørlegger (*rūr*-leh-gerr) *m* plumber

røyk (rur^(ew)k) *m* smoke

røyke (*rurew*-ker) *v* smoke; røyking forbudt no smoking

røykekupé (*rurew*-ker-kew-pāy) *m* smoking compartment, smoker

røyker (*rurew*-kerr) *m* smoker

røykfri (rur^(ew)k-frēē) *adj* smoke-free

rå (raw) *adj* raw

råd (rawd) *nt* advice; counsel, council; *ha ~ til *can afford

råde (*raw*-der) *v* advise

rådgiver (*rawd*-ʸee-verr) *m* counsellor

rådhus (*rawd*-hēwss) *nt* (pl ~) town hall

rådslagning (*rawd*-shlaag-ning) *m* deliberation

*rådslå (*rawd*-shlaw) *v* deliberate

rådsmedlem (*rawds*-māyd-lerm) *nt* (pl ~mer) councillor

*rådspørre (*rawd*-spur-rer) *v* consult

råmateriale (*raw*-mah-ter-ri-aa-ler) *nt* raw material

råtten (*rot*-tern) *adj* rotten

S

safe (sayf) *m* safe

safir (sah-*feer*) *m* sapphire

saft (sahft) *c* juice

saftig (*sahf*-ti) *adj* juicy

sag (saag) *c* saw

sagbruk (*saag*-brōōk) *nt* (pl ~) sawmill

sagflis (*saag*-fleess) *c* sawdust

sak (saak) *c* matter, cause; case; issue

sakfører (*saak*-fūr-rerr) *m* solicitor

sakkyndig (*saak*-khewn-di) *adj* expert

saks (sahks) *c* scissors *pl*

sakte (*sahk*-ter) *adj* slow

sal (saal) *m* hall; saddle

salat (sah-*laat*) *m* salad, lettuce

saldo (*sahl*-doo) *m* balance

salg (sahlg) *nt* sale; **til salgs** for sale

salgbar (*sahlg*-baar) *adj* saleable

salme (*sahl*-mer) *m* hymn

salmiakk (sahl-mi-*ahkk*) *m* ammonia

salong (sah-*longng*) *m* salon; lounge, drawing room

salt (sahlt) *nt* salt; *adj* salty

saltkar (*sahlt*-kaar) *nt* (pl ~) salt cellar, salt shaker *Am*

salve (*sahl*-ver) *c* ointment

samarbeid (*sahm*-mahr-

bayd) *nt* co-operation

samarbeide (*sahm*-mahr-bay-der) *v* collaborate

samarbeidsvillig (*sahm*-mahr-bayds-vi-li) *adj* co-operative

same (*saa*-mer) *m* Saami (aborigines of Northern Scandinavia)

samfunn (*sahm*-fewn) *nt* (pl ~) society; community; **samfunns-** social

samle (*sahm*-ler) *v* collect; gather; assemble; compile; ~ **inn** collect

samler (*sahm*-lerr) *m* collector

samles (*sahm*-lerss) *v* gather

samling (*sahm*-ling) *c* collection

samme (*sahm*-mer) *adj* same

sammen (*sahm*-mern) *adv* together

sammendrag (*sahm*-mern-draag) *nt* (pl ~) summary

sammenføye (*sahm*-mern-fūr^(ew)-er) *v* join

sammenheng (*sahm*-mern-hehng) *m* connection; coherence

sammenkomst (*sahm*-mern-komst) *m* meeting, assembly

sammenligne (*sahm*-mern-

ling-ner) *v* compare
sammenligning (*sahm-mern-ling-ning*) *m* comparison; **uten ~** by far
sammensetning (*sahm-mern-seht-ning*) *m* composition
sammensmelting (*sahm-mern-smehlt-ning*) *m* merger
sammenstille (*sahm-mern-sti-ler*) *v* combine
sammenstøt (sahm-mern-st[̈u]rt) *nt* (pl ~) collision
sammenvergelse (*sahm-mern-svær-gel-ser*) *m* plot
sammenverge seg (*sahm-mern-svær-ger*) conspire
sammentreff (*sahm-mern-trehf*) *nt* (pl ~) coincidence
samordne (*sahm-mor-dner*) *v* co-ordinate
samtale (*sahm-taa-ler*) *m* talk, conversation; discussion
samtale venter (*sahm-taa-ler vehn-ter*) *c* call waiting
samtidig[1] (*sahm-tee-di*) *adj* simultaneous; contemporary; *adv* simultaneously
samtidig[2] (*sahm-tee-di*) (pl ~e) contemporary
samtykke (*sahm-tew-ker*) *v* consent; *nt* consent
samvittighet (sahm-*vit*-ti-h[̄a]yt) *c* conscience
sanatorium (sah-nah-*tōō*-ri-ewm) *nt* (pl -ier) sanatorium

sand (sahnn) *m* sand
sandal (sahn-*daal*) *c* sandal
sanddyne (*sahn-dēw*-ner) *c* dune
sandet (*sahn*-nert) *adj* sandy
sandpapir (*sahn*-pah-peer) *nt* sandpaper
sang (sahngng) *m* song
sanger (*sahng*-ngerr) *m* vocalist, singer
sanitetsbind (sah-ni-*tāyts*-bin) *nt* (pl ~) sanitary towel
sanitær (sah-ni-*tæær*) *adj* sanitary
sann (sahnn) *adj* true
sannferdig (sahn-*fær*-di) *adj* truthful
sannhet (*sahn*-h[̄a]yt) *c* truth
sannsynlig (sahn-*sēwn*-li) *adj* probable, likely
sannsynligvis (sahn-*sēwn*-li-veess) *adv* probably
sans (sahns) *m* sense
sardin (sah-*deen*) *m* sardine
satellitt (sah-ter-*litt*) *m* satellite; **~-TV** satellite tv
satellittoverføring (sah-ter-*litt*-aw-verr-*fūr*-ing) *c* satellite television
satelittradio (sah-ter-*litt*-rah-di-ōō) *c* satelite radio
sateng (sah-*tehngng*) *m* satin
sau (sou) *m* sheep
Saudi-Arabia (*sou*-di-ah-rah-bi-ah) Saudi Arabia
saudiarabisk (*sou*-di-ah-raa-bisk) *adj* Saudi

Arabian

saus (souss) *m* sauce

savn (sahvn) *nt* lack

savne (sahv-ner) *v* miss; lack; **savnet person** missing person

scene (*say*-ner) *m* stage; scene; shot

*se (say) *v* *see; look; notice; ~ **opp** look out; ~ **på** look at; ~ **ut** look

sebra (*sayb*-rah) *m* zebra

seder (*say*-derr) *pl* customs; morals

sedvane (*sayd*-vaa-ner) *m* usage

sedvanlig (sehd-*vaan*-li) *adj* customary

seer (*say*-err) *m* spectator

seg (say) *pron* himself, herself, itself, oneself; themselves

segl (sayl) *nt* seal

seier (*say*-err) *m* victory

seig (say) *adj* tough

seil (sayl) *nt* sail

seilbar (*sayl*-baar) *adj* navigable

seilbåt (*sayl*-bawt) *m* sailing boat

seilduk (*sayl*-dewk) *m* canvas

seile (*say*-ler) *v* sail

seilforening (*sayl*-fo-ray-ning) *c* yacht club

seilsport (*sayl*-spot) *m* yachting

sekk (sehkk) *m* sack

sekretær (sehk-rer-*tæær*) *m* secretary; clerk

seks (sehks) *num* six

seksjon (sehk-*shoon*) *m* section

seksten (*sayss*-tern) *num* sixteen

sekstende (*sayss*-ter-ner) *num* sixteenth

seksti (*sehks*-ti) *num* sixty

seksualitet (sehk-sew-ah-li-*tayt*) *m* sexuality

seksuell (sehk-sew-*ehll*) *adj* sexual

sekund (seh-*kewnn*) *nt* second

sekundær (seh-kewn-*dæær*) *adj* secondary; subordinate

sel (sayl) *m* seal

*selge (*sehl*-ler) *v* *sell

selleri (seh-ler-*ree*) *m* celery

selskap (*sehl*-skaap) *nt* party, company; society

selskapsantrekk (*sehl*-skaap-sahn-trehk) *nt* (pl ~) evening dress

selters (*sehl*-tersh) *m* soda water

selv (sehll) *pron* myself, yourself, herself, himself, itself, oneself, ourselves, yourselves, themselves, self, selves; ~ **om** though, although

selvbetjening (*sehl*-beh-t*ay*-ning) *c* self-service

selvbetjeningsvaskeri (*sehl*-beh-t*ay*-nings-vahss-ker-ree) *nt* launderette

selvfølgelig (sehl-*furl*-ger-li) *adv* naturally, of course

selvgod (*sehl*-goo) *adj* conceited

selvisk (*sehl*-visk) *adj* selfish

selvmord (*sehl*-moord) *nt* (pl ~) suicide

selvmordsangrep (*sehl*-morts-*ahn*-grayp) *nt* (pl ~) suicide attack

selvmordsbomber (*sehl*-morts-*boom*-ber) *c* (pl ~e) suicide bomber

selvopptatt (*sehl*-lop-taht) *adj* self-centered *Am*, self-centred

selvstendig (sehl-*stehn*-di) *adj* independent; self-employed

selvstyre (*sayl*-stew-rer) *nt* self-government

selvstyrt (*sehl*-stewt) *adj* autonomous

sement (seh-*mehnt*) *m* cement

semikolon (seh-mi-*koo*-lon) *nt* semi-colon

sen (sayn) *adj* late; **for sent** too late; **senere** afterwards

senat (seh-*naat*) *nt* senate

senator (seh-*naa*-toor) *m* senator

sende (*sehn*-ner) *v* *send; transmit; ~ **av sted** dispatch; *send off; ~ **bort** dismiss; ~ **tilbake** *send back

sendemann (*sehn*-ner-mahn) *m* (pl -menn) envoy

sender (*sehn*-nerr) *c* transmitter

sending (*sehn*-ning) *c* consignment; transmission

sene (*say*-ner) *c* sinew, tendon

seng (sehngng) *c* bed

sengeteppe (*sehng*-nger-teh-per) *nt* bedspread

sengetøy (*sehng*-nger-tur^(ew)) *nt* bedding

senil (seh-*neel*) *adj* senile

senit (*say*-nit) *nt* zenith

senke (*sehng*-ker) *v* lower

sennep (*sehn*-nerp) *m* mustard

sensasjon (sehn-sah-*shoon*) *m* sensation

sensasjonell (sehn-sah-shoo-*nehll*) *adj* sensational

sensur (sehn-*sewr*) *m* censorship

sentimental (sehn-ti-mehn-*taal*) *adj* sentimental

sentral (sehn-*traal*) *adj* central

sentralbord (sehn-*traal*-boor) *nt* (pl ~) switchboard

sentralfyring (sehn-*traal*-few-ring) *c* central heating

sentralisere (sehn-trah-li-*say*-rer) *v* centralize

sentralstasjon (sehn-*traal*-stah-shoon) *m* central station

sentrum (*sehn*-trewm) *nt* (pl -ra) town center *Am*, town centre, center *Am*, centre

separat (seh-pah-*raat*) *adv* apart, separately

separere (seh-pah-*ray*-rer) *v* separate

september (sehp-*tehm*-berr) September

septisk (*sehp*-tisk) *adj* septic

seremoni (seh-reh-moo-*nee*) *m* ceremony

serie (*sāy*-ri-er) *m* series, sequence

seriøs (seh-ri-*ūrss*) *adj* serious

servere (sær-*vāy*-rer) *v* serve

serveringsavgift (sær-*vāy*-ring-saav-*ỹift*) *c* service charge

serviett (sær-vi-*ehtt*) *m* napkin, serviette

servise (sær-*vee*-ser) *nt* dinner service

servitør (sær-vi-*thūr*) *m* waiter, waitress

sesjon (seh-*shōōn*) *m* session

sesong (seh-*songng*) *m* season; **utenfor sesongen** off season

sesongkort (seh-*song*-kot) *nt* (pl ~) season ticket

sete (*sāy*-ter) *nt* seat; chair

setning (*seht*-ning) *m* sentence

sett (sehtt) *nt* set

***sette** (*seht*-ter) *v* *lay, place, *set; ~ **i gang** launch; ~ **inn** insert; ~ **i stand** enable; ~ **opp** *make up; *draw up; ~ **på** turn on; ~ **sammen** compose, assemble; ~ **seg** *sit down

severdighet (*sāy*-vær-di-hāyt) *c* sight; scenic place

sex (sehks) *m* sex

shorts (shawts) *m* (pl ~) shorts (pl)

***si** (see) *v* *say, *tell

siamesisk (si-ah-*māy*-sisk) *adj* Siamese

side (*see*-der) *c* page; side; **på den andre siden** across; **på den andre siden av** across, beyond; **til** ~ **aside**; **til siden** sideways; aside; **ved siden av** next to, beside

sidegate (*see*-der-gaa-ter) *c* sidestreet

siden (*see*-dern) *adv* since; *prep* since; *conj* since; **for … siden** ago

siffer (*sif*-ferr) *nt* (pl ~, sifre) digit

sigar (si-*gaar*) *m* cigar

sigarett (si-gah-*rehtt*) *m* cigarette

sigarettetui (si-gah-*reht*-teh-tew-ee) *nt* cigarette case

sigarettobakk (si-gah-*reht*-too-bahk) *m* cigarette tobacco

signal (sing-*naal*) *nt* signal

signalement (sing-nah-ler-*mahngng*) *nt* description

signalere (sing-nah-*lāy*-rer) *v* signal

signatur (sing-nah-*tēwr*) *m* signature

sikker (*sik*-kerr) *adj* secure, safe; certain, sure

sikkert (*sik*-kerrt) *adv*
certainly

sikkerhet (*sik*-kerr-hāyt) *c*
security, safety

sikkerhetsbelte (*sik*-kerr-
hāyts-behl-ter) *nt* seat belt,
safety belt

sikkerhetsforanstaltning
(*sik*-kerr-hāyts-fo-rahn-
stahlt-ning) *m* precaution

sikkerhetsnål (*sik*-kerr-
hāyts-nawl) *c* safety pin

sikkert (*sik*-kert) *adv* surely;
helt ~ without fail

sikre seg (*sik*-rer) secure

sikring (*sik*-ring) *c* fuse

sikt (sikt) *m* visibility

sikte[1] (*sik*-ter) *nt* aim; *ta ~
på aim at

sikte[2] (*sik*-ter) *v* aim; ~ på
aim at

sil (seel) *m* sieve, strainer

sild (sill) *c* (pl ~) herring

sile (*see*-ler) *v* strain

silke (*sil*-ker) *m* silk

simpel (*sim*-perl) *adj*
common; vulgar

simpelthen (*sim*-pehlt-
hehn) *adv* simply

simulere (si-mew-*lāy*-rer) *v*
simulate

sindig (*sin*-di) *adj* sedate,
soberminded

sink (singk) *m* zinc

sinke (*sing*-ker) *v* impede

sinn (sinn) *nt* mind

sinne (*sin*-ner) *nt* anger,
temper

sinnsbevegelse (*sins*-beh-
vāy-gerl-ser) *m* emotion

sinnsforvirring (*sins*-for-vi-
ring) *c* insanity

sinnssyk (*sin*-sēwk) *adj*
insane, mad, crazy

sint (sint) *adj* cross, angry

sirene (si-*rāy*-ner) *c* siren

siriss (si-*riss*) *m* cricket

sirkel (*seer*-kerl) *m* (pl
-kler) circle

sirkulasjon (seer-kew-lah-
shōōn) *m* circulation

sirkus (*seer*-kewss) *nt* circus

sirup (*seer*-rewp) *m* syrup

sist (sist) *adj* last

siste (*siss*-ter) *adj* ultimate;
i det ~ lately

sitat (si-*taat*) *nt* quotation

sitere (si-*tāy*-rer) *v* quote

sitron (si-*trōōn*) *m* lemon

*sitte (*sit*-ter) *v* *sit

sitteplass (*sit*-ter-plahss) *m*
seat

situasjon (si-tew-ah-*shōōn*)
m position, situation

siv (seev) *nt* rush, reed

sivil (si-*veel*) *adj* civil;
civilian

sivilisasjon (si-vi-li-sah-
shōōn) *m* civilization

sivilisert (si-vi-li-*sāyt*) *adj*
civilized

sivilperson (si-*veel*-pæ-
shōōn) *m* civilian

sivilrett (si-*veel*-reht) *m* civil
law

sjakk (shahkk) *m* chess;
sjakk! check!

sjakkbonde (*shahk*-boo-
ner) *m* (pl -bønder) pawn

sjakkbrett (*shahk*-breht) *nt*

(pl ~) chessboard;
checkerboard *nAm*

sjal (shaal) *nt* shawl

sjalu (shah-*lew*) *adj* jealous;
envious

sjalusi (shah-lew-*see*) *m*
jealousy

sjampinjong (shahm-pin-*yongng*) *m* mushroom

sjampo (shahm-poo) *m*
shampoo

sjanse (*shahng*-ser) *m*
chance

sjargong (shaa-*gongng*) *m*
slang; jargon

sjarlatan (shaa-lah-tahn) *m*
quack

sjarm (shahrm) *m* charm;
glamour, attraction

sjarmerende (shahr-*may*-rer-ner) *adj* charming

sjef (shayf) *m* manager,
boss, chief

sjekk (shehkk) *m* cheque;
check *nAm*

sjekke (*shehk*-ker) *v* check

sjel (shayl) *c* soul

sjelden (*shehl*-dern) *adv*
rarely, seldom; *adj* rare,
uncommon, infrequent

sjenere (sheh-*nay*-rer) *v*
embarrass

sjenert (sheh-*nayt*) *adj* shy

sjenerthet (sheh-*nayt*-hayt)
c timidity

sjetong (sheh-*tong*) *m*
token

sjette (*sheht*-ter) *num* sixth

sjofel (*shoof*-erl) *adj* mean

sjokk (shokk) *nt* shock

sjokkere (sho-*kay*-rer) *v*
shock

sjokkerende (sho-*kay*-rer-ner) *adj* shocking

sjokolade (shoo-koo-*laa*-der) *m* chocolate

sju (shew) *num* seven

sjuende (*shew*-er-ner) *num*
seventh

sjusket (*shewss*-kert) *adj*
slovenly

sjø (shūr) *m* sea

sjøfugl (*shūr*-fewl) *m* seabird

sjøkart (*shūr*kaht) *nt* chart

sjømann (*shūr*-mahn) *m* (pl
-menn) sailor, seaman

sjøpinnsvin (*shūr*-pin-sveen) *nt* (pl ~) sea urchin

sjøreise (*shūr*-ray-ser) *c*
cruise

sjørøver (*shūr*-rūr-verr) *m*
pirate

sjøsetning (*shūr*-seht-ning)
m launching

sjøsyk (*shūr*-sewk) *adj*
seasick

sjøsyke (*shūr*-sew-ker) *m*
seasickness

sjøvann (*shūr*-vahn) *nt* sea
water

sjåfør (sho-*fūrr*) *m*
chauffeur

skade (skaa-der) *m* injury,
damage; harm, mischief; *v*
*hurt, harm, injure;
damage

skadelig (*skaa*-der-li) *adj*
harmful, hurtful

skadeserstatning (skaa-

der-sææsh-taht-ning) *m*
compensation, indemnity

skadet (*skaa*-dert) *adj*
injured

skaffe (*skahf*-fer) *v* provide,
furnish

skaft (skahft) *nt* handle

skala (*skaa*-lah) *m* scale

skall (skahll) *nt* shell; skin

skalldyr (*skahl*-dewr) *nt* (pl
∼) shellfish

skalle (*skahl*-ler) *m* skull

skallet (*skahl*-lert) *adj* bald

skam (skahmm) *c* shame,
disgrace

skamfull (*skahm*-fewl) *adj*
ashamed

skamme seg (*skahm*-mer)
*be ashamed

skandale (skahn-*daa*-ler) *m*
scandal

skandinav (skahn-di-*naav*)
m Scandinavian

Skandinavia (skahn-di-*naa*-
vi-ah) Scandinavia

skandinavisk (skahn-di-
naa-visk) *adj* Scandinavian

skanne (*skahn*-ner) *v* scan

skanner (*skahn*-nerr) *c* (pl
∼e) scanner

skap (skaap) *nt* cupboard;
closet; locker

skape (*skaaper*) *v* create

skapende (*skaa*-pene) *adj*
creative

skapning (*skaap*-ning) *m*
creature

skarlagenrød (skah-*laa*-
gern-rur) *adj* scarlet

skarp (skahrp) *adj* sharp;

keen; bright

skatt (skahtt) *m* treasure;
tax; darling

skattefri (*skaht*-ter-free) *adj*
tax-free

*skattelegge** (*skaht*-leh-ger)
v tax

ski (shee) *c* (pl ∼) ski; *gå på
∼ ski

skibukse (*shee*-book-ser) *c*
ski pants

skifer (*shee*-ferr) *m* slate

skift (shift) *nt* shift

skifte (*shif*-ter) *v* switch;
change

skiftenøkkel (*shif*-ter-nur-
kerl) *m* (pl -nøkler)
monkey wrench *Am*

skiheis (*shee*-hayss) *m* ski
lift

skihopp (*shee*-hop) *nt* (pl ∼)
ski jump

skikk (shikk) *m* custom

skikkelse (*shi*-kerl-ser) *m*
figure

skille (*shil*-ler) *v* separate,
part; divide

skilles (*shil*-lerss) *v* divorce

skillevegg (*shil*-ler-vehg) *m*
partition

skillevei (*shil*-ler-vay) *m*
road fork

skilpadde (*shil*-pah-der) *c*
turtle

skilsmisse (*shils*-mi-ser) *c*
divorce

skiløper (*shee*-lūr-perr) *m*
skier

skiløping (*shee*-lūr-ping) *c*
skiing

skimte

skimte (*shim*-ter) v glimpse

skinke (*shing*-ker) c ham

skinn (shinn) nt skin; hide; glare; **semsket ~** suede; **skinn-** leather

skinne¹ (*shin*-ner) v *shine

skinne² (*shin*-ner) c rail; track

skinnende (*shin*-ner-ner) adj bright

skinnhellig (*shin*-heh-li) adj hypocritical

skip (sheep) nt boat, ship

skipe (*shee*-per) v ship

skipsfart (*ships*-faht) m navigation, navigation; shipping

skipsreder (*ships*-rāȳ-derr) m shipowner

skipsverft (*ships*-værft) nt shipyard

skisse (*shiss*-ser) c sketch

skissere (shi-*sāȳ*-rer) v sketch

skistaver (*shee*-staa-verr) pl ski sticks; ski poles Am

skistøvler (*shee*-sturv-lerr) pl ski boots

skitt (shitt) m dirt

skitten (*shit*-tern) adj filthy, dirty, foul; soiled

skive (*shee*-ver) c disc; slice

skiveprolaps (*shee*-ver-pro-lahps) m slipped disc

skje¹ (shāȳ) v occur, happen

skje² (shāȳ) c spoon

skjebne (*shāȳb*-ner) m destiny, fate; fortune, luck

skjebnesvanger (*shāȳb*-ner-svah-ngerr) adj fatal

skjefull (*shāȳ*-fewl) m spoonful

skjegg (shehgg) nt beard

skjelett (sheh-*lehtt*) nt skeleton

skjell (shehll) nt shell, sea-shell; scale

skjelle (*shehl*-ler) v scold; **~ ut** call names

skjelne (*shehl*-ner) v distinguish

***skjelve** (*shehl*-ver) v tremble, shiver

skjeløyd (*shāȳl*-ur^{ew}d) adj cross-eyed

skjema (*shāȳ*-mah) nt scheme; form

skjemme bort (*shehm*-mer boot) *spoil

skjenke (*shehng*-ker) v pour; donate

skjenne på (*shehn*-ner) v scold

skjerf (shærf) nt scarf

skjerm (shærm) m screen

skjermbrett (*shærm*-breht) nt folding screen

skjev (shāȳv) adj slanting

skjorte (*shoot*-ter) c shirt

skjul (shēwl) nt cover

skjule (*shēw*-ler) v *hide, conceal

skjær (shæær) adj sheer; nt rock

***skjære** (*shææ*-rer) v *cut; carve; **~ av** *cut off; **~ i** carve; **~ ned** *cut; **~ ut** carve

skjødesløs (*shūr*-derss-lūrss) adj careless

skjønn (shurnn) *adj* wonderful, lovely

skjønne (*shurn*-ner) *v* *understand, *see

skjønnhet (*shurn*-hāyt) *c* beauty

skjønnhetspleie (shurn-hāyts-play-er) *m* beauty treatment

skjønnhetssalong (shurn-hāyt-sah-long) *m* beauty parlo(u)r, beauty salon

skjønt (shurnt) *conj* though, although

skjør (shurr) *adj* fragile

skjørt (shurtt) *nt* skirt

skjøteledning (*shūr*-ter-lāyd-ning) *m* extension cord

skli (sklee) *v* slip

sko (skoo) *m* (pl ~) shoe

skog (skoog) *m* wood, forest

skogkledd (*skoog*-klehd) *adj* wooded

skogsområde (skoogs-oom-raw-der) *nt* woodland

skokrem (*skoo*-krāym) *m* shoe polish

skole (*skoo*-ler) *m* school; **videregående ~** secondary school

skolebestyrer (*skoo*-ler-beh-stēw-rerr) *m* principal

skolegutt (*skoo*-ler-gewt) *m* schoolboy

skolepike (*skoo*-ler-pee-ker) *m* schoolgirl

skolisse (*skoo*-li-ser) *c* shoe-lace

skomaker (*skoo*-maa-kerr) *m* shoemaker

skorpe (*skor*-per) *c* crust

skorstein (*skosh*-tayn) *m* chimney

skotsk (skotsk) *adj* Scottish

Skottland (*skot*-lahn) Scotland

skotøy (*skoo*-tur^{cw}) *nt* footwear

skotøyforretning (*skoo*-tur^{cw}-fo-reht-ning) *c* shoe shop

skramme (*skrahm*-mer) *c* scratch

skrap (skraap) *nt* junk

skrape (*skraa*-per) *v* scrape, scratch

skravle (*skrahv*-ler) *v* chat

skravlebøtte (*skrahv*-ler-bur-ter) *c* chatterbox

skredder (*skrehd*-derr) *m* tailor

skreddersydd (*skrehd*-der-shewd) *adj* tailor-made

skrekk (skrehkk) *m* fright

skrekkelig (skreh-ker-li) *adj* horrible, grim

skrell (skrehll) *nt* peel

skrelle (*skrehl*-ler) *v* peel

skremme (*skrehm*-mer) *v* scare, terrify

skremmende (skrehm-mer-ner) *adj* terrifying

skremt (skrehmt) *adj* frightened

skrifte (*skrif*-ter) *v* confess

skriftemål (*skrif*-ter-mawl) *nt* (pl ~) confession

skriftlig (*skrift*-li) *adj* in

writing; written

skrik (skreek) *nt* scream, cry

***skrike** (skree-ker) *v* shout, scream, cry; shriek

skritt (skritt) *nt* step, pace, move

***skrive** (skree-ver) *v* *write; ~ inn book; ~ ned *write down; ~ på data type; ~ seg inn check in; ~ ut print out

skriveblokk (skree-ver-blok) *c*; writing pad

skrivebord (skree-ver-boor) *nt* desk, bureau

skrivemaskin (skree-ver-mah-sheen) *m* typewriter

skrivemaskinpapir (skree-ver-mah-sheen-pah-peer) *nt* typing paper

skrivepapir (skree-ver-pah-peer) *nt* writing paper

skriver (skree-verr) *m* printer

skru (skrew) *v* screw; ~ av turn off; ~ på turn on

skrubbe (skrewb-ber) *v* scrub

skrubbsår (skrewb-sawr) (pl ~) graze

skrue (skrew-er) *m* screw

skruestikke (skrew-er-sti-ker) *m* clamp

skrujern (skrew-ᵞæn) *nt* (pl ~) screw-driver

skrukke (skrook-ker) *v* crease

skrunøkkel (skrew-nur-kerl) *m* (pl -nøkler) wrench

***skryte** (skrew-ter) *v* boast

skrøne (skrur-ner) *v* *tell tall tales

skrøpelig (skrur-per-li) *adj* fragile

skrå (skraw) *adj* slanting

skråne (skraw-ner) *v* slant

skrånende (skraw-ner-ner) *adj* sloping, slanting

skråning (skraw-ning) *m* incline, slope

skudd (skewdd) *nt* shot

skuddår (skewd-dawr) *nt* (pl ~) leap year

skue (skoo-er) *nt* sight

skuespill (skew-er-spil) *nt* (pl ~) drama

skuespiller (skew-er-spil-lerr) *m* actor, actress *m*; comedian

skuespillforfatter (skew-er-spil-for-fah-terr) *m* playwright

skuff (skooff) *m* drawer

skuffe (skewf-fer) *v* disappoint; *være skuffet *be disappointed

skuffelse (skewf-ferl-ser) *m* disappointment

skulder (skewl-derr) *c* (pl -drer) shoulder

skulke (skewl-ker) *v* play truant

***skulle** (skewl-ler) *v* *shall; *should

skulptur (skewlp-tewr) *m* sculpture

skum (skoomm) *nt* foam, lather

skumgummi (skoom-gew-mi) *m* foam rubber

skumme (*skoom*-mer) *v* foam

skumring (*skoom*-ring) *c* twilight

skur (skēwr) *nt* shed; *m* shower

skurd (skewrd) *m* carving

skurk (skewrk) *m* bastard, villain, rascal

skvette (*skvehl*-ter) *v* splash

sky (shēw) *c* cloud; *adj* shy

skyet (*shēw*-ert) *adj* cloudy

skyffel (*shewf*-ferl) *m* (pl skyfler) shovel

skygge (*shewg*-ger) *m* shadow, shade

skyggefull (*shewg*-ger-fewl) *adj* shady

skyggelue (*shewg*-er-*lew*-er) *c* cap

skyhet (*shēw*-hāyt) *c* shyness

skyld (shewll) *c* blame, guilt

skylde (*shewl*-ler) *v* owe

skyldig (*shewl*-di) *adj* guilty; due; *være ~ owe

skylle (*shewl*-ler) rinse

skylling (*shewl*-ling) *c* rinse

skynde seg (*shewn*-ner) hurry, hasten

skyskraper (*shēw*-skraa-perr) *m* skyscraper

skyte (*shēw*-ter) *v* fire, *shoot

skyteskive (*shēw*-ter-shee-ver) *c* mark, target

skyve (*shēw*-ver) *v* push

skyvedør (*shēw*-ver-dūrr) *c* sliding door

skøyeraktig (*skurew*-er-rahk-ti) *adj* mischievous

skøyte (*shurew*-ter) *c* skate; *gå på skøyter skate

skøytebane (*shurew*-ter-baa-ner) *m* skating rink

skøyteløping (*shurew*-ter-lūr*-ping) *c* skating

skål (skawl) *c* saucer; *m* toast

sladder (*shlahd*-derr) *m* gossip

sladre (*shlahd*-rer) *v* gossip

slag (shlaag) *nt* blow; smash; breed; battle; lapel

slaganfall (*shlaagahn*-fahl) *nt* (pl ~) stroke

slagord (*shlaa*-gōōr) *nt* (pl ~) slogan

slags (shlahks) *m/nt* sort; alle ~ all sorts of

slakter (*shlahk*-terr) *m* butcher

slange (*shlahng*-nger) *m* snake

slang (shlahng) *m* slang

slank (shlahngk) *adj* slender, slim

slanke seg (shlahng-ker) slim

slapp (shlahpp) *adj* limp

slappe av (*shlahp*-per) relax

slave (*shlaa*-ver) *m* slave

slede (*shlāy*-er) *m* sleigh, sledge

sleip (shlayp) *adj* slippery

slekt (shlehkt) *m* family; relatives

slektning (*shlehkt*-ning) *m*

relation, relative

slem (*shlehmm*) *adj* naughty, bad

slenge (*shlehng*-nger) *v* *throw

slentre (*shlehn*-trer) *v* stroll

slepe (*shlāy*-per) *v* haul, drag

slepebåt (*shlāy*-per-bawt) *m* tug

slette (*shleht*-ter) *c* plain

slettvar (*shleht*-vaar) *m* brill

slik (*sleek*) *pron* such; *adv* thus, so, such; ~ at so that; ~ **som** such as

slikke (*shlik*-ker) *v* lick, lap

slips (*shlips*) *nt* tie, necktie

***slite** (*shlee*-ter) *v* labo(u)r; ~ **ut** wear out

sliten (*shlee*-tern) *adj* weary, worn out

slitt (*shlitt*) *adj* worn

slokke (*shlook*-ker) *v* *put out, extinguish

slott (*shlott*) *nt* castle

slu (*shlēw*) *adj* sly, cunning

sludder (*shlewd*-derr) *nt* rubbish

sluke (*shlēw*-ker) *v* swallow

slukt (*shlewkt*) *m* gorge

slum (*shlewmm*) *m* slum

slump (*shloomp*) *m* chance; **på** ~ by chance

slurk (*shlewrk*) *m* sip

slurvet (*shlewr*-vert) *adj* sloppy

sluse (*shlēw*-ser) *m* lock

slutning (*shlewt*-ning) *m* conclusion; end

slutt (*shlewtt*) *m* finish, end;

til ~ at last; eventually

slutte (*shlewt*-ter) *v* finish, end; quit; ~ **seg til** join

sluttresultat (*shlewt*-reh-sewl-taat) *nt* final result

slyngel (*shlewng*-ngerl) *m* (pl -gler) rascal

slør (*shlūrr*) *nt* veil

sløse bort (*shlūr*-ser boot) waste

sløseri (*shlūr*-ser-*ree*) *nt* waste

sløv (*shlūrv*) *adj* dull, blunt

sløyfe (*shlurew*-fer) *c* bow; bow tie

slå (*shlaw*) *m* bolt

slå (*shlaw*) *v* *strike, *beat, *hit; punch; bruise; dial; ~ **av** switch off; ~ **hakk i** chip; ~ **igjen slam**; ~ **i hjel** kill; ~ **i stykker** crack; ~ **ned** knock down; ~ **opp** look up; ~ **på** switch on; ~ **seg** settle down; ~ **til** *strike

slående (*shlaw*-er-ner) *adj* striking

***slåss** (*shloss*) *v* *fight; struggle

smak (*smaak*) *m* taste; flavo(u)r; *sette ~ **på** flavo(u)r

smake (*smaa*-ker) *v* taste; ~ **på** taste

smakløs (*smaak*-lūrss) *adj* tasteless

smal (*smaal*) *adj* narrow

smaragd (*smah-rahgd*) *m* emerald

smart (*smaat*) *adj* smart, lur

smed (*smay*) *m* smith

smekke (*smehk*-ker) *v* smack

smell (smehll) *nt* crack

*smelle (*smehl*-ler) *v* crack

smelte (*smehl*-ter) *v* melt; thaw

smerte (*smæt*-ter) *m* pain; grief, sorrow

smertefri (*smæt*-ter-free) *adj* painless

smertefull (*smæ*-ter-fool) *adj* painful

smertestillende middel (*smæ*-ter-stil-lene *mid*-del) *nt* painkiller

*smette (*smeht*-ter) *v* slip

smidig (*smee*-di) *adj* supple

smil (smeel) *nt* smile

smile (*smee*-ler) *v* smile

sminke (*sming*-ker) *c* make-up

smitte (*smit*-ter) *v* infect

smittende (*smi*-ter-ner) *adj* contagious

smittsom (*smit*-som) *adj* infectious, contagious

smoking (*smaw*-king) *m* dinner jacket; tuxedo *nAm*

smug (*smewg*) *nt* alley, lane

smugle (*smewg*-ler) *v* smuggle

smul (smewl) *adj* smooth

smule (*smew*-ler) *m* crumb; bit

smykke (*smewk*-ker) *nt* piece of jewellery (*Am* jewelry)

smør (smurr) *nt* butter

smørbrød (*smūrr*-brūr) *nt*

(pl ~) open sandwich

*smøre (*smūr*-rer) *v* grease; lubricate

smøreolje (*smūr*-rer-ol-ᵞer) *c* lubrication oil

smøring (*smūr*-ring) *c* lubrication

små (smaw) (pl liten) *adj* small

småbarn (*smaw*-baan) *nt* toddler

smågris (smaw-greess) *m* piglet

småkake (*smaw*-kaa-ker) *c* biscuit; cookie *nAm*

smålig (*smaw*-li) *adj* stingy

småpenger (*smaw*-peh-ngerr) *pl* petty cash, change

småstein (*smaw*-stayn) *m* pebble

snakke (*snahk*-ker) *v* *speak, talk

snakkesalig (*snahk*-ker-saa-li) *adj* talkative

snart (snaat) *adv* presently, soon, shortly; så ~ som as soon as

snegl (snayl) *m* snail

snekker (*snehk*-kerr) *m* carpenter

snever (*snay*-verr) *adj* narrow, restricted

sneversynt (*snay*-ver-shewnt) *adj* narrow-minded

snikskytter (*sneek*-shew-terr) *m* sniper

snill (snill) *adj* good, nice, kind

snitte (*snit*-ter) v *cut, slice
snitsel (*snit*-tsel) m cutlet
sno (snoo) v twist; ~ seg
   *wind
snor (snoor) c string; cord
snorke (*snor*-ker) v snore
snorkel (*snor*-kerl) m (pl
   -kler) snorkel
snu (snew) v turn round; ~
   om invert; ~ seg turn
   round
snuble (*snewb*-ler) v
   stumble
snurre (*snewr*-rer) v *spin
snute (*snew*-ter) c snout
*snyte (*snew*-ter) v cheat
snø (snür) v snow; m snow
snøskred (*snür*-skräyd) nt
   (pl ~) avalanche
snøslaps (*snur*-shlahps) nt
   slush
snøstorm (*snür*-storm) m
   blizzard, snowstorm
sodavann (*soo*-dah-vahn)
   nt soda water
sofa (*soof*-fah) m sofa
software (*sooft*-vehr) m
   software
sogn (songn) nt parish
sogneprest (*song*-ner-
   prehst) m rector, vicar
sokk (sokk) m sock
sol (sool) c sun
solbrent (*sool*-brehnt) adj
   sunburned
solbriller (*sool*-bri-lerr) pl
   sun-glasses pl
solbær (*sool*-bæær) nt (pl ~)
   black-currant
soldat (sool-*daat*) m soldier

sole seg (*soo*-ler) sunbathe
solid (soo-*leed*) adj solid,
   firm
solistkonsert (soo-*list*-
   koon-sæt) m recital
sollys (*sool*-lēwss) nt
   sunlight
solnedgang (*sool*-nāy-
   gahng) m sunset
sololje (*soo*-lol-¹yer) c
   suntan oil
soloppgang (*soo*-lop-
   gahng) m sunrise
solrik (*sool*-reek) adj sunny
solseil (*sool*-sayl) nt (pl ~)
   awning
solskinn (*sool*-shin) nt
   sunshine
solstikk (*sool*-stik) nt (pl ~)
   sunstroke
solsystem (*sool*-sewss-
   tāym) nt solar system
som (somm) pron who, that,
   which; conj as; ~ om as if
somletog (*soom*-ler-tawg)
   nt (pl ~) slow train; milk
   train Am
sommer (*som*-merr) m (pl
   somrer) summer
sommerfugl (*som*-merr-
   fēwl) m butterfly
sommertid (*som*-mer-teed)
   c summer time
sone (*soo*-ner) c zone;
   trådløs ~ wireless internet
   hotspot
sopp (sopp) m mushroom;
   toadstool
sorg (sorg) c sorrow, grief;
   mourning

sort (sott) *m* kind, sort

sortere (so-*tay*-rer) *v* sort, assort

sortiment (so-ti-*mahngng*) *nt* assortment

sosial (soo-si-*aal*) *adj* social

sosialisme (soo-si-ah-*liss*-mer) *m* socialism

sosialist (soo-si-ah-*list*) *m* socialist

sosialistisk (soo-si-ah-*liss*-tisk) *adj* socialist

sosiologi (soo-si-oo-loo-*gee*) *m* sociology

****sove** (*saw*-ver) *v* *sleep

sovende (*saw*-ver-ner) *adj* asleep

sovepille (*saw*-ver-pi-ler) *c* sleeping pill

sovepose (*saw*-ver-pōō-ser) *m* sleeping bag

sovesal (*saw*-ver-saal) *m* dormitory

sovevogn (*saw*-ver-vongn) *c* sleeping car; Pullman

soveværelse (*saw*-ver-vææ-rerl-ser) *nt* bedroom

sovne (*sov*-ner) *v* *fall asleep

spade (*spaa*-er) *m* spade

spalte (*spahl*-ter) *c* column

spandere (spahn-*day*-rer) *v* *spend

Spania (*spaa*-ni-ah) Spain

spanier (*spaa*-ni-err) *m* Spaniard

spanjol (spahn-ᵞ*ōōl*) *m* Spaniard

spann (spahnn) *nt* pail, bucket

spansk (spahnsk) *adj* Spanish

spare (*spaa*-rer) *v* save; economize

sparebank (*spaa*-rer-bahngk) *m* savings bank

sparegris (*spaa*-rer-gris) *m* piggy bank

sparepenger (*spaa*-rer-peh-ngerr) *pl* savings *pl*

spark (spahrk) *nt* kick

sparke (*spahr*-ker) *v* kick; **gi sparken dismiss

sparsommelig (spaa-*shom*-mer-li) *adj* thrifty, economical

spasere (spah-*say*-rer) *v* walk

spaserstokk (spah-*say*-shtok) *m* walking stick

spasertur (spah-*say*-tewr) *m* stroll, walk

spedalskhet (speh-*daalsk*-hāyt) *c* leprosy

spedbarn (*spāy*-baan) *nt* (pl ∼) infant

speider (*spay*-derr)*m*girl scout; boy scout

speil (spayl) *nt* looking--glass, mirror

speilbilde (*spayl*-bil-der) *nt* reflection

spekulere (speh-kew-*lāy*-rer) *v* speculate

spenne (*spayn*-ner) *c* buckle

spennende (*spehn*-ner-ner) *adj* exciting

spenning (*spehn*-ning) *m* tension; voltage

sperre (*spehr*-rer) *v* block; ~
  inne lock up
spesialisere seg (speh-si-
  ah-li-*say*-rer) specialize
spesialist (speh-si-ah-*list*)
  m specialist
spesialitet (speh-si-ah-li-
  tayt) *m* speciality
spesiell (speh-si-*ehll*) *adj*
  particular, special
spesifikk (speh-si-*fikk*) *adj*
  specific
spidd (spidd) *nt* spit
spiker (*spee*-kerr) *m* (pl ~,
  -krer) nail
spill (spill) *nt* game
spille (*spil*-ler) *v* play; act
spillemerke (*spil*-ler-mær-
  ker) *nt* chip
spiller (*spil*-lerr) *m* player
spillkort (*spil*-kot) *nt* (pl ~)
  playing card
spillopper (spi-*lop*-perr) *pl*
  mischief
spinat (spi-*naat*) *m* spinach
spindelvev (*spin*-derl-*vayv*)
  m (pl ~) spider's web
***spinne** (*spin*-ner) *v* *spin
spion (spi-*oon*) *m* spy
spir (speer) *nt* spire
spirituosa (spi-ri-tew-*oo*-
  sah) *pl* spirits
spise (*spee*-ser) *v* *eat
spisekart (*spee*-ser-kaht) *nt*
  menu
spiselig (*spee*-ser-li) *adj*
  edible
spisesal (*spee*-ser-saal) *m*
  dining room
spiseskje (*spee*-ser-*shay*) *c*

  tablespoon
spisestue (*spee*-ser-*stew*-er)
  c dining room
spisevogn (*spee*-ser-vongn)
  c dining car
spiss (spiss) *adj* pointed,
  sharp; *m* tip, point
spissborgerlig (*spiss*-bor-
  ger-li) *adj* bourgeois
spisse (*spiss*-ser) *v* sharpen
splint (splint) *m* splinter
splinter ny (*splin*-terr *new*)
  brand-new
spole (*spoo*-ler) *m* spool
spor (spoor) *nt* trace; trail,
  track
sport (spott) *m* sport
sports og nyttekjøretøy
  (*spotts*-aw-*newt*-teh-*khur*-
  er-turew) *c* (pl ~) SUV
sportsbil (*spotsh*-beel) *m*
  sports car
sportsklær (*spotsh*-klæær)
  pl sportswear
sprang (sprahng) *nt* jump
spray (spray) *m* atomizer;
  spray
sprayflaske (*spray*-flahss-
  ker) *c* atomizer
spre (spray) *v* *spread;
  scatter; *shed
sprekk (sprehkk) *m* crack
***sprekke** (*sprehk*-ker) *v*
  *burst; crack
sprenge (*sprehng*-er) *v*
  blow up
sprengstoff (*sprehng*-stof)
  nt explosive
springvann (*spring*-vahn)
  nt (pl ~) fountain

sprit (spreet) *m* liquor

spritapparat (*spree*-tah-pah-raat) *nt* spirit stove

sprut (sprewt) *m* squirt

sprute (sprēwt-er) *v* squirt; spray

sprø (sprür) *adj* crisp

sprøyte (sprūrew-ter) *c* syringe; shot

språk (sprawk) *nt* language

spurv (spewrv) *m* sparrow

spyd (spēwd) *nt* spear

spytt (spewtt) *nt* spit

spytte (*spewt*-ter) *v* *spit

spøk (spürk) *m* joke

spøkelse (*spür*-kerl-ser) *nt* ghost; spirit

*spørre (*spurr*-rer) *v* ask

spørrelek (*spurr*-rer-lāyk) *m* quiz

spørsmål (*spursh*-mawl) *nt* (pl ∼) question; matter, issue

spørsmålstegn (*spursh*-mawls-tayn) *nt* (pl ∼) question mark

spå (spaw) *v* predict, tell fortunes

sta (staa) *adj* head-strong, stubborn, pig-headed, obstinate

stabel (*staa*-berl) *m* (pl -bler) stack

stabil (stah-*beel*) *adj* stable

stable (*stahb*-ler) *v* pile

stadig (*staa*-di) *adj* continual, frequent

stadion (*staa*-di-oon) *nt* stadium

stadium (*staa*-di-ewm) *nt*

(pl -ier) stage, phase

stakitt (stah-*kitt*) *nt* picket fence

stall (stahll) *m* stable

stallkar (*stahll*-kahrr) *m* groom

stamme (*stahm*-mer) *m* trunk; tribe; *v* stammer

stamcelle (*stahm*-sehl-ler) *c* stem cell

stampe (*stahm*-per) *v* stamp

stand¹ (stahnn) *m* (pl stender) state; *gjøre i ∼ mend; i ∼ til able

stand² (stahnn) *m* stand

standard- (*stahn*-dahr) standard

standhaftig (stahn-*hahf*-ti) *adj* steadfast

stang (stahngng) *c* (pl stenger) bar, pole; rod

stanse (*stahn*-ser) *v* stop, halt, pull up

start (staat) *m* take-off; beginning, start

startbane (*staat*-baa-ner) *m* runway

starte (*staht*-ter) *v* start, *begin

stasjon (stah-*shōōn*) *m* station; depot *nAm*

stat (staat) *m* state; stats-national

statistikk (stah-ti-*stikk*) *m* statistics *pl*

statsborgerskap (*staats*-bor-ger-shkaap) *nt* citizenship

statskasse (*staats*-kahs-ser) *c* treasury

statsminister (*staats*-mi-niss-terr) *m* (pl ~e, -trer) premier, Prime Minister

statsoverhode (*staat*-saw-verr-hōō-der) *nt* head of state

statsråd (*staats*-rawd) *m* minister

statstjenestemann (*staats*-t'āy-ner-ster-mahn) *m* (pl -menn) civil servant

statue (*staa*-tew-er) *m* statue

stave (*staa*-ver) *v* *spell

stavelse (*staa*-verl-ser) *m* syllable

stavemåte (*staa*-ver-maw-ter) *m* spelling

stearinlys (steh-ah-*reen*-lēwss) *nt* (pl ~) candle

stebarn (*stāy*-baan) *nt* (pl ~) stepchild

sted (stāy) *nt* spot, site, place; locality

stedfortreder (*stāy*-fo-trāy-derr) *m* substitute; deputy

stedlig (*stāyd*-li) *adj* local; resident

stefar (*stāy*-faar) *m* (pl -fedre) stepfather

steg (stāyg) *nt* step

steil (stayl) *adj* steep

stein (stayn) *m* stone; **stein-stone**

steinbrudd (*stayn*-brewd) *nt* (pl ~) quarry

steinet (*stay*-nert) *adj* rocky

steintøy (*stayn*-tur^(ew)) *nt* stoneware, crockery

steke (*stāy*-ker) *v* fry; roast

stekeovn (*stāy*-ker-ovn) *m* oven

stekepanne (*stāy*-ker-pah-ner) *c* frying pan

stemme (*stehm*-mer) *m* voice; vote; *v* vote; ~ **overens agree**

stemmerett (*stehm*-mer-reht) *m* franchise, suffrage

stemning (*stehm*-ning) *m* atmosphere; mood

stemor (*stāy*-mōōr) *c* (pl -mødre) stepmother

stempel (*stehm*-perl) *nt* (pl ~, -pler) stamp; piston

stenge (*stehng*-nger) *v* close; ~ **av turn off**; *cut off; ~ **inne** *shut in

stengt (stehngt) *adj* closed, shut

stereo (*stāyh*-rāyoo) *m* stereo

stereoanlegg (*stāyh*-rāyoo-ahn-lehg) *nt* stereo (unit)

steril (steh-*reel*) *adj* sterile

sterilisere (steh-ri-li-*sāy*-rer) *v* sterilize

sterk (stærk) *adj* strong; powerful

sti (stee) *m* trail, path

stift (stift) *m* staple

stifte (*stif*-ter) *v* found, institute

stiftelse (*stif*-terl-ser) *m* foundation

stige (*stee*-ger) *m* ladder

*stige (*stee*-ger) *v* ascend, *rise; ~ **av** *get off; ~ **opp** ascend; ~ **på** *get on

stigning (*steeg*-ning) *m*

increase; ascent

stikk (stikk) *nt* bite, sting; picture, engraving

***stikke** (*stik*-ker) *v* *sting

stikkelsbær (*stik*-kerls-bæær) *nt* (pl ~) gooseberry

stikkontakt (*stik*-koon-tahkt) *m* plug

stikkord (*stikk*-oor) *nt* catchword

stikkpille (*stik*-pi-ler) *c* suppository

stil (steel) *m* style; essay

stilk (stilk) *m* stem

stillas (sti-*laass*) *nt* scaffolding

stille (*stil*-ler) *adj* calm, quiet, still; silent; *v* place, *put; ~ **inn** tune in

Stillehavet (*stil*-ler-haa-ver) Pacific Ocean

stillestående (*stil*-ler-staw-er-ner) *adj* stationary

stillferdig (stil-*fæædi*) *adj* quiet

stillhet (*stil*-hãyt) *c* silence, quiet

stilling (*stil*-ling) *c* position; job

stimulans (sti-mew-*lahngs*) *m* stimulant

stimulere (sti-mew-*lãy*-rer) *v* stimulate

sting (stingng) *nt* stitch

***stinke** (*sting*-ker) *v* *smell, *stink

stipend (sti-*pehnd*) *nt* grant, scholarship

stirre (*steer*-rer) *v* stare, gaze

stiv (steev) *adj* stiff

***stjele** (*st'ãy*-ler) *v* *steal

stjerne (*st'ææ*-ner) *c* star

stoff (stoff) *nt* cloth, material, fabric; matter

stokk (stokk) *m* cane, stick

stokke (*stok*-ker) *v* shuffle

stol (stool) *m* chair

stola (*stoo*-lah) *m* stole

stole på (*stoo*-ler) trust; rely on

stolpe (*stol*-per) *m* post; pillar

stolt (stolt) *adj* proud

stolthet (*stolt*-hãyt) *c* pride

stopp! (stopp) stop!

stoppe (*stop*-per) *v* stop; quit; darn

stor (stoor) *adj* great, major, big; large

storartet (*stoor*-raa-tert) *adj* superb, grand, terrific

Storbritannia (*stoor*-bri-tah-ni-ah) Great Britain

stork (stork) *m* stork

storm (storm) *m* gale; storm

stormagasin (*stoor*-mah-gah-seen) *nt* department store

stormfull (*storm*-fewl) *adj* stormy

stormlykt (*storm*-lewkt) *c* hurricane lamp

storslått (*stoo*-shlot) *adj* magnificent

Stortinget (*stoor*-ti-nger) Norwegian Parliament

stortingsrepresentant (*stoo*-tings-reh-preh-sern-tahnt) *m* Member of (the

Norwegian) Parliament

straff (strahff) *m* punishment; penalty

straffe (strahf-fer) *v* punish

strafferett (strahf-fer-reht) *m* criminal law

straffespark (strahf-fer-spahrk) *nt* (pl ~) penalty kick

straks (strahks) *adv* instantly, at once, immediately

stram (strahmm) *adj* tight

stramme (strahm-mer) *v* tighten; **strammes** to be tightened

strand (strahnn) *c* (pl strender) beach

strebe (strāy-ber) *v* aspire; ~ etter pursue, aim at

streife omkring (stray-fer) roam

streik (strayk) *m* strike

streike (stray-ker) *v* *strike

strek (strāyk) *m* line

strekning (strehk-ning) *m* stretch; distance

streng (strehngng) *adj* strict, severe, harsh; *m* string

stress (strehss) *nt* stress

strid (streed) *m* contest; fight, battle, struggle

***strides** (stree-derss) *v* dispute

strikk (strikk) *m* rubber band

strikke (strik-ker) *v* *knit

strimmel (strim-merl) *m* (pl strimler) strip

stripe (stree-per) *c* stripe

stripet (stree-pert) *adj* striped

strofe (strōō-fer) *m* stanza

struktur (strewk-tewr) *m* structure; texture, fabric

strupekatarr (strewper-kah-tahr) *m* laryngitis

struts (strewts) *m* ostrich

***stryke** (strew-ker) *v* iron; *strike; fail an exam

strykefri (strew-ker-free) *adj* drip-dry, wash and wear

strykejern (strew-ker-ᵞæn) *nt* (pl ~) iron

strøm (strurmm) *m* (pl ~mer) electricity; current, stream; med strømmen downstream; mot strømmen upstream

strømfordeler (sturm-fo-dāy-lerr) *m* distributor

strømme (sturm-mer) *v* flow, stream

strømpe (sturm-per) *c* stocking

strømpebukse (sturm-per-book-ser) *c* tights *pl*, panty hose

stråle (straw-ler) *m* beam, ray; spout, jet; *v* *shine

strålende (straw-ler-ner) *adj* brilliant; glorious

student (stew-dehnt) *m* student

studere (stew-dāy-rer) *v* study

studium (stēw-di-oom) *nt* (pl -ier) study; studies

stue (stēw-er) *c* sitting room

stuert (*stoo*-ert) *m* steward

stum (stewmm) *adj* mute, dumb

stund (stewnn) *c* while

stup (stewp) *nt* precipice

stupe (*stew*-per) *v* dive

stusse (stewss-ser) *v* trim

stygg (stewgg) *adj* ugly

stykke (stewk-ker) *nt* piece, fragment, lump, part; *gå i stykker* *break down; i stykker broken; stort ~ chunk

styrbord (stewr-*boor*) starboard

styre (*stew*-rer) *v* direct; steer; *nt* board, direction; government; rule

styrke (stewr-ker) *m* power, strength; force; *væpnede styrker* armed forces

styrte (stewt-ter) *v* crash; rush, dash

stær (stæær) *m* starling

stø (stūr) *adj* steady

stønne (sturn-ner) *v* groan

støpejern (*stūr*-per-Yææn) *nt* (pl ~) cast iron

størkne (sturr-kner) *v* harden

størrelse (sturr-rerl-ser) *m* size; *stor ~* outsize

størsteparten (stursh-ter-pah-tern) *m* bulk, the greater part of

støt (stūrt) *nt* bump

støtdemper (*stūrt*-dehm-perr) *m* shock absorber

støte (*stūr*-ter) *v* bump; ~ *på* run into, *come across;

knock against; ~ *sammen* bump

støtfanger (*stūrt*-fah-ngerr) *m* bumper

støtte (sturt-ter) *v* *hold up; *m* support

støv (stūrv) *nt* dust

støvel (sturv-verl) *m* (pl -vler) boot

støvet (*stūr*-vert) *adj* dusty

støvsuge (*stūrv*-sew-ger) *v* hoover; vacuum *vAm*

støvsuger (*stūrv*-sew-gerr) *m* vacuum cleaner

støy (stur^ew) *m* noise

støyende (sturew-er-ner) *adj* noisy

***stå** (staw) *v* *stand; ~ *opp* *get up; *rise

stående (staw-er-ner) *adj* erect

stål (stawl) *nt* steel; *rustfritt ~* stainless steel

ståltråd (*stawl*-traw) *m* wire

subjekt (sewb-Yehkt) *nt* subject

substans (sewb-stahns) *m* substance

substansiell (sewb-stahn-si-*ehl*) *adj* substantial

substantiv (*sewp*-stahn-teev) *nt* noun

subtil (sewb-*teel*) *adj* subtle

suge (*sew*-ger) *v* suck

suite (*svit*-ter) *m* suite

sukke (sewk-ker) *v* sigh

sukker (sook-kerr) *nt* sugar

sukkerbit (sook-kerr-beet) *m* lump of sugar

sukkersyke (sook-ker-shew̄-ker) *m* diabetes

sukkersykepasient *(sook-ker-shew̄-ker-pah-si-ehnt)* *m* diabetic

sukkertøy *(sook-ker-tur^(ew))* *nt* sweet; candy *nAm*

sukre *(sook-rer)* *v* sweeten

suksess *(sewk-sehss)* *m* success; hit

sult *(sewlt)* *m* hunger

sulten *(sewl-tern)* *adj* hungry

sum *(sewmm)* *m* (pl ~mer) sum; amount

summing *(sewm-ming)* *c* buzz

sump *(soomp)* *m* marsh

sunn *(sewnn)* *adj* healthy; wholesome

superlativ *(sew-pæl-lah-teev)* *m* superlative

supermarked *(sew̄-perr-mahr-kerd)* *nt* supermarket

suppe *(sewp-per)* *c* soup

suppeskje *(sewp-per-shaȳ)* *c* soup spoon

suppetallerken *(sewp-per-tah-lær-kern)* *m* soup plate

sur *(sew̄r)* *adj* sour

surfe *(sewr-fer)* *v* surf

surfingbrett *(surr-fing-breht)* *nt* surf-board

surstoff *(sew̄-shtof)* *nt* oxygen

suspendere *(sewss-pahng-daȳ-rer)* *v* suspend

suvenir *(sew-ver-neer)* *m* souvenir

svak *(svaak)* *adj* weak, feeble; faint; slight

svakhet *(svaak-hāyt)* *c* weakness

svale *(svaa-ler)* *c* swallow

svamp *(svahmp)* *m* sponge

svane *(svaa-ner)* *c* swan

svangerskap *(svahng-ngerr-skaap)* *nt* pregnancy

svar *(svaar)* *nt* answer, reply; **som ~** in reply

svare *(svaa-rer)* *v* answer, reply; **~ til** correspond

svart *(svahtt)* *adj* dirty; black

svartebørs *(svaht-ter-būrsh)* *m* black market

svarttrost *(svaht-rost)* *m* blackbird

sveise *(svay-ser)* *v* weld

Sveits *(svayts)* Switzerland

sveitser *(svayt-serr)* *m* Swiss

sveitsisk *(svayt-sisk)* *adj* Swiss

svelge *(svehl-ger)* *v* swallow

svelle *(svehl-ler)* *v* *swell

svensk *(svehnsk)* *adj* Swedish

svenske *(svehn-sker)* *m* Swede

sverd *(sværd)* *nt* sword

***sverge** *(svær-ger)* *v* vow, *swear

Sverige *(svær-ʸer)* Sweden

svette *(sveht-ter)* *v* perspire, sweat; *m* perspiration, sweat

***svi** *(svee)* *v* *burn

svigerdatter *(svee-gerr-dah-terr)* *c* daughter-in-law

svigerfar *(svee-gerr-faar)* *m*

symaskin

(pl -fedre) father-in-law

svigerforeldre (*svee-gerr-fo-rehl-drer*) *pl* parents-in-law *pl*

svigerinne (*svee-ger-rin-ner*) *c* sister-in-law

svigermor (*svee-gerr-mōōr*) *c* (pl -mødre) mother-in-law

svigersønn (*svee-ger-shurn*) *m* son-in-law

svikte (*svik-ter*) *v* *let down

svimmel (*svim-merl*) *adj* dizzy, giddy

svimmelhet (*svim-merl-hāyt*) *c* dizziness, giddiness

svindel (*svin-derl*) *m* swindle

svindle (*svin-dler*) *v* swindle

svindler (*svin-dlerr*) *m* swindler

svinekjøtt (*svee-ner-khurt*) *nt* pork

svinelær (*svee-ner-læær*) *nt* pigskin

sving (svingng) *m* turning, bend, turn

svingdør (*sving-dūrr*) *c* revolving door

svinge (*sving-nger*) *v* turn; *swing

sviske (*sviss-ker*) *c* prune

svoger (*svaw-gerr*) *m* (pl ~e, -grer) brother-in-law

svulst (svewlst) *m* tumo(u)r, growth

svær (svæær) *adj* huge

svært (svæær) *adv* very

svømme (*svurm-mer*) *v*

*swim

svømmebasseng (*svurm-mer-bah-sehng*) *nt* swimming pool

svømmer (svurm-merr) *m* swimmer

svømmevest (*svurm-me-vest*) *m* life jacket

svømming (*svurm-ming*) *c* swimming

swahili (svah-*hee*-li) *m* Swahili

sy (sēw) *v* *sew; ~ sammen *sew up

syd (sēwd) *m* south

sydlig (*sēwd*-li) *adj* southerly

Sydpolen (*sēwd*-pōō-lern) South Pole

syk (sēwk) *adj* sick, ill

sykdom (*sēwk*-dom) *m* (pl ~mer) sickness, illness; disease

sykebil (*sēw*-ker-beel) *m* ambulance

sykehus (*sēw*-ker-hēwss) *nt* (pl ~) hospital

sykepleier (*sēw*-ker-play-er) *m* nurse

sykkel (*sewk*-kerl) *m* (pl sykler) bicycle, cycle, bike

sykle (*sewk*-kler) *v* bicycle, cycle, bike

syklist (sewk-*list*) *m* cyclist

syklus (*sēwk*-lewss) *m* cycle

sylinder (sew-*lin*-derr) *m* (pl ~e, -drer) cylinder

syltetøy (*sewl*-ter-tur^(ew)) *nt* jam

symaskin (*sēw*-mah-sheen)

m sewing machine

symbol (sewm-*bool*) *nt* symbol

symfoni (sewm-foo-*nee*) *m* symphony

sympati (sewm-pah-*tee*) *m* sympathy

sympatisk (sewm-*paa*-tisk) *adj* nice

symptom (sewm-*toom*) *nt* symptom

syn (sewn) vision; outlook, view; sight, spectacle

synagoge (sew-nah-*goo*-ger) *m* synagogue

synd (sewnn) *m* sin; **så synd!** what a pity!; **synes ~ på** pity

synde (sewnn-der) *v* sin

syndebukk (sewn-der-book) *m* scapegoat

synder (sewnn-derr) *m* sinner

synes (*sew*-nerss) *v* appear, look, seem; **jeg ~ I** think; **I find**

*synge (sewng-nger) *v* *sing

*synke (sewng-ker) *v* *sink

synlig (*sewn*-li) *adj* visible

synonym (sew-noo-*newm*) *nt* synonym

synspunkt (*sewns*-poongt) *nt* point of view

syntetisk (sewn-*tay*-tisk) *adj* synthetic

syrer (*sew*-rerr) *m* Syrian

Syria (*sew*-ri-ah) Syria

syrisk (*sew*-risk) *adj* Syrian

system (sewss-*taym*) *nt* system

systematisk (sewss-teh-*maa*-tisk) *adj* systematic

sytten (*surt*-tern) *num* seventeen

syttende (*surt*-ter-ner) *num* seventeenth

sytti (*surt*-ti) *num* seventy

syv (sewv) *num* seven

syvende (*sew*-ver-ner) *num* seventh

sær (sæær) *adj* queer

særdeles (sæ-*day*-lerss) *adv* quite

særdeleshet: i ~ (ee sæ-***ay-lerss-*hayt*) in particular

særegen (*sææ*-reh-gern) *adj* particular

særlig (*sæær*-li) *adv* especially

særskilt (*sææ*-shilt) *adj* separate

søke (*sur*-ker) *v* *seek, apply

søker (*sur*-kerr) *m* view-finder

søknad (*sur*k-nah) *m* application

søle (*sur*-ler) *v* *spill; *m* mud

sølet (*sur*-lert) *adj* muddy

sølv (surll) *nt* silver; **sølv-** silver

sølvsmed (surl-smay) *m* silversmith

sølvtøy (*surl*-tur^(ew)) *nt* silverware

søm (surmm) *m* (pl ~mer) seam

sømmelig (*surm*-mer-li) *adj*

proper

søndag (*surn*-daa) *m* Sunday

sønn (surn) *m* son

søppel (*surp*-perl) *nt* garbage, litter

søppelbøtte (*surp*-perl-bur-ter) *c* rubbish bin; waste basket *Am*

søppelkasse (*surp*-perl-kah-ser) *c* dustbin; trash can *Am*

sør (sūrr) *m* south

Sør-Afrika (*sūr*-rahf-ri-kah) South Africa

sørge (surr-ger) *v* grieve; mourn; ~ **for** see to, look after

sørlig (*sūr*-li) *adj* southern

sørvest (surr-*vehst*) *m* south-west

sørøst (surr-*urst*) *m* south-east

søster (surss-terr) *c* (pl -tre) sister

søt (sūrt) *adj* sweet

søtsaker (*sūrt*-saa-kerr) *pl* candy *nAm*

søvn (survn) *m* sleep

søvnig (surv-ni) *adj* sleepy

søvnløs (survn-*lūrss*) *adj* sleepless

søvnløshet (survn-*lūrss*-hāyt) *c* insomnia

søyle (surew-ler) *c* column

så (saw) *adv* so; then; *conj* so, so that; *v* *sow; ~ **vel som** as well as; ~ **vidt** barely; as much

såkalt (*saw*-kahlt) *adj* so--called

såle (*saw*-ler) *m* sole

sånn (sonn) *adj* such

såpe (*saw*-per) *c* soap

sår (sawr) *nt* wound; ulcer, sore; *adj* sore

sårbar (*sawr*-baar) *adj* vulnerable

såre (*saw*-rer) *v* wound; *hurt

***ta** (taa) *v* *take; ~ **bort** *take out; ~ **ille opp** resent; * ~ **imot** accept; ~ **inn** stay; ~ **med** *bring; ~ **med seg** *take away; ~ **opp** pick up; *bring up; ~ **på** *put on; ~ **seg av** attend to, *deal with; ~ **vare på** *take care of; ~ **vekk** *take away

T

tabell (tah-*behll*) *m* chart, table

tablett (tahb-*lehtt*) *m* tablet

tabu (*taa*-bew) *nt* taboo

tak (taak) *nt* roof; ceiling; grip

takk (tahkk) thank you

takke (*tahk*-ker) *v* thank; ***ha å** ~ **for** owe

takknemlig (tahk-*nehm*-li) *adj* grateful, thankful

takknemlighet (tahk-*nehm*-

li-hāyt) c gratitude
taksameter (tahk-sah-*māy*-terr) nt (pl ~, -tre) taxi-meter
taksere (tahk-*sāy*-rer) v value, estimate
takstein (*taak*-stayn) m tile
taktikk (tahk-*tikk*) m tactics pl
tale (*taa*-ler) m speech
talent (tah-*lehnt*) nt talent
talerstol (*taa*-ler-shtōōl) m pulpit
talkum (*tahl*-kewm) m talc powder
tall (tahll) nt figure, number
tallerken (tah-*lær*-kern) m plate, dish
tallord (*tahl*-lōōr) nt (pl ~) numeral
tallrik (*tahl*-reek) adj numerous
tam (tahmm) adj tame
tampong (tahm-*pongng*) m tampon
tang (tahngng) c (pl tenger) tongs pl, pliers pl
tank (tahngk) m tank
tankbåt (*tahngk*-bawt) m tanker
tanke (*tahng*-ker) m thought, idea
tankefull (*tahng*-ker-fewl) adj thoughtful
tankestrek (*tahng*-ker-strāyk) m dash
tann (tahnn) c (pl tenner) tooth
tannbørste (*tahn*-bursh-ter) m toothbrush

tannkjøtt (*tahn*-khurt) nt gum
tannkrem (*tahnn*-krāym) m toothpaste
tannlege (*tahn*-lāy-ger) m dentist
tannpasta (*tahn*-pahss-tah) m toothpaste
tannpine (*tahn*-pee-ner) c toothache
tannpirker (*tahn*-peer-kerr) m toothpick
tannregulering (*tahn*-reh-gew-*lāy*-ring) c brace
tannverk (*tahn*-værk) m toothache
tante (*tahn*-ter) c aunt
tap (taap) nt loss
tape (*taa*-per) v *lose
taper (*taa*-perr) m loser
tapet (tah-*pāyt*) nt wallpaper
tapper (*tahp*-perr) adj brave, courageous
tapperhet (*tahp*-perr-hāyt) c courage
tariff (tah-*riff*) m rate, tariff
tarm (tahrm) m intestine, gut; tarmer bowels pl, intestines
tast (tahst) m key
tastatur (tahsta-*tewr*) nt keyboard
taste (*tahs*-ter) v dial, type
tau (tou) nt cord
taue (*tou*-er) v tow, tug
taus (touss) adj silent
tavle (*tahv*-ler) c blackboard; board
taxi (*tahk*-si) m taxi

te (*tay*) *m* tea

teater (teh-*aa*-terr) *nt* (pl ~, -tre) theater *Am*, theatre

teaterstykke (teh-*aa*-ter-shtew-ker) *nt* play

tegn (tayn) *nt* sign, token, signal; indication

tegne (*tay*-ner) *v* *draw; sketch; ~ opp design

tegnefilm (*tay*-ner-film) *m* cartoon

tegnestift (*tay*-ner-stift) *m* drawing pin; thumbtack *nAm*

tegning (*tay*-ning) *c* sketch, drawing

tekanne (*tāy*-kah-ner) *c* teapot

tekniker (*tehk*-ni-kerr) *m* technician

teknikk (tehk-*nikk*) *m* technique

teknisk (*tehk*-nisk) *adj* technical

teknisk støtte (*tehk*-nisk sturt-ter) *c* technical support

teknologi (tehk-noo-loo-gee) *m* technology

teknologisk (tehk-noo-*loo*-gee) *adj* technological

tekopp (*tāy*-kop) *m* teacup

tekst (tehkst) *m* text; subtitle

tekstil (tehk-*steel*) *m*/*nt* textile

telefaks (*teh*-ler-fahks) *m* fax; sende en ~ send a fax

telefon (teh-ler-*fōōn*) *m* phone, telephone

telefonere (teh-ler-foo-*nāy*-rer) *v* phone

telefonkatalog (teh-ler-*fōōn*-kah-tah-lawg) *m* telephone directory; telephone book *Am*

telefonkiosk (teh-ler-*fōōn*-khosk) *m* telephone booth

telefonkort (teh-ler-*fōōn*-kot)*nt* phone card

telefonrør (teh-ler-*fōōn*-rürr) *nt* (pl ~) receiver

telefonsamtale (teh-ler-*fōōn*-sahm-taa-ler) *m* telephone call

telefonsentral (teh-ler-*fōōn*-sehn-traal) *m* telephone exchange

telefonsvarer (teh-ler-*fōōn*-svaa-rerr) *m* answering machine

telekommunikasjon (teh-ler-koo-mewn-ni-kah-*shōōn*) *c* telecommunications

telekort (*tel*-ler-kōōt) *nt* (pl ~) phone card

teleobjektiv (*tāy*-ler-ob-ʸehk-teev) *nt* telephoto lens

telepati (teh-ler-pah-*tee*) *c* telepathy

*telle (*tehl*-ler) *v* count; ~ opp count

telt (tehlt) *nt* tent

tema (*tāy*-mah) *nt* theme

temme (*tehm*-mer) *v* tame

temmelig (*tehm*-mer-li) *adv* rather, pretty, fairly, quite

tempel (*tehm*-perl) *nt* (pl ~,

-pler) temple

temperatur (tehm-per-rah-*tewr*) *m* temperature

tempo (*tehm*-poo) *nt* pace

tendens (tehn-*dehns*) *m* tendency; *ha ~ til* tend

tenke (*tehng*-ker) *v* *think; *~ over* *think over; *~ på* *think of; *~ seg* imagine, fancy; *~ ut* conceive

tenker (*tehng*-kerr) *m* thinker

tenne (*tehn*-ner) *v* *light

tenning (*tehn*-ning) *c* ignition

tennis (*tehn*-niss) *m* tennis

tennisbane (*tehn*-niss-baa-ner) *m* tennis court

tennissko (*tehn*-ni-skōō) *pl* tennis shoes

tennplugg (*tehn*-plewg) *m* sparking plug

tennspole (*tehn*-spōō-ler) *m* ignition coil

tenåring (*tāy*-naw-ring) *m* teenager

teologi (teh-oo-loo-*gee*) *m* theology

teoretisk (teh-oo-*rāy*-tisk) *adj* theoretical

teori (teh-oo-*ree*) *m* theory

teppe (*tehp*-per) *nt* blanket; carpet; curtain

terapi (teh-rah-*pee*) *m* therapy

termin (tær-*meen*) *m* term

termometer (tær-moo-*māy*-terr) *nt* (pl ~, -tre) thermometer

termosflaske (*tær*-mooss-flahss-ker) *c* thermos flask

termostat (tær-moo-*staat*) *m* thermostat

terning (*tææ*-ning) *m* cube; dice *pl*

terpentin (tær-pehn-*teen*) *m* turpentine

terrasse (tæ-*rahss*-ser) *c* terrace

terreng (tæ-*rehngng*) *nt* terrain

terror (*tær*-roor) *m* terror

terrorisme (tæ-roo-*riss*-mer) *m* terrorism

terrorist (tæ-roo-*rist*) *m* terrorist

terskel (*tæsh*-kerl) *m* threshold

tesalong (*tāy*-sah-long) *m* tea-shop

tese (*tāy*-ser) *m* thesis

teservise (*tāy*-sær-vee-ser) *nt* tea set

teskje (*tāy*-shāy) *c* teaspoon

test (tehst) *m* test

testamente (tehss-tah-*mehn*-ter) *nt* will

teste (*tehss*-ter) *v* test

tett (tehtt) *adj* dense, thick

tettpakket (*teht*-pah-kert) *adj* crowded

Thailand (*tigh*-lahn) Thailand

thailandsk (*tigh*-lahnsk) *adj* Thai

thailender (*tigh*-leh-nerr) *m* Thai

ti (tee) *num* ten

tid (teed) *c* time; period; *hele tiden* all the time; *i*

tide in time
tidevann (*tee*-der-vahn) *nt*
tide
tidlig (*tee*-li) *adj* early;
tidligere before, former,
previous, formerly, *adv*
before; past
tidsbesparende (*tits*-beh-
spaa-rer-ner) *adj* time-
-saving
tidsfordriv (*tits*-for-driv)*nt*
pastime
tidsskrift (*tit*-skrift) *nt*
magazine, periodical,
review, journal
tie (*tee*-er) *v* *be silent,
*keep quiet
tiende (*tee*-er-ner) *num*
tenth
tiger (*tee*-gerr) *m* tiger
tigge (*tig*-ger) *v* beg
tigger (*tig*-gerr) *m* beggar
til (till) *prep* to; for; until,
till; en ~ another; ~ og
med even
tilbake (til-*baa*-ker) *adv*
back; *gå ~ *get back
tilbakebetale (til-*baa*-ker-
beh-taa-ler) *v* reimburse,
*repay
tilbakebetaling (til-*baa*-
ker-beh-taa-ling) *c*
repayment, refund
tilbakegang (til-*baa*-ker-
gahng) *m* recession
tilbakekalle (til-*baa*-ker-
kah-ler) *v* recall
tilbakekomst (til-*baa*-ker-
komst) *m* return
tilbakereise (til-*baa*-ker-

ray-ser) *c* return journey
tilbakevei (til-*baa*-ker-vay)
m way back
tilbakevise (til-*baa*-ker-vee-
ser) *v* reject
*tilbe (til-*bay*) *v* worship
tilbehør (*til*-beh-hurr) *nt*
accessories *pl*
tilberede (til-beh-*ray*-der) *v*
prepare; cook
*tilbringe (til-*bri*-nger) *v*
*spend
tilbud (*til*-bewd) *nt* (pl ~)
offer; supply; bid
*tilby (*til*-bew) *v* offer; *bid
tilbøyelig (til-*burew*-er-li)
adj inclined; *være ~ til
tend to
tilbøyelighet (til-*burew*-er-
li-hayt) *c* inclination,
tendency
tildele (til-*day*-ler) *v* award;
assign to; administer
tilfeldig (til-*fehl*-di) *adj*
incidental, accidental,
casual
tilfeldighet (til-*fehl*-di-hayt)
c chance, coincidence
tilfeldigvis (til-*fehl*-di-
veess) *adv* by chance
tilfelle (*til*-feh-ler) *nt* case,
instance; chance;
coincidence; i ~ av in case
of
tilfluktssted (*til*-flewkt-
steh) *nt* shelter
tilfreds (til-*frehts*) *adj*
content; satisfied
tilfredshet (til-*frehts*-hayt) *c*
contentment

tilfredsstille (*til*-freht-sti-ler) *v* satisfy

tilfredsstillelse (*til*-freht-sti-lerl-ser) *m* satisfaction

tilfredsstillende (*til*-freht-sti-lerl-ner) *adj* satisfactory

tilfredsstilt (*til*-freht-stilt) *adj* satisfied

tilførsel (*til*-fur-sherl) *m* (pl -sler) supply

tilføye (*til*-fur^ew-er) *v* add; inflict

tilføyelse (*til*-fur^ew-erl-ser) *m* addition

tilgang (*til*-gahng) *m* access

***tilgi** (*til*-^yee) *v* *forgive

tilgivelse (*til*-^yee-verl-ser) *m* pardon

tilgjengelig (til-^yehng-nger-li) *adj* available; accessible

tilhenger (*til*-heh-ngerr) *m* trailer; supporter

tilhøre (*til*-hūr-rer) *v* belong, belong to

tilhører (*til*-hūr-rerr) *m* auditor

***tilintetgjøre** (ti-*lin*-tert-^yūr-rer) *v* destroy; ruin

***tillate** (*til*-laa-ter) *v* permit, allow; *være tillatt *be allowed

tillatelse (*til*-laa-terl-ser) *m* permission, authorization; permit; *gi ~ license

tillegg (*til*-lehg) *nt* (pl ~) supplement; surcharge; annex

tillit (*til*-leet) *m* faith, confidence, trust

tillitsfull (*til*-leets-fewl) *adj* confident

tilpasse (*til*-pah-ser) *v* adapt, suit; adjust; accommodate

tilrettevise (til-*reht*-ter-vee-ser) *v* reprimand

tilråde (*til*-raw-der) *v* recommend

tilsiktet (*til*-sik-tert) *adj* intentional

***tilskrive** (*til*-skree-ver) *v* assign to

tilskudd (*til*-skewd) *nt* (pl ~) subsidy; grant

tilskuer (*til*-skēw-errr) *m* spectator

tilsluttet (*til*-shlew-tert) *adj* affiliated

tilstand (*til*-stahn) *m* condition

tilstedeværelse (til-*stay*-der-væ-rerl-ser) *m* presence

tilstedeværende (til-*stay*-der-væ-rer-ner) *adj* present

tilstrekkelig (*til*-streh-ker-li) *adj* enough, sufficient; adequate; *være ~ suffice; *do

tilstøtende (*til*-stūr-ter-ner) *adj* neighbo(u)ring; adjacent

***tilstå** (*til*-staw) *v* confess, admit

tilståelse (*til*-staw-erl-ser) *m* confession

tilsvare (*til*-svaa-rer) *v* correspond

tilsvarende (*til*-svaa-rer-

tonn

ner) *adj* equivalent

tilsynelatende (til-*sew*-ner-laa-ter-ner) *adj* apparent

*tilta (*til*-taa) *v* increase

tiltakende (*til*-taa-ker-ner) *adj* progressive

*tiltrekke (*til*-treh-ker) *v* attract

tiltrekkende (*til*-treh-ker) *adj* attractive

tiltrekning (*til*-trehk-ning) *m* attraction

time (*tee*-mer) *m* hour; lesson; hver ~ hourly

timeplan (*ti*-mer-plaan) *m* schedule

timian (*tee*-mi-ahn) *m* thyme

tind (tinn) *m* peak

tine (*tee*-ner) *v* thaw

ting (tingng) *m* (pl ~) thing

tinn (tinn) *nt* pewter, tin

tinning (tin-ning) *m* temple

tirsdag (*teesh*-dah) *m* Tuesday

tispe (*tiss*-per) *c* bitch

tistel (*tiss*-terl) *m* (pl -tler) thistle

tittel (*tit*-terl) *m* (pl titler) title

tiur (*tee*-ewr) *m* wood grouse

tjene (*t'ay*-ner) *v* earn; *make

tjener (*t'ay*-nerr) *m* boy, servant, domestic

tjeneste (*t'ay*-nerss-ter) *m* favo(u)r; service

tjue (*khew*-er) *num* twenty

tjuende (*khew*-er-ner) *num*

twentieth

tjære (*khææ*-rer) *c* tar

to (too) *num* two

toalett (too-ah-*leht*) *nt* bathroom, lavatory, toilet; washroom, rest room *Am*

toalettpapir (too-ah-*leht*-pah-peer) *nt* toilet paper

toalettsaker (too-ah-*leht*-saa-kerr) *pl* toiletry

toalettveske (too-ah-*leht*-vehss-ker) *c* toilet case

tobakk (too-*bahkk*) *m* tobacco

tobakksforretning (too-*bahks*-fo-reht-ning) *c* tobacconist's

todelt (*too*-dehlt) *adj* two-piece

tog (tawg) *nt* train, parade

tolk (tolk) *m* interpreter

tolke (*tol*-ker) *v* interpret

toll (toll) *m* customs duty; customs *pl*

tollavgift (*tol*-laav-'ift) *c* customs duty

toller (*tol*-lerr) *m* customs officer

tollfri (*toll*-free) *adj* duty-free

tolv (toll) *num* twelve

tolvte (*tol*-ter) *num* twelfth

tom (tomm) *adj* empty

tomat (too-*maat*) *m* tomato

tomme (*tom*-me) *m* inch

tommelfinger (*tom*-merl-fi-ngerr) *m* (pl -gre) thumb

tomt (tomt) *c* grounds, plot

tone (*too*-ner) *m* note, sound

tonn (tonn) *nt* ton

topp (topp) *m* summit, top; peak

topplokk (*top*-lok) *nt* (pl ~) cylinder head

torden (*too*-dern) *m* thunder

tordenvær (*too*-dern-væær) *nt* (pl ~) thunderstorm

tordne (*tood*-ner) *v* thunder

torg (torg) *nt* market-place

torn (*toon*) *m* thorn

torsdag (*tawsh*-dah) *m* Thursday

torsk (toshk) *m* (pl ~) cod

tortur (too-*tewr*) *m* torture

torturere (too-tew-*rāy*-rer) *v* torture

tosk (tosk) *m* fool

tospråklig (*tōō*-sprawk-li) *adj* bilingual

total (too-*taal*) *adj* total; overall; utter

totalisator (too-tah-li-*saa*-toor) *m* bookmaker

totalitær (too-tah-li-*tæær*) *adj* totalitarian

totalsum (too-*taal*-sewm) *m* (pl ~mer) total

totalt (too-*taalt*) *adv* completely

tradisjon (trah-di-*shōōn*) *m* tradition

tradisjonell (trah-di-shoo-*nehll*) *adj* traditional

trafikk (trah-*fikk*) *m* traffic

trafikk-kork (trah-*fik*-kork) *m* jam, traffic jam

trafikklys (trah-*fik*-lēwss) *nt* (pl ~) traffic light

trafikkraseri (trah-fikk-*rāā*-ser-*rēē*) *nt* road rage

tragedie (trah-*gāy*-di-er) *m* tragedy

tragisk (*traa*-gisk) *adj* tragic

trakt (trahkt) *c* region; funnel

traktat (trahk-*taat*) *m* treaty

traktor (*trahk*-toor) *m* tractor

trang (trahngng) *adj* tight, narrow; *m* urge

transaksjon (trahn-sahk-*shōōn*) *m* deal, transaction

transatlantisk (*trahn*-saht-lahn-tisk) *adj* transatlantic

transformator (trahns-for-*maa*-toor) *m* transformer

transpirasjon (trahn-spi-rah-*shōōn*) *m* perspiration

transpirere (trahn-spi-*rāy*-rer) *v* perspire

transport (trahns-*pott*) *m* transport, transportation

transportabel (trahns-po-*taa*-berl) *adj* portable

transportere (trahns-po-*tāy*-rer) *v* transport

trapp (trahpp) *c* stairs *pl*, staircase

travel (*traa*-verl) *adj* busy

travelhet (*traa*-verl-*hāyt*) *c* bustle

*tre¹ (*trāy*) *v* step; thread

tre¹ (*trāy*) *num* three

tre² (*trāy*) *nt* (pl trær) tree; wood; tre- wooden

tredje (*trāyd*-)ᵉ) *num* third

*treffe (*trehf*-fer) *v* *hit; *meet

treg (*trayg*) *adj* slack

trekant (*tray*-kahnt) *m* triangle

trekantet (*tray*-kahn-tert) *adj* triangular

trekk (trehkk) *nt* move; trait; *m* draught

*trekke (*trehk*-ker) *v* pull, *draw; upholster; ~ fra deduct; subtract; ~ opp *wind; uncork; ~ tilbake *withdraw; ~ ut extract

trekning (*trehk*-ning) *m* draw

trekull (*tray*-kewl) *nt* charcoal

trene (*tray*-ner) *v* drill; train

trener (*tray*-nerr) *m* coach; trainer

trenge (*trehng*-nger) *v* need; ~ seg frem push

trening (*tray*-ning) *c* training

treskjærerarbeid (*tray*-shææ-rerr-ahr-bayd) *nt* wood carving

tresko (*tray*-skoo) *m* (pl ~) wooden shoe

trett (trehtt) *adj* tired, weary

trette (*reht*-ter) *v* argue, quarrel; tire; *m* quarrel

tretten (*treht*-tern) *num* thirteen

trettende (*reht*-ter-ner) *num* thirteenth; *adj* tiring

tretti (*treht*-ti) *num* thirty

trettiende (*treht*-ti-er-ner) *num* thirtieth

trevle opp (*trehv*-ler) fray

tribune (tri-*bew*-ner) *m* stand

trick (trikk) *nt* trick

trikk (trikk) *m* tram; streetcar *nAm*

trillebår (*tril*-ler-bawr) *c* wheelbarrow

trinn (trinn) *nt* step

trinse (*trin*-ser) *c* pulley

trist (trist) *adj* sad

triumf (tri-*ewmf*) *m* triumph

triumfere (tri-ewm-*fay*-rer) *v* triumph

triumferende (tri-ewm-*fay*-rer-ner) *adj* triumphant

tro (troo) *v* believe; reckon; *c* belief, faith; *adj* faithful

trofast (*troo*-fahst) *adj* faithful, true

trolig (*troo*-li) *adj* credible

trolldom (*trol*-dom) *m* magic

tromme (*troom*-mer) *c* drum

trommehinne (*troom*-mer-hi-ner) *c* ear-drum

trompet (troom-*payt*) *m* trumpet

trone (*troo*-ner) *c* throne

tropene (*troo*-per-ner) *pl* tropics *pl*

tropisk (*troo*-pisk) *adj* tropical

tropper (*trop*-perr) *pl* troops *pl*

tross (tross) *prep* in spite of, despite; til ~ for in spite of

trost (trost) *m* thrush

true (*trew*-er) *v* threaten

truende (*trew*-er-ner) *adj*

trumf

threatening

trumf (trewmf) *m* trump, trump card

trupp (trewpp) *m* band; company

truse (trew-ser) *c* briefs *pl*, panties *pl*; underpants *plAm*

trussel (trewss-serl) *m* (*pl* -sler) threat

trygle (trew-ger-ler) *v* plead, beseech, beg

trykk[1] (trewkk) *nt* pressure

trykk[2] (trewkk) *nt* engraving, print

trykk[3] (trewkk) *nt* stress; *legge ~ på* stress

trykke[1] (trewk-ker) *v* press; *~ på* press

trykke[2] (trewk-ker) *v* print

trykkende (trewk-ker-ner) *adj* stuffy

trykknapp (trewk-knahp) *m* push button; press-stud

trykkoker (trewk-kōō-kerr) *m* pressure cooker

tryllekunstner (trewl-ler-kewnst-nerr) *m* magician

trøbbel (trurb-berl) *nt* trouble

trøffel (trur-ferl) *m* truffle

trøst (trurst) *c* comfort

trøste (trurss-ter) *v* comfort

trøstepremie (trurss-ter-prāy-mi-er) *m* consolation prize

trå (traw) *v* step

tråd (traw) *m* thread

trådløs (trawd-lūrss) *adj* wireless

tube (tēw-ber) *m* tube

tuberkulose (tew-bær-kew-lōō-ser) *m* tuberculosis

tulipan (tew-li-paan) *m* tulip; *~løk* tulip bulb

tull (tewll) *nt* rubbish

tunfisk (tēwn-fisk) *m* tuna

tung (toongng) *adj* heavy

tunge (toong-nger) *c* tongue

tungnem (toong-nehm) *adj* slow

tunika (tēw-ni-kah) *m* tunic

Tunisia (tew-nee-si-ah) Tunisia

tunisier (tew-nee-si-err) *m* Tunisian

tunisisk (tew-nee-sisk) *adj* Tunisian

tunnel (tew-nehll) *m* tunnel

tur (tēwr) *m* ride, trip; turn

turbin (tewr-been) *m* turbine

turbojet (tewr-boo-^yeht) *m* turbojet

turgjenger (tēwr-^yeh-ngerr) *m* walker

turist (tew-rist) *m* tourist

turistklasse (tew-rist-klah-ser) *c* tourist class

turistkontor (tew-rist-koon-tōōr) *nt* tourist office

turisttrafikk (tew-riss-trah-fik) *m* tourism

turner (tew-nerr) *m* gymnast

turnering (tew-nāy-ring) *c* tournament

turnsko (tēwn-skōō) *pl* gym shoes; sneakers *plAm*

tur-retur (tēwr-reh-tēwr)

round trip
tusen (*tew*-sern) *num*
thousand
tusmørke (*tewss*-murr-ker)
nt dusk
tut (*tewt*) *m* nozzle
tute (*tew*-ter) *v* hoot; honk
vAm, toot *vAm*
TV (te**wehr) *m colloquial*
TV
tvang (tvahng) *m*
constraint; force
tverr (tværr) *adj* cross
tvert imot (*tvæt* i-*mōōt*) on
the contrary
tvert om (*tvæt* om) the
other way round
tvetydig (*rvāy*-tēw-di) *adj*
ambiguous
tvil (tveel) *m* doubt; **uten ~**
without doubt
tvile (*rvee*-ler) *v* doubt
tvillinger (*tvil*-li-ngerr) *pl*
twins *pl*
tvilsom (*tveel*-som) *adj*
doubtful
*tvinge (*tving*-nger) *v* force
tvist (tvist) *m* dispute
tydelig (*tēw*-der-li) *adj*
clear, distinct, plain;
evident, apparent; explicit
tyfus (*tēw*-fewss) *m* typhoid
tygge (*tewg*-ger) *v* chew
tyggegummi (*tewg*-ger-
gew-mi) *m* chewing gum
tykk (tewkk) *adj* thick;
corpulent, big
tykkelse (*tewk*-kerl-ser) *m*
thickness
tykkfallen (*tewk*-fah-lern)

adj stout
tykne (*tewk*-ner) *v* thicken
tyngde (*tewng*-der) *m*
weight
tyngdekraft (*tewng*-der-
krahft) *c* gravity
tynge (*tewng*-nger) *v*
oppress
tynn (tewnn) *adj* thin; sheer;
weak
type (*tēw*-per) *m* type
typisk (*tēw*-pisk) *adj* typical
tyr (tēwr) *m* bull
tyrann (tew-*rahnn*) *m* tyrant
tyrefektning (*tēw*-rer-fehkt-
ning) *m* bullfight
Tyrkia (*tewr*-ki-ah) Turkey
tyrkisk (*tewr*-kisk) *adj*
Turkish
tysk (tewsk) *adj* German
tysker (*tewss*-kerr) *m*
German
Tyskland (*tewsk*-lahn)
Germany
tyv (tēwv) *m* thief
tyve (*tēw*-ver) *num* twenty
tyvende (*tēw*-ver-ner) *num*
twentieth
tyveri (tēw-ver-*ree*) *nt*
robbery, theft
tøffel (*turf*-ferl) *m* (pl
tøfler) slipper
tømme (*turm*-mer) *v* empty
tømmer (*turm*-merr) *nt*
timber
tømmermenn (*turm*-merr-
mehn) *pl* hangover
tømming (*turm*-ming) *c*
emptying
tønne (*turn*-ner) *c* cask,

barrel

tørke (*turr*-ker) *c* drought; *v* wipe, dry; ~ av wipe; ~ bort wipe

tørkeapparat (*turr*-ker-ah-paat) *nt* dryer

tørr (turrr) *adj* dry

tørst (tursht) *adj* thirsty; *m* thirst

tøvær (*tūr*-væær) *nt* thaw

tøye (*turew*-er) *v* stretch

tøyelig (*turew*-er-li) *adj* elastic

tøyelighet (*turew*-er-li-hāyt) *c* elasticity

tøyle (*turew*-ler) *v* curb; restrain

tå (taw) *c* (pl tær) toe

tåke (*taw*-ker) *c* mist, fog

tåkelykt (*taw*-ker-lewkt) *c* foglamp

tåket (*taw*-kert) *adj* foggy

tålmodig (tol-*mōō*-di) *adj* patient

tålmodighet (tol-*mōō*-di-hāyt) *c* patience

tåpelig (*taw*-per-li) *adj* silly, foolish; crazy

tåre (*taw*-rer) *c* tear

tårn (tawn) *nt* tower

U

uakseptabel (*ew*-ahk-sep-taabel) *adj* unacceptable

ualminnelig (ew-ahl-*mi*-ner-li) *adj* unusual

uanselig (ew-ahn-*sāy*-li) *adj* inconspicuous, insignificant

uanstendig (*ew*-ahn-stehn-di) *adj* indecent; obscene

uavbrutt (*ew*-ahv-brewt) *adj* continuous

uavhengig (*ew*-ahv-heh-ngi) *adj* independent

uavhengighet (*ewahv*-heh-ngi-hāyt) *c* independence

ubebodd (*ew*-beh-bood) *adj* uninhabited

ubeboelig (*ew*-beh-*bōō*-er-li) *adj* uninhabitable

ubegrenset (*ew*-beh-grehn-sert) *adj* unlimited

ubehagelig (*ew*-beh-haa-ger-li) *adj* disagreeable, unpleasant; nasty

ubekvem (*ew*-beh-kvehm) *adj* uncomfortable

ubekymret (*ew*-beh-khewm-rert) *adj* carefree

ubeleilig (*ew*-beh-lay-li) *adj* inconvenient

ubeleilighet (*ew*-beh-lay-li-hāyt) *c* inconvenience

ubesindig (*ew*-beh-sin-di) *adj* rash

ubeskjeden (*ew*-beh-shāy-dern) *adj* immodest

ubeskyttet (*ew*-beh-shew-tert) *adj* unprotected

ubestemt (*ew*-beh-stehmt) *adj* indefinite

ubesvart (*ew*-beh-svaat) *adj* unanswered

ubetydelig (ēw-beh-*tēw*-der-li) *adj* insignificant; slight, petty

ubevisst (ew-ber-vist) *adj* unconscious

ubotelig (ew-*bōō*-ter-li) *adj* irreparable

ubåt (ew-bawt) *m* submarine

udugelig (ew-*dēw*-ger-li) *adj* incapable

udyrket (ew-dewr-kert) *adj* uncultivated

uegnet (ēw-ay-nert) *adj* unsuitable, unfit

uekte (ēw-ehk-ter) *adj* false

uendelig (ew-*ehn*-ner-li) *adj* endless, infinite

uenig: *være ~ (væe*-rer ew-*āy*-ni) disagree

uerfaren (ēw-ær-faa-rern) *adj* inexperienced

ufaglært (ēw-faag-læært) *adj* unskilled

uflaks (ēw-flahks) *m* bad luck

uforklarlig (ēw-for-*klaa*-li) *adj* unaccountable

uformell (ēw-for-mehll) *adj* casual, informal

uforskammet (ēw-fo-shkah-mert) *adj* insolent, impertinent, impudent; rude, *colloquial* cheeky

uforskammethet (ēw-fo-shkah-mert-hāyt) *c* insolence

uforståelig (ēw-fo-shtaw-er-li) *adj* puzzling

ufortjent (ēw-fo-t'āynt) *adj*

unearned

ufremkommelig (ēw-frehm-ko-mer-li) *adj* impassable

ufullkommen (ēw-fewl-ko-mern) *adj* imperfect

ufullstendig (ēw-fewl-stehn-di) *adj* incomplete

ufølsom (ēw-fur-l-som) *adj* insensitive

ufør (ēw-fūr) *adj* disabled

ugift (ēw-ʸift) *adj* single

ugjenkallelig (ew-ʸehn-*kahl*-ler-li) *adj* irrevocable

ugle (ewg-ler) *c* owl

ugress (ēw-grehss) *nt* weed

ugunstig (ēw-gewn-sti) *adj* unfavo(u)rable

ugyldig (ēw-ʸewl-di) *adj* invalid, void

uhelbredelig (ēw-hehl-*brāy*-der-li) *adj* incurable

uheldig (ew-*hehl*-di) *adj* unfortunate, unlucky

uheldigvis (ew-*hehl*-di-veess) *adv* unfortunately

uhell (ēw-hehl) *nt* misfortune; accident; mishap

uhyggelig (ew-*hew*-ger-li) *adj* creepy; ominous

uhøflig (ew-*hurf*-li) *adj* impolite

ujevn (ēw-ʸehvn) *adj* uneven

uke (ēw-ker) *c* week

ukentlig (ēw-kernt-li) *adj* weekly

ukjent (ēw-khehnt) *adj* unknown, unfamiliar

uklar (ēw-klaar) *adj* obscure, dim

uklok (ēw-klōōk) *adj* unwise

uknuselig (ew-knēw-ser-li) *adj* unbreakable

ukvalifisert (ēw-kvah-li-fi-sāyt) *adj* unqualified

uleilighet (ew-*lay*-li-hāyt) *c* trouble

ulempe (ēw-lehm-per) *m* disadvantage

uleselig (ew-*lay*-ser-li) *adj* illegible

ulik (ēw-leek) *adj* unequal, uneven

ulike (ēw-lee-ker) *adj* odd

ull (ewll) *c* wool; **ull-wool(l)en**

ulljakke (ewl-ᵞah-ker) *c* sweater, cardigan

ulovlig (ēw-lawv-li) *adj* illegal, unlawful

ultrafiolett (ewl-trah-fi-oo-leht) *adj* ultraviolet

ulv (ewlv) *m* wolf

ulykke (ēw-lew-ker) *c* accident, misfortune; calamity, disaster; misery

ulykkelig (ew-*lewk*-ker-li) *adj* unhappy; miserable

ulærd (ēw-læærd) *adj* uneducated

umake (ēw-maa-ker) *m* pains; *være umaken verd* *be worthwhile

umiddelbart (ēw-mi-derl-baat) *adv* immediately, instantly

umoderne (ēw-moo-dææ-ner) *adj* out of date; old--fashioned

umulig (ew-mēw-li) *adj*

impossible

umyndig (ēw-mewn-di) *adj* under age

umåtelig (ew-*maw*-ter-li) *adj* vast, immense

under[1] (ewn-derr) *nt* wonder

under[2] (ewn-nerr) *prep* below, during, beneath, under; *adv* beneath

underbukse (ewn-nerr-book-ser) *c* panties *pl*, drawers, pants *pl*; shorts *plAm*

underdrive (ewn-nerr-driver) *v* understate

underdrivelse (ewn-nerr-driv-erl-ser) *n* understatement

underernæring (ewn-nerr-æ-næ-ring) *c* malnutrition

undergang (ewn-nerr-gahng) *m* ruin, destruction

undergrunnsbane (ewn-nerr-grewns-baa-ner) *m* underground; subway *nAm*

*underholde (ewn-nerr-ho-ler) *v* entertain, amuse

underholdende (ewn-nerr-ho-ler-ner) *adj* entertaining

underholdning (ewn-nerr-hol-ning) *m* entertainment

underjordisk (ewn-nerr-ᵞoor-disk) *adj* underground

underkaste seg (ewn-nerr-kahss-ter) submit

underkue (ewn-nerr-kēwer) v subject

underlegen (ewn-ner-lāy-gern) adj inferior

underlig (ewn-der-li) adj odd, strange, queer; peculiar

underordnet (ewn-ner-oord-nert) adj subordinate; minor, secondary; additional

underretning (ewn-ner-reht-ning) m notice

underrette (ewn-ner-reh-ter) v inform; notify

underskrift (ewn-nerr-skrift) c signature

underskudd (ewn-ner-shkewd) nt (pl ~) deficit

understreke (ewn-ner-shtrāy-ker) v underline; emphasize

understrøm (ewn-ner-shtrurm) m (pl ~mer) undercurrent

undersøke (ewn-ner-shūr-ker) v enquire; examine

undersøkelse (ewn-ner-shūr-kerl-ser) m investigation, enquiry; check-up, examination

undersått (ewn-ner-shot) m subject

undertegne (ewn-ner-tay-ner) v sign

undertrykke (ewn-ner-trewk-ker) v oppress, suppress

undertøy (ewn-ner-tur^(ew)) pl underwear

undervanns- (ewn-nerr-vahns) underwater

undervise (ewn-nerr-vee-ser) v *teach; instruct

undervisning (ewn-nerr-veess-ning) c tuition, instruction

undervurdere (ewn-nerr-vew-dāy-rer) v underestimate

undre seg (ewn-drer) wonder; marvel

ung (oongng) adj young

ungarer (oong-gaa-rerr) m Hungarian

Ungarn (ewng-gaan) Hungary

ungarsk (ewng-gaashk) adj Hungarian

ungdom (oong-dom) m (pl ~mer) youth; ungdoms-juvenile

ungdomsherberge (oong-doms-hær-bær-ger) nt youth hostel

unge (oong-nger) m kid

ungkar (oong-kaar) m bachelor

uniform (ew-ni-form) c uniform

union (ew-ni-ōōn) m union

univers (ew-ni-væshsh) nt universe

universell (ew-ni-væ-shehll) adj universal

universitet (ew-ni-væ-shi-tāyt) nt university

***unngå** (ewn-gaw) v avoid; escape

unnskyld! (ewn-shewl) sorry!

unnskylde (ewn-shew-ler) v

excuse

unnskyldning (*ewn-shewl-ning*) *m* apology, excuse; *be om ~ apologize

*unnslippe (*ewn-shli-per*) *v* escape

unntak (*ewn-taak*) *nt* (pl ~) exception

unntaksvis (*ewn-taaks-vis*) *adv* for a change

unntatt (*ewn-taht*) *prep* except

*unnvike (*ewn-vee-ker*) *v* avoid

*unnvære (*ewn-væær*) *v* spare

unyttig (*ew*-new-ti) *adj* useless

unødvendig (*ew*-nurd-vern-di) *adj* unnecessary

unøyaktig (*ew*-nur^ew-ahk-ti) *adj* inaccurate

uoffisiell (*ew*-o-fi-si-erl) *adj* unofficial

uopphørlig (*ew*-oop-hūr-li) *adv* continually

uorden (*ew*-o-dern) *m* disorder; i ~ out of order; broken

uordentlig (*ew*-ont-li) *adj* untidy

uoverkommelig (*ew*-o-verr-ko-mer-li) *adj* prohibitive, insurmountable

uovertruffen (*ew*-o-ver-troo-fern) *adj* unsurpassed

upartisk (*ew*-paa-tisk) *adj* impartial

upassende (*ew*-pah-ser-ner) *adj* improper

upersonlig (*ew*-pæ-shōon-li) *adj* impersonal

upopulær (*ew*-poo-pew-læær) *adj* unpopular

upålitelig (*ew*-po-lee-ter-li) *adj* unreliable, untrustworthy

ur (*ewr*) *nt* watch

uregelmessig (*ew*-rāy-gerl-meh-si) *adj* irregular

urett (*ew*-reht) *m* wrong, injustice; *gjøre ~ wrong; *ha ~ *be wrong

urettferdig (*ew*-reht-fæ-di) *adj* unfair, unjust

uriktig (ew-rik-ti) *adj* incorrect, wrong

urimelig (*ew*-ree-mer-li) *adj* unreasonable; absurd

urin (ew-*reen*) *m* urine

urmaker (*ewr*-maa-kerr) *m* watch-maker

uro (*ew*-rōō) *m* unrest

urolig (ew-*rōō*-li) *adj* restless; uneasy

urskog (*ew*-shkōōg) *m* jungle; primeval forest

urt (ewtt) *c* herb

urtids- (*ew*-tits) *adj* ancient

Uruguay (ew-rew-gew-*igh*) Uruguay

uruguayaner (ew-rew-gew-igh-*aa*-nerr) *m* Uruguayan

uruguayansk (ew-rew-gew-igh-*aansk*) *adj* Uruguayan

usann (*ew*-sahn) *adj* untrue

usannsynlig (*ew*-sahn-sēwn-li) *adj* improbable, unlikely

usedvanlig (ew-sehd-*vaan*-

li) *adj* uncommon,
extraordinary, exceptional
uselvisk (*ew*-sehl-visk) *adj*
unselfish
usikker (*ew*-si-kerr) *adj*
uncertain; doubtful;
unsafe
uskadd (*ew*-skahd) *adj*
unhurt; whole
uskadelig (ew-*skaa*-der-li)
adj harmless
uskikkelig (ew-*shik*-ker-li)
adj naughty
uskyld (*ew*-shewl) *c*
innocence
uskyldig (ew-*shewl*-di) *adj*
innocent
uspiselig (ew-*spee*-ser-li)
adj inedible
ustabil (*ew*-stah-beel) *adj*
unstable
ustadig (ew-*staa*-di) *adj*
unsteady
ustø (*ew*-stūr) *adj* unsteady
usunn (*ew*-sewn) *adj*
unhealthy, unsound
usympatisk (*ew*-sewm-paa-
tisk) *adj* unpleasant
usynlig (ew-*sewn*-li) *adj*
invisible
ut (*ewt*) *adv* out; *~gå ~ *go
out; *~ over* beyond
utad (*ew*-taad) *adv* outwards
utakknemlig (*ew*-tahk-
nehm-li) *adj* ungrateful
utbre (*ewt*-*bray*) *v* expand
utbredelse (*ewt*-bred-ehl-
ser) *m* expansion
utbrudd (*ewt*-brewd) *nt* (pl
~) outbreak

*utbryte (*ewt*-brew-ter) *v*
exclaim
utbytte (*ewt*-bew-ter) *nt*
benefit; profit; **ha ~ av*
profit
utdanne (*ewt*-dah-ner) *v*
educate
utdannelse (*ewt*-dah-nerl-
ser) *m* education;
background
utdele (*ewt*-dāy-ler) *v*
distribute
utdrag (*ewt*-draag) *nt* (pl ~)
extract, excerpt
utdype (*ewt*-dew-per) *v*
elaborate
ute (*ew*-ter) *adv* out
*utelate (*ew*-ter-laa-ter) *v*
omit, **leave out*
utelukke (*ew*-ter-loo-ker) *v*
exclude
utelukkende (*ew*-ter-loo-
ker-ner) *adv* solely,
exclusively
uten (*ew*-tern) *prep* without
utenat (*ew*-ter-naht) *adv* by
heart
utendørs (*ew*-tern-dūrsh)
adv outdoors
utenfor (*ew*-tern-for) *prep*
outside; *adv* outside
utenkelig (ew-*tehng*-ker-li)
adj inconceivable
utenlands (*ew*-tern-lahns)
adv abroad
utenlandsk (*ew*-tern-
lahnsk) *adj* alien, foreign
utflukt (*ewt*-flookt) *c* trip,
excursion, outing
utfolde (*ewt*-fo-ler) *v*

unfold, display

utfordre (ēwt-foord-rer) v
challenge; dare;
utfordrende challenging,
defiant

utforske (ēwt-fosh-ker) v
explore

utføre (ēwt-fūr-rer) v
execute, perform,
implement, carry out;
export

utførlig (ewt-fūr-li) adj
detailed

utførsel (ēwt-fur-sherl) m
(pl -sler) export

utgang (ēwt-gahng) m way
out, exit; outcome

utgangspunkt (ēwt-gahngs-
poongt) nt starting point

utgave (ēwt-gaa-ver) c
edition

*__utgi__ (ēwt-ʸee) v publish;
issue; edit

utgift (ēwt-ʸift) c expense;
utgifter expenditure

utgravning (ēwt-graav-
ning) m excavation

*__utgyte__ (ēwt-ʸew-ter) v
*shed

*__utholde__ (ēwt-ho-ler) v
endure

utholdelig (ēwt-ho-ler-li)
adj tolerable

utilfreds (ēw-til-frehts) adj
dissatisfied

utilfredsstillende (ēw-til-
freht-sti-ler-ner) adj
unsatisfactory

utilgjengelig (ēw-til-ʸeh-
nger-li) adj inaccessible

utilsiktet (ēw-til-sik-tert) adj
unintentional

utilstrekkelig (ēw-til-streh-
ker-li) adj insufficient;
inadequate

utiltalende (ēw-til-taa-ler-
ner) adj unpleasant

utjevne (ēwt-ʸehv-ner) v
equalize

utkant (ēwt-kahnt) m
outskirts pl

utkast (ēwt-kahst) nt draft

utkjørsel (ēwt-khur-sherl) m
exit, driveway

utkople (ēwt-kop-ler) v
disconnect

utlede (ēwt-lāy-der) v
deduce, infer

utlending (ēwt-lehn-ing) m
alien, foreigner

utligne (ēwt-ling-ner) v level

utluftning (ēwt-lewft-ning)
m ventilation

utløp (ēwt-lūrp) nt (pl ~)
expiry

*__utløpe__ (ēwt-lūr-per) v
expire

utløpt (ēwt-lurpt) adj
expired

utmatte (ēwt-mah-ter) v
exhaust

utmattet (ēwt-mah-tert) adj
tired

utmerke seg (ēwt-mær-ker)
excel

utmerket (ēwt-mær-kert) adj
fine, excellent

utnevne (ēwt-nehv-ner) v
appoint

utnevnelse (ēwt-nehv-nerl-

ser) *m* nomination,
appointment

utnytte (*ēwt*-new-ter) *v*
exploit

utpresse (*ēwt*-preh-ser) *v*
extort

utpressing (*ēwt*-preh-sing)
c extortion

utregning (*ēwt*-ray-ning) *c*
calculation

utrivelig (ew-*tree*-ver-li) *adj*
unpleasant

utro (*ēw*-trōō) *adj* unfaithful

utrolig (ew-*trōō*-li) *adj*
incredible; amazing

utrop (*ēwt*-rōōp) *nt* (pl ~)
exclamation

utruste (*ēwt*-rewss-ter) *v*
equip

utrustning (*ēwt*-rewst-ning)
m outfit

utsalg (*ēwt*-sahlg) *nt* (pl ~)
sales

utseende (*ēwt*-sāy-er-ner)
nt look, appearance;
semblance

utsending (*ēwt*-seh-ning) *m*
delegate

*****utsette** (*ēwt*-seh-ter) *v*
postpone; expose; **utsatt
for** liable to; subject to

utsettelse (*ēwt*-seh-terl-ser)
m delay

utside (*ēwt*-seeer) *c* outside;
exterior

utsikt (*ēwt*-sikt) *m* view;
prospect, outlook

utskeielse (*ēwt*-shay-erl-
ser) *m* excess

utskrift (*ēwt*-skrift) *c*

printout

utslett (*ēwt*-sleht) *nt* rash

utslitt (*ēwt*-shlit) *adj* worn-
out

utsolgt (*ēwt*-solt) *adj* sold
out

utstedelse (*ēwt*-stāy-derl-
ser) *m* issue

utstikker (*ēwt*-sti-kerr) *m*
pier

utstille (*ēwt*-sti-ler) *v* *show,
exhibit; display

utstilling (*ēwt*-sti-ling) *c*
exposition, exhibition,
show, display

utstillingsdukke (*ēwt*-sti-
lings-dew-ker) *c*
mannequin

utstillingslokale (*ēwt*-sti-
lings-loo-kaa-ler) *nt*
showroom

utstillingsvindu (*ēwt*-sti-
lings-vin-dew) *nt* shop-
window

utstrakt (*ēwt*-strahkt) *adj*
extensive, broad

utstyr (*ēwt*-stēwr) *nt*
equipment; kit, gear

utstyre (*ēwt*-stēw-rer) *v*
equip

utsøkt (*ēwt*-surkt) *adj*
exquisite, select

uttale (*ēw*-taa-ler) *m*
pronunciation; *v*
pronounce; ~ **galt**
mispronounce

uttrykk (*ēw*-trewk) *nt* (pl ~)
expression; phrase; term;
*****gi ~ for** express

uttrykke (*ēw*-trew-ker) *v*

express

uttrykkelig (ew-*trewk*-ker-li) *adj* explicit, express

utvalg ($\overline{ewt}$-vahlg) *nt* (pl ∼) choice, selection; variety, assortment; committee

utvalgt ($\overline{ewt}$-vahlt) *adj* select

utvandre ($\overline{ewt}$-vahn-drer) *v* emigrate

utvei ($\overline{ewt}$-vay) *m* way out; course

utveksle ($\overline{ewt}$-vehk-shler) *v* exchange

utveksling ($\overline{ewt}$-vehk-shling) *c* exchange

*****utvelge** ($\overline{ewt}$-vehl-ger) *v* select

utvendig ($\overline{ewt}$-vehn-di) *adj* external, outward

utvide ($\overline{ewt}$-vee-der) *v* widen; extend, expand, enlarge

utvidelse ($\overline{ewt}$-vee-derl-ser) *m* extension; expansion

utvikle ($\overline{ewt}$-vik-ler) *v* develop

utvikling ($\overline{ewt}$-vik-ling) *c* development

utvilsomt (ew-*tveel*-somt) *adv* undoubtedly

utvise ($\overline{ewt}$-vee-ser) *v* expel

utvungenhet ($\overline{ew}$-tvoo-ngern-hāyt) *c* ease

utydelig (ew-*tew*-der-li) *adj* dim

utøve ($\overline{ew}$-tūr-ver) *v* exercise

utålelig (ew-*taw*-ler-li) *adj* intolerable

utålmodig ($\overline{ew}$-tol-mōō-di) *adj* eager, impatient

uunngåelig (ew-ewng-*gaw*-er-li) *adj* unavoidable, inevitable

uunnværlig (ew-ewn-*vææ*-li) *adj* essential

uutholdelig (ew-ewt-*hol*-ler-li) *adj* unbearable

uvanlig (ew-*vahn*-li) *adj* unusual

uvant ($\overline{ew}$-vahnt) *adj* unaccustomed

uvedkommende ($\overline{ew}$-vāyd-ko-mer-ner) *m* (pl ∼) trespasser

uvel ($\overline{ew}$-vehl) *adj* unwell

uvennlig ($\overline{ew}$-vehn-li) *adj* unkind, unfriendly

uventet ($\overline{ew}$-vehn-tert) *adj* unexpected

uvesentlig (ew-*vāy*-sernt-li) *adj* insignificant

uviktig ($\overline{ew}$-vik-ti) *adj* unimportant

uvillig ($\overline{ew}$-vi-li) *adj* unwilling; averse

uvirkelig ($\overline{ew}$-veer-ker-li) *adj* unreal

uvirksom ($\overline{ew}$-veerk-som) *adj* idle

uviss (ew-*viss*) *adj* uncertain

uvitende ($\overline{ew}$-vi-ter-ner) *adj* ignorant

uvurderlig ($\overline{ew}$-vew-*dāy*-li) *adj* priceless

uvær (ew-*vær*) *nt* (pl ∼) tempest

uærlig ($\overline{ew}$-ææ-li) *adj* dishonest; crooked

uønsket ($\overline{ew}$-urn-skert) *adj* undesirable

V

vaffel (*vahf*-ferl) *m* (pl vafler) waffle

vag (vaag) *adj* vague, faint

vakker (*vahk*-kerr) *adj* handsome, fair, beautiful

vakle (*vahk*-ler) *v* falter

vaklende (*vahk*-ler-ner) *adj* shaky

vaksinasjon (vahk-si-nah-*shōōn*) *m* inoculation

vaksinere (vahk-si-*nāy*-rer) *v* vaccinate, inoculate

vaksinering (vahk-si-*nāy*-ring) *c* vaccination

vakt (vahkt) *m* guard; attendant

vaktel (*vahk*-terl) *m* (pl -tler) quail

vaktmester (*vahkt*-mehss-terr) *m* (pl ⁓e, -trer) caretaker, janitor

vakuum (*vaa*-kewm) *nt* vacuum

valen (*vaa*-lern) *adj* numb

valg (vahlg) *nt* choice, pick; election

valgfri (*vahlg*-free) *adj* optional

valgkrets (*vahlg*-krehts) *m* constituency

valgspråk (*vahlg*-sprawk) *nt* (pl ⁓) slogan

valmue (*vahl*-mēwer) *m* poppy

valnøtt (*vaal*-nurt) *c* walnut

vals (vahls) *m* waltz

valuta (vah-*lewt*-tah) *m* currency

valutakurs (vah-*lewt*-tah-kēwsh) *m* rate of exchange, exchange rate

vandre (*vahn*-drer) *v* wander

vandrerhjem (*vahn*-drer-ʸehmm) *nt* youth hostel

vane (*vaa*-ner) *m* custom, habit

vanilje (vah-*nil*-ʸer) *m* vanilla

vanlig (*vaan*-li) *adj* common, usual, ordinary, habitual; customary, regular, simple

vanligvis (*vaan*-li-veess) *adv* as a rule, usually

vann (vahnn) *nt* water; innlagt ⁓ running water

vannfarge (*vahn*-fahr-ger) *m* watercolo(u)r

vannkopper (*vahn*-ko-perr) *pl* chickenpox

vannkran (*vahn*-kraan) *c* faucet *nAm*

vannmelon (*vahn*-meh-lōōn) *m* watermelon

vannski (*vahn*-shee) *c* water ski

vannstoff (*vahn*-stof) *nt* hydrogen; ⁓ hyperoksyd peroxide

vanntett (*vahn*-teht) *adj* waterproof

vanskapt (*vahn*-skahpt) *adj* deformed

vanskelig (*vahn*-sker-li) *adj* difficult; hard

vanskelighet (*vahn*-sker-li-hāyt) *c* difficulty

vant (vahnt) *adj* accustomed; **være ~ til* ***be used to

vanvidd (*vahn*-vid) *nt* lunacy

vanvittig (*vahn*-vi-ti) *adj* mad

vaporisator (vah-poo-ri-*saa*-toor) *m* atomizer

vare (*vaa*-rer) *v* last; *c* ware

varebil (*vaa*-rer-beel) *m* pick-up van, van, delivery van

varehus (*vaa*-rer-hēwss) *nt* (pl ~) department store

varemerke (*vaa*-rer-mær-ker) *nt* trademark

varemesse (*vaa*-rer-meh-ser) *c* fair

vareopptelling (*vaa*-rer-oop-teh-ling) *c* inventory

vareprøve (*vaarer*-prūr-ver) *c* sample

varer (*vaa*-rerr) *pl* merchandise, wares *pl*, goods *pl*

varetekt (*vaa*-rer-tehkt) *c* custody

variabel (vah-ri-*aa*-berl) *adj* variable

variere (vah-ri-*āy*-rer) *v* vary

variert (vah-ri-*āyt*) *adj* varied

varig (*vaa*-ri) *adj* lasting; permanent

varighet (*vaa*-ri-hāyt) *c* duration

varm (vahrm) *adj* hot, warm

varme (*vahr*-mer) *m* heat, warmth; *v* warm; *~ opp* heat

varmeflaske (*vahr*-mer-flahss-ker) *c* hot-water bottle

varmeovn (*vahr*-mer-ovn) *m* heater

varmepute (*vahr*-mer-pēw-ter) *c* heating pad

varsle (*vahsh*-ler) *v* forecast; notify

vase (*vaa*-ser) *m* vase

vask (vahsk) *m* washing; laundry; sink

vaskbar (*vahsk*-baar) *adj* washable

vaske (*vahss*-ker) *v* wash; *~ opp* wash up

vaskemaskin (*vahss*-ker-mah-sheen) *m* washing machine

vaskepulver (*vahss*-ker-pewl-verr) *nt* washing powder

vaskeri (vahss-ker-*ree*) *nt* laundry

vasse (*vahss*-ser) *v* wade

vatt (vahtt) *m* cotton wool

vatt-teppe *nt* quilt

ved (vāy) *m* firewood; *prep* by; on; *~ siden av* beside, next to

vedde (*vehd*-der) *v* *bet

veddeløp (*vehd*-der-lūrp) *nt*

race

veddeløpsbane (*vehd-der-lūrps-baa-ner*) *m* race-course; racetrack

veddeløpshest (*vehd-der-lūrps-hehst*) *m* race-horse

veddemål (*vehd-der-mawl*) *nt* (pl ~) bet

vedlegg (*vāy-lehg*) *nt* enclosure; attachment

***vedlegge** (*vāy-leh-ger*) *v* attach, enclose

vedlikehold (*veh-lee-ker-hol*) *nt* maintenance, upkeep

vedrøre (*vāy-rūr-rer*) *v* affect

vedrørende (*vāy-rūr-rer-ner*) *prep* with reference to, concerning

***vedta** (*vāy-taa*) *v* adopt, decide

vedvarende (*vāy-vaa-rer-ner*) *adj* permanent

veg (vay) *m* road; way

vegetarianer (*veh-ger-tah-ri-aa-nerr*) *m* vegetarian

vegg (vehgg) *m* wall

veggedyr (*vehg-ger-dēwr*) *nt* (pl ~) bug

vei (vay) *m* road; way; **på ~ til** bound for

veiarbeid (*vay-ahr-bayd*) *nt* road work

veidekke (*vay-deh-ker*) *nt* pavement

veie (*vay-er*) *v* weigh

veikant (*vay-kahnt*) *m* roadside, wayside

veikart (*vay-kaht*) *nt* road map

veikryss (*vay-krewss*) *nt* (pl ~) intersection, junction

veilede (*vay-lāy-der*) *v* direct

veinett (*vay-neht*) *nt* (pl ~) road system

veiskilt (*vay-shilt*) *nt* road sign

veiviser (*vay-vee-serr*) *m* signpost

vekk (vehkk) *adv* off; away

vekke (*vehk-ker*) *v* *wake, *awake

vekkeklokke (*vehk-ke-klo-ker*) *c* alarm-clock

vekselstrøm (*vehk-serl-strurm*) *m* alternating current

vekselvis (*vehk-sherl-veess*) *adv* alternate

veksle (*vehk-shler*) *v* change; exchange

vekslepenge (*vehk-shler-peh-ngerr*) *pl* change

vekslingskontor (*vehk-shlings-koon-tōōr*) *nt* money exchange, exchange office

vekst (vehkst) *m* growth

vekt (vehkt) *c* weight; scales *pl*; ***legge ~ på** stress

vektstang (*vehkt-stahng*) *c* (pl -tenger) lever

velbegrunnet (*vehl-beh-grew-nert*) *adj* well-founded

velbehag (*vehl-beh-haag*) *nt* pleasure

veldig (*vehl-di*) *adj* huge;

immense

velferd (*vehl-fæær*) *m*
welfare

*velge (*vehl-ger*) *v* *choose;
pick; elect; ~ ut select

velgjørenhet (*vehl-ᵞūr-rern-hāyt*) *c* charity

velhavende (*vehl-haa-ver-ner*) *adj* well-to-do

velkjent (*vehl-khehnt*) *adj*
familiar; well-known

velkommen (*vehl-kom-mern*) *adj* welcome; hilse ~
welcome

velkomst (*vehl-komst*) *m*
welcome

vellykket (*vehl-lew-kert*) *adj*
successful

velsigne (*vehl-sing-ner*) *v*
bless

velsignelse (*vehl-sing-nerl-ser*) *m* blessing

velsmakende (*vehl-smaa-ker-ner*) *adj* tasty,
savo(u)ry

velstand (*vehl-stahn*) *m*
prosperity

velstående (*vehl-stawer-ner*) *adj* prosperous

velvære (*vehl-væe-rer*) *nt*
comfort

vemmelig (*vehm-mer-li*)
adj nasty

vemod (*vāy-mōōd*) *nt*
sadness

vemodig (*vāy-mōō-di*) *adj*
sad

vende (*vehn-ner*) *v* turn; ~
om turn over; ~ tilbake
return; *go back, turn back

vendepunkt (*vehn-ner-pewngt*) *nt* turning point

vending (*vehn-ning*) *c* turn

Venezuela (veh-neh-sew-āy-lah) Venezuela

venezuelaner (veh-neh-sew-eh-*laa*-nerr) *m*
Venezuelan

venezuelansk (veh-neh-sew-eh-*laansk*) *adj*
Venezuelan

venn (vehnn) *m* (male,
female) friend

venne (*vehn-ner*) *v*
accustom

venninne (veh-*nin*-ner) *c*
(female) friend

vennlig (*vehn-li*) *adj* kind,
friendly; med ~ hilsen,
mvh best regards; yours
sincerely

vennligst (*vehn-likst*)
please

vennskap (*vehn-skaap*) *nt*
friendship

vennskapelig (vehn-*skaa-per-li*) *adj* friendly

venstre (*vehn-strer*) *adj*
left; left-hand

vente (*vehn-ter*) *v* wait;
expect; ~ på await

venteliste (*vehn-ter-liss-ter*)
c waitinglist

ventet (*vehn-tert*) *adj* due

venteværelse (*vehn-ter-væe-rerl-ser*) *nt* waiting
room

ventil (vehn-*teel*) *m* valve

ventilasjon (vehn-ti-lah-*shōōn*) *m* ventilation

ventilator (vehn-ti-*laa*-toor) *m* ventilator

ventilere (vehn-ti-*lay*-rer) *v* ventilate

venting (*vehn*-ting) *m* waiting

veps (vehps) *m* wasp

veranda (væ-*rahn*-dah) *m* veranda

verb (værb) *nt* verb

verd (værd) *nt* worth; ***være ~** *be worth

verden (*vær*-dern) *m* world

verdensberømt (*vær*-derns-beh-rurmt) *adj* world-famous

verdensdel (*vær*-derns-dayl) *m* continent

verdenskrig (*vær*-derns-kreeg) *m* world war

verdensomfattende (*vær*-dern-soom-fah-ter-ner) *adj* global

verdensomspennende (*vær*-dern-soom-speh-ner-ner) *adj* world-wide

verdensrom (*vær*-derns-room) *nt* space

verdi (væ-*dee*) *m* value

verdifull (væ-*dee*-fewl) *adj* valuable

verdig (*væ*-di) *adj* dignified; worthy of

verdighet (*væ*-di-hayt) *c* dignity

verdiløs (væ-*dee*-lurss) *adj* worthless

verdipapirer (væ-*dee*-pah-pee-rerr) *pl* stocks and shares

verdisaker (væ-*dee*-saa-kerr) *pl* valuables *pl*

***verdsette** (*værd*-seh-ter) *v* appreciate estimate

verdsettelse (*værd*-seh-terl-ser) *m* appreciation

verk (værk) *m* ache; pus

verke (*vær*-ker) *v* ache

verken ... eller (*vær*-kern ... ehl-err) neither ... nor

verksted (*værk*-stay) *nt* workshop

verktøy (*værk*-tur^(ew)) *nt* implement, tool

vern (væærn) *nt* defense *Am*, defence

vernepliktig (*væææ*-ner-plik-ti) *m* conscript

verre (*vær*-rer) *adv* worse; *adj* worse; **verst** worst

vers (væshsh) *m* verse

versjon (væ-*shoon*) *m* version

vert (vætt) *m* host; landlord

vertikal (væ-ti-*kaal*) *adj* vertical

vertinne (væ-*tin*-ner) *c* hostess; landlady

vertshus (*væts*-hewss) *nt* (*pl* ~) public house; inn; *m* roadside restaurant

vesen (*vay*-sern) *nt* being; essence

vesentlig (*vay*-sernt-li) *adj* essential; vital

veske (*vehss*-ker) *c* bag

vest (vehst) *m* west; waistcoat; vest *nAm*

vestlig (*vehst*-li) *adj* western, westerly

veterinær (veh-ter-ri-*næær*) *m* veterinary surgeon

vett (vehtt) *nt* brains, sense

vev (vāyv) *m* loom; *nt* tissue

veve (*vāy*-ver) *v* *weave

vi (vee) *pron* we

via (*vee*-ah) *prep* via

viadukt (vi-ah-*dewkt*) *m* viaduct

vibrasjon (vi-brah-*shōōn*) *m* vibration

vibrere (vi-*brāy*-rer) *v* vibrate

vid (vee) *adj* wide

vidd (vidd) *nt* wit

vidde (vee-er) *c* plateau

videokamera (*vid*-eoo-kah-meh-raa) *nt* video camera

videokassett (*vid*-eoo-kah-sehtt) *m* video cassette

videospiller (*vid*-eoo-spil-lerr) *m* video recorder

videre (*vee*-der-rer) *adj* further; farther; **og så ~** and so on, etcetera

vidstrakt (*vee*-strahkt) *adj* vast, broad

vidunder (vi-*dewn*-derr) *nt* (pl ~, ~e) marvel

vidunderlig (vi-*dewn*-der-li) *adj* wonderful, marvel(l)ous

vie (vee-er) *v* marry; devote; dedicate

vielse (*vee*-erl-ser) *m* wedding

vielsesring (*vee*-erl-serss-ring) *m* wedding ring

vifte (*vif*-ter) *c* fan

vifterem (*vif*-ter-rehm) *c* fan belt

vik (veek) *c* inlet, creek

vikle (*vik*-ler) *v* *wind

viktig (vik-ti) *adj* important; big, capital

viktighet (*vik*-ti-hāyt) *c* importance

vilje (*vil*-^yer) *m* will; **med ~** on purpose

viljestyrke (*vil*-^yer-stewr-ker) *m* will-power

vilkår (*vil*-kawr) *nt* condition

vilkårlig (vil-*kaw*-li) *adj* arbitrary

vill (vill) *adj* savage, wild; fierce; **gått ~** lost

villa (*vil*-lah) *m* villa

***ville** (*vil*-ler) *v* *will, want

villig (*vil*-li) *adj* willing

vilt (vilt) *nt* game, quarry

vin (veen) *m* wine

vind (vinn) *m* wind

vindebro (*vin*-ner-brōō) *c* drawbridge

vindhard (*vin*-haar) *adj* windy

vindkast (*vin*-kahst) *nt* (pl ~) blow, gust

vindmølle (*vin*-mur-ler) *c* windmill

vindu (*vin*-dew) *nt* window

vindusvisker (*vin*-dewss-viss-kerr) *m* windscreen wiper; windshield wiper *Am*

vinge (vingng-er) *m* wing

vink (vingk) *nt* sign

vinkart (*veen*-kaht) *nt* wine list

vitenskapskvinne

vinke (*ving*-ker) *v* wave

vinkel (*ving*-kerl) *m* (pl -kler) angle

vinkjeller (*veen*-kheh-lerr) *m* wine cellar

vinmonopol (*veen*-moo-noo-*pool*) *nt* off-licence, *Am* liquor store

*****vinne** (*vin*-ner) *v* gain, *win

vinnende (*vin*-ner-ner) *adj* winning

vinner (*vin*-nerr) *m* winner

vinranke (*veen*-rahng-ker) *m* vine

vinter (*vin*-terr) *m* (pl -trer) winter

vintersport (*vin*-ter-shpot) *m* winter sports

vipe (*vee*-per) *c* pewit

vippe (*vip*-per) *c* seesaw

virke (*veer*-ker) *v* work; operate

virkelig (*veer*-ker-li) *adj* actual, real; very, true; substantial; *adv* indeed, really

virkelighet (*veer*-ker-li-hāyt) *c* reality; **i virkeligheten** as a matter of fact

virkemåte (*veer*-ker-maw-ter) *m* mode of operation

virkning (*veerk*-ning) *m* effect

virkningsfull (*veerk*-nings-fewl) *adj* effective, efficient

virkningsløs (*veerk*-nings-lūrss) *adj* inefficient,

ineffective

virksom (*veerk*-som) *adj* active

virksomhet (*veerk*-som-hāyt) *c* enterprise, business

virus (*vēer*-rews) *nt* (pl ∼) virus

virvar (*veer*-vahr) *nt* muddle

vis (veess) *adj* wise; *nt* way, manner

visdom (*veess*-dom) *m* wisdom

vise (*vee*-ser) *v* *show; point out; display; ∼ **frem** *show; ∼ **seg** appear; prove

visepresident (*vee*-ser-preh-si-dehnt) *m* vice president

visitere (vi-si-*tāy*-rer) *v* search

visitt (vi-*sitt*) *m* call, visit

visittkort (vi-*sit*-kot) *nt* (pl ∼) card, business card

viskelær (*viss*-ker-læær) *nt* (pl ∼) rubber, eraser

vispe (*viss*-per) *v* whip

viss (viss) *adj* certain

visse (*viss*-ser) *pron* some

visum (*vee*-sewm) *nt* (pl visa) visa

vitamin (vi-tah-*meen*) *nt* vitamin

*****vite** (*vee*-ter) *v* *know

vitebegjærlig (*vee*-ter-beh-ʸææ-li) *adj* curious

vitenskap (*vee*-tern-skaap) *m* science

vitenskapelig (*vee*-tern-skaaper-li) *adj* scientific

vitenskapskvinne (*vee*-

tern-skaaps-kvin-ner) *c* (female) scientist

vitenskapsmann (*vee*-tern-skaaps-mahn) *v* (pl -menn) (male) scientist

vitne (*vit*-ner) *nt* witness; *v* testify

vitnesbyrd (*vit*-nerss-bewrd) *nt* certificate

vits (vits) *m* joke

vittig (*vit*-ti) *adj* humorous, witty

vogn (voangn) *c* carriage

vokal (voo-*kaal*) *m* vowel; *adj* vocal

voks (voks) *m* wax

vokse (*vok*-ser) *v* *grow

voksen[1] (*vok*-sern) *m* (pl -sne) adult, grown-up

voksen[2] (*vok*-sern) *adj* adult, grown-up

vokskabinett (*voks*-kah-bi-neht) *nt* waxworks *pl*

vokte seg (*vok*-ter) beware

vold (voll) *m* violence; force

volde (*vol*-ler) *v* cause

voldsom (*vol*-som) *adj* violent

***voldta** (*vol*-taa) *v* rape

voldtekt (*vol*-tekt) *c* rape

voligrav (*vol*-graav) *c* moat

volt (volt) *m* volt

volum (voo-*lewm*) *nt* volume

vond (voonn) *adj* bad, painful; evil; *gjøre vondt *hurt; *ha vondt *have a pain

vorte (*vor*-ter) *c* wart

votter (*vot*-terr) *pl* mittens

pl

vrak (vraak) *nt* wreck

vrengt (vrehngt) *adj* inside out

***vri** (vree) *v* twist, wrench; ~ om turn

vridning (*vreed*-ning) *m* twist

vrien (*vree*-ern) *adj* difficult

vrøvle (*vrurv*-ler) *v* talk rubbish

vugge (*vewg*-ger) *c* cradle

vulgær (vewl-*gæær*) *adj* vulgar

vulkan (vewl-*kaan*) *m* volcano

vær (væær) *nt* weather

***være** (*vææ*-rer) *v* *be; vær så god here you are

værelse (*vææ*-rerl-ser) *nt* room; ~ med frokost bed and breakfast

værelsesbetjening (*vææ*-rerl-serss-beh-t'*ay*-ning) *c* room service

værelsestemperatur (*vææ*-rerl-serss-tehm-peh-rah-tewr) *m* room temperature

værmelding (*væær*-meh-ling) *c* weather forecast

væske (*vehss*-ker) *c* fluid

våge (*vaw*-ger) *v* dare; venture

vågemot (*vaw*-ger-*moot*) *nt* guts

våken (*vaw*-kern) *adj* awake

våkne (*vok*-ner) *v* wake up
våningshus (*vaw*-nings-hēwss) *nt* (pl ∼) farmhouse
våpen (*vaw*-pern) *nt* (pl ∼) arm, weapon
våpenstillstand (*vaw*-pern-

still-stann) *m* ceasefire
vår[1] (vawr) *pron* our; ours
vår[2] (vawr) *m* spring; springtime
våt (vawt) *adj* wet; moist

W

watt (vahtt) *m* watt

Y

ydmyk (ēwd-mēwk) *adj* humble
ynde (ewn-der) *m* grace
yndig (ewn-di) *adj* lovely, graceful
yndling (ewnd-ling) *m* favo(u)rite; **yndlings-** pet, favo(u)rite
ynkelig (ewng-ker-li) *adj* lamentable
yrke (ewr-ker) *nt* trade; occupation
yte (ēw-ter) *v* yield, produce

ytre (ewt-rer) *v* utter; express; *adj* exterior
ytterlig (ewt-ter-li) *adj* extreme
ytterligere (ewt-ter-li-er-rer) *adj* additional, further
ytterlighet (ewt-ter-li-hāyt) *c* extreme
ytterside (ewt-ter-shee-der) *c* outside
ytterst (ewt-tersht) *adj* utmost, extreme

Z

zoo (sōō) *m* zoo; **zoologisk hage** zoological gardens
zoologi (soo-loo-*gi*) *m* zoology

zoomlinse (*sōōm*-lin-ser) *c* zoom lens

Æ

ærbødig (ær-*bur*-di) *adj* respectful

ærbødighet (ær-*bur*-di-hāyt) *c* respect

ære (*ææ*-rer) *c* honour; glory; *v* honour

ærefull (*ææ*-rer-fewl) *adj* honourable

ærend (*ææ*-rern) *nt* errand

æresfølelse (*ææ*-rerss-*fūr*-erl-ser) *m* sense of honour

ærgjerrig (ær-*ᵞær*-ri) *adj* ambitious

ærgjerrighet (ær-*ᵞær*-ri-hāyt) *c* ambition

ærlig (*ææ*-li) *adj* honest; straight

ærlighet (*ææ*-li-hāyt) *c* honesty

ærverdig (ær-*vær*-di) *adj* venerable

Ø

øde (*ūr*-der) *adj* desert; waste

***ødelegge** (*ūr*-der-leh-ger) *v* wreck; smash; destroy; ruin; *spoil

ødeleggelse (*ūr*-der-leh-gerl-ser) *m* destruction

ødsel (urt-serl) *adj* wasteful; lavish

øke (*ūr*-ker) *v* increase; raise

økning (*ūrk*-ning) *m* increase

økologi (ur-koo-loo-*gee*) *m* ecology

økologisk (ur-koo-*loo*-gisk) *adj* ecologic; ecological

økonom (ur-koo-*nōōm*) *m* economist

økonomi (ur-koo-noo-*mee*) *m* economy

økonomisk (ur-koo-*nōō*-misk) *adj* economic; economical

økoturist (*ūr*-koo-tēw-rist) *c* eco-tourist

øks (urks) *c* axe

øl (urll) *nt* beer; ale

øm (urmm) *adj* sore; gentle, tender

ønske (*urns*-ker) *v* wish, want, desire; *nt* wish, desire; ~ **til lykke** congratulate

ønskelig (*urns*-ker-li) *adj* desirable

øre (*ūr*-rer) *nt* ear

øredobb (*ūr*-rer-dob) *m* earring

øreverk (*ūr*-rer-værk) *m* earache

ørken (*urr*-kern) *m* desert

ørn (*ūrn*) c eagle

ørret (*urr*-rert) m trout

øsregn (*ūrss*-rayn) nt downpour

øst (urst) m east

Østerrike (*urss*-ter-ree-ker) Austria

østerriker (*urss*-ter-ree-kerr) m Austrian

østerriksk (*urss*-ter-reeksk) adj Austrian

østers (*urss*-tersh) m (pl ∼) oyster

østlig (*urst*-li) adj eastern

østre (*urst*-rer) adj eastern

øve (*ūr*-ver) v exercise; ∼ seg practise

øvelse (*ūr*v-erl-ser) m exercise

øverst (*ūr*-versht) adj top

øvre (*ūr*-rer) adj upper

for øvrig (for *ūr*v-ri) moreover

øy (ur^ew) c island

øye (*urew*-er) nt (pl øyne) eye

øyeblikk (*urew*-er-blik) nt instant, second, moment

øyeblikkelig (ur^ew-er-*blik*-li) adv instantly, immediately; adj immediate

øyenbryn (*urew*-ern-brēwn) nt (pl ∼) eyebrow

øyenbrynsblyant (*urew*-ern-brēwns-blew-ahnt) m eyebrow pencil

øyenlege (*urew*-ern-*lay*-ger) m oculist

øyenlokk (*urew*-ern-lok) nt eyelid

øyenskygge (*urew*-ern-shew-ger) m eye shadow

øyensverte (*urew*-ern-svæ-ter) c mascara

øyensynlig (ur^ew-ern-*sēwn*-li) adv apparently

øyenvippe (*urew*-ern-vi-per) m eyelash

øyenvitne (*urew*-ern-vit-ner) nt eye-witness

Å

åbor (*ob*-boor) m bass, perch

åk (awk) nt yoke

åker (*aw*-kerr) m (pl åkrer) field

ål (awl) m eel

ånd (onn) m spirit; ghost

åndedrett (*on*-der-dreht) nt breathing, respiration

åndelig (*on*-der-li) adj spiritual

åpen (*aw*-pern) adj open

åpenbare (*aw*-pern-baa-rer) v reveal

åpenbart (*aw*-pern-baat) adv apparently

åpenhjertig (*aw*-pern-^yæ-ti) adj open

åpne (*awp*-ner) v open; *undo

åpning (*awp*-ning) *c* opening; breach, gap

åpningstid (*awp*-nings-teed) *c* business hours

år (awr) *nt* year; per ~ per annum

årbok (*awr*-book) *c* (pl -bøker) annual

åre (*aw*-rer) *c* oar; vein

åreknute (*aw*-rer-knew-ter) *m* varicose vein

århundre (*awr*-hewn-drer) *nt* century

årlig (*aw*-li) *adj* yearly, annual

årsak (*aw*-shaak) *c* reason, cause

årsdag (*awsh*-daag) *m* anniversary

årstid (*awsh*-teed) *c* season

årvåken (*awr*-vaw-kern) *adj* vigilant

åtte (*ot*-ter) *num* eight

åttende (*ot*-ter-ner) *num* eighth

åtti (*ot*-ti) *num* eighty

English–Norwegian
Engelsk–Norsk

A

a [ei, ə] *art* (an) en; ei; et *art*

abbey ['æbi] *n* abbedi *nt*

abbreviation [ə,briːviˈeiʃən] *n* forkortelse *m*

ability [əˈbiləti] *n* dyktighet *c*; evne *c*

able ['eibəl] *adj* i stand til, dyktig; *be ~ to *være i stand til; *kunne

aboard [əˈbɔːd] *adv* om bord

abolish [əˈbɔliʃ] *v* avskaffe

abortion [əˈbɔːʃən] *n* abort *m*

about [əˈbaut] *prep* om; angående; rundt; *adv* omtrent, omkring

above [əˈbʌv] *prep* over; ovenfor; *adv* over; ovenfor

abroad [əˈbrɔːd] *adv* utenlands

abscess ['æbses] *n* byll *m*

absence ['æbsəns] *n* fravær *nt*

absent ['æbsənt] *adj* fraværende

absolutely ['æbsəluːtli] *adv* absolutt

abstain from [əbˈstein] *avholde seg fra

abstract ['æbstrækt] *adj*

abstrakt

absurd [əbˈsəːd] *adj* urimelig, absurd

abundance [əˈbʌndəns] *n* overflod *m*

abundant [əˈbʌndənt] *adj* rikelig

abuse [əˈbjuːs] *n* misbruk *nt*

academy [əˈkædəmi] *n* akademi *nt*

accelerate [əkˈseləreit] *v* akselerere, øke farten

accelerator [əkˈseləreitə] *n* gasspedal *m*

accent ['æksənt] *n* aksent *m*; betoning *c*

accept [əkˈsept] *v* akseptere, *ta imot, *motta

access ['ækses] *n* tilgang *m*

accessible [əkˈsesəbəl] *adj* tilgjengelig

accessories [əkˈsesəriz] *pl* tilbehør *nt*

accident ['æksidənt] *n* ulykke *c*, uhell *nt*

accidental [,æksiˈdentəl] *adj* tilfeldig

accommodate [əˈkɔmədeit] *v* tilpasse; skaffe husrom

accommodation [ə,kɔməˈdeiʃən] *n* husrom

nt, losji *nt*

accompany [əˈkʌmpəni] *v*
følge; akkompagnere

accomplish [əˈkʌmpliʃ] *v*
fullende; fullføre

accordance: in ~ with [in
əˈkɔːdəns wið] i
overensstemmelse med

according to [əˈkɔːdiŋ tuː]
ifølge; i overensstemmelse
med

account [əˈkaunt] *n* konto
m; redegjørelse *m*; **~ for**
avlegge regnskap for; **on ~**
of på grunn av

accurate [ˈækjurət] *adj*
nøyaktig

accuse [əˈkjuːz] *v* beskylde;
anklage

accused [əˈkjuːzd] *n*
anklagede *m*

accustom [əˈkʌstəm] *v*
venne; **accustomed** vant

ache [eik] *v* verke; *n* verk *m*

achieve [əˈtʃiːv] *v* oppnå;
prestere

achievement [əˈtʃiːvmənt]
n prestasjon *m*

acknowledge [əkˈnɒlidʒ] *v*
erkjenne; innrømme;
bekrefte

acne [ˈækni] *n* filipens *m*

acorn [ˈeikɔːn] *n* eikenøtt *c*

acquaintance
[əˈkweintəns] *n* bekjent *m*

acquire [əˈkwaiə] *v* erverve

acquisition [ˌækwiˈziʃən] *n*
ervervelse *m*

acquittal [əˈkwitəl] *n*
frifinnelse *m*

across [əˈkrɒs] *prep* over;
på den andre siden av; *adv*
på den andre siden

act [ækt] *n* handling *c*; akt
m; nummer *nt*; *v* handle,
oppføre seg; spille

action [ˈækʃən] *n* handling
c, aksjon *m*

active [ˈæktiv] *adj* aktiv;
virksom

activewear [ˈæktiˌweə] *n*
sportsklær *pl*

activity [ækˈtivəti] *n*
aktivitet *m*

actor [ˈæktə] *n* skuespiller
m

actress [ˈæktris] *n*
skuespiller *m*

actual [ˈæktʃuəl] *adj* faktisk,
virkelig

actually [ˈæktʃuəli] *adv*
faktisk

acute [əˈkjuːt] *adj* akutt

adapt [əˈdæpt] *v* tilpasse

adaptor [əˈdæptə] *n* adapter
m

add [æd] *v* *legge sammen;
tilføye

addition [əˈdiʃən] *n*
addisjon *m*; tilføyelse *m*

additional [əˈdiʃənəl] *adj*
ekstra; ytterligere

address [əˈdres] *n* adresse
c; *v* adressere; henvende
seg til

addressee [ˌædreˈsiː] *n*
adressat *m*

adequate [ˈædikwət] *adj*
tilstrekkelig; passende,
adekvat

adjective ['ædʒiktiv] n
adjektiv nt
adjust [ə'dʒʌst] v justere;
tilpasse
administer [əd'ministə] v
bestyre; tildele
administration
[əd,mini'streiʃən] n
administrasjon m; ledelse
m
administrative
[əd'ministrətiv] adj
administrerende;
forvaltende; ~ law
forvaltningsrett m
admiration [,ædmə'reiʃən]
n beundring c
admire [əd'maiə] v beundre
admission [əd'miʃən] n
adgang m; opptak nt
admit [əd'mit] v *oppta;
innrømme, erkjenne
admittance [əd'mitəns] n
adgang m; no ~ adgang
forbudt
adopt [ə'dɒpt] v adoptere;
*vedta
adorable [ə'dɔːrəbəl] adj
henrivende
adult ['ædʌlt] n voksen m;
adj voksen
advance [əd'vɑːns] n
fremskritt nt; forskudd nt;
v *gjøre fremskritt; betale
på forskudd; in ~ på
forhånd, på forskudd
advanced [əd'vɑːnst] adj
avansert
advantage [əd'vɑːntidʒ] n
fordel m

advantageous
[,ædvən'teidʒəs] adj
fordelaktig
adventure [əd'ventʃə] n
eventyr nt
adverb ['ædvəːb] n adverb
nt
advertisement
[əd'vəːtismənt] n annonse
m
advertising ['ædvətaiziŋ] n
reklame m
advice [əd'vais] n råd nt
advise [əd'vaiz] v råde
advocate ['ædvəkət] n
talsmann m
aerial ['eəriəl] n antenne c
aeroplane ['eərəplein] n fly
nt
affair [ə'feə] n anliggende
nt; affære m, forhold nt
affect [ə'fekt] v påvirke;
vedrøre
affected [ə'fektid] adj
affektert
affection [ə'fekʃən] n
hengivenhet c
affectionate [ə'fekʃənit] adj
hengiven, kjærlig
affiliated [ə'filieitid] adj
tilsluttet
affirm [ə'fəːm] v bedyre;
bekrefte
affirmative [ə'fəːmətiv] adj
bekreftende
afford [ə'fɔːd] v *ha råd til
afraid [ə'freid] adj redd,
engstelig; *be ~ *være redd
Africa ['æfrikə] Afrika
African ['æfrikən] adj

afrikansk; *n* afrikaner *m*

after ['ɑːftə] *prep* etter; *conj* etter at

afternoon [,ɑːftə'nuːn] *n* ettermiddag *m*; **this** ~ **i** ettermiddag

afterwards ['ɑːftəwədz] *adv* senere; etterpå

again [ə'gen] *adv* igjen; ~ **and again** gang på gang

against [ə'genst] *prep* mot

age [eidʒ] *n* alder *m*; alderdom *m*; **of** ~ myndig; **under** ~ umyndig

aged ['eidʒid] *adj* gammel

agency ['eidʒənsi] *n* agentur *m*; byrå *nt*

agenda [ə'dʒendə] *n* dagsorden *m*

agent ['eidʒənt] *n* agent *m*, representant *m*

aggressive [ə'gresiv] *adj* aggressiv

ago [ə'gou] *adv* for ... siden

agree [ə'griː] *v* *være enig; *gå med på; stemme overens

agreeable [ə'griːəbəl] *adj* behagelig

agreement [ə'griːmənt] *n* kontrakt *m*; overenskomst *m*, avtale *m*; overensstemmelse *m*

agriculture ['ægrikʌltʃə] *n* jordbruk *nt*

ahead [ə'hed] *adv* fremover; ~ **of** foran; *go ~ *gå videre; **straight** ~ rett frem

aid [eid] *n* hjelp *c*; *v* *hjelpe, *bistå

AIDS [eidz] *n* AIDS

aim [eim] *n* sikte *nt*; ~ **at** rette mot, sikte på; strebe etter, *ta sikte på

air [ɛə] *n* luft *c*; *v* lufte

airbag ['ɛə bæg] *n* airbag *m*

air conditioning ['ɛəkən,diʃəniŋ] *n* luftkondisjonering *c*; **air-conditioned** *adj* luftkondisjonert

airfield ['ɛəfiːld] *n* flyplass *m*

airline ['ɛəlain] *n* flyselskap *nt*

airmail ['ɛəmeil] *n* luftpost *m*

airplane ['ɛəplein] *nAm* fly *nt*

airport ['ɛəpɔːt] *n* lufthavn *c*, flyplass *m*

airsickness ['ɛə,siknəs] *n* luftsyke *m*

airtight ['ɛətait] *adj* lufttett

airy ['ɛəri] *adj* luftig

aisle [ail] *n* sideskip *nt*; midtgang *m*

alarm [ə'lɑːm] *n* alarm *m*; *v* alarmere, forurolige; ~ **clock** vekkeklokke *c*

album ['ælbəm] *n* album *nt*

alcohol ['ælkəhɔl] *n* alkohol *m*

alcoholic [,ælkə'hɔlik] *adj* alkoholholdig

ale [eil] *n* øl *nt*

algebra ['ældʒibrə] *n* algebra *m*

Algeria [æl'dʒiəriə] Algerie *n*

Algerian [æl'dʒiəriən] *adj*

algerisk; n algerier m

alien ['eilian] n utlending m; adj utenlandsk

alike [ə'laik] adj likedan, lik; adv likedan

alive [ə'laiv] adj levende

all [ɔːl] adj all; ~ in alt inkludert; ~ right! fint!, årlreit; at ~ overhodet

allergic [ə'ləʒik] adj allergisk

allergy ['ælədʒi] n allergi m

alley ['æli] n smug nt

alliance [ə'laiəns] n allianse m

allow [ə'lau] v *tillate, bevilge; ~ to *la; *be allowed *være tillatt; *be allowed to *ha lov til

allowance [ə'lauəns] n bidrag nt

almond ['ɑːmənd] n mandel m

almost ['ɔːlmoust] adv nesten

alone [ə'loun] adv alene

along [ə'lɔŋ] prep langs

aloud [ə'laud] adv høyt

alphabet ['ælfəbet] n alfabet nt

already [ɔːl'redi] adv allerede

also ['ɔːlsou] adv også; dessuten, likeledes

altar ['ɔːltə] n alter nt

alter ['ɔːltə] v forandre, endre

alteration [ˌɔːltə'reiʃən] n forandring c, endring c

alternate [ɔːl'təːnət] adj

vekselvis

alternative [ɔːl'təːnətiv] n alternativ nt

although [ɔːl'ðou] conj skjønt

altitude ['æltitjuːd] n høyde m

alto ['æltou] n (pl ~s) alt m

altogether [ˌɔːltə'geðə] adv fullstendig; i det hele

always ['ɔːlweiz] adv alltid

am [æm] v (pr be)

amaze [ə'meiz] v forbause, forundre

amazement [ə'meizmənt] n forbauselse m

amazing [ə'meiziŋ] adj forbausende

ambassador [æm'bæsədə] n ambassadør m

amber ['æmbə] n rav nt

ambiguous [æm'bigjuəs] adj tvetydig

ambition [æm'biʃən] n ærgjerrighet c

ambitious [æm'biʃəs] adj ærgjerrig

ambulance ['æmbjuləns] n ambulanse m, sykebil m

ambush ['æmbuʃ] n bakhold nt

America [ə'merikə] n Amerika

American [ə'merikən] adj amerikansk; n amerikaner m

amethyst ['æmiθist] n ametyst m

amid [ə'mid] prep blant, midt i

ammonia [ə'məuniə] n
salmiakk m

amnesty ['æmnisti] n
amnesti m

among [ə'mʌŋ] prep blant,
mellom; ~ other things
blant annet

amount [ə'maunt] n
mengde m; beløp nt, sum
m; ~ to *beløpe seg til

amuse [ə'mju:z] v more,
*underholde

amusement [ə'mju:zmənt]
n fornøyelse m, atspredelse
m

amusing [ə'mju:ziŋ] adj
morsom, gøyal

anaemia [ə'ni:miə] n anemi
m

anaesthesia [,ænis'θi:ziə] n
bedøvelse m

anaesthetic [,ænis'θetik] n
bedøvelsesmiddel nt

analyse ['ænəlaiz] v
analysere

analysis [ə'næləsis] n (pl
-ses) analyse m

analyst ['ænəlist] n
analytiker m;
psykoanalytiker m

anarchy ['ænəki] n anarki nt

anatomy [ə'nætəmi] n
anatomi m

ancestor ['ænsestə] n
forfader m

anchor ['æŋkə] n anker nt

anchovy ['æntʃəvi] n ansjos
m

ancient ['einʃənt] adj
gammel; foreldet,

gammeldags; urtids-

and [ænd, ənd] conj og

angel ['eindʒəl] n engel m

anger ['æŋgə] n sinne nt;
raseri m

angle ['æŋgəl] v fiske; n
vinkel m

angry ['æŋgri] adj sint

animal ['æniməl] n dyr nt

ankle ['æŋkəl] n ankel m

annex[1] ['æneks] n anneks
nt; tillegg nt

annex[2] [ə'neks] v annektere

anniversary [,æni'və:səri] n
årsdag m, bryllupsdag m

announce [ə'nauns] v
*kunngjøre, *bekjentgjøre

announcement
[ə'naunsmənt] n
kunngjøring c,
bekjentgjørelse m

annoy [ə'nɔi] v ergre,
irritere

annoyance [ə'nɔiəns] n
ergrelse m

annoying [ə'nɔiiŋ] adj
ergerlig, irriterende

annual ['ænjuəl] adj årlig; n
årbok c

anonymous [ə'nɔniməs] adj
anonym

another [ə'nʌðə] adj en til;
en annen

answer ['ɑ:nsə] v svare;
besvare; n svar nt

answering machine
['ɑ:nsəriŋ mə'ʃi:n] n
telefonsvarer m

ant [ænt] n maur m

antibiotic [, æntibai'ɔtik] n

appreciate

antibiotikum *nt*

anticipate [æn'tisipeit] *v*
*forutse, *foregripe

antifreeze ['æntifri:z] *n*
frysevæske *c*

antipathy [æn'tipəθi] *n*
motvilje *c*

antique [æn'ti:k] *adj* antikk;
n antikvitet *m*; ~ dealer
antikvitetshandler *m*

anxiety [æŋ'zaiəti] *n*
bekymring *c*

anxious ['æŋkʃəs] *adj* ivrig;
engstelig

any ['eni] *adj* hvilke som
helst

anybody ['enibɔdi] *pron*
hvem som helst

anyhow ['enihau] *adv* på
hvilken som helst måte

anyone ['eniwʌn] *pron*
enhver

anything ['eniθiŋ] *pron* hva
som helst

anyway ['eniwei] *adv* i hvert
fall

anywhere ['eniwɛə] *adv*
hvor som helst

apart [ə'pa:t] *adv* atskilt,
separat; ~ from bortsett fra

apartment [ə'pa:tmənt]
nAm leilighet *c*; ~ house
Am leiegård *m*

aperitif [ə'perətiv] *n*
aperitiff *m*

apologize [ə'pɔlədʒaiz] *v*
*be om unnskyldning

apology [ə'pɔlədʒi] *n*
unnskyldning *m*

apparatus [ˌæpə'reitəs] *n*
apparat *nt*

apparent [ə'pærənt] *adj*
tilsynelatende; tydelig

apparently [ə'pærəntli] *adv*
åpenbart; øyensynlig

appeal [ə'pi:l] *n* appell *m*

appear [ə'piə] *v* *se ut til;
synes; *fremgå; vise seg;
*fremtre

appearance [ə'piərəns] *n*
fremtoning *m*; utseende *nt*;
opptreden *m*

appendicitis
[əˌpendi'saitis] *n*
blindtarmbetennelse *m*

appendix [ə'pendiks] *n* (pl
-dices, -dixes) blindtarm *m*

appetite ['æpətait] *n* matlyst
c, appetitt *m*

appetizer ['æpətaizə] *n*
appetittvekker *m*

appetizing ['æpətaiziŋ] *adj*
appetittlig

applause [ə'plɔ:z] *n*
applaus *m*

applaud [ə'plɔ:d] *v*
applaudere

apple ['æpəl] *n* eple *nt*

appliance [ə'plaiəns] *n*
apparat *nt*

application [ˌæpli'keiʃən] *n*
anvendelse *m*; søknad *m*

apply [ə'plai] *v* anvende,
bruke; søke; *gjelde

appoint [ə'pɔint] *v* utnevne

appointment [ə'pɔintmənt]
n avtale *m*, møte *nt*;
utnevnelse *m*

appreciate [ə'pri:ʃieit] *v*
*verdsette; påskjønne

appreciation [ə‚priːʃiˈeiʃən] *n* vurdering *c*; verdsettelse *m*

apprentice [əˈprentis] *n* lærling *m*

approach [əˈproutʃ] *v* nærme seg; *n* fremgangsmåte *m*

appropriate [əˈproupriət] *adj* formålstjenlig, passende, rett

approval [əˈpruːvəl] *n* godkjennelse *m*; billigelse *m*

approve [əˈpruːv] *v* godkjenne

approximate [əˈprɔksimət] *adj* omtrentlig

approximately [əˈprɔksimətli] *adv* cirka, omtrent

apricot [ˈeiprikɔt] *n* aprikos *m*

April [ˈeiprəl] april

apron [ˈeiprən] *n* forkle *nt*

Arab [ˈærəb] *adj* arabisk; *n* araber *m*

arbitrary [ˈɑːbitrəri] *adj* vilkårlig

arcade [ɑːˈkeid] *n* buegang *m*, arkade *m*

arch [ɑːtʃ] *n* bue *m*; hvelv *nt*

archaeologist [‚ɑːkiˈɔlədʒist] *n* arkeolog *m*

archaeology [‚ɑːkiˈɔlədʒi] *n* arkeologi *m*

arched [ɑːtʃt] *adj* bueformet

architect [ˈɑːkitekt] *n*

arkitekt *m*

architecture [ˈɑːkitektʃə] *n* byggekunst *m*, arkitektur *m*

archives [ˈɑːkaivz] *pl* arkiv *nt*

are [ɑː] *v* (pr be)

area [ˈɛəriə] *n* område *nt*; areal *m*; ~ **code** retningsnummer *nt*

Argentina [‚ɑːdʒənˈtiːnə] Argentina

Argentinian [‚ɑːdʒənˈtiniən] *adj* argentinsk; *n* argentiner *m*

argue [ˈɑːgjuː] *v* diskutere, debattere, argumentere; trette

argument [ˈɑːgjumənt] *n* argument *nt*; diskusjon *m*

*arise [əˈraiz] *v* *oppstå

arithmetic [əˈriθmətik] *n* regning *c*

arm [ɑːm] *n* arm *m*; våpen *nt*; *v* bevæpne

armchair [ˈɑːmtʃɛə] *n* lenestol *m*

armed [ɑːmd] *adj* bevæpnet; ~ **forces** væpnede styrker

armour [ˈɑːmə] *n* rustning *m*

army [ˈɑːmi] *n* armé *m*

aroma [əˈroumə] *n* aroma *m*

around [əˈraund] *prep* omkring; *adv* rundt

arrange [əˈreindʒ] *v* ordne; arrangere

arrangement [əˈreindʒmənt] *n* ordning *c*

arrest [əˈrest] *v* arrestere; *n* arrestasjon *m*, pågripelse

m

arrival [ə'raivəl] *n* ankomst *m*

arrive [ə'raiv] *v* *ankomme

arrow ['ærou] *n* pil *c*

art [ɑːt] *n* kunst *m*; ~ kunstferdighet *m*; ~ collection kunstsamling *m*; ~ exhibition kunstutstilling *c*; ~ gallery kunstgalleri *nt*; ~ history kunsthistorie *c*; arts and crafts kunst og håndverk; ~ school kunstakademi *nt*

artery ['ɑːtəri] *n* pulsåre *c*

artichoke ['ɑːtitʃouk] *n* artisjokk *m*

article ['ɑːtikəl] *n* gjenstand *m*; artikkel *m*

artificial [,ɑːti'fiʃəl] *adj* kunstig

artist ['ɑːtist] *n* kunstner *m*

artistic [ɑː'tistik] *adj* kunstnerisk, artistisk

as [æz] *conj* liksom, som; like; fordi, ettersom; ~ from fra; fra og med; ~ if som om; ~ som om

asbestos [æz'bestɔs] *n* asbest *m*

ascend [ə'send] *v* *stige; *stige opp; *bestige

ascent [ə'sent] *n* stigning *m*; oppstigning *m*

ascertain [,æsə'tein] *v* konstatere; forvisse seg om, *fastslå

ash [æʃ] *n* aske *c*

ashamed [ə'ʃeimd] *adj* skamfull; *be ~ skamme

seg

ashore [ə'ʃɔː] *adv* i land

ashtray ['æʃtrei] *n* askebeger *nt*

Asia ['eiʃə] Asia

Asian ['eiʃən] *adj* asiatisk; *n* asiat *m*

aside [ə'said] *adv* til siden, til side

ask [ɑːsk] *v* *spørre; *be; *invitere

asleep [ə'sliːp] *adj* sovende

asparagus [ə'spærəgəs] *n* asparges *m*

aspect ['æspekt] *n* utseende *nt*; aspekt *nt*

asphalt ['æsfælt] *n* asfalt *m*

aspire [ə'spaiə] *v* strebe

aspirin ['æspərin] *n* aspirin *m*

assassination [ə,sæsi'neiʃən] *n* mord *nt*

assault [ə'sɔːlt] *v* *angripe; *overfalle

assemble [ə'sembəl] *v* samle, *sette sammen

assembly [ə'sembli] *n* forsamling *c*, sammenkomst *m*

assignment [ə'sainmənt] *n* oppdrag *nt*

assign to [ə'sain] *v* tildele; *tilskrive

assist [ə'sist] *v* *bistå, *hjelpe; ~ at *hjelpe til med

assistance [ə'sistəns] *n* hjelp *c*; assistanse *m*, understøttelse *m*

assistant [ə'sistənt] *n*

assistent *m*

associate[1] [ə'souʃiət] *n*
partner *m*, kompanjong *m*;
forbundsfelle *m*; medlem
nt

associate[2] [ə'souʃieit] *v*
*forbinde; ~ with *omgås

association [ə,sousi'eiʃən]
n forening *c*

assort [ə'sɔ:t] *v* sortere

assortment [ə'sɔ:tmənt] *n*
utvalg *nt*, sortiment *nt*

assume [ə'sju:m] *v* *anta,
formode

assure [ə'ʃuə] *v* forsikre

asthma ['æsmə] *n* astma *m*

astonish [ə'stɔniʃ] *v*
forbløffe, forbause

astonishing [ə'stɔniʃiŋ] *adj*
forbausende

astonishment
[ə'stɔniʃmənt] *n*
forbauselse *m*

astronaut ['æstrənɔːt] *n*
astronaut *m*

astronomy [ə'strɔnəmi] *n*
astronomi *m*

asylum [ə'sailəm] *n* asyl *nt*

at [æt] *prep* på, hos, i

ate [et] *v* (p eat)

atheist ['eiθiist] *n* ateist *m*

athlete ['æθliːt] *n*
idrettsutøver *m*

athletics [æθ'letiks] *pl*
friidrett *m*

Atlantic [ət'læntik]
Atlanterhavet

ATM [,eiti'em] *n* minibank
m

atmosphere ['ætməsfiə] *n*

atmosfære *m*; stemning *m*

atom ['ætəm] *n* atom *nt*

atomic [ə'tɔmik] *adj* atom-

atomizer ['ætəmaizə] *n*
sprayflaske *c*; spray *m*,
vaporisator *m*

attach [ə'tætʃ] *v* feste;
*vedlegge; **attached to**
knyttet til

attachment [ə'tætʃmənt] *n*
vedlegg *m*

attack [ə'tæk] *v* *angripe; *n*
angrep *nt*

attain [ə'tein] *v* oppnå

attainable [ə'teinəbəl] *adj*
oppnåelig

attempt [ə'tempt] *v* forsøke,
prøve; *n* forsøk *nt*

attend [ə'tend] *v* overvære;
~ **on** betjene; ~ **to** *ta hånd
om, *ta seg av; *være
oppmerksom på

attendance [ə'tendəns] *n*
deltakelse *m*

attendant [ə'tendənt] *n* vakt
c

attention [ə'tenʃən] *n*
oppmerksomhet *c*; *pay ~
*være oppmerksom

attentive [ə'tentiv] *adj*
oppmerksom

attest [ə'test] *v* attestere,
bevitne

attic ['ætik] *n* loft *nt*

attitude ['ætitjuːd] *n*
holdning *m*

attorney [ə'tɔːni] *n* advokat
m

attract [ə'trækt] *v* *tiltrekke

attraction [ə'trækʃən] *n*

attraksjon *m*; tiltrekning *m*, sjarm *m*

attractive [ə'træktiv] *adj* tiltrekkende

auction ['ɔːkʃən] *n* auksjon *m*

audible ['ɔːdibəl] *adj* hørbar

audience ['ɔːdiəns] *n* publikum *nt*

auditor ['ɔːditə] *n* tilhører *m*

auditorium [,ɔːdi'tɔːriəm] *n* auditorium *nt*

August ['ɔːgəst] august

aunt [ɑːnt] *n* tante *c*

Australia [ɔ'streiliə] Australia

Australian [ɔ'streiliən] *adj* australsk; *n* australier *m*

Austria ['ɔstriə] Østerrike

Austrian ['ɔstriən] *adj* østerriksk; *n* østerriker *m*

authentic [ɔː'θentik] *adj* autentisk; ekte

author ['ɔːθə] *n* forfatter *m*

authoritarian [ɔː,θɔri'teəriən] *adj* autoritær

authority [ɔː'θɔrəti] *n* autoritet *m*; myndighet *c*

authorization [,ɔːθərai'zeiʃən] *n* tillatelse *m*; autorisasjon *m*

automatic [,ɔːtə'mætik] *adj* automatisk; ~ teller minibank *m*

automation [,ɔːtə'meiʃən] *n* automatisering *c*

automobile ['ɔːtəməbiːl] *n* bil *m*; ~ club

automobilklubb *m*

autonomous [ɔː'tɔnəməs] *adj* selvstyrt

autopsy ['ɔːtɔpsi] *n* obduksjon *m*

autumn ['ɔːtəm] *n* høst *m*

available [ə'veiləbəl] *adj* tilgjengelig, disponibel, for hånden

avalanche ['ævəlɑːnʃ] *n* snøskred *nt*

avenue ['ævənjuː] *n* aveny *m*; gate *c*

average ['ævəridʒ] *adj* gjennomsnittlig; *n* gjennomsnitt *nt*; on the ~ i gjennomsnitt

averse [ə'vəːs] *adj* uvillig

aversion [ə'vəːʃən] *n* motvilje *m*

avoid [ə'vɔid] *v* *unngå; *unnvike

await [ə'weit] *v* vente på, avvente

awake [ə'weik] *adj* våken

***awake** [ə'weik] *v* vekke

award [ə'wɔːd] *n* pris *m*; *v* tildele

aware [ə'weə] *adj* klar over

away [ə'wei] *adv* bort; *go ~ reise bort

awful ['ɔːfəl] *adj* forferdelig, redselsfull

awkward ['ɔːkwəd] *adj* pinlig; klosset

awning ['ɔːniŋ] *n* markise *m*

axe [æks] *n* øks *c*

axle ['æksəl] *n* aksel *m*

B

baby ['beibi] n baby m; ~ carriage Am barnevogn c

babysitter ['beibi,sitə] n barnevakt c

bachelor ['bætʃələ] n ungkar m

back [bæk] n rygg m; adv tilbake; *go ~ vende tilbake

backache ['bækeik] n ryggsmerter pl

backbone ['bækboun] n ryggrad m

background ['bækgraund] n bakgrunn m

backwards ['bækwədz] adv baklengs

bacon ['beikən] n bacon nt

bacterium [bæk'ti:riəm] n (pl -ria) bakterie m

bad [bæd] adj dårlig; alvorlig; slem

bag [bæg] n pose m; veske c, håndveske c; reiseveske c

baggage ['bægidʒ] n bagasje m; ~ deposit office Am bagasjeoppbevaring c; hand ~ håndbagasje m

bail [beil] n kausjon m

bait [beit] n agn nt

bake [beik] v bake

baker ['beikə] n baker m

bakery ['beikəri] n bakeri nt

balance ['bæləns] n likevekt c; balanse m; saldo m

balcony ['bælkəni] n balkong m

bald [bɔːld] adj skallet

ball [bɔːl] n ball m; ball nt

ballet ['bælei] n ballett m

balloon [bə'luːn] n ballong m

ballpoint pen ['bɔːlpɔintpen] n kulepenn m

banana [bə'nɑːnə] n banan m

band [bænd] n orkester nt; bånd nt

bandage ['bændidʒ] n bandasje m

bank [bæŋk] n bredd m; bank m; v *sette i banken; ~ account bankkonto m

banknote ['bæŋknout] n pengeseddel m

bank rate ['bæŋkreit] n diskonto m

bankrupt ['bæŋkrʌpt] adj konkurs, fallitt

banner ['bænə] n banner nt

banquet ['bæŋkwit] n bankett m

baptism ['bæptizəm] n dåp m

baptize [bæp'taiz] v døpe

bar [baː] n bar m; stang c

barbecue ['baːbikjuː] n grillfest m, grilling c; v grille

barbed wire ['baːbd waiə] n piggtråd m

barber ['baːbə] n frisør m

bare [beə] *adj* naken, bar

barely ['beəli] *adv* så vidt

bargain ['bɑːgin] *n* godt kjøp; *v* *kjøpslå, prute

baritone ['bæritoun] *n* baryton *m*

bark [bɑːk] *n* bark *m*; *v* gjø

barley ['bɑːli] *n* bygg *nt*

barn [bɑːn] *n* låve *m*

barometer [bə'rɔmitə] *n* barometer *nt*

baroque [bə'rɔk] *adj* barokk

barracks ['bærəks] *pl* kaserne *m*

barrel ['bærəl] *n* fat *nt*, tønne *c*

barrier ['bæriə] *n* barriere *m*; bom *m*

barrister ['bæristə] *n* advokat *m*

bartender ['bɑː,tendə] *n* bartender *m*

base [beis] *n* base *m*, basis *m*; fundament *nt*; *v* basere

baseball ['beisbɔːl] *n* baseball *m*

basement ['beismənt] *n* kjelleretasje *m*

basic ['beisik] *adj* grunnleggende; basics *npl* grunnlag *nt* / *pl*

basilica [bə'zilikə] *n* basilika *m*

basin ['beisən] *n* bolle *m*

basis ['beisis] *n* (pl bases) basis *m*, grunnlag *nt*

basket ['bɑːskit] *n* kurv *m*

bass[1] [beis] *n* bass *m*

bass[2] [bæs] *n* (pl ~) åbor *m*

bastard ['bɑːstəd] *n* bastard *m*; skurk *m*

batch [bætʃ] *n* bunke *m*

bath [bɑːθ] *n* bad *nt*; ~ towel badehåndkle *nt*

bathe [beið] *v* bade

bathing cap ['beiðiŋkæp] *n* badehette *c*

bathing suit ['beiðiŋsuːt] *n* badedrakt *c*; badebukse *c*

bathrobe ['bɑːθroub] *n* badekåpe *c*

bathroom ['bɑːθruːm] *n* bad *nt*, badeværelse *nt*; toalett *nt*

batter ['bætə] *n* deig *m*

battery ['bætəri] *n* batteri *nt*

battle ['bætəl] *n* slag *nt*; kamp *m*, strid *m*; *v* kjempe

bay [bei] *n* bukt *c*; *v* gjø

*be [biː] *v* *være

beach [biːtʃ] *n* strand *c*; nudist ~ nudistbadestrand *c*

bead [biːd] *n* perle *c*; beads *pl* perlekjede *nt*; rosenkrans *m*

beak [biːk] *n* nebb *nt*

beam [biːm] *n* stråle *m*; bjelke *m*

bean [biːn] *n* bønne *c*

bear [beə] *n* bjørn *m*

*bear [beə] *v* *bære; tåle; *holde ut

beard [biəd] *n* skjegg *nt*

bearer ['beərə] *n* innehaver *m*

beast [biːst] *n* dyr *nt*; ~ of prey rovdyr *nt*

beat [biːt] *n* rytme *m*; slag *nt*

*beat [biːt] *v* *slå

beautiful ['bju:tifəl] *adj*
vakker

beauty ['bju:ti] *n* skjønnhet
c; ~ parlo/u/r *n*
skjønnhetssalong *m*; ~
treatment skjønnhetspleie
m

beaver ['bi:və] *n* bever *m*

because [bi'kɔz] *conj* fordi;
ettersom; ~ of på grunn av

*become [bi'kʌm] *v* *bli; kle

bed [bed] *n* seng *c*; ~ and
board kost og losji,
helpensjon *m*; ~ and
breakfast værelse med
frokost

bedding ['bediŋ] *n* sengetøy
nt

bedroom ['bedru:m] *n*
soveværelse *nt*

bee [bi:] *n* bie *c*

beech [bi:tʃ] *n* bøk *m*

beef [bi:f] *n* oksekjøtt *nt*

beefburger [bi:fbə:gə] *n*
hamburger *m*

beehive ['bi:haiv] *n* bikube
m

been [bi:n] *v* (pp be)

beer [biə] *n* øl *nt*

beetle ['bi:təl] *n* bille *m*

beetroot ['bi:tru:t] *n*
rødbete *c*

before [bi'fɔ:] *prep* før;
foran; *conj* før; *adv*
tidligere

beg [beg] *v* tigge;
*bønnfalle; *be

beggar ['begə] *n* tigger *m*

*begin [bi'gin] *v* begynne;
starte

beginner [bi'ginə] *n*
nybegynner *m*

beginning [bi'giniŋ] *n*
begynnelse *m*; start *m*

behalf: on ~ of [ɔn bi'hɑ:f
ɔv] på vegne av; til fordel
for

behave [bi'heiv] *v* oppføre
seg

behavio/u/r [bi'heivjə] *n*
oppførsel *m*

behind [bi'haind] *prep* bak;
adv bak

beige [beiʒ] *adj* beige

being ['bi:iŋ] *n* vesen *nt*

Belgian ['beldʒən] *adj*
belgisk; *n* belgier *m*

Belgium ['beldʒəm] Belgia

belief [bi'li:f] *n* tro *c*

believe [bi'li:v] *v* tro

bell [bel] *n* klokke *c*;
ringeklokke *c*

bellboy ['belbɔi] *n* pikkolo
m

belly ['beli] *n* mage *m*

belong [bi'lɔŋ] *v* tilhøre

belongings [bi'lɔŋiŋz] *pl*
eiendeler

beloved [bi'lʌvd] *adj* elsket

below [bi'lou] *prep*
nedenfor; under; *adv* nede

belt [belt] *n* belte *nt*

bench [bentʃ] *n* benk *m*

bend [bend] *n* sving *m*,
bøyning *m*; krumning *m*

*bend [bend] *v* bøye; ~
down bøye seg

beneath [bi'ni:θ] *prep*
under; *adv* nede

benefit ['benifit] *n* utbytte

nt; fordel *m*; *v* *ha fordel
av

bent [bent] *adj* (pp bend)
bøyd

berry ['beri] *n* bær *nt*

beside [bi'said] *prep* ved
siden av

besides [bi'saidz] *adv*
dessuten; forresten; *prep*
foruten

best [best] *adj* best

bet [bet] *n* veddemål *nt*;
innsats *m*

***bet** [bet] *v* vedde

betray [bi'trei] *v* forråde

better ['betə] *adj* bedre

between [bi'twi:n] *prep*
mellom

beverage ['bevəridʒ] *n*
drikk *m*

beware [bi'weə] *v* vokte seg

beyond [bi'jɔnd] *prep*
hinsides; på den andre
siden av; ut over; *adv*
bortenfor

bible ['baibəl] *n* bibel *m*

bicycle ['baisikəl] *n* sykkel
m

bid [bid] *n* bud *nt*; tilbud *nt*

***bid** [bid] *v* *tilby; *by

big [big] *adj* stor;
omfangsrik; tykk; viktig

bike [baik] *n colloquial*
sykkel *m*; *v* sykle

bile [bail] *n* galle *m*

bilingual [bai'liŋgwəl] *adj*
tospråklig

bill [bil] *n* regning *c*, nota *m*;
v fakturere

billiards ['biljədz] *pl* biljard

m

billion ['biljən] *n* milliard *m*

***bind** [baind] *v* *binde

binding ['baindiŋ] *n*
bokbind *nt*

binoculars [bi'nɔkjələz] *pl*
kikkert *m*

biodegradable
[,baioudi'greidəbəl] *adj*
biologisk nedbrytbar

biology [bai'ɔlədʒi] *n*
biologi *m*

bipolar [,bai'poulə] *adj*
bipolar

birch [bə:tʃ] *n* bjørk *c*

bird [bə:d] *n* fugl *m*

birth [bə:θ] *n* fødsel *m*

birthday ['bə:θdei] *n*
fødselsdag *m*

biscuit ['biskit] *n* småkake *c*

bishop ['biʃəp] *n* biskop *m*

bit [bit] *n* bit *m*; smule *m*

bitch [bitʃ] *n* tispe *c*

bite [bait] *n* bit *m*; stikk *nt*

***bite** [bait] *v* *bite

bitter ['bitə] *adj* bitter

black [blæk] *adj* svart; ~
market svartebørs *m*

blackberry ['blækbəri] *n*
bjørnebær *c*

Blackberry® ['blækbəri] *n*
Blackberry *c*

blackbird ['blækbə:d] *n*
svarttrost *m*

blackboard ['blækbɔ:d] *n*
tavle *c*

blackcurrant [,blæk'kʌrənt]
n solbær *nt*

blackmail ['blækmeil] *n*
pengeutpresning *m*; *v*

presse penger av
blacksmith ['blæksmiθ] *n* grovsmed *m*
bladder ['blædə] *n* blære *c*
blade [bleid] *n* blad *nt*; ~ of **grass** gresstrå *nt*
blame [bleim] *n* skyld *c*; bebreidelse *m*; *v* klandre, bebreide
blank [blæŋk] *adj* blank
blanket ['blæŋkit] *n* ullteppe *nt*; teppe *nt*
blast [blɑːst] *n* eksplosjon *m*
bleach [bliːtʃ] *v* bleke
bleak [bliːk] *adj* ødslig, barsk
***bleed** [bliːd] *v* blø; flå
bless [bles] *v* velsigne
blessing ['blesiŋ] *n* velsignelse *m*
blind [blaind] *n* persienne *m*, rullegardin *c* / *nt*; *adj* blind; *v* blende
blister ['blistə] *n* blemme *c*, gnagsår *nt*
blizzard ['blizəd] *n* snøstorm *m*
block [blɔk] *v* sperre, blokkere; *n* kloss *m*; kvartal *nt*; ~ of flats leiegård *m*
blog [blɔg] *n* (Nett)blogg *c*
blond [blɔnd] *adj* blond
blonde [blɔnd] *n* blondine *c*, blond person *m*
blood [blʌd] *n* blod *nt*; ~ **poisoning** blodforgiftning *m*; ~ **pressure** blodtrykk *nt*; ~ **vessel** blodkar *nt*
bloody [blʌdi] *adj* blodig;

colloquial fordømt
blossom ['blɔsəm] *n* blomst *m*; *v* blomstre
blot [blɔt] *n* flekk *m*
blouse [blauz] *n* bluse *c*
blow [blou] *n* fik *m*, slag *nt*; vindkast *nt*
***blow** [blou] *v* blåse; ~ **up** sprenge; eksplodere
blowout ['blauaut] *n* punktering *c*; utblåsning *m*
blue [bluː] *adj* blå; nedtrykt
blunt [blʌnt] *adj* sløv; butt
blush [blʌʃ] *v* rødme
board [bɔːd] *n* planke *m*; tavle *c*; oppslagstavle *c*; pensjon *m*; styre *nt*; ~ **and lodging** kost og losji, helpensjon *m*
boardinghouse ['bɔːdiŋhaus] *n* pensjonat *nt*
boarding school ['bɔːdiŋskuːl] *n* pensjonatskole *m*
boast [boust] *v* *skryte
boat [bout] *n* båt *m*, skip *nt*
body ['bɔdi] *n* kropp *m*; legeme *nt*
bodyguard ['bɔdigɑːd] *n* livvakt *c*
body-work ['bɔdiwɜːk] *n* karosseri *m*
bog [bɔg] *n* myr *c*
boil [bɔil] *v* koke; *n* byll *m*
bold [bould] *adj* dristig; frekk
Bolivia [bə'liviə] Bolivia
Bolivian [bə'liviən] *adj* boliviansk; *n* bolivianer *m*

bolt [boult] n slå c; bolt m

bomb [bom] n bombe c; v bombardere

bond [bond] n obligasjon m

bone [boun] n bein nt; fiskebein nt; v skjære ut bein

bonnet ['bonit] n bilpanser nt

book [buk] n bok c; v reservere, bestille; bokføre

booking ['bukiŋ] n bestilling c, reservasjon m

bookmaker ['buk,meikə] n totalisator m

bookseller ['buk,selə] n bokhandler m

bookstand ['bukstænd] n bokstand m

bookstore ['buksto:] n bokhandel m

boot [bu:t] n støvel m; bagasjerom nt

booth [bu:ð] n bu c; bås m

booze [bu:z] n colloquial alkohol m; v drikke alkohol

border ['bo:də] n grense c; kant m

bore¹ [bo:] v kjede; bore; n kjedelig person m

bore² [bo:] v (p bear)

boring ['bo:riŋ] adj kjedelig

born [bo:n] adj født

borrow ['borou] v låne

bosom ['buzəm] n barm m; bryst nt

boss [bos] n boss m, sjef m

botany ['botəni] n botanikk m

both [bouθ] adj begge; both ... and både ... og

bother ['boðə] v plage; bry seg; n bry nt

bottle ['botəl] n flaske c; ~ opener flaskeåpner m; hot-water ~ varmeflaske c

bottleneck ['botəlnek] n flaskehals m

bottom ['botəm] n bunn m; akterspeil nt, bak m; adj underste

bought [bo:t] v (p, pp buy)

boulder ['bouldə] n rullestein m

bound [baund] n grense c; *be ~ to *måtte; ~ for på vei til

boundary ['baundəri] n grense c

bouquet [bu'kei] n bukett m

bourgeois ['buəʒwa:] adj spissborgerlig

boutique [bu'ti:k] n butikk m

bow¹ [bau] v bukke

bow² [bou] n bue m; ~ tie sløyfe c

bowels [bauəlz] pl tarmer

bowl [boul] n bolle m

bowling ['bouliŋ] n bowling m; ~ alley bowlingbane m

box¹ [boks] v bokse; boxing match boksekamp m

box² [boks] n eske c

box office ['boks,ofis] n billettluke c, billettkontor nt

boy [boi] n gutt m; tjener m

boyfriend ['boifrend] n

kjæreste *m*

bra [brɑ:] *n* brystholder *m*,
behå *m*

brace [breis] *n*
(tann-)regulering *c*

bracelet ['breislit] *n*
armbånd *nt*

braces ['breisiz] *pl*
bukseseler *pl*;

brain [brein] *n* hjerne *m*;
forstand *m*;~ **wave** innfall
nt

brake [breik] *n* brems *m*; ~
drum bremsetrommel *m*;~
lights bremselys *pl*

branch [brɑ:ntʃ] *n* gren *m*;
filial *m*

brand [brænd] *n* merke *nt*;
brennemerke *nt*

brand-new [,brænd'nju:]
adj splinter ny

brass [brɑ:s] *n* messing *m*; ~
band hornorkester *nt*

brave [breiv] *adj* modig,
tapper

Brazil [brə'zil] Brasil

Brazilian [brə'ziljən] *adj*
brasiliansk; *n* brasilianer *m*

breach [bri:tʃ] *n* åpning *c*

bread [bred] *n* brød *nt*;
wholemeal ~ helkornbrød
nt

breadth [bredθ] *n* bredde *m*

break [breik] *n* brudd *nt*; *m*
pause *m*; frikvarter *m*

*****break** [breik] *v* *bryte; ~
down *gå i stykker;
inndele

breakdown ['breikdaun] *n*
maskinskade *m*,

motorstopp *m* / *nt*

breakfast ['brekfəst] *n*
frokost *m*

breast [brest] *n* bryst *nt*

breaststroke ['breststrouk]
n brystsvømming *c*

breath [breθ] *n* pust *m*

breathe [bri:ð] *v* puste

breathing ['bri:ðiŋ] *n*
åndedrett *nt*

breed [bri:d] *n* rase *m*; slag
nt

*****breed** [bri:d] *v* ale opp,
oppdrette

breeze [bri:z] *n* bris *m*

brew [bru:] *v* brygge

brewery ['bru:əri] *n*
bryggeri *n*

bribe [braib] *v* *bestikke

bribery ['braibəri] *n*
bestikkelse *m*

brick [brik] *n* murstein *m*

bricklayer ['brikleiə] *n*
murer *m*

bride [braid] *n* brud *c*

bridegroom ['braidgru:m] *n*
brudgom *m*

bridge [bridʒ] *n* bro *c*;
bridge *m*

brief [bri:f] *adj* kort;
kortfattet

briefcase ['bri:fkeis] *n*
dokumentmappe *c*

briefs [bri:fs] *pl* truse *c*

bright [brait] *adj* skinnende;
oppvakt

brighten ['braitən] *v* lyse
opp

brill [bril] *n* slettvar *m*

brilliant ['briljənt] *adj*

strålende; begavet
brim [brim] n rand m
*bring [briŋ] v *ta med,
*bringe; *medbringe; ~
back *bringe tilbake; ~ up
*oppdra; *ta opp
brisk [brisk] adj livlig
Britain ['britən] Britannia
British ['britiʃ] adj britisk
Briton ['britən] n brite m
broad [brɔːd] adj bred;
utstrakt, vidstrakt; allmenn
broadband ['brɔːdæbænd] n
bredbånd nt
broadcast ['brɔːdkɑːst] n
sending c
*broadcast ['brɔːdkɑːst] v
kringkaste
brochure ['brouʃuə] n
brosjyre m
broke¹ [brouk] v (p break)
broke² [brouk] adj blakk
broken ['broukən] adj (pp
break) knust, i stykker; i
uorden
broker ['broukə] n megler m
bronchitis [brɔŋ'kaitis] n
bronkitt m
bronze [brɔnz] n bronse m;
adj bronse-
brooch [broutʃ] n brosje c
brook [bruk] n bekk m
broom [bruːm] n kost m
brothel ['brɔθəl] n bordell m
brother ['brʌðə] n bror m
brother-in-law
['brʌðərinlɔː] n (pl
brothers-) svoger m
brought [brɔːt] v (p, pp
bring)

brown [braun] adj brun
bruise [bruːz] n blått merke;
v *slå
brunette [bruː'net] n
brunette c
brush [brʌʃ] n børste m;
pensel m; v børste
brutal ['bruːtəl] adj brutal
bubble ['bʌbəl] n boble c
buck [bʌk] n bukk m;
colloquial dollar m
bucket ['bʌkit] n spann nt
buckle ['bʌkəl] n spenne c
bud [bʌd] n knopp m
buddy ['bʌdi] n colloquial
kamerat m
budget ['bʌdʒit] n budsjett
nt
buffet ['bufei] n koldtbord
nt
bug [bʌg] n veggedyr nt;
bille m; insekt nt
*build [bild] v bygge
building ['bildiŋ] n bygning
m
bulb [bʌlb] n blomsterløk
m; light ~ lyspære c
Bulgaria [bʌl'geəriə]
Bulgaria
Bulgarian [bʌl'geəriən] adj
bulgarsk; n bulgarer m
bulk [bʌlk] n last c; masse
m; størsteparten m
bulky ['bʌlki] adj fyldig,
omfangsrik
bull [bul] n tyr m, okse m
bullet ['bulit] n kule c
bulletin ['bulitin] n
bekjentgjørelse m, oppslag
nt

bullfight ['bulfait] n
tyrefektning m

bump [bʌmp] v støte; støte
sammen; dunke; n støt nt

bumper ['bʌmpə] n
støtfanger m

bumpy ['bʌmpi] adj humpet

bun [bʌn] n hvetebolle m

bunch [bʌntʃ] n bukett m;
flokk m

bundle ['bʌndəl] n bunt m;
v bunte, *binde sammen

bunk [bʌŋk] n køye c

buoy [bɔi] n bøye m

burden ['bəːdən] n byrde m

bureau ['bjuərou] n (pl ~x,
~s) skrivebord nt;
kommode m

bureaucracy [bjuə'rɔkrəsi]
n byråkrati nt

burger ['bəːgə] n hamburger

burglar ['bəːglə] n
innbruddstyv m

burgle ['bəːgəl] v *begå
innbrudd

burial ['beriəl] n begravelse
m

burn [bəːn] n brannsår nt

*burn [bəːn] v *brenne; *svi

*burst [bəːst] v *sprekke;
*briste

bury ['beri] v begrave; grave
ned

bus [bʌs] n buss m

bush [buʃ] n busk m

business ['biznəs] n
forretninger pl, handel m;
virksomhet c, forretning c;

yrke nt; ~ card visittkort nt;
~ hours åpningstid c,
kontortid c; ~ trip
forretningsreise c; on ~ i
forretninger

business-like ['biznislaik]
adj forretningsmessig

businessman ['biznəsmən]
n (pl -men)
forretningsmann m

businesswoman
['biznəswumən] n (pl
-women) forretningskvinne
c

bust [bʌst] n byste c

bustle ['bʌsəl] n travelhet c

busy ['bizi] adj opptatt;
travel

but [bʌt] conj men; dog;
prep unntatt

butcher ['butʃə] n slakter m

butter ['bʌtə] n smør nt

butterfly ['bʌtəflai] n
sommerfugl m; ~ stroke
butterfly c

buttock ['bʌtək] n
rumpeballe m

button ['bʌtən] n knapp m;
v knappe

*buy [bai] v kjøpe; anskaffe

buyer ['baiə] n kjøper m

buzz [bʌz] n summing c

by [bai] prep av; med; ved

bye-bye [bai'bai] colloquial
ha det!

by-pass ['baipɑːs] n ringvei
m; bypass m; v *omgå

C

cab [kæb] n drosje c, taxi m
cabaret ['kæbəreɪ] n kabaret m; nattklubb m
cabbage ['kæbɪdʒ] n kål m
cab driver ['kæb,draɪvə] n drosjesjåfør m, taxisjåfør m
cabin ['kæbɪn] n kabin m; hytte c; omkledningskabin m; lugar m
cable ['keɪbəl] n kabel m; ~ tv kabelfjernsyn, nt kabel-TV nt
café ['kæfeɪ] n kafé m
cafeteria [,kæfə'tɪərɪə] n kafeteria m
caffeine ['kæfiːn] n kaffein m
cage [keɪdʒ] n bur nt
cake [keɪk] n kake c
calamity [kə'læmətɪ] n ulykke c, katastrofe m
calcium ['kælsɪəm] n kalsium nt
calculate ['kælkjʊleɪt] v regne ut
calculation [,kælkjʊ'leɪʃən] n utregning c
calculator ['kælkjʊleɪtə] n kalkulator m, lommeregner m
calendar ['kæləndə] n kalender m
calf [kɑːf] n (pl calves) kalv m; legg m; ~skin kalveskinn nt
call [kɔːl] v rope; kalle;

ringe opp; n rop nt; besøk nt, visitt m; oppringning m; *be called *hete; ~ names skjelle ut; ~ on besøke; ~ up ringe opp
call waiting ['kɔːl,weɪtɪŋ] n samtale venter c
caller ID ['kɔːlər,aɪ'diː] n nummervisning c
calm [kɑːm] adj stille, rolig; ~ down berolige; roe seg, falle til ro
calorie ['kælərɪ] n kalori m
came [keɪm] v (p come)
camel ['kæməl] n kamel m
camera ['kæmərə] n fotografiapparat nt; filmkamera nt; ~ shop fotoforretning c
camp [kæmp] n leir m; v campe; ~ bed feltseng c
campaign [kæm'peɪn] n kampanje m
camper ['kæmpə] n campinggjest m; bobil m
camping ['kæmpɪŋ] n camping m; ~ site campingplass m
can [kæn] n boks m; ~ opener boksåpner m
***can** [kæn] v *kan
Canada ['kænədə] Canada
Canadian [kə'neɪdɪən] adj kanadisk; n kanadier m
canal [kə'næl] n kanal m
canary [kə'neərɪ] n

kanarifugl *m*

cancel ['kænsəl] *v*
annullere; avbestille

cancellation [,kænsə'leiʃən]
n avbestilling *c*

cancer ['kænsə] *n* kreft *m*

candid ['kændid] *adj* åpen,
oppriktig

candidate ['kændidət] *n*
kandidat *m*

candle ['kændəl] *n*
stearinlys *nt*

candy ['kændi] *nAm*
sukkertøy *nt*; godter *pl*,
søtsaker *pl*

cane [kein] *n* rør *nt*; stokk *m*

canister ['kænistə] *n* boks
m

canoe [kə'nu:] *n* kano *c*

canteen [kæn'ti:n] *n*
kantine *c*

canvas ['kænvəs] *n* lerret
nt, seilduk *m*

cap [kæp] *n* lue *c*, skyggelue
c

capable ['keipəbəl] *adj*
dyktig, kompetent

capacity [kə'pæsəti] *n*
kapasitet *m*; evne *c*

cape [keip] *n* cape *m*; kapp
nt

capital ['kæpitəl] *n*
hovedstad *m*; kapital *m*;
adj viktig, hoved-; ~ letter
stor bokstav

capitalism ['kæpitəlizəm] *n*
kapitalisme *m*

capitulation
[kə,pitju'leiʃən] *n*
kapitulasjon *m*

capsule ['kæpsju:l] *n* kapsel
m

captain ['kæptin] *n* kaptein
m; flykaptein *m*

capture ['kæptʃə] *v* fange,
*ta til fange; erobre; *n*
arrestasjon *m*; erobring *c*

car [ka:] *n* bil *m*; ~ hire
bilutleie *m*; ~ park
parkeringsplass *m*; ~ rental
Am bilutleie *c*

carjacking ['ka:,dʒækiŋ] *n*
biltyveri *nt*

caramel ['kærəməl] *n*
karamell *m*

carat ['kærət] *n* karat *m*

caravan ['kærəvæn] *n* bobil
m

carburettor [,ka:bju'retə] *n*
forgasser *m*

card [ka:d] *n* kort *nt*;
visittkort *nt*

cardboard ['ka:dbɔ:d] *n*
papp *m*; *adj* kartong-

cardigan ['ka:digən] *n*
ulljakke *c*

cardinal ['ka:dinəl] *n*
kardinal *m*; *adj* hoved-; ~
number grunntall *nt*

care [keə] *n* omsorg *c*;
bekymring *c*; ~ about
bekymre seg om; ~ for bry
seg om; *take ~ of passe på,
*ta vare på

career [kə'riə] *n* karriere *m*

carefree ['keəfri:] *adj*
ubekymret

careful ['keəfəl] *adj*
forsiktig; omhyggelig,
nøyaktig

careless ['keələs] adj
likegyldig, skjødesløs

caretaker ['keə,teikə] n
vaktmester m

cargo ['ka:gou] n (pl ~es)
last c, frakt c

carnival ['ka:nivəl] n
karneval nt

carp [ka:p] n (pl ~) karpe m

carpenter ['ka:pintə] n
snekker m

carpet ['ka:pit] n gulvteppe
nt, teppe nt

carriage ['kæridʒ] n
hestevogn c, vogn c

carriageway ['kæridʒwei] n
kjørebane m

carrot ['kærət] n gulrot c

carry ['kæri] v *bære; føre; ~
on *fortsette; ~ out utføre

carrycot ['kærikət] n
babybag m

cart [ka:t] n kjerre c

cartilage ['ka:tilidʒ] n brusk
m

carton ['ka:tən] n kartong
m

cartoon [ka:'tu:n] n
tegnefilm c

cartridge ['ka:tridʒ] n
patron m

carve [ka:v] v *skjære;
*skjære i, *skjære ut

carving ['ka:viŋ] n
utskjæring c, skurd m

case [keis] n tilfelle nt; sak
c; koffert m; etui nt;
attaché ~ dokumentmappe
c; in ~ hvis

cash [kæʃ] n kontanter pl; v

innkassere, heve; ~
dispenser minibank m

cashier [kæ'ʃiə] n kasserer
m

cashmere ['kæʃmiə] n
kasjmir m

casino [kə'si:nou] n (pl ~s)
kasino nt

cask [ka:sk] n fat nt, tønne c

cassette [kə'set] n kassett
m

cast [ka:st] n kast nt

*cast [ka:st] v kaste; cast
iron støpejern nt

castle ['ka:səl] n slott nt,
borg c

casual ['kæʒuəl] adj
uformell; tilfeldig, flyktig

casualty ['kæʒuəlti] n
ulykke c; offer nt

cat [kæt] n katt m

catacomb ['kætəkoum] n
katakombe m

catalogue ['kætələg] n
katalog m

catarrh [kə'ta:] n katarr m

catastrophe [kə'tæstrəfi] n
katastrofe m

*catch [kætʃ] v fange;
*gripe; overrumple; nå,
*rekke

catchword [kætʃwə:d] n
stikkord nt

category ['kætigəri] n
kategori m

caterer [,keitərər] n catering
m

cathedral [kə'θi:drəl] n
katedral m, domkirke c

catheter [kə'θi:dər] n

kateter *nt*

catholic ['kæθəlik] *adj*
katolsk

cattle ['kætəl] *pl* kveg *nt*

caught [kɔːt] *v* (p, pp catch)

cauliflower ['kɔliflauə] *n*
blomkål *m*

cause [kɔːz] *n* forårsake;
volde; *n* årsak *c*; grunn *m*;
sak *c*; ~ to *få til å

caution ['kɔːʃən] *n*
forsiktighet *c*; *v* advare

cautious ['kɔːʃəs] *adj*
forsiktig

cave [keiv] *n* grotte *c*; hule *c*

cavern ['kævən] *n* hule *c*

caviar ['kævɪɑː] *n* kaviar *m*

cavity ['kævəti] *n* hulrom *nt*

CD [siː'diː] *n* CD *m*; ~
player CD-spiller

CD (-ROM) [siː'diː(rɔm)] *n*
CD-ROM *m*

cease [siːs] *v* opphøre

ceasefire [siːs'faiə] *n*
våpenstillstand *m*

ceiling ['siːliŋ] *n* tak *nt*

celebrate ['selibreit] *v* feire

celebration [,seli'breiʃən] *n*
feiring *c*

celebrity [si'lebrəti] *n*
berømmelse *m*

celery ['seləri] *n* selleri *m*

cell [sel] *n* celle *c*

cellar ['selə] *n* kjeller *m*

cellphone ['selfoun] *n*
mobil(-telefon) *m*

cement [si'ment] *n* sement
m

cemetery ['semitri] *n*
gravlund *m*

censorship ['sensəʃip] *n*
sensur *m*

center ['sentə] *nAm*
sentrum *nt*; midtpunkt *nt*

centigrade ['sentigreid] *adj*
celsius

centimeter *Am*, **centimetre**
['sentimiːtə] *n* centimeter
m

central ['sentrəl] *adj* sentral;
~ heating sentralfyring *c*; ~
station sentralstasjon *m*

centralize ['sentrəlaiz] *v*
sentralisere

centre, center *Am* ['sentə]
n sentrum *nt*; midtpunkt *nt*

century ['sentʃəri] *n*
århundre *nt*

ceramics [si'ræmiks] *pl*
keramikk *m*

ceremony ['serəməni] *n*
seremoni *m*

certain ['səːtən] *adj* sikker;
viss

certainly ['səːtənli] *adv*
sikkert; klart

certificate [sə'tifikət] *n*
attest *m*; vitnesbyrd *nt*,
diplom *nt*, dokument *nt*

chain [tʃein] *n* kjede *nt* ,
kjetting *m*

chair [tʃeə] *n* stol *m*; sete *nt*

chairman ['tʃeəmən] *n* (pl
-men) formann *m*, leder *m*

chairwoman ['tʃeəwumən]
n (pl -women) formann *m*,
leder *m*

chalet ['ʃælei] *n* hytte *c*

chalk [tʃɔːk] *n* kritt *nt*

challenge ['tʃæləndʒ] *v*

utfordre; *n* utfordring *c*

chamber ['tʃeimbə] *n* rom *nt*

champagne [ʃæm'pein] *n* champagne *c*

champion ['tʃæmpjən] *n* mester *m*; forkjemper *m*

chance [tʃɑːns] *n* slump *m*; sjanse *m*, anledning *m*; risiko *m*; tilfelle *nt*; by ~ tilfeldigvis

change [tʃeindʒ] *v* forandre; veksle; kle seg om; skifte; *n* forandring *c*, endring *c*; småpenger *pl*, vekslepenger *pl*; vekslepenger *pl*; **for a** ~ til avveksling; unntaksvis

channel ['tʃænəl] *n* kanal *m*; **English Channel** Den engelske kanal

chaos ['keiɔs] *n* kaos *nt*

chaotic [kei'ɔtik] *adj* kaotisk

chap [tʃæp] *n* fyr *m*

chapel ['tʃæpəl] *n* kapell *nt*, kirke *c*

chaplain ['tʃæplin] *n* kapellan *m*

character ['kærəktə] *n* karakter *m*

characteristic [,kærəktə'ristik] *adj* betegnende, karakteristisk; *n* kjennetegn *nt*; karaktertrekk *nt*

characterize ['kærəktəraiz] *v* karakterisere

charcoal ['tʃɑːkoul] *n* trekull *nt*

charge [tʃɑːdʒ] *v* kreve; *pålegge; anklage; laste; *n* pris *m*; ladning *m*, byrde *m*, belastning *m*; anklage *m*; **free of** ~ kostfri; **in** ~ **of** ansvarlig for; *take* ~ **of** *påta seg

charity ['tʃærəti] *n* velgjørenhet *c*

charm [tʃɑːm] *n* sjarm *m*; amulett *m*

charming ['tʃɑːmiŋ] *adj* sjarmerende

chart [tʃɑːt] *n* tabell *m*; diagram *nt*; sjøkart *nt*; **conversion** ~ omregningstabell *m*

chase [tʃeis] *v* *forfølge; jage bort, *fordrive; *n* jakt *c*

chasm ['kæzəm] *n* kløft *c*

chassis ['ʃæsi] *n* (pl ~) chassis *c*

chaste [tʃeist] *adj* kysk

chat [tʃæt] *v* prate, skravle; *n* prat *m* / *nt*

chatterbox ['tʃætəbɔks] *n* skravlebøtte *c*

chauffeur ['ʃoufə] *n* sjåfør *m*

cheap [tʃiːp] *adj* billig; gunstig

cheat [tʃiːt] *v* jukse, *snyte

check [tʃek] *v* sjekke, kontrollere; *n* rute *c*; regning *c*; sjekk *m*; **check!** sjakk!; ~ **in** sjekke inn; ~ **out** sjekke ut

checkbook ['tʃekbuk] *nAm* sjekkhefte *nt*

checkerboard ['tʃekəbɔːd]
nAm sjakkbrett nt

checkers ['tʃekəz] plAm
damspill nt

checkroom ['tʃekruːm]
nAm garderobe m

checkup ['tʃekʌp] n
undersøkelse m

cheek [tʃiːk] n kinn nt

cheekbone ['tʃiːkboun] n
kinnbein nt

cheeky ['tʃiːki] adj
colloquial frekk,
uforskammet

cheer [tʃiə] v hylle, juble; ~
up oppmuntre

cheerful ['tʃiəfəl] adj lystig,
glad

cheese [tʃiːz] n ost m

chef [ʃef] n kjøkkensjef m

chemical ['kemikəl] adj
kjemisk

chemist ['kemist] n
apoteker m; chemist's
apotek nt

chemistry ['kemistri] n
kjemi m

cheque [tʃek] n sjekk m

cherry ['tʃeri] n kirsebær nt

chess [tʃes] n sjakk m

chest [tʃest] n bryst nt;
brystkasse c; kiste c; ~ of
drawers kommode m

chestnut ['tʃesnʌt] n
kastanje m

chew [tʃuː] v tygge

chewing gum ['tʃuːiŋgʌm]
n tyggegummi m

chicken ['tʃikin] n kylling m

chickenpox ['tʃikinpɔks] n

vannkopper pl

chief [tʃiːf] n sjef m; adj
hoved-, over-

chieftain ['tʃiːftən] n
høvding m

child [tʃaild] n (pl children)
barn nt

childbirth ['tʃaildbəːθ] n
fødsel m

childhood ['tʃaildhud] n
barndom m

Chile ['tʃili] Chile

Chilean ['tʃilien] adj
chilensk; n chilener m

chill [tʃil] n kuldegysning m

chilly ['tʃili] adj kjølig

chimes [tʃaimz] pl
klokkespill nt

chimney ['tʃimni] n
skorstein m

chin [tʃin] n hake c

China ['tʃainə] Kina

china ['tʃainə] n porselen nt

Chinese [tʃaiˈniːz] adj
kinesisk; n kineser m

chip [tʃip] n flis c; chip m;
brikke c; v *slå hakk i,
snitte; chips pommes frites

chisel ['tʃizəl] n meisel m

chives [tʃaivz] pl gressløk
m

chlorine ['klɔːriːn] n klor m

chocolate ['tʃɔklət] n
sjokolade m; konfekt m

choice [tʃɔis] n valg nt;
utvalg nt

choir [kwaiə] n kor nt

choke [tʃouk] v kveles;
kvele; n choke m

*choose [tʃuːz] v *velge

chop [tʃɔp] n kotelett m; v
hakke
Christ [kraist] Kristus
christen ['krisən] v døpe
christening ['krisəniŋ] n
dåp m
Christian ['kristʃən] adj
kristen; ~ name fornavn nt
Christmas ['krisməs] n jul c
chronic ['krɔnik] adj
kronisk
chronological
[,krɔnə'lɔdʒikəl] adj
kronologisk
chuckle ['tʃʌkəl] v klukke,
*le
chunk [tʃʌŋk] n stort stykke
church [tʃəːtʃ] n kirke c
churchyard ['tʃəːtʃjaːd] n
kirkegård m
cigar [si'gaː] n sigar m
cigarette [,sigə'ret] n
sigarett m; ~ case
sigarettetui nt; ~ lighter
[,sigə'ret,laitə] n lighter m
cinema ['sinəmə] n kino m
cinnamon ['sinəmən] n
kanel m
circle ['səːkəl] n sirkel m;
krets m; balkong m; v
*omgi, omringe
circulation [,səːkju'leiʃən]
n sirkulasjon m;
blodomløp nt; omløp nt
circumstance
['səːkəmstæns] n
omstendighet c
circus ['səːkəs] n sirkus nt
citizen ['sitizən] n borger m
citizenship ['sitizənʃip] n

statsborgerskap nt
city ['siti] n by m
civic ['sivik] adj borger-
civil ['sivəl] adj sivil; høflig;
~ law sivilrett m; ~ servant
statstjenestemann m
civilian [si'viljən] adj sivil; n
sivilperson m
civilization [,sivəlai'zeiʃən]
n sivilisasjon m
civilized ['sivəlaizd] adj
sivilisert
claim [kleim] v kreve;
*påstå; n krav nt, fordring c
clamp [klæmp] n krampe m;
skruestikke c
clap [klæp] v klappe,
applaudere
clarify ['klærifai] v
*klarlegge, *klargjøre
class [klaːs] n klasse c
classical ['klæsikəl] adj
klassisk
classify ['klæsifai] v
gruppere
classmate ['klaːsmeit] n
klassekamerat m
classroom ['klaːsruːm] n
klasseværelse c
clause [klɔːz] n klausul m
claw [klɔː] n klo c
clay [klei] n leire c
clean [kliːn] adj ren; v
rense, gjøre rent
cleaning ['kliːniŋ] n
rengjøring c; ~ fluid
vaskemiddel nt
clear [kliə] adj klar; tydelig;
v rydde
clearing ['kliəriŋ] n lysning

m

cleft [kleft] n kløft c

clergyman ['klə:dʒimən] n (pl -men) prest m

clerk [klɑ:k] n sekretær m, kontorpersonale nt

clever ['klevə] adj intelligent; flink, begavet, klok

click [klik] v klikke; ~ into place følge på plass

client ['klaiənt] n kunde m; klient m

cliff [klif] n klippe m

climate ['klaimit] n klima nt

climb [klaim] v klatre; n klatring c

cling ['kliŋ] v klistre, klenge; ~ to klamre seg til

clinic ['klinik] n klinikk m

cloak [klouk] n kappe c

cloakroom ['kloukru:m] n garderobe m

clock [klɔk] n klokke c; at ... o'clock klokken / klokka ...

cloister ['klɔistə] n kloster nt

clone [kloun] v klone; n kloning c

close¹ [klouz] v lukke; closed adj stengt, lukket

close² [klous] adj nær

closet ['klɔzit] nAm skap nt; garderobeskap nt

close-up ['klousʌp] n nærbilde nt

cloth [klɔθ] n stoff nt; klut m

clothes [klouðz] pl klær pl

clothing ['klouðiŋ] n klær pl

cloud [klaud] n sky c

cloudberry [klaudbəri] n molte c, multe c

cloudy ['klaudi] adj skyet, overskyet

clover ['klouvə] n kløver m

clown [klaun] n klovn m

club [klʌb] n klubb m, forening c; kølle c, klubbe c

clumsy ['klʌmzi] adj klosset

clutch [klʌtʃ] n clutch m; grep nt

coach [koutʃ] n buss m; jernbanevogn c; trener m

coal [koul] n kull nt

coarse [kɔ:s] adj grov

coast [koust] n kyst m

coat [kout] n frakk m, kåpe c; kappe c; ~ hanger kleshenger

cocaine [kou'kein] n kokain m / nt

cock [kɔk] n hane m

cocktail ['kɔkteil] n cocktail m

coconut ['koukənʌt] n kokosnøtt c

cod [kɔd] n (pl ~) torsk m

code [koud] n kode m

coffee ['kɔfi] n kaffe m

cognac ['kɔnjæk] n konjakk m

coherence [kou'hiərəns] n sammenheng n

coin [kɔin] n mynt m

coincide [,kouin'said] v *falle sammen med

coincidence [,kouin'sidens]

m tilfelle *nt*, tilfeldighet *c*
cold [kould] *adj* kald; *n*
kulde *c*; forkjølelse *m*;
*catch a ~ *bli forkjølet
collaborate [kə'læbəreit] *v*
samarbeide
collapse [kə'læps] *v* *bryte
sammen
collar ['kɔlə] *n* halsbånd *nt*;
krage *m*
collarbone ['kɔləboun] *n*
kragebein *nt*
colleague ['kɔli:g] *n* kollega
m
collect [kə'lekt] *v* samle;
hente, avhente; samle inn
collection [kə'lekʃən] *n*
samling *c*; kolleksjon *m*
collective [kə'lektiv] *adj*
kollektiv
collector [kə'lektə] *n*
samler *m*; innsamler *m*
college ['kɔlidʒ] *n* høyere
læreinstitusjon; høyskole *m*
collide [kə'laid] *v* kollidere
collision [kə'liʒən] *n*
sammenstøt *nt*, kollisjon *m*
Colombia [kə'lɔmbiə]
Colombia
Colombian [kə'lɔmbiən] *adj*
colombiansk; *n*
colombianer *m*
colonel ['kə:nəl] *n* oberst *m*
colony ['kɔləni] *n* koloni *m*
colo(u)r ['kʌlə] *n* farge *m*; *v*
farge
colo(u)r-blind ['kʌləblaind]
adj fargeblind
colo(u)red ['kʌləd] *adj*
farget

colo(u)rful ['kʌləfəl] *adj*
fargerik
column ['kɔləm] *n* søyle *c*,
spalte *c*; kolonne *m*
coma ['koumə] *n* koma *m*
comb [koum] *v* gre; *n* kam
m
combat ['kɔmbæt] *n* kamp
m; *v* bekjempe, kjempe
combination
[,kɔmbi'neiʃən] *n*
kombinasjon *m*
combine [kəm'bain] *v*
kombinere; sammenstille
*come [kʌm] *v* *komme; ~
across støte på; *komme
over
comedian [kə'mi:diən] *n*
skuespiller *m*; komiker *m*
comedy ['kɔmədi] *n*
komedie *m*, lystspill *nt*
comfort ['kʌmfət] *n*
komfort *m*,
bekvemmelighet *c*, velvære
nt; trøst *m*; *v* trøste
comfortable ['kʌmfətəbəl]
adj bekvem, komfortabel
comic ['kɔmik] *adj* komisk
comics ['kɔmiks] *pl*
tegneserie *m*
coming ['kʌmiŋ] *n* komme
nt; *adj* kommende
comma ['kɔmə] *n* komma *nt*
command [kə'mɑ:nd] *v*
befale; *n* befaling *c*
commander [kə'mɑ:ndə] *n*
befalshavende *m*
commemoration
[kə,memə'reiʃən] *n*
minnefest *m*; in ~ of til

minne om
commence [kə'mens] v
begynne
comment ['kɔment] n
kommentar m; v
kommentere
commerce ['kɔmə:s] n
handel m
commercial [kə'mɔ:ʃəl] adj
handels-, kommersiell; n
reklame m; ~ law
handelsrett m
commission [kə'miʃən] n
kommisjon m
commit [kə'mit] v *overlate,
betro; *begå
committee [kə'miti] n
komité m
common ['kɔmən] adj
felles; vanlig, alminnelig;
simpel
commune ['kɔmju:n] n
kommune m
communicate
[kə'mju:nikeit] v meddele
communication
[kə,mju:ni'keiʃən] n
kommunikasjon m;
meddelelse m
communism ['kɔmjunizəm]
n kommunisme m
communist ['kɔmjunist] n
kommunist m
community [kə'mju:nəti] n
samfunn nt
commuter [kə'mju:tə] n
pendler m
compact ['kɔmpækt] adj
kompakt
companion [kəm'pænjən] n

ledsager m ; guide m
company ['kʌmpəni] n
selskap nt, firma nt
comparative [kəm'pærətiv]
adj relativ
compare [kəm'peə] v
sammenligne
comparison [kəm'pærisən]
n sammenligning c
compartment
[kəm'pɑ:tmənt] n kupé m
compass ['kʌmpəs] n
kompass m / nt; passer m
compel [kəm'pel] v tvinge,
nøde
compensate ['kɔmpənseit]
v kompensere, erstatte
compensation
[,kɔmpən'seiʃən] n
kompensasjon m;
skadeserstatning m
compete [kəm'pi:t] v
konkurrere
competition [,kɔmpə'tiʃən]
n konkurranse m
competitor [kəm'petitər] n
konkurrent m
compile [kəm'pail] v samle
complain [kəm'plein] v
klage
complaint [kəm'pleint] n
klage c
complete [kəm'pli:t] adj
fullstendig, komplett; v
fullende
completely [kəm'pli:tli] adv
helt, totalt
complex ['kɔmpleks] n
kompleks nt; adj innviklet
complexion [kəm'plekʃən]

n hudfarge *m*

complicated ['kɔmplikeitid]
adj komplisert, innviklet

compliment ['kɔmplimənt]
n kompliment *m*; *v*
komplimentere

compose [kəm'pouz] *v*
*sette sammen;
komponere

composer [kəm'pouzə] *n*
komponist *m*

composition
[ˌkɔmpə'ziʃən] *n*
komposisjon *m*;
sammensetning *m*

comprehensive
[ˌkɔmpri'hensiv] *adj*
omfattende

comprise [kəm'praiz] *v*
innbefatte, omfatte

compromise ['kɔmprəmaiz]
n kompromiss *nt*

compulsory [kəm'pʌlsəri]
adj obligatorisk

computer [kəm'pjutə] *n*
datamaskin *m*, PC *m*

conceal [kən'siːl] *v* skjule

conceited [kən'siːtid] *adj*
selvgod; innbilsk *colloquial*

conceive [kən'siːv] *v*
oppfatte, tenke ut;
forestille seg

concentrate ['kɔnsəntreit]
v konsentrere

concentration
[ˌkɔnsən'treiʃən] *n*
konsentrasjon *m*

conception [kən'sepʃən] *n*
forestilling *c*; befruktning
m

concern [kən'səːn] *v*
*gjelde, *angå; *n*
bekymring *c*; anliggende
nt; bedrift *m*, foretak *nt*,
konsern *nt*

concerned [kən'səːnd] *adj*
bekymret; innblandet

concerning [kən'səːniŋ]
prep angående, vedrørende

concert ['kɔnsət] *n* konsert
m; ~ hall konsertsal *m*

concession [kən'seʃən] *n*
konsesjon *m*

concierge [ˌkɔ-si'ɛəʒ] *n*
portner *m*

concise [kən'sais] *adj*
konsis

conclusion [kəŋ'kluːʒən] *n*
konklusjon *m*, slutning *m*

concrete ['kɔŋkriːt] *adj*
konkret; *n* betong *m*

concurrence [kəŋ'kʌrəns] *n*
overensstemmelse *m*

concussion [kəŋ'kʌʃən] *n*
hjernerystelse *m*

condition [kən'diʃən] *n*
vilkår *nt*; kondisjon *m*,
tilstand *m*; omstendighet *c*

conditional [kən'diʃənəl]
adj betinget

conditioner [kən'diʃənə] *n*
hårbalsam *m*

condom ['kɔndəm] *n*
kondom *nt*

conduct¹ ['kɔndʌkt] *n*
oppførsel *m*

conduct² [kən'dʌkt] *v*
ledsage; dirigere

conductor [kən'dʌktə] *n*
leder *m*; dirigent *m*

conference ['kɔnfərəns] n
konferanse m

confess [kən'fes] v *tilstå;
skrifte; bekjenne

confession [kən'feʃən] n
tilståelse m; skriftemål nt

confidence ['kɔnfidəns] n
tillit m

confident ['kɔnfidənt] adj
tillitsfull

confidential [,kɔnfi'denʃəl]
adj konfidensiell

confirm [kən'fəːm] v
bekrefte

confirmation
[,kɔnfə'meiʃən] n
bekreftelse m

confiscate ['kɔnfiskeit] v
*beslaglegge, konfiskere

conflict ['kɔnflikt] n
konflikt m

confuse [kən'fjuːz] v
forvirre

confusion [kən'fjuːʒən] n
forvirring c

congratulate
[kən'grætʃuleit] v
gratulere

congratulation
[kən,grætʃu'leiʃən] n
gratulasjon m,
lykkønskning m

congregation
[,kɔŋgri'geiʃən] n
menighet c; forsamling c

congress ['kɔŋgres] n
kongress m

connect [kə'nekt] v
*forbinde; kople; kople til

connection [kə'nekʃən] n

forbindelse m;
sammenheng m

connoisseur [,kɔnə'səː] n
kjenner m

conquer ['kɔŋkə] v erobre;
beseire

conqueror ['kɔŋkərə] n
erobrer m

conquest ['kɔŋkwest] n
erobring c

conscience ['kɔnʃəns] n
samvittighet c

conscious ['kɔnʃəs] adj
bevisst

consciousness
['kɔnʃəsnəs] n bevissthet c

conscript ['kɔnskript] n
verneplikting m

consent [kən'sent] v
samtykke; bifalle;
samtykke nt

consequence
['kɔnsikwəns] n følge m,
konsekvens m

consequently
['kɔnsikwəntli] adv altså

conservative [kən'səːvətiv]
adj konservativ

consider [kən'sidə] v
betrakte; overveie; *anse,
mene

considerable
[kən'sidərəbəl] adj
betraktelig; betydelig,
anselig

considerate [kən'sidərət]
adj hensynsfull

consideration
[kən,sidə'reiʃən] n
overveielse m; omtanke m;

contraceptive

hensyn *nt*

considering [kən'sidəriŋ]
prep i betraktning av

consignment
[kən'sainmənt] *n* sending *c*

consist of [kən'sist] *bestå
av

conspire [kən'spaiə] *v*
sammensverge seg

constant ['kɔnstənt] *adj*
konstant

constipation
[,kɔnsti'peiʃən] *n*
forstoppelse *m*

constituency
[kən'stitʃuənsi] *n* valgkrets
m

constitution
[,kɔnsti'tju:ʃən] *n*
grunnlov *m*

construct [kən'strʌkt] *v*
konstruere; bygge, oppføre

construction
[kən'strʌkʃən] *n*
konstruksjon *m*; oppførelse
m, bygning *m*

consul ['kɔnsəl] *n* konsul *m*

consulate ['kɔnsjulət] *n*
konsulat *nt*

consult [kən'sʌlt] *v*
*rådspørre

consultation
[,kɔnsəl'teiʃən] *n*
konsultasjon *m*

consume [kən'sju:m] *v*
konsumere, forbruke;
*ødelegge

consumer [kən'sju:mə] *n*
forbruker *m*

consumption

[kən'sumpʃən] *n* forbruk
nt, konsum *nt*

contact ['kɔntækt] *n*
kontakt *m*; *v* kontakte; ~
lenses kontaktlinser *pl*

contagious [kən'teidʒəs]
adj smittsom, smittende

contain [kən'tein] *v*
*inneholde; romme

container [kən'teinə] *n*
beholder *m*; container *m*

contemporary
[kən'tempərəri] *adj*
samtidig

contempt [kən'tempt] *n*
ringeakt *m*, forakt *m*

content [kən'tent] *adj*
tilfreds

contentment
[kən'tentmənt] *n*
tilfredshet *c*

contents ['kɔntents] *pl*
innhold *nt*

contest ['kɔntest] *n* strid *m*;
konkurranse *m*

continent ['kɔntinənt] *n*
kontinent *nt*, verdensdel *m*

continental [,kɔnti'nentəl]
adj kontinental

continual [kən'tinjuəl] *adj*
stadig; continually *adv*
uopphørlig

continue [kən'tinju:] *v*
*fortsette

continuous [kən'tinjuəs]
adj uavbrutt, kontinuerlig

contour ['kɔntuə] *n* omriss
nt

contraceptive
[,kɔntrə'septiv] *n*

prevensjonsmiddel *nt*
contract[1] ['kɔntrækt] *n* kontrakt *m*
contract[2] [kən'trækt] *v* *pådra seg
contractor [kən'træktə] *n* entreprenør *m*
contradict [,kɔntrə'dikt] *v* *motsi
contradictory [,kɔntrə'diktəri] *adj* motstridende
contrary ['kɔntrəri] *n* det motsatte; *adj* motsatt; on the ~ tvert imot
contrast ['kɔntra:st] *n* kontrast *m*, motsetning *m*
contribution [,kɔntri'bju:ʃən] *n* bidrag *nt*
control [kən'troul] *n* kontroll *m*; *v* kontrollere
controversial [,kɔntrə'və:ʃəl] *adj* kontroversiell, omstridt
convenience [kən'vi:njəns] *n* bekvemmelighet *c*
convenient [kən'vi:njənt] *adj* bekvem; passende, egnet, beleilig
convent ['kɔnvənt] *n* nonnekloster *nt*
conversation [,kɔnvə'seiʃən] *n* samtale *m*
convert [kən'və:t] *v* omvende; omregne
convict[1] [kən'vikt] *v* *finne skyldig
convict[2] ['kɔnvikt] *n*

domfelt *m*
conviction [kən'vikʃən] *n* overbevisning *m*; domfellelse *m*
convince [kən'vins] *v* overbevise
convulsion [kən'vʌlʃən] *n* krampetrekning *m*
cook [kuk] *n* kokk *m*; *v* lage mat, tilberede
cookbook ['kukbuk] *nAm* kokebok *c*
cooker ['kukə] *n* komfyr *m*; **gas** ~ gasskomfyr *m*
cookery book ['kukəribuk] *n* kokebok *c*
cookie ['kuki] *nAm* småkake *c*
cool [ku:l] *adj* kjølig
cooperation [kou,ɔpə'reiʃən] *n* samarbeid *nt*; medvirkning *m*
co-operative [kou'ɔpərətiv] *adj* kooperativ; samarbeidsvillig
coordinate [kou'ɔ:dineit] *v* samordne
coordination [kou,ɔ:di'neiʃən] *n* koordinasjon *m*
cope [koup] *v* greie, mestre
copper ['kɔpə] *n* kopper *nt*
copy ['kɔpi] *n* kopi *m*; eksemplar *nt*; *v* kopiere; etterligne
coral ['kɔrəl] *n* korall *m*
cord [kɔ:d] *n* tau *nt*; snor *c*
cordial ['kɔ:diəl] *adj* hjertelig

corduroy ['kɔːdərɔi] n
kordfløyel m

core [kɔː] n kjerne m;
kjernehus nt

cork [kɔːk] n kork m

corkscrew ['kɔːkskruː] n
korketrekker m

corn [kɔːn] n korn nt;
liktorn m; ~ **on the cob**
maiskolbe m

corner ['kɔːnə] n hjørne nt

cornfield ['kɔːnfiːld] n
kornåker m

corpse [kɔːps] n lik nt

corpulent ['kɔːpjulənt] adj
korpulent; tykk, fyldig

correct [kə'rekt] adj
korrekt, riktig; v rette,
korrigere

correction [kə'rekʃən] n
rettelse m

correctness [kə'rektnəs] n
nøyaktighet c

correspond [ˌkɔri'spɔnd] v
brevveksle; svare til,
tilsvare

correspondence
[ˌkɔri'spɔndəns] n
korrespondanse m,
brevveksling c

correspondent
[ˌkɔri'spɔndənt] n
korrespondent m

corridor ['kɔridɔː] n
korridor m

corrupt [kə'rʌpt] adj
korrupt; v *bestikke

corruption [kə'rʌpʃən] n
bestikkelse m

corset ['kɔːsit] n korsett nt

cosmetics [kɔz'metiks] pl
kosmetika pl

cost [kɔst] n kostnad m; pris
m

***cost** [kɔst] v koste

cosy ['kouzi] adj koselig

cot [kɔt] nAm feltseng c

cottage ['kɔtidʒ] n hytte c

cotton ['kɔtən] n bomull m;
bomulls-; ~ **wool** n vatt m

couch [kautʃ] n sofa m

cough [kɔf] n hoste m; v
hoste

could [kud] v (p can)

council ['kaunsəl] n råd nt;
rådsforsamling c

councillor ['kaunsələ] n
rådsmedlem nt

counsel ['kaunsəl] n råd nt

counsellor ['kaunsələ] n
rådgiver m

count [kaunt] v *telle; *telle
opp; medregne; *anse; n
greve m

counter ['kauntə] n disk m

counterfeit ['kauntəfiːt] v
forfalske

countess ['kauntis] n
grevinne c

country ['kʌntri] n land nt;
landområde nt; ~ **house**
landsted nt

countryman ['kʌntrimən] n
(pl -men) landsmann m

county ['kaunti] n grevskap
nt

couple ['kʌpəl] n par nt

coupon ['kuːpɔn] n kupong
m

courage ['kʌridʒ] n

tapperhet *c*, mot *nt*
courageous [kə'reidʒəs] *adj* tapper, modig
course [kɔːs] *n* kurs *m*; rett *m*; løp *nt*; kurs *nt*; **intensive ~** intensivkurs *nt*; **of ~** naturligvis, selvfølgelig
court [kɔːt] *n* domstol *m*; hoff *nt*; gårdsplass *m*
courteous [ˈkəːtiəs] *adj* høflig
cousin [ˈkʌzən] *n* kusine *c*, fetter *m*
cover [ˈkʌvə] *v* dekke; *n* ly *nt*, skjul *nt*; lokk *nt*; perm *m*; **~ charge** kuvertavgift *c*
cow [kau] *n* ku *c*
coward [ˈkauəd] *n* feiging *m*
cowardly [ˈkauədli] *adj* feig
crab [kræb] *n* krabbe *c*
crack [kræk] *n* smell *nt*; sprekk *m*; *v* *smelle; *slå i stykker, *knekke, *sprekke
cracker [ˈkrækə] *nAm* kjeks *m*
cradle [ˈkreidəl] *n* vugge *c*
cramp [kræmp] *n* krampe *c*
crane [krein] *n* kran *c*
crap [kræp] *n* *vulgar* dritt *m*
crash [kræʃ] *n* kollisjon *m*; *v* kollidere; styrte; **~ barrier** barriere *m*
crate [kreit] *n* kasse *c*
crater [ˈkreitə] *n* krater *nt*
crawl [krɔːl] *v* krabbe; *n* crawl *m*
craze [kreiz] *n* mani *m*
crazy [ˈkreizi] *adj* gal; sinnssyk
creak [kriːk] *v* knirke

cream [kriːm] *n* krem *m*; fløte *m*; *adj* kremgul
creamy [ˈkriːmi] *adj* fløteaktig
crease [kriːs] *v* skrukke, krølle; *n* fold *m*; rynke *c*; press *m*
create [kriˈeit] *v* skape; kreere
creative [kriˈeitiv] *adj* kreativ, skapende
creature [ˈkriːtʃə] *n* skapning *m*
credible [ˈkredibəl] *adj* troverdig
credit [ˈkredit] *n* kreditt *m*; *v* *godskrive; **~ card** kredittkort *nt*
creditor [ˈkreditə] *n* kreditor *m*
credulous [ˈkredjuləs] *adj* godtroende
creek [kriːk] *n* vik *c*
***creep** [kriːp] *v* *krype
creepy [ˈkriːpi] *adj* nifs, uhyggelig
cremate [kriˈmeit] *v* kremere
crew [kruː] *n* mannskap *nt*
cricket [ˈkrikit] *n* cricket *m*; siriss *m*
crime [kraim] *n* forbrytelse *m*
criminal [ˈkriminəl] *n* forbryter *m*; *adj* forbrytersk, kriminell; **~ law** strafferett *m*
criminality [ˌkrimiˈnæləti] *n* kriminalitet *m*
crimson [ˈkrimzən] *adj*

høyrød
crisis ['kraisis] n (pl crises)
krise c
crisp [krisp] adj sprø
critic ['kritik] n kritiker m
critical ['kritikəl] adj kritisk;
risikabel
criticism ['kritisizəm] n
kritikk m
criticize ['kritisaiz] v
kritisere
crochet ['krouʃei] v hekle
crockery ['krɔkəri] n
steintøy nt
crocodile ['krɔkədail] n
krokodille c
crooked ['krukid] adj
kroket, fordreid; uærlig
crop [krɔp] n avling c
cross [krɔs] v *gå over; adj
tverr, sint; n kors nt
cross-eyed ['krɔsaid] adj
skjeløyd
crossing ['krɔsiŋ] n overfart
m; kryss nt;
fotgjengerovergang m;
jernbaneovergang m
crossroads ['krɔsroudz] n
gatekryss nt
crosswalk ['krɔswɔːk] nAm
fotgjengerovergang m
crow [krou] n kråke c
crowbar ['kroubɑː] n
brekkjern nt
crowd [kraud] n mengde m,
folkemengde m
crowded ['kraudid] adj
overfylt; tettpakket
crown [kraun] n krone c; v
krone

crucifix ['kruːsifiks] n
krusifiks nt
crucifixion [,kruːsi'fikʃən]
n korsfestelse m
crucify ['kruːsifai] v
korsfeste
cruel [kruəl] adj grusom
cruise [kruːz] n sjøreise c,
cruise nt
crumb [krʌm] n smule m
crusade [kruː'seid] n
korstog nt
crust [krʌst] n skorpe c
crutch [krʌtʃ] n krykke c
cry [krai] v *gråte; *skrike;
rope; n skrik nt; rop nt
crystal ['kristəl] n krystall
m / nt; adj krystall-
Cuba ['kjuːbə] Cuba
Cuban ['kjuːbən] adj
kubansk; n kubaner m
cube [kjuːb] n kube m;
terning m
cuckoo ['kukuː] n gjøk m
cucumber ['kjuːkəmbə] n
agurk m
cuddle ['kʌdəl] v kjæle
med; klemme
cuff [kʌf] n mansjett m; ~
links pl mansjettknapper
pl
cul-de-sac ['kʌldəsæk] n
blindgate c
cultivate ['kʌltiveit] v dyrke
culture ['kʌltʃə] n kultur m
cultured ['kʌltʃəd] adj
kultivert
cunning ['kʌniŋ] adj slu
cup [kʌp] n kopp m; pokal
m

cupboard ['kʌbəd] *n* skap
nt
curb [kə:b] *n* fortauskant *m*;
v tøyle
cure [kjuə] *v* helbrede, lege;
n kur *m*; helbredelse *m*
curiosity [,kjuəri'ɔsəti] *n*
nysgjerrighet *c*
curious ['kjuəriəs] *adj*
vitebegjærlig, nysgjerrig;
merkverdig
curl [kə:l] *v* krølle; *n* krøll *m*
curly ['kə:li] *adj* krøllet
currant ['kʌrənt] *n* rips *m*;
solbær *m*
currency ['kʌrənsi] *n* valuta
m; **foreign ~** utenlandsk
valuta
current ['kʌrənt] *n* strøm *m*;
adj nåværende, aktuell;
alternating ~ vekselstrøm
m; **direct ~** likestrøm *m*
curry ['kʌri] *n* karri *m*
curse [kə:s] *v* banne;
forbanne; *n* banning *c*;
forbannelse *m*
curtain ['kə:tən] *n* gardin
m / *nt*; teppe *nt*
curve [kə:v] *n* kurve *m*;
krumning *m*

curved [kə:vd] *adj* krum,
buet
cushion ['kuʃən] *n* pute *c*
custody ['kʌstədi] *n*
varetekt *c*; forvaring *c*;
formynderskap *nt*
custom ['kʌstəm] *n* vane *m*;
skikk *m*
customary ['kʌstəməri] *adj*
alminnelig, sedvanlig,
vanlig
customer ['kʌstəmə] *n*
kunde *m*
customs ['kʌstəmz] *pl* toll
m; **~ duty** tollavgift *c*; **~
officer** toller *m*
cut [kʌt] *n* kutt *nt*
***cut** [kʌt] *v* *skjære; klippe;
*skjære ned; **~ off** *skjære
av; klippe av; stenge av
cutlery ['kʌtləri] *n* bestikk
nt
cutlet ['kʌtlət] *n* snitsel *m*
cycle ['saikəl] *n* sykkel *m*;
kretsløp *nt*, syklus *m*
cycling ['saikliŋ] *n* sykling *c*
cyclist ['saiklist] *n* syklist *m*
cylinder ['silində] *n* sylinder
m; **~ head** topplokk *nt*

D

dad [dæd], **daddy** ['dædi] *n*
pappa *m*
daffodil ['dæfədil] *n*
påskelilje *c*
daily ['deili] *adj* daglig; *n*
dagsavis *c*

dairy ['dɛəri] *n* meieri *nt*;
melkebutikk *m*
dam [dæm] *n* demning *m*
damage ['dæmidʒ] *n* skade
m; *v* skade
damn [dæm] *v* forbanne; **~!**

faen *colloquial*

damp [dæmp] *adj* fuktig; *n* fuktighet *c*; *v* fukte

dance [dɑːns] *v* danse; *n* dans *m*

dandelion ['dændilaiən] *n* løvetann *c*

dandruff ['dændrəf] *n* flass *nt*

Dane [dein] *n* danske *m*

danger ['deindʒə] *n* fare *m*

dangerous ['deindʒərəs] *adj* farlig

Danish ['deiniʃ] *adj* dansk; ~ pastry wienerbrød *nt*

dare [deə] *v* *tore, våge; utfordre

daring ['deəriŋ] *adj* dristig

dark [dɑːk] *adj* mørk; *n* mørke *nt*

darling ['dɑːliŋ] *n* kjæreste *m*, skatt *m*

darn [dɑːn] *v* stoppe

dash [dæʃ] *v* styrte; *n* tankestrek *m*

dashboard ['dæʃbɔːd] *n* instrumentbord *nt*

data ['deitə] *pl* data *pl*

date¹ [deit] *n* dato *m*; avtale *m*; stevnemøte *nt*; *v* datere; out of ~ umoderne

date² [deit] *n* daddel *m*

daughter ['dɔːtə] *n* datter *c*

daughter-in-law ['dɔːtərinlɔː] *n* (*pl* daughters-) svigerdatter *c*

dawn [dɔːn] *n* daggry *nt*

day [dei] *n* dag *m*; by ~ om dagen; ~ trip dagstur *m*; per ~ per dag; the ~ before

yesterday i forgårs

daybreak ['deibreik] *n* daggry *c*

daylight ['deilait] *n* dagslys *nt*; ~ saving time sommertid *c*

day spa ['dei,spɑː] *n* dagsspa *c*

dead [ded] *adj* død

deaf [def] *adj* døv

deal [diːl] *n* transaksjon *m*, handel *m*

*deal [diːl] *v* dele ut; ~ with *ta seg av; handle med

dealer ['diːlə] *n* forhandler *m*; dealer *m*

dear [diə] *adj* kjær; dyr; dyrebar

death [deθ] *n* død *m*; ~ penalty dødsstraff *m*

debate [di'beit] *n* debatt *m*

debit ['debit] *n* debet *m*

debit card ['debit,kɑːd] *n* debetkort *nt*

debt [det] *n* gjeld *c*

decaffeinated [diː'kæfineitid] *adj* kaffeinfri

deceit [di'siːt] *n* bedrag *nt*

deceive [di'siːv] *v* *bedra

December [di'sembə] desember

decency ['diːsənsi] *n* anstendighet *c*

decent ['diːsənt] *adj* anstendig

decide [di'said] *v* *avgjøre

decision [di'siʒən] *n* beslutning *m*, avgjørelse *m*

deck [dek] *n* dekk *nt*; ~

chair fluktstol *m*

declaration [,deklə'reiʃən] *n* erklæring *c*; deklarasjon *m*

declare [di'kleə] *v* erklære; *oppgi; deklarere

decorate [,dekə'reit] *v* pynte; innrede

decoration [,dekə'reiʃən] *n* dekorasjon *m*

decrease [di:'kri:s] *v* minke, minske; *avta; *n* nedgang *m*

dedicate [,dedikeit] *v* vie

deduce [di'dju:s] *v* utlede; avlede; konkludere

deduct [di'dʌkt] *v* *trekke fra

deed [di:d] *n* handling *c*, gjerning *c*

deep [di:p] *adj* dyp

deep-freeze [,di:p'fri:z] *n* dypfryser *m*

deer [diə] *n* (pl ~) hjort *m*

defeat [di'fi:t] *v* *overvinne; *n* nederlag *nt*

defective [di'fektiv] *adj* mangelfull

defence, defense *Am* [di'fens] *n* forsvar *nt*; vern *nt*

defend [di'fend] *v* forsvare

deficiency [di'fiʃənsi] *n* mangel *m*

deficit ['defisit] *n* underskudd *nt*

define [di'fain] *v* bestemme, definere

definite ['definit] *adj* bestemt

definition [,defi'niʃən] *n* definisjon *m*

deformed [di'fɔ:md] *adj* misdannet, vanskapt

degree [di'gri:] *n* grad *m*

delay [di'lei] *v* forsinke; *utsette; *n* forsinkelse *m*; utsettelse *m*

delegate ['deligət] *n* utsending *m*

delegation [,deli'geiʃən] *n* delegasjon *m*

deliberate[1] [di'libəreit] *v* overveie; *rådslå

deliberate[2] [di'libərət] *adj* overlagt

deliberation [di,libə'reiʃən] *n* overveielse *m*, rådslagning *m*

delicacy ['delikəsi] *n* lekkerbisken *m*; finfølelse *m*

delicate ['delikət] *adj* delikat

delicatessen [,delikə'tesən] *n* delikatesse *m*; matvareforretning *m*

delicious [di'liʃəs] *adj* deilig, lekker

delight [di'lait] *n* glede *c*, fryd *m*; *v* glede; I'm ~ed gleder meg

delightful [di'laitfəl] *adj* henrivende, herlig

deliver [di'livə] *v* levere, avlevere

delivery [di'livəri] *n* levering *c*, leveranse *m*; nedkomst *m*; ~ van varebil *m*

demand [di'mɑ:nd] v
behøve, forlange; n krav
nt; etterspørsel m
democracy [di'mɔkrəsi] n
demokrati nt
democratic [,demə'krætik]
adj demokratisk
demolish [di'mɔliʃ] v *rive
ned; *ødelegge
demolition [,demə'liʃən] n
nedrivning m
demonstrate ['demənstreit]
v bevise; demonstrere
demonstration
[,demən'streiʃən] n
demonstrasjon m
den [den] n hi nt; hule c
Denmark ['denmɑ:k]
Danmark
denomination
[di,nɔmi'neiʃən] n
benevnelse m; trosretning
m; verdienhet m
dense [dens] adj tett
dent [dent] n bulk m
dentist ['dentist] n tannlege
m
denture ['dentʃə] n gebiss nt
deny [di'nai] v benekte;
nekte
deodorant [di:'oudərənt] n
deodorant m
depart [di'pɑ:t] v reise bort,
*gå sin vei; *avgå ved
døden
department [di'pɑ:tmənt] n
avdeling c, departement nt;
~ store stormagasin nt,
varehus nt
departure [di'pɑ:tʃə] n

avreise c; avgang m
dependant [di'pendənt] adj
avhengig
depend on [di'pend] bero
på; that depends det
kommer an på
deposit [di'pɔzit] n
depositum nt; pant m;
bunnfall nt, avleiring c; v
deponere
depot ['depou] n lagerplass
m; stasjon c
depress [di'pres] v tynge
ned
depressing [di'presiŋ] adj
deprimerende
depression [di'preʃən] n
depresjon m; lavtrykk nt;
nedgang m
deprive of [di'praiv] *frata
depth [depθ] n dybde m
deputy ['depjuti] n deputert
m; stedfortreder m
descend [di'send] v *gå ned
descendant [di'sendənt] n
etterkommer m
descent [di'sent] n
nedstigning m
describe [di'skraib] v
*beskrive
description [di'skripʃən] n
beskrivelse m; signalement
nt
desert¹ ['dezət] n ørken m;
adj øde
desert² [di'zə:t] v desertere;
*forlate
deserve [di'zə:v] v fortjene
design [di'zain] v tegne
opp; n design m; utkast nt;

hensikt *m*

designate ['dezigneit] *v*
peke ut

desirable [di'zaiərəbəl] *adj*
attråverdig, ønskelig

desire [di'zaiə] *n* ønske *nt*;
lyst *c*, begjær *nt*; *v* ønske,
begjære

desk [desk] *n* skrivebord *nt*;
kateter *nt*; pult *m*

despair [di'speə] *n*
håpløshet *c*; *v* fortvile

despatch [di'spætʃ] *v*
avsende

desperate ['despərət] *adj*
fortvilet

despise [di'spaiz] *v* forakte

despite [di'spait] *prep* tross

dessert [di'zə:t] *n* dessert *m*

destination [,desti'neiʃən]
n bestemmelsessted *nt*

destine ['destin] *v*
bestemme

destiny ['destini] *n* skjebne
m, lodd *m*

destroy [di'strɔi] *v*
*ødelegge, *tilintetgjøre

destruction [di'strʌkʃən] *n*
ødeleggelse *m*; undergang
m

detach [di'tætʃ] *v* løsne

detail ['di:teil] *n* detalj *m*

detailed ['di:teild] *adj*
detaljert, utførlig

detect [di'tekt] *v* oppdage

detective [di'tektiv] *n*
detektiv *m*; ~ story krim *m*

detergent [di'tə:dʒənt] *n*
vaskepulver *nt*

determine [di'tə:min] *v*

*fastsette, bestemme

determined [di'tə:mind] *adj*
bestemt

detest [di'test] *v* avsky, hate

detour ['di:tuə] *n* omvei *m*;
omkjøring *c*

devaluation
[,di:vælju'eiʃən] *n*
devaluering *c*

devalue [,di:'vælju:] *v*
devaluere

develop [di'veləp] *v* utvikle;
fremkalle

development
[di'veləpmənt] *n* utvikling
c

deviate ['di:vieit] *v* *avvike

devil ['devəl] *n* djevel *m*

devote [di'vout] *v* *hengi

dew [dju:] *n* dugg *m*

diabetes [,daiə'bi:ti:z] *n*
sukkersyke *m*, diabetes *m*

diabetic [,daiə'betik] *n*
diabetiker *m*,
sukkersykepasient *m*

diagnose [,daiəg'nouz] *v*
stille en diagnose;
konstatere

diagnosis [,daiəg'nousis] *n*
(pl -ses) diagnose *m*

diagonal [dai'ægənəl] *n*
diagonal *m*; *adj* diagonal

diagram ['daiəgræm] *n*
diagram *nt*; grafisk
fremstilling

dial ['daiəl] *n* urskive *c*; *v*
slå, taste

dialect ['daiəlekt] *n* dialekt
m

diamond ['daiəmənd] *n*

diamant *m*
diaper ['daɪəpə] *n Am* bleie *c*
diaphragm ['daɪəfræm] *n*
mellomgulv *nt*
diarrh(o)ea [daɪə'rɪə] *n*
diaré *m*
diary ['daɪəri] *n* almanakk
m; dagbok *c*
dictate [dɪk'teɪt] *v* diktere
dictator [dɪk'teɪtə] *n*
diktator *m*
dictionary ['dɪkʃənəri] *n*
ordbok *c*
did [dɪd] *v* (p do)
die [daɪ] *v* dø
diesel ['diːzəl] *n* diesel *m*
diet ['daɪət] *n* diett *m*
differ ['dɪfə] *v* *være
forskjellig
difference ['dɪfərəns] *n*
forskjell *m*
different ['dɪfərənt] *adj*
forskjellig; annerledes
difficult ['dɪfɪkəlt] *adj*
vanskelig; vrien
difficulty ['dɪfɪkəlti] *n*
vanskelighet *c*
*dig [dɪg] *v* grave
digest [dɪ'dʒest] *v* fordøye
digestible [dɪ'dʒestəbəl] *adj*
fordøyelig
digestion [dɪ'dʒestʃən] *n*
fordøyelse *m*
digit ['dɪdʒɪt] *n* siffer *nt*
digital ['dɪdʒɪtəl] *adj* digital
digital camera
['dɪdʒɪtəl 'kæmərə] *n*
digitalkamera *nt*
digital photo
['dɪdʒɪtəl 'foutou] *n*

digitalbilde *nt*
digital projector
['dɪdʒɪtəl prə'dʒektə] *n*
Digital prosjektør *n*
dignified ['dɪgnɪfaɪd] *adj*
verdig
dignity ['dɪgniti] *n* verdighet
c
dilapidated [dɪ'læpɪdeɪtɪd]
adj forfallen
diligence ['dɪlɪdʒəns] *n* flid
m
diligent ['dɪlɪdʒənt] *adj*
flittig
dilute [daɪ'ljuːt] *v* fortynne
dim [dɪm] *adj* dunkel, matt;
uklar, utydelig
din [dɪn] *v* bråk *nt*
dine [daɪn] *v* spise middag
dinghy ['dɪŋgi] *n* jolle *c*
dining car ['daɪnɪŋkɑː] *n*
spisevogn *c*
dining room ['daɪnɪŋruːm]
n spisestue *c*; spisesal *m*
dinner ['dɪnə] *n* middag *m*;
lunsj *m*, aftensmat *m*; ~
jacket smoking *m*; ~
service servise *nt*
diphtheria [dɪf'θɪərɪə] *n*
difteri *m*
diploma [dɪ'ploumə] *n*
diplom *nt*
diplomat ['dɪpləmæt] *n*
diplomat *m*
direct [1] [dɪ'rekt] *adj* direkte,
likefrem
direct [2] [dɪ'rekt] *v* rette;
veilede; styre; regissere
direction [dɪ'rekʃən] *n*
retning *m*; direktiv *nt*; regi

m; styre *nt*, veiledning *m*;
directional signal *Am*
retningsviser *m*; **directions
for use** bruksanvisning *m*
directive [di'rektiv] *n*
direktiv *nt*
director [di'rektə] *n*
direktør *m*; regissør *m*
directory [di'rektəri] *n*
adressebok *c*;
telefonkatalog *m*
dirt [də:t] *n* skitt *m*
dirty ['də:ti] *adj* skitten,
svart
disabled [di'seibəld] *adj*
funksjonshemmet, ufør
disadvantage
[,disəd'va:ntidʒ] *n* ulempe
m
disagree [,disə'gri:] *v* *være
uenig
disagreeable
[,disə'gri:əbəl] *adj*
ubehagelig
disappear [,disə'piə] *v*
*forsvinne
disappoint [,disə'pɔint] *v*
skuffe
disappointment
[,disə'pɔintmənt] *n*
skuffelse *m*
disapprove [,disə'pru:v] *v*
misbillige
disaster [di'za:stə] *n*
katastrofe *m*; ulykke *c*
disastrous [di'za:strəs] *adj*
katastrofal
disc [disk] *n* skive *c*; plate *c*;
slipped ~ skiveprolaps *m*
discard [di'ska:d] *v* kassere

discharge [dis'tʃa:dʒ] *v*
lesse av, losse; **~ of** *frita
for
discipline ['disiplin] *n*
disiplin *m*
discolo(u)r [di'skʌlə] *v*
farge av
disconnect [,diskə'nekt] *v*
utkople; *ta ut kontakten
discontented
[,diskən'tentid] *adj*
misfornøyd
discontinue [,diskən'tinju:]
v stanse, opphøre
discount ['diskaunt] *n*
rabatt *m*, avslag *nt*
discourage [di'skʌrədʒ] *v*
*ta motet fra, avskrekke
discover [di'skʌvə] *v*
oppdage
discovery [di'skʌvəri] *n*
oppdagelse *m*
discuss [di'skʌs] *v*
diskutere; debattere
discussion [di'skʌʃən] *n*
diskusjon *m*; samtale *m*,
debatt *m*
disease [di'zi:z] *n* sykdom
m
disembark [,disim'ba:k] *v*
*gå fra borde, *gå i land
disgrace [dis'greis] *n* skam
c
disguise [dis'gaiz] *v* forkle
seg; *n* forkledning *m*
disgust [dis'gʌst] *n* avsky *m*
disgusting [dis'gʌstiŋ] *adj*
motbydelig, avskyelig
dish [diʃ] *n* tallerken *m*; fat
nt; rett *m*; **dirty dishes**

oppvask *m*

dishonest [dis'ɔnist] *adj* uærlig

dishwasher [dis'wɔʃə] *n* oppvaskmaskin *m*

disinfect [,disin'fekt] *v* desinfisere

disinfectant [,disin'fektənt] *n* desinfiserende middel

disk drive ['disk,,draiv] *n* diskstasjon *c*

dislike [dis'laik] *v* mislike, avsky; *n* motvilje *m*, avsky *m*, antipati *m*

dislocated ['disləkeitid] *adj* gått av ledd

dismiss [dis'mis] *v* sende bort; *gi sparken, avskjedige

disorder [dis'ɔːdə] *n* uorden *m*

dispatch [dis'pætʃ] *v* avsende, sende av sted

display [dis'splei] *v* utstille; vise; *n* utstilling *c*

disposable [dis'spouzəbəl] *adj* engangs-

disposal [dis'spouzəl] *n* disposisjon *m*

dispose of [dis'spouz] kvitte seg med

dispute [dis'spjuːt] *n* ordstrid *m*; krangel *m* / *nt*, tvist *m*; *v* *strides, *bestride

dissatisfied [dis'sætisfaid] *adj* utilfreds

dissolve [di'zolv] *v* oppløse

dissuade from [di'sweid] fraråde

distance ['distəns] *n* avstand *m*; strekning *m*; ~ in kilometres (kilometers *Am*) kilometertall *nt*

distant ['distənt] *adj* fjern

distinct [dis'tiŋkt] *adj* tydelig; forskjellig

distinction [dis'tiŋkʃən] *n* forskjell *m*

distinguish [dis'tiŋgwiʃ] *v* skjelne, *gjøre forskjell

distinguished [dis'tiŋgwiʃt] *adj* fremstående

distress [dis'stres] *n* nød *c*; bedrøvelse *m*; ~ signal nødsignal *nt*

distribute [dis'stribjuːt] *v* utdele

distributor [dis'stribjutə] *n* eneforhandler *m*; strømfordeler *m*

district ['distrikt] *n* distrikt *nt*; kvartal *m*

disturb [dis'stəːb] *v* forstyrre

disturbance [dis'stəːbəns] *n* forstyrrelse *m*; forvirring *c*

ditch [ditʃ] *n* grøft *c*

dive [daiv] *v* dukke, stupe

diversion [dai'vəːʃən] *n* omkjøring *c*; atspredelse *m*

divide [di'vaid] *v* dele; fordele; skille

divine [di'vain] *adj* guddommelig

division [di'viʒən] *n* deling *c*; atskillelse *m*; avdeling *c*

divorce [di'vɔːs] *n* skilsmisse *m*; *v* skilles

dizziness ['dizinəs] *n*

dizzy
254

svimmelhet c

dizzy ['dizi] adj svimmel

*do [du:] v *gjøre; *være tilstrekkelig

dock [dɔk] n dokk m; kai c; v *dokksette; *legge til kai

docker ['dɔkə] n havnearbeider m

doctor ['dɔktə] n lege m; doktor m

document ['dɔkjumənt] n dokument nt

dog [dɔg] n hund m

doll [dɔl] n dukke c

dollar ['dɔlə] n dollar c

dome [doum] n kuppel m

domestic [də'mestik] adj hus-; innenlands; ~ animal husdyr nt

domicile ['dɔmisail] n bopel m

dominate [,dɔmi'neit] v dominere

dominion [də'minjən] n herredømme nt

donate [dou'neit] v skjenke

donation [dou'neiʃən] n donasjon m

done [dʌn] v (pp do)

donkey ['dɔŋki] n esel nt

donor ['dounə] n donator m; giver m

door [dɔ:] n dør c; revolving ~ svingdør c; sliding ~ skyvedør c

doorbell ['dɔ:bel] n ringeklokke c

doorkeeper ['dɔ:,ki:pə] n dørvokter m

doorman ['dɔ:mən] n (pl

-men) portier m

dormitory ['dɔ:mitri] n sovesal m

dose [dous] n dose m

dot [dɔt] n punkt nt, punktum nt, prikk m

double ['dʌbl] adj dobbel; ~ bed dobbeltseng c

doubt [daut] v tvile, betvile; n tvil m; without ~ uten tvil

doubtful ['dautfəl] adj tvilsom; usikker

dough [dou] n deig m; colloquial penger pl

down¹ [daun] adv ned, nedover; over ende; adj nedslått; prep nedover, langs; ~ payment nedbetaling c

down² [daun] n dun nt

download ['daun,loud] n nedlasting c

downpour ['daunpɔ:] n øsregn nt

downstairs [,daun'stɛəz] adv nedenunder

downstream [,daun'stri:m] adv med strømmen

down-to-earth [,dauntu'ə:θ] adj nøktern

downwards ['daunwɔdz] adv nedover

dozen ['dʌzən] n (pl ~, ~s) dusin nt

draft [drɑ:ft] n utkast nt

drag [dræg] v slepe

dragon ['drægən] n drake m

drain [drein] v drenere; n avløp m

drama ['drɑ:mə] n drama nt;

skuespill *nt*

dramatic [drə'mætik] *adj*
dramatisk

drank [dræŋk] *v* (p drink)

draught [drɑːft] *n* trekk *m*;
~ beer fatøl *nt*; draughts
damspill *nt*

draw [drɔː] *n* trekning *m*

*draw [drɔː] *v* tegne;
*trekke; heve; ~ up avfatte,
*sette opp

drawbridge ['drɔːbridʒ] *n*
vindebro *c*

drawer ['drɔːə] *n* skuff *m*;
drawers underbukse *c*

drawing ['drɔːiŋ] *n* tegning
c; ~ pin tegnestift *m*; ~
room salong *m*

dread [dred] *v* frykte; *n*
frykt *m*

dreadful ['dredfəl] *adj*
fryktelig, forferdelig

dream [driːm] *n* drøm *m*

*dream [driːm] *v* drømme

dress [dres] *v* kle på; kle på
seg, kle seg; *forbinde; *n*
kjole *m*

dressing gown
['dresiŋgaun] *n*
morgenkåpe *c*

dressmaker ['dres,meikə] *n*
skredder *c*

drill [dril] *v* bore; trene; *n*
bor *nt*; drilling platform
boreplattform *nt*

drink [driŋk] *n* drink *m*;
drikk *m*

*drink [driŋk] *v* *drikke

drinking water
['driŋkiŋ,wɔːtə] *n*

drikkevann *nt*

drip-dry [,drip'drai] *adj*
strykefri

drive [draiv] *n* vei *m*;
kjøretur *m*

*drive [draiv] *v* kjøre; føre

driver ['draivə] *n* fører *m*,
sjåfør *m*

driver's license *nAm*,
driving licence *n* førerkort
nt

drizzle ['drizəl] *n* duskregn
nt

drop [drɔp] *v* *la falle; *n*
dråpe *m*

drought [draut] *n* tørke *c*

drown [draun] *v* drukne;
*be drowned drukne

drug [drʌg] *n* narkotika *m*;
medisin *m*; ~ addict
narkoman *m*

drugstore ['drʌgstɔː] *nAm*
apotek *nt*

drum [drʌm] *n* tromme *c*

drunk [drʌŋk] *adj* (pp
drink) full, beruset

dry [drai] *adj* tørr; *v* tørke

dry-clean [,drai'kliːn] *v*
rense

dry cleaner's [,drai'kliːnəz]
n renseri *m*

dryer ['draiə] *n*
tørketrommel *m*,
tørkeapparat *nt*

duchess [dʌtʃis] *n*
hertuginne *c*

duck [dʌk] *n* and *c*

due [djuː] *adj* ventet;
skyldig; forfalt til betaling

dues [djuːz] *pl* avgifter *pl*

dug [dʌg] v (p, pp dig)

duke [djuːk] n hertug m

dull [dʌl] adj kjedelig; matt;
sløv

dumb [dʌm] adj stum; dum

dune [djuːn] n sanddyne c

dung [dʌŋ] n gjødsel c

duration [djuˈreiʃən] n
varighet c

during [ˈdjuəriŋ] prep
under, i løpet av

dusk [dʌsk] n tusmørke nt

dust [dʌst] n støv nt

dustbin [ˈdʌstbin] n
søppelkasse c

dusty [ˈdʌsti] adj støvet

Dutch [dʌtʃ] adj hollandsk,

nederlandsk

Dutchman [ˈdʌtʃmən] n (pl
-men) nederlender m,
hollender m

duty [ˈdjuːti] n plikt m;
oppgave c; innførselstoll
m; customs ~ tollavgift c

duty-free [ˌdjuːtiˈfriː] adj
tollfri

DVD [diviˈdiː] n DVD m

DVD-ROM [ˈdiːviːdiːˈrɔm] n
DVD-rom c

dwarf [dwɔːf] n dverg m

dye [dai] v farge; n farge m

dynamo [ˈdainəmou] n (pl
~s) dynamo m

E

each [iːtʃ] adj hver; ~ other
hverandre

eager [ˈiːgə] adj ivrig,
utålmodig

eagle [ˈiːgəl] n ørn c

ear [iə] n øre nt

earache [ˈiəreik] n øreverk
m

eardrum [ˈiədrʌm] n
trommehinne c

earl [əːl] n greve m

early [ˈəːli] adj tidlig

earn [əːn] v tjene; fortjene

earnest [ˈəːnist] n alvor nt

earnings [ˈəːniŋz] pl inntekt
c

earring [ˈiəriŋ] n øredobb m

earth [əːθ] n jord c; bakke m

earthquake [ˈəːθkweik] n

jordskjelv m / nt

ease [iːz] n letthet c,
utvungenhet c

east [iːst] n øst m

Easter [ˈiːstə] påske c

eastern [ˈiːstən] adj østlig,
østre

easy [ˈiːzi] adj lett; bekvem;
~ chair lenestol m

easy-going [ˈiːziˌgouiŋ] adj
avslappet

*eat [iːt] v spise

eavesdrop [ˈiːvzdrɔp] v
sniklytte

ebony [ˈebəni] n ibenholt
m / nt

eccentric [ikˈsentrik] adj
eksentrisk

echo [ˈekou] n (pl ~es)

gjenlyd *m*, ekko *nt*

eclipse [i'klips] *n* formørkelse *m*

economic [,i:kə'nɔmik] *adj* økonomisk

economical [,i:kə'nɔmikəl] *adj* økonomisk, sparsommelig

economist [i'kɔnəmist] *n* økonom *m*

economize [i'kɔnəmaiz] *v* spare

economy [i'kɔnəmi] *n* økonomi *m*; næring *c*, næringsliv *nt*

eco-tourist [i:kou,tu:rist] *n* økoturist *c*

ecstasy ['ekstəzi] *n* ekstase *m*

Ecuador ['ekwədɔ:] Ecuador

Ecuadorian [,ekwə'dɔ:riən] *n* ecuadorianer *m*

eczema ['eksimə] *n* eksem *m* / *nt*

edge [edʒ] *n* kant *m*

edible ['edibəl] *adj* spiselig

edit ['edit] *v* utgi, redigere

edition [i'diʃən] *n* utgave *c*; opplag *nt*; morning ~ morgenutgave *c*

editor ['editə] *n* redaktør *m*

educate ['edʒukeit] *v* *oppdra, utdanne

education [,edʒu'keiʃən] *n* utdannelse *m*; oppdragelse *m*

eel [i:l] *n* ål *m*

effect [i'fekt] *n* effekt *m*, virkning *m*; *v* *frembringe;

in ~ faktisk

effective [i'fektiv] *adj* effektiv, virkningsfull

efficient [i'fiʃənt] *adj* virkningsfull, effektiv

effort ['efət] *n* anstrengelse *m*; bestrebelse *m*; prestasjon *m*

egg [eg] *n* egg *nt*; ~ yolk eggeplomme *c*

eggplant ['egplɑ:nt] *n* aubergine *c*

Egypt ['i:dʒipt] Egypt

Egyptian [i'dʒipʃən] *adj* egyptisk; *n* egypter *m*

eiderdown ['aidədaun] *n* ederdun *c*; dyne *c*

eight [eit] *num* åtte

eighteen [,ei'ti:n] *num* atten

eighteenth [,ei'ti:nθ] *num* attende

eighth [eitθ] *num* åttende

eighty ['eiti] *num* åtti

either ['aiðə] *pron* den ene eller den andre; either ... or enten ... eller

elaborate [i'læbəreit] *v* utdype

elastic [i'læstik] *adj* elastisk; tøyelig; ~ band strikk *m*

elasticity [,elæ'stisəti] *n* tøyelighet *c*

elbow ['elbou] *n* albue *m*

elder ['eldə] *adj* eldre

elderly ['eldəli] *adj* eldre

elect [i'lekt] *v* *velge

election [i'lekʃən] *n* valg *nt*

electric [i'lektrik] *adj* elektrisk; ~ cord ledning

m; ~ **razor** barbermaskin *m*
electrician [,ilek'triʃən] *n*
elektriker *m*
electricity [,ilek'trisəti] *n*
elektrisitet *m*
electronic [ilek'trɔnik] *adj*
elektronisk
elegance ['eligəns] *n*
eleganse *m*
elegant ['eligənt] *adj*
elegant
element ['elimənt] *n*
element *nt*, bestanddel *m*
elephant ['elifənt] *n* elefant
m
elevator ['eliveitə] *nAm*
heis *m*
eleven [i'levən] *num* elleve
eleventh [i'levənθ] *num*
ellevte
elf [elf] *n* (pl elves) alv *m*
eliminate [i'limineit] *v*
fjerne; avskaffe
elm [elm] *n* alm *m*
else [els] *adv* ellers
elsewhere [,el'swɛə] *adv*
annetsteds
elucidate [i'lu:sideit] *v*
*klargjøre
e-mail ['i: meil] *n* e-post *m*;
v sende (med) e-post
emancipation
[i,mænsi'peiʃən] *n*
frigjøring *c*
embankment
[im'bæŋkmənt] *n* bredd *m*;
demning *m*
embargo [em'bɑ:gou] *n* (pl
~es) beslag *nt*;
handelsforbud *nt*

embark [im'bɑ:k] *v* *gå om
bord
embarkation
[,embɑ:'keiʃən] *n*
innskipning *m*
embarrass [im'bærəs] *v*
*gjøre brydd, *gjøre
forlegen; sjenere;
embarrassed brydd, flau,
forlegen; **embarrassing**
pinlig; **embarrassment**
forlegenhet *c*
embassy ['embəsi] *n*
ambassade *m*
emblem ['embləm] *n*
emblem *nt*; symbol *nt*
embrace [im'breis] *v*
omfavne; *n* omfavnelse *m*
embroider [im'brɔidə] *v*
brodere
embroidery [im'brɔidəri] *n*
broderi *m*
emerald ['emərəld] *n*
smaragd *m*
emergency [i'mə:dʒənsi] *n*
krisesituasjon *m*,
nødstilfelle *nt*; ~ **exit**
nødutgang *m*
emigrant ['emigrənt] *n*
utvandrer *m*
emigrate ['emigreit] *v*
utvandre
emigration [,emi'greiʃən] *n*
emigrasjon *m*
emotion [i'mouʃən] *n*
sinnsbevegelse *m*, følelse
m
emperor ['empərə] *n* keiser
m
emphasize ['emfəsaiz] *v*

understreke
empire ['empaiə] *n*
imperium *nt*, keiserdømme
nt
employ [im'plɔi] *v* *ansette;
anvende
employee [,emplɔi'i:] *n*
lønnstaker *m*, ansatt *m*
employer [im'plɔiə] *n*
arbeidsgiver *m*
employment [im'plɔimənt]
n beskjeftigelse *m*, arbeid
nt; ~ **exchange**
arbeidsformidling *c*
empress ['empris] *n*
keiserinne *c*
empty ['empti] *adj* tom; *v*
tømme
enable [i'neibəl] *v* *sette i
stand
enamel [i'næməl] *n* emalje
m
enamelled [i'næməld] *adj*
emaljert
enchanting [in'tʃɑːntiŋ] *adj*
bedårende, henrivende
encircle [in'sɜːkəl] *v*
omringe, *omgi; innsirkle
enclose [iŋ'klouz] *v*
*vedlegge
enclosure [iŋ'klouʒə] *n*
vedlegg *nt*
encounter [iŋ'kauntə] *v*
møte; *n* møte *nt*
encourage [iŋ'kʌridʒ] *v*
oppmuntre
encyclop(a)edia
[en,saiklə'piːdiə] *n*
leksikon *nt*
end [end] *n* ende *m*, slutt *m*;

v slutte; opphøre
ending ['endiŋ] *n* avslutning
m
endless ['endləs] *adj*
uendelig
endorse [in'dɔːs] *v*
endossere
endure [in'djuə] *v* *utholde
enemy ['enəmi] *n* fiende *m*
energetic [,enə'dʒetik] *adj*
energisk
energy ['enədʒi] *n* energi *m*;
kraft *c*
engage [iŋ'geidʒ] *v*
*ansette; bestille; forplikte
seg; **engaged** forlovet;
opptatt
engagement [iŋ'geidʒmənt]
n forlovelse *m*; forpliktelse
m; avtale *m*; ~ **ring**
forlovelsesring *m*
engine ['endʒin] *n* maskin
m, motor *m*; lokomotiv *nt*
engineer [,endʒi'niə] *n*
ingeniør *m*
England ['iŋglənd] England
English ['iŋgliʃ] *adj* engelsk
Englishman ['iŋgliʃmən] *n*
(pl -men) engelskmann *m*
engrave [iŋ'greiv] *v* gravere
engraving [iŋ'greiviŋ] *n*
trykk *nt*; kopperstikk *nt*
enigma [i'nigmə] *n* gåte *c*
enjoy [in'dʒɔi] *v* *nyte, *ha
glede av
enjoyable [in'dʒɔiəbəl] *adj*
behagelig, hyggelig,
morsom; deilig
enjoyment [in'dʒɔimənt] *n*
nytelse *m*

enlarge [in'lɑːdʒ] v
forstørre; utvide
enlargement [in'lɑːdʒmənt]
n forstørrelse m
enormous [i'nɔːməs] adj
enorm, kolossal
enough [i'nʌf] adv nok; adj
tilstrekkelig
enquire [iŋ'kwaiə] v
*forespørre; undersøke
enquiry [iŋ'kwaiəri] n
forespørsel m;
undersøkelse m;
rundspørring c
enter ['entə] v *gå inn, *tre
inn i; *innskrive
enterprise ['entəpraiz] n
virksomhet c; driftighet c
entertain [,entə'tein] v
*underholde, more;
beverte
entertainer [,entə'teinə] n
underholder m
entertaining [,entə'teiniŋ]
adj morsom,
underholdende
entertainment
[,entə'teinmənt] n
underholdning m,
forlystelse m
enthusiasm
[in'θjuːziæzəm] n
entusiasme m
enthusiastic
[in,θjuːzi'æstik] adj
entusiastisk
entire [in'taiə] adj hel
entirely [in'taiəli] adv helt
entrails ['entreilz] n
innvoller

entrance ['entrəns] n
inngang m; adgang m;
inntreden m; ~ fee
inngangspenger pl
entry ['entri] n inngang m,
adgang m; oppføring c; no
~ adgang forbudt
envelop [in'veləp] v pakke
inn, omslutte
envelope ['envəloup] n
konvolutt m
envious ['enviəs] adj sjalu,
misunnelig
environment
[in'vaiərənmənt] n miljø
nt; omgivelser pl;
environmental protection
miljøvern nt
envoy ['envɔi] n sendemann
m
envy ['envi] n misunnelse
m; v misunne
epic ['epik] n epos nt; adj
episk
epidemic [,epi'demik] n
epidemi m
epilepsy ['epilepsi] n
epilepsi m
epilogue ['epilɔg] n epilog
m
episode ['episoud] n
episode m
equal ['iːkwəl] adj lik; n
likemann m; v måle seg
med
equality [i'kwɔləti] n likhet
c
equalize ['iːkwəlaiz] v
utjevne
equally ['iːkwəli] adv like

equator [i'kweitə] *n* ekvator *m*

equip [i'kwip] *v* utruste, utstyre

equipment [i'kwipmənt] *n* utstyr *nt*

equivalent [i'kwivələnt] *adj* motsvarende, tilsvarende

eraser [i'reizə] *n* viskelær *m*

erect [i'rekt] *v* reise; *adj* oppreist, stående

err [ə:] *v* feile

errand ['erənd] *n* ærend *nt*

error ['erə] *n* feiltakelse *m*, feil *m*

escalator ['eskəleitə] *n* rulletrapp *c*

escape [i'skeip] *v* *unnslippe; *unngå, flykte; *n* flukt *c*

escort¹ ['eskɔ:t] *n* eskorte *m*

escort² [i'skɔ:t] *v* ledsage

especially [i'speʃəli] *adv* især, først og fremst, særlig

essay ['esei] *n* essay *nt*; stil *m*, avhandling *c*

essence ['esəns] *n* essens *m*; vesen *nt*, kjerne *m*

essential [i'senʃəl] *adj* uunnværlig; vesentlig

essentially [i'senʃəli] *adv* først og fremst

establish [i'stæbliʃ] *v* etablere; *fastslå

estate [i'steit] *n* eiendom *m*

esteem [i'sti:m] *n* aktelse *m*, respekt *m*; *v* akte

estimate¹ ['estimeit] *v* vurdere, taksere,

estimate² ['estimət] *n* vurdering *c*

estuary ['estʃuəri] *n* elvemunning *m*

etcetera [et'setərə] og så videre

etching ['etʃiŋ] *n* radering *c*

eternal [i'tə:nəl] *adj* evig

eternity [i'tə:nəti] *n* evighet *c*

ether ['i:θə] *n* eter *m*

Ethiopia [iθi'oupiə] Etiopia

Ethiopian [iθi'oupiən] *adj* etiopisk; *n* etiopier *m*

e-ticket ['i:,tikət] *n* e-billett *c*

EU ['i:'ju] EU, den europeiske union *c*

Euro ['ju:rou] *n* euro *m*

Europe ['juərəp] Europa

European [,juərə'pi:ən] *adj* europeisk; *n* europeer *m*

evacuate [i'vækjueit] *v* evakuere

evaluate [i'væljueit] *v* vurdere

evaporate [i'væpəreit] *v* fordampe

even ['i:vən] *adj* jevn, like, plan; konstant; *adv* til og med

evening ['i:vniŋ] *n* kveld *m*; ~ **dress** selskapsantrekk *nt*

event [i'vent] *n* begivenhet *c*

eventual [i'ventʃuəl] *adj* mulig; endelig

eventually [i'ventʃuəli] *adv* endelig; til slutt

ever ['evə] *adv* noen gang;

*verdsette

alltid
every ['evri] *adj* hver
everybody ['evri,bɒdi] *pron* enhver
everyday ['evridei] *adj* daglig
everyone ['evriwʌn] *pron* enhver
everything ['evriθiŋ] *pron* alt
everywhere ['evriweə] *adv* overalt
evidence ['evidəns] *n* bevis *nt*
evident ['evidənt] *adj* tydelig
evil ['i:vəl] *n* onde *nt*; *adj* ondsinnet, ond
evolution [,i:və'lu:ʃən] *n* evolusjon *m*
exact [ig'zækt] *adj* nøyaktig
exactly [ig'zæktli] *adv* akkurat
exaggerate [ig'zædʒəreit] *v* *overdrive
exam [ig'zæm] *colloquial*, **examination** [ig,zæmi'neiʃən] eksamen *m*; undersøkelse *m*; forhør *nt*
examine [ig'zæmin] *v* undersøke
example [ig'zɑːmpəl] *n* eksempel *nt*; **for ~** for eksempel
excavation [,ekskə'veiʃən] *n* utgravning *m*
exceed [ik'si:d] *v* *overskride; *overgå
excel [ik'sel] *v* utmerke seg

excellent ['eksələnt] *adj* fremragende, utmerket
except [ik'sept] *prep* unntatt
exception [ik'sepʃən] *n* unntak *nt*
exceptional [ik'sepʃənəl] *adj* usedvanlig, enestående
excerpt ['eksɔːpt] *n* utdrag *nt*
excess [ik'ses] *n* utskeielse *m*; overdrivelse *m*
excessive [ik'sesiv] *adj* overdreven
exchange [iks'tʃeindʒ] *v* bytte, veksle, utveksle; *n* bytte *nt*; børs *m*; **~ office** vekslingskontor *nt*; **~ rate** valutakurs *m*
excite [ik'sait] *v* opphisse
excited [ik'saitəd] *adj* opphisset
excitement [ik'saitmənt] *n* opphisselse *m*; spenning *m*
exciting [ik'saitiŋ] *adj* spennende
exclaim [ik'skleim] *v* *utbryte
exclamation [,eksklə'meiʃən] *n* utrop *nt*
exclude [ik'sklu:d] *v* utelukke
exclusive [ik'sklu:siv] *adj* eksklusiv
exclusively [ik'sklu:sivli] *adv* utelukkende
excursion [ik'skɔ:ʃən] *n* utflukt *c*
excuse[1] [ik'skju:s] *n* unnskyldning *m*

excuse² [ik'skju:z] v
unnskylde
execute ['eksikju:t] v utføre
execution [,eksi'kju:ʃən] n
henrettelse m
executioner
[,eksi'kju:ʃənə] n bøddel
m
executive [ig'zekjutiv] adj
administrerende; n
utøvende makt; direktør m
exempt [ig'zempt] v *frita;
adj fritatt
exemption [ig'zempʃən] n
fritak nt
exercise ['eksəsaiz] n
øvelse m; oppgave c; v øve;
utøve
exhale [eks'heil] v puste ut
exhaust [ig'zo:st] n
eksosrør nt; v utmatte; ~
gases eksos m
exhibit [ig'zibit] v utstille;
fremvise, oppvise
exhibition [,eksi'biʃən] n
utstilling c
exile ['eksail] n eksil nt;
landflyktig m
exist [ig'zist] v eksistere
existence [ig'zistəns] n
eksistens m
exit ['eksit] n utgang m;
utkjørsel m
exotic [ig'zɔtik] adj eksotisk
expand [ik'spænd] v utvide;
utbre; utfolde
expansion [ik'spænʃən] n
utbredelse; utvidelse,
ekspansjon
expect [ik'spekt] v vente

expectation
[,ekspek'teiʃən] n
forventning m
expedition [,ekspə'diʃən] n
ekspedisjon m
expel [ik'spel] v utvise
expenditure [ik'spenditʃə]
n forbruk m
expense [ik'spens] n utgift
c; expenses pl
omkostninger pl, kostnader
pl
expensive [ik'spensiv] adj
dyr; kostbar
experience [ik'spiəriəns] n
erfaring c; v oppleve,
erfare; experienced
erfaren
experiment [ik'sperimənt] n
eksperiment nt, forsøk nt;
v eksperimentere
expert ['ekspə:t] n fagmann
m, ekspert m; adj
sakkyndig
expire [ik'spaiə] v *utløpe,
opphøre; utånde; expired
utløpt
explain [ik'splein] v forklare
explanation
[,eksplə'neiʃən] n
forklaring c
explicit [ik'splisit] adj
tydelig, uttrykkelig
explode [ik'sploud] v
eksplodere
exploit [ik'splɔit] v utnytte
explore [ik'splɔ:] v utforske
explosion [ik'splouʒən] n
eksplosjon m
explosive [ik'splousiv] adj

eksplosiv; *n* sprengstoff *nt*
export[1] [ik'spɔːt] *v*
eksportere, utføre
export[2] ['ekspɔːt] *n* eksport
m, utførsel *m*
expose [ik'spouz] *v* utsette;
avsløre; eksponere
exposition [,ekspə'ziʃən] *n*
utstilling *c*
exposure [ik'spouʒə] *n*
utsatthet *c*; eksponering *c*;
~ **meter** lysmåler *m*
express [ik'spres] *v*
uttrykke; *gi uttrykk for,
ytre; *adj* ekspress-;
uttrykkelig; ~ **train**
hurtigtog *nt*
expression [ik'spreʃən] *n*
uttrykk *nt*
exquisite [ik'skwizit] *adj*
utsøkt
extend [ik'stend] *v* forlenge;
utvide; bevilge
extension [ik'stenʃən] *n*
forlengelse *m*; utvidelse *m*;
linje *c*; ~ **cord**
skjøteledning *m*
extensive [ik'stensiv] *adj*
omfangsrik; utstrakt,
omfattende
extent [ik'stent] *n* omfang
nt
exterior [ek'stiəriə] *adj* ytre;
n utside *c*

external [ek'stə:nəl] *adj*
utvendig
extinguish [ik'stiŋgwiʃ] *v*
slokke
extort [ik'stɔːt] *v* utpresse
extortion [ik'stɔːʃən] *n*
utpressing *c*
extra ['ekstrə] *adj* ekstra
extract[1] [ik'strækt] *v*
*trekke ut
extract[2] ['ekstrækt] *n*
utdrag *nt*
extradite ['ekstrədait] *v*
utlevere en forbryter
extraordinary
[ik'strɔːdənri] *adj*
usedvanlig
extravagant [ik'strævəgənt]
adj ekstravagant,
overdreven
extreme [ik'striːm] *adj*
ekstrem; ytterst, ytterlig; *n*
ytterlighet *c*
exuberant [ig'zjuːbərənt]
adj overstrømmende
eye [ai] *n* øye *nt*; ~ **shadow**
øyenskygge *m*
eyebrow ['aibrau] *n*
øyenbryn *nt*
eyelash ['ailæʃ] *n* øyenvippe
m
eyelid ['ailid] *n* øyenlokk *nt*
eyewitness ['ai,witnəs] *n*
øyenvitne *nt*

F

fable ['feibəl] n fabel m;
sagn nt

fabric ['fæbrik] n stoff nt;
struktur m

façade [fə'saːd] n fasade m

face [feis] n ansikt nt; v
konfrontere; ~ **cream**
ansiktskrem m

facilities [fə'silətis] pl
innretning(er) pl; **cooking**
~ mulighet til å lage mat

facing overfor

fact [fækt] n kjensgjerning
c, faktum nt; **in** ~ **faktisk**

factor ['fæktə] n faktor m

factory ['fæktəri] n fabrikk
m

factual ['fæktʃuəl] adj
faktisk

faculty ['fækəlti] n evne c;
begavelse m, anlegg nt;
fakultet m

fade [feid] v blekne, falme

fail [feil] v mislykkes;
mangle; forsømme;
dumpe; *stryke; **without** ~
helt sikkert

failure ['feiljə] n fiasko m

faint [feint] v besvime; adj
svak, vag

fair [fɛə] n basar m;
varemesse c; adj rettferdig;
lyshåret, blond; vakker

fairly ['fɛəli] adv nokså,
temmelig, ganske

fairy ['fɛəri] n fe m

fairytale ['fɛəriteil] n
eventyr nt

faith [feiθ] n tro c; tillit m

faithful ['feiθful] adj trofast

fake [feik] n forfalskning m

fall [fɔːl] n fall nt; høst m

***fall** [fɔːl] v *falle

false [fɔːls] adj falsk; gal,
uekte; ~ **teeth** gebiss nt

falter ['fɔːltə] v vakle;
stamme

fame [feim] n berømmelse
m; rykte nt

familiar [fə'miljə] adj
velkjent; fortrolig

family ['fæməli] n familie m;
slekt c; ~ **name** etternavn
nt

famous ['feiməs] adj
berømt

fan [fæn] n vifte c; beundrer
m; ~ **belt** vifterem c

fanatical [fə'nætikəl] adj
fanatisk

fancy ['fænsi] v *ha lyst til,
like; tenke seg, forestille
seg; n lune nt; fantasi m

fantastic [fæn'tæstik] adj
fantastisk

fantasy ['fæntəzi] n fantasi
m

far [faː] adj fjern; adv
meget; **by** ~ uten
sammenligning; **so** ~ hittil;
~ **away** langt borte

fare [fɛə] n billettpris m;

kost *m*
farm [fɑːm] *n* bondegård *m*
farmer ['fɑːmə] *n* bonde *m*
farmhouse ['fɑːmhaus] *n*
våningshus *nt*
far-off ['fɑːrɔf] *adj* fjern
farther ['fɑːðə] *adj* videre
fascinate ['fæsineit] *v*
fengsle, fjetre
fascism ['fæʃizəm] *n*
fascisme *m*
fascist ['fæʃist] *adj*
fascistisk; *n* fascist *m*
fashion ['fæʃən] *n* mote *m*;
måte *m*
fashionable ['fæʃənəbəl]
adj moderne
fast [fɑːst] *adj* rask, hurtig;
fast
fasten ['fɑːsən] *v* feste,
stenge
fastener ['fɑːsənə] *n*
festeinnretning *m*
fat [fæt] *adj* tykk, fet; *n* fett
nt; ~ free *adj* fettfri
fatal ['feitəl] *adj* dødelig,
skjebnesvanger, fatal
fate [feit] *n* skjebne *m*
father ['fɑːðə] *n* far *m*; pater
m
father-in-law ['fɑːðərinlɔː]
n (pl fathers-) svigerfar *m*
fatigue [fəˈtiːg] *n* utmattelse
m, tretthet *c*
fatty ['fæti] *adj* fettholdig
faucet ['fɔːsit] *nAm*
vannkran *c*
fault [fɔːlt] *n* feil *m*, defekt
m
faultless ['fɔːltləs] *adj*

feilfri; perfekt
faulty ['fɔːlti] *adj* defekt,
mangelfull
favo(u)r ['feivə] *n* tjeneste
m; *v* privilegere,
begunstige
favo(u)rable ['feivərəbəl]
adj gunstig
favo(u)rite ['feivərit] *n*
favoritt *m*, yndling *m*; *adj*
yndlings-
fax [fæks] *n* telefaks *m*, faks
m; send a ~ sende en faks
fear [fiə] *n* frykt *m*,
engstelse *m*; *v* frykte
feasible ['fiːzəbəl] *adj*
mulig, gjennomførbart
feast [fiːst] *n* fest *m*
feat [fiːt] *n* prestasjon *m*
feather ['feðə] *n* fjær *c*
feature ['fiːtʃə] *n*
kjennemerke *nt*;
ansiktstrekk *nt*
February ['februəri] februar
federal ['fedərəl] *adj*
forbunds-
federation [,fedəˈreiʃən] *n*
forbundsstat *m*
fee [fiː] *n* honorar *nt*; gebyr
nt
feeble ['fiːbəl] *adj* svak
*feed [fiːd] *v* mate; fed up
with lei av
*feel [fiːl] *v* føle; ~ like *ha
lyst til
feeling ['fiːliŋ] *n* følelse *m*
feet (pl foot)
fell [fel] *v* (p fall)
fellow ['felou] *n* fyr *m*
felt¹ [felt] *n* filt *m*

felt² [felt] v (p, pp feel)

female ['fi:meil] adj hunn-

feminine ['feminin] adj feminin

fence [fens] n gjerde nt; stakitt nt; v fekte

ferment [fə:'ment] v gjære

ferry-boat ['feribout] n ferge c; ferje c

fertile ['fə:tail] adj fruktbar

festival ['festivəl] n festival m

festive ['festiv] adj festlig

fetch [fetʃ] v hente *innbringe

feudal ['fju:dəl] adj føydal

fever ['fi:və] n feber m

feverish ['fi:vəriʃ] adj feberaktig

few [fju:] adj få

fiancé [fi'ɑ:nsei] n forlovede m

fiancée [fi'ɑ:nsei] n forlovede m

fibre ['faibə] n fiber m

fiction ['fikʃən] n skjønnlitteratur m, oppdiktning m

field [fi:ld] n mark c, åker m; felt nt; ~ glasses feltkikkert m

fierce [fiəs] adj vill; heftig

fifteen [,fif'ti:n] num femten

fifteenth [,fif'ti:nθ] num femtende

fifth [fifθ] num femte

fifty ['fifti] num femti

fig [fig] n fiken c

fight [fait] n strid m, kamp m

*fight [fait] v kjempe, *slåss

figure ['figə] n skikkelse m, figur m; tall nt

file [fail] n kartotek nt, fil m; dokumentsamling c; rekke c

fill [fil] v fylle; ~ in fylle ut; ~ out Am fylle ut; ~ up fylle opp; filling station bensinstasjon m

filling ['filiŋ] n plombe m; fyll nt

film [film] n film m; v filme

filter ['filtə] n filter nt

filthy ['filθi] adj skitten

final ['fainəl] adj endelig

finally ['fainəli] adv endelig, til slutt

finance [fai'næns] v finansiere

finances [fai'nænsiz] pl finanser pl

financial [fai'nænʃəl] adj finansiell

finch [fintʃ] n finke m

*find [faind] v *finne

fine [fain] n mulkt c; adj fin; pen; skjønn, utmerket; ~ arts skjønne kunster

finger ['fiŋgə] n finger m; little ~ lillefinger m

fingerprint ['fiŋgəprint] n fingeravtrykk nt

finish ['finiʃ] v fullende, avslutte, slutte; opphøre; n slutt m; mållinje c; finished ferdig

Finland ['finlənd] Finland

Finn [fin] n finne m

Finnish ['finiʃ] adj finsk

fire [faiə] n ild m; brann m;
v *skyte; avskjedige; ~
alarm brannalarm m; ~
brigade brannvesen nt; ~
escape branntrapp c; ~
extinguisher brannslokker
m

firefighter ['faiə,faitə] n
brannmannskap nt

fireplace ['faiəpleis] n peis
m

fireproof ['faiəpru:f] adj
brannsikker; ildfast

firewall ['faiə‿,wɔ:l] n
brannmur c

firm [fə:m] adj fast; solid; n
firma nt

first [fə:st] num første; at ~
først; i begynnelsen; ~
name fornavn nt

first aid [,fə:st'eid] n
førstehjelp c; ~ kit
førstehjelpsutstyr nt; ~
post førstehjelpsstasjon m

first-class [,fə:st'klɑ:s] adj
førsteklasses

first-rate [,fə:st'reit] adj
førsteklasses, førsterangs

fir tree ['fə:tri:] n nåletre nt,
gran c

fish¹ [fiʃ] n (pl ~, ~es) fisk
m; ~ shop fiskeforretning c

fish² [fiʃ] v fiske; fishing
gear fiskeutstyr nt; fishing
hook fiskekrok m; fishing
industry fiskeri nt; fishing
license Am, fishing
licence fiskekort nt;
fishing line fiskesnøre nt;
fishing net fiskegarn nt;

fishing rod fiskestang c;
fishing tackle fiskeredskap
nt

fishbone ['fiʃboun] n
fiskebein nt

fisherman ['fiʃəmən] n (pl
-men) fisker m

fist [fist] n knyttneve m

fit [fit] adj egnet; n anfall nt;
v passe; fitting room
prøverom nt

five [faiv] num fem

fix [fiks] v reparere, ordne

fixed [fikst] adj fast

fizz [fiz] n brusing c

fjord [fjɔ:d] n fjord

flag [flæg] n flagg nt

flame [fleim] n flamme m

flamingo [flə'miŋgou] n (pl
~s, ~es) flamingo m

flannel ['flænəl] n flanell m

flash [flæʃ] n glimt nt; ~
bulb blitzlampe c

flashlight ['flæʃlait] n
lommelykt c

flask [flɑ:sk] n flaske c;
thermos ~ termosflaske c

flat [flæt] adj flat, plan; n
leilighet c; ~ tyre
punktering c

flavo(u)r ['fleivə] n smak m;
v *sette smak på

flaw [flɔ:] n sprekk m;
svakhet c

flee [fli:] v flykte, rømme

fleet [fli:t] n flåte m

flesh [fleʃ] n kjøtt nt

flew [flu:] v (p fly)

flex [fleks] n ledning m; v
bøye

flexible ['fleksibəl] *adj* bøyelig

flight [flait] *n* flytur *m*; charter ~ chartertur *m*

flint [flint] *n* flintstein *m*

float [flout] *v* *flyte; *n* flottør *m*

flock [flɔk] *n* flokk *m*

flood [flʌd] *n* oversvømmelse *m*; flo *m*

floor [flɔ:] *n* gulv *nt*; etasje *m*; first ~ annen etasje; *Am* første etasje; ~ show floor- -show *nt*

florist ['flɔrist] *n* blomsterhandler *m*

flour [flauə] *n* mel *nt*

flow [flou] *v* strømme, *flyte

flower [flauə] *n* blomst *m*; ~ shop blomsterforretning *c*

flowerbed ['flauəbed] *n* blomsterbed *nt*

flown [floun] *v* (pp fly)

flu [flu:] *n* influensa *m*

fluent ['flu:ənt] *adj* flytende

fluid ['flu:id] *adj* flytende; *n* væske *c*

flute [flu:t] *n* fløyte *c*

fly [flai] *n* flue *c*; buksesmekk *m*

*fly [flai] *v* *fly

foam [foum] *n* skum *nt*; *v* skumme; ~ rubber skumgummi *m*

focus ['foukəs] *n* brennpunkt *nt*

fog [fɔg] *n* tåke *c*

foggy ['fɔgi] *adj* tåket

foglamp ['fɔglæmp] *n* tåkelykt *c*

fold [fould] *v* brette, folde; folde sammen; *n* fold *m*

folk [fouk] *n* folk *nt*; ~ dance folkedans *m*; ~ song folkevise *c*

folklore ['fouklɔ:] *n* folklore *c*

follow ['fɔlou] *v* *følge; following *adj* neste, følgende

fond: *be ~ of [bi: fɔnd ɔv] like

food [fu:d] *n* mat *m*; føde *c*; ~ poisoning matforgiftning *c*

foodstuffs ['fu:dstʌfs] *pl* matvarer *pl*

fool [fu:l] *n* tosk *m*; *v* narre

foolish ['fu:liʃ] *adj* fjollet, tåpelig; dum

foot [fut] *n* (pl feet) fot *m*; on ~ til fots

football ['futbɔ:l] *n* fotball *m*; ~ match fotballkamp *m*

foot brake ['futbreik] *n* fotbrems *m*

footpath ['futpa:θ] *n* gangsti *m*

footwear ['futwεə] *n* skotøy *nt*

for [fɔ:, fə] *prep* til; i; på grunn av, av, for; *conj* for

*forbid [fə'bid] *v* *forby

force [fɔ:s] *v* *tvinge; forsere; *n* kraft *c*, styrke *m*; vold *m*; by ~ nødtvunget; driving ~ drivkraft *c*

forecast ['fɔ:ka:st] *n* varsel *nt*; *v* *forutsi, varsle

foreground ['fɔ:graund] *n*

forgrunn *m*

forehead ['fɔred] *n* panne *c*

foreign ['fɔrin] *adj*
utenlandsk; fremmed

foreigner ['fɔrinə] *n*
utlending *m*

foreman ['fɔ:mən] *n* (pl
-men) formann *m*

foremost ['fɔ:moust] *adj*
fremst, forrest

forest ['fɔrist] *n* skog *m*

forester ['fɔristə] *n*
forstmann *m*

forever, for ever [fə'revə]
adv for alltid; stadig

forge [fɔ:dʒ] *v* forfalske

***forget** [fə'get] *v* glemme

forgetful [fə'getfəl] *adj*
glemsom

***forgive** [fə'giv] *v* *tilgi

fork [fɔ:k] *n* gaffel *m*;
skillevei *m*; *v* dele seg

form [fɔ:m] *n* form *c*;
blankett *m*; skjema *nt*;
klasse *c*; *v* forme

formal ['fɔ:məl] *adj* formell

formality [fɔ:'mæləti] *n*
formalitet *m*

former ['fɔ:mə] *adj*
forhenværende; tidligere;
formerly før i tiden

formula ['fɔ:mjulə] *n* (pl ~e,
~s) formel *m*

fortnight ['fɔ:tnait] *n*
fjorten dager

fortress ['fɔ:tris] *n* festning
m

fortunate ['fɔ:tʃənət] *adj*
heldig

fortunately ['fɔ:tʃənətli]

adv heldigvis

fortune ['fɔ:tʃu:n] *n* formue
m; skjebne *m*, lykke *c*

forty ['fɔ:ti] *num* førti

forward ['fɔ:wəd] *adv* frem,
fremad; *v* ettersende

foster parents
['fɔstə,pεərənts] *pl*
pleieforeldre *pl*

fought [fɔ:t] *v* (p, pp fight)

foul [faul] *adj* skitten;
gemen

found¹ [faund] *v* (p, pp
find)

found² [faund] *v*
*grunnlegge, opprette,
stifte

foundation [faun'deiʃən] *n*
grunnlag *nt*; stiftelse *m*

fountain ['fauntin] *n*
springvann *nt*; kilde *m*

fountain pen ['fauntinpen]
n fyllepenn *m*

four [fɔ:] *num* fire

fourteen [,fɔ:'ti:n] *num*
fjorten

fourteenth [,fɔ:'ti:nθ] *num*
fjortende

fourth [fɔ:θ] *num* fjerde

fowl [faul] *n* (pl ~s, ~)
fjærkre *nt*

fox [fɔks] *n* rev *m*

foyer ['fɔiei] *n* foajé *m*

fraction ['frækʃən] *n*
brøkdel *m*

fracture ['fræktʃə] *v*
*brekke; *n* brudd *nt*

fragile ['frædʒail] *adj* skjør;
skrøpelig

fragment ['frægmənt] *n*

bruddstykke *nt*; stykke *nt*
frame [freim] *n* ramme *c*;
innfatning *m*
France [frɑːns] Frankrike
franchise [ˈfræntʃaiz] *n*
stemmerett *m*
frank [fræŋk] *adj* oppriktig
fraternity [frəˈtəːnəti] *n*
brorskap *m*
fraud [frɔːd] *n* bedrageri *nt*
fray [frei] *v* trevle opp
free [friː] *adj* fri; gratis; ~ **of
charge** gratis; ~ **ticket**
fribillett *m*
freedom [ˈfriːdəm] *n* frihet *c*
*****freeze** [friːz] *v* *fryse; fryse
freezer [ˈfriːzə] *n* fryser *m*,
fryseboks *m*
freezing [ˈfriːziŋ] *adj* iskald
freezing point
[ˈfriːziŋpɔint] *n* frysepunkt
nt
freight [freit] *n* last *c*, frakt *c*
freight train [ˈfreittrein]
nAm godstog *nt*
French [frentʃ] *adj* fransk;
the ~ *pl* franskmennene; ~
fries *pl* pommes frites
Frenchman [ˈfrentʃmən] *n*
(pl -men) franskmann *m*
frequency [ˈfriːkwənsi] *n*
frekvens *m*; hyppighet *c*
frequent [ˈfriːkwənt] *adj*
stadig, hyppig; **frequently**
ofte
fresh [freʃ] *adj* fersk;
forfriskende; ~ **water**
ferskvann *nt*
friction [ˈfrikʃən] *n* friksjon
m

Friday [ˈfraidi] fredag *m*
fridge [fridʒ] *n* kjøleskap *nt*
friend [frend] *n* venn *m*;
venninne *c*
friendly [ˈfrendli] *adj*
vennlig; vennskapelig
friendship [ˈfrendʃip] *n*
vennskap *nt*
fright [frait] *n* skrekk *m*,
angst *m*
frighten [ˈfraitən] *v*
forskrekke
frightened [ˈfraitənd] *adj*
skremt; ***be** ~ ***bli**
forskrekket
frightful [ˈfraitfəl] *adj*
forferdelig, forskrekkelig
fringe [frindʒ] *n* frynse *c*
frock [frɔk] *n* kjole *m*
frog [frɔg] *n* frosk *m*
from [frɔm] *prep* fra; av; fra
og med
front [frʌnt] *n* forside *c*; **in** ~
of foran
frontier [ˈfrʌntiə] *n* grense *c*
frost [frɔst] *n* frost *m*
frozen [ˈfrouzən] *adj*
frossen; ~ **food** dypfryst
mat
fruit [fruːt] *n* frukt *c*
fry [frai] *v* steke
frying pan [ˈfraiiŋpæn] *n*
stekepanne *c*
fuck [fʌk] *v vulgar* knulle,
pule
fuel [ˈfjuːəl] *n* brensel *nt*;
bensin *m*; ~ **pump** *Am*
bensinpumpe *c*
full [ful] *adj* full; ~ **board**
helpensjon *m*; ~ **stop**

punktum *nt*; ~ up fullsatt
fun [fʌn] *n* moro *c*, gøy *m* /
nt
function ['fʌŋkʃən] *n*
funksjon *m*
fund [fʌnd] *n* fond *nt*
fundamental
[,fʌndə'mentəl] *adj*
fundamental
funeral ['fju:nərəl] *n*
begravelse *m*
funnel ['fʌnəl] *n* trakt *c*
funny ['fʌni] *adj* pussig,
komisk; merkelig
fur [fə:] *n* pels *m*; ~ **coat**
pelskåpe *c*
furious ['fjuəriəs] *adj*
rasende
furnace ['fə:nis] *n* ovn *m*

furnish ['fə:niʃ] *v* forsyne,
skaffe; møblere, innrette; ~
with forsyne med
furniture ['fə:nitʃə] *n*
møbler *pl*
furrier ['fʌriə] *n* buntmaker
m
further ['fə:ðə] *adj* videre;
ytterligere
furthermore ['fə:ðəmɔ:]
adv dessuten
furthest ['fə:ðist] *adj*
fjernest; lengst
fuse [fju:z] *n* sikring *c*;
lunte *c*
fuss [fʌs] *n* bråk *nt*; oppstyr
nt, mas *nt*
future ['fju:tʃə] *n* fremtid *c*;
adj fremtidig

G

gable ['geibəl] *n* gavl *m*
gadget ['gædʒit] *n*
innretning *m*, apparat *nt*
gain [gein] *v* *vinne; *n*
fortjeneste *m*
gale [geil] *n* storm *m*
gall [gɔ:l] *n* galle *m*; ~
bladder galleblære *c*
gallery ['gæləri] *n* galleri *nt*;
kunstgalleri *c*
gallon ['gælən] *n* gallon *m*
(Brit 4,55 l; Am 3,79 l)
gallop ['gæləp] *n* galopp *m*
gallows ['gæləuz] *pl* galge
m
gallstone ['gɔ:lstoun] *n*
gallestein *m*

game [geim] *n* spill *nt*; vilt
nt
gang [gæŋ] *n* bande *m*;
gjeng *m*
gangway ['gæŋwei] *n*
landgang *m*
gap [gæp] *n* åpning *c*
garage ['gæra:ʒ] *n* garasje
m; *v* *sette i garasje
garbage ['ga:bidʒ] *n* avfall
nt, søppel *nt*
garden ['ga:dən] *n* hage *m*;
public ~ offentlig
parkanlegg; **zoological**
gardens zoologisk hage
gardener ['ga:dənə] *n*
gartner *m*

gargle ['gɑ:gəl] v gurgle

garlic ['gɑ:lik] n hvitløk m

garment [,gɑ:mənt] n klesplagg m

gas [gæs] n gass m; bensin m; ~ cooker gasskomfyr m; ~ pump Am bensinpumpe c; ~ station bensinstasjon m; ~ stove gasovn m

gasoline ['gæsəli:n] nAm bensin m

gastric ['gæstrik] adj mage-; ~ ulcer magesår nt

gasworks ['gæswə:ks] n gassverk nt

gate [geit] n port m; grind c

gather ['gæðə] v samle; samles; høste

gauge [geidʒ] n måleinstrument nt

gave [geiv] v (p give)

gay [gei] adj munter; fargerik; colloquial homofil

gaze [geiz] v stirre

gear [giə] n gir nt; utstyr nt; change ~ skifte gir; ~ lever girstang c

gearbox ['giəbɔks] n girkasse c

geese [gi:z] n (pl goose) gjess pl

gem [dʒem] n edelsten m, juvel m; klenodie nt

gender ['dʒendə] n kjønn nt

general ['dʒenərəl] adj generell; n general m; ~ practitioner allmennpraktiserende lege; in ~ som regel

generate ['dʒenəreit] v *frembringe

generation [,dʒenə'reiʃən] n generasjon m

generator ['dʒenəreitər] n generator m

generosity [,dʒenə'rɔsəti] n gavmildhet c

generous ['dʒenərəs] adj gavmild

genital ['dʒenitəl] adj kjønns-

genius ['dʒi:niəs] n geni nt

gentle ['dʒentəl] adj mild; lett, øm; forsiktig

gentleman ['dʒentəlmən] n (pl -men) herre m

genuine ['dʒenjuin] adj ekte

geography [dʒi'ɔgrəfi] n geografi m

geology [dʒi'ɔlədʒi] n geologi m

geometry [dʒi'ɔmətri] n geometri m

germ [dʒə:m] n basill m; kim m

German ['dʒə:mən] adj tysk; n tysker m

Germany ['dʒə:məni] Tyskland

gesticulate [dʒi'stikjuleit] v gestikulere

get-together sammenkomst m

*get [get] v *få; hente; *bli; ~ back *gå tilbake; ~ off *stige av; ~ on *stige på; *gjøre fremskritt; ~ up *stå opp

ghost

ghost [goust] *n* spøkelse *nt*; ånd *m*

giant ['dʒaiənt] *n* kjempe *m*

giddiness ['gidinəs] *n* svimmelhet *c*

giddy ['gidi] *adj* svimmel

gift [gift] *n* presang *m*, gave *c*; evne *c*; ~ **card** *n* gavekort *nt*

gifted ['giftid] *adj* begavet

gigantic [dʒai'gæntik] *adj* enorm

giggle ['gigəl] *v* fnise

gill [gil] *n* gjelle *c*

gilt [gilt] *adj* forgylt

ginger ['dʒindʒə] *n* ingefær *m*

girl [gə:l] *n* pike *m*

girlfriend ['gə:lfrend] *n* kjæreste *m*

***give** [giv] *v* *gi; *gave, *overrekke; ~ **away** røpe; ~ **in** *gi seg, *gi etter; ~ **up** *oppgi, *gi opp

glacier ['glæsiə] *n* isbre *m*

glad [glæd] *adj* fornøyd, glad; **gladly** med glede, gjerne

gladness ['glædnəs] *n* glede *c*

glamorous ['glæmərəs] *adj* betagende, fortryllende

glamour ['glæmə] *n* sjarm *m*

glance [glɑ:ns] *n* blikk *nt*; *v* kaste et blikk

gland [glænd] *n* kjertel *m*

glare [gleə] *n* skarpt lys; skinn *nt*

glaring ['gleəriŋ] *adj* blendende

glass [glɑ:s] *n* glass *nt*; glass-; **glasses** briller *pl*; **magnifying** ~ forstørrelsesglass *nt*

glaze [gleiz] *v* glasere

glide [glaid] *v* *gli

glider ['glaidə] *n* glidefly *nt*

glimpse [glimps] *n* glimt *nt*; *v* skimte

global ['gloubəl] *adj* verdensomfattende; ~ **warming** *n* global oppvarming *c*

globalization [,gloubəli'zeiʃən] *n* globalisering *c*

globalize ['gloubə,laiz] *v* globalisere

globe [gloub] *n* globus *m*, jordklode *m*

gloom [glu:m] *n* mørke *nt*

gloomy ['glu:mi] *adj* dyster

glorious ['glɔ:riəs] *adj* strålende

glory ['glɔ:ri] *n* ære *c*, berømmelse *m*; ros *m*, heder *m*

gloss [glɔs] *n* glans *m*

glossy ['glɔsi] *adj* blank

glove [glʌv] *n* hanske *m*

glow [glou] *v* gløde; *n* glød *m*

glue [glu:] *n* lim *nt*

***go** [gou] *v* *gå; reise; ~ **ahead** *fortsette; ~ **away** reise bort; ~ **back** vende tilbake; ~ **home** *gå hjem; ~ **in** *gå inn; ~ **on** *fortsette, *gå videre; ~ **out**

*gå ut; ~ **through**
*gjennomgå, *gå igjennom
goal [goul] *n* mål *nt*
goalkeeper ['goul,ki:pə] *n*
målmann *m*
goat [gout] *n* geit *c*
god [gɔd] *n* gud *m*
goddess ['gɔdis] *n* gudinne
c
godmother ['gɔd,mʌðə] *n*
gudmor *c*; fadder *m*
godfather ['gɔd,fɑ:ðə] *n*
gudfar *m*; fadder *m*
goggles ['gɔgəlz] *pl*
dykkerbriller *pl*, snøbriller
pl
gold [gould] *n* gull *nt*; ~ **leaf**
bladgull *nt*
golden ['gouldən] *adj* gyllen
goldsmith ['gouldsmiθ] *n*
gullsmed *m*
golf [gɔlf] *n* golf *m*; ~
course golfbane *m*; ~ **links**
golfbane *m*
golfclub ['gɔlfklʌb] *n*
golfkølle *c*; golfklubb *m*
gondola ['gɔndələ] *n*
gondol *m*
gone [gɔn] *adv* (pp go)
borte
good [gud] *adj* bra, god;
snill
goodbye [,gud'bai] adjø
good-humo(u)red
[,gud'hju:məd] *adj* godlynt
good-looking [,gud'lukiŋ]
adj pen
good-natured
[,gud'neitʃəd] *adj*
godmodig

goods [gudz] *pl* varer *pl*; ~
train godstog *nt*
good-tempered
[,gud'tempəd] *adj*
godmodig
goodwill [,gud'wil] *n*
godvilje *m*
goose [gu:s] *n* (pl geese)
gås *c*; ~ **flesh** gåsehud *c*
gooseberry ['guzbəri] *n*
stikkelsbær *m*
gorge [gɔ:dʒ] *n* kløft *c*; *v*
proppe seg
gorgeous ['gɔ:dʒəs] *adj*
praktfull
gospel ['gɔspəl] *n*
evangelium *nt*
gossip ['gɔsip] *n* sladder *m*;
v sladre
got [gɔt] *v* (p, pp get)
gout [gaut] *n* gikt *c*
govern ['gʌvən] *v* regjere
government ['gʌvənmənt]
n styre *nt*, regjering *c*
governor ['gʌvənə] *n*
guvernør *m*
gown [gaun] *n* kjole *m*
GPS ['dʒi:pi:'es], **global
positioning system** *n* GPS
nt, globalt posisjonssystem
nt
grace [greis] *n* ynde *m*;
nåde *n*
graceful ['greisfəl] *adj*
yndig, grasiøs
grade [greid] *n* grad *m*;
klasse *c*, *v* klassifisere;
gradere
gradient ['greidiənt] *n*
helling *c*

gradual ['grædʒuəl] *adj*
gradvis

graduate ['grædʒueit] *v* *ta
avsluttende eksamen

grain [grein] *n* korn *nt*

gram [græm] *n* gram *nt*

grammar ['græmə] *n*
grammatikk *m*; ~ book
grammatikk *m*

grammatical [grə'mætikəl]
adj grammatisk

grand [grænd] *adj* storartet

grandchild ['græn,tʃaild] *n*
barnebarn *nt*

granddad ['grændæd],
grandfather ['græn,fɑ:ðə]
n farfar *m*; morfar *m*;
bestefar *m*

grandma ['grænmɑ],
grandmother
['græn,mʌðə] *n* farmor *c*;
mormor *c*; bestemor *c*

grandparents
['græn,peərənts] *pl*
besteforeldre *pl*

granite ['grænit] *n* granitt *m*

grant [grɑ:nt] *v* bevilge;
innvilge; *n* stipend *nt*,
tilskudd *nt*

grapefruit ['greipfru:t] *n*
grapefrukt *c*

grapes [greips] *pl* druer *pl*

graph [græf] *n* diagram *nt*

graphic ['græfik] *adj* grafisk

grasp [grɑ:sp] *v* *gripe; *n*
grep *nt*

grass [grɑ:s] *n* gress *nt*

grasshopper ['grɑ:s,hɔpə]
n gresshoppe *c*

grate [greit] *n* rist *c*; *v* raspe

grateful ['greitfəl] *adj*
takknemlig

grater ['greitə] *n* rivjern *nt*;
rasp *c*

gratis ['grætis] *adj* gratis

gratitude ['grætitju:d] *n*
takknemlighet *c*

gratuity [grə'tju:əti] *n*
drikkepenger *pl*

grave [greiv] *n* grav *c*; *adj*
alvorlig

gravel ['grævəl] *n* grus *m*

gravestone ['greivstoun] *n*
gravstein *m*

graveyard ['greivjɑ:d] *n*
kirkegård *m*

gravity ['grævəti] *n*
tyngdekraft *c*; alvor *nt*

gravy ['greivi] *n* saus *m*

graze [greiz] *v* beite; *n*
skrubbsår *nt*

grease [gri:s] *n* fett *nt*; *v*
*smøre

greasy ['gri:si] *adj* fettet

great [greit] *adj* stor; Great
Britain Storbritannia

Greece [gri:s] Hellas

greed [gri:d] *n* griskhet *c*

greedy ['gri:di] *adj* grisk;
grådig

Greek [gri:k] *adj* gresk; *n*
greker *m*

green [gri:n] *adj* grønn; ~
card grønt kort

greengrocer ['gri:n,grousə]
n grønnsakhandler *m*

greenhouse ['gri:nhaus] *n*
drivhus *nt*

greens [gri:nz] *pl*
grønnsaker *pl*

greet [griːt] v hilse

greeting ['griːtiŋ] n hilsen m

grey [grei] adj grå

greyhound ['greihaund] n mynde m

grief [griːf] n sorg c; smerte m

grieve [griːv] v sørge

grill [gril] n grill m; v grille

grim [grim] adj grusom, skrekkelig

grin [grin] v glise, smile bredt; n glis nt

*grind [graind] v male; finmale

grip [grip] v *gripe; n grep nt, tak nt

grit [grit] n grus m; fasthet c

groan [groun] v stønne

grocer ['grousə] n matvarehandler m; grocer's matvareforretning c

groceries ['grousəriz] pl matvarer pl

groin [grɔin] n lyske m

groom [gruːm] n hestepleier m, stallkar m; brudgom m; v pleie

groove [gruːv] n fure m

gross [grous] adj grov; brutto

grotto ['grɔtou] n (pl ~es, ~s) grotte c

ground¹ [graund] n jord c, grunn m; ~ floor første etasje; grounds tomt m

ground² [graund] v (p, pp grind)

group [gruːp] n gruppe c

grouse [graus] n (pl ~) rype c

grove [grouv] n lund m

*grow [grou] v vokse; dyrke; *bli

growl [graul] v brumme

grown-up ['grounʌp] adj voksen; n voksen m

growth [grouθ] n vekst m; svulst m

grudge [grʌdʒ] v misunne

grumble ['grʌmbəl] v knurre, klage

guarantee [,gærən'tiː] n garanti m; kausjon m; v garantere

guard [gɑːd] n vakt c; v bevokte

guardian ['gɑːdiən] n formynder m

guess [ges] v gjette; *anta; n formodning m

guest [gest] n gjest m; ~ room gjesteværelse nt

guesthouse ['gesthaus] n pensjonat nt

guide [gaid] n guide m; v vise vei

guidebook ['gaidbuk] n reisehåndbok c

guide dog ['gaiddɔg] n førerhund m

guideline ['gaidlain] n retningslinje c

guilt [gilt] n skyld c

guilty ['gilti] adj skyldig

guinea pig ['ginipig] n marsvin nt; forsøksdyr nt

guitar [gi'tɑː] n gitar m

gulf [gʌlf] *n* golf *m*; vik *c*
gull [gʌl] *n* måke *c*
gum [gʌm] *n* tannkjøtt *nt*;
gummi *m*; lim *nt*
gun [gʌn] *n* revolver *m*,
gevær *nt*; kanon *m*
gunpowder ['gʌn,paudə] *n*
krutt *nt*
gust [gʌst] *n* vindkast *nt*
gusty ['gʌsti] *adj* blåsende
gut [gʌt] *n* tarm *m*; **guts**
vågemot *nt*
gutter ['gʌtə] *n* rennestein

m
guy [gai] *n* kar *m*
gymnasium [dʒim'neiziəm]
n (pl ~s, -sia)
gymnastikksal *m*
gymnast ['dʒimnæst] *n*
turner *m*
gymnastics [dʒim'næstiks]
pl gymnastikk *m*
gynaecologist
[,gainə'kɔlədʒist] *n*
kvinnelege *m*, gynekolog *m*

H

habit ['hæbit] *n* vane *m*
habitable ['hæbitəbəl] *adj*
beboelig
habitual [hə'bitʃuəl] *adj*
vanemessig
had [hæd] *v* (p, pp have)
haddock ['hædək] *n* (pl ~)
kolje *c*
h(a)emorrhage ['heməridʒ]
n blødning *m*
haemorrhoids ['hemərɔidz]
pl hemorroider *pl*
hail [heil] *n* hagl *nt*
hair [hεə] *n* hår *nt*; ~ **gel**
hårgelé
hairbrush ['hεəbrʌʃ] *n*
hårbørste *c*
haircut ['hεəkʌt] *n* hårklipp

m
hairdo ['hεədu:] *n* frisyre *m*
hairdresser ['hεə,dresə] *n*
frisør *m*
hairdrier, hairdryer

['hεədraiə] *n* hårtørrer *m*
hairpin ['hεəpin] *n*
hårspenne *c*
hair spray ['hεəsprei] *n*
hårlakk *m*
hairy ['hεəri] *adj* håret
half[1] [hɑ:f] *adj* halv
half[2] [hɑ:f] *n* (pl halves)
halvdel *m*
half time [,hɑ:f'taim] *n*
halvtid *c*
halfway [,hɑ:f'wei] *adv*
halvveis
halibut ['hælibət] *n* (pl ~)
kveite *c*
hall [hɔ:l] *n* vestibyle *m*; sal
m
halt [hɔ:lt] *v* stanse
halve [hɑ:v] *v* halvere
ham [hæm] *n* skinke *c*
hamlet ['hæmlət] *n* liten
landsby
hammer ['hæmə] *n* hammer

hasty

m

hammock ['hæmək] *n*
hengekøye *c*
hamper ['hæmpə] *n* kurv *m*
hand [hænd] *n* hånd *c*; *v*
*overrekke; ~ **cream**
håndkrem *m*
handbag ['hændbæg] *n*
håndveske *c*
handbook ['hændbuk] *n*
håndbok *c*
handbrake ['hændbreik] *n*
håndbrems *m*
handcuffs ['hændkʌfs] *pl*
håndjern *pl*
handful ['hændful] *n*
håndfull *m*
handheld ['hand,held] *adj*
håndholdt
handicraft ['hændikrɑ:ft] *n*
håndverk *nt*;
kunsthåndverk *nt*
handicap ['hændikæp] *n*
handikap *nt*;
funksjonshemming *c*
handkerchief ['hæŋkətʃif]
n lommetørkle *nt*
handle ['hændəl] *n* skaft *nt*,
håndtak *nt*; *v* håndtere;
behandle
hand-made [,hænd'meid]
adj håndlaget
handshake ['hændʃeik] *n*
håndtrykk *nt*
handsome ['hænsəm] *adj*
pen
handwork ['hændwə:k] *n*
håndarbeid *nt*
handwriting ['hænd,raitiŋ]
n håndskrift *c*

handy ['hændi] *adj* hendig
***hang** [hæŋ] *v* *henge
hanger ['hæŋə] *n* henger *m*
hangover ['hæŋ,ouvə] *n*
bakrus *m*, tømmermenn *pl*
happen ['hæpən] *v* hende,
skje
happening ['hæpəniŋ] *n*
hendelse *m*, begivenhet *c*
happiness ['hæpinəs] *n*
lykke *c*
happy ['hæpi] *adj* lykkelig,
glad
harbour ['hɑ:bə] *n* havn *c*
hard [hɑ:d] *adj* hard;
vanskelig; ~ **disk** harddisk;
hardly neppe
hardware ['hɑ:dwɛə] *n*
jernvarer *pl*; ~ **store**
jernvarehandel *m*
hare [hɛə] *n* hare *m*
harm [hɑ:m] *n* skade *m*;
fortred *m*; *v* skade
harmful ['hɑ:mfəl] *adj*
skadelig
harmless ['hɑ:mləs] *adj*
uskadelig; harmløs
harmony ['hɑ:məni] *n*
harmoni *c*
harp [hɑ:p] *n* harpe *c*
harpsichord ['hɑ:psikɔ:d] *n*
cembalo *m*
harsh [hɑ:ʃ] *adj* streng;
grusom
harvest ['hɑ:vist] *n* avling *c*
has [hæz] *v* (pr have)
haste [heist] *n* hast *m*
hasten ['heisən] *v* skynde
seg
hasty ['heisti] *adj* hurtig;

forhastet
hat [hæt] *n* hatt *m*
hatch [hætʃ] *n* luke *c*; *v* ruge ut
hate [heit] *v* avsky; hate; *n* hat *nt*
hatred ['heitrid] *n* hat *nt*
haughty ['hɔːti] *adj* hovmodig
haul [hɔːl] *v* slepe
*have [hæv] *v* *ha; *få; ~ to *måtte
hawk [hɔːk] *n* hauk *m*; falk *m*
hay [hei] *n* høy *nt*; ~ fever høysnue *m*
hazard ['hæzəd] *n* risiko *m*
haze [heiz] *n* dis *m*
hazelnut ['heizəlnʌt] *n* hasselnøtt *c*
hazy ['heizi] *adj* disig
he [hiː] *pron* han
head [hed] *n* hode *nt*; *v* lede; ~ of state statsoverhode *nt*; ~ teacher overlærer *m*; ~ waiter hovmester *m*
headache ['hedeik] *n* hodepine *c*
heading ['hediŋ] *n* overskrift *c*
headlamp ['hedlæmp] *n* frontlys *nt*
headlight ['hedlait] *n* frontlys *nt*
headline ['hedlain] *n* overskrift *c*
headmaster [,hed'mɑːstə] *n* overlærer *m*; rektor *m*
headquarters

[,hed'kwɔːtəz] *pl* hovedkvarter *nt*
headrest ['hedrest] *n* nakkestøtte *m*
head-strong ['hedstrɔŋ] *adj* sta
heal [hiːl] *v* hele, lege
health [helθ] *n* helse *c*; ~ certificate helseattest *m*
healthy ['helθi] *adj* sunn
heap [hiːp] *n* hop *m*, haug *m*
*hear [hiə] *v* høre
hearing ['hiəriŋ] *n* hørsel *m*
heart [hɑːt] *n* hjerte *nt*; kjerne *m*; by ~ utenat; ~ attack hjerteanfall *nt*
heartburn ['hɑːtbəːn] *n* halsbrann *m*
hearth [hɑːθ] *n* ildsted *nt*
heartless ['hɑːtləs] *adj* hjerteløs
hearty ['hɑːti] *adj* hjertelig
heat [hiːt] *n* hete *m*, varme *m*; *v* varme opp; heating pad varmepute *c*
heater ['hiːtə] *n* varmeovn *m*
heath [hiːθ] *n* hei *c*
heathen ['hiːðən] *n* hedning *m*; *adj* hedensk
heather ['heðə] *n* lyng *m*
heating ['hiːtiŋ] *n* fyring *c*
heaven ['hevən] *n* himmel *m*
heavy ['hevi] *adj* tung
Hebrew ['hiːbruː] *n* hebraisk *nt*
hedge [hedʒ] *n* hekk *m*
hedgehog ['hedʒhɔg] *n* pinnsvin *nt*

heel [hi:l] *n* hæl *m*

height [hait] *n* høyde *m*; høydepunkt *nt*

heir [eə] *n* arving *m*

heiress [eəres] *n* kvinnelig arving *m*

helicopter ['helikɔptə] *n* helikopter *nt*

hell [hel] *n* helvete *nt*

hello! [he'lou] hei!, hallo!; say hello to hilse på

helm [helm] *n* ror *nt*

helmet ['helmit] *n* hjelm *m*

helmsman ['helmzmən] *n* rormann *m*

help [help] *v* *hjelpe; *n* hjelp *c*

helper ['helpə] *n* hjelper *m*

helpful ['helpfəl] *adj* hjelpsom

helping ['helpiŋ] *n* porsjon *m*

hem [hem] *n* fald *m*; søm *m*

hemp [hemp] *n* hamp *m*

hen [hen] *n* høne *c*

her [hɔ:] *pron* henne; hennes

herb [hɔ:b] *n* urt *c*

herd [hɔ:d] *n* flokk *m*; bøling *m*

here [hiə] *adv* her; ~ you are! vær så god!

hereditary [hi'reditəri] *adj* arvelig

hernia ['hɔ:niə] *n* brokk *m* / *nt*

hero ['hiərou] *n* (pl ~es) helt *m*

heron ['herən] *n* hegre *m*

herring ['heriŋ] *n* (pl ~, ~s) sild *c*

herself [hɔ:'self] *pron* seg; selv

hesitate ['heziteit] *v* nøle

heterosexual [,hetərə'sekʃuəl] *adj* heteroseksuell

hiccup ['hikʌp] *n* hikke *m*

hide [haid] *n* skinn *nt*

*hide [haid] *v* gjemme; skjule

hideous ['hidiəs] *adj* avskyelig

hierarchy ['haiərɑ:ki] *n* hierarki *n*

high [hai] *adj* høy

highway ['haiwei] *n* riksvei *m*; motorvei *m*

hijack ['haidʒæk] *v* kapre

hijacker ['haidʒækə] *n* kaprer *m*

hike [haik] *v* *gå fottur

hill [hil] *n* bakke *m*

hillside ['hilsaid] *n* li *c*; bakke *m*

hilltop ['hiltɔp] *n* bakketopp *m*

hilly ['hili] *adj* kupert

him [him] *pron* han, ham

himself [him'self] *pron* seg; selv

hinder ['hində] *v* hindre

hinge [hindʒ] *n* hengsel *nt*

hint [hint] *n* hint; antydning *c*

hip [hip] *n* hofte *c*

hip-hop ['hip,hɔp] *n* hiphop *c*

hire [haiə] *v* leie; for ~ til leie

hire purchase

[ˌhaiəˈpɔːtʃəs] n
avbetalingskjøp nt

his [hiz] adj hans

historian [hiˈstɔːriən] n
historiker m

historic [hiˈstɔrik] adj
historisk

historical [hiˈstɔrikəl] adj
historisk

history [ˈhistəri] n historie c

hit [hit] n suksess m; slag nt;
treff nt

*hit [hit] v *slå; ramme,
*treffe

hitchhike [ˈhitʃhaik] v haike

hitchhiker [ˈhitʃˌhaikə] n
haiker m

hoarse [hɔːs] adj hes

hobby [ˈhɔbi] n hobby m

hobbyhorse [ˈhɔbihɔːs] n
kjepphest m

hockey [ˈhɔki] n hockey m

hoist [hɔist] v heise

hold [hould] n lasterom nt

*hold [hould] v *holde,
*holde på; *beholde; ~ on
*holde seg fast; ~ up
*holde oppe, støtte

hold-up [ˈhouldʌp] n
overfall nt

hole [houl] n hull nt

holiday [ˈhɔlədi] n ferie m;
helligdag m; ~ camp
ferieleir m; ~ resort
feriested nt; on ~ på ferie

Holland [ˈhɔlənd] Holland

hollow [ˈhɔlou] adj hul

holy [ˈhouli] adj hellig

homage [ˈhɔmidʒ] n hyllest
m

home [houm] n hjem nt;
pleiehjem nt; adv
hjemover, hjemme; at ~
hjemme

homework [ˈhoumwəːk] n
hjemmelekser pl, lekser pl

home-made [ˌhoumˈmeid]
adj hjemmelaget

homesickness
[ˈhoumˌsiknəs] n
hjemlengsel m

homosexual
[ˌhouməˈsekʃuəl] adj
homoseksuell; homofil

honest [ˈɔnist] adj ærlig;
oppriktig

honesty [ˈɔnisti] n ærlighet
c

honey [ˈhʌni] n honning m

honeymoon [ˈhʌnimuːn] n
hvetebrødsdager pl,
bryllupsreise c

honk [hʌŋk] vAm tute

honour [ˈɔnə] n ære c; v
hedre, ære

honourable [ˈɔnərəbəl] adj
ærefull, hederlig;
rettskaffen

hood [hud] n hette c;
motorpanser nt

hoof [huːf] n hov m

hook [huk] n krok m

hoot [huːt] v tute

hooter [ˈhuːtə] n bilhorn nt

hop¹ [hɔp] v hoppe; n hopp
nt

hop² [hɔp] n humle c

hope [houp] n håp nt; v
håpe

hopeful [ˈhoupfəl] adj

håpefull
hopeless ['houpləs] *adj*
håpløs
horizon [hə'raizən] *n*
horisont *m*
horizontal [,hɔri'zɔntəl] *adj*
horisontal
horn [hɔːn] *n* horn *nt*;
signalhorn *nt*
horrible ['hɔribəl] *adj*
redselsfull; grusom,
avskyelig, skrekkelig
horror ['hɔrə] *n* gru *m*,
redsel *m*
hors d'oeuvre [ɔː'dəːvr] *n*
forrett *m*
horse [hɔːs] *n* hest *m*
horseman ['hɔːsmən] *n* (pl
-men) rytter *m*
horsepower ['hɔːs,pauə] *n*
hestekraft *c*
horserace ['hɔːsreis] *n*
hestevddeløp *nt*
horseradish ['hɔːs,rædiʃ] *n*
pepperrot *c*
horseshoe ['hɔːsʃuː] *n*
hestesko *m*
hospitable ['hɔspitəbəl] *adj*
gjestfri
hospital ['hɔspitəl] *n*
sykehus *nt*, hospital *nt*
hospitality [,hɔspi'tæləti] *n*
gjestfrihet *c*
host [houst] *n* vert *m*
hostage ['hɔstidʒ] *n* gissel
nt
hostess ['houstis] *n*
vertinne *c*
hostile ['hɔstail] *adj*
fiendtlig

hot [hɔt] *adj* het, varm
hotel [hou'tel] *n* hotell *nt*
hotspot ['hɔt,spɔt] *n*
(*internet*) trådløs sone *c*
hot-tempered
[,hɔt'tempəd] *adj* hissig
hour [auə] *n* time *m*
hourly ['auəli] *adj* hver time
house [haus] *n* hus *nt*; bolig
m; ~ **agent**
eiendomsmegler *m*; ~
block *Am* kvartal *nt*;
public ~ vertshus *nt*
houseboat ['hausbout] *n*
husbåt *m*
household ['haushould] *n*
husstand *m*
housekeeper ['haus,kiːpə]
n husholderske *c*
housekeeping
['haus,kiːpiŋ] *n*
husholdning *m*
housemaid ['hausmeid] *n*
hushjelp *c*
housewife ['hauswaif] *n*
husmor *c*
housework ['hauswəːk] *n*
husarbeid *nt*
how [hau] *adv* hvordan;
hvor; ~ **many** hvor mange;
~ **much** hvor mye
however [hau'evə] *conj*
likevel
hug [hʌg] *v* omfavne;
klemme; *n* klem *m*
huge [hjuːdʒ] *adj* svær,
veldig, enorm
hum [hʌm] *v* nynne
human ['hjuːmən] *adj*
menneskelig; ~ **being**

menneske *nt*
humanity [hju'mænəti] *n*
menneskehet *c*
humble ['hʌmbəl] *adj*
ydmyk
humid ['hju:mid] *adj* fuktig
humidity [hju'midəti] *n*
fuktighet *c*
humorous ['hju:mərəs] *adj*
vittig, morsom,
humoristisk
humo(u)r ['hju:mə] *n*
humor *m*
hundred ['hʌndrəd] *n*
hundre
Hungarian [hʌŋ'gɛəriən]
adj ungarsk; *n* ungarer *m*
Hungary ['hʌŋgəri] Ungarn
hunger ['hʌŋgə] *n* sult *m*
hungry ['hʌŋgri] *adj* sulten
hunt [hʌnt] *v* jakte; *n* jakt *c*;
~ **for** lete etter
hunter ['hʌntə] *n* jeger *m*
hurricane ['hʌrikən] *n*
orkan *m*; ~ **lamp** stormlykt
c

hurry ['hʌri] *v* forte seg,
skynde seg; *n* hastverk *nt*;
in a ~ i full fart
***hurt** [hə:t] *v* *gjøre vondt,
skade; såre
hurtful ['hə:tfəl] *adj*
skadelig
husband ['hʌzbənd] *n*
ektemann *m*; mann *m*
hut [hʌt] *n* hytte *c*
hygiene ['haidʒi:n] *n*
hygiene *m*
hygienic [hai'dʒi:nik] *adj*
hygienisk
hymn [him] *n* hymne *m*,
salme *m*
hyphen ['haifən] *n*
bindestrek *m*
hypocrisy [hi'pɔkrəsi] *n*
hykleri *nt*
hypocrite ['hipəkrit] *n*
hykler *m*
hypocritical [,hipə'kritikəl]
adj hyklersk, skinnhellig
hysterical [hi'sterikəl] *adj*
hysterisk

I

I [ai] *pron* jeg
ice [ais] *n* is *m*; ~ **cream**
iskrem *m*
Iceland ['aislənd] Island
Icelander ['aisləndə] *n*
islending *m*
Icelandic [ais'lændik] *adj*
islandsk
icon ['aikɔn] *n* ikon *m* / *nt*
ID [ai'di:] *n* identitetskort *nt*

idea [ai'diə] *n* idé *m*; tanke
m, innfall *nt*; begrep *nt*,
forestilling *c*
ideal [ai'diəl] *adj* ideell; *n*
ideal *nt*
identical [ai'dentikəl] *adj*
identisk
identification
[ai,dentifi'keiʃən] *n*
identifisering *c*

impediment

identify [ai'dentifai] v
identifisere

identity [ai'dentəti] n
identitet m; ~ card
identitetskort nt

idiom ['idiəm] n idiom nt

idiomatic [,idiə'mætik] adj
idiomatisk

idiot ['idiət] n idiot m

idiotic [,idi'ɔtik] adj idiotisk

idle ['aidəl] adj uvirksom;
lat; nyttesløs

idol ['aidəl] n avgud m; idol
nt

if [if] conj hvis; om

ignition [ig'niʃən] n tenning
c; ~ coil tennspole c

ignorant ['ignərənt] adj
uvitende

ignore [ig'nɔ:] v ignorere

ill [il] adj syk; dårlig

illegal [i'li:gəl] adj illegal,
ulovlig

illegible [i'ledʒəbəl] adj
uleselig

illiterate [i'litərət] n
analfabet m

illness ['ilnəs] n sykdom m

illuminate [i'lu:mineit] v
opplyse, belyse

illumination [i,lu:mi'neiʃən]
n belysning m

illusion [i'lu:ʒən] n illusjon
m; fantasifoster nt

illustrate ['iləstreit] v
illustrere

illustration [,ilə'streiʃən] n
illustrasjon m

image ['imidʒ] n bilde nt

imaginary [i'mædʒinəri] adj

innbilt

imagination
[i,mædʒi'neiʃən] n fantasi
m

imagine [i'mædʒin] v
forestille seg; innbille seg;
tenke seg

imitate ['imiteit] v imitere,
etterligne

imitation [,imi'teiʃən] n
imitasjon m, etterligning c

immediate [i'mi:djət] adj
øyeblikkelig

immediately [i'mi:djətli]
adv straks, øyeblikkelig,
umiddelbart

immense [i'mens] adj
enorm, veldig, umåtelig

immigrant ['imigrənt] n
innvandrer m

immigrate ['imigreit] v
immigrere

immigration [,imi'greiʃən]
n immigrasjon m

immodest [i'mɔdist] adj
ubeskjeden

immunity [i'mju:nəti] n
immunitet m

immunize ['imjunaiz] v
*gjøre immun

impartial [im'pa:ʃəl] adj
upartisk

impassable [im'pa:səbəl]
adj ufremkommelig

impatient [im'peiʃənt] adj
utålmodig

impede [im'pi:d] v hindre,
sinke

impediment [im'pedimənt]
n hindring c

imperfect [im'pə:fikt] adj
ufullkommen

imperial [im'piəriəl] adj
keiserlig; riks-

impersonal [im'pə:sənəl]
adj upersonlig

impertinence
[im'pə:tinəns] n frekkhet c

impertinent [im'pə:tinənt]
adj uforskammet, nesevis

implement¹ ['implimənt] n
verktøy nt

implement² ['impliment] v
iverksette, implementere

imply [im'plai] v antyde;
*innebære

impolite [,impə'lait] adj
uhøflig

import¹ [im'pɔ:t] v
importere, innføre

import² [im'pɔ:t] n innførsel
m, importvarer pl, import
m; ~ duty importavgift c

importance [im'pɔ:təns] n
viktighet c, betydning m

important [im'pɔ:tənt] adj
betydningsfull, viktig

importer [im'pɔ:tə] n
importør m

imposing [im'pouziŋ] adj
imponerende

impossible [im'pɔsəbəl] adj
umulig

impotence ['impətəns] n
impotens m

impotent ['impətənt] adj
impotent; avmektig

impress [im'pres] v *gjøre
inntrykk på, imponere

impression [im'preʃən] n

inntrykk nt

impressive [im'presiv] adj
imponerende

imprison [im'prizən] v
fengsle

imprisonment
[im'prizənmənt] n
fangenskap nt

improbable [im'prɔbəbəl]
adj usannsynlig

improper [im'prɔpə] adj
upassende

improve [im'pru:v] v
forbedre

improvement
[im'pru:vmənt] n
forbedring c

improvise ['imprəvaiz] v
improvisere

impudent ['impjudənt] adj
uforskammet

impulse ['impʌls] n impuls
m; innskytelse m

impulsive [im'pʌlsiv] adj
impulsiv

in [in] prep i; om; adv inn

inaccessible
[i,næk'sesəbəl] adj
utilgjengelig

inaccurate [i'nækjurət] adj
unøyaktig

inadequate [i'nædikwət]
adj utilstrekkelig

incapable [iŋ'keipəbəl] adj
udugelig

incense ['insens] n røkelse
m

inch [intʃ] n tomme m (2,54
cm)

incident ['insidənt] n

hendelse *m*
incidental [ˌinsi'dentəl] *adj* tilfeldig
incite [in'sait] *v* anspore, egge
inclination [ˌiŋkli'neiʃən] *n* tilbøyelighet *c*
incline [in'klain] *n* skråning *m*
inclined [in'klaind] *adj* tilbøyelig
include [in'kluːd] *v* innbefatte, omfatte; included inkludert
inclusive [in'kluːsiv] *adj* inklusive
income ['iŋkəm] *n* inntekt *c*; ~ tax inntektsskatt *m*
incompetent [in'kɔmpətənt] *adj* inkompetent; udugelig
incomplete [ˌinkəm'pliːt] *adj* ufullstendig
inconceivable [ˌinkən'siːvəbəl] *adj* utenkelig
inconspicuous [ˌinkən'spikjuəs] *adj* uanselig
inconvenience [ˌinkən'viːnjəns] *n* ubeleilighet *c*, besvær *nt*
inconvenient [ˌinkən'viːnjənt] *adj* ubeleilig; besværlig
incorrect [ˌinkə'rekt] *adj* uriktig, feil
increase[1] [iŋ'kriːs] *v* øke; forsterke, *tilta
increase[2] ['iŋkriːs] *n* vekst

m; stigning *m*
incredible [iŋ'kredəbəl] *adj* utrolig
incurable [iŋ'kjuərəbəl] *adj* uhelbredelig
indecent [in'diːsənt] *adj* uanstendig
indeed [in'diːd] *adv* virkelig
indefinite [in'definit] *adj* ubestemt; uklar
indemnity [in'demnəti] *n* skadeserstatning *m*; erstatning *m*
independence [ˌindi'pendəns] *n* uavhengighet *c*
independent [ˌindi'pendənt] *adj* uavhengig; selvstendig
index ['indeks] *n* fortegnelse *m*, register *nt*; ~ finger pekefinger *m*
India ['indiə] India
Indian ['indiən] *adj* indisk; indiansk; *n* inder *m*; indianer *m*
indicate ['indikeit] *v* antyde, anvise, *angi
indication [ˌindi'keiʃən] *n* tegn *nt*
indicator ['indikeitə] *n* blinklys *nt*
indifferent [in'difərənt] *adj* likegyldig
indigestion [ˌindi'dʒestʃən] *n* dårlig fordøyelse
indignation [ˌindig'neiʃən] *n* forargelse *m*
indirect [ˌindi'rekt] *adj* indirekte

individual [ˌindi'vidʒuəl]
adj individuell, enkelt; n
enkeltperson *m*, individ *nt*
Indonesia [ˌində'niːziə]
Indonesia
Indonesian [ˌində'niːziən]
adj indonesisk; *n*
indoneser *m*
indoor ['indɔː] *adj*
innendørs
indoors [ˌin'dɔːz] *adv* inne
indulge [in'dʌldʒ] *v* *gi
etter; *hengi seg til
industrial [in'dʌstriəl] *adj*
industriell; ~ area
industriområde *nt*
industrious [in'dʌstriəs]
adj flittig
industry ['indəstri] *n*
industri *m*; næring *c*
inedible [i'nedibəl] *adj*
uspiselig
inefficient [ˌini'fiʃənt] *adj*
udugelig; ineffektiv
inevitable [i'nevitəbəl] *adj*
uunngåelig
inexpensive [ˌinik'spensiv]
adj billig
inexperienced
[ˌinik'spiəriənst] *adj*
uerfaren
infant ['infənt] *n* spedbarn
nt
infantry ['infəntri] *n*
infanteri *nt*
infect [in'fekt] *v* infisere,
smitte
infection [in'fekʃən] *n*
smitte *m*
infectious [in'fekʃəs] *adj*

smittsom
infer [in'fəː] *v* utlede
inferior [in'fiəriə] *adj*
dårligere, underlegen;
mindreverdig; nedre
infinite ['infinət] *adj*
uendelig
infinitive [in'finitiv] *n*
infinitiv *m*
inflammable [in'flæməbəl]
adj ildsfarlig
inflammation
[ˌinflə'meiʃən] *n*
betennelse *m*
inflatable [in'fleitəbəl] *adj*
oppblåsbar
inflate [in'fleit] *v* blåse opp
inflation [in'fleiʃən] *n*
inflasjon *m*
inflict [in'flikt] *v* tilføye
influence ['influəns] *n*
innflytelse *m*; *v* påvirke
influential [ˌinflu'enʃəl] *adj*
innflytelsesrik
influenza [ˌinflu'enzə] *n*
influensa *m*
inform [in'fɔːm] *v* opplyse,
informere; underrette,
meddele
informal [in'fɔːməl] *adj*
uformell
information [ˌinfə'meiʃən]
n informasjon *m*;
meddelelse *m*, opplysning
m; ~ bureau
informasjonskontor *nt*
infra-red [ˌinfrə'red] *adj*
infrarød
infrequent [in'friːkwənt]
adj sjelden

ingredient [iŋ'gri:diənt] *n*
bestanddel *m*, ingrediens
m

inhabit [in'hæbit] *v* bebo

inhabitable [in'hæbitəbəl]
adj beboelig

inhabitant [in'hæbitənt] *n*
innbygger *m*; beboer *m*

inhale [in'heil] *v* innånde

inherit [in'herit] *v* arve

inheritance [in'heritəns] *n*
arv *m*

inhibit [in'hibit] *v* hemme;
forhindre

initial [i'niʃəl] *adj*
opprinnelig, begynnelses-;
n forbokstav *m*; *v* merke
med initialer

initiate [i'niʃieit] *v* innføre;
*ta initiativet til

initiative [i'niʃətiv] *n*
initiativ *nt*

inject [in'dʒekt] *v*
innsprøyte

injection [in'dʒekʃən] *n*
injeksjon *m*

injure ['indʒə] *v* skade,
kveste; krenke

injury ['indʒəri] *n* skade *m*;
krenkelse *m*

injustice [in'dʒʌstis] *n* urett
m

ink [iŋk] *n* blekk *nt*

inlet ['inlet] *n* vik *c*

inn [in] *n* vertshus *nt*

inner ['inə] *adj* indre

innkeeper ['in,ki:pə] *n*
vertshusholder *m*

innocence ['inəsəns] *n*
uskyld *c*

innocent ['inəsənt] *adj*
uskyldig

inoculate [i'nɔkjuleit] *v*
vaksinere

inoculation [i,nɔkju'leiʃən]
n vaksinasjon *m*

inquire [iŋ'kwaiə] *v*
*forespørre, forhøre seg

inquiry [iŋ'kwaiəri] *n*
forespørsel *m*;
etterforskning *m*; ~ **office**
informasjonskontor *nt*

inquisitive [iŋ'kwizətiv] *adj*
nysgjerrig

insane [in'sein] *adj* sinnssyk

inscription [in'skripʃən] *n*
inskripsjon *m*

insect ['insekt] *n* insekt *nt*;
~ **repellent** insektmiddel *nt*

insecticide [in'sektisaid] *n*
insektmiddel *nt*

insensitive [in'sensətiv] *adj*
ufølsom

insert [in'sə:t] *v* *sette inn,
*innskyte

inside [,in'said] *n* innside *c*;
adj indre; *adv* inne; inni;
prep innen, innenfor; ~ **out**
vrengt; **insides** innvoller *pl*

insight ['insait] *n* innsikt *m*

insignificant
[,insig'nifikənt] *adj*
ubetydelig; intetsigende,
uanselig; uvesentlig

insist [in'sist] *v* insistere;
*fastholde

insolence ['insələns] *n*
uforskammethet *c*

insolent ['insələnt] *adj*
uforskammet, frekk

insomnia [in'sɔmniə] *n*
søvnløshet *c*

inspect [in'spekt] *v*
inspisere

inspection [in'spekʃən] *n*
inspeksjon *m*; kontroll *m*

inspector [in'spektə] *n*
inspektør *m*

inspire [in'spaiə] *v* inspirere

install [in'stɔːl] *v* installere

installation [,instə'leiʃən] *n*
installasjon *m*

instal(l)ment [in'stɔːlmənt]
n avdrag *nt*; **installment
plan** *Am* avbetalingskjøp
nt

instance ['instəns] *n*
eksempel *nt*; tilfelle *nt*; **for
~ for** eksempel

instant ['instənt] *n* øyeblikk
nt

instant message
['instənt͵'mesədʒ] *n*
lynmelding *c*

instantly ['instəntli] *adv*
øyeblikkelig, straks,
umiddelbart

instead of [in'sted ɔv]
istedenfor

instinct ['instiŋkt] *n* instinkt
nt

institute ['institjuːt] *n*
institutt *nt*; forordning *m*; *v*
opprette, stifte

institution [,insti'tjuːʃən] *n*
institusjon *m*, stiftelse *m*

instruct [in'strʌkt] *v*
undervise

instruction [in'strʌkʃən] *n*
undervisning *c*; veiledning

instructive [in'strʌktiv] *adj*
lærerik

instructor [in'strʌktə] *n*
instruktør *m*

instrument ['instrumənt] *n*
instrument *nt*; **musical ~**
musikkinstrument *nt*

insufficient [,insə'fiʃənt]
adj utilstrekkelig

insulate ['insjuleit] *v* isolere

insulation [,insju'leiʃən] *n*
isolasjon *m*

insulator ['insjuleitə] *n*
isolator *m*

insult[1] [in'sʌlt] *v* fornærme

insult[2] ['insʌlt] *n*
fornærmelse *m*

insurance [in'ʃuərəns] *n*
forsikring *c*; **~ policy**
forsikringspolise *m*

insure [in'ʃuə] *v* forsikre

intact [in'tækt] *adj* intakt

integrate ['intəgreit] *v*
integrere; innlemme

intellect ['intəlekt] *n*
intellekt *nt*, forstand *m*

intellectual [,intə'lektʃuəl]
adj intellektuell

intelligence [in'telidʒəns] *n*
intelligens *m*

intelligent [in'telidʒənt] *adj*
intelligent

intend [in'tend] *v* *ha til
hensikt

intense [in'tens] *adj* intens

intention [in'tenʃən] *n*
hensikt *m*

intentional [in'tenʃənəl] *adj*
tilsiktet

intercourse ['intəkɔːs] *n*
omgang *m*
interest ['intrəst] *n*
interesse *m*; rente *c*; *v*
interessere
interested ['intristid] *adj*
interessert
interesting ['intrəstiŋ] *adj*
interessant
interfere [,intə'fiə] *v* *gripe
inn; ~ **with** blande seg inn i
interference [,intə'fiərəns]
n innblanding *c*
interim ['intərim] *n*
mellomtid *c*; *adj* foreløpig
interior [in'tiəriə] *n* innside
c
interlude ['intəluːd] *n*
mellomspill *nt*
intermediary
[,intə'miːdjəri] *n*
mellommann *m*
intermission [,intə'miʃən] *n*
pause *m*
internal [in'təːnəl] *adj* indre
international
[,intə'næʃənəl] *adj*
internasjonal
Internet ['intənet] *n*
Internett *nt*, nett *nt*
interpret [in'təːprit] *v* tolke
interpreter [in'təːpritə] *n*
tolk *m*
interrogate [in'terəgeit] *v*
forhøre
interrogation
[in,terə'geiʃən] *n* forhør *nt*
interrupt [,intə'rʌpt] *v*
*avbryte
interruption [,intə'rʌpʃən]

n avbrytelse *m*
intersection [,intə'sekʃən]
n veikryss *nt*
interval ['intəvəl] *n* pause
m; intervall *nt*
intervene [,intə'viːn] *v*
*gripe inn
interview ['intəvjuː] *n*
intervju *nt*
intestine [in'testin] *n* tarm
m; **intestines** tarmer
intimate ['intimət] *adj* intim
into ['intu] *prep* inn i
intolerable [in'tɔlərəbəl] *adj*
utålelig
intoxicated [in'tɔksikeitid]
adj beruset
intrigue [in'triːg] *n* intrige
m
introduce [,intrə'djuːs] *v*
introdusere, presentere,
innføre
introduction [,intrə'dʌkʃən]
n presentasjon *m*;
innledning *m*
invade [in'veid] *v* trenge inn
invalid¹ ['invəliːd] *n*
funksjonshemmet *m*, ufør
m; *adj* funksjonshemmet,
ufør
invalid² [in'vælid] *adj*
ugyldig
invasion [in'veiʒən] *n*
invasjon *m*
invent [in'vent] *v*
*oppfinne, *oppdikte
invention [in'venʃən] *n*
oppfinnelse *m*
inventive [in'ventiv] *adj*
oppfinnsom

inventor [in'ventə] *n*
oppfinner *m*

inventory ['invəntri] *n*
inventar *nt*; inventarliste *c*

invert [in'vəːt] *v* snu om

invest [in'vest] *v* investere

investigate [in'vestigeit] *v*
etterforske

investigation
[in,vesti'geiʃən] *n*
undersøkelse *m*;
etterforskning *m*

investment [in'vestmənt] *n*
investering *c*;
kapitalanbringelse *m*,
pengeanbringelse *m*

invisible [in'vizəbəl] *adj*
usynlig

invitation [,invi'teiʃən] *n*
innbydelse *m*

invite [in'vait] *v* *innby,
invitere

invoice ['invɔis] *n* faktura *m*

involve [in'vɔlv] *v*
innblande

inwards ['inwədz] *adv*
innover

iodine ['aiədiːn] *n* jod *m*

Iran [i'rɑːn] Iran

Iranian [i'reiniən] *adj* iransk;
n iraner *m*

Iraq [i'rɑːk] Irak

Iraqi [i'rɑːki] *adj* irakisk; *n*
iraker *m*

Ireland ['aiələnd] Irland

Irish ['aiəriʃ] *adj* irsk

iron ['aiən] *n* jern *nt*;
strykejern *nt*; jern-; *v*
*stryke

ironical [ai'rɔnikəl] *adj*

ironisk

irony ['aiərəni] *n* ironi *m*

irregular [i'regjulə] *adj*
uregelmessig

irreparable [i'repərəbəl] *adj*
ubotelig

irrevocable [i'revəkəbəl]
adj ugjenkallelig

irritable ['iritəbəl] *adj*
irritabel

irritate ['iriteit] *v* irritere,
ergre

is [iz] *v* (pr be)

island ['ailənd] *n* øy *c*

isolate ['aisəleit] *v* isolere

isolation [,aisə'leiʃən] *n*
isolasjon *m*

Israel ['izreil] Israel

Israeli [iz'reili] *adj* israelsk;
n israeler *m*

issue ['iʃuː] *v* utstede; *utgi;
n utstedelse *m*; utgivelse
m; spørsmål *nt*, sak *c*;
utgang *m*, resultat *nt*, følge
m, sluttresultat *nt*; utvei *m*

it [it] *pron* det

Italian [i'tæljən] *adj*
italiensk; *n* italiener *m*

Italy ['itəli] Italia

itch [itʃ] *n* kløe *m*; *v* klø

item ['aitəm] *n* post *m*;
punkt *m*

itinerary [ai'tinərəri] *n*
reiserute *c*, reiseplan *m*

its [its] *pron* dens, dets

itself [it'self] *pron* seg; seg
selv; selv; by ~ alene; av
seg selv

ivory ['aivəri] *n* elfenbein *nt*

ivy ['aivi] *n* eføy *m*

J

jack [dʒæk] n jekk m
jacket ['dʒækit] n
  dressjakke c, jakke c;
  omslag nt
jade [dʒeid] n jade m
jail [dʒeil] n fengsel nt
jam [dʒæm] n syltetøy nt;
  trafikkork m
janitor ['dʒænitə] n
  vaktmester m
January ['dʒænjuəri] januar
Japan [dʒə'pæn] Japan
Japanese [,dʒæpə'ni:z] adj
  japansk; n japaner m
jar [dʒɑ:] n krukke c
jargon [dʒɑ:gən] n sjargong
  m
jaundice ['dʒɔ:ndis] n
  gulsott m
jaw [dʒɔ:] n kjeve m
jealous ['dʒeləs] adj sjalu
jealousy ['dʒeləsi] n sjalusi
  m
jeans [dʒi:nz] pl
  dongeribukse c, jeans m,
  olabukse c
jelly ['dʒeli] n gelé m
jellyfish ['dʒelifiʃ] n manet
  m
jersey ['dʒə:zi] n jersey m;
  genser m
jet [dʒet] n stråle m; jetfly nt
jet lag ['jet‿læg] n jetlag c
jetty ['dʒeti] n molo m
Jew [dʒu:] n jøde m
jewel ['dʒu:əl] n smykke nt

jewelry ['dʒu:əlri] nAm
  smykker pl
jeweller ['dʒu:ələ] n
  gullsmed m
jewellery ['dʒu:əlri] n
  smykker pl
Jewish ['dʒu:iʃ] adj jødisk
job [dʒɔb] n jobb m; stilling
  c
jobless ['dʒɔbles] adj
  arbeidsløs
jockey ['dʒɔki] n jockey m
join [dʒɔin] v *forbinde;
  slutte seg til; forene,
  sammenføye
joint [dʒɔint] n ledd nt; adj
  felles, forent; ~ venture
  fellesprosjekt nt
jointly ['dʒɔintli] adv i
  fellesskap
joke [dʒɔuk] n vits m, spøk
  m
jolly ['dʒɔli] adj lystig
Jordan ['dʒɔ:dən] Jordan
Jordanian [dʒɔ:'deiniən]
  adj jordansk; n jordaner m
journal ['dʒə:nəl] n
  tidsskrift nt
journalism ['dʒə:nəlizəm] n
  journalistikk m
journalist ['dʒə:nəlist] n
  journalist m
journey ['dʒə:ni] n reise c
joy [dʒɔi] n glede c, fryd m
joyful ['dʒɔifəl] adj glad
jubilee ['dʒu:bili:] n

jubileum nt

judge [dʒʌdʒ] n dommer m;
v dømme; bedømme

judgment ['dʒʌdʒmənt] n
dom m

jug [dʒʌg] n mugge c

juice [dʒuːs] n saft m

juicy ['dʒuːsi] adj saftig

July [dʒuˈlai] juli

jump [dʒʌmp] v hoppe; n
hopp nt, sprang nt

junction ['dʒʌŋkʃən] n
veikryss nt; knutepunkt nt

June [dʒuːn] juni

jungle ['dʒʌŋgəl] n urskog

m, jungel m

junior ['dʒuːnjə] adj junior

junk [dʒʌŋk] n skrap nt

jurisdiction [dʒuərisdikʃən]
n jurisdiksjon m

jury ['dʒuəri] n jury m

just [dʒʌst] adj rettferdig,
passende; riktig; adv
nettopp; akkurat

justice ['dʒʌstis] n rett m;
rettferdighet c

justify ['dʒʌstifai] v
rettferdiggjøre

juvenile ['dʒuːvənail] adj
ungdoms-

K

kangaroo [ˌkæŋgəˈruː] n
kenguru m

kayak ['kaijæk] n kajakk m

keel [kiːl] n kjøl m

keen [kiːn] adj begeistret;
skarp

*keep [kiːp] v *holde;
bevare; *holde på med; ~
away from mmholde seg
borte fra; ~ **off** *la være; ~
on *fortsette; ~ **quiet** tie; ~
up *holde ut; ~ **up with**
*holde følge med

kennel ['kenəl] n hundehus
nt; kennel m

Kenya ['kenjə] Kenya

kerosene ['kerəsiːn] n
petroleum m; kerosin m,
flybensin m

kettle ['ketəl] n kjele m

key [kiː] n nøkkel m

keyhole ['kiːhoul] n
nøkkelhull nt

khaki ['kaːki] n kaki m

kick [kik] v sparke; n spark
nt

kickoff [ˌkiˈkɔf] n avspark nt

kid [kid] n barn nt, unge m;
v skrøne

kidney ['kidni] n nyre c

kill [kil] v drepe, *slå i hjel

kilogram ['kiləgræm] n kilo
m / nt

kilometer Am, **kilometre**
['kiləˌmiːtə] n kilometer m

kind [kaind] adj snill,
vennlig; god; n sort m

kindergarten
['kindəˌgaːtən] n
barnehage m, førskole m

king [kiŋ] n konge m

kingdom ['kiŋdəm] n

kongerike *nt*; rike *nt*
kiosk ['kiːɔsk] *n* kiosk *m*
kiss [kis] *n* kyss *nt*; *v* kysse
kit [kit] *n* utstyr *nt*
kitchen ['kitʃin] *n* kjøkken
nt; ~ **garden** kjøkkenhage
m; ~ **towel** kjøkkenhåndkle
nt
knapsack ['næpsæk] *n*
ryggsekk *m*; ransel *m*
knave [neiv] *n* knekt *m*
knee [niː] *n* kne *nt*
kneecap ['niːkæp] *n* kneskål
c
*kneel [niːl] *v* knele
knew [njuː] *v* (p know)

knife [naif] *n* (pl knives)
kniv *m*
knight [nait] *n* ridder *m*
*knit [nit] *v* strikke; **knitting
wool** garn *nt*
knob [nɔb] *n* knott *m*
knock [nɔk] *v* banke; *n* bank
nt; ~ **against** støte på; ~
down *slå ned
knot [nɔt] *n* knute *m*; *v*
knytte
*know [nou] *v* *vite;
*kunne, kjenne
knowledge ['nɔlidʒ] *n*
kjennskap *nt*; kunnskap *m*
knuckle ['nʌkəl] *n* knoke *m*

L

label ['leibəl] *n* etikett *m*; *v*
*sette merkelapp på
laboratory [lə'bɔrətəri] *n*
laboratorium *nt*
labo(u)r ['leibə] *n* arbeid *nt*;
fødselsveer *pl*; *v* *slite,
anstrenge seg; **labor
permit** *Am*
arbeidstillatelse *m*
labo(u)rer ['leibərə] *n*
arbeider *m*
labo(u)r-saving
['leibə,seiviŋ] *adj*
arbeidsbesparende
labyrinth ['læbərinθ] *n*
labyrint *m*
lace [leis] *n* kniplinger *pl*;
lisse *c*
lack [læk] *n* savn *nt*, mangel
m; *v* mangle

lacquer ['lækə] *n* lakk *m*
lactose ['læktous] *n* laktose
c
lactose intolerant
['læktous ˌin'tɔlərənt] *adj*
laktoseintolerant
lad [læd] *n* gutt *m*
ladder ['lædə] *n* stige *m*
lady ['leidi] *n* dame *c*;
ladies' room dametoalett
nt
lagoon [lə'guːn] *n* lagune *m*
lake [leik] *n* innsjø *m*
lamb [læm] *n* lam *nt*;
lammekjøtt *nt*
lame [leim] *adj* lam, halt
lamentable ['læməntəbəl]
adj beklagelig
lamp [læmp] *n* lampe *c*
lampshade ['læmpʃeid] *n*

lampeskjerm *m*

land [lænd] *n* land *nt*; *v* lande; *gå i land

landlady ['lænd,leidi] *n* vertinne *c*

landlord ['lændlɔːd] *n* vert *m*, huseier *m*; husvert *m*

landmark ['lændmɑːk] *n* landemerke *nt*

landscape ['lændskeip] *n* landskap *nt*

lane [lein] *n* smug *nt*, smal vei; fil *m*

language ['læŋgwidʒ] *n* språk *m*

lantern ['læntən] *n* lykt *c*

lap [læp] *n* fang *nt*; runde *m*; *v* slikke

lapel [lə'pel] *n* jakkeslag *nt*

laptop ['læp,tɔp] *n* bærbar PC *c*

large [lɑːdʒ] *adj* stor; rommelig

lark [lɑːk] *n* lerke *c*

laryngitis [,lærin'dʒaitis] *n* strupekatarr *m*

last [lɑːst] *adj* sist; forrige; *v* vare; at ~ til slutt

lasting ['lɑːstiŋ] *adj* varig

latchkey ['lætʃkiː] *n* entrénøkkel *m*

late [leit] *adj* sen; for sent

lately ['leitli] *adv* i det siste, nylig

lather ['lɑːðə] *n* skum *nt*

Latin America ['lætin ə'merikə] Latin-Amerika

Latin-American [,lætinə'merikən] *adj* latinamerikansk

latitude ['lætitjuːd] *n* breddegrad *m*

laugh [lɑːf] *v* *le; in latter *m*

laughter ['lɑːftə] *n* latter *m*

launch [lɔːntʃ] *v* *sette i gang; *skyte opp; *n* motorbåt *m*

launching ['lɔːntʃiŋ] *n* sjøsetning *m*

launderette [,lɔːndə'ret] *n* selvbetjeningsvaskeri *nt*

laundry ['lɔːndri] *n* vaskeri *nt*; vask *m*

lavatory ['lævətəri] *n* toalett *nt*

lavish ['læviʃ] *adj* ødsel

law [lɔː] *n* lov *m*; rett *m*; ~ court domstol *m*

lawful ['lɔːfəl] *adj* lovlig

lawn [lɔːn] *n* gressplen *m*

lawsuit ['lɔːsuːt] *n* rettssak *c*

lawyer ['lɔːjə] *n* advokat *m*; jurist *m*

laxative ['læksətiv] *n* avføringsmiddel *nt*

*lay [lei] *v* plassere, *legge, *sette; ~ bricks mure

layer [leiə] *n* lag *nt*

layman ['leimən] *n* lekmann *m*

lazy ['leizi] *adj* doven; lat

*lead [liːd] *v* lede

lead¹ [liːd] *n* forsprang *nt*; ledelse *m*; hunderem *c*

lead² [led] *n* bly *nt*

leader ['liːdə] *n* fører *m*, anfører *m*

leadership ['liːdəʃip] *n* ledelse *m*; lederskap *nt*

leading ['liːdiŋ] *adj* ledende

leaf [liːf] *n* (pl leaves) blad *nt*

league [liːg] *n* forbund *nt*; liga *m*

leak [liːk] *v* lekke; *n* lekkasje *m*

leaky ['liːki] *adj* lekk

lean [liːn] *adj* mager

***lean** [liːn] *v* lene seg

leap [liːp] *n* hopp *nt*

*leap** [liːp] *v* hoppe

leap year ['liːpjiə] *n* skuddår *nt*

*learn** [ləːn] *v* lære

learner ['ləːnə] *n* nybegynner *m*

lease [liːs] *n* leiekontrakt *m*; forpaktning *m*; *v* forpakte bort, leie ut; leie; lease

leash [liːʃ] *n* koppel *nt*, bånd *nt*

least [liːst] *adj* minst; **at ~ i** det minste; minst

leather ['leðə] *n* lær *nt*; skinn-, lær-

leave [liːv] *n* permisjon *m*

*leave** [liːv] *v* *forlate, *gå bort; *legge igjen; *etterlate; ~ **behind** *etterlate; ~ **out** *utelate

Lebanese [ˌlebə'niːz] *adj* libanesisk; *n* libaneser *m*

Lebanon ['lebənən] Libanon

lecture ['lektʃə] *n* foredrag *nt*, forelesning *m*

left[1] [left] *adj* venstre

left[2] [left] *v* (p, pp leave)

left-hand ['lefthænd] *adj* venstre

left-handed [ˌleft'hændid] *adj* keivhendt

leg [leg] *n* bein *nt*

legacy ['legəsi] *n* legat *nt*

legal ['liːgəl] *adj* legal; rettslig; juridisk

legalization [ˌliːgəlai'zeiʃən] *n* legalisering *c*

legation [liˈgeiʃən] *n* legasjon *m*

legible ['ledʒibəl] *adj* leselig

legitimate [liˈdʒitimət] *adj* lovlig

leisure ['leʒə] *n* fritid *c*; ro og mak

lemon ['lemən] *n* sitron *m*

lemonade [ˌlemə'neid] *n* limonade *m*; brus *m*

*lend** [lend] *v* låne bort

length [leŋθ] *n* lengde *c*

lengthen ['leŋθən] *v* forlenge

lengthways ['leŋθweiz] *adv* på langs

lens [lenz] *n* linse *c*; **telephoto ~** teleobjektiv *nt*; **zoom ~** zoomlinse *c*

leprosy ['leprəsi] *n* spedalskhet *c*

lesbian ['lesbiən] *adj* lesbisk

less [les] *adv* mindre

lessen ['lesən] *v* minske, forminske

lesson ['lesən] *n* leksjon *m*, time *m*

*let** [let] *v* *la; leie ut; ~ **down** svikte

lethal ['liːðəl] *adj* dødelig

letter ['letə] *n* brev *nt*;

letterbox 298

bokstav *m*; ~ **of credit**
akkreditiv *nt*; ~ **of
recommendation**
anbefalingsbrev *nt*
letterbox ['letəbɔks] *n*
postkasse *c*
lettuce ['letis] *n* bladsalat *m*
level ['levəl] *adj* jevn; plan;
n plan *nt*, nivå *nt*; *v*
nivellere, utligne; ~
crossing planovergang *m*
lever ['li:və] *n* vektstang *c*
liability [,laiə'biləti] *n*
ansvar *nt*; forpliktelse *m*
liable ['laiəbəl] *adj*
ansvarlig; ~ **to** utsatt for
liar ['laiə] *n* løgner *m*
liberal ['libərəl] *adj* liberal;
rundhåndet, gavmild
liberation [,libə'reiʃən] *n*
befrielse *m*
Liberia [lai'biəriə] Liberia
Liberian [lai'biəriən] *adj*
liberisk; *n* liberier *m*
liberty ['libəti] *n* frihet *c*
library ['laibrəri] *n* bibliotek
nt
licence ['laisəns] *n*, **license**
nAm bevilling *c*; tillatelse
m; **driving** ~, **driver's** ~
Am førerkort *nt*; ~ **number**
Am registreringsnummer
nt; ~ **plate** nummerskilt *nt*
license ['laisəns] *v* *gi
tillatelse
lick [lik] *v* slikke
lid [lid] *n* lokk *nt*
lie [lai] *v* lyve; *n* løgn *c*
*lie [lai] v *ligge; ~ down
*legge seg ned

life [laif] *n* (pl lives) liv *nt*; ~
insurance livsforsikring *c*;
~ **jacket** svømmevest *m*
lifebelt ['laifbelt] *n* livbelte
nt
lifetime ['laiftaim] *n* levetid
c
lift [lift] *v* løfte; *n* heis *m*
light [lait] *n* lys *nt*; *adj* lett;
lys; ~ **bulb** lyspære *c*
*light [lait] v tenne
lighter ['laitə] *n* lighter *m*
lighthouse ['laithaus] *n*
fyrtårn *nt*
lighting ['laitiŋ] *n* belysning
m
lightning ['laitniŋ] *n* lyn *nt*
like [laik] *v* like; *adj* lik; *conj*
liksom; *prep* liksom
likely ['laikli] *adj* sannsynlig
like-minded [,laik'maindid]
adj likesinnet
likewise ['laikwaiz] *adv*
likeså, likeledes
lily ['lili] *n* lilje *c*
limb [lim] *n* lem *nt*; gren *c*
lime [laim] *n* kalk *m*; lind *m*;
limett *m*
limetree ['laimtri:] *n*
lindetre *m*
limit ['limit] *n* grense *c*; *v*
begrense
limp [limp] *v* halte; *adj* slapp
line [lain] *n* linje *c*; strek *m*;
line *c*; kø *m*; **stand in** ~
Am stå i kø
linen ['linin] *n* lin *nt*, lintøy
nt
liner ['lainə] *n* passasjerbåt
m

long

lingerie ['lɔ-ʒəriː] n dameundertøy m

lining ['lainiŋ] n fôr nt

link [liŋk] v *forbinde; n (computer) lenke m; ledd nt; link m

lion ['laiən] n løve m

lip [lip] n leppe c; ~ **balm** leppepomade m

liposuction ['lipou,sʌkʃən] n fettsuging c

lipstick ['lipstik] n leppestift m

liqueur [li'kjuə] n likør m

liquid ['likwid] adj flytende; n væske c

liquor ['likə] n sprit m; brennevin nt; ~ **store** Am alkoholutsalg nt

liquorice ['likəris] n lakris m

list [list] n liste c; v *innskrive, regne opp

listen ['lisən] v lytte

listener ['lisnə] n lytter m

liter ['liːtə] nAm liter m

literary ['litrəri] adj litterær

literature ['litrətʃə] n litteratur m

litre ['liːtə] n liter m

litter ['litə] n avfall nt, søppel nt; kull nt

little ['litəl] adj liten; lite

live¹ [liv] v leve; bo

live² [laiv] adj levende; direkte

livelihood ['laivlihud] n levebrød nt

lively ['laivli] adj livlig

liver ['livə] n lever c

living ['liviŋ] n liv nt; levebrød nt; adj levende; ~ **room** dagligstue c; stue c

lizard ['lizəd] n firfisle c

load [loud] n last c; bør c; v laste

loaf [louf] n (pl loaves) brød nt

loan [loun] n lån nt

lobby ['lɔbi] n vestibyle m; foajé m; lobby m

lobster ['lɔbstə] n hummer c

local ['loukəl] adj lokal, stedlig; ~ **call** lokalsamtale m; ~ **train** lokaltog nt

locality [lou'kæləti] n sted nt

locate [lou'keit] v lokalisere

location [lou'keiʃən] n beliggenhet c

lock [lɔk] v låse; n lås m; sluse c; ~ **up** låse opp, sperre inne

locker ['lɔkə] n skap nt

locomotive [,loukə'moutiv] n lokomotiv nt

lodge [lɔdʒ] v huse; n hytte c

lodger ['lɔdʒə] n leieboer m

lodgings ['lɔdʒiŋz] pl losji nt

log [lɔg] n kubbe m; ~ **in** v logge inne; ~ **off** v logge ut

logic ['lɔdʒik] n logikk m

logical ['lɔdʒikəl] adj logisk

lonely ['lounli] adj ensom

long [lɔŋ] adj lang; langvarig; ~ **for** lengte etter; **no longer** ikke nt lenger

longing ['lɒŋiŋ] *n* lengsel *m*

longitude ['lɒndʒitjuːd] *n* lengdegrad *m*

look [luk] *v* *se; synes, *se ut; *n* blikk *nt*; utseende *nt*; ~ **after** sørge for, passe; ~ **at** *se på; ~ **for** lete etter; ~ **out** *se opp, passe seg for; ~ **up** *slå opp

looking-glass ['lukiŋglɑːs] *n* speil *nt*

loop [luːp] *n* løkke *c*

loose [luːs] *adj* løs

loosen ['luːsən] *v* løsne

lord [lɔːd] *n* lord *m*; herre *m*

lorry ['lɒri] *n* lastebil *m*

*lose [luːz] *v* tape, miste

loser ['luːzə] *n* taper *m*

loss [lɒs] *n* tap *nt*

lost [lɒst] *adj* gått vill; forsvunnet; ~ **and found** hittegods *nt*; ~ **property office** hittegodskontor *nt*

lot [lɒt] *n* lodd *m*; mengde *m*, hop *m*

lotion ['louʃən] *n* hudkrem *m*; **aftershave** ~ barbervann *nt*

lottery ['lɒtəri] *n* lotteri *nt*

loud [laud] *adj* høylydt, høy

loudspeaker [,laud'spiːkə] *n* høyttaler *m*

lounge [laundʒ] *n* salong *m*; vestibyle *m*

louse [laus] *n* (pl lice) lus *c*

love [lʌv] *v* elske, *være glad i; *n* kjærlighet *c*; **in** ~ forelsket

lovely ['lʌvli] *adj* yndig,

herlig, skjønn

lover ['lʌvə] *n* elsker *m*

love story ['lʌv,stɔːri] *n* kjærlighetshistorie *c*

low [lou] *adj* lav; dyp; nedstemt; ~ **tide** fjære *c*

lower ['louə] *v* senke; *adj* lavere

lowlands ['louləndz] *pl* lavland *nt*

loyal ['lɔiəl] *adj* lojal

lubricate ['luːbrikeit] *v* *smøre

lubrication [,luːbri'keiʃən] *n* smøring *c*; ~ **oil** smøreolje *c*

luck [lʌk] *n* hell *nt*; tilfeldighet *c*; **bad** ~ uflaks *m*; **good** ~! lykke til!

lucky ['lʌki] *adj* heldig; ~ **charm** amulett *m*

ludicrous ['luːdikrəs] *adj* latterlig

luggage ['lʌgidʒ] *n* bagasje *m*; **hand** ~ håndbagasje *m*; **left** ~ **office** bagasjeoppbevaring *c*; ~ **rack** bagasjehylle *c*; ~ **van** bagasjevogn *c*

lukewarm ['luːkwɔːm] *adj* lunken

lumbago [lʌm'beigou] *n* lumbago *m*

luminous ['luːminəs] *adj* lysende

lump [lʌmp] *n* klump *m*, stykke *nt*; kul *m*; ~ **of sugar** sukkerbit *m*; ~ **sum** rund sum

lumpy ['lʌmpi] *adj* klumpet

malaria

lunch [lʌntʃ] n
formiddagsmat m, lunsj m
luncheon ['lʌntʃən] n lunsj
m
lung [lʌŋ] n lunge c

lust [lʌst] n begjær nt
luxurious [lʌg'ʒuəriəs] adj
luksuriøs
luxury ['lʌkʃəri] n luksus m

M

machine [mə'ʃiːn] n maskin
m, apparat nt
machinery [mə'ʃiːnəri] n
maskineri nt
mackerel ['mækrəl] n (pl ~)
makrell m
mackintosh ['mækintɔʃ] n
regnfrakk m
mad [mæd] adj gal,
vanvittig, rasende
madam ['mædəm] n frue c
madness ['mædnəs] n
galskap m
magazine [,mægə'ziːn] n
tidsskrift nt
magic ['mædʒik] n magi m,
trolldom m; adj magisk
magician [mə'dʒiʃən] n
tryllekunstner m
magistrate ['mædʒistreit] n
dommer m
magnetic [mæg'netik] adj
magnetisk
magnificent [mæg'nifisənt]
adj praktfull, storslått
magnify [mæg'nifai] v
forstørre, overdrive
maid [meid] n hushjelp c
maiden name ['meidən
neim] pikenavn nt
mail [meil] n post m; v

poste; ~ order Am
postanvisning m
mailbox ['meilbɔks] nAm
postkasse c
main [mein] adj hoved-;
størst; ~ deck øverste dekk
nt; ~ road hovedvei m; ~
street hovedgate c
mainland ['meinlənd] n
fastland nt
mainly ['meinli] adv
hovedsakelig
mains [meinz] pl
hovedledning m
maintain [mein'tein] v
*opprettholde
maintenance ['meintənəns]
n vedlikehold nt
maize [meiz] n mais m
major ['meidʒə] adj større;
eldre; n major m; dur m
majority [mə'dʒɔrəti] n
flertall nt
*make [meik] v lage; tjene;
nå; ~ do with nøye seg
med; ~ good *godtgjøre; ~
up *sette opp
make-up ['meikʌp] n
sminke c
malaria [mə'lɛəriə] n
malaria m

Malay [mə'lei] *n* malaysier *m*

Malaysia [mə'leiziə] Malaysia

Malaysian [mə'leiziən] *adj* malaysisk

male [meil] *adj* hann-

malicious [mə'liʃəs] *adj* ondskapsfull

malignant [mə'lignənt] *adj* ondartet

mall [mɔːl] *nAm* kjøpesenter *nt*

mallet ['mælit] *n* kølle *c*

malnutrition [ˌmælnjuˈtriʃən] *n* underernæring *c*

mammal ['mæməl] *n* pattedyr *nt*

man [mæn] *n* (pl men) mann *m*; menneske *nt*; **men's room** herretoalett *nt*

manage ['mænidʒ] *v* bestyre; lykkes

manageable ['mænidʒəbəl] *adj* håndterlig

management ['mænidʒmənt] *n* ledelse *m*; administrasjon *m*

manager ['mænidʒə] *n* sjef *m*, direktør *m*

mandarin ['mændərin] *n* mandarin *m*

mandate ['mændeit] *n* mandat *nt*

manger ['meindʒə] *n* krybbe *c*

manicure ['mænikjuə] *n* manikyr *m*

mankind [mænˈkaind] *n*

menneskehet *c*

mannequin ['mænəkin] *n* utstillingsdukke *c*

manner ['mænə] *n* måte *m*, vis *nt*; **manners** *pl* manerer *pl*

man-of-war [ˌmænəvˈwɔː] *n* krigsskip *nt*

manor house ['mænəhaus] *n* herregård *m*

mansion ['mænʃən] *n* herregård *m*

manual ['mænjuəl] *adj* hånd-, manuell

manufacture [ˌmænjuˈfæktʃə] *v* fabrikkere

manufacturer [ˌmænjuˈfæktʃərə] *n* fabrikant *m*

manure [mə'njuə] *n* gjødsel *c*

manuscript ['mænjuskript] *n* manuskript *nt*

many ['meni] *adj* mange

map [mæp] *n* kart *nt*

maple ['meipəl] *n* lønn *c*

marble ['mɑːbəl] *n* marmor *m*; klinkekule *c*

March [mɑːtʃ] mars

march [mɑːtʃ] *v* marsjere; marsj *m*

mare [mɛə] *n* hoppe *c*

margarine [ˌmɑːdʒəˈriːn] *n* margarin *m*

margin ['mɑːdʒin] *n* marg *m*

maritime ['mæritaim] *adj* maritim

mark [mɑːk] *v* markere; merke; kjennetegne; *n*

merke nt; karakter m;
skyteskive c
market ['ma:kit] n marked
nt
marketplace ['ma:kitpleis]
n torg nt
marmalade ['ma:məleid] n
marmelade m
marriage ['mærid3] n
ekteskap nt
marrow ['mærou] n marg m
marry ['mæri] v gifte seg;
married couple ektepar nt
marsh [ma:ʃ] n sump m
martyr ['ma:tə] n martyr m
marvel ['ma:vəl] n vidunder
nt; v undre seg
marvel(l)ous ['ma:vələs]
adj vidunderlig
mascara [mæ'ska:rə] n
øyensverte c
masculine ['mæskjulin] adj
maskulin
mash [mæʃ] v mose;
mashed potatoes npl
potetstappe c
mask [ma:sk] n maske c
Mass [mæs] n messe m
mass [mæs] n mengde m; ~
production
masseproduksjon m
massage ['mæsa:3] n
massasje m; v massere
masseur [mæ'sə:] n massør
m
massive ['mæsiv] adj
massiv
mast [ma:st] n mast c
master ['ma:stə] n mester
m; lektor m, lærer m; v

mestre, beherske
masterpiece ['ma:stəpi:s] n
mesterverk nt
mat [mæt] n matte c; adj
glansløs, matt
match [mætʃ] n fyrstikk m;
kamp m; v passe til
matchbox ['mætʃbɔks] n
fyrstikkeske c
material [mə'tiəriəl] n
materiale nt; stoff nt; adj
materiell
mathematical
[,mæθə'mætikəl] adj
matematisk
mathematics
[,mæθə'mætiks] n
matematikk m
matrimony ['mætriməni] n
ekteskap nt
matter ['mætə] n stoff nt;
spørsmål nt, sak c; v *være
av betydning; **as a ~ of fact**
faktisk, i virkeligheten
matter-of-fact
[,mætərəv'fækt] adj
realistisk
mattress ['mætrəs] n
madrass m
mature [mə'tjuə] adj moden
maturity [mə'tjuərəti] n
modenhet c
mausoleum [,mɔ:sə'li:əm]
n mausoleum nt
mauve [mouv] adj lilla
May [mei] mai
***may** [mei] v *kunne
maybe ['meibi:] adv kanskje
mayor [mɛə] n borgermester
m

maze [meiz] *n* labyrint *m*

me [mi:] *pron* meg

meadow ['medou] *n* eng *c*

meal [mi:l] *n* måltid *nt*

mean [mi:n] *adj* sjofel; *n* gjennomsnitt *nt*

***mean** [mi:n] *v* bety; mene

meaning ['mi:niŋ] *n* mening *m*

meaningless ['mi:niŋləs] *adj* meningsløs

means [mi:nz] *n* middel *nt*; **by no ~** på ingen måte

meantime: in the ~ [in ðə 'mi:ntaim] i mellomtiden, imens

meanwhile ['mi:nwail] *adv* i mellomtiden, imens

measles ['mi:zəlz] *n* meslinger *pl*

measure ['meʒə] *v* måle; *n* mål *nt*; foranstaltning *m*

meat [mi:t] *n* kjøtt *nt*

mechanic [mi'kænik] *n* mekaniker *m*

mechanical [mi'kænikəl] *adj* mekanisk

mechanism ['mekənizəm] *n* mekanisme *m*

medal ['medəl] *n* medalje *m*

media ['mi:diə] *pl* media *pl*

mediaeval [,medi'i:vəl] *adj* middelaldersk

mediate ['mi:dieit] *v* megle

mediator ['mi:dieitə] *n* megler *m*

medical ['medikəl] *adj* medisinsk

medicine ['medsin] *n* medisin *m*; legevitenskap *m*

meditate ['mediteit] *v* meditere

Mediterranean [,meditə'reiniən] Middelhavet

medium ['mi:diəm] *adj* gjennomsnittlig, middels

***meet** [mi:t] *v* møte; *treffe

meeting ['mi:tiŋ] *n* møte *nt*, sammenkomst *m*

meeting place ['mi:tiŋpleis] *n* møtested *nt*

melancholy ['melənkəli] *n* melankoli *m*

mellow ['melou] *adj* bløt; moden

melodrama ['melə,drɑ:mə] *n* melodrama *nt*

melody ['melədi] *n* melodi *m*

melon ['melən] *n* melon *m*

melt [melt] *v* smelte

member ['membə] *n* medlem *nt*; **Member of Parliament** parlamentsrepresentant *m*

membership ['membəʃip] *n* medlemskap *nt*

memo ['memou] *n* (pl ~s) memorandum *nt*

memorable ['memərəbəl] *adj* minneverdig

memorial [mə'mɔ:riəl] *n* minnestein *m*

memorize ['meməraiz] *v* lære utenat

memory ['meməri] *n* hukommelse *m*; minne *nt*

mend [mend] *v* reparere,

*gjøre i stand
menstruation
[,menstru'eiʃən] n
menstruasjon m
mental ['mentəl] adj mental
mention ['menʃən] v nevne;
n omtale m
menu ['menju:] n spisekart
nt, meny m
merchandise
['mə:tʃəndaiz] n varer pl,
handelsvare m
merchant ['mə:tʃənt] n
kjøpmann m
merciful ['mə:sifəl] adj
barmhjertig
mercury ['mə:kjuri] n
kvikksølv nt
mercy ['mə:si] n
barmhjertighet c, nåde m
merely ['miəli] adv bare
merge ['mə:dʒ] v
sammensmelte; fusjonere
merger ['mə:dʒə] n
sammensmeltning m;
fusjon m
merit ['merit] v fortjene; n
fortjeneste m
merry ['meri] adj munter
merry-go-round
['merigou,raund] n
karusell m
mesh [meʃ] n nett nt, maske
c
mess [mes] n rot nt; ~ up
rote til
message ['mesidʒ] n
beskjed m
message board
['mesədʒ‿bɔːd] n

oppslagstavle c
messenger ['mesindʒə] n
budbringer m
metal ['metəl] n metall nt;
metall-
meter ['mi:tə] n måler m
method ['meθəd] n metode
m, fremgangsmåte m;
ordning c
methodical [mə'θɔdikəl] adj
metodisk
metre ['mi:tə] n meter m
metric ['metrik] adj metrisk
Mexican ['meksikən] adj
meksikansk; n meksikaner
m
Mexico ['meksikou] Mexico
mice (pl mouse)
microphone ['maikrəfoun]
n mikrofon m
microwave oven
['maikrəweiv 'ʌvən] n
mikrobølgeovn m
midday ['middei] n middag
m; midt på dagen
middle ['midəl] n midte m;
adj mellomste; **Middle
Ages** middelalderen; ~
class middelklasse c;
middle-class adj borgerlig
midnight ['midnait] n
midnatt c
midst [midst] n midte m
midsummer ['mid,sʌmə] n
midtsommer m
midwife ['midwaif] n (pl
-wives) jordmor c
might [mait] n makt c
might [mait] v *kunne
mighty ['maiti] adj mektig

migraine ['miːɡreɪn] n
migrene c

mild [maɪld] adj mild

mildew ['mɪldjuː] n mugg m

mile [maɪl] n engelsk mil

milage ['maɪlɪdʒ] n distanse
m

milepost ['maɪlpoʊst] n
veiskilt nt

milestone ['maɪlstoʊn] n
milestein m

milieu ['miːljəː] n miljø m

military ['mɪlɪtəri] adj
militær-; ~ **force** krigsmakt
c

milk [mɪlk] n melk c

milkshake ['mɪlkʃeɪk] n
milkshake m

milky ['mɪlki] adj melkaktig

mill [mɪl] n mølle c; fabrikk
m

million ['mɪljən] n million m

millionaire [ˌmɪljəˈneə] n
millionær m

mince [mɪns] v finhakke

mind [maɪnd] n sinn nt; v
*ha noe imot; passe på,
passe seg for, bry seg om

mine [maɪn] n gruve c

miner ['maɪnə] n
gruvearbeider m

mineral ['mɪnərəl] n mineral
nt; ~ **water** naturlig
mineralvann c

mingle ['mɪŋɡl] v blande
(seg) med; blande seg inn

miniature ['mɪnjətʃə] n
miniatyr m

minimum ['mɪnɪməm] n
minimum nt

mining ['maɪnɪŋ] n
gruvedrift c

minister ['mɪnɪstə] n
statsråd m; prest m; **Prime
Minister** statsminister m

ministry ['mɪnɪstri] n
departement nt;
prestegjerning c

mink [mɪŋk] n mink m

minor ['maɪnə] adj mindre,
liten; underordnet; n
mindreårig m; moll m

minority [maɪˈnɒrəti] n
mindretall m

mint [mɪnt] n mynte c

minus ['maɪnəs] prep minus

minute[1] ['mɪnɪt] n minutt
nt; **minutes** referat nt

minute[2] [maɪˈnjuːt] adj
bitte liten

miracle ['mɪrəkəl] n mirakel
nt

miraculous [mɪˈrækjʊləs]
adj mirakuløs

mirror ['mɪrə] n speil nt

misbehave [ˌmɪsbɪˈheɪv] v
oppføre seg dårlig

miscarriage [mɪsˈkærɪdʒ] n
spontan abort m

miscellaneous
[ˌmɪsəˈleɪnɪəs] adj diverse

mischief ['mɪstʃif] n
spillopper pl; ugagn m,
skade m

mischievous ['mɪstʃivəs]
adj skøyeraktig

miserable ['mɪzərəbəl] adj
elendig, ulykkelig

misery ['mɪzəri] n
elendighet c, ulykke c; nød

c
misfortune [mis'fɔ:tʃen] *n*
ulykke *c*, uhell *nt*
mishap ['mishæp] *n* ulykke
c, uhell *nt*
*****mislay** [mis'lei] *v* *****forlegge
misplaced [mis'pleist] *adj*
malplassert; mistet
mispronounce
[,misprə'nauns] *v* uttale
galt
miss [mis] *v* miste
missing ['misiŋ] *adj*
manglende; **~ person**
savnet person
mist [mist] *n* dis *m*, tåke *c*
mistake [mi'steik] *n*
feiltakelse *m*, feil *m*
*****mistake** [mi'steik] *v*
forveksle
mistaken [mi'steikən] *adj*
feilaktig; *****be ~ **ta feil
mister ['mistə] herr, herre *m*
(*obsolete*)
mistress ['mistrəs] *n* frue *c*;
bestyrer *m*; elskerinne *c*
mistrust [mis'trʌst] *v*
mistro
misty ['misti] *adj* disig
*****misunderstand**
[,misʌndə'stænd] *v*
*****misforstå
misunderstanding
[,misʌndə'stændiŋ] *n*
misforståelse *m*
misuse [mis'ju:s] *n* misbruk
nt
mitten ['mitən] *n* vott *m*
mix [miks] *v* blande; **~ with**
*****omgås med

mixed [mikst] *adj* blandet
mixer ['miksə] *n* mikser *m*
mixture ['mikstʃə] *n*
blanding *c*
moan [moun] *v* jamre
moat [mout] *n* vollgrav *c*
mobile ['moubail] *adj*
bevegelig, mobil; **~**
(phone) mobil(telefon) *m*
mock [mɔk] *v* håne
mockery ['mɔkəri] *n* hån *m*
model ['mɔdəl] *n* modell *m*;
mannekeng *m*; *v*
modellere, forme
modem ['moudem] *n*
modem *nt*
moderate ['mɔdərət] *adj*
moderat; middelmådig
modern ['mɔdən] *adj*
moderne
modest ['mɔdist] *adj*
beskjeden
modesty ['mɔdisti] *n*
beskjedenhet *c*
modify ['mɔdifai] *v*
modifisere, endre
moist [mɔist] *adj* fuktig, våt
moisten ['mɔisən] *v* fukte
moisture ['mɔistʃə] *n*
fuktighet *c*; **moisturizing
cream** fuktighetskrem *m*
molar ['moulə] *n* jeksel *m*
mom ['mɔm], **mommy**
['mɔmi] mamma *m*
moment ['moumənt] *n*
øyeblikk *nt*
momentary ['mouməntəri]
adj kortvarig
monarch ['mɔnək] *n*
monark *m*

monarchy ['mɔnəki] n
monarki nt

monastery ['mɔnəstri] n
kloster nt

Monday ['mʌndi] mandag m

monetary ['mʌnitəri] adj
penge-; ~ unit myntenhet
m

money ['mʌni] n penger pl;
~ exchange
vekslingskontor nt; ~ order
postanvisning m

monk [mʌŋk] n munk m

monkey ['mʌŋki] n ape c

monologue ['mɔnələg] n
monolog m

monopoly [mə'nɔpəli] n
monopol nt

monotonous [mə'nɔtənəs]
adj monoton

month [mʌnθ] n måned m

monthly ['mʌnθli] adj
månedlig

monument ['mɔnjumənt] n
monument nt,
minnesmerke nt

mood [muːd] n humør nt,
stemning m

moon [muːn] n måne m

moonlight ['muːnlait] n
måneskinn nt

moose [muːs] n (pl ~, ~s)
elg m

moped ['mouped] n moped
m

moral ['mɔrəl] n moral m;
adj moralsk, sedelig

morality [mə'ræləti] n moral
m

more [mɔː] adj mer; once ~

en gang til

moreover [mɔː'rouvə] adv
dessuten, for øvrig

morning ['mɔːniŋ] n
morgen m, formiddag m; ~
paper morgenavis c; this ~
i morges

Moroccan [mə'rɔkən] adj
marokkansk; n
marokkaner m

Morocco [mə'rɔkou] n
Marokko

morphine ['mɔːfiːn] n
morfin m

morsel ['mɔːsəl] n bit m

mortal ['mɔːtəl] adj dødelig

mortgage ['mɔːgidʒ] n
pantelån nt

mosaic [mə'zeiik] n
mosaikk m

mosque [mɔsk] n moské m

mosquito [mə'skiːtou] n (pl
~es) mygg m; moskito m; ~
net myggnett nt

moss [mɔs] n mose m

most [moust] adj flest; at ~
høyst; ~ of all mest

mostly ['moustli] adv for
det meste

motel [mou'tel] n motell nt

moth [mɔθ] n møll m;
nattsvermer m

mother ['mʌðə] n mor c; ~
of pearl perlemor m; ~
tongue morsmål nt

mother-in-law ['mʌðərinlɔː]
n (pl mothers-) svigermor c

motion ['mouʃən] n
bevegelse m; forslag nt

motive ['moutiv] n motiv nt

municipality

motivate ['moutiveit] v
motivere

motor ['mouta] n motor m;
v bile; ~ body nAm
karosseri nt; starter ~
starter m

motorbike ['moutabaik]
nAm moped m

motorboat ['moutabout] n
motorbåt m

motorcycle ['mouta,saikal]
n motorsykkel m

motoring ['moutariŋ] n
bilkjøring c

motorist ['moutarist] n
bilist m

motorway ['moutawei] n
motorvei m

motto ['mɔtou] n (pl ~es, ~s)
motto nt

mouldy ['mouldi] adj
muggen

mound [maund] n haug m

mount [maunt] v *bestige; n
berg nt

mountain ['mauntin] n fjell
nt; ~ pass pass nt; ~ range
fjellkjede m

mountaineering
[,maunti'niəriŋ] n
fjellklatring c

mountainous ['mauntinəs]
adj fjellendt

mourning ['mɔ:niŋ] n sorg c

mouse [maus] n (pl mice)
mus c; ~ pad musmatte c

moustache [mə'sta:ʃ] n
bart m

mouth [mauθ] n munn m;
kjeft m, gap nt; munning m

mouthwash ['mauθwɔʃ] n
munnvann m

movable ['mu:vəbəl] adj
flyttbar

move [mu:v] v bevege;
flytte; røre seg; n trekk nt,
skritt nt; flytting c

movement ['mu:vmənt] n
bevegelse m; sats m

movie ['mu:vi] n film m;
movies plAm kino m; ~
theater kino m

much [mʌtʃ] adj mange,
mye; adv mye; as ~ like
mye; så vidt

mud [mʌd] n søle c

muddle ['mʌdəl] n
forvirring c, rot nt, virvar
nt; v rote

muddy ['mʌdi] adj sølet

muffler ['mʌflə] nAm
lydpotte c

mug [mʌg] n krus nt

mule [mju:l] n mulesel nt,
muldyr m

multicultural
[,mʌlti'kʌltʃərəl] adj
multikulturell

multiplex ['mʌlti,pleks] n
multiplex nt

multiplication
[,mʌltipli'keiʃən] n
multiplikasjon c

multiply ['mʌltiplai] v
multiplisere

mumps [mʌmps] n kusma
m

municipal [mju:'nisipəl] adj
kommunal, by-

municipality

[mju:nisi'pæləti] n
kommune m

murder ['mə:də] n mord nt;
v myrde

murderer ['mə:dərə] n
morder m

muscle ['mʌsəl] n muskel m

muscular ['mʌskjulə] adj
muskuløs

museum [mju:'zi:əm] n
museum nt

mushroom ['mʌʃru:m] n
sjampinjong m; sopp m

music ['mju:zik] n musikk
m; ~ **academy**
konservatorium nt; ~ **hall**
revyteater m

musical ['mju:zikəl] adj
musikalsk; n musikal m

musician [mju:'ziʃən] n
musiker m

mussel ['mʌsəl] n blåskjell

nt

Muslim ['mʌslim] n muslim
m

*****must** [mʌst] v *måtte

mustard ['mʌstəd] n sennep
m

mute [mju:t] adj stum

mutiny ['mju:tini] n mytteri
nt

mutton ['mʌtən] n fårekjøtt
nt

mutual ['mju:tʃuəl] adj
gjensidig

my [mai] adj min

myself [mai'self] pron meg;
selv

mysterious [mi'stiəriəs] adj
gåtefull, mystisk

mystery ['mistəri] n
mysterium nt

myth [miθ] n myte m

N

nail [neil] n negl m; spiker
m; ~ **file** neglefil c; ~ **polish**
neglelakk m; ~ **scissors** pl
neglesaks c

naïve [na:'i:v] adj naiv

naked ['neikid] adj naken;
bar

name [neim] n navn nt; v
oppkalle, kalle; **in the ~ of**
i ...s navn

namely ['neimli] adv nemlig

nap [næp] n lur m

napkin ['næpkin] n serviett
m

nappy ['næpi] n bleie c

narcosis [na:'kousis] n (pl
-ses) narkose m

narcotic [na:'kɔtik] n
narkotisk middel

narrow ['nærou] adj trang,
smal, snever

narrow-minded
[,nærou'maindid] adj
sneversynt

nasty ['na:sti] adj
ubehagelig, vemmelig;
ekkel

nation ['neiʃən] n nasjon m;

folk *nt*

national ['næʃənəl] *adj*
nasjonal; folke-; stats-; ~
anthem nasjonalsang *m*; ~
dress nasjonaldrakt *c*;
bunad *m*; ~ park
nasjonalpark *m*

nationality [ˌnæʃə'næləti] *n*
nasjonalitet *m*

nationalize ['næʃənəlaiz] *v*
nasjonalisere

native ['neitiv] *n* innfødt *m*;
adj født; ~ country
fedreland *nt*; hjemland *nt*;
~ language morsmål *nt*

natural ['nætʃərəl] *adj*
naturlig; medfødt

naturally ['nætʃərəli] *adv*
selvfølgelig, naturligvis

nature ['neitʃə] *n* natur *m*

naughty ['nɔːti] *adj*
uskikkelig, slem

nausea ['nɔːsiə] *n* kvalme *m*

naval ['neivəl] *adj* marine-

navel ['neivəl] *n* navle *m*

navigable ['nævigəbəl] *adj*
seilbar

navigate ['nævigeit] *v*
navigere

navigation [ˌnævi'geiʃən] *n*
navigasjon *m*; seilas *m*

navy ['neivi] *n* flåte *m*

near [niə] *prep* nær; *adj* nær

nearby ['niəbai] *adj*
nærliggende, tilstøtende

nearly ['niəli] *adv* nesten

neat [niːt] *adj* nett, ordentlig

necessary ['nesəsəri] *adj*
nødvendig

necessity [nə'sesəti] *n*

nødvendighet *c*

neck [nek] *n* hals *m*; nape of
the ~ nakke *m*

necklace ['nekləs] *n*
halskjede *nt*

necktie ['nektai] *n* slips *nt*

need [niːd] *v* behøve,
trenge; *n* behov *nt*;
nødvendighet *c*; ~ to
*måtte

needle ['niːdəl] *n* nål *c*

needlework ['niːdəlwəːk] *n*
håndarbeid *nt*

negative ['negətiv] *adj*
negativ, benektende; *n*
negativ *nt*

neglect [ni'glekt] *v*
forsømme; *n* forsømmelse
m

negligee ['negliʒei] *n*
neglisjé *m* / *nt*

negotiate [ni'gouʃieit] *v*
forhandle

negotiation [niˌgouʃi'eiʃən]
n forhandling *c*

neighbo(u)r ['neibə] *n*
granne *m*, nabo *m*

neighbo(u)rhood
['neibəhud] *n* nabolag *nt*

neighbo(u)ring ['neibəriŋ]
adj tilstøtende,
nærliggende

neither ['naiðə] *pron* ingen
av dem; neither ... nor
verken ... eller

nephew ['nefjuː] *n* nevø *m*

nerve [nəːv] *n* nerve *m*;
dristighet *c*

nervous ['nəːvəs] *adj*
nervøs

nest   312

nest [nest] *n* rede *nt*
net [net] *n* nett *nt*; *adj* netto
Netherlands: the ~
['neðələndz] Nederland
network ['netwə:k] *n*
nettverk *nt*
networking ['net,wə:kiŋ] *n*
nettverksbygging *c*
neuralgia [njuə'rældʒə] *n*
nevralgi *m*
neurosis [njuə'rousis] *n*
nevrose *m*
neuter ['nju:tə] *adj*
intetkjønns-
neutral ['nju:trəl] *adj*
nøytral
never ['nevə] *adv* aldri
nevertheless [,nevəðə'les]
adv ikke desto mindre
new [nju:] *adj* ny; New Year
nyttår *nt*
news [nju:z] *n* nyheter *pl*,
nyhet *c*
newspaper ['nju:z,peipə] *n*
avis *c*
newsstand ['nju:zstænd] *n*
aviskiosk *m*
New Zealand [nju: 'zi:lənd]
Ny-Zealand
next [nekst] *adj* neste; ~ to
ved siden av
next-door [,nekst'dɔ:] *adv*
ved siden av, nabo-
nice [nais] *adj* koselig, snill,
pen; lekker; sympatisk
nickel ['nikəl] *n* nikkel *m*;
5-cent-mynt
nickname ['nikneim] *n*
kjælenavn *nt*
nicotine ['nikəti:n] *n*

nikotin *m*
niece [ni:s] *n* niese *c*
Nigeria [nai'dʒiəriə] Nigeria
Nigerian [nai'dʒiəriən] *adj*
nigeriansk; *n* nigerianer *m*
night [nait] *n* natt *c*; kveld
m; by ~ om natten; ~ rate
natt-takst *m*; ~ train natt-
-tog *nt*
nightclub ['naitklʌb] *n*
nattklubb *m*
night cream ['naitkri:m] *n*
nattkrem *m*
nightingale ['naitiŋgeil] *n*
nattergal *m*
nightly ['naitli] *adj* nattlig
nil [nil] ingenting; null
nine [nain] *num* ni
nineteen [,nain'ti:n] *num*
nitten
nineteenth [,nain'ti:nθ]
num nittende
ninety ['nainti] *num* nitti
ninth [nainθ] *num* niende
nitrogen ['naitrədʒən] *n*
kvelstoff *nt*
no [nou] nei; *adj* ingen; ~
one ingen
nobility [nou'biləti] *n* adel
m
noble ['noubəl] *adj* adelig;
edel
nobody ['noubɔdi] *pron*
ingen
nod [nɔd] *n* nikk *nt*; *v* nikke
noise [nɔiz] *n* lyd *m*; bulder
nt, larm *m*, støy *m*
noisy ['nɔizi] *adj* støyende
nominal ['nɔminəl] *adj*
nominell

nowhere

nominate ['nɔmineit] v
nominere

nomination [,nɔmi'neiʃən]
n nominasjon m;
utnevnelse m

none [nʌn] pron ingen

nonsense ['nɔnsəns] n
nonsens nt

non-smoker [,nɔn'smoukə]
n ikke-røyker m

noodles [nu:dəls] pl nudler
pl, pasta m

noon [nu:n] n klokken
(klokka) tolv

normal ['nɔ:məl] adj normal

north [nɔ:θ] n nord m; adj
nordlig; North Pole
Nordpolen

north-east [,nɔ:θ'i:st] n
nordøst m

northern ['nɔ:ðən] adj
nordlig

north-west [,nɔ:θ'west] n
nordvest m

Norway ['nɔ:wei] Norge

Norwegian [nɔ:'wi:dʒən]
adj norsk; n nordmann (pl
–menn) m

nose [nouz] n nese c

nosebleed ['nouzbli:d] n
neseblod nt

nostril ['nɔstril] n nesebor
nt

nosy ['nouzi] adj colloquial
nysgjerrig

not [nɔt] adv ikke

notary ['noutəri] n notar m

note [nout] n merknad m,
notis m; notat nt; tone m; v
notere; bemerke,

konstatere

notebook ['noutbuk] n
notisbok c

noted ['noutid] adj kjent

notepaper ['nout,peipə] n
brevpapir nt

nothing ['nʌθiŋ] n
ingenting, intet nt

notice ['noutis] v merke,
bemerke, *legge merke til,
oppdage; *se; n
underretning m,
kunngjøring c;
oppmerksomhet c

noticeable ['noutisəbəl] adj
merkbar;
bemerkelsesverdig

notify ['noutifai] v meddele;
underrette; varsle

notion ['nouʃən] n anelse m,
begrep nt

notorious [nou'tɔ:riəs] adj
beryktet

nought [nɔ:t] n null m / nt

noun [naun] n substantiv nt

nourishing ['nʌriʃiŋ] adj
nærende

nourishment ['nʌriʃmənt] n
næring c

novel ['nɔvəl] n roman m

novelist ['nɔvəlist] n
romanforfatter m

November [nou'vembə]
november

now [nau] adv nå; from ~ on
heretter; ~ and then nå og
da

nowadays ['nauədeiz] adv
nåtildags

nowhere ['nouweə] adv

ingensteds, ingen steder
nozzle ['nɔzəl] *n* tut *m*
nuance [nju:'ɑ:s] *n* nyanse *m*
nuclear ['nju:kliə] *adj* kjerne-; ~ **energy** kjernekraft *c*
nucleus ['nju:kliəs] *n* kjerne *m*
nude [nju:d] *adj* naken; *n* akt *m*
nuisance ['nju:səns] *n* plage *m*
numb [nʌm] *adj* følelsesløs; valen
number ['nʌmbə] *n* nummer *nt*; tall *nt*, antall *nt*
numeral ['nju:mərəl] *n* tallord *nt*

numerous ['nju:mərəs] *adj* tallrik
nun [nʌn] *n* nonne *c*
nurse [nə:s] *n* sykepleier *m*; barnepike *m*; *v* pleie; amme
nursery ['nə:səri] *n* barneværelse *nt*; planteskole *m*
nut [nʌt] *n* nøtt *c*; mutter *m*
nutcrackers ['nʌt,krækəz] *pl* nøtteknekker *m*
nutmeg ['nʌtmeg] *n* muskatnøtt *c*
nutritious [nju:'triʃəs] *adj* nærende
nutshell ['nʌtʃel] *n* nøtteskall *c*

O

oak [ouk] *n* eik *c*
oar [ɔ:] *n* åre *c*
oasis [ou'eisis] *n* (pl oases) oase *m*
oath [ouθ] *n* ed *m*
oats [outs] *pl* havre *m*
obedience [ə'bi:diəns] *n* lydighet *c*
obedient [ə'bi:diənt] *adj* lydig
obese [ou'bi:s] *adj* fet
obesity [ou'bi:siti] *n* fedme *m*
obey [ə'bei] *v* *adlyde
object[1] ['ɔbdʒikt] *n* objekt *nt*; gjenstand *m*; formål *nt*
object[2] [əb'dʒekt] *v*

protestere, innvende
objection [əb'dʒekʃən] *n* innvending *c*
objective [əb'dʒektiv] *adj* objektiv; *n* formål *nt*
obligatory [ə'bligətəri] *adj* obligatorisk
oblige [ə'blaidʒ] *v* forplikte; *be obliged to* *være forpliktet til; *være nødt til
obliging [ə'blaidʒiŋ] *adj* imøtekommende
oblong ['ɔblɔŋ] *adj* avlang; *n* rektangel *nt*
obscene [əb'si:n] *adj* uanstendig; obskøn
obscure [əb'skjuə] *adj*

uklar, mørk

observation [,ɔbzə'veiʃən]
n iakttakelse *m*,
observasjon *m*

observatory [əb'zɔːvətri] *n*
observatorium *nt*

observe [əb'zɔːv] *v* *iakttta,
observere

obsession [əb'seʃən] *n*
besettelse *m*

obstacle ['ɔbstəkəl] *n*
hindring *c*

obstinate ['ɔbstinət] *adj* sta;
hardnakket

obtain [əb'tein] *v* erverve,
*få

obtainable [əb'teinəbəl] *adj*
oppnåelig

obvious ['ɔbviəs] *adj*
innlysende

occasion [ə'keiʒən] *n*
tilfelle *nt*; foranledning *m*

occasionally [ə'keiʒənəli]
adv av og til, nå og da

occupant ['ɔkjupənt] *n*
beboer *m*

occupation [,ɔkju'peiʃən] *n*
beskjeftigelse *m*;
okkupasjon *m*

occupy ['ɔkjupai] *v*
*besette; beskjeftige;
occupied *adj* opptatt

occur [ə'kəː] *v* hende,
*forekomme, skje

occurrence [ə'kʌrəns] *n*
hendelse *m*

ocean ['ouʃən] *n* hav *nt*

October [ɔk'toubə] oktober

octopus ['ɔktəpəs] *n*
blekksprut *m*

oculist ['ɔkjulist] *n*
øyenlege *m*

odd [ɔd] *adj* underlig, rar;
ulike

odo(u)r ['oudə] *n* lukt *c*

of [ɔv, əv] *prep* av; fra; i

off [ɔf] *adv* av; vekk; *prep* av

offence [ə'fens] *n* forseelse
m; krenkelse *m*; anstøt *nt*,
fornærmelse *m*

offend [ə'fend] *v* krenke,
fornærme; *forgå seg

offense [ə'fens] *nAm*
forseelse *m*; krenkelse *m*;
anstøt *nt*, fornærmelse *m*

offensive [ə'fensiv] *adj*
offensiv; støtende,
krenkende

offer ['ɔfə] *v* *tilby; yte; *n*
tilbud *nt*

office ['ɔfis] *n* kontor *nt*;
embete *nt*; ~ **hours**
kontortid *c*

officer ['ɔfisə] *n* offiser *m*

official [ə'fiʃəl] *adj* offisiell

off-licence ['ɔf,laisəns] *n*
alkoholutsalg *nt*

often ['ɔfən] *adv* ofte

oil [ɔil] *n* olje *c*; **fuel** ~
brenselolje *c*; ~ **drilling
platform** boreplattform *nt*;
~ **filter** oljefilter *nt*; ~
painting oljemaleri *nt*; ~
pressure oljetrykk *nt*; ~
refinery oljeraffineri *nt*; ~
well oljebrønn *m*

oily ['ɔili] *adj* oljet; glatt

ointment ['ɔintmənt] *n*
salve *c*

okay!, **OK!** [,ou'kei] greit!

ok!

old [ould] *adj* gammel; ~ age alderdom *m*

old-fashioned [,ould'fæʃənd] *adj* gammeldags

olive ['ɔliv] *n* oliven *m*; ~ oil olivenolje *c*

omelette ['ɔmlət] *n* omelett *m*

ominous ['ɔminəs] *adj* illevarslende

omit [ə'mit] *v* *utelate

omnipotent [ɔm'nipətənt] *adj* allmektig

on [ɔn] *prep* på; ved

once [wʌns] *adv* en gang; at ~ straks; for ~ for en gangs skyld; ~ more en gang til

oncoming ['ɔn,kʌmiŋ] *adj* kommende; møtende

one [wʌn] *num* en; *pron* man

oneself [wʌn'self] *pron* selv

one-way ['wʌn-wei] *adj* enkel

only ['ounli] *adj* eneste; *adv* bare, alene, kun; *conj* men

onwards ['ɔnwədz] *adv* fremover

onyx ['ɔniks] *n* onyks *m*

opal ['oupəl] *n* opal *m*

open ['oupən] *v* åpne; *adj* åpen; åpenhjertig

opener ['oupənə] *n* (flaske-)åpner *m*; åpningsnummer *nt*

opening ['oupəniŋ] *n* åpning *c*

opera ['ɔpərə] *n* opera *m*; ~ house opera *m*

operate ['ɔpəreit] *v* virke, *drive; operere

operation [,ɔpə'reiʃən] *n* virksomhet *c*; operasjon *m*

operator ['ɔpəreitə] *n* operatør *m*

opinion [ə'pinjən] *n* oppfatning *m*, mening *m*

opponent [ə'pounənt] *n* motstander *m*

opportunity [,ɔpə'tju:nəti] *n* leilighet *c*, anledning *m*

oppose [ə'pouz] *v* *motsette seg, opponere

opposite ['ɔpəzit] *prep* overfor; *adj* motsatt

opposition [,ɔpə'ziʃən] *n* opposisjon *m*

oppress [ə'pres] *v* undertrykke, knuge

optician [ɔp'tiʃən] *n* optiker *m*

optimism ['ɔptimizəm] *n* optimisme *m*

optimist ['ɔptimist] *n* optimist *m*

optimistic [,ɔpti'mistik] *adj* optimistisk

optional ['ɔpʃənəl] *adj* valgfri

or [ɔ:] *conj* eller

oral ['ɔ:rəl] *adj* muntlig

orange ['ɔrindʒ] *n* appelsin *m*; *adj* oransje

orbit ['ɔ:bit] *n* omløp *nt*

orchard ['ɔ:tʃəd] *n* frukthage *m*

orchestra ['ɔ:kistrə] *n* orkester *nt*; ~ seat *Am*

orkesterplass *m*
order ['ɔ:də] *v* beordre;
bestille; *n* rekkefølge *m*,
orden *m*; ordre *m*, befaling
c; bestilling *c*; in ~ i orden;
in ~ to for å; made to ~
laget på bestilling; out of ~
i uorden
ordinary ['ɔ:dənri] *adj*
vanlig, dagligdags
ore [ɔ:] *n* malm *m*
organ ['ɔ:gən] *n* organ *nt*;
orgel *nt*
organic [ɔ:'gænik] *adj*
organisk
organization
[ˌɔ:gənai'zeiʃən] *n*
organisasjon *m*
organize ['ɔ:gənaiz] *v*
organisere
Orient ['ɔ:riənt] *n* Orienten
oriental [ˌɔ:ri'entəl] *adj*
orientalsk
orientate [ˈɔ:rienteit] *v*
orientere seg
origin ['ɔridʒin] *n*
avstamning *m*, opphav *nt*;
herkomst *m*
original [əˈridʒinəl] *adj*
original, opprinnelig
originally [əˈridʒinəli] *adv* i
begynnelsen
ornament ['ɔ:nəmənt] *n*
utsmykning *m*
ornamental [ˌɔ:nəˈmentəl]
adj dekorativ
orphan ['ɔ:fən] *n*
foreldreløst barn
orthodox ['ɔ:θədɔks] *adj*
ortodoks

ostrich ['ɔstritʃ] *n* struts *m*
other ['ʌðə] *adj* annen
otherwise ['ʌðəwaiz] *conj*
ellers; *adv* annerledes
*ought to [ɔ:t] *burde
ounce [auns] *n* vektenhet,
ca 30 g
our, ours [auə] *adj* vår
ourselves [auəˈselvz] *pron*
oss; selv
out [aut] *adv* ute, ut; ~ of
sluppet opp for
outbreak ['autbreik] *n*
utbrudd *nt*
outcome ['autkʌm] *n*
resultat *nt*
*outdo [ˌaut'du:] *v* *overgå
outdoors [ˌaut'dɔ:z] *adv*
utendørs
outer ['autə] *adj* ytre
outfit ['autfit] *n* utrustning
m; klesdrakt *c*
outing ['autiŋ] *n* utflukt *c*
outline ['autlain] *n* kontur
m, omriss *nt*; *v* gi et omriss
av
outlook ['autluk] *n* utsikt *m*;
syn *nt*
output ['autput] *n*
produksjon *m*
outrage ['autreidʒ] *n*
fornærmelse *m*; krenkelse
m
outside [ˌaut'said] *adv*
utenfor; *prep* utenfor; *n*
utside *c*, ytterside *c*
outsize ['autsaiz] *n* stor
størrelse
outskirts ['autskə:ts] *pl*
utkant *m*

outstanding [ˌautˈstændiŋ] adj fremtredende, fremragende

outward [ˈautwəd] adj utvendig

outwards [ˈautwədz] adv utad

oval [ˈouvəl] adj oval

oven [ˈʌvn] n stekeovn m

over [ˈouvə] prep over, ovenfor; adv over; over ende; ~ there der borte

overall [ˌouvərɔːl] adj total

overalls [ˈouvərɔːlz] pl overall m

overcast [ˈouvəkɑːst] adj overskyet

overcoat [ˈouvəkout] n frakk m

*__overcome__ [ˌouvəˈkʌm] v *overvinne

overdo [ˌouvəˈduː] v overdrive

overdraft [ˈouvədrɑːft] n overtrekk nt

overdue [ˌouvəˈdjuː] adj forsinket; forfalt

overgrown [ˌouvəˈgroun] adj overgrodd

overhaul [ˌouvəˈhɔːl] v overhale

overhead [ˌouvəˈhed] adv ovenfor

*__overlook__ [ˌouvəˈluk] v *overse

overnight [ˌouvəˈnait] adv natten over

overseas [ˌouvəˈsiːz] adj oversjøisk

oversight [ˈouvəsait] n forglemmelse m

*__oversleep__ [ˌouvəˈsliːp] v *forsove seg

overstrung [ˌouvəˈstrʌŋ] adj overspent

*__overtake__ [ˌouvəˈteik] v kjøre forbi; no overtaking forbikjøring forbudt

over-tired [ˌouvəˈtaiəd] adj overtrett

overture [ˈouvətʃə] n ouverture m

overweight [ˈouvəweit] n overvekt c; adj overvektig

overwhelm [ˌouvəˈwelm] v overvelde

overwork [ˌouvəˈwəːk] v overanstrenge seg

owe [ou] v *være skyldig, skylde; *ha å takke for; owing to på grunn av

owl [aul] n ugle c

own [oun] v eie; adj egen

owner [ˈounə] n eier m, innehaver m

ox [ɔks] n (pl oxen) okse m

oxygen [ˈɔksidʒən] n surstoff nt

oyster [ˈɔistə] n østers m

ozone [ˈouzoun] n ozon nt

pace [peis] n skritt nt; tempo nt

Pacific Ocean [pə'sifik 'ouʃən] Stillehavet

pacifism ['pæsifizəm] n pasifisme m

pacifist ['pæsifist] n pasifist m; pasifistisk

pack [pæk] v pakke; nAm kortstokk m; ~ up pakke ned

package ['pækidʒ] n pakke c

packet ['pækit] n liten pakke, småpakke c

packing ['pækiŋ] n innpakning m

pact [pækt] n pakt c; kontrakt m

pad [pæd] n pute m; notisblokk c

paddle ['pædəl] n padleåre c

padlock ['pædlɔk] n hengelås m / nt

pagan ['peigən] adj hedensk; n hedning m

page [peidʒ] n side c

pail [peil] n spann nt

pain [pein] n smerte m; pains umake m

painful ['peinfəl] adj smertefull

painkiller ['peinkilə] n smertestillende middel nt

painless ['peinləs] adj smertefri

paint [peint] n maling c; v male

paintbox ['peintbɔks] n malerskrin nt

paintbrush ['peintbrʌʃ] n pensel m

painter ['peintə] n maler m

painting ['peintiŋ] n maleri nt

pair [pɛə] n par nt

Pakistan [ˌpɑːki'stɑːn] Pakistan

Pakistani [ˌpɑːki'stɑːni] adj pakistansk; n pakistaner m

palace ['pæləs] n palass nt

pale [peil] adj blek; lysere

palm [pɑːm] n palme m; håndflate c

palpable ['pælpəbəl] adj følelig, merkbar

palpitation [ˌpælpi'teiʃən] n hjerteklapp m

pan [pæn] n panne c; kasserolle m

pane [pein] n vindusrute c

panel ['pænəl] n panel nt

panelling ['pænəliŋ] n panelverk nt

panic ['pænik] n panikk m

pant [pænt] v pese

panties ['pæntiz] pl underbukse c, truse c

pants [pænts] pl underbukse c; bukse c

pant suit ['pæntsuːt] n buksedrakt c, buksedress

m

panty hose ['pæntihouz] *n* strømpebukse *c*

paper ['peipə] *n* papir *nt*; avis *c*; papir-; ~ **bag** papirpose *m*; ~ **knife** papirkniv *m*; ~ **napkin** papirserviett *m*; **wrapping** ~ innpakningspapir *nt*

paperback ['peipəbæk] *n* billigbok *c*

parade [pə'reid] *n* parade *m*; tog *nt*

paradise [pærədais] *n* paradis *m*

paraffin ['pærəfin] *n* parafin *m m*

paragraph ['pærəgrɑ:f] *n* avsnitt *nt*; paragraf *m*

parakeet ['pærəki:t] *n* papegøye *m*

parallel ['pærəlel] *adj* parallell; *n* parallell *m*

paralyse ['pærəlaiz] *v* lamme

parcel ['pɑ:səl] *n* pakke *c*

pardon ['pɑ:dən] *n* tilgivelse *m*; benådning *m*

parent ['peərənt] *n* forelder *m*

parents ['peərənts] *pl* foreldre *pl*

parents-in-law ['peərəntsinlɔ:] *pl* svigerforeldre *pl*

parish ['pærif] *n* sogn *nt*

park [pɑ:k] *n* park *m*; *v* parkere

parking ['pɑ:kiŋ] *n* parkering *c*; **no** ~ parkering

forbudt; ~ **fee** parkeringsavgift *c*; ~ **light** parkeringslys *nt*; ~ **lot** *Am* parkeringsplass *m*; ~ **meter** parkometer *nt*; ~ **zone** parkeringssone *c*

parliament ['pɑ:ləmənt] *n* parlament *nt*

parliamentary [,pɑ:lə'mentəri] *adj* parlamentarisk

parrot ['pærət] *n* papegøye *m*

parsley ['pɑ:sli] *n* persille *c*

parson ['pɑ:sən] *n* prest *m*

parsonage ['pɑ:sənidʒ] *n* prestegård *m*

part [pɑ:t] *n* del *m*; stykke *nt*; *v* skille; **spare** ~ reservedel *m*

partial ['pɑ:fəl] *adj* delvis; partisk

participant [pɑ:'tisipənt] *n* deltaker *m*

participate [pɑ:'tisipeit] *v* *delta

particular [pə'tikjulə] *adj* spesiell, særegen; kresen; **in** ~ i særdeleshet

parting ['pɑ:tiŋ] *n* avskjed *m*; hårskill *m*

partition [pɑ:'tifən] *n* skillevegg *m*

partly ['pɑ:tli] *adv* delvis

partner ['pɑ:tnə] *n* partner *m*; kompanjong *m*

partridge ['pɑ:tridʒ] *n* rapphøne *c*

party ['pɑ:ti] *n* parti *nt*; selskap *nt*; gruppe *c*

pass [pɑːs] v *forløpe, passere; *rekke; *bestå; no passing Am forbikjøring forbudt; ~ by *gå forbi; ~ through *gå gjennom

passage ['pæsidʒ] n passasje m; overfart m; avsnitt nt; gjennomreise c

passenger ['pæsəndʒə] n passasjer m; ~ train persontog nt

passer-by [ˌpɑːsə'bai] n forbipasserende m

passion ['pæʃən] n lidenskap m

passionate ['pæʃənət] adj lidenskapelig

passive ['pæsiv] adj passiv

passport ['pɑːspɔːt] n pass nt; ~ control passkontroll m; ~ photograph passfoto nt

password ['pɑːswəːd] n passord nt

past [pɑːst] n fortid c; adj forrige, tidligere; prep forbi, langs

paste [peist] n lim nt; v klistre

pastime ['pɑːstaim] n tidsfordriv nt

pastry ['peistri] n finere bakverk nt; ~ shop konditori m

pasture ['pɑːstʃə] n beite nt

pasty ['peisti] n postei m

patch [pætʃ] n lapp m

patent ['peitənt] n patent nt

path [pɑːθ] n sti m

patience ['peiʃəns] n tålmodighet c

patient ['peiʃənt] adj tålmodig; n pasient m

patriot ['peitriət] n patriot m

patrol [pə'troul] n patrulje m; v patruljere; overvåke

pattern ['pætən] n mønster nt, motiv nt

pause [pɔːz] n pause m; v *holde pause

pave [peiv] v *legge veidekke; *brolegge

pavement ['peivmənt] n fortau nt; veidekke nt

pavilion [pə'viljən] n paviljong m

paw [pɔː] n pote m

pawn [pɔːn] v *pantsette; n sjakkbonde m

pawnbroker ['pɔːnˌbroukə] n pantelåner m

pay [pei] n gasje m, lønn c

*pay [pei] v betale; lønne seg; ~ attention to *være oppmerksom på; ~ off nedbetale; ~ on account avbetale; paying lønnsom

pay desk ['peidesk] n kasse c

payment ['peimənt] n betaling c

pea [piː] n ert c

peace [piːs] n fred m

peaceful ['piːsfəl] adj fredelig

peach [piːtʃ] n fersken m

peacock ['piːkɔk] n påfugl m

peak [piːk] n tind m; topp

m; ~ **hour** rushtid *c*; ~
season høysesong *m*
peanut ['pi:nʌt] *n* peanøtt
m c
pear [peə] *n* pære *c*
pearl [pə:l] *n* perle *c*
peasant ['pezənt] *n* bonde
m
pebble ['pebəl] *n* småstein
m
peculiar [pi'kju:ljə] *adj*
underlig; eiendommelig
peculiarity [pi,kju:li'ærəti]
n eiendommelighet *c*
pedal ['pedəl] *n* pedal *m*
pedestrian [pi'destriən] *n*
fotgjenger *m*; ~ **crossing**
fotgjengerovergang *m*; **no
pedestrians** ikke for
fotgjengere
peel [pi:l] *v* skrelle; *n* skrell
nt
peep [pi:p] *v* kikke
peg [peg] *n* knagg *m*
pelican ['pelikən] *n* pelikan
m
pelvis ['pelvis] *n* bekken *nt*
pen [pen] *n* penn *m*
penalty ['penəlti] *n* bot *c*;
straff *m*; ~ **kick** straffespark
nt
pencil ['pensəl] *n* blyant *m*;
~ **sharpener** blyantspisser
m
penetrate ['penitreit] *v*
trenge gjennom
penguin ['peŋgwin] *n*
pingvin *m*
penicillin [,peni'silin] *n*
penicillin *nt*

peninsula [pə'ninsjulə] *n*
halvøy *c*
penknife ['pennaif] *n* (pl
-knives) lommekniv *m*
penny ['peni] *n* (pl pennies,
pence) penny *m*
pension[1] ['pɑ:sio:] *n*
pensjonat *nt*
pension[2] ['penʃən] *n*
pensjon *m*
Pentecost ['pentikəst] *n*
pinse *c*
people ['pi:pəl] *pl* folk *pl*; *n*
folk *nt*, folkeslag *nt*
pepper ['pepə] *n* pepper *m*
peppermint ['pepəmint] *n*
peppermynte *c*
per [pə:] *prep* per, pr.; ~ **cent**
prosent
perceive [pə'si:v] *v*
fornemme
percent [pə'sent] *n* prosent
m
percentage [pə'sentidʒ] *n*
prosentsats *m*
perceptible [pə'septibəl]
adj merkbar
perception [pə'sepʃən] *n*
fornemmelse *m*
perch [pə:tʃ] (pl ~) åbor *m*
percolator ['pə:kəleitə] *n*
kaffetrakter *m*
perfect ['pə:fikt] *adj*
fullkommen, perfekt
perfection [pə'fekʃən] *n*
perfeksjon *m*,
fullkommenhet *c*
perform [pə'fɔ:m] *v* utføre;
*opptre; utøve
performance [pə'fɔ:məns]

n forestilling *c*

perfume ['pəːfjuːm] *n* parfyme *m*

perhaps [pə'hæps] *adv* kanskje; muligens

peril ['peril] *n* fare *m*

perilous ['periləs] *adj* livsfarlig

period ['piəriəd] *n* periode *m*, tid *c*; punktum *nt*

periodical [,piəri'ɔdikəl] *n* tidsskrift *nt*; *adj* periodevis

perish ['periʃ] *v* *omkomme; *forgå

perishable ['periʃəbəl] *adj* bedervelig

perjury ['pəːdʒəri] *n* mened *m*

permanent ['pəːmənənt] *adj* varig, permanent, vedvarende, fast

permission [pə'miʃən] *n* tillatelse *m*; lov *m*

permit[1] [pə'mit] *v* *tillate

permit[2] ['pəːmit] *n* tillatelse *m*, permisjon *m*

peroxide [pə'rɔksaid] *n* vannstoff hyperoksyd

perpendicular [,pəːpən'dikjulə] *adj* loddrett

persecute ['pəːsikjuːt] *v* *forfølge, plage

Persia ['pəːʃə] Persia

Persian ['pəːʃən] *adj* persisk; *n* perser *m*

person ['pəːsən] *n* person *m*; per ~ per person

personal ['pəːsənəl] *adj* personlig

personality [,pəːsə'næləti] *n* personlighet *c*

personnel [,pəːsə'nel] *n* personale *nt*

perspective [pə'spektiv] *n* perspektiv *nt*

perspiration [,pəːspə'reiʃən] *n* svette *m*

perspire [pə'spaiə] *v* transpirere, svette

persuade [pə'sweid] *v* overtale; overbevise

persuasion [pə'sweiʒən] *n* overbevisning *m*; overtaling *c*

pessimism ['pesimizəm] *n* pessimisme *m*

pessimist ['pesimist] *n* pessimist *m*

pessimistic [,pesi'mistik] *adj* pessimistisk

pet [pet] *n* kjæledyr *nt*; kjæledegge *m*; *adj* yndlings-

petal ['petəl] *n* kronblad *nt*

petition [pi'tiʃən] *n* bønn *m*; petisjon *m*

petrol ['petrəl] *n* bensin *m*; unleaded ~ blyfri bensin; ~ pump bensinpumpe *c*; ~ station bensinstasjon *m*; ~ tank bensintank *m*

petroleum [pi'trouliəm] *n* petroleum *m*

petty ['peti] *adj* smålig, ubetydelig, liten; ~ cash småpenger *pl*

phantom ['fæntəm] *n* fantasibilde *nt*; gjenferd *nt*

pharmacology

[,fɑːməˈkɔlədʒi] n
farmakologi m
pharmacy [ˈfɑːməsi] n
apotek m
phase [feiz] n fase m
Philippine [ˈfilipain] adj
filippinsk
Philippines [ˈfilipiːnz] pl
Filippinene
philosopher [fiˈlɔsəfə] n
filosof m
philosophy [fiˈlɔsəfi] n
filosofi m
phone [foun] n telefon m; v
telefonere, ringe; ~ card
telefonkort nt
phonetic [fəˈnetik] adj
fonetisk
phoney [ˈfouni] adj falsk; n
bløffmaker m
photo [ˈfoutou] n (pl ~s)
fotografi m
photo message
[ˈfoutou,mesədʒ] n
bildemelding c
photocopy [ˈfoutəkɔpi] n
fotokopi m; v (foto)kopiere
photograph [ˈfoutəgrɑːf] n
fotografi nt; v fotografere
photographer [fəˈtɔgrəfə]
n fotograf m
photography [fəˈtɔgrəfi] n
fotografering c
phrase [freiz] n uttrykk nt
phrase book [ˈfreizbuk] n
parlør m
physical [ˈfizikəl] adj fysisk
physician [fiˈziʃən] n lege
m
physicist [ˈfizisist] n fysiker

m
physics [ˈfiziks] n fysikk m
physiology [,fiziˈɔlədʒi] n
fysiologi m
pianist [ˈpiːənist] n pianist
m
piano [piˈænou] n piano nt;
grand ~ flygel nt
pick [pik] v plukke; *velge;
n valg nt; ~ up *ta opp;
hente; pick-up van varebil
m
picnic [ˈpiknik] n piknik m;
v *dra på piknik
picture [ˈpiktʃə] n maleri nt;
illustrasjon m, stikk nt;
bilde nt; ~ postcard
prospektkort nt; pictures
kino m
picturesque [,piktʃəˈresk]
adj pittoresk, malerisk
piece [piːs] n stykke nt, bit
m; brikke c
pier [piə] n utstikker m
pierce [piəs] v gjennombore
pig [pig] n gris m
pigeon [ˈpidʒən] n due c
piggy bank [ˈpigibæŋk] n
sparegris m
pig-headed [,pigˈhedid] adj
sta
piglet [ˈpiglət] n smågris m
pigskin [ˈpigskin] n svinelær
nt
pike [paik] (pl ~) gjedde c
pile [pail] n haug m; v
stable; piles pl
hemorroider pl
pilgrim [ˈpilgrim] n pilegrim
m

pilgrimage ['pilgrimidʒ] n pilegrimsreise c

pill [pil] n pille c

pillar ['pilə] n søyle c

pillar-box ['piləbɔks] n postkasse c

pillow ['pilou] n pute c, hodepute c

pillowcase ['piloukeis] n putevar nt

pilot ['pailət] n pilot m; los m

pimple ['pimpəl] n kvise c

pin [pin] n knappenål c; v feste med nål; **bobby ~** Am hårspenne c

PIN [pin], **personal identification number** n PIN, kode c

pincers ['pinsəz] pl knipetang c

pinch [pintʃ] v *klype

pineapple ['pai,næpəl] n ananas m

ping-pong ['piŋpɔŋ] n bordtennis m

pink [piŋk] adj lyserød, rosa

pioneer [,paiə'niə] n nybygger m; pioner m

pious ['paiəs] adj from

pip [pip] n kjerne m

pipe [paip] n pipe c; rør nt; **~ cleaner** piperenser m; **~ tobacco** pipetobakk m

pirate ['paiərət] n sjørøver m

pistol ['pistəl] n pistol m

piston ['pistən] n stempel nt

pit [pit] n grop c; gruve c

pitcher ['pitʃə] n krukke c

pity ['piti] n medlidenhet c; v synes synd på, *ha medlidenhet med; **what a pity!** så synd!

placard ['plækɑːd] n plakat m

place [pleis] n sted nt; v *sette, stille; **~ of birth** fødested nt; ***take ~** *finne sted

plague [pleig] n plage c; pest m

plaice [pleis] n (pl ~) rødspette c

plain [plein] adj tydelig; alminnelig, enkel; n slette c

plan [plæn] n plan m; v *planlegge

plane [plein] adj flat; n fly nt; **~ crash** flyulykke c

planet ['plænit] n planet m

planetarium [,plæni'teəriəm] n planetarium c

plank [plæŋk] n planke m

plant [plɑːnt] n plante c; fabrikk m; v plante

plantation [plæn'teiʃən] n plantasje c

plaster ['plɑːstə] n murpuss m, gips m; plaster nt

plastic ['plæstik] adj plastikk-; n plastikk m

plate [pleit] n tallerken m; plate c

plateau ['plætou] n (pl ~x, ~s) vidde c; høyslette c

platform ['plætfɔːm] n perrong m

platinum ['plætinəm] n

platina *m*
play [plei] *n* lek *m*;
teaterstykke *nt*; *v* leke;
spille; one-act ~ enakter
m; ~ truant skulke
player ['pleiə] *n* spiller *m*
playground ['pleigraund] *n*
lekeplass *m*
playing card ['pleiiŋkɑːd] *v*
spillkort *nt*
playwright ['pleirait] *n*
skuespillforfatter *m*
plea [pliː] *n* påstand *m*;
bønn *m*
plead [pliːd] *v* føre en sak;
trygle
pleasant ['plezənt] *adj*
hyggelig, deilig
please [pliːz] vennligst; *v*
glede; pleased fornøyd;
pleasing behagelig
pleasure ['pleʒə] *n* behag
nt, fornøyelse *m*
plentiful ['plentifəl] *adj*
rikelig
plenty ['plenti] *n* rikelighet
c; overflod *m*
pliers [plaiəz] *pl* tang *c*
plot [plɔt] *n* komplott *nt*,
sammensvergelse *m*;
handling *c*; plott *nt*
plough [plau] *n* plog *m*; *v*
pløye
plucky ['plʌki] *adj* modig
plug [plʌg] *n* stikkontakt *m*;
~ in sette i kontakten,
plugge inn
plum [plʌm] *n* plomme *c*
plumber ['plʌmə] *n*
rørlegger *m*

plump [plʌmp] *adj* lubben
plural ['pluərəl] *n* flertall *nt*
plus [plʌs] *prep* pluss
pneumatic [njuː'mætik] *adj*
luft..., pneumatisk
pneumonia [njuː'mouniə] *n*
lungebetennelse *m*
poach [poutʃ] *v* ~ed eggs
pocherte egg
pocket ['pɔkit] *n* lomme *c*
pocketbook ['pɔkitbuk]
nAm lommebok *c*
pocketknife ['pɔkitnaif] *n*
(pl -knives) lommekniv *m*
poem ['pouim] *n* dikt *nt*
poet ['pouit] *n* dikter *m*
poetry ['pouitri] *n* poesi *m*
point [pɔint] *n* punkt *nt*;
spiss *m*; *v* peke; ~ of view
synspunkt *nt*; ~ out vise
pointed ['pɔintid] *adj* spiss
poison ['pɔizən] *n* gift *c*; *v*
forgifte
poisonous ['pɔizənəs] *adj*
giftig
Poland ['poulənd] Polen
pole [poul] *n* stang *c*
police [pə'liːs] *pl* politi *nt*; ~
station politistasjon *m*
policeman [pə'liːsmən] *n*
(pl -men) politibetjent *m*
policewoman
[pə'liːswumən] *n* (pl
-women) politibetjent *m*
policy ['pɔlisi] *n* politikk *m*;
polise *m*
Polish ['pouliʃ] *adj* polsk
polish ['pɔliʃ] *v* pusse,
polere
polite [pə'lait] *adj* høflig

political [pə'litikəl] adj
politisk
politician [,pɔli'tiʃən] n
politiker m
politics ['pɔlitiks] n politikk
m
poll [poul] n meningsmåling
c; valg; go to the polls
velge
pollute [pə'luːt] v forurense
pollution [pə'luːʃən] n
forurensning m
pond [pɔnd] n dam m
pony ['pouni] n ponni m
pool [puːl] n dam m;
svømmebasseng nt; ~
attendant badevakt m
poor [puə] adj fattig;
fattigslig; dårlig
pope [poup] n pave m
pop music [pɔp 'mjuːzik]
popmusikk m
poppy ['pɔpi] n valmue m
popular ['pɔpjulə] adj
populær; folke-
population [,pɔpju'leiʃən] n
befolkning m
populous ['pɔpjuləs] adj
folkerik
porcelain ['pɔːsəlin] n
porselen nt
porcupine ['pɔːkjupain] n
pinnsvin nt
pork [pɔːk] n svinekjøtt nt
port [pɔːt] n havn c; babord
portable ['pɔːtəbəl] adj
transportabel
porter ['pɔːtə] n bærer m;
portier m
porthole ['pɔːthoul] n

kuøye nt
portion ['pɔːʃən] n porsjon
m
portrait ['pɔːtrit] n portrett
nt
Portugal ['pɔːtjugəl]
Portugal
Portuguese [,pɔːtju'giːz]
adj portugisisk; n
portugiser m
position [pə'ziʃən] n
posisjon m; situasjon m;
holdning m; stilling c
positive ['pɔzətiv] adj
positiv; n positivt bilde
possess [pə'zes] v eie;
possessed adj besatt
possession [pə'zeʃən] n
besittelse m; possessions
eiendeler pl
possibility [,pɔsə'biləti] n
mulighet c
possible ['pɔsəbəl] adj
mulig; eventuell
post [poust] n stolpe m;
post m; v boste; post-
-office postkontor nt
postage ['poustidʒ] n porto
m; ~ paid portofri; ~ stamp
frimerke nt
postcard ['poustkɑːd] n
postkort nt; prospektkort
nt
poster ['poustə] n plakat m
poste restante [poust
re'stɑ..ːt] poste restante
postman ['poustmən] n (pl
-men) postbud nt
post-paid [,poust'peid] adj
frankert

postpone [pə'spoun] v
*utsette

pot [pɔt] n gryte c

potato [pə'teitou] n (pl ~es)
potet m

pottery ['pɔtəri] n keramikk
m; steintøy nt

pouch [pautʃ] n pung m

poultry ['poultri] n fjærkre
nt

pound [paund] n pund nt

pour [pɔː] v helle, skjenke

poverty ['pɔvəti] n
fattigdom m

powder ['paudə] n pudder
nt

power [pauə] n kraft c,
styrke m; energi m; makt c;
~ station kraftverk nt

powerful ['pauəfəl] adj
mektig; sterk

powerless ['pauələs] adj
maktesløs

practical ['præktikəl] adj
praktisk

practically ['præktikli] adv
praktisk talt

practice ['præktis] n praksis
m

practise ['præktis] v
praktisere; øve seg

praise [preiz] v rose; n ros
m

pram [præm] n barnevogn c

prawn [prɔːn] n reke c

pray [prei] v *be

prayer [prɛə] n bønn m

preach [priːtʃ] v preke

precarious [pri'kɛəriəs] adj
risikabel; utrygg

precaution [pri'kɔːʃən] n
forsiktighet c;
sikkerhetstiltak nt

precede [pri'siːd] v *gå
forut for

preceding [pri'siːdiŋ] adj
foregående

precious ['preʃəs] adj
kostbar; dyrebar; ~ stone
edelstein m

precipice ['presipis] n stup
nt

precipitation
[pri,sipi'teiʃən] n nedbør
m

precise [pri'sais] adj presis,
nøyaktig; pertentlig

predecessor ['priːdisesə] n
forgjenger m

predict [pri'dikt] v spå

prefer [pri'fəː] v *foretrekke

preferable ['prefərəbəl] adj
til å foretrekke

preference ['prefərəns] n
forkjærlighet c

prefix ['priːfiks] n
forstavelse m

pregnant ['pregnənt] adj
gravid

pregnancy ['pregnənsi] n
svangerskap nt

prejudice ['predʒədis] n
fordom m

preliminary [pri'liminəri]
adj innledende;
forberedende

premature ['prematʃuə] adj
forhastet; for tidlig

premier ['premiə] n
statsminister m

premises ['premisiz] *pl* eiendom *m*

premium ['pri:miəm] *n* forsikringspremie *m*

prepaid [,pri:'peid] *adj* forhåndsbetalt

preparation [,prepə'rei∫ən] *n* forberedelse *m*

prepare [pri'peə] *v* forberede; tilberede

prepared [pri'peəd] *adj* beredt

preposition [,prepə'zi∫ən] *n* preposisjon *m*

prescribe [pri'skraib] *v* *foreskrive

prescription [pri'skrip∫ən] *n* resept *m*

presence ['prezəns] *n* nærvær *nt*; tilstedeværelse *m*

present¹ ['prezənt] *n* presang *m*, gave *c*; nåtid *c*; *adj* nåværende; tilstedeværende

present² [pri'zent] *v* presentere; *forelegge

presentation [pri'zent'ei∫ən] *v* presentasjon

presently ['prezəntli] *adv* snart

preservation [,prezə'vei∫ən] *n* konservering *c*

preserve [pri'zə:v] *v* konservere; hermetisere

president ['prezidənt] *n* president *m*; formann *m*

press [pres] *n* presse *m*; *v*

trykke på, trykke; presse; ~ **conference** pressekonferanse *m*

pressing ['presiŋ] *adj* presserende, inntrengende

pressure ['pre∫ə] *n* trykk *nt*; press *nt*; atmospheric ~ lufttrykk *nt*; ~ **cooker** trykkoker *m*

prestige [pre'sti:ʒ] *n* prestisje *m*

presumable [pri'zju:məbəl] *adj* antakelig

presumptuous [pri'zʌmp∫əs] *adj* overmodig; anmassende

pretence [pri'tens] *n* påskudd *nt*

pretend [pri'tend] *v* *foregi, *late som

pretext ['pri:tekst] *n* påskudd *nt*

pretty ['priti] *adj* pen; *adv* ganske, temmelig

prevent [pri'vent] *v* avverge, forhindre; forebygge

preventive [pri'ventiv] *adj* forebyggende

preview ['privju:] *n* forhåndsvisning *m*

previous ['pri:viəs] *adj* foregående, tidligere, forrige

price [prais] *n* pris *m*; *v* prise

priceless ['praisləs] *adj* uvurderlig

price list ['prais,list] *n* prisliste *c*

pride [praid] *n* stolthet *c*

priest [pri:st] n katolsk prest

primary ['praiməri] adj primær; hoved-, første; elementær

primeval forest [praim'i:vəl 'fɔrist] n urskog m

prince [prins] n prins m

princess [prin'ses] n prinsesse c

principal ['prinsəpəl] adj hoved-; n rektor m, skolebestyrer m

principle ['prinsəpəl] n prinsipp nt, grunnsetning m

print [print] v trykke; n avtrykk nt; trykk nt

printer ['printə] n printer m, skriver m

printout ['printaut] n utskrift c

prior ['praiə] adj forutgående

priority [prai'ɔrəti] n fortrinnsrett m, prioritet m

prison ['prizən] n fengsel m

prisoner ['prizənə] n fange m, innsatt m; ~ of war krigsfange m

privacy ['praivəsi] n privatliv n

private ['praivit] adj privat; personlig

privilege ['priviliʤ] n privilegium n

prize [praiz] n premie m; belønning c

probable ['prɔbəbəl] adj sannsynlig

probably ['prɔbəbli] adv sannsynligvis

problem ['prɔbləm] n problem nt; spørsmål nt

procedure [prə'si:dʒə] n fremgangsmåte m

proceed [prə'si:d] v *fortsette; *gå til verks

process ['prouses] n prosess m, fremgangsmåte m; rettergang m

procession [prə'seʃən] n opptog m, prosesjon m

proclaim [prə'kleim] v *kunngjøre

produce[1] [prə'dju:s] v fremstille, produsere

produce[2] ['prɔdju:s] n landbruksprodukter pl; avling c

producer [prə'dju:sə] n produsent m

product ['prɔdʌkt] n produkt nt

production [prə'dʌkʃən] n produksjon m

profession [prə'feʃən] n yrke nt; fag nt

professional [prə'feʃənəl] adj profesjonell

professor [prə'fesə] n professor m

profit ['prɔfit] n fortjeneste c, fordel m; v *ha utbytte av

profitable ['prɔfitəbəl] adj innbringende

profound [prə'faund] adj dypsindig; grundig

programme ['prougræm] n

program *nt*
progress¹ ['prougres] *n*
fremskritt *nt*
progress² [prə'gres] *v*
*gjøre fremskritt
progressive [prə'gresiv] *adj*
progressiv,
fremadstrebende;
tiltagende
prohibit [prə'hibit] *v* *forby
prohibition [,proui'biʃən] *n*
forbud *nt*
prohibitive [prə'hibitiv] *adj*
uoverkommelig
project ['prɔdʒekt] *n* plan
m, prosjekt *nt*
promenade [,promə'nɑːd] *n*
promenade *m*
promise ['promis] *n* løfte *nt*;
v love
promote [prə'mout] *v*
forfremme, fremme
promotion [prə'mouʃən] *n*
forfremmelse *m*
prompt [prompt] *adj*
omgående, straks
pronoun ['prounaun] *n*
pronomen *nt*
pronounce [prə'nauns] *v*
uttale
pronunciation
[,prənʌnsi'eiʃən] *n* uttale
m
proof [pruːf] *n* bevis *nt*
propaganda [,propə'gændə]
n propaganda *m*
propel [prə'pel] *v* *drive
frem
propeller [prə'pelə] *n*
propell *m*

proper ['propə] *adj*
passende; sømmelig, riktig
property ['propəti] *n*
eiendeler *pl*, eiendom *m*;
egenskap *m*
prophet ['profit] *n* profet *m*
proportion [prə'pɔːʃən] *n*
proporsjon *m*
proportional [prə'pɔːʃənəl]
adj forholdsmessig
proposal [prə'pouzəl] *n*
forslag *nt*
propose [prə'pouz] *v*
*foreslå
proposition [,propə'ziʃən] *n*
forslag *nt*
proprietor [prə'praiətə] *n*
eier *m*
prosecute ['prosikjuːt] *v*
saksøke, anklage
prospect ['prospekt] *n*
utsikt *m*
prosperity [prə'sperəti] *n*
fremgang *m*, velstand *m*
prosperous ['prospərəs] *adj*
velstående
prostitute ['prostitjuːt] *n*
prostituert *m*
protect [prə'tekt] *v* beskytte
protection [prə'tekʃən] *n*
beskyttelse *m*
protein ['proutiːn] *n* protein
nt
protest¹ ['proutest] *n*
protest *m*
protest² [prə'test] *v*
protestere
Protestant ['protistənt] *adj*
protestantisk
proud [praud] *adj* stolt;

hovmodig

prove [pru:v] *v* bevise; vise seg

proverb ['prɔvə:b] *n* ordspråk *nt*

provide [prə'vaid] *v* forsyne, skaffe; **provided that** forutsatt at

province ['prɔvins] *n* fylke *nt*; provins *m*

provincial [prə'vinʃəl] *adj* provinsiell

provisional [prə'viʒənəl] *adj* foreløpig

provisions [prə'viʒənz] *pl* proviant *m*

prudent ['pru:dənt] *adj* klok; varsom

prune [pru:n] *n* sviske *c*

psychiatrist [sai'kaiətrist] *n* psykiater *m*

psychic ['saikik] *adj* psykisk

psychoanalyst [,saikou'ænəlist] *n* psykoanalytiker *m*

psychological [,saikə'lɔdʒikəl] *adj* psykologisk

psychologist [sai'kɔlədʒist] *n* psykolog *m*

psychology [sai'kɔlədʒi] *n* psykologi *m*

pub [pʌb] *n* kro *c*, kneipe *c*, pub *m*

public ['pʌblik] *adj* offentlig; allmenn; *n* publikum *nt*; ~ **garden** offentlig parkanlegg; ~ **house** vertshus *nt*

publication [,pʌbli'keiʃən]

n offentliggjørelse *m*

publicity [pʌ'blisəti] *n* publisitet *m*

publish ['pʌbliʃ] *v* *utgi, *offentliggjøre

publisher ['pʌbliʃə] *n* forlegger *m*

puddle ['pʌdəl] *n* pytt *m*

pull [pul] *v* *trekke; ~ **out** *trekke seg; *dra av sted; ~ **up** stanse

pulley ['puli] *n* (pl ~s) trinse *c*

Pullman ['pulmən] *n* sovevogn *c*

pullover ['pu,louvə] *n* genser *m*

pulpit ['pulpit] *n* prekestol *m*, talerstol *m*

pulse [pʌls] *n* puls *m*

pump [pʌmp] *n* pumpe *c*; *v* pumpe

pun [pʌn] *n* ordspill *nt*

punch [pʌntʃ] *v* *slå; *n* knyttneveslag *nt*; punsj *m*

punctual ['pʌŋktʃuəl] *adj* punktlig, presis

puncture ['pʌŋktʃə] *n* punktering *c*

punctured ['pʌŋktʃəd] *adj* punktert

punish ['pʌniʃ] *v* straffe

punishment ['pʌniʃmənt] *n* straff *m*

pupil ['pju:pəl] *n* elev *m*

puppet-show ['pʌpitʃou] *n* dukketeater *m*

purchase ['pə:tʃəs] *v* kjøpe; *n* kjøp *nt*, anskaffelse *m*; ~ **price** kjøpesum *m*; ~ **tax**

moms *m*

purchaser ['pɔːtʃəsə] *n*
kjøper *m*

pure [pjuə] *adj* ren

purple ['pɔːpəl] *adj*
purpurfarget, lilla

purpose ['pɔːpəs] *n* hensikt
m, formål *nt*; on ~ med
vilje

purse [pɔːs] *n* pengepung
m, håndveske *c*

pursue [pə'sjuː] *v* *forfølge;
strebe etter

pus [pʌs] *n* verk *m*; materie
m

push [puʃ] *n* dytt *m*, støt *nt*;
v *skyve; trenge seg frem

push button ['puʃ,bʌtn] *n*
trykknapp *m*

*put [put] *v* stille, *legge,
plassere; putte; ~ away
rydde vekk; ~ off *utsette;
~ on *ta på; ~ out slokke

puzzle ['pʌzəl] *n* puslespill
nt; gåte *c*; *v* volde hodebry;
jigsaw ~ puslespill *nt*

puzzling ['pʌzliŋ] *adj*
uforståelig

pyjamas [pə'dʒɑːməz] *pl*
pyjamas *m*

Q

quack [kwæk] *n* sjarlatan *m*,
kvakksalver *m*

quail [kweil] *n* (pl ~, ~s)
vaktel *m*

quaint [kweint] *adj*
eiendommelig;
gammeldags

qualification
[,kwɔlifi'keiʃən] *n*
kvalifikasjon *m*; forbehold
nt, innskrenkning *m*

qualified ['kwɔlifaid] *adj*
kvalifisert; kompetent

qualify ['kwɔlifai] *v*
kvalifisere seg

quality ['kwɔləti] *n* kvalitet
m; egenskap *m*

quantity ['kwɔntəti] *n*
kvantitet *m*; antall *nt*

quarantine ['kwɔrəntiːn] *n*
karantene *m*

quarrel ['kwɔrəl] *v* trette,
krangle; *n* krangel *m* / *nt*,
trette *c*

quarry ['kwɔri] *n* steinbrudd
nt

quarter ['kwɔːtə] *n* kvart;
kvartal *nt*; kvarter *nt*; *Am*
25-cent-mynt; ~ of an hour
kvarter *nt*

quarterly ['kwɔːtəli] *adj*
kvartals-

quay [kiː] *n* kai *c*

queen [kwiːn] *n* dronning *c*

queer [kwiə] *adj* merkelig,
underlig; sær

query ['kwiəri] *n* forespørsel
m; *v* *forespørre; betvile

question ['kwestʃən] *n*
spørsmål *m*, problem *nt*; *v*
*spørre ut; *dra i tvil; ~
mark spørsmålstegn *nt*

queue [kjuː] n kø m; v *stå i
kø

quick [kwik] adj hurtig

quick-tempered
[‚kwik'tempəd] adj hissig

quiet ['kwaiət] adj stille,
rolig, stillferdig; n stillhet c,
ro m

quilt [kwilt] n vatt-teppe nt

quit [kwit] v slutte, stoppe

quite [kwait] adv helt;
ganske, temmelig, særdeles

quiz [kwiz] n (pl ~zes)
spørrelek m; prøve c

quota ['kwoutə] n kvote m

quotation [kwou'teiʃən] n
sitat nt; ~ marks
anførselstegn pl

quote [kwout] v sitere

R

rabbit ['ræbit] n kanin m

rabies ['reibiz] n
hundegalskap m, rabies m

race [reis] n kappløp nt,
veddeløp nt; rase m

racecourse ['reiskɔːs] n
veddeløpsbane m

racehorse ['reishɔːs] n
veddeløpshest m

racetrack ['reistræk] n
veddeløpsbane m

racial ['reiʃəl] adj rase-

racket ['rækit] n rabalder nt;
racket m

radiator ['reidieitə] n
radiator m

radical ['rædikəl] adj radikal

radio ['reidiou] n radio m

radish ['rædiʃ] n reddik m

radius ['reidiəs] n (pl radii)
radius m

raft [rɑːft] n flåte m

rag [ræg] n fille c

rage [reidʒ] n raseri nt; v
rase

raid [reid] n angrep nt

rail [reil] n gelender nt,
rekkverk nt

railing ['reiliŋ] n gelender nt

railroad ['reilroud] nAm
jernbane m

railway ['reilwei] n jernbane
m; skinnegang m

rain [rein] n regn nt; v regne

rainbow ['reinbou] n
regnbue m

raincoat ['reinkout] n
regnfrakk m

rainy ['reini] adj regnfull

raise [reiz] v heve; øke;
dyrke, *oppdra, ale opp;
*pålegge; nAm lønnstillegg
nt

raisin ['reizən] n rosin c

rake [reik] n rake m

rally ['ræli] n rally nt; opptog
nt; v samle seg

ramp [ræmp] n rampe c

ramshackle ['ræm‚ʃækəl]
adj falleferdig

rancid ['rænsid] adj harsk

rang [ræŋ] v (p ring)

range [reindʒ] n rekkevidde
c; ~ finder avstandsmåler
m

rank [ræŋk] n rang m; rekke
c

ransom ['rænsəm] n
løsepenger pl

rap [ræp] n rap c

rape [reip] v *voldta; n
voldtekt c

rapid ['ræpid] adj hurtig

rapids ['ræpidz] pl elvestryk
nt

rare [rɛə] adj sjelden;
lettstekt, blodig

rarely ['rɛəli] adv sjelden

rascal ['rɑːskəl] n skurk m,
slyngel m

rash [ræʃ] n utslett nt; adj
forhastet, ubesindig

raspberry ['rɑːzbəri] n
bringebær nt

rat [ræt] n rotte c

rate [reit] n tariff m, pris m;
fart m; at any ~ i alle fall, i
hvert fall; ~ of exchange
valutakurs m

rather ['rɑːðə] adv
temmelig, ganske, riktig;
heller

ration ['ræʃən] n rasjon m

raven ['reivən] n ravn m

raw [rɔː] adj rå; ~ material
råmateriale m

ray [rei] n stråle m

razor ['reizə] n barberhøvel
m; ~ blade barberblad nt

reach [riːtʃ] v nå; n
rekkevidde c

react [ri'ækt] v reagere

reaction [ri'ækʃən] n
reaksjon m

*read [riːd] v lese

reading ['riːdiŋ] n lesning m

reading lamp ['riːdiŋlæmp]
n leselampe c

reading room ['riːdiŋruːm]
n lesesal m

ready ['redi] adj klar, parat;
ferdig

real [riəl] adj virkelig

reality [ri'æləti] n
virkelighet c

realizable [riəlaizəbəl] adj
mulig

realize ['riəlaiz] v virkelig-
*ha klart for seg; realisere

really ['riəli] adv virkelig,
faktisk; egentlig

rear [riə] n bakside c; v
*oppdra; heve; ~ light
baklykt c

reason ['riːzən] n årsak c,
grunn m; fornuft m,
forstand m; v resonnere

reasonable ['riːzənəbəl] adj
fornuftig; rimelig

reassure [ˌriːə'ʃuə] v
berolige

rebate ['riːbeit] n fradrag nt,
rabatt m

rebellion [ri'beljən] n
oppstand m, opprør nt

recall [ri'kɔːl] v erindre,
minnes; tilbakekalle;
annullere

receipt [ri'siːt] n kvittering
c; mottakelse m

receive [ri'siːv] v *få,
*motta

receiver [ri'si:və] n
telefonrør nt

recent ['ri:sənt] adj ny

recently ['ri:səntli] adv
forleden, nylig

reception [ri'sepʃən] n
mottakelse m; ~ office
resepsjon m

receptionist [ri'sepʃənist] n
resepsjonist m

recession [ri'seʃən] n
tilbakegang m

recipe ['resipi] n oppskrift c

recital [ri'saitəl] n
solistkonsert m

reckon ['rekən] v regne; tro

recognition [,rekəg'niʃən] n
anerkjennelse m;
gjenkjennelse m

recognize ['rekəgnaiz] v
kjenne igjen; anerkjenne

recollect [,rekə'lekt] v
huske

recommend [,rekə'mend] v
anbefale; tilråde

recommendation
[,rekəmen'deiʃən] n
anbefaling c

reconciliation
[,rekənsili'eiʃən] n
forsoning c

record¹ ['rekɔ:d] n plate c;
rekord m; protokoll m

record² [ri'kɔ:d] v registrere

recorder [ri'kɔ:də] n
kassettspiller m

recording [ri'kɔ:diŋ] n
opptak m

recover [ri'kʌvə] v *finne
igjen; bli frisk, *komme

seg

recovery [ri'kʌvəri] n
helbredelse m, bedring c

recreation [,rekri'eiʃən] n
atspredelse m, rekreasjon
m; ~ center Am, ~ centre
rekreasjonssenter nt

recruit [ri'kru:t] n rekrutt m

rectangle ['rektæŋgəl] n
rektangel m

rectangular [rek'tæŋgjulə]
adj rektangulær

rector ['rektə] n sogneprest
m

rectum ['rektəm] n
endetarm m

recyclable [ri'saikləbəl] adj
resirkulerbar

recycle [ri'saikəl] v
resirkulere

red [red] adj rød; red tape
papirmølle c, byråkrati nt

redeem [ri'di:m] v frelse

reduce [ri'dju:s] v redusere,
minske

reduction [ri'dʌkʃən] n
reduksjon m, avslag nt

redundant [ri'dʌndənt] adj
overflødig

reed [ri:d] n siv nt

reef [ri:f] n rev nt

reference ['refrəns] n
referanse m, henvisning m;
forbindelse m; with ~ to
vedrørende

refer to [ri'fə:] henvise til

referee [,refə'ri:] n dommer
m

refill ['ri:fil] n refill m

refinery [ri'fainəri] n

raffineri nt

reflect [ri'flekt] v reflektere;
gjenspeile

reflection [ri'flekʃən] n
refleks m; speilbilde nt

reflector [ri'flektə] n
reflektor m

refresh [ri'freʃ] v forfriske

refreshment [ri'freʃmənt] n
forfriskning m

refrigerator [ri'fridʒəreitə]
n kjøleskap nt

refugee [,refju'dʒi:] n
flyktning m

refund¹ [ri'fʌnd] v
refundere

refund² ['ri:fʌnd] n
tilbakebetaling c

refusal [ri'fju:zəl] n avslag
nt

refuse¹ [ri'fju:z] v *avslå

refuse² ['refju:s] n avfall nt

regard [ri'gɑ:d] v *anse;
betrakte; n respekt m; as
regards angående, med
hensyn til; best ~ med
vennlig hilsen, mvh

regarding [ri'gɑ:diŋ] prep
med hensyn til; angående

regatta [ri'gætə] n regatta m

régime [rei'ʒi:m] n regime
nt

region ['ri:dʒən] n egn m;
område nt

regional ['ri:dʒənəl] adj
regional

register ['redʒistə] v
*innskrive seg; bokføre;
registered letter
rekommandert brev

registration
[,redʒi'streiʃən] n
registrering c; ~ number
registreringsnummer nt; ~
plate nummerskilt nt

regret [ri'gret] v beklage; n
beklagelse m

regular ['regjulə] adj
regelmessig; normal, vanlig

regulate ['regjuleit] v
regulere

regulation [,regju'leiʃən] n
regel m, bestemmelse m;
regulering c

rehabilitation
[,ri:hə,bili'teiʃən] n
rehabilitering c

rehearsal [ri'hə:səl] n prøve
c; øvelse m

rehearse [ri'hə:s] v prøve;
øve

reign [rein] n regjeringstid c;
v herske

reimburse [,ri:im'bə:s] v
tilbakebetale

reindeer ['reindiə] n (pl ~)
reinsdyr nt

reject [ri'dʒekt] v
tilbakevise, avvise; forkaste

relate [ri'leit] v *fortelle

related [ri'leitid] adj
beslektet

relation [ri'leiʃən] n forhold
nt, forbindelse m; slektning
m

relative ['relətiv] n slektning
m; adj relativ

relax [ri'læks] v slappe av

relaxation [,rilæk'seiʃən] n
avslapning m

reliable [ri'laiəbəl] *adj*
pålitelig

relic ['relik] *n* relikvie *m*

relief [ri'li:f] *n* lindring *c*,
lettelse *m*; hjelp *c*; relieff
nt

relieve [ri'li:v] *v* lindre;
avløse

religion [ri'lidʒən] *n* religion
m

religious [ri'lidʒəs] *adj*
religiøs

rely on [ri'lai] stole på

remain [ri'mein] *v* *forbli,
*bli igjen

remainder [ri'meində] *n* rest
m

remaining [ri'meiniŋ] *adj*
resterende

remark [ri'ma:k] *n*
bemerkning *m*; *v* bemerke

remarkable [ri'ma:kəbəl]
adj bemerkelsesverdig

remedy ['remədi] *n*
legemiddel *nt*; botemiddel
nt

remember [ri'membə] *v*
huske

remembrance
[ri'membrəns] *n* erindring
c, minne *nt*

remind [ri'maind] *v* minne

remit [ri'mit] *v* overføre

remittance [ri'mitəns] *n*
remisse *m*

remnant ['remnənt] *n* rest
m, levning *m*

remote [ri'mout] *adj* fjern,
avsides

remote control

[ri'mout‿kən'troul] *n*
fjernkontroll *c*

removal [ri'mu:vəl] *n*
fjerning *c*

remove [ri'mu:v] *v* fjerne

remuneration
[ri‚mju:nə'reiʃən] *n*
godtgjørelse *m*

renew [ri'nju:] *v* fornye

renewable [ri'nju:əbəl] *adj*
fornybar

rent [rent] *v* leie; *n* leie *c*

repair [ri'peə] *v* reparere; *n*
reparasjon *m*

reparation [‚repə'reiʃən] *n*
reparasjon *m*

*repay [ri'pei] *v*
tilbakebetale

repayment [ri'peimənt] *n*
tilbakebetaling *c*

repeat [ri'pi:t] *v* *gjenta

repellent [ri'pelənt] *adj*
frastøtende

repentance [ri'pentəns] *n*
anger *m*

repertory ['repətəri] *n*
repertoar *nt*

repetition [‚repə'tiʃən] *n*
gjentakelse *m*

replace [ri'pleis] *v* erstatte

reply [ri'plai] *v* svare; *n* svar
nt; in ~ som svar

report [ri'pɔ:t] *v* rapportere;
melde; melde seg; *n*
rapport *m*, melding *c*

reporter [ri'pɔ:tə] *n* reporter
m

represent [‚repri'zent] *v*
representere; forestille

representation

respite

[ˌreprizenˈteiʃən] n
representasjon m
representative
[ˌrepriˈzentətiv] adj
representativ
reprimand [ˈreprimɑːnd] v
*irettesette
reproach [riˈproutʃ] n
bebreidelse m; v bebreide
reproduce [ˌriːprəˈdjuːs] v
reprodusere
reproduction
[ˌriːprəˈdʌkʃən] n
reproduksjon m
reptile [ˈreptail] n krypdyr
nt
republic [riˈpʌblik] n
republikk m
republican [riˈpʌblikən] adj
republikansk
repulsive [riˈpʌlsiv] adj
frastøtende
reputation [ˌrepjuˈteiʃən] n
rykte nt; anseelse m
request [riˈkwest] n
anmodning, bønn m; v
anmode, be*
require [riˈkwaiə] v kreve;
behøve
requirement [riˈkwaiəmənt]
n krav nt
requisite [ˈrekwizit] adj
påkrevd
rescue [ˈreskjuː] v redde; n
redning m
research [riˈsəːtʃ] n
forskning m
resemblance [riˈzembləns]
n likhet c
resemble [riˈzembəl] v likne

resent [riˈzent] v *ta ille
opp
reservation [ˌrezəˈveiʃən] n
reservasjon m; forbehold nt
reserve [riˈzəːv] v reservere;
bestille; n reserve m
reserved [riˈzəːvd] adj
reservert
reservoir [ˈrezəvwɑː] n
reservoar nt
reside [riˈzaid] v bo
residence [ˈrezidəns] n
bolig m; ~ permit
oppholdstillatelse m
resident [ˈrezidənt] n
fastboende m; adj bosatt;
stedlig
resign [riˈzain] v *fratre;
*gå av
resignation [ˌrezigˈneiʃən]
n avskjedssøknad m;
avskjed m
resist [riˈzist] v *gjøre
motstand mot
resistance [riˈzistəns] n
motstand m
resolute [ˈrezəluːt] adj
bestemt, besluttsom
respect [riˈspekt] n respekt
m; ærbødighet c, aktelse
m; v respektere
respectable [riˈspektəbəl]
adj respektabel
respectful [riˈspektfəl] adj
ærbødig
respective [riˈspektiv] adj
respektiv
respiration [ˌrespəˈreiʃən] n
åndedrett nt
respite [ˈrespait] n henstand

m

responsibility
[ri,spɔnsə'biləti] *n* ansvar
nt

responsible [ri'spɔnsəbəl]
adj ansvarlig

rest [rest] *n* hvile *m*; rest *m*;
v hvile

restaurant ['restɔrɔ:ŋ] *n*
restaurant *m*

restful ['restfəl] *adj*
beroligende

rest home ['resthoum] *n*
hvilehjem *nt*

restless ['restləs] *adj* urolig;
rastløs

restrain [ri'strein] *v* tøyle

restriction [ri'strikʃən] *n*
innskrenkning *m*

rest room ['restru:m] *nAm*
toalett *nt*

result [ri'zʌlt] *n* resultat *nt*;
følge *m*; *v* resultere

resume [ri'zju:m] *v*
*gjenoppta

résumé ['rezjumei] *n*
resymé *nt*

retail ['ri:teil] *n* ~ trade
detaljhandel *m*

retina ['retinə] *n* netthinne *c*

retire [ri'taiə] *v* trekke seg
tilbake; gå av med pensjon

retired [ri'taiəd] *adj*
pensjonert

retirement [ri'taiəmənt] *n*
pensjon *m*

return [ri'tə:n] *v* vende
tilbake, *komme tilbake; *n*
tilbakekomst *m*; ~ flight
tilbaketur *m*; ~ journey

hjemreise *m*, tilbakereise *c*

reunite [,ri:ju:'nait] *v*
gjenforene

reveal [ri'vi:l] *v* åpenbare,
avsløre

revelation [,revə'leiʃən] *n*
avsløring *c*

revenge [ri'vendʒ] *n* hevn *m*

revenue ['revənju:] *n*
inntekter *pl*, toll *m*

reverse [ri'və:s] *n*
motsetning *m*; bakside *c*;
revers *m*; motgang *m*;
omslag *nt*; *adj* motsatt; *v*
rygge

review [ri'vju:] *n*
anmeldelse *m*; tidsskrift *nt*

revise [ri'vaiz] *v* revidere

revision [ri'viʒən] *n* revisjon *m*

revival [ri'vaivəl] *n*
gjenopplivelse *m*

revolt [ri'voult] *v* *gjøre
opprør; *n* oppstand *m*,
opprør *nt*

revolting [ri'voultiŋ] *adj*
motbydelig, frastøtende,
opprørende

revolution [,revə'lu:ʃən] *n*
revolusjon *m*; omdreining
m

revolutionary
[,revə'lu:ʃənəri] *adj*
revolusjonær

revolver [ri'vɔlvə] *n*
revolver *m*

revue [ri'vju:] *n* revy *m*

reward [ri'wɔ:d] *n*
belønning *c*; *v* belønne

rheumatism ['ru:mətizəm]

n reumatisme *m*

rhinoceros [rai'nɔsərəs] *n* (pl ~, ~es) neshorn *nt*

rhubarb ['ru:ba:b] *n* rabarbra *m*

rhyme [raim] *n* rim *nt*

rhythm ['riðəm] *n* rytme *m*

rib [rib] *n* ribbein *nt*

ribbon ['ribən] *n* bånd *nt*

rice [rais] *n* ris *m*

rich [ritʃ] *adj* rik

riches ['ritʃiz] *pl* rikdom *m*

rid [rid] *v* befri (of fra); **get ~ of** bli kvitt

riddle ['ridəl] *n* gåte *c*

ride [raid] *n* tur *m*

***ride** [raid] *v* kjøre; *ride

rider ['raidə] *n* rytter *m*

ridge [ridʒ] *n* høydedrag *nt*

ridicule ['ridikju:l] *v* *latterliggjøre

ridiculous [ri'dikjuləs] *adj* latterlig

riding ['raidiŋ] *n* ridning *m*; ~ **school** rideskole *m*

rifle ['raifəl] *v* gevær *nt*

right [rait] *n* rettighet *c*; *adj* rett, riktig; høyre; rettferdig; **all right!** bra!; ***be ~** *ha rett; ~ **of way** forkjørsrett *m*

righteous ['raitʃəs] *adj* rettskaffen

right-hand ['raithænd] *adj* på høyre side, høyre

rightly ['raitli] *adv* med rette

rim [rim] *n* felg *m*; kant *m*

ring [riŋ] *n* ring *m*; krets *m*; manesje *m*

***ring** [riŋ] *v* ringe; ~ **up** ringe opp

rinse [rins] *v* skylle; *n* skylling *c*

riot ['raiət] *n* oppløp *nt*

rip [rip] *v* *rive i stykker

ripe [raip] *adj* moden

rise [raiz] *n* pålegg *nt*, høyde *m*; oppstigning *m*; opprinnelse *m*

***rise** [raiz] *v* reise seg; *stå opp; *stige

rising ['raiziŋ] *n* oppstand *m*

risk [risk] *n* risiko *m*; fare *m*; *v* risikere

risky ['riski] *adj* risikabel, dristig

rival ['raivəl] *n* rival *m*; konkurrent *m*; *v* rivalisere

rivalry ['raivəlri] *n* rivalitet *m*; konkurranse *m*

river ['rivə] *n* elv *m*; ~ **bank** elvebredd *m*

riverside ['rivəsaid] *n* elvebredd *m*

roach [routʃ] *n* (pl ~) mort *m*

road [roud] *n* gate *c*, vei *m*; ~ **fork** veiskille *m*; ~ **map** veikart *nt*; ~ **system** veinett *nt*; ~ **up** veiarbeid *nt*

roadhouse ['roudhaus] *n* veikro *c*

roadrage ['roud,reidʒ] *n* trafikkraseri *m*

roadside ['roudsaid] *n* veikant *m*; ~ **restaurant** vertshus *m*

roadway ['roudwei] *nAm*

kjørebane *m*
roam [roum] *v* streife omkring
roar [rɔ:] *v* brøle, bruse; *n* dur *m*, brøl *nt*
roast [roust] *v* steke, riste; *n* stek *c*
rob [rɔb] *v* rane
robber ['rɔbə] *n* ransmann *m*
robbery ['rɔbəri] *n* plyndring *c*, ran *nt*, tyveri *nt*; overfall *nt*
robe [roub] *n* lang kjole; embetsdrakt *c*
robin ['rɔbin] *n* rødstrupe *m*
robust [rou'bʌst] *adj* robust
rock [rɔk] *n* klippe *m*; *v* gynge
rocket ['rɔkit] *n* rakett *m*
rocky ['rɔki] *adj* steinet
rod [rɔd] *n* stang *c*
roe [rou] *n* rogn *c*
roll [roul] *v* rulle; *n* rull *m*; rundstykke *nt*
Rollerblade® ['roulə,bleid] *n* (inline) rulleskøyter *c*
roller-skating ['roulə,skeitiŋ] *n* rulleskøyteløping *c*
Roman Catholic ['roumən 'kæθəlik] romersk-katolsk
romance [rə'mæns] *n* romanse *m*
romantic [rə'mæntik] *adj* romantisk
roof [ru:f] *n* tak *nt*; thatched ~ halmtak *m*
room [ru:m] *n* rom *nt*, værelse *nt*; plass *m*; ~ and

board kost og losji; ~ **service** værelsesbetjening *c*; ~ **temperature** værelsestemperatur *m*
roomy ['ru:mi] *adj* rommelig
root [ru:t] *n* rot *c*
rope [roup] *n* rep *nt*
rosary ['rouzəri] *n* rosenkrans *c*
rose [rouz] *n* rose *c*; *adj* rosa
rotten ['rɔtən] *adj* råtten
rouge [ru:ʒ] *n* rouge *m*
rough [rʌf] *adj* ru
roulette [ru:'let] *n* rulett *m*
round [raund] *adj* rund; *prep* om, omkring; *n* runde *m*; ~ **trip** *Am* tur-retur
roundabout ['raundəbaut] *n* rundkjøring *c*
rounded ['raundid] *adj* avrundet
route [ru:t] *n* rute *c*
routine [ru:'ti:n] *n* rutine *m*
row¹ [rou] *n* rad *m*; *v* ro
row² [rau] *n* krangel *m / n*
rowdy ['raudi] *adj* ståkende, voldsom
rowing boat ['rouiŋbout] *n* robåt *m*
royal ['rɔiəl] *adj* kongelig
rub [rʌb] *v* *gni
rubber ['rʌbə] *n* gummi *m*; viskelær *nt*; ~ **band** strikk *m*
rubbish ['rʌbiʃ] *n* avfall *nt*; tull *nt*, sludder *nt*; **talk** ~ vrøvle; ~ **bin** søppelbøtte *c*
ruby ['ru:bi] *n* rubin *m*
rucksack ['rʌksæk] *n*

ryggsekk *m*

rudder ['rʌdə] *n* ror *nt*

rude [ru:d] *adj* uforskammet

rug [rʌg] *n* rye *m*

ruin ['ru:in] *v* *ødelegge;
undergang *m*; ruins ruin *m*

rule [ru:l] *n* regel *m*; styre *nt*,
makt *c*, regjering *c*; *v*
regjere, herske; as a ~ som
regel, vanligvis

ruler ['ru:lə] *n* regent *m*,
monark *m*; linjal *m*

Rumania [ru:'meiniə] *n*
Romania

Rumanian [ru:'meiniən] *adj*
rumensk; *n* rumener *m*

rumour ['ru:mə] *n* rykte *nt*

*run [rʌn] *v* *løpe; *renne; ~
into støte på

runaway ['rʌnəwei] *n*
rømling *m*

rung [rʌn] *v* (pp ring)

runner ['rʌnə] *n* løper *m*

runway ['rʌnwei] *n*
startbane *m*

rural ['ruərəl] *adj* landlig

ruse [ru:z] *n* list *c*

rush [rʌʃ] *v* styrte; *n* siv *nt*

rush hour ['rʌʃauə] *n*
rushtid *c*

Russia ['rʌʃə] Russland

Russian ['rʌʃən] *adj* russisk;
n russer *m*

rust [rʌst] *n* rust *m*

rustic ['rʌstik] *adj* landsens,
rustikal

rusty ['rʌsti] *adj* rusten

S

sack [sæk] *n* sekk *m*

sacred ['seikrid] *adj* hellig

sacrifice ['sækrifais] *n* offer
nt; *v* ofre

sacrilege ['sækrilidʒ] *n*
helligbrøde *m*

sad [sæd] *adj* bedrøvet;
vemodig, bedrøvelig, trist

saddle ['sædəl] *n* sal *m*

sadness ['sædnəs] *n* vemod
nt

safe [seif] *adj* sikker; *n* safe
m, pengeskap *nt*

safety ['seifti] *n* sikkerhet *c*;
~ belt sikkerhetsbelte *nt*;
bilbelte *nt*; ~ pin
sikkerhetsnål *c*; ~ razor

barberhøvel *m*

sail [seil] *v* seile; *n* seil *nt*

sailing boat ['seiliŋbout] *n*
seilbåt *m*

sailor ['seilə] *n* sjømann *m*

saint [seint] *n* helgen *m*

salad ['sæləd] *n* salat *m*

salad-oil ['sælədɔil] *n*
matolje *c*

salary ['sæləri] *n* gasje *m*,
lønn *c*

sale [seil] *n* salg *nt*; for ~ til
salgs; sales utsalg *nt*; sales
tax moms *m*

saleable ['seiləbəl] *adj*
salgbar

salesman ['seilzmən] *n* (pl

-men) ekspeditør *m*,
butikkselger *m*
salmon ['sæmən] *n* (pl ~)
laks *m*
salon ['sælɔ:] *n* salong *m*
saloon [sə'lu:n] *n* bar *m*
salt [sɔ:lt] *n* salt *nt*; ~ cellar,
Am ~ shaker *n* saltkar *nt*
salty ['sɔ:lti] *adj* salt
salute [sə'lu:t] *v* hilse
same [seim] *adj* samme
sample ['sɑ:mpəl] *n*
vareprøve *c*
sanatorium [,sænə'tɔ:riəm]
n (pl ~s, -ria) sanatorium *nt*
sand [sænd] *n* sand *m*
sandal ['sændəl] *n* sandal *m*
sandpaper ['sænd,peipə] *n*
sandpapir *nt*
sandy ['sændi] *adj* sandet
sanitary ['sænitəri] *adj*
sanitær; ~ towel, *Am* ~
napkin (sanitets)bind *nt*
sapphire ['sæfaiə] *n* safir *m*
sardine [sɑ:'di:n] *n* sardin
m
satchel ['sætʃəl] *n* ransel *m*
satellite ['sætəlait] *n*
satellitt *m*; ~ dish
parabolantenne *c*; ~ radio
n satelittradio *c*; ~ tv
satellittoverføring *c*,
satellitt-TV *m*
satin ['sætin] *n* sateng *m*
satisfaction [,sætis'fækʃən]
n tilfredsstillelse *m*,
tilfredshet *c*
satisfactory [,sætis'fæktəri]
adj tilfredsstillende
satisfy ['sætisfai] *v*

tilfredsstille; **satisfied**
tilfreds, tilfredsstilt
Saturday ['sætədi] lørdag *m*
sauce [sɔ:s] *n* saus *m*
saucepan ['sɔ:spən] *n*
kasserolle *m*, gryte *c*
saucer ['sɔ:sə] *n* skål *c*
Saudi Arabia
[,saudiə'reibiə] Saudi-
-Arabia
Saudi Arabian
[,saudiə'reibiən] *adj*
saudiarabisk
sauna ['sɔ:nə] *n* badstue *c*
sausage ['sɔsidʒ] *n* pølse *c*
savage ['sævidʒ] *adj* vill
save [seiv] *v* redde; spare
savings ['seiviŋz] *pl*
sparepenger *pl*; ~ bank
sparebank *m*
saviour ['seivjə] *n* frelser *m*
savo(u)ry ['seivəri] *adj*
velsmakende; pikant
saw[1] [sɔ:] *v* (p see)
saw[2] [sɔ:] *n* sag *c*
sawdust ['sɔ:dʌst] *n* sagflis
c
sawmill ['sɔ:mil] *n* sagbruk
nt
***say** [sei] *v* *si
scaffolding ['skæfəldiŋ] *n*
stillas *nt*
scale [skeil] *n* målestokk *m*;
skala *m*; skjell *nt*; **scales** *pl*
vekt *c*
scan [skæn] *v* skanne
scandal ['skændəl] *n*
skandale *m*
Scandinavia
[,skændi'neiviə]

Skandinavia
Scandinavian
[,skændi'neiviən] adj
skandinavisk; n skandinav
m

scanner ['skænə] n skanner
c

scapegoat ['skeipgout] n
syndebukk m

scar [ska:] n arr nt

scarce [skɛəs] adj knapp

scarcely ['skɛəsli] adv
knapt

scarcity ['skɛəsəti] n
knapphet c

scare [skɛə] v skremme; n
panikk m

scarf [ska:f] n (pl ~s,
scarves) skjerf nt

scarlet ['ska:lət] adj
skarlagenrød

scary ['skɛəri] adj
foruroligende; nifs

scatter ['skætə] v spre

scene [si:n] n scene m

scenery ['si:nəri] n
landskap nt

scenic ['si:nik] adj
naturskjønn

scent [sent] n duft m

schedule ['fedju:l] n
ruteplan m, timeplan m

scheme [ski:m] n skjema
nt; plan m

scholar ['skɔlə] n
akademiker; student m;
elev m

scholarship ['skɔləfip] n
stipend nt

school [sku:l] n skole m

schoolboy ['sku:lbɔi] n
skolegutt m

schoolgirl ['sku:lgə:l] n
skolepike m

schoolmaster
['sku:l,ma:stə] n lærer m

schoolteacher
['sku:l,ti:tʃə] n lærer m

science ['saiəns] n
(natur)vitenskap c

scientific [,saiən'tifik] adj
vitenskapelig

scientist ['saiəntist] n
vitenskapskvinne c;
vitenskapsmann (pl
–menn) m

scissors ['sizəz] pl saks c

scold [skould] v skjenne på;
skjelle

scooter ['sku:tə] n scooter
m; sparksykkel m

score [skɔ:] n poengsum m;
v markere

scorn [skɔ:n] n hån m,
forakt m; v forakte

Scotland ['skɔtlənd]
Skottland

Scottish ['skɔtiʃ] adj skotsk

scout [skaut] n speider m

scrap [skræp] n bit m

scrape [skreip] v skrape

scratch [skrætʃ] v skrape,
rispe; n risp nt, skramme c

scream [skri:m] v *skrike,
hyle; n hyl nt, skrik nt

screen [skri:n] n
skjermbrett nt; skjerm m,
filmlerret nt

screw [skru:] n skrue m; v
skru

screwdriver ['skru:ˌdraivə] n skrujern m

scrub [skrʌb] v skrubbe; n kratt m

sculptor ['skʌlptə] n billedhogger m

sculpture ['skʌlptʃə] n skulptur m

sea [si:] n sjø m; ~ urchin sjøpinnsvin nt; ~ water sjøvann nt

seabird ['si:bɔ:d] n sjøfugl m

seacoast ['si:koust] n kyst m

seagull ['si:gʌl] n havmåke c

seal [si:l] n segl nt; sel m, kobbe m

seam [si:m] n søm m

seaman ['si:mən] n (pl -men) sjømann m

seaport ['si:pɔ:t] n havneby m

search [sɔ:tʃ] v lete etter; ransake; n leting c

searchlight ['sɔ:tʃlait] n lyskaster m

seascape ['si:skeip] n bilde med maritimt motiv

seashell ['si:ʃel] n skjell nt

seashore ['si:ʃɔ:] n strand c; kyst m

seasick ['si:sik] adj sjøsyk

seasickness ['si:ˌsiknəs] n sjøsyke m

seaside ['si:said] n kyst m; ~ resort badested nt

season ['si:zən] n sesong m, årstid c; high ~ høysesong

m; low ~ lavsesong m; off ~ utenfor sesongen; ~ ticket sesongkort nt

seat [si:t] n sete nt; plass m, sitteplass m; ~ belt sikkerhetsbelte nt

second ['sekənd] num annen; n sekund nt; øyeblikk nt

secondary ['sekəndəri] adj sekundær, underordnet; ~ school høyere skole

second-hand [ˌsekənd'hænd] adj brukt

secret ['si:krət] n hemmelighet c; adj hemmelig

secretary ['sekrətri] n sekretær m

section ['sekʃən] n seksjon m, avdeling c

secure [si'kjuə] adj sikker; v sikre seg

security [si'kjuərəti] n sikkerhet c; kausjon m

sedative ['sedətiv] n beroligende middel

seduce [si'dju:s] v forføre

*see [si:] v *se; *innse, *begripe; *forstå; ~ to sørge for

seed [si:d] n frø nt

*seek [si:k] v søke

seem [si:m] v *late til, synes

seen [si:n] v (pp see)

seesaw ['si:sɔ:] n vippe c

seize [si:z] v *gripe

seldom ['seldəm] adv sjelden

select [si'lekt] v *utvelge,

*velge ut; adj utsøkt, utvalgt

selection [si'lekʃən] n utvalg nt

self [self] selves; n selv, jeg; selv…

self-centered Am, self--centred [,self'sentəd] adj selvopptatt

self-employed [,selfim'plɔid] adj selvstendig næringsdrivende

self-evident [,sel'fevidənt] adj opplagt

self-government [,self'gʌvəmənt] n selvstyre nt

selfish ['selfiʃ] adj selvisk

selfishness ['selfiʃnəs] n egoisme m

self-service [self'sə:vis] n selvbetjening c; ~ restaurant kafeteria m

*sell [sel] v *selge

semblance ['semblans] n utseende nt; likhet c

semi- ['semi] halv-

semicircle ['semi,sə:kəl] n halvsirkel m

semicolon [,semi'koulən] n semikolon nt

senate ['senət] n senat nt

senator ['senətə] n senator m

*send [send] v sende; ~ back sende tilbake, returnere; ~ for sende bud etter; ~ off sende av sted

sender ['sendə] n sender m; avsender m

senile ['si:nail] adj senil

sensation [sen'seiʃən] n sensasjon m; fornemmelse m, følelse m

sensational [sen'seiʃənəl] adj sensasjonell, oppsiktsvekkende

sense [sens] n sans m; fornuft m; mening m, betydning m; v merke; ~ of honour æresfølelse m

senseless ['senslas] adj meningsløs

sensible ['sensəbəl] adj fornuftig

sensitive ['sensitiv] adj følsom

sentence ['sentəns] n setning m; dom m; v dømme

sentimental [,senti'mentəl] adj sentimental

separate¹ ['sepəreit] v skille, separere

separate² ['sepərət] adj særskilt, atskilt

separately ['sepərətli] adv separat

September [sep'tembə] september

septic ['septik] adj septisk; *become ~ *gå betennelse i

sequel ['si:kwəl] n fortsettelse m

sequence ['si:kwəns] n rekkefølge m; serie m

serene [sə'ri:n] adj rolig; klar

series ['siəri:z] n (pl ~) serie m

serious ['siəriəs] adj seriøs, alvorlig

seriousness ['siəriəsnəs] n alvor nt

sermon ['sə:mən] n preken m

servant ['sə:vənt] n tjener m

serve [sə:v] v servere

service ['sə:vis] n tjeneste m; betjening c; ~ charge serveringsavgift c; ~ station bensinstasjon m

serviette [,sə:vi'et] n serviett m

session ['seʃən] n sesjon m

set [set] n klikk m; sett nt

*set [set] v *sette; ~ menu fast meny; ~ out *dra av sted

setting ['setiŋ] n omgivelser pl

settle ['setəl] v ordne, avslutte; ~ down *slå seg ned

settlement ['setəlmənt] n ordning c, overenskomst m

seven ['sevən] num sju, syv

seventeen [,sevən'ti:n] num sytten

seventeenth [,sevən'ti:nθ] num syttende

seventh ['sevənθ] num sjuende, syvende

seventy ['sevənti] num sytti

several ['sevərəl] adj atskillige, flere

severe [si'viə] adj heftig,

streng

*sew [sou] v sy; ~ up sy sammen

sewer ['su:ə] n kloakk m

sewing machine ['souiŋmə,ʃi:n] n symaskin m

sex [seks] n kjønn nt; sex m

sexual ['sekʃuəl] adj seksuell

sexuality [,sekʃu'æləti] n seksualitet m

shade [ʃeid] n skygge m; nyanse m

shadow ['ʃædou] n skygge m

shady ['ʃeidi] adj skyggefull

*shake [ʃeik] v riste, ryste

shaky ['ʃeiki] adj vaklende

*shall [ʃæl] v *skal

shallow ['ʃælou] adj grunn

shame [ʃeim] n skam c; shame! fy!

shampoo [ʃæm'pu:] n sjampo m

shape [ʃeip] n form c; v forme

share [ʃeə] v dele; n del m; aksje m

shark [ʃɑ:k] n hai m

sharp [ʃɑ:p] adj spiss

sharpen ['ʃɑ:pən] v spisse

shave [ʃeiv] v barbere seg

shaver ['ʃeivə] n barbermaskin m

shaving brush ['ʃeiviŋbrʌʃ] n barberkost m

shaving foam ['ʃeiviŋfoum] n barberskum m

shawl [ʃɔ:l] n sjal nt

349

showcase

she [ʃiː] *pron* hun

shed [ʃed] *n* skur *nt*

*shed [ʃed] *v* *utgyte; spre

sheep [ʃiːp] *n* (pl ~) sau *m*

sheer [ʃiə] *adj* pur, absolutt; skjær, gjennomsiktig, tynn

sheet [ʃiːt] *n* laken *nt*; ark *nt*; plate *c*

shelf [ʃelf] *n* (pl shelves) hylle *c*

shell [ʃel] *n* skjell *nt*; skall *nt*

shellfish [ˈʃelfiʃ] *n* skalldyr *nt*

shelter [ˈʃeltə] *n* ly, tilfluktssted *nt*; *v* *gi ly

shepherd [ˈʃepəd] *n* gjeter *m*

shift [ʃift] *n* skift *nt*

*shine [ʃain] *v* skinne; glinse, stråle

ship [ʃip] *n* skip *nt*; *v* skipe

shipowner [ˈʃi,pounə] *n* skipsreder *m*

shipyard [ˈʃipjɑːd] *n* skipsverft *nt*

shirt [ʃɜːt] *n* skjorte *c*

shiver [ˈʃivə] *v* *skjelve, hutre; *n* skjelven *m*

shock [ʃɔk] *n* sjokk *nt*; *v* sjokkere; ~ absorber støtdemper *m*

shocking [ˈʃɔkiŋ] *adj* sjokkerende

shoe [ʃuː] *n* sko *m*; ~ polish skokrem *m*; ~ shop skotøyforretning *c*; gym shoes turnsko *pl*

shoelace [ˈʃuːleis] *n* skolisse *c*

shoemaker [ˈʃuː,meikə] *n*

skomaker *m*

shook [ʃuk] *v* (p shake)

*shoot [ʃuːt] *v* *skyte

shop [ʃɔp] *n* forretning *c*; *v* handle; ~ assistant ekspeditør *m*, butikkselger *m*; shopping bag handlebag *m*; shopping centre kjøpesenter *nt*

shopkeeper [ˈʃɔp,kiːpə] *n* kjøpmann *m*

shopwindow [ˌʃɔpˈwindou] *n* utstillingsvindu *nt*

shore [ʃɔː] *n* bredd *m*, kyst *m*

short [ʃɔːt] *adj* kort; liten; ~ circuit kortslutning *c*

shortage [ˈʃɔːtidʒ] *n* knapphet *c*, mangel *m*

shorten [ˈʃɔːtən] *v* forkorte

shortly [ˈʃɔːtli] *adv* snart, i nær fremtid

shorts [ʃɔːts] *pl* shorts *m*; underbukse *c*

short-sighted [ˌʃɔːtˈsaitid] *adj* nærsynt

shot [ʃɔt] *n* skudd *nt*; sprøyte *c*; scene *m*

*should [ʃud] *v* *skulle

shoulder [ˈʃouldə] *n* skulder *c*

shout [ʃaut] *v* *skrike, rope; *n* rop *nt*

shovel [ˈʃʌvəl] *n* skuffe *c*

show [ʃou] *n* oppførelse *m*, forestilling *c*; utstilling *c*

*show [ʃou] *v* vise; utstille, vise frem; bevise

showcase [ˈʃoukeis] *n* monter *m*

shower 350

regnskur *m*, skur *m*

showroom ['ʃouru:m] *n*
utstillingslokale *c*

shriek [ʃri:k] *v* *skrike; *n*
hvin *nt*

shrimp [ʃrimp] *n* reke *c*

shrine [ʃrain] *n* helgenskrin
nt, helligdom *m*

*shrink [ʃriŋk] *v* krympe

shrinkproof ['ʃriŋkpru:f]
adj krympefri

shrub [ʃrʌb] *n* busk *m*

shudder ['ʃʌdə] *n* gys *nt*

shuffle ['ʃʌfəl] *v* stokke

*shut [ʃʌt] *v* lukke; shut
stengt, lukket; ~ in stenge
inne

shutter ['ʃʌtə] *n* vinduslem
m, skodde *m*

shy [ʃai] *adj* sjenert, sky

shyness ['ʃainəs] *n* skyhet *c*

Siamese [ˌsaiə'mi:z] *adj*
siamesisk

sick [sik] *adj* syk; kvalm

sickness ['siknəs] *n*
sykdom *m*; kvalme *m*

side [said] *n* side *c*; parti *nt*;
one-sided *adj* ensidig

sideburns ['saidbə:nz] *pl*
kinnskjegg *nt*

side street ['saidstri:t] *n*
sidegate *c*

sidewalk ['saidwɔ:k] *nAm*
fortau *nt*

sideways ['saidweiz] *adv* til
siden

siege [si:dʒ] *n* beleiring *c*

sieve [siv] *n* sil *m*; *v* sikte,
sile

sight [sait] *n* syne *nt*; skue
nt, syn; severdighet *c*

sign [sain] *n* tegn *nt*; vink *nt*,
gest *m*; *v* undertegne

signal ['signəl] *n* signal *nt*;
tegn *nt*; *v* signalisere

signature ['signətʃə] *n*
underskrift *c*, signatur *m*

significant [sig'nifikənt] *adj*
betydningsfull

signpost ['sainpoust] *n*
veiviser *m*

silence ['sailəns] *n* stillhet
c; *v* få til å tie

silencer ['sailənsə] *n*
lydpotte *c*

silent ['sailənt] *adj* stille,
taus; *be ~ tie

silk [silk] *n* silke *m*

silly ['sili] *adj* dum, tåpelig

silver ['silvə] *n* sølv *nt*; sølv-

silversmith ['silvəsmiθ] *n*
sølvsmed *m*

silverware ['silvəweə] *n*
sølvtøy *nt*

similar ['similə] *adj*
liknende

similarity [ˌsimi'lærəti] *n*
likhet *c*

simple ['simpəl] *adj*
likefrem, enkel; vanlig

simply ['simpli] *adv*
simpelthen

simulate ['simjuleit] *v*
etterligne

simultaneous
[ˌsiməl'teiniəs] *adj*
samtidig

sin [sin] *n* synd *c*

since [sins] *prep* siden; *adv*

siden; *conj* siden; fordi
sincere [sin'siə] *adj*
oppriktig; yours sincerely
med vennlig hilsen, mvh
sinew ['sinju:] *n* sene c
*sing [siŋ] *v* *synge
singer ['siŋə] *n* sanger *m*;
sangerinne c
single ['siŋgəl] *adj* enkel;
ugift; ~ room enkeltrom *nt*
singular ['siŋgjulə] *n* entall
nt; *adj* enestående
sinister ['sinistə] *adj*
illevarslende
sink [siŋk] *n* vask *m*
*sink [siŋk] *v* *synke
sip [sip] *n* slurk *m*
sir [sə:] min herre
siren ['saiərən] *n* sirene c
sister ['sistə] *n* søster c
sister-in-law ['sistərinlo:] *n*
(pl sisters-) svigerinne c
*sit [sit] *v* *sitte; ~ down
*sette seg
site [sait] *n* sted *nt*;
beliggenhet c
sitting room ['sitiŋru:m] *n*
stue c
situated ['sitʃueitid] *adj*
beliggende
situation [,sitʃu'eiʃən] *n*
situasjon *m*; stilling c
six [siks] *num* seks
sixteen [,siks'ti:n] *num*
seksten
sixteenth [,siks'ti:nθ] *num*
sekstende
sixth [siksθ] *num* sjette
sixty ['siksti] *num* seksti
size [saiz] *n* størrelse *m*,

dimensjon *m*; format *nt*
skate [skeit] *v* *gå på
skøyter; *n* skøyte c
skating ['skeitiŋ] *n*
skøyteløping c; ~ rink
skøytebane *m*
skeleton ['skelitən] *n*
skjelett *nt*
sketch [sketʃ] *n* skisse c,
utkast *nt*; *v* tegne, skissere
ski¹ [ski:] *v* *gå på ski
ski² [ski:] *n* (pl ~, ~s) ski c; ~
boots skistøvler *pl*; ~ jump
skihopp *nt*; hoppbakke *m*;
~ lift skiheis *m*; ~ pants
skibukse c; ~ poles *Am*
skistaver *pl*; ~ sticks
skistaver *pl*
skid [skid] *v* *gli
skier ['ski:ə] *n* skiløper *m*
skiing ['ski:iŋ] *n* skiløping c
skil(l)ful ['skilfəl] *adj*
kyndig, flink, dyktig
skill [skil] *n* dyktighet c
skilled [skild] *adj* kyndig,
dreven; faglært
skin [skin] *n* hud c, skinn *nt*;
skall *nt*
skip [skip] *v* hoppe; hoppe
over
skirt [skə:t] *n* skjørt *nt*
skull [skʌl] *n* skalle *m*
sky [skai] *n* himmel *m*; luft c
skyscraper ['skai,skreipə] *n*
skyskraper *m*
slack [slæk] *adj* treg; slapp
slacks [slæks] *pl* bukse c,
bukser *pl*
slam [slæm] *v* *slå igjen
slander ['sla:ndə] *n*

bakvaskelse *m*

slang [slæŋ] *n* slang *m*; sjargong *m*

slant [slɑːnt] *v* skråne

slanting ['slɑːntiŋ] *adj* skjev, skrånende, skrå

slap [slæp] *v* fike; *n* fik *m*

slate [sleit] *n* skifer *m*

slave [sleiv] *n* slave *m*

sledge [sledʒ] *n* slede *m*, kjelke *m*

sleep [sliːp] *n* søvn *m*

*sleep [sliːp] *v* *sove

sleeping bag ['sliːpiŋbæg] *n* sovepose *m*

sleeping car ['sliːpiŋkɑː] *n* sovevogn *c*

sleeping pill ['sliːpiŋpil] *n* sovepille *c*

sleepless ['sliːpləs] *adj* søvnløs

sleepy ['sliːpi] *adj* søvnig

sleet [sliːt] *n* sludd *nt*

sleeve [sliːv] *n* erme *nt*; omslag *nt*

sleigh [slei] *n* kjelke *m*, slede *m*

slender ['slendə] *adj* slank

slice [slais] *n* skive *c*

slide [slaid] *n* rutsjebane *m*; lysbilde *nt*

*slide [slaid] *v* *gli

slight [slait] *adj* ubetydelig; svak

slim [slim] *adj* slank; *v* slanke seg

slip [slip] *v* *gli, skli; *smette; *n* feiltrinn *nt*

slipper ['slipə] *n* tøffel *m*

slippery ['slipəri] *adj* glatt,

sleip

slogan ['slougən] *n* slagord *nt*, valgspråk *nt*

slope [sloup] *n* skråning *m*; *v* helle

sloping ['sloupiŋ] *adj* skrånende

sloppy ['slɔpi] *adj* slurvet

slot [slɔt] *n* myntsprekk *m*; åpning *c*; ~ **machine** automat *m*

slovenly ['slʌvənli] *adj* sjusket

slow [slou] *adj* tungnem, langsom, sakte; ~ **down** *sette ned farten, saktne farten; bremse

slum [slʌm] *n* slum *m*

slump [slʌmp] *n* prisfall *nt*

slush [slʌʃ] *n* snøslaps *nt*

sly [slai] *adj* slu

smack [smæk] *v* smekke; *n* dask *m*

small [smɔːl] *adj* liten; ringe

smallpox ['smɔːlpɔks] *n* kopper *pl*

smart [smɑːt] *adj* fiks; smart, flink, lur

smash [smæʃ] *n* hardt slag *m*; *v* knuse; ødelegge

smell [smel] *n* lukt *c*

*smell [smel] *v* lukte; *stinke

smelly ['smeli] *adj* illeluktende

smile [smail] *v* smile; *n* smil *nt*

smith [smiθ] *n* smed *m*

smoke [smouk] *v* røyke; *n* røyk *m*; **no smoking**

røyking forbudt
smoke-free ['smouk,fri:] adj røykfri
smoker ['smoukə] n røyker m; røykekupé m
smoking compartment ['smoukiŋkəm,pa:tmənt] n røykekupé m
smooth [smu:ð] adj jevn, smul, glatt; myk
smuggle ['smʌgəl] v smugle
snack [snæk] n matbit m
snail [sneil] n snegl m
snake [sneik] n slange m
snapshot ['snæpʃɔt] n øyeblikksfotografi nt, snapshot nt
sneakers ['sni:kəz] plAm tennissko pl, joggesko pl
sneeze [sni:z] v *nyse
sniper ['snaipə] n snikskytter m
snooty ['snu:ti] adj hoven
snore [snɔ:] v snorke
snorkel ['snɔ:kəl] n snorkel m
snout [snaut] n snute c
snow [snou] n snø m; v snø
snowstorm ['snoustɔ:m] n snøstorm m
so [sou] conj så; adv slik; så, i den grad; and ~ on og så videre; ~ far hittil; ~ that så, slik at
soak [souk] v gjennombløte, bløte
soap [soup] n såpe c
sober ['soubə] adj edru; nøktern
so-called [,sou'kɔ:ld] adj

såkalt
soccer ['sɔkə] n fotball m; ~ team fotball-lag nt
social ['souʃəl] adj samfunns-, sosial
socialism ['souʃəlizəm] n sosialisme m
socialist ['souʃəlist] adj sosialistisk; n sosialist m
society [sə'saiəti] n samfunn nt; selskap nt, forening c
sock [sɔk] n sokk m
socket ['sɔkit] n pæreholder m; stikkontakt m
soda ['soudə]: ~ pop nAm colloquial brus m; ~ water soda m, selters m; naturlig mineralvann m
sofa ['soufə] n sofa m
soft [sɔft] adj myk; ~ drink alkoholfri drikk
soften ['sɔfən] v *bløtgjøre
software ['sɔftweə] n programvare m
soil [sɔil] n jord m; jordbunn m; jordsmonn nt
soiled [sɔild] adj skitten
solar ['soulə] adj sol...; ~ system solsystem nt
sold [sould] v (p, pp sell); ~ out utsolgt
soldier ['souldʒə] n soldat m
sole¹ [soul] adj eneste
sole² [soul] n såle m; flyndre c
solely ['soulli] adv utelukkende
solemn ['sɔləm] adj

høytidelig

solicitor [sə'lisitə] n
sakfører m, advokat m

solid ['sɔlid] adj solid;
massiv; n fast stoff

soluble ['sɔljubəl] adj
oppløselig

solution [sə'lu:ʃən] n
løsning c; oppløsning c

solve [sɔlv] v løse

somber Am, sombre
['sɔmbə] adj dyster

some [sʌm] adj noen; pron
visse, enkelte; litt; ~ day en
gang; ~ more litt mer; ~
time en gang

somebody ['sʌmbədi] pron
noen

somehow ['sʌmhau] adv på
en eller annen måte

someone ['sʌmwʌn] pron
noen

something ['sʌmθiŋ] pron
noe

sometimes ['sʌmtaimz] adv
av og til

somewhat ['sʌmwɔt] adv
nokså

somewhere ['sʌmwɛə] adv
etsteds

son [sʌn] n sønn m

song [sɔŋ] n sang m

son-in-law ['sʌninlɔ:] n (pl
sons-) svigersønn m

soon [su:n] adv fort, snart;
as ~ as så snart som

sooner ['su:nə] adv heller

sore [sɔ:] adj sår, øm; n ømt
sted; sår nt; ~ throat
halsesyke m

sorrow ['sɔrou] n sorg c

sorry ['sɔri] adj lei for;
sorry! unnskyld!, beklager!

sort [sɔ:t] v ordne, sortere;
n sort m, slags m / nt; all
sorts of alle slags

soul [soul] n sjel c

sound [saund] n klang m,
lyd m; v *lyde; adj sunn;
pålitelig

soundproof ['saundpru:f]
adj lydtett

soup [su:p] n suppe c; ~
plate suppetallerken m; ~
spoon suppeskje c

sour [sauə] adj sur

source [sɔ:s] n kilde m

south [sauθ] n syd m, sør m;
South Pole Sydpolen

South Africa [sauθ 'æfrikə]
Sør-Afrika

South America [sauθ
ə'merikə] Sør-Amerika

southeast [,sauθ'i:st] n
sørøst m

southerly ['sʌðəli] adj sørlig

southern ['sʌðən] adj sørlig

southwest [,sauθ'west] n
sørvest m

souvenir ['su:vəniə] n
suvenir m

sovereign ['sɔvrin] n
hersker m

*sow [sou] v så

spa [spa:] n kursted nt

space [speis] n rom nt;
verdensrom nt; avstand m,
mellomrom nt; v sette
mellomrom n; ~ shuttle
romferge c

spacious ['speiʃəs] adj
rommelig

spade [speid] n spade m

Spain [spein] Spania

Spaniard ['spænjəd] n
spanjol m, spanier m

Spanish ['spæniʃ] adj
spansk

spanking ['spæŋkiŋ] n
juling c; ris nt

spare [speə] adj reserve-,
ekstra; v *unnvære; ~ part
reservedel m; ~ room
gjesteværelse nt; ~ time
fritid c; ~ tyre reservedekk
nt; ~ wheel reservehjul nt

spark [spɑ:k] n gnist m

spark(ing) plug
['spɑ:kiŋplʌg] n tennplugg
m

sparkling ['spɑ:kliŋ] adj
funklende; musserende

sparrow ['spærou] n spurv
m

*speak [spi:k] v snakke

speaker phone
['spi:kə‚foun] n
høytalertelefon c

spear [spiə] n spyd nt

special ['speʃəl] adj
spesiell; ~ delivery
ekspress

specialist ['speʃəlist] n
spesialist m

speciality [ˌspeʃi'æləti] n
spesialitet m

specialize ['speʃəlaiz] v
spesialisere seg

specially ['speʃəli] adv i
særdeleshet

species ['spi:ʃi:z] n (pl ~)
art m

specific [spə'sifik] adj
spesifikk

specimen ['spesimən] n
prøve c, eksemplar nt

speck [spek] n flekk m

spectacle ['spektəkəl] n
skue nt, syn nt; spectacles
briller pl

spectator [spek'teitə] n
tilskuer m

speculate ['spekjuleit] v
spekulere

speech [spi:tʃ] n tale m

speechless ['spi:tʃləs] adj
målløs

speed [spi:d] n hastighet c;
fart m; cruising ~ marsjfart
m; ~ dial(ing) n
hurtigtaster c; ~ limit
fartsgrense c

*speed [spi:d] v kjøre fort;
kjøre for fort

speeding ['spi:diŋ] n
råkjøring c

speedometer [spi:'dɔmitə]
n fartsmåler m

spell [spel] n fortryllelse m

*spell [spel] v stave

spelling ['speliŋ] n
stavemåte m

*spend [spend] v bruke,
spandere; *tilbringe

sphere [sfiə] n kule c;
område nt

spice [spais] n krydder nt;
spices krydderier pl

spiced [spaist] adj krydret

spicy ['spaisi] adj krydret

spider ['spaidə] n
edderkopp m; spider's
web spindelvev m

*spill [spil] v søle

*spin [spin] v *spinne;
snurre

spinach ['spinidʒ] n spinat
m

spine [spain] n ryggrad m

spire [spaiə] n spir nt

spirit ['spirit] n ånd m;
spøkelse nt; ~ stove
spritapparat nt; spirits
pl, spirituosa pl,
alkoholholdige drikker;
humør nt

spiritual ['spirit∫uəl] adj
åndelig

spit [spit] n spytt nt; spidd
nt

*spit [spit] v spytte

spite [spait] n
ondskapsfullhet c; v være
ekkel mot; in ~ of til tross
for

spiteful ['spaitfəl] adj
ondskapsfull

splash [splæ∫] v skvette

splendid ['splendid] adj
praktfull, glimrende

splendo(u)r ['splendə] n
prakt m

splint [splint] n beinskinne
c

splinter ['splintə] n splint m

*split [split] v kløyve

*spoil [spoil] v *ødelegge;
skjemme bort

spoke¹ [spouk] v (p speak)

spoke² [spouk] n eike c

sponge [spʌndʒ] n svamp m

spool [spu:l] n spole m

spoon [spu:n] n skje c

spoonful ['spu:nful] n
skjefull m

sport [spɔ:t] n sport m

sports car ['spɔ:tska:] n
sportsbil m

sportsman ['spɔ:tsmən] n
(pl -men) idrettsmann m

sportswear ['spɔ:tswɛə] n
sportsklær pl

sportswoman
['spɔ:tswumən] n (pl
-women) idrettskvinne c

spot [spɔt] n flekk m; sted
nt

spotless ['spɔtləs] adj
plettfri

spotlight ['spɔtlait] n
prosjektør m

spotted ['spɔtid] adj flekket

spout [spaut] n tut m

sprain [sprein] v forstue; n
forstuing c

spray [sprei] n sprut m;
spray m; v sprøyte
(planter), sprute, spraye

*spread [spred] v spre

spring [spriŋ] n vår m; fjær
c; kilde m

springtime ['spriŋtaim] n
vår m

sprouts [sprauts] pl
rosenkål m

spy [spai] n spion m

square [skwɛə] adj
kvadratisk; n kvadrat nt;
plass m

squash [skwɔ∫] n fruktsaft

steel

c; squash m; v kryste
squeeze [skwi:z] v presse (saft); trykke
squirrel ['skwirəl] n ekorn nt
squirt [skwə:t] n sprut m
stable ['steibəl] adj stabil; n stall m
stack [stæk] n stabel m
stadium ['steidiəm] n stadion nt
staff [stɑ:f] n personale nt
stage [steidʒ] n scene m; stadium nt, fase m; etappe m
stain [stein] v flekke; n flekk m; stained glass window glassmaleri nt; ~ remover flekkfjerner m
stainless ['steinləs] adj plettfri; ~ steel rustfritt stål
staircase ['steəkeis] n trapp c
stairs [steəz] pl trapp c
stale [steil] adj ~ bread gammelt brød; ~ air dårlig luft
stall [stɔ:l] n utsalgsbord nt; orkesterplass m
stamp [stæmp] n frimerke nt; stempel nt; v frankere; trampe; ~ machine frimerkeautomat m
stand [stænd] n stand m; tribune m
*stand [stænd] v *stå
standard ['stændəd] n norm m; standard-; ~ of living levestandard m
stanza ['stænzə] n strofe m;

vers nt
staple ['steipəl] n stift m
star [stɑ:] n stjerne c
starboard ['stɑ:bəd] n styrbord
stare [steə] v stirre
starling ['stɑ:liŋ] n stær m
start [stɑ:t] v begynne; n start m
starting point ['stɑ:tiŋpoint] n utgangspunkt m
state [steit] n stat m; stand m; v erklære; the States [ðə steits] De forente stater
statement ['steitmənt] n erklæring c
station ['steiʃən] n stasjon m; posisjon m
stationary ['steiʃənəri] adj stillestående
stationer's ['steiʃənəz] n papirhandel m
stationery ['steiʃənəri] n papirvarer pl
statistics [stə'tistiks] pl statistikk m
statue ['stætʃu:] n statue m
stay [stei] v *bli; *opphold seg, *ta inn; n opphold nt
steadfast ['stedfɑ:st] adj standhaftig
steady ['stedi] adj stø
steak [steik] n biff m
*steal [sti:l] v *stjele
steam [sti:m] n damp m
steamer ['sti:mə] n dampskip m
steel [sti:l] n stål nt

steep [sti:p] *adj* bratt, steil

steeple ['sti:pəl] *n* kirketårn *nt*

steer [stiə] *v* styre

steering column ['stiəriŋ,kɔləm] *n* rattstamme *m*

steering wheel ['stiəriŋwi:l] *n* ratt *nt*

steersman ['stiəzmən] *n* (pl -men) rorgjenger *m*

stem [stem] *n* stilk *m*

stem cell ['stem,sel] *n* stamcelle *c*

step [step] *n* skritt *nt*, steg *nt*; trinn *nt*; *v* *tre, trå

stepchild ['steptʃaild] *n* (pl -children) stebarn *nt*

stepfather ['step,fɑ:ðə] *n* stefar *m*

stepmother ['step,mʌðə] *n* stemor *c*

stereo [steriou] *n* stereo *m*; *colloquial* stereoanlegg *nt*

sterile ['sterail] *adj* steril

sterilize ['sterilaiz] *v* sterilisere

steward ['stjuːəd] *n* stuert *m*; flyvert *m*

stewardess ['stjuːədes] *n* flyvertinne *c*

stick [stik] *n* stokk *m*

*stick [stik] *v* klebe

sticker [stikə] *n* klistremerke *nt*

sticky [stiki] *adj* klebrig

stiff [stif] *adj* stiv

still [stil] *adv* fremdeles; likevel; *adj* stille

stimulant ['stimjulənt] *n*

stimulans *m*

stimulate ['stimjuleit] *v* stimulere

sting [stiŋ] *n* stikk *nt*

*sting [stiŋ] *v* *stikke

stingy ['stindʒi] *adj* gjerrig; smålig

*stink [stiŋk] *v* *stinke

stipulate ['stipjuleit] *v* *fastsette

stipulation [,stipju'leiʃən] *n* betingelse *m*

stir [stəː] *v* røre

stitch [stitʃ] *n* sting *nt*; hold *nt*

stock [stɔk] *n* forsyning *c*; *v* lagre; ~ exchange fondsbørs *m*, børs *m*; ~ market fondsmarked *nt*; stocks and shares verdipapirer *pl*

stocking ['stɔkiŋ] *n* strømpe *c*

stole¹ [stoul] *v* (p steal)

stole² [stoul] *n* stola *m*

stomach ['stʌmək] *n* mage *m*; ~ ache magesmerter *pl*

stone [stoun] *n* stein *m*; edelsten *m*; stein-; pumice ~ pimpstein *m*

stood [stud] *v* (p, pp stand)

stop [stɔp] *v* stoppe; avslutte, *holde opp med; *n* holdeplass *m*; stop! stopp!

stopper ['stɔpə] *n* kork *m*

storage ['stɔːridʒ] *n* lagring *c*

store [stɔː] *n* lagerbeholdning *m*;

forretning c; v lagre; ~
house lagerbygning m
stor(e)y ['stɔ:ri] n etasje m
stork [stɔ:k] n stork m
storm [stɔ:m] n storm m
stormy ['stɔ:mi] adj
stormfull
story ['stɔ:ri] n fortelling c
stout [staut] adj korpulent,
tykkfallen
stove [stouv] n ovn m;
komfyr m
straight [streit] adj rak;
ærlig; adv rett; ~ ahead rett
frem; ~ away med en gang;
~ on rett frem
strain [strein] n
anstrengelse m;
anspennelse m; v
overanstrenge; sile
strainer ['streinə] n sil m;
dørslag n
strange [streindʒ] adj
fremmed; underlig
stranger ['streindʒə] n
fremmed m
strangle ['stræŋgəl] v kvele
strap [stræp] n rem c
straw [strɔ:] n halm m
strawberry ['strɔ:bəri] n
jordbær m
stream [stri:m] n bekk m;
strøm m; v strømme
street [stri:t] n gate c
streetcar ['stri:tka:] nAm
trikk m
strength [streŋθ] n styrke m
stress [stres] n stress m;
trykk nt; v belaste, *legge
vekt på

stretch [stretʃ] v tøye; n
strekning m
strict [strikt] adj streng
strike [straik] n streik m
*strike [straik] v *slå; *slå
til; streike; *stryke
striking ['straikiŋ] adj
påfallende,
oppsiktsvekkende, slående
string [striŋ] n snor c; streng
m
strip [strip] n strimmel m
stripe [straip] n stripe c
striped [straipt] adj stripet
stroke [strouk] n slaganfall
nt
stroll [stroul] v slentre; n
spasertur m
strong [strɔŋ] adj sterk;
kraftig
stronghold ['strɔŋhould] n
tilfluktssted nt; høyborg c
structure ['strʌktʃə] n
struktur m
struggle ['strʌgəl] n strid
m, kamp m; v *slåss,
kjempe
stubborn ['stʌbən] adj sta
student ['stju:dənt] n
student m; elev m
studies ['stʌdiz] pl studium
nt
study ['stʌdi] v studere; n
studium nt; arbeidsværelse
nt
stuff [stʌf] n materiale nt;
saker pl
stuffed [stʌft] adj fylt
stuffing ['stʌfiŋ] n fyll nt
stuffy ['stʌfi] adj trykkende;

snerpet

stumble ['stʌmbəl] v snuble

stung [stʌŋ] v (p, pp sting)

stupid ['stjuːpid] adj dum

style [stail] n stil m

subject¹ ['sʌbdʒikt] n subjekt nt; undersått m; gjenstand m; emne nt; ~ to utsatt for

subject² [səb'dʒekt] v underkue

sublet [,sub'let] v fremleie

submarine ['sʌbməriːn] n ubåt m

submit [səb'mit] v underkaste seg

subordinate [sə'bɔːdinət] adj underordnet; sekundær

subscriber [səb'skraibə] n abonnent m

subscription [səb'skripʃən] n abonnement nt

subsequent ['sʌbsikwənt] adj følgende

subsidy ['sʌbsidi] n tilskudd nt

substance ['sʌbstəns] n substans m

substantial [səb'stænʃəl] adj substansiell; virkelig; anselig

substitute ['sʌbstitjuːt] v erstatte; n erstatning m; stedfortreder m

subtitle ['sʌb,taitəl] n undertekst m

subtle ['sʌtəl] adj subtil

subtract [səb'trækt] v *trekke fra

suburb ['sʌbəːb] n forstad m

suburban [sə'bəːbən] adj forstads-

subway ['sʌbwei] nAm undergrunnsbane m

succeed [sək'siːd] v lykkes; *etterfølge

success [sək'ses] n suksess m

successful [sək'sesfəl] adj vellykket

succumb [sə'kʌm] v bukke under

such [sʌtʃ] adj sånn, slik; adv slik; ~ as slik som

suck [sʌk] v suge

sudden ['sʌdən] adj plutselig

suddenly ['sʌdənli] adv plutselig

suede [sweid] n semsket skinn

suffer ['sʌfə] v *lide; *gjennomgå

suffering ['sʌfəriŋ] n lidelse m

suffice [sə'fais] v *være tilstrekkelig

sufficient [sə'fiʃənt] adj tilstrekkelig

suffrage ['sʌfridʒ] n stemmerett m

sugar ['ʃugə] n sukker nt

suggest [sə'dʒest] v *foreslå

suggestion [sə'dʒestʃən] n forslag m

suicide ['suːisaid] n selvmord nt; ~ attack n selvmordangrep nt; ~

suppository

bomber *n*
selvmordsbomber *c*

suit [su:t] *v* passe; tilpasse;
kle; *n* dress *m*

suitable ['su:təbəl] *adj*
egnet

suitcase ['su:tkeis] *n*
koffert *m*

suite [swi:t] *n* suite *m*

sum [sʌm] *n* sum *m*

summary ['sʌməri] *n*
sammendrag *nt*

summer ['sʌmə] *n* sommer
m; ~ time sommertid *c*

summit ['sʌmit] *n* topp *m*

sun [sʌn] *n* sol *c*

sunbathe ['sʌnbeið] *v* sole
seg

sunburn ['sʌnbə:n] *n*
solbrenthet *c*

Sunday ['sʌndi] søndag *m*

sunglasses ['sʌn,glɑ:siz] *pl*
solbriller *pl*

sunlight ['sʌnlait] *n* sollys
nt

sunny ['sʌni] *adj* solrik

sunrise ['sʌnraiz] *n*
soloppgang *m*

sunset ['sʌnset] *n*
solnedgang *m*

sunshade ['sʌnʃeid] *n*
parasoll *m*

sunshine ['sʌnʃain] *n*
solskinn *nt*

sunstroke ['sʌnstrouk] *n*
solstikk *nt*

suntan ['sʌntæn] brunfarge
m

suntan oil ['sʌntænɔil]
sololje *c*

super ['sjupə] *adj colloquial*
flott, bra; kul, kult

superb [su'pə:b] *adj*
storartet

superficial [,su:pə'fiʃəl] *adj*
overfladisk

superfluous [su'pə:fluəs]
adj overflødig

superior [su'piəriə] *adj*
høyere, overlegen, bedre,
større

supermarket
['su:pə,mɑ:kit] *n*
supermarked *m*

superstition [,su:pə'stiʃən]
n overtro *c*

supervise ['su:pəvaiz] *v*
overvåke

supervision [,su:pə'viʒən]
n overoppsyn *nt*, oppsyn *nt*

supervisor ['su:pəvaizə] *n*
kontrollør *m*

supper ['sʌpə] *n* aftensmat
m

supple ['sʌpəl] *adj* bøyelig,
smidig, myk

supplement ['sʌplimənt] *n*
tillegg *nt*

supply [sə'plai] *n* tilførsel
m, levering *c*; forråd *nt*;
tilbud *nt*; *v* forsyne

support [sə'pɔ:t] *v* *bære,
*hjelpe; *n* støtte *m*

supporter [sə'pɔ:tə] *n*
tilhenger *m*; forsørger *m*

suppose [sə'pouz] *v* *anta;
supposing that forutsatt
at

suppository [sə'pɔzitəri] *n*
stikkpille *c*

suppress [sə'pres] v
undertrykke

surcharge ['sə:tʃɑ:dʒ] n
ekstragebyr nt

sure [ʃuə] adj sikker

surely ['ʃuəli] adv sikkert

surface ['sə:fis] n overflate
c

surf (the Net) [sə:f] v surfe

surfboard ['sə:fbɔ:d] n
surfingbrett nt

surgeon ['sə:dʒən] n kirurg
m; veterinary ~ veterinær
m

surgery ['sə:dʒəri] n
operasjon m; legekontor
nt; reconstructive ~
rekonstruktiv kirurgi c

surname ['sə:neim] n
etternavn nt

surplus ['sə:pləs] n
overskudd nt

surprise [sə'praiz] n
overraskelse m; v
overraske; forbause

surrender [sə'rendə] v
*overgi seg; n overgivelse
m

surround [sə'raund] v
*omgi, omringe

surrounding [sə'raundiŋ]
adj omkringliggende

surroundings [sə'raundiŋz]
pl omegn m

survey ['sə:vei] n oversikt
m

surveillance [sə:'veiəns] n
overvåking c

survival [sə'vaivəl] n
overleving c

survive [sə'vaiv] v overleve

suspect¹ [sə'spekt] v
mistenke; ane

suspect² ['sʌspekt] n
mistenkt m

suspend [sə'spend] v
suspendere

suspenders [sə'spendəz]
plAm bukseseler pl

suspension [sə'spenʃən] n
fjæring c; ~ bridge
hengebro c

suspicion [sə'spiʃən] n
mistanke m;
mistenksomhet c; anelse m

suspicious [sə'spiʃəs] adj
mistenkelig; mistenksom,
mistroisk

sustain [sə'stein] v orke;
*opprettholde

SUV ['esyu:'vi:], sport
utility vehicle n SUV nt,
sports og nyttekjøretøy

Swahili [swə'hi:li] n swahili
m

swallow ['swolou] v svelge,
sluke; n svale c

swam [swæm] v (p swim)

swamp [swomp] n myr c

swan [swon] n svane c

swap [swop] v bytte

*swear [sweə] v *sverge;
banne

sweat [swet] n svette m; v
svette

sweater ['swetə] n ulljakke
c; genser m

sweatshirt ['swetʃə:t] n
(bomulls)genser

Swede [swi:d] n svenske m

systematic

Sweden ['swi:dən] Sverige
Swedish ['swi:diʃ] adj
svensk
*sweep [swi:p] v feie
sweet [swi:t] adj søt; n
sukkertøy nt; dessert m;
sweets sukkertøy pl;
godter pl
sweeten ['swi:tən] v sukre
sweetheart ['swi:tha:t] n
elskling m
swell [swel] adj flott
*swell [swel] v svelle
swelling ['sweliŋ] n hevelse
m
swift [swift] adj rask
*swim [swim] v svømme
swimmer ['swimə] n
svømmer m
swimming ['swimiŋ] n
svømming c; ~ pool
svømmebasseng nt
swimmingtrunks
['swimiŋtrʌŋks] pl
badebukse c
swimsuit ['swimsu:t], n
swimming suit nAm
badedrakt c
swindle ['swindəl] v
svindle; n svindel m
swindler ['swindlə] n
svindler m
swing [swiŋ] n huske c
*swing [swiŋ] v svinge;
huske
Swiss [swis] adj sveitsisk; n
sveitser m
switch [switʃ] n bryter m; v

skifte; ~ off *slå av; ~ on
*slå på
switchboard ['switʃbɔ:d] n
sentralbord nt
Switzerland ['switsələnd] n
Sveits
sword [sɔ:d] n sverd nt
swum [swʌm] v (pp swim)
syllable ['siləbəl] n stavelse
m
symbol ['simbəl] n symbol
nt
sympathetic [,simpə'θetik]
adj deltakende,
medfølende
sympathy ['simpəθi] n
sympati m; medfølelse m
symphony ['simfəni] n
symfoni m
symptom ['simtəm] n
symptom nt
synagogue ['sinəgɔg] n
synagoge m
synonym ['sinənim] n
synonym nt
synthetic [sin'θetik] adj
syntetisk
Syria ['siriə] Syria
Syrian ['siriən] adj syrisk; n
syrer m
syringe [si'rindʒ] n sprøyte
c
syrup ['sirəp] n sirup m
system ['sistəm] n system
nt; decimal ~
desimalsystem nt
systematic [,sistə'mætik]
adj systematisk

T

table ['teibəl] n bord nt; tabell m; ~ of contents innholdsfortegnelse m; ~ tennis bordtennis m
tablecloth ['teibəlklɔθ] n duk c
tablespoon ['teibəlspu:n] n spiseskje c
tablet ['tæblit] n tablett m; plate c
taboo [tə'bu:] n tabu nt
tactics ['tæktiks] pl taktikk m
tag [tæg] n merkelapp m
tail [teil] n hale m
taillight ['teillait] n baklys nt
tailor ['teilə] n skredder m
tailor-made ['teiləmeid] adj skreddersydd
*take [teik] v *ta; *gripe; *følge; skjønne, *forstå, *begripe; ~ away *ta med seg; fjerne, *ta vekk; ~ off *ta av; lette; ~ out *ta bort; ~ over *overta; ~ place *finne sted; ~ up *oppta
take-off ['teikɔf] n start m
tale [teil] n fortelling m, eventyr nt
talent ['tælənt] n begavelse m, talent nt
talented ['tæləntid] adj begavet
talk [tɔ:k] v snakke; n samtale m
talkative ['tɔ:kətiv] adj snakkesalig
tall [tɔ:l] adj høy, lang
tame [teim] adj tam; v temme
tampon ['tæmpən] n tampong m
tangerine [,tændʒə'ri:n] n mandarin m
tangible ['tændʒibəl] adj følbar
tank [tæŋk] n tank m
tanker ['tæŋkə] n tankbåt m
tanned [tænd] adj brun
tap [tæp] n kran c; lett slag; v banke
tape [teip] n lydbånd nt; bånd nt; adhesive ~ limbånd nt, tape m; ~ measure målebånd nt; ~ recorder båndopptaker m
tar [ta:] n tjære c
target ['ta:git] n skyteskive c, mål nt
tariff ['tærif] n tariff m
task [ta:sk] n oppgave c
taste [teist] n smak m; v smake; smake på
tasteless ['teistləs] adj smakløs
tasty ['teisti] adj velsmakende
taught [tɔ:t] v (p, pp teach)
tavern ['tævən] n kro c
tax [tæks] n skatt m; v *skattlegge

taxation [tæk'seiʃən] n
beskatning m

tax-free ['tæksfri:] adj
skattefri

taxi ['tæksi] n taxi m, drosje
c; ~ driver drosjesjåfør m; ~
rank drosjeholdeplass m; ~
stand nAm
drosjeholdeplass m

taximeter ['tæksi,mi:tə] n
taksameter nt

tea [ti:] n te m; ~ set
teservise nt

*teach [ti:tʃ] v lære,
undervise

teacher ['ti:tʃə] n lærer m,
lektor m

teachings ['ti:tʃiŋz] pl lære
c

tea cloth ['ti:klɔθ] n
kjøkkenhåndkle nt

teacup ['ti:kʌp] n tekopp m

team [ti:m] n lag nt

teapot ['ti:pɔt] n tekanne c

*tear [tɛə] v *rive

tear¹ [tiə] n tåre c

tear² [tɛə] n rift c

tease [ti:z] v erte

tea-shop ['ti:ʃɔp] n tesalong
m

teaspoon ['ti:spu:n] n
teskje c

technical ['teknikəl] adj
teknisk; ~ support teknisk
støtte

technician [tek'niʃən] n
tekniker m

technique [tek'ni:k] n
teknikk m

technological

[,teknə'lɔdʒikəl] adj
teknologisk

technology [tek'nɔlədʒi] n
teknologi m

teenager ['ti:,neidʒə] n
tenåring m

telecommunications
[,telikəmju:ni'keiʃənz] n
telekommunikasjon c

telepathy [ti'lepəθi] n
telepati m

telephone ['telifoun] n
telefon m; ~ book Am
telefonkatalog m; ~ booth
telefonkiosk m; ~ call
telefon m, telefonsamtale
m; ~ directory
telefonkatalog m; ~
exchange telefonsentral m

television ['teliviʒən] n
fjernsyn nt; ~ set
fjernsynsapparat nt

*tell [tel] v *si; *fortelle

telly ['teli] n colloquial
fjernsyn nt, TV m

temper ['tempə] n sinne nt

temperature ['temprətʃə] n
temperatur m

tempest ['tempist] n storm
m

temple ['tempəl] n tempel
nt; tinning m

temporary ['tempərəri] adj
midlertidig, foreløpig

tempt [tempt] v friste

temptation [temp'teiʃən] n
fristelse m

ten [ten] num ti

tenant ['tenənt] n leieboer
m

tend [tend] v *ha tendens
til; passe; ~ to *være
tilbøyelig til

tendency ['tendənsi] n
tendens m, tilbøyelighet c

tender ['tendə] adj øm,
myk; mør

tendon ['tendən] n sene c

tennis ['tenis] n tennis m; ~
court tennisbane m; ~
shoes tennissko pl;
joggesko pl

tense [tens] adj anspent

tension ['tenʃən] n
spenning m

tent [tent] n telt nt

tenth [tenθ] num tiende

tepid ['tepid] adj lunken

term [təːm] n uttrykk nt;
frist m, termin m;
betingelse m

terminal ['təːminəl] n
endestasjon m; terminal m

terrace ['terəs] n terrasse m

terrain [te'rein] n terreng nt

terrible ['teribəl] adj
fryktelig, forferdelig,
grusom

terrific [tə'rifik] adj storartet

terrify ['terifai] v skremme;
terrifying skremmende

territory ['teritəri] n område
nt

terror ['terə] n redsel m

terrorism ['terərizəm] n
terror m, terrorisme m

terrorist ['terərist] n
terrorist m

terry(cloth) ['teri(klɔθ)] n
frotté m

test [test] n prøve c, test m;
v teste

testify ['testifai] v vitne

text [tekst] n tekst m

textbook ['teksbuk] n
lærebok c

textile ['tekstail] n tekstil
m / nt

texture ['tekstʃə] n struktur
m

Thai [tai] adj thailandsk; n
thailender m

Thailand ['tailænd] n
Thailand

than [ðæn] conj enn

thank [θæŋk] v takke; ~
you! takk !

thankful ['θæŋkfəl] adj
takknemlig

that [ðæt] pron den, det;
som; conj at

thaw [θɔː] v tine, smelte; n
tøvær nt

the [ðə,ði] art -en, -a; -et;
the ... the jo ... jo

theater Am, theatre ['θiətə]
n teater nt

theft [θeft] n tyveri nt

their [ðeə] adj deres

them [ðem] pron dem

theme [θiːm] n tema nt,
emne nt

themselves [ðəm'selvz]
pron seg; selv

then [ðen] adv da; deretter,
så

theology [θi'ɔlədʒi] n
teologi m

theoretical [θiə'retikəl] adj
teoretisk

theory ['θiəri] n teori m

therapy ['θerəpi] n terapi m

there [ðɛə] adv der; dit

therefore ['ðɛəfɔː] conj derfor

thermometer [θəˈmɔmitə] n termometer nt

thermostat ['θɔːməstæt] n termostat m

these [ðiːz] adj disse

thesis ['θiːsis] n (pl theses) tese m; avhandling c

they [ðei] pron de

thick [θik] adj tykk; tett

thicken ['θikən] v tykne

thickness ['θiknəs] n tykkelse m

thief [θiːf] n (pl thieves) tyv m

thigh [θai] n lår nt

thimble ['θimbəl] n fingerbøl m

thin [θin] adj tynn; mager

thing [θiŋ] n ting m

*think [θiŋk] v tenke; tenke etter; ~ of tenke på; *komme på; ~ over tenke over

thinker ['θiŋkə] n tenker m

third [θɔːd] num tredje

thirst [θɔːst] n tørst m

thirsty ['θɔːsti] adj tørst

thirteen [,θɔːˈtiːn] num tretten

thirteenth [,θɔːˈtiːnθ] num trettende

thirtieth ['θɔːtiəθ] num trettiende

thirty ['θɔːti] num tretti

this [ðis] adj denne; pron denne

thistle ['θisəl] n tistel m

thorn [θɔːn] n torn m

thorough ['θʌrə] adj omhyggelig, grundig

thoroughfare ['θʌrəfɛə] n ferdselsåre c, hovedvei m

those [ðouz] pron de

though [ðou] conj selv om, skjønt; adv imidlertid

thought¹ [θɔːt] v (p, pp think)

thought² [θɔːt] n tanke m

thoughtful ['θɔːtfəl] adj tankefull; omtenksom

thousand ['θauzənd] num tusen

thread [θred] n tråd m; v *tre

threadbare ['θredbɛə] adj loslitt

threat [θret] n trussel m

threaten ['θretən] v true

three [θriː] num tre

three-quarter [,θriːˈkwɔːtə] adj tre fjerdedels

threshold ['θreʃould] n terskel m

threw [θruː] v (p throw)

thrifty ['θrifti] adj sparsommelig

throat [θrout] n hals m; strupe m

throne [θroun] n trone c

throttle ['θrɔtəl] n choke m

through [θruː] prep gjennom

throughout [θruːˈaut] adv overalt; heltigjennom

throw [θrou] n kast nt

throw

*throw [θrou] v slenge, kaste

thrush [θrʌʃ] n trost m

thumb [θʌm] n tommelfinger m

thumbtack ['θʌmtæk] nAm tegnestift m

thump [θʌmp] v dunke

thunder ['θʌndə] n torden m; v tordne

thunderstorm ['θʌndəstɔːm] n tordenvær nt

Thursday ['θəːzdi] torsdag m

thus [ðʌs] adv slik

thyme [taim] n timian m

tick [tik] n merke nt; ~ off krysse av

ticket ['tikit] n billett m; lapp m; ~ machine billettautomat m

tickle ['tikəl] v kile

tide [taid] n tidevann nt; high ~ høyvann nt; low ~ lavvann nt

tidy ['taidi] adj ordentlig; ~ up rydde opp

tie [tai] v *binde, knytte; n slips nt

tiger ['taigə] n tiger m

tight [tait] adj stram; trang; adv fast

tighten ['taitən] v stramme; strammes

tights [taits] pl strømpebukse c

tile [tail] n gulvflis c; takstein m

till [til] prep inntil, til; conj inntil

timber ['timbə] n tømmer nt

time [taim] n tid c; gang m; takt m; all the ~ hele tiden; in ~ i tide; ~ of arrival ankomsttid c; ~ of departure avgangstid c

time-saving ['taim,seivin] adj tidsbesparende

timetable ['taim,teibəl] n ruteplan m

timid ['timid] adj blyg

timidity [ti'midəti] n sjenerthet c

tin [tin] n tinn nt; boks m, hermetikkboks m; tinned food hermetikk m; ~ opener hermetikkåpner m

tiny ['taini] adj bitte liten

tip [tip] n spiss m; drikkepenger pl

tire¹ [taiə] n dekk nt

tire² [taiə] v *bli trett

tired [taiəd] adj utmattet, trett; ~ of lei av

tiring ['taiərin] adj trettende

tissue ['tiʃuː] n vev nt; papirlommetørkle nt

title ['taitəl] n tittel m

to [tuː] prep til, på; for å

toad [toud] n padde c

toadstool ['toudstuːl] n fluesopp m; giftig sopp

toast [toust] n ristet brød; skål m; v riste

tobacco [tə'bækou] n (pl ~s) tobakk m

tobacconist's tobakksforretning c

today [tə'dei] adv i dag

toddler ['tɔdlə] n småbarn

nt

toe [tou] *n* tå *c*

toffee ['tɔfi] *n* en slags karamell

together [təˈgeðə] *adv* sammen

toilet ['tɔilət] *n* toalett *nt*, *colloquial* do *m* / *nt*; ~ case toalettveske *c*; ~ paper toalettpapir *nt*

toiletry ['tɔilətri] *n* toalettsaker *pl*

token ['toukən] *n* tegn *nt*; bevis *nt*; sjetong *m*

told [tould] *v* (p, pp tell)

tolerable ['tɔlərəbəl] *adj* utholdelig

toll [toul] *n* bompenger *pl*; gebyr *nt*

tomato [təˈmɑːtou] *n* (pl ~es) tomat *m*

tomb [tuːm] *n* grav *c*

tombstone ['tuːmstoun] *n* gravstein *m*

tomorrow [təˈmɔrou] *adv* i morgen

ton [tʌn] *n* tonn *nt*

tone [toun] *n* tone *m*; klang *m*

tongs [tɔŋz] *pl* tang *c*

tongue [tʌŋ] *n* tunge *c*

tonight [təˈnait] *adv* i kveld, i natt

tonsilitis [,tɔnsəˈlaitis] *n* betente mandler

tonsils ['tɔnsəlz] *pl* mandler *pl*

too [tuː] *adv* altfor; også

took [tuk] *v* (p take)

tool [tuːl] *n* verktøy *nt*, redskap *nt*

toot [tuːt] *vAm* tute

tooth [tuːθ] *n* (pl teeth) tann *c*

toothache ['tuːθeik] *n* tannverk *m*; tannpine *c*

toothbrush ['tuːθbrʌʃ] *n* tannbørste *c*

toothpaste ['tuːθpeist] *n* tannkrem *c*

toothpick ['tuːθpik] *n* tannpirker *m*

top [tɔp] *n* topp *m*; overside *c*; lokk *nt*; øverst; on ~ of oppå; ~ side overside *c*

topic ['tɔpik] *n* emne *nt*

topical ['tɔpikəl] *adj* aktuell

torch [tɔːtʃ] *n* fakkel *m*; lommelykt *c*

torment¹ [tɔːˈment] *v* pine

torment² [ˈtɔːment] *n* pine *c*

torture ['tɔːtʃə] *n* tortur *m*; *v* torturere

toss [tɔs] *v* kaste

tot [tɔt] *n* lite barn

total ['toutəl] *adj* total; fullstendig; *n* totalsum *m*

totalitarian [,toutæliˈtɛəriən] *adj* totalitær

touch [tʌtʃ] *v* røre, berøre; *n* kontakt *m*, berøring *c*; følesans *m*

touching ['tʌtʃiŋ] *adj* rørende

tough [tʌf] *adj* seig

tour [tuə] *n* rundreise *c*, tur *m*

tourism ['tuərizəm] *n* turisttrafikk *m*

tourist ['tuərist] n turist m;
~ class turistklasse c; ~
office turistkontor nt

tournament ['tuənəmənt] n
turnering c

tow [tou] v taue

towards [tə'wɔːdz] prep
mot; overfor

towel [tauəl] n håndkle nt

towel(l)ing ['tauəliŋ] n
frotté c

tower [tauə] n tårn nt

town [taun] n by m; ~ center
Am, ~ centre sentrum nt; ~
hall rådhus nt

townspeople ['taunz,piːpəl]
pl byfolk pl

toxic ['tɔksik] adj giftig

toy [tɔi] n leketøy nt

toyshop ['tɔiʃɔp] n
leketøysforretning c

trace [treis] n spor nt; v
ettersporre, oppspore

track [træk] n spor nt; bane
m

tracksuit [træksuːt] n
treningsdrakt c

tractor ['træktə] n traktor m

trade [treid] n handel m;
yrke nt; v *drive handel

trademark ['treidmɑːk] n
varemerke nt

trader ['treidə] n kjøpmann
m

tradesman ['treidzmən],
tradeswoman
[,treidz'wumən], n (pl
-men, -women) butikkeier
m

trade union [,treid'juːnjən]

n fagforening c

tradition [trə'diʃən] n
tradisjon m

traditional [trə'diʃənəl] adj
tradisjonell

traffic ['træfik] n trafikk m;
~ jam trafikk-kork m; ~
light trafikklys nt

tragedy ['trædʒədi] n
tragedie m

tragic ['trædʒik] adj tragisk

trail [treil] n sti m, spor nt

trailer ['treilə] n tilhenger
m; campingvogn c

train [trein] n tog nt; v
dressere, trene; stopping ~
somletog nt; through ~
hurtigtog nt; ~ ferry
jernbaneferje c

trainee [trei'niː] n lærling;
trainee

trainer ['treinə] n trener m

training ['treiniŋ] n trening
c

trait [treit] n trekk nt

traitor ['treitə] n forræder m

tram [træm] n trikk m

tramp [træmp] n landstryker
m; go for a ~ gå på tur

tranquil ['træŋkwil] adj
rolig

tranquillizer ['træŋkwilaizə]
n beroligende middel

transaction [træn'zækʃən]
n transaksjon c

transatlantic
[,trænzət'læntik] adj
transatlantisk

transfer [træns'fəː] v
overføre

transform [træns'fɔːm] v forvandle, omdanne

transformer [træns'fɔːmə] n transformator m

transition [træn'siʃən] n overgang m

translate [træns'leit] v *oversette

translation [træns'leiʃən] n oversettelse m

translator [træns'leitə] n oversetter m

transmission [trænz'miʃən] n sending c

transmit [trænz'mit] v sende

transmitter [trænz'mitə] n sender m

transparent [træn'speərənt] adj gjennomsiktig

transport¹ ['trænspɔːt] n transport m

transport² [træn'spɔːt] v transportere

transportation [,trænspɔː'teiʃən] n transport m

trap [træp] n felle c

trash [træʃ] n rask nt, skrap nt; ~ can Am søppelkasse c

travel ['trævəl] v reise; ~ agency, ~ agent reisebyrå nt; ~ insurance reiseforsikring c; travelling expenses reiseutgifter pl

travel(l)er ['trævələ] n reisende m; travel(l)er's cheque reisesjekk m

tray [trei] n brett nt

treason ['triːzən] n

forræderi nt

treasure ['treʒə] n skatt m

treasurer ['treʒərə] n kasserer m

treasury ['treʒəri] n statskasse c

treat [triːt] v behandle

treatment ['triːtmənt] n behandling c

treaty ['triːti] n traktat m

tree [triː] n tre nt

tremble ['trembəl] v *skjelve; dirre

tremendous [tri'mendəs] adj kolossal

trendy ['trendi] adj colloquial moderne

trespass ['trespəs] v krenke annens eiendom

trespasser ['trespəsə] n uvedkommende c

trial [traiəl] n rettssak c; forsøk nt

triangle ['traiæŋgəl] n trekant m

triangular [trai'æŋgjulə] adj trekantet

tribe [traib] n stamme m

tributary ['tribjutəri] n bielv c

tribute ['tribjuːt] n hyllest m

trick [trik] n knep nt; trick nt

trigger ['trigə] n avtrekker m

trim [trim] v klippe, stusse

trip [trip] n reise c, utflukt c, tur m

triumph ['traiəmf] n triumf m; v triumfere

triumphant [trai'ʌmfənt] *adj* triumferende

troops [truːps] *pl* tropper *pl*

tropical ['trɔpikəl] *adj* tropisk

tropics ['trɔpiks] *pl* tropene *pl*

trouble ['trʌbəl] *n* trøbbel *nt*, uleilighet *c*, besvær *nt*; *v* bry

troublesome ['trʌbəlsəm] *adj* brysom

trousers ['trauzəz] *pl* bukse *c*; trouser... bukse...

trout [traut] *n* (pl ~) ørret *m*

truck [trʌk] *nAm* lastebil *m*

true [truː] *adj* sann; ekte, virkelig; trofast, tro

trumpet ['trʌmpit] *n* trompet *m*

trunk [trʌŋk] *n* koffert *m*, stamme *m*; bagasjerom *nt*

trust [trʌst] *v* stole på; *n* tillit *m*

trustworthy ['trʌst,wəː(ð)i] *adj* pålitelig

truth [truːθ] *n* sannhet *c*

truthful ['truːθfəl] *adj* sannferdig

try [trai] *v* prøve, forsøke, anstrenge seg; *n* forsøk *nt*; ~ on prøve

tube [tjuːb] *n* rør *nt*; tube *m*

tuberculosis [tjuːˌbəːkjuˈlousis] *n* tuberkulose *m*

Tuesday ['tjuːzdi] tirsdag *m*

tug [tʌg] *v* taue; *n* slepebåt *m*; rykk *m*

tuition [tjuːˈiʃən] *n* undervisning *c*; skolepenger *pl*

tulip ['tjuːlip] *n* tulipan *m*

tumo(u)r ['tjuːmə] *n* svulst *m*

tuna ['tjuːnə] *n* (pl ~, ~s) tunfisk *m*

tune [tjuːn] *n* melodi *m*; ~ in stille inn

tuneful ['tjuːnfəl] *adj* melodisk

tunic ['tjuːnik] *n* tunika *m*

Tunisia [tjuːˈniziə] Tunisia

Tunisian [tjuːˈnizien] *adj* tunisisk; *n* tunisier *m*

tunnel ['tʌnəl] *n* tunnel *m*

turbine ['təːbain] *n* turbin *m*

turbojet [ˌtəːbouˈdʒet] *n* turbojet *m*

Turkey ['təːki] Tyrkia

turkey ['təːki] *n* kalkun *m*

Turkish ['təːkiʃ] *adj* tyrkisk; ~ bath romerbad *nt*

turn [təːn] *v* dreie; vende, svinge, *vri om; *n* dreining *m*, vending *c*; sving *m*; tur *m*; ~ back vende tilbake; ~ down forkaste; ~ into forvandles til; ~ off stenge av; ~ on *sette på; skru på; ~ over vende om; ~ round snu; snu seg

turning ['təːniŋ] *n* sving *m*

turning point ['təːniŋpoint] *n* vendepunkt *nt*

turnover ['təːˌnouvə] *n* omsetning *m*; ~ tax moms *m*

turnpike ['təːnpaik] *nAm* bomvei *m*

turpentine ['tə:pəntain] n
terpentin n

turtle ['tə:təl] n skilpadde c

tutor ['tju:tə] n huslærer m

tuxedo [tʌk'si:dou] nAm (pl
~s, ~es) smoking m

TV [,ti'vi:] n colloquial TV
m; on ~ på TV

tweed [twi:d] n tweed m

tweezers ['twi:zəz] pl
pinsett m

twelfth [twelfθ] num tolvte

twelve [twelv] num tolv

twentieth ['twentiəθ] num
tyvende

twenty ['twenti] num tyve

twice [twais] adv to ganger

twig [twig] n kvist m

twilight ['twailait] n
skumring c

twine [twain] n hyssing m

twins [twinz] pl tvillinger pl

twist [twist] v sno; *vri;
vridning m

two [tu:] num to

two-piece [,tu:'pi:s] adj
todelt

type [taip] v *skrive på data;
taste; n type m

typhoid ['taifɔid] n tyfus m

typical ['tipikəl] adj typisk

tyrant ['taiərənt] n tyrann m

tyre [taiə] n dekk nt; ~
pressure lufttrykk nt

U

ugly ['ʌgli] adj stygg

ulcer ['ʌlsə] n magesår nt

ultimate ['ʌltimət] adj siste

ultraviolet [,ʌltrə'vaiələt]
adj ultrafiolett

umbrella [ʌm'brelə] n
paraply m

umpire ['ʌmpaiə] n dommer
m

unable [ʌ'neibəl] adj ute av
stand til

unacceptable
[,ʌnək'septəbəl] adj
uakseptabel

unaccountable
[,ʌnə'kauntəbəl] adj
uforklarlig; uansvarlig

unaccustomed
[,ʌnə'kʌstəmd] adj uvant

unanimous [ju:'næniməs]
adj enstemmig

unanswered [,ʌ'nɑ:nsəd]
adj ubesvart

unauthorized
[,ʌ'nɔ:θəraizd] adj uten
fullmakt

unavoidable
[,ʌnə'vɔidəbəl] adj
uunngåelig

unaware [,ʌnə'weə] adj
ubevisst

unbearable [ʌn'beərəbəl]
adj uutholdelig

unbreakable [ʌn'breikəbəl]
adj uknuselig

unbroken [,ʌn'broukən] adj
intakt

unbutton [,ʌn'bʌtən] v

knappe opp
uncertain [ʌn'sɜːtən] adj
uviss, usikker
uncle ['ʌŋkəl] n onkel m
uncomfortable
[ʌn'kʌmfətəbəl] adj
ubekvem
uncommon [ʌn'kɔmən] adj
usedvanlig, sjelden
unconditional
[ʌnkən'diʃənəl] adj
betingelsesløs
unconscious [ʌn'kɔnʃəs]
adj bevisstløs
uncork [ʌn'kɔːk] v *trekke
opp
uncover [ʌn'kʌvə] v
avdekke
uncultivated
[ʌn'kʌltiveitid] adj
udyrket
under ['ʌndə] prep under,
nedenfor
undercurrent
['ʌndəˌkʌrənt] n
understrøm m
underestimate
[ʌndə'restimeit] v
undervurdere
underground
['ʌndəgraund] adj
underjordisk; n
undergrunnsbane m
underline [ʌndə'lain] v
understreke
underneath [ʌndə'niːθ] adv
nedenunder
underpants ['ʌndəpænts]
plAm truse c
*understand [ʌndə'stænd]

v *forstå, fatte
understanding
[ʌndə'stændiŋ] n
forståelse m
understate [ʌndə'steit] v
underdrive
understatement
[ʌndə'steitmənt] n
underdrivelse m
*undertake [ʌndə'teik] v
*gå i gang med
undertaking [ʌndə'teikiŋ]
n foretak nt
underwater ['ʌndəˌwɔːtə]
adj undervanns-
underwear ['ʌndəweə] n
undertøy pl
undesirable
[ʌndi'zaiərəbəl] adj
uønsket
*undo [ʌn'duː] v åpne, løse
opp
undoubtedly [ʌn'dautidli]
adv utvilsomt
undress [ʌn'dres] v kle av
seg
unearned [ʌ'nɜːnd] adj
ufortjent
uneasy [ʌ'niːzi] adj urolig
uneducated
[ʌ'nedjukeitid] adj uten
utdannelse
unemployed [ʌnim'plɔid]
adj arbeidsløs; arbeidsledig
unemployment
[ʌnim'plɔimənt] n
arbeidsløshet c;
arbeidsledighet c
unequal [ʌ'niːkwəl] adj
ulik

uneven [ˌʌ'niːvən] adj ulik, ujevn

unexpected [ˌʌnik'spektid] adj uventet

unfair [ʌn'feə] adj urettferdig

unfaithful [ˌʌn'feiθfəl] adj utro

unfamiliar [ˌʌnfə'miljə] adj ukjent

unfasten [ˌʌn'fɑːsən] v løse, løsne

unfavo(u)rable [ˌʌn'feivərəbəl] adj ugunstig

unfit [ˌʌn'fit] adj uegnet

unfold [ʌn'fould] v brette ut, folde ut

unfortunate [ʌn'fɔːtʃənət] adj uheldig

unfortunately [ʌn'fɔːtʃənətli] adv uheldigvis, dessverre

unfriendly [ˌʌn'frendli] adj uvennlig

ungrateful [ʌn'greitfəl] adj utakknemlig

unhappy [ʌn'hæpi] adj ulykkelig

unhealthy [ʌn'helθi] adj usunn

unhurt [ˌʌn'hɜːt] adj uskadd

uniform ['juːnifɔːm] n uniform c; adj ensartet

unimportant [ˌʌnim'pɔːtənt] adj uviktig

uninhabitable [ˌʌnin'hæbitəbəl] adj ubeboelig

uninhabited [ˌʌnin'hæbitid]

adj ubebodd

unintentional [ˌʌnin'tenʃənəl] adj utilsiktet

union ['juːnjən] n fagforening c; union m, forbund nt

unique [juː'niːk] adj enestående

unit ['juːnit] n enhet m

unite [juː'nait] v forene; united adj forent

United States [juː'naitid steits] De forente stater

unity ['juːnəti] n enhet m

universal [ˌjuːni'vɜːsəl] adj universell, generell

universe ['juːnivɜːs] n univers nt

university [ˌjuːni'vɜːsəti] n universitet nt

unjust [ʌn'dʒʌst] adj urettferdig

unkind [ʌn'kaind] adj uvennlig; ukjærlig

unknown [ˌʌn'noun] adj ukjent

unlawful [ˌʌn'lɔːfəl] adj ulovlig

unless [ən'les] conj med mindre

unlike [ˌʌn'laik] adj forskjellig

unlikely [ʌn'laikli] adj usannsynlig

unlimited [ʌn'limitid] adj grenseløs, ubegrenset

unload [ˌʌn'loud] v lesse av

unlock [ˌʌn'lɔk] v lukke opp; låse opp

unlucky

376

unlucky [ʌnˈlʌki] adj
uheldig

unnecessary [ʌnˈnesəsəri]
adj unødvendig

unoccupied [ʌˈnɔkjupaid]
adj ledig

unofficial [ˌʌnəˈfiʃəl] adj
uoffisiell

unpack [ʌnˈpæk] v pakke
opp

unpleasant [ʌnˈplezənt] adj
utrivelig, ubehagelig;
usympatisk, utiltalende

unpopular [ˌʌnˈpɔpjulə] adj
upopulær

unprotected [ˌʌnprəˈtektid]
adj ubeskyttet

unqualified [ˌʌnˈkwɔlifaid]
adj ukvalifisert

unreal [ˌʌnˈriəl] adj
uvirkelig

unreasonable
[ʌnˈriːzənəbəl] adj urimelig

unreliable [ˌʌnriˈlaiəbəl] adj
upålitelig

unrest [ˌʌnˈrest] n uro m;
rastløshet c

unsafe [ˌʌnˈseif] adj
usikker, utrygg

unsatisfactory
[ˌʌnsætisˈfæktəri] adj
utilfredsstillende

unscrew [ˌʌnˈskruː] v skru
løs

unselfish [ˌʌnˈselfiʃ] adj
uselvisk

unskilled [ˌʌnˈskild] adj
ufaglært

unsound [ˌʌnˈsaund] adj
usunn

unstable [ˌʌnˈsteibəl] adj
ustabil

unsteady [ˌʌnˈstedi] adj
ustø; ustadig

unsuccessful
[ˌʌnsəkˈsesfəl] adj
mislykket

unsuitable [ˌʌnˈsuːtəbəl]
adj uegnet

unsurpassed [ˌʌnsəˈpɑːst]
adj uovertruffen

untidy [ˌʌnˈtaidi] adj
uordentlig

untie [ˌʌnˈtai] v knytte opp

until [ənˈtil] prep inntil, til

untrue [ˌʌnˈtruː] adj usann

untrustworthy
[ˌʌnˈtrʌstˌwəːði] adj
upålitelig

unusual [ʌnˈjuːʒuəl] adj
uvanlig, ualminnelig

unwell [ˌʌnˈwel] adj uvel

unwilling [ˌʌnˈwiliŋ] adj
uvillig

unwise [ˌʌnˈwaiz] adj uklok

unwrap [ˌʌnˈræp] v pakke
opp

up [ʌp] adv opp, oppover

upholster [ʌpˈhoulstə] v
*trekke, polstre

upkeep [ˈʌpkiːp] n
vedlikehold nt

uplands [ˈʌpləndz] pl
høyland nt

upload [ˈʌpˌloud] v laste
opp

upon [əˈpɔn] prep på

upper [ˈʌpə] adj øvre, over-

upright [ˈʌprait] adj rank;
rett; loddrett

*upset [ʌp'set] v forstyrre; adj opprørt

upside down [,ʌpsaid'daun] adv på hodet; opp ned

upstairs [,ʌp'stɛəz] adv ovenpå

upstream [,ʌp'striːm] adv mot strømmen

upwards ['ʌpwədz] adv oppover

urban ['əːbən] adj by-

urge [əːdʒ] v formane; n trang m

urgency ['əːdʒənsi] n innstendighet c; viktighet c

urgent ['əːdʒənt] adj presserende

urine ['juərin] n urin m

Uruguay ['juərəgwai] Uruguay

Uruguayan [,juərə'gwaiən] adj uruguayansk; n uruguayaner m

us [ʌs] pron oss

usable ['juːzəbəl] adj

anvendelig

usage ['juːzidʒ] n sedvane m; bruk m

use¹ [juːz] v bruke; *be used to *være vant til; ~ up bruke opp

use² [juːs] n bruk m; nytte c; *be of ~ *være til nytte

useful ['juːsfəl] adj nyttig, brukbar

useless ['juːsləs] adj unyttig

user ['juːzə] n bruker m

usher ['ʌʃə] n vise veien

usual ['juːʒuəl] adj vanlig

usually ['juːʒuəli] adv vanligvis

utensil [juː'tensəl] n redskap m; kjøkkenredskap nt

utility [juː'tiləti] n nytte c

utilize ['juːtilaiz] v anvende

utmost ['ʌtmoust] adj ytterst

utter ['ʌtə] adj total, fullstendig; v ytre

V

vacancy ['veikənsi] n ledig stilling

vacant ['veikənt] adj ledig

vacation [və'keiʃən] n ferie m

vaccinate ['væksineit] v vaksinere

vaccination [,væksi'neiʃən] n vaksinering c

vacuum ['vækjuəm] n

vakuum nt; vAm støvsuge; ~ cleaner støvsuger m

vague [veig] adj vag

vain [vein] adj forfengelig; forgjeves; in ~ forgjeves

valid ['vælid] adj gyldig

valley ['væli] n dal m

valuable ['væljubəl] adj verdifull; valuables pl verdisaker pl

value ['vælju:] n verdi m; v
taksere, vurdere

valve [vælv] n ventil m

van [væn] n varebil m

vanilla [və'nilə] n vanilje m

vanish ['væniʃ] v *forsvinne

vapo(u)r ['veipə] n damp m

variable ['vɛəriəbəl] adj
variabel

variation [,vɛəri'eiʃən] n
avveksling c; forandring c

variety [və'raiəti] n utvalg nt

various ['vɛəriəs] adj
forskjellige, diverse

varnish ['vɑ:niʃ] n lakk m; v
lakkere

vary ['vɛəri] v variere;
forandre; *være forskjellig

vase [vɑ:z] n vase m

vast [vɑ:st] adj vidstrakt,
umåtelig

vault [vɔ:lt] n hvelving m;
bankhvelv nt

veal [vi:l] n kalvekjøtt nt

vegetable ['vedʒətəbəl] n
grønnsak c; ~ merchant
grønnsakshandler m

vegetarian [,vedʒi'tɛəriən]
n vegetarianer m

vegetation [,vedʒi'teiʃən] n
vegetasjon m

vehicle ['vi:əkəl] n kjøretøy
nt

veil [veil] n slør nt

vein [vein] n åre c; varicose
~ åreknute m

velvet ['velvit] n fløyel m

velveteen [,velvi'ti:n] n
bomullsfløyel m

venerable ['venərəbəl] adj
ærverdig

venereal disease [vi'niəriəl
di'zi:z] kjønnssykdom m

Venezuela [,veni'zweilə]
Venezuela

Venezuelan [,veni'zweilən]
adj venezuelansk; n
venezuelaner m

ventilate ['ventileit] v
ventilere; lufte, lufte ut

ventilation [,venti'leiʃən] n
ventilasjon m; utluftning m

ventilator ['ventileitə] n
ventilator m

venture ['ventʃə] v våge

veranda [və'rændə] n
veranda m

verb [və:b] n verb nt

verbal ['və:bəl] adj muntlig

verdict ['və:dikt] n
kjennelse m, dom m

verify ['verifai] v kontrollere

verse [və:s] n vers nt

version ['və:ʃən] n versjon
m

versus ['və:səs] prep kontra

vertical ['və:tikəl] adj
vertikal

very ['veri] adv svært,
meget; adj eksakt, virkelig;
absolutt

vessel ['vesəl] n fartøy nt;
kar nt

vest [vest] n undertrøye c;
vest m

veterinary surgeon
['vetrinəri 'sə:dʒən]
dyrlege m

via [vaiə] prep via

vibrate [vai'breit] v vibrere

vibration [vai'breiʃən] n
vibrasjon m

vicar ['vikə] n sogneprest m

vicarage ['vikəridʒ] n
prestegård m

vice president
[,vais'prezidənt] n
visepresident m

vicinity [vi'sinəti] n nabolag
nt, nærhet c

vicious ['viʃəs] adj
ondskapsfull

victim ['viktim] n offer nt

victory ['viktəri] n seier m

video camera
['vidiou'kæmərə] n video-
kamera nt

video cassette
['vidiou'kæset] n
videokassett m

video recorder ['vidiou
ri'kɔːdə] n video-spiller m

view [vjuː] n utsikt m;
oppfatning m, syn; v
betrakte

viewfinder ['vjuː,faində] n
søker m

vigilant ['vidʒilənt] adj
årvåken

villa ['vilə] n villa m

village ['vilidʒ] n landsby m;
bygd c

villain ['vilən] n skurk m

vine [vain] n vinranke c

vinegar ['vinigə] n eddik m

vintage ['vintidʒ] n vinhøst
m; årgang m

violation [vaiə'leiʃən] n
krenkelse m

violence ['vaiələns] n vold

m

violent ['vaiələnt] adj
voldsom, heftig

violet ['vaiələt] n fiol m; adj
fiolett, lilla

violin [vaiə'lin] n fiolin m

virgin ['vəːdʒin] n jomfru c

virtue ['vəːtʃuː] n dyd m

virus ['vairəs] n virus nt

visa ['viːzə] n visum nt

visibility [,vizə'biləti] n sikt
m

visible ['vizəbəl] adj synlig

vision ['viʒən] n syn

visit ['vizit] v besøke; n
besøk nt, visitt m; visiting
hours besøkstid c

visitor ['vizitə] n besøkende
m

vital ['vaitəl] adj vesentlig

vitamin ['vitəmin] n vitamin
nt

vivid ['vivid] adj livfull

vocabulary [və'kæbjuləri] n
ordforråd nt; ordliste c

vocal ['voukəl] adj vokal

vocalist ['voukəlist] n
sanger m

voice [vɔis] n stemme m

voice mail ['vɔis,meil] n
voicemail c

void [vɔid] adj ugyldig

volcano [vɔl'keinou] n (pl
~es, ~s) vulkan m

volt [voult] n volt m

voltage ['voultidʒ] n
spenning m

volume ['vɔljum] n volum
nt; bind nt

voluntary ['vɔləntəri] adj

frivillig

volunteer [ˌvɔlən'tiə] *n*
frivillig *m*

vomit ['vɔmit] *v* kaste opp,
*brekke seg

vote [vout] *v* stemme; *n*
stemme *m*; avstemning *m*

voucher ['vautʃə] *n* bong *m*

vow [vau] *n* løfte *nt*, ed *m*; *v*

*sverge

vowel [vauəl] *n* vokal *m*

voyage ['vɔiidʒ] *n* reise *c*

vulgar ['vʌlgə] *adj* vulgær;
simpel, ordinær

vulnerable ['vʌlnərəbəl] *adj*
sårbar

vulture ['vʌltʃə] *n* gribb *m*

W

wade [weid] *v* vasse

waffle ['wɔfəl] *n* vaffel *m*

wages ['weidʒiz] *pl* lønn *c*

wag(g)on ['wægən] *n*
godsvogn *c*; vogn *c*

waist [weist] *n* midje *c*

waistcoat ['weiskout] *n* vest
m

wait [weit] *v* vente; ~ **on**
oppvarte

waiter ['weitə] *n* kelner *m*,
servitør *m*

waiting ['weitiŋ] *n* venting
c; ~ **list** venteliste *c*; ~
room venteværelse *nt*

waitress ['weitris] *n*
(kvinnelig) servitør *m*

wake [weik] *v* vekke; ~ **up**
våkne

walk [wɔ:k] *v* *gå; spasere; *n*
spasertur *m*; gange *m*;
walking til fots

walker ['wɔ:kə] *n* turgjenger
m

walking stick ['wɔ:kiŋstik]
n spaserstokk *m*

wall [wɔ:l] *n* mur *m*; vegg *m*

wallet ['wɔlit] *n* lommebok
c

wallpaper ['wɔ:l,peipə] *n*
tapet *nt*

walnut ['wɔ:lnʌt] *n* valnøtt *c*

waltz [wɔ:ls] *n* vals *m*

wander ['wɔndə] *v* flakke,
vandre

want [wɔnt] *v* *ville; ønske;
n behov *nt*; mangel *m*

war [wɔ:] *n* krig *m*

wardrobe ['wɔ:droub] *n*
klesskap *nt*, garderobe *m*

warehouse ['wɛəhaus] *n*
pakkhus *nt*, lagerbygning
m

wares [wɛəz] *pl* varer *pl*

warm [wɔ:m] *adj* varm; *v*
varme

warmth [wɔ:mθ] *n* varme *m*

warn [wɔ:n] *v* advare

warning ['wɔ:niŋ] *n*
advarsel *m*

wary ['wɛəri] *adj* forsiktig

was [wɔz] *v* (p be)

wash [wɔʃ] *v* vaske; ~ **and
wear** strykefri; ~ **up** vaske

opp

washable ['wɔʃəbəl] *adj* vaskbar

washbasin ['wɔʃ,beisən] *n* håndvask *m*

washing ['wɔʃiŋ] *n* vask *m*; ~ **machine** vaskemaskin *m*; ~ **powder** vaskepulver *nt*

washroom ['wɔʃru:m] *nAm* toalett *nt*

wasp [wɔsp] *n* veps *m*

waste [weist] *v* sløse bort; *n* sløseri *nt*; *adj* øde; ~ **separation** kildesortering *c*

wasteful ['weistfəl] *adj* ødsel

wastepaper basket [weist'peipə,bɑ:skit] *n* papirkurv *m*

watch [wɔtʃ] *v* betrakte, *iaktta; bevokte; *n* ur *nt*; ~ **for** *holde utkikk etter; ~ **out** *være forsiktig

watchmaker ['wɔtʃ,meikə] *n* urmaker *m*

watchstrap ['wɔtʃstræp] *n* klokkerem *c*

water ['wɔ:tə] *n* vann *nt*; iced ~ isvann *nt*; running ~ innlagt vann; ~ **ski** vannski *c*

watercolo(u)r ['wɔ:tə,kʌlə] *n* vannfarge *m*; akvarell *m*

waterfall ['wɔ:təfɔ:l] *n* foss *m*

watermelon ['wɔ:tə,melən] *n* vannmelon *m*

waterproof ['wɔ:təpru:f] *adj* vanntett

watt [wɔt] *n* watt *m*

wave [weiv] *n* bølge *c*; *v* vinke

wavelength ['weivleŋθ] *n* bølgelengde *m*

wavy ['weivi] *adj* bølget

wax [wæks] *n* voks *m*

waxworks ['wækswɔ:ks] *pl* vokskabinett *nt*

way [wei] *n* vis *nt*, måte *m*; vei *m*; retning *m*; avstand *m*; any ~ på hvilken som helst måte; by the ~ forresten; out of the ~ avsides; the other ~ round tvert om; ~ **back** fjern fortid; ~ **in** inngang *m*; ~ **out** utgang *m*; one-way traffic enveiskjøring *c*

wayside ['weisaid] *n* veikant *m*

we [wi:] *pron* vi

weak [wi:k] *adj* svak; tynn

weakness ['wi:knəs] *n* svakhet *c*

wealth [welθ] *n* rikdom *m*

wealthy ['welθi] *adj* rik

weapon ['wepən] *n* våpen *nt*

wear [wɛə] *v* *ha på seg; ~ **out** *slite ut

weary ['wiəri] *adj* trett, sliten

weather ['weðə] *n* vær *nt*; ~ **forecast** værmelding *c*

weave [wi:v] *v* veve

website ['web,sait] *n* nettsted *nt*

wedding ['wediŋ] *n* vielse *m*, bryllup *nt*; ~ **ring** vielsesring *m*

wedge [wedʒ] *n* kile *m*

Wednesday ['wenzdi] onsdag *m*

weed [wi:d] n ugress nt

week [wi:k] n uke c

weekday ['wi:kdei] n
hverdag m

weekend ['wi:kend] n helg c

weekly ['wi:kli] adj ukentlig

*weep [wi:p] v *gråte

weigh [wei] v veie

weight [weit] n vekt c

Welch [welʃ] adj walisisk

welcome ['welkəm] adj
velkommen; n velkomst m;
v hilse velkommen

weld [weld] v sveise

welfare ['welfɛə] n velferd m

well¹ [wel] adv godt; adj
frisk; as ~ også; as ~ as så
vel som; well! ja vel!

well² [wel] n kilde m; brønn
m

well-founded [,wel'faundid]
adj velbegrunnet

well-known ['welnoun] adj
velkjent

well-to-do [,weltə'du:] adj
velhavende

went [went] v (p go)

were [wə:] v (p be)

west [west] n vest m

westerly ['westəli] adj
vestlig

western ['westən] adj
vestlig

wet [wet] adj våt; fuktig

whale [weil] n hval m

wharf [wɔ:f] n (pl ~s,
wharves) kai c

what [wɔt] pron hva; ~ for
hvorfor

whatever [wɔ'tevə] pron

wheat [wi:t] n hvete m

wheel [wi:l] n hjul nt

wheelbarrow ['wi:l,bærou]
n trillebår c

wheelchair ['wi:ltʃɛə] n
rullestol m

when [wen] adv når; conj
når, da

whenever [we'nevə] conj
når enn; alltid når

where [wɛə] adv hvor; conj
hvor

wherever [wɛə'revə] conj
hvor enn

whether ['weðə] conj om;
whether ... or om ... eller

which [witʃ] pron hvilken;
som

whichever [wi'tʃevə] adj
hvilken som helst

while [wail] conj mens; n
stund c

whim [wim] n innfall nt,
nykke nt

whip [wip] n pisk m; v vispe

whiskers ['wiskəz] pl
kinnskjegg nt

whisper ['wispə] v hviske; n
hvisking c

whistle ['wisəl] v plystre; n
fløyte c

white [wait] adj hvit

whiting ['waitiŋ] n (pl ~)
hvitting c

wit [wit] n vidd nt

who [hu:] pron hvem; som

whoever [hu:'evə] pron
hvem (som) enn

whole [houl] adj fullstendig,

hel; uskadd; n hele nt

wholesale ['houlseil] n
engroshandel m; ~ dealer
grosserer m

wholesome ['houlsəm] adj
sunn

wholly ['houlli] adv helt

whom [hu:m] pron til hvem

whore [hɔ:] n hore c

whose [hu:z] pron hvis

why [wai] adv hvorfor

wicked ['wikid] adj ond

wide [waid] adj bred, vid

widen ['waidən] v utvide

widow ['widou] n enke c

widower ['widouə] n
enkemann m

width [widθ] n bredde m

wife [waif] n (pl wives) kone c

wig [wig] n parykk m

wild [waild] adj vill

will [wil] n vilje m;
testamente nt

*will [wil] v *vil

willing ['wiliŋ] adj villig

willow ['wilou] n pil c

willpower ['wilpauə] n
viljestyrke m

*win [win] v *vinne

wind [wind] n vind m

*wind [waind] v sno seg;
*trekke opp, vikle

winding ['waindiŋ] adj
buktet

windmill ['windmil] n
vindmølle c

window ['windou] n vindu
nt

windowsill ['windousil] n
vinduskarm m

windscreen ['windskri:n] n
frontrute c; ~ wiper
vindusvisker m

windshield ['windʃi:ld]
nAm frontrute c; ~ wiper
Am vindusvisker m

windy ['windi] adj vindhard

wine [wain] n vin m; ~ cellar
vinkjeller m; ~ list vinkart
nt

wing [wiŋ] n vinge m

winner ['winə] n vinner m

winning ['winiŋ] adj
vinnende; winnings pl
gevinst m

winter ['wintə] n vinter m; ~
sports vintersport m

wipe [waip] v tørke, tørke
bort; tørke av

wire [waiə] n wire m, vaier
m; ståltråd m

wireless ['waiələs] adj
trådløs

wisdom ['wizdəm] n visdom
m

wise [waiz] adj vis

wish [wiʃ] v lenges etter,
ønske; n ønske nt, lengsel
m

witch [witʃ] n heks c

with [wið] prep med; hos; av

*withdraw [wið'drɔ:] v
*trekke tilbake

*withhold [wið'hould] v
*holde tilbake

within [wi'ðin] prep
innenfor; adv innvendig;
innen

without [wi'ðaut] prep uten

witness ['witnəs] n vitne nt

wits [wits] *pl* forstand *m*

witty ['witi] *adj* vittig;
spirituell

WMD ['dʌbəlju:'em'di:] *n*,
weapons of mass
destruction
masseødeleggelsesvåpen *nt*

wolf [wulf] *n* (pl wolves) ulv
m

woman ['wumən] *n* (pl
women) kvinne *c*

womb [wu:m] *n* livmor *c*

won [wʌn] *v* (p, pp win)

wonder ['wʌndə] *n* under
nt; forundring *c*; *v* undre
seg

wonderful ['wʌndəfəl] *adj*
skjønn, vidunderlig; herlig

wood [wud] *n* trevirke *nt*;
skog *m*; ~ carving
treskjærerarbeid *nt*

wooded ['wudid] *adj*
skogkledd

wooden ['wudən] *adj* tre-; ~
shoe tresko *m*

woodland ['wudlənd] *n*
skogsområde *nt*

wool [wul] *n* ull *c*

wool(l)en ['wulən] *adj* ull-

word [wə:d] *n* ord *nt*

wore [wɔ:] *v* (p wear)

work [wə:k] *n* arbeid *nt*; *v*
arbeide; virke, fungere;
working day arbeidsdag
m; ~ of art kunstverk *nt*; ~
permit arbeidstillatelse *m*

workaholic [,wə:kə'holik] *n*
arbeidsnarkoman *c*

worker ['wə:kə] *n* arbeider
m

workman ['wə:kmən] *n* (pl
-men) arbeider *m*

works [wə:ks] *pl* fabrikk *m*

workshop ['wə:kʃɔp] *n*
verksted *nt*

world [wə:ld] *n* verden *m*; ~
war verdenskrig *m*

world-famous
[,wə:ld'feiməs] *adj*
verdensberømt

world-wide ['wə:ldwaid] *adj*
verdensomspennende

worm [wə:m] *n* mark *m*

worn [wɔ:n] *adj* (pp wear)
slitt

worn-out [,wɔ:n'aut] *adj*
utslitt

worried ['wʌrid] *adj*
bekymret

worry ['wʌri] *v* bekymre
seg; *n* bekymring *c*

worse [wə:s] *adj* verre; *adv*
verre

worship ['wə:ʃip] *v* *tilbe; *n*
gudstjeneste *m*

worst [wə:st] *adj* verst; *adv*
verst

worth [wə:θ] *n* verd *nt*; *be ~
*være verd; *be worth-
while *være umaken verd

worthless ['wə:θləs] *adj*
verdiløs

worthy of ['wə:ði ɔv] verdig

would [wud] *v* (p will)

wound¹ [wu:nd] *n* sår *nt*; *v*
såre

wound² [waund] *v* (p, pp
wind)

wrap [ræp] *v* pakke inn

wreck [rek] *n* vrak *nt*; *v*

*ødelegge
wrench [rentʃ] *n*
skrunøkkel *m*; rykk *nt*; *v*
*vri
wrinkle ['riŋkəl] *n* rynke *c*
wrist [rist] *n* håndledd *nt*
wristwatch ['ristwɔtʃ] *n*
armbåndsur *nt*
*write [rait] *v* *skrive; in
writing skriftlig; ~ down
*skrive ned

writer ['raitə] *n* forfatter *m*
writing pad ['raitiŋpæd] *n*
skriveblokk *c*
writing paper ['raitiŋ,peipə]
n skrivepapir *nt*
written ['ritən] *adj* (pp
write) skriftlig
wrong [rɔŋ] *adj* gal, uriktig;
n urett *m*; *v* *gjøre urett;
*be ~ *ta feil
wrote [rout] *v* (p write)

X

Xmas ['krisməs] jul *c*
X-ray ['eksrei] *n*

røntgenbilde *nt*; *v*
røntgenfotografere

Y

yacht [jɔt] *n* lystbåt *m*; ~
club seilforening *c*
yachting ['jɔtiŋ] *n* seilsport
m
yard [jɑːd] *n* gårdsplass *m*;
hage *c*
yarn [jɑːn] *n* garn *nt*
yawn [jɔːn] *v* gjespe
year [jiə] *n* år *nt*
yearly ['jiəli] *adj* årlig
yeast [jiːst] *n* gjær *m*
yell [jel] *v* hyle; *n* hyl *nt*
yellow ['jelou] *adj* gul
yes [jes] ja
yesterday ['jestədi] *adv* i
går
yet [jet] *adv* ennå; *conj*
likevel, allikevel
yield [jiːld] *v* yte; *vike

yoghurt ['jɔgət] *n* yoghurt,
jogurt *m*
yoke [jouk] *n* åk *nt*
yolk [jouk] *n* eggeplomme *c*
you [juː] *pron* du; deg; dere
young [jʌŋ] *adj* ung
your [jɔː] *pron* din; dine,
deres
yours [jɔːz] *pron* din; dine,
deres
yourself [jɔː'self] *pron* deg;
selv
yourselves [jɔː'selvz] *pron*
dere; selv
youth [juːθ] *n* ungdom *m*; ~
hostel ungdomsherberge
nt; vandrerhjem *nt*
yuppie ['jʌpi] *n* japp *c*

Z

zeal [zi:l] *n* iver *m*

zealous ['zeləs] *adj* ivrig

zebra ['zi:brə] *n* sebra *m*

zenith ['zeniθ] *n* senit *nt*; høydepunkt *nt*

zero ['ziərou] *n* (pl ~s) null *nt*

zest [zest] *n* lyst *c*; iver *m*

zinc [ziŋk] *n* sink *m*

zip [zip] *n* glidelås *m*; ~ code *Am* postnummer *nt*

zipper ['zipə] *n* glidelås *m*

zodiac ['zoudiæk] *n* dyrekretsen

zone [zoun] *n* sone *c*; område *nt*

zoo [zu:] *n* (pl ~s) dyrehage *m*

zoology [zou'ɔlədʒi] *n* zoologi *m*

Some Basic Phrases	Noen vanlige uttrykk
Hello!	Hei!
Please.	Vær så snill.
Thank you very much.	Tusen takk.
Don't mention it.	Ingen årsak.
Good morning.	God morgen.
Good afternoon.	God dag.
Good evening.	God kveld.
Good night.	God natt.
Good-bye.	Ha det (bra)!
See you later.	Vi ses!
Where is/Where are…?	Hvor er…?
What do you call this?	Hva heter (kalles) dette?
What does that mean?	Hva betyr det?
Do you speak English?	Snakker du engelsk?
Do you speak German?	Snakker du tysk?
Do you speak French?	Snakker du fransk?
Do you speak Spanish?	Snakker du spansk?
Do you speak Italian?	Snakker du italiensk?
Could you speak more slowly, please?	Kunne du snakke litt langsommere?
I don't understand.	Jeg forstår ikke.
Can I have…?	Kan jeg få…?
Can you show me…?	Kan du vise meg…?
Can you tell me…?	Kan du si meg…?
Can you help me, please?	Kan du være så vennlig å hjelpe meg?
I'd like…	Jeg ville gjerne ha…
We'd like…	Vi ville gjerne ha…
Please give me…	Vær så snill å gi meg…
Please bring me…	Vær så snill å la meg få…
I'm hungry.	Jeg er sulten.
I'm thirsty.	Jeg er tørst.
I'm lost.	Jeg har gått meg vill.
Hurry up!	Skynd deg!
There is/There are…	Det finnes…
There isn't/There aren't…	Det finnes ikke…

Arrival

Your passport, please.
Have you anything to
declare?
No, nothing at all.
Can you help me with my
luggage, please?
Where's the bus to the centre
of town, please?
This way, please.
Where can I get a taxi?

What's the fare to…?
Take me to this address,
please.
I'm in a hurry.

Hotel

My name is…
Have you a reservation?
I'd like a room with a bath.

What's the price per night?
May I see the room?
What's my room number,
please?
There's no hot water.
May I see the manager,
please?
Did anyone telephone me?

Is there any mail for me?
May I have my bill (check),
please?

Eating out

Do you have a fixed-price
menu?

Ankomst

Passet, takk.
Har du noe å fortolle?

Nei, ingenting.
Kan du hjelpe meg med
bagasjen?
Hvor tar man bussen til
sentrum?
Denne veien.
Hvor kan jeg få tak i en
drosje?
Hva koster det til…?
Vær så snill å kjøre meg til
denne adressen.
Jeg har det travelt.

Hotell

Mitt navn er…
Har du bestilt?
Jeg vil gjerne ha et rom med
bad.
Hva koster det for en natt?
Kan jeg få se rommet?
Hvilket værelsesnummer har
jeg?
Det er ikke noe varmt vann.
Kan jeg få snakke med
direktøren?
Har det vært noen telefon til
meg?
Er det noe post til meg?
Kan jeg få regningen, takk.

Restaurant

Har dere en fast meny?

May I see the menu?	Kan jeg få se spisekartet?
May we have an ashtray, please?	Kan vi få et askebeger, takk?
Where's the toilet, please?	Hvor er toalettet?
I'd like an hors d'œuvre (starter).	Jeg vil gjerne ha en forrett.
Have you any soup?	Har dere suppe?
I'd like some fish.	Jeg vil gjerne ha fisk.
What kind of fish do you have?	Hva slags fisk har dere?
I'd like a steak.	Jeg vil gjerne ha en biff.
What vegetables have you got?	Hvilke grønnsaker har dere?
Nothing more, thanks.	Takk, jeg er forsynt.
What would you like to drink?	Hva vil du ha å drikke?
I'll have a beer, please.	Jeg vil gjerne ha en øl, takk.
I'd like a bottle of wine.	Jeg vil gjerne ha en flaske vin.
May I have the bill (check), please?	Regningen, takk!
Is service included?	Er service inkludert?
Thank you, that was a very good meal.	Takk. Det smakte utmerket.

Travelling

På reise

Where's the railway station, please?	Hvor er jernbanestasjonen?
Where's the ticket office, please?	Unnskyld, kan du si meg hvor billettluken er?
I'd like a ticket to…	Jeg vil gjerne ha en billett til…
First or second class?	Første eller annen klasse?
First class, please.	Første, takk.
Single or return (one way or roundtrip)?	Enkeltbillett eller tur-retur?
Do I have to change trains?	Må jeg bytte tog?
What platform does the train for… leave from?	Fra hvilken plattform går toget til…?

Where's the nearest underground (subway) station?	Hvor er nærmeste undergrunnsstasjon?
Where's the bus station, please?	Hvor er buss-stasjonen?
When's the first bus to…?	Når går den første bussen til…?
Please let me off at the next stop.	Kan du slippe meg av på neste holdeplass?

Meeting people

Bekjentskap

How do you do.	God dag.
How are you?	Hvordan står det til?
Very well, thank you. And you?	Bare bra, takk. Og med deg?
May I introduce…?	Kan jeg få presentere…?
My name is…	Mitt navn er…
I'm very pleased to meet you.	Gleder meg (å treffe deg).
How long have you been here?	Hvor lenge har du vært her?
It was nice meeting you.	Det var hyggelig å treffe deg.
Do you mind if I smoke?	Har du noe imot at jeg røyker?
Do you have a light, please?	Unnskyld, kan du gi meg fyr?
May I get you a drink?	Kan jeg by deg på en drink?
May I invite you for dinner tonight?	Vil du spise middag med meg i kveld?
Where shall we meet?	Hvor skal vi møtes?

Emergencies

Ulykker

Call a doctor quickly.	Tilkall en lege – fort.
Call an ambulance.	Ring etter en sykebil.
Please call the police.	Tilkall politiet.

Norwegian Abbreviations

adm.dir.	*administrerende direktør*	managing director
alm.	*alminnelig(het)*	general(ly)
A/S	*aksjeselskap*	Ltd., Inc.
dvs.	*det vil si*	i.e.
e.Kr.	*etter Kristi fødsel*	A.D.
el.	*eller*	or
EU	*Den europeiske union*	European Union
f.eks.	*for eksempel*	e.g.
fj.	*fjord*	fjord
f.Kr.	*før Kristi fødsel*	B.C.
flt.	*flertall*	plural
FN	*De forente nasjoner*	UN, United Nations
gen.sekr.	*generalsekretær*	secretary general
...gt.	*gate*	street
iflg.	*ifølge*	according to
KFUK	*Kristelig Forening av Unge Kvinner*	YWCA, Young Women's Christian Association
KFUM	*Kristelig Forening av Unge Menn*	YMCA, Young Men's Christian Association
kl.	*klokken*	hour, o'clock
KNM	*Den Kongelige Norske Marine*	Royal Norwegian Navy
kr	*krone*	crown (currency)
LO	*Landsorganisasjonen i Norge*	Association of Norwegian Trade Unions
mht.	*med hensyn til*	concerning
moms	*meromsetningsskatt*	VAT, value added tax
mots.	*motsatt*	contrary
N	*Norge*	Norway
nr.	*nummer*	number
NRK	*Norsk Rikskringkasting*	Norwegian Broadcasting Service
NSB	*Norges Statsbaner*	Norwegian National Railways
NTB	*Norsk Telegrambyrå*	Norwegian News Agency

NUH	*Norske*	Norwegian Youth
	ungdomsherberger	Hostels
o.a.	*og annet, og andre*	etc., and others
osv.	*og så videre*	etc., and so on
stk.	*stykke(r)*	piece(s)
tlf.	*telefon*	telephone
...vn.	*veien, vegen*	road
årh.	*århundre*	century

Engelske forkortelser

A.D.	*anno Domini*	e.Kr.
Am.	*America; American*	Amerika; amerikansk
a.m.	*ante meridiem (before noon)*	mellom kl. 00.00 og 12.00
Amtrak	*American railroad corporation*	sammenslutning av private amerikanske jernbaneselskaper
Ave.	*avenue*	aveny
B.C.	*before Christ*	f.Kr.
Blvd.	*boulevard*	boulevard
B.R.	*British Rail*	Britiske statsbaner
Brit.	*Britain; British*	Storbritannia; britisk
Bros.	*brothers*	brødrene (i firmanavn)
¢	*cent*	1/100 dollar
Can.	*Canada; Canadian*	Canada; kanadisk
CID	*Criminal Investigation Department*	Det britiske kriminalpoliti
CNR	*Canadian National Railway*	Kanadiske statsbaner
c/o	*(in) care of*	adressert
Co.	*company*	kompani
Corp.	*corporation*	aksjeselskap *Am*
CPR	*Canadian Pacific Railways*	et privat kanadisk jernbaneselskap
D.C.	*District of Columbia*	Columbia-distriktet (Washington, D.C.)

DDS	Doctor of Dental Science	tannlege
e.g.	for instance	f.eks.
Eng.	England; English	England; engelsk
EU	European Union	Den europeiske union
ft.	foot/feet	fot (30,5 cm)
GB	Great Britain	Storbritannia
H.H.	His Holiness	Hans Hellighet
H.M.	His/her Majesty	Hans/Hennes Majestet
H.M.S.	Her Majesty's ship	britisk marineskip
hp	horsepower	hestekraft
i.e.	that is to say	dvs.
in.	inch	tomme (2,54 cm)
Inc.	incorporated	A/S
£	pound sterling	engelsk pund
L.A.	Los Angeles	Los Angeles
Ltd.	limited	A/S
M.D.	Doctor of Medicine	lege
M.P.	Member of Parliament	medlem av Det britisk parlament
mph	miles per hour	eng. mil i timen
Mr.	Mister	herr
Mrs.	Missis	fru
Ms.	Missis/Miss	fru/frk.
nat.	national	nasjonal
No.	number	nr.
N.Y.C.	New York City	byen New York
p.	page; penny/pence	side; $^1/_{100}$ pund
p.a.	per annum	pr. år
Ph.D.	Doctor of Philosophy	dr. philos.
p.m.	post meridiem (after noon)	mellom kl. 12.00 og 24.00
PO	Post Office	postkontor
P.T.O.	please turn over	vennligst bla om
RCMP	Royal Canadian Mounted Police	Det kongelige kanadiske ridende politi
Rd.	road	vei, veg
ref.	reference	referanse
Rev.	reverend	pastor
RFD	rural free delivery	postboks (på landsbygda)

RR	*railroad*	jernbane
RSVP	*please reply*	vennligst svar
$	*dollar*	dollar
Soc.	*society*	selskap
St.	*saint; street*	sankt; gate
STD	*Subscriber Trunk Dialling*	automattelefon
UN	*United Nations*	FN
US	*United States*	USA
USS	*United States Ship*	amerikansk marineskip
VAT	*value added tax*	med moms
VIP	*very important person*	betydningsfull person
Xmas	*Christmas*	jul
yd.	*yard*	yard (91,44 cm)
YMCA	*Young Men's Christian Association*	KFUM
YWCA	*Young Women's Christian Association*	KFUK
ZIP	*ZIP code*	postnummer

Mini Norwegian Grammar

Articles

Norwegian nouns are either masculine, feminine or neuter. The majority of feminine nouns also have a masculine form, so we have chosen to use the denotations *m* (masculine), *c* (common) and *n* (neuter). In this way, you will have to learn only two sets of articles, as masculine and common words can have the same article:

1. Indefinite article (a/an)

masculine*:	**en bil**	*a* car
common*:	**en dør**	*a* door
neuter:	**et eple**	*an* apple

2. Definite article (the)

Where we, in Engllsh, say "the house" Norwegians tag the definite article onto the end of the noun and say "house-the". In masculine and common nouns "the" is -**(e)n**, in neuter nouns -**(e)t**.

masculine:	**bilen**	*the* car
common*:	**døren**	*the* door
neuter:	**eplet**	*the* apple

Nouns

The plural of most nouns is formed by an -**(e)r** ending (indefinite plural) and an -**(e)ne** ending (definite plural).

masculine:	**biler**	cars	**bilene**	*the* cars
common*:	**dører**	doors	**dørene**	*the* doors
neuter:	**epler**	apples	**eplene**	*the* apples

Many monosyllabic nouns have irregular plurals.

en mann	a man	**menn**	men	**mennene**	the men
en sko	a shoe	**sko**	shoes	**skoene**	the shoes

---

* In the feminine form "a door, the door" would be *ei dør, døra*; the common form is *en dør, døren*. In plural there is no difference.

Adjectives

1. Adjectives agree with the noun in gender and number. For the indefinite form, the neuter is generally formed by adding **-t**, the plural by adding **-e**.

(en) stor hund	(a) big dog	**store hunder**	big dogs
(et) stort hus	(a) big house	**store hus**	big houses

2. The ending **-e** (masculine, common, neuter and plural) is used when the adjective is preceded by **den, det, de** (the definite article used with adjectives) or by a demonstrative or a possessive adjective.

den store hunden the big dog **det store huset** the big house
de store hundene the big dogs **de store husene** the big houses

3. Comparative and superlative

The comparative and superlative are normally formed either by adding the endings **-(e)re** and **-(e)st**, respectively, to the adjective or by putting **mer** (more) and **mest** (most) before the adjective.

stor/større/størst	big/bigger/biggest
lett/lettere/lettest	easy/easier/easiest
imponerende/*mer* imponerende/*mest* imponerende	impressive/more impressive/the most impressive

4. Possessive adjectives agree in number and gender with the noun they modify, i.e. with the thing possessed and not the possessor.

	common	neuter	plural
my	**min**	**mitt**	**mine**
your	**din**	**ditt**	**dine**
his	**sin, hans**	**sitt, hans**	**sine, hans**
her	**sin, hennes**	**sitt, hennes**	**sine, hennes**
its	**sin, dens/dets***	**sitt, dens/dets**	**sine, dens/dets**
our	**vår**	**vårt**	**våre**
their	**sin, deres**	**sitt, deres**	**sine, deres**

---

* Use **dens** if "it" is of common gender and **dets** if "it" is neuter.

Personal pronouns

	subject	object	genitive
I	jeg	meg	–
you	du	deg	–
he	han	ham/han	hans
she	hun	henne	hennes
it	den/det	den/det	dens/dets
we	vi	oss	–
you (plural)	dere	dere	–
they	de	dem	deres

Verbs

The present tense is simple, because it has the same form for all persons.

	to ask	to buy	to go	to do
Infinitive	å spørre	å kjøpe	å gå	å gjøre
Present tense	spør	kjøper	går	gjør
Imperative	spør	kjøp	gå	gjør

There is no equivalent to the English present continuous tense. Thus:

Jeg reiser. I travel/I am travelling.

Negation is expressed by using the adverb **ikke** (not). It is usually placed immediately after the verb in a main clause. In compound tenses, **ikke** appears between the auxiliary and the main verb.

Jeg snakker norsk. I speak Norwegian.
Jeg snakker ikke norsk. I do not speak Norwegian.

Irregular Verbs

There is a large number of prefixes in Norwegian, like *an-, av-, be-, etter-, for-, fra-, frem-, inn-, med-, ned-, om-, opp-, over-, på-, til-, under-, unn-, unna-, ut-, ved-*, etc. A prefixed verb is conjugated in the same way as the stem verb.

Infinitive	Preterite	Past participle	
be	ba	bedt	*ask, pray*
binde	bandt	bundet	*bind, tie*
bite	bet	bitt	*bite*
bli	ble	blitt	*become, remain*
brekke	brakk	brukket	*break*
brenne	brant/brente*	brent	*burn*
bringe	brakte	brakt	*bring*
briste	brast	bristet	*burst*
bryte	brøt	brutt	*break*
by	bydde/bød	budt	*offer; command*
bære	bar	båret	*bear*
dra	dro(g)	dradd/dratt	*pull; go, travel*
drikke	drakk	drukket	*drink*
drive	drev	drevet	*lead, manage; drift*
ete	åt	ett	*eat (animals)*
falle	falt	falt	*fall*
fare	fór	faret/fart	*go away, leave*
finne	fant	funnet	*find*
fly	fløy	fløyet	*fly*
flyte	fløt	flytt	*flow, float*
forstå	forsto(d)	forstått	*understand*
forsvinne	forsvant	forsvunnet	*disappear*
fortelle	fortalte	fortalt	*tell, relate*
fryse	frøs	frosset	*be cold, freeze*
følge	fulgte	fulgt	*follow*
få	fikk	fått	*get*

---

* These verbs are regular when used transitively, i.e. when they take an object.

gi	ga(v)	gitt	give
gjelde	gjaldt	gjeldt	concern; be valid
gjøre	gjorde	gjort	do, make
gli	gled	glidd	slide, glide
gnage	gnagde/gnog	gnagd	gnaw
gni	gnidde/gned	gnidd	rub
grave	gravde/grov	gravd	dig
gripe	grep	grepet	catch, seize
gråte	gråt	grått	weep, cry
gyte	gytte/gjøt	gytt	spawn
gå	gikk	gått	walk, go
ha	hadde	hatt	have
henge	hang/hengte*	hengt	hang
hete	het/hette	hett	be called
hive	hev	hevet	throw
hjelpe	hjalp	hjulpet	help
holde	holdt	holdt	hold
klinge	klang	kling(e)t	ring
klype	klypte/kløp	klypt/kløpet	pinch
klyve	kløv	kløvet	climb
knekke	knakk/knekte*	knekt/knekket	crack, break
knipe	knep	knepet	pinch
komme	kom	kommet	come
krype	krøp	krøpet	creep, crawl
kunne (kan)	kunne	kunnet	can
kveppe	kvapp	kveppet	startle
la(te)	lot	latt	let
le	lo	ledd	laugh
legge	la	lagt	lay, put
lide	led	lidd	suffer
ligge	lå	ligget	lie
lyde	lød	lydt	sound
lyge	løy	løyet	tell a lie
løpe	løp	løpt	run
måtte (må)	måtte	måttet	must
nyse	nyste/nøs	nyst	sneeze

---

* These verbs are regular when used transitively, i.e. when they take an object.

nyte	nøt	nytt	*enjoy*
pipe	pep	pepet	*chirp*
rekke	rakte/rakk	rakt/rukket	*reach; hand*
renne	rant/rente*	rent	*run, flow*
ri(de)	red	ridd	*ride*
rive	rev	revet	*tear*
ryke	røk	røket	*smoke*
se	så	sett	*see*
selge	solgte	solgt	*sell*
sette	satte	satt	*set*
si	sa	sagt	*say*
sitte	satt	sittet	*sit*
skjelve	skalv	skjelvet	*tremble*
skjære	skar	skåret	*cut*
skri(de)	skred	skredet/skridd	*stride, stalk*
skrike	skrek	skreket	*scream*
skrive	skrev	skrevet	*write*
skryte	skrøt	skrytt	*boast*
skulle (skal)	skulle	skullet	*shall*
skvette	skvatt/skvettet*	skvettet	*startle; splash*
skyte	skjøt	skutt	*shoot*
skyve	skjøv	skjøvet	*push, shove*
slenge	slang/slengte*	slengt	*throw, fling*
slippe	slapp	sluppet	*let go, drop*
slite	slet	slitt	*pull, tear*
slå	slo	slått	*strike, beat*
slåss	sloss	slåss	*fight*
smelle	smalt/smelte*	smelt	*smack, slam*
smette	smatt	smettet	*slip away*
smøre	smurte	smurt	*smear*
snike	snek	sneket	*sneak*
snyte (seg)	snøt	snytt	*blow one's nose; cheat*
sove	sov	sovet	*sleep*
spinne	spant	spunnet	*spin; purr*
sprekke	sprakk	sprukket	*burst*
sprette	spratt	sprettet	*bound*

---

* These verbs are regular when used transitively, i.e. when they take an object.

springe	sprang	sprunget	*run; jump*
spørre	spurte	spurt	*ask*
stige	steg	steget	*rise, climb*
stikke	stakk	stukket	*sting*
stjele	stjal	stjålet	*steal*
strekke	strakk	strukket	*stretch*
stri(de)	stridde/stred	stridd	*quarrel*
stryke	strøk	strøket	*iron; cross out*
stå	sto	stått	*stand*
sverge	sverget/svor	sverget/svoret	*swear*
svi	sved/svidde*	svidd	*singe*
svike	svek	sveket	*betray, disappoint*
svinge	svang	sving(e)t/ svunget	*swing*
synge	sang	sunget	*sing*
synke	sank	sunket	*sink*
ta	tok	tatt	*take*
telle	talte/telte	talt/telt	*count*
tie	tidde	tidd	*be/keep silent*
tigge	tigget/tagg	tigget/tigd	*beg*
tre	trådte	trådt	*tread, step*
treffe	traff	truffet	*meet; hit*
trekke	trakk	trukket	*pull*
tvinge	tvang	tvunget	*force*
tygge	tygde	tygd	*chew*
vekke	vakte	vakt	*wake*
velge	valgte	valgt	*choose, elect*
vike	vek	veket	*yield*
ville (vil)	ville	villet	*will*
vinde	vandt	vundet	*wind*
vinne	vant	vunnet	*win*
vite	visste	visst	*know*
vri	vred	vridd	*wrench, twist*
være	var	vært	*be*

Engelsk minigrammatikk

Artikler

Den **bestemte** artikkel har samme form i entall og flertall: **the.**

the room – the rooms   rommet – rommene

Den **ubestemte** artikkel har to former: **a**, som brukes foran ord som begynner med en konsonant, og **an**, som brukes foran vokal eller stum **h**.

a coat   en kåpe/frakk
an umbrella   en paraply
an hour   en time

Some angir en ubestemt mengde eller et ubestemt antall. Det anvendes foran substantiv i både entall og flertall, og tilsvarer på norsk «noen», «noe», «litt».

I'd like some tea, please.   Jeg vil gjerne ha litt te.
Give me some stamps, please.   Gi meg noen frimerker, er du
                                     snill.

Any betyr «noen»/«hvilken som helst», og brukes ofte i nektende og spørrende setninger.

There isn't any soap.   Det er ikke noe såpe her.
Do you have any stamps?   Har du frimerker?
Is there any mail for me?   Er det kommet noe post til meg?

Substantiver

Flertall dannes som regel ved å føye **-(e)s** til entallsformen.

cup – cups   kopp – kopper
dress – dresses   kjole – kjoler

Obs! Hvis et substantiv slutter på **-y** i entall, endres stavemåten til **-ies** i flertall hvis **y** kommer etter en konsonant. Kommer den etter en vokal, anvendes den normale flertallsendelsen **-s**.

lady – ladies   dame – damer
day – days   dag – dager

Men ingen regel unten unntak…

man – men	mann – menn
woman – women	kvinne – kvinner
child – children	barn – barn
foot – feet	fot – føtter
knife – knives	kniv – kniver

Genitiv

1. Når eieren er et levende vesen og når substantivet ikke slutter på **-s**, føyer man til **'s**.

the boy's room	guttens rom
Anne's dress	Annes kjole

Hvis substantivet slutter på **-s**, føyer man kun til apostrofen (').

the boy's room	guttenes rom

2. Hvis eieren ikke er et levende vesen, brukes preposisjonen **of**.

the end of the journey	reisens slutt (slutten på reisen)

Adjektiver

Adjektivet forblir uendret både foran substantivet og når det står alene.

a large brown suitcase	en stor brun koffert
Komparativ og **superlativ**	kan dannes på to måter.

1. Adjektiver med én stavelse og de fleste adjektiver med to stavelser får endelsen **-(e)r** og **-(e)st**.

small – smaller – smallest	liten – mindre – minst
pretty – prettier – prettiest	søt – søtere – søtest

Obs! **-y** etter konsonant endres til **i** foran **-er** og **-est**.

2. Adjektiver med flere enn to stavelser og enkelte adjektiver med to stavelser (f.eks. de som slutter på **-ful** eller **-less**) danner komparativ og superlativ ved hjelp av **more** og **most**.

expensive (dyr) – more expensive – most expensive
careful (forsiktig) – more careful – most careful

404

Følgende adjektiver er uregelmessige:

good (bra) – **better** – **best**   **much** (mye) }
bad (dårlig) – **worse** – **worst** **many** (mange) } – **more** – **most**
little (lite) – **less** – **least**

Pronomener

	personlige pronomen nominativ	pronomen akkusativ	eiendomspronomener 1)	2)
jeg	**I**	**me**	**my**	**mine**
du	**you**	**you**	**your**	**yours**
han	**he**	**him**	**his**	**his**
hun	**she**	**her**	**her**	**hers**
den/det	**it**	**it**	**its**	–
vi	**we**	**us**	**our**	**ours**
dere	**you**	**you**	**your**	**yours**
de	**they**	**them**	**their**	**theirs**

Verb

Tre viktige **hjelpeverb** i presens:

to be (å være)

	sammentrukket form	sammentrukket nektende form	
I am	**I'm**	**I'm not**	–
you are	**you're**	**you're not**	**you aren't**
he is	**he's**	**he's not**	**he isn't**
she is	**she's**	**she's not**	**she isn't**
it is	**it's**	**it's not**	**it isn't**
we are	**we're**	**we're not**	**we aren't**
you are	**you're**	**you're not**	**you aren't**
they are	**they're**	**they're not**	**they aren't**

Spørreform: **Am I? – Is he? – Are they?**
Obs! I dagligtale brukes så å si bare de sammentrukne formene.

to have (å ha)

	sammentrukket form	sammentrukket nektende form
I have	I've	I haven't
you have	you've	you haven't
he/she/it has	he's/she's/it's	he/she/it hasn't
we have	we've	we haven't
you have	you've	you haven't
they have	they've	they haven't

Spørrende: **Have you? – Has he?**

to do (å gjøre)

I do, you, he/she/it does, we do, you do, they do

Nektende: **I do not (I don't) – He does not (He doesn't)**
Spørrende: **Do you? – Does she?**

For alle hjelpeverb gjelder:

1. Nektende form dannes med **not** (ikke).
2. Spørrende form dannes ved å sette verbet foran subjektet.

Andre verb
Engelske verb beholder samme form i alle personer i **presens**, med unntak av 3. person entall der man legger til **-(e)s.**

	to speak (å snakke)	to ask (å spørre)	to go (å gå)
I	speak	ask	go
you	speak	ask	go
he/she/it	speaks	asks	goes
we/you/they	speak	ask	go

Imperfektum og **perfektum partisipp** dannes for regelmessige verb ved å føye til endelsen **-d** eller **-ed**.

Presens partisipp dannes ved å føye til endelsen **-ing** til infinitivsformen.

Nektende form dannes med hjelpeverbet **do** + **not** + infinitiv:
I do not (don't) like this hotel.   Jeg liker ikke dette hotellet.

Spørrende form dannes med hjelpeverbet **do** + subjekt + infinitiv:
Do you drink wine?   Drikker du vin?

Progressiv (pågående) form
Denne formen finnes ikke på norsk, men motsvarer «holder på med å», og dannes med hjelpeverbet **to be** fulgt av presens partisipp av verbet.

infinitiv	presens partisipp	progressiv form
to read	reading	I'm reading.
to sing	singing	She's singing.

What are you doing?   Hva er det du holder på med (å gjøre)?
I'm writing a letter.   Jeg holder på (med) å skrive et brev.

Uregelmessige verb

Her er en liste over uregelmessige engelske verb. Sammensatte verb, eller verb som har prefiks, bøyes etter samme mønster som det enkle verbet; eks.: *overdrive* bøyes som *drive*, *mistake* som *take*.

Infinitiv	Imperfektum	Perfektum partisipp	
arise	arose	arisen	stå opp
awake	awoke	awoken/ awaked	vekke; våkne
be	was	been	være
bear	bore	borne	bære
beat	beat	beaten	slå
become	became	become	bli
begin	began	begun	begynne
bend	bent	bent	bøye
bet	bet	bet	vedde
bid	bade/bid	bidden/bid	by (befale)
bind	bound	bound	binde
bite	bit	bitten	bite
bleed	bled	bled	blø
blow	blew	blown	blåse
break	broke	broken	brekke
breed	bred	bred	ale opp
bring	brought	brought	bringe
build	built	built	bygge
burn	burnt/burned	burnt/burned	brenne
burst	burst	burst	briste
buy	bought	bought	kjøpe
can*	could	–	kunne
cast	cast	cast	kaste
catch	caught	caught	gripe
choose	chose	chosen	velge
cling	clung	clung	klamre seg til
clothe	clothed/clad	clothed/clad	kle på
come	came	come	komme
cost	cost	cost	koste

* presens indikativ

creep	crept	crept	*krype*
cut	cut	cut	*skjære*
deal	dealt	dealt	*handle*
dig	dug	dug	*grave*
do (he does*)	did	done	*gjøre*
draw	drew	drawn	*trekke*
dream	dreamt/	dreamt/	*drømme*
	dreamed	dreamed	
drink	drank	drunk	*drikke*
drive	drove	driven	*kjøre*
dwell	dwelt	dwelt	*bo*
eat	ate	eaten	*spise*
fall	fell	fallen	*falle*
feed	fed	fed	*fôre*
feel	felt	felt	*føle*
fight	fought	fought	*slåss*
find	found	found	*finne*
flee	fled	fled	*flykte*
fling	flung	flung	*kaste*
fly	flew	flown	*fly*
forsake	forsook	forsaken	*svikte*
freeze	froze	frozen	*fryse*
get	got	got	*få*
give	gave	given	*gi*
go (he goes*)	went	gone	*gå*
grind	ground	ground	*male, knuse*
grow	grew	grown	*gro*
hang	hung	hung	*henge*
have (he has*)	had	had	*ha*
hear	heard	heard	*høre*
hew	hewed	hewed/hewn	*hugge*
hide	hid	hidden	*gjemme*
hit	hit	hit	*slå*
hold	held	held	*holde*
hurt	hurt	hurt	*såre*
keep	kept	kept	*beholde*
kneel	knelt	knelt	*knele*
knit	knitted/knit	knitted/knit	*strikke*

---

* presens indikativ

know	knew	known	*vite*
lay	laid	laid	*legge*
lead	led	led	*lede*
lean	leant/leaned	leant/leaned	*lene*
leap	leapt/leaped	leapt/leaped	*hoppe*
learn	learnt/learned	learnt/learned	*lære*
leave	left	left	*forlate*
lend	lent	lent	*låne (ut)*
let	let	let	*la; leie ut*
lie	lay	lain	*ligge*
light	lit/lighted	lit/lighted	*tenne*
lose	lost	lost	*miste*
make	made	made	*lage*
may*	might	–	*kunne (få lov)*
mean	meant	meant	*mene*
meet	met	met	*møte*
mow	mowed	mowed/mown	*slå (gress)*
must*	must	–	*måtte*
ought* (to)	ought	–	*burde*
pay	paid	paid	*betale*
put	put	put	*legge*
read	read	read	*lese*
rid	rid	rid	*befri*
ride	rode	ridden	*ride*
ring	rang	rung	*ringe*
rise	rose	risen	*reise seg*
run	ran	run	*løpe*
saw	sawed	sawn	*sage*
say	said	said	*si*
see	saw	seen	*se*
seek	sought	sought	*søke*
sell	sold	sold	*selge*
send	sent	sent	*sende*
set	set	set	*sette*
sew	sewed	sewed/sewn	*sy*
shake	shook	shaken	*riste*
shall*	should	–	*skulle*
shed	shed	shed	*felle*

---

* presens indikativ

shine	shone	shone	*skinne*
shoot	shot	shot	*skyte*
show	showed	shown	*vise*
shrink	shrank	shrunk	*krympe*
shut	shut	shut	*lukke*
sing	sang	sung	*synge*
sink	sank	sunk	*synke*
sit	sat	sat	*sitte*
sleep	slept	slept	*sove*
slide	slid	slid	*gli*
sling	slung	slung	*kaste*
slink	slunk	slunk	*luske*
slit	slit	slit	*flenge*
smell	smelled/smelt	smelled/smelt	*lukte*
sow	sowed	sown/sowed	*så*
speak	spoke	spoken	*snakke*
speed	sped/speeded	sped/speeded	*haste*
spell	spelt/spelled	spelt/spelled	*stave*
spend	spent	spent	*gi ut; tilbringe*
spill	spilt/spilled	spilt/spilled	*søle, spille*
spin	spun	spun	*spinne*
spit	spat	spat	*spytte*
split	split	split	*splitte*
spoil	spoilt/spoiled	spoilt/spoiled	*ødelegge; skjemme bort*
spread	spread	spread	*spre*
spring	sprang	sprung	*hoppe opp*
stand	stood	stood	*stå*
steal	stole	stolen	*stjele*
stick	stuck	stuck	*klebe*
sting	stung	stung	*stikke*
stink	stank/stunk	stunk	*stinke*
strew	strewed	strewed/strewn	*strø*
stride	strode	stridden	*skride*
strike	struck	struck/stricken	*slå*
string	strung	strung	*tre på snor*
strive	strove	striven	*streve*
swear	swore	sworn	*banne; sverge*
sweep	swept	swept	*feie*

swell	swelled	swollen/	*hovne*
		swelled	
swim	swam	swum	*svømme*
swing	swung	swung	*svinge*
take	took	taken	*ta*
teach	taught	taught	*undervise*
tear	tore	torn	*rive*
tell	told	told	*fortelle*
think	thought	thought	*tenke*
throw	threw	thrown	*kaste*
thrust	thrust	thrust	*støte*
tread	trod	trodden	*trå*
wake	woke/waked	woken/waked	*våkne; vekke*
wear	wore	worn	*ha på seg*
weave	wove	woven	*veve*
weep	wept	wept	*gråte*
will*	would	–	*ville*
win	won	won	*vinne*
wind	wound	wound	*sno*
wring	wrung	wrung	*vri*
write	wrote	written	*skrive*

---

* presens indikativ

Numerals

Cardinal numbers	Ordinal numbers
0 null	1. første
1 en	2. annen
2 to	3. tredje
3 tre	4. fjerde
4 fire	5. femte
5 fem	6. sjette
6 seks	7. syvende/sjuende
7 syv/sju	8. åttende
8 åtte	9. niende
9 ni	10. tiende
10 ti	11. ellevte
11 elleve	12. tolvte
12 tolv	13. trettende
13 tretten	14. fjortende
14 fjorten	15. femtende
15 femten	16. sekstende
16 seksten	17. syttende
17 sytten	18. attende
18 atten	19. nittende
19 nitten	20. tyvende/tjuende
20 tyve/tjue	21. enogtyvende/
	tjueførste
21 enogtyve/tjueen	22. toogtyvende/tjueandre
30 tredve/tretti	23. treogtyvende/
	tjuetredje
31 enogtredve/trettien	24. firogtyvende/
	tjuefjerde
40 førti	25. femogtyvende/
	tjuefemte
41 enogførti/førtien	26. seksogtyvende/
	tjuesjette
50 femti	27. syvogtyvende/
51 enogfemti/femtien	tjuesjuende
60 seksti	28. åtteogtyvende/
61 enogseksti/sekstien	tjueåttende
70 sytti	29. niogtyvende/
	tjueniende
71 enogsytti/syttien	30. tredevte/trettiende
80 åtti	40. førtiende
81 enogåtti/åttien	50. femtiende
90 nitti	60. sekstiende
91 enognitti/nittien	70. syttiende
100 hundre	80. åttiende
101 hundre og en	90. nittiende
1 000 tusen	100. hundrede
1 000 000 en million	1 000. tusende

Tall

Grunntall		Ordenstall	
0	zero	1st	first
1	one	2nd	second
2	two	3rd	third
3	three	4th	fourth
4	four	5th	fifth
5	five	6th	sixth
6	six	7th	seventh
7	seven	8th	eighth
8	eight	9th	ninth
9	nine	10th	tenth
10	ten	11th	eleventh
11	eleven	12th	twelfth
12	twelve	13th	thirteenth
13	thirteen	14th	fourteenth
14	fourteen	15th	fifteenth
15	fifteen	16th	sixteenth
16	sixteen	17th	seventeenth
17	seventeen	18th	eighteenth
18	eighteen	19th	nineteenth
19	nineteen	20th	twentieth
20	twenty	21st	twenty-first
21	twenty-one	22nd	twenty-second
22	twenty-two	23rd	twenty-third
23	twenty-three	24th	twenty-fourth
24	twenty-four	25th	twenty-fifth
25	twenty-five	26th	twenty-sixth
30	thirty	27th	twenty-seventh
40	forty	28th	twenty-eighth
50	fifty	29th	twenty-ninth
60	sixty	30th	thirtieth
70	seventy	40th	fortieth
80	eighty	50th	fiftieth
90	ninety	60th	sixtieth
100	a/one hundred	70th	seventieth
230	two hundred and thirty	80th	eightieth
1,000	a/one thousand	90th	ninetieth
10,000	ten thousand	100th	hundredth
100,000	a/one hundred thousand	230th	two hundred and thirtieth
1,000,000	a/one million	1,000th	thousandth

Time

Although official time in Norway is based on the 24-hour clock, the 12-hour system is used in conversation.

If you have to indicate that it is a.m. or p.m., add *om morgenen, om formiddagen, om ettermiddagen, om kvelden, om natten*.

Thus:

klokken syv om morgenen	7 a.m.
klokken elleve om formiddagen	11 a.m.
klokken to om ettermiddagen	2 p.m.
klokken åtte om kvelden	8 p.m.
klokken to om natten	2 a.m.

Days of the week

søndag	Sunday	*torsdag*	Thursday
mandag	Monday	*fredag*	Friday
tirsdag	Tuesday	*lørdag*	Saturday
onsdag	Wednesday		

Klokken

Både engelskmennene og amerikanerne anvender uttrykkene a.m. (ante meridiem) om tiden etter midnatt frem til kl. 12, og p.m. (post meridiem) om tiden etter kl. 12 frem til midnatt. I England går man imidlertid mer og mer over til å bruke 24-timerssystemet.

Eksempler:

I'll come at seven a.m.   Jeg kommer kl. 7 om morgenen.
I'll come at two p.m.   Jeg kommer kl. 2 om ettermiddagen.
I'll come at eight p.m.   Jeg kommer kl. 8 om kvelden.

Dagene

Sunday	søndag	*Thursday*	torsdag
Monday	mandag	*Friday*	fredag
Tuesday	tirsdag	*Saturday*	lørdag
Wednesday	onsdag		

Conversion tables/Omregningstabeller

Metres and feet

The figure in the middle stands for both metres and feet, e.g.
1 metre = 3.281 ft. and 1 foot = 0.30 m.

Meter og fot

Tallene i midten gjelder både for meter og fot, dvs. 1 meter =
3,281 fot, og 1 fot = 0,30 meter.

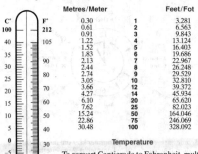

C°	F°	Metres/Meter		Feet/Fot
100	212	0.30	1	3.281
		0.61	2	6.563
40	105	0.91	3	9.843
		1.22	4	13.124
35	90	1.52	5	16.403
		1.83	6	19.686
30		2.13	7	22.967
	80	2.44	8	26.248
25		2.74	9	29.529
	70	3.05	10	32.810
20		3.66	12	39.372
		4.27	14	45.934
15	60	6.10	20	65.620
		7.62	25	82.023
10	50	15.24	50	164.046
		22.86	75	246.069
5	40	30.48	100	328.092

Temperature

To convert Centigrade to Fahrenheit, multiply by 1.8 and add 32.
To convert Fahrenheit to Centigrade, subtract 32 from Fahrenheit and divide by 1.8.

Temperatur

For å regne om fra celsius- til fahrenheitgrader, ganger en med 1,8 og legger til 32.
Omvendt – for å regne om fra fahrenheittil celsiusgrader – trekker en fra 32 og deler med 1,8.